MPs
IN DUBLIN

Rochfort (1806)
Speaker: Robert Rochfort, 1652–1727
Time as Speaker: 1695–1703
Unknown artist

MPs
IN DUBLIN

COMPANION TO
HISTORY OF THE
IRISH PARLIAMENT
1692–1800

EDITH MARY JOHNSTON-LIIK

ULSTER HISTORICAL
FOUNDATION

Ulster Historical Foundation is pleased to acknowledge the contribution of
the Office of the Taoiseach, Dublin, towards this publication;
also the Department of Culture, Arts and Leisure, Belfast, for their support of
the digitisation project of which this book is the companion volume.

First published 2006
by Ulster Historical Foundation
www.ancestryireland.com

© Edith Mary Johnston-Liik, 2006

ISBN 13: 978 1 903688 60 1
ISBN 10: 1903688 60 4

Copyediting by Moira Johnston
Design by December Publications
Cover design by Dunbar Design
Printed by ColourBooks Ltd

Set in Adobe Garamond
11 point text on 13.5 leading

'Objects material in their day produced hostility
between our ancestors.
The causes of that hostility have ceased to exist.
Let the enmity too perish.'

DECLARATION OF THE CATHOLIC COMMITTEE,
OCTOBER 1792

May Ireland, North and South,
have peace and prosperity.

Edith Mary Johnston-Liik was born in Belfast and educated at Richmond Lodge and Victoria College. She has an MA and a PhD from the University of St Andrews and a Diploma in Education from the Queen's University of Belfast. From 1956 to 1976 she was a Lecturer and Senior Lecturer in the University of Sheffield and foundation warden of Tapton University Hall of Residence. From 1976 to 1993 she was Professor of History at Macquarie University, Sydney, Australia. She has also taught in the United States as Land Grant Centennial Lecturer in the University of Delaware and as Visiting Lecturer at the University of Michigan at Ann Arbor. In Canada she taught at McMaster University and Queen's University in Ontario and at the University of Alberta at Edmonton. She was awarded a Fulbright Fellowship from 1961 to 1963 and a Commonwealth Fellowship in 1973.

Professor Johnston-Liik's publications include *Great Britain and Ireland: a study in Political Administration* (1963, reprinted in USA 1978); *Ireland in the Eighteenth Century* (1974); with G. Liik and R.G. Ward, *A Measure of Greatness: the Origins of the Australian Iron and Steel Industry* (1998). She has also published articles in *Irish Historical Studies* and the *Proceedings of the Royal Irish Academy* and she has contributed chapters to various books including O. MacDonagh *et al.*, *Irish Culture and Nationalism*, vols I & II and P. Roebuck, ed., *Macartney of Lisanoure*.

REVIEWS

of

History of the Irish Parliament 1692–1800:
Commons, Constituencies and Statutes

Professor Johnston-Liik is better aware than most of the impossibility of achieving perfection in any work of this scale and nature. Her aim, modestly expressed in the acknowledgements, is to 'provide a platform from which other scholars can advance'. This she has done. Indeed, the strongest impression that I am left with in respect of this large and ambitious work is not disappointment at its limitations, but sheer admiration for an author who overcame such formidable financial and other obstacles to bring it to completion. In doing so she has not only honoured the memory of those before her who tried in their own way to produce a 'picture of parliament', but she has also triumphed over the generations of suspicion that frustrated its achievement during the twentieth century.

Irish Historical Studies, xxxiii, no. 130, Nov. 2002

... the *History of the Irish Parliament* should be regarded primarily as the single most useful reference source for anyone interested in Irish history in the period from the Williamite war to the Act of Union. This collection will be the standard starting point for researchers for decades to come ... It is difficult to think of a publication, primarily the work of a single individual, which has or will make a comparable contribution to the development of Irish historical research ... A striking feature of the collection is its very high quality presentation.

Parliamentary History, Vol. 23, Part 3, 2004

Once the fresh information from the biographies and constituencies is digested, it should be possible to pursue more effectively some of the themes which have started to interest the quizzical: notably how those outside the conventional circles of privilege – catholics, women, the middling sort – made their preferences felt. Embedded in some of the biographies are hints of the influences that women occasionally exercised over the electoral process ... All concerned with Irish history, even those who content themselves roaming in the undemanding foothills, must recognise the accomplishment. The information never before assembled, not only allows, but demands, new efforts to make better sense of Hanoverian Ireland.

The English Historical Review, Vol. CXVIII, No. 478, Sep. 2003

The *History of the Irish Parliament* represents the work of an entire academic career ... [its] significance, and it is significant, lies in the materials painstakingly collected and presented by Edith Mary Johnston-Liik. The thoroughness of her scholarship and her familiarity with her subject are particularly noticeable ... Tackling the intricacies of eighteenth-century Irish parliamentary politics and the peculiarities of Ireland's electoral processes was no mean feat. Johnston-Liik gives her readers a straightforward and illuminating general introduction to these subjects as well as case studies for all of Ireland's eighteenth-century constituencies. This coupled with the meticulously researched biographical entries, makes the *History of the Irish Parliament* one of the most significant contributions to Irish Studies in recent decades.

The Irish Literary Supplement, Vol. 22, No. 1, Spring 2003

The published work certainly looks the part and will stand long as a monument to the persistence and endeavour of its author ... this is a superb testimony to the art of book design as well as to an exceptional scholar's capacity to conceive and bring a major project to completion.

Irish Historical Studies, xxxiii, no. 130, Nov. 2002

CONTENTS

PREFACE

This handbook is a continuation of the *History of the Irish Parliament* (see www.historyoftheirishparliament.com) intended for those who wish to use the on-line version. It contains two new chapters which examine the motivation of the MPs, one on the general background against which they operated and a more personal one on particular issues of individual concern to the MPs. It is not and cannot be a substitute for the *History* itself, to which reference should be made not only for the hard-copy but also for a further expansion of detail on the various topics referred to in this volume. The most important difference is the omission of the Survey. Considerations of space and finance have imposed these limitations. Similarly it has not proved possible to revise the biographies (apart from one branch of the Trench family which was omitted in the original). However, the bibliography has been expanded to include a large number of the books which appeared during or after the publication of the *History*. These are particularly relevant as reference has been made to as many of them as possible in the new chapters. It is intended to revise the biographies in the not too distant future.

The acknowledgments and preface in the original *History* are equally relevant here. It would have been impossible to attempt such a project 10,000 miles from the sources without the loyal support of the various researchers who have been involved from time to time. In the early years, 1978 to 1981, continuity was a problem for, being funded annually, it was not possible to offer any hope of employment beyond the current year. The original research was financed by a patchwork of annual, often small, grants. It has been made viable by the generous financial support of the Australian Research Council, the Leverhulme Trust, the British Academy, the Esme Mitchel Trust and the School of Irish Studies Fund under its administrator, Professor K. B. Nolan. The research was greatly assisted by the generosity of the Research Funds of the University of Sheffield and Macquarie University. I acknowledge with gratitude the support over many years of both universities. I am most grateful to the Northern Ireland and Irish governments for supporting its publication and to its publishers, the Ulster Historical Foundation and Fintan Mullan, and the team who undertook the actual publication.

I would like once again briefly to acknowledge the contribution to the *History of the Irish Parliament* of those who worked on it. Fuller acknowledgements have been made in the original *History* to them and others less closely involved. In 1978 Dr Peter Smyth was seconded to the project from the PRONI. Mrs Patricia Simpson came from Australia for some months in 1979. Mrs Simpson was succeeded by Mr David Jackson, who then joined the staff in the PRONI. Mrs Sally Wheeler, who had previously worked with the *Oxford English Dictionary*, assisted on a part-time basis, but by the time David Jackson left it was clear that without the continuity only possible with full-time research further progress was unlikely. Then in 1981 Mr Colin Wisdom was appointed Research Assistant to the project, and from that time the work advanced steadily. By 1983 we urgently needed secretarial assistance and we obtained our first ACE (Action for Community Employment) worker, Mrs Eileen Sharpe. Mrs Sharpe was an experienced legal secretary who wished to gain skills in what was then new technology. She put the work on a primitive microcomputer that I had brought from Australia, where Dean Davidson (now at the University of New England) and the Macquarie University Computing Centre made the entry and transfer of data possible. Mrs Sharpe's successors, Mary McCoy, Eileen Burns, Elizabeth Belshaw, Claire McCagherty, Diane Jones, Michele Ford and Siobhan Parr, all contributed substantially to the accurate and careful recording of the research. Anne McNamara and Linda Davidson became part of our establishment, undertaking various research tasks in addition to their secretarial duties. Their work on the microfilms of the *Belfast News Letter* and the *Dublin Journal* has made an important contribution to the project. The ACE workers were not historians and supervising their work on the microcomputers took up a considerable amount of time. For 18 months in 1984–5 Dr David Lammey, now of the PRONI, assisted with the research and supervision. From 1989 to 1992 Macquarie University offered Colin Wisdom a University Research Fellowship to work on the project, and his place in Belfast was taken by Mr David Luke, who proved to be another devoted researcher and efficient manager. The success of a project like this depends not only on its ability to attract funds but also on the calibre and enthusiasm of the researchers. On both counts I have been very fortunate and I am grateful to all whose skills – and faith – have made the project, which many declared impossible, possible.

The project was made viable by the practical support of three institutions, the Public Record Office of Northern Ireland, The Queen's University of Belfast and the Department of Economic Development N.I. The Public Record Office not only gave the researchers accommodation but also provided or made available much of the essential research material. Since the foundation of the PRONI successive heads of the institution have given priority to the discovery and cataloguing of such archives in Great Britain and Ireland as might, in some measure, compensate for the terrible destruction of the Irish Record Office in 1922. They have been amazingly successful, none more so than PRONI's former head, Dr A. P. W. Malcomson, who was actively engaged in reviving the *History* and worked on it in its early years. His scholarship, enthusiasm for and unrivalled knowledge of eighteenth-century Irish documents have made an enormous personal contribution to the research. He ensured that much material of great historical value was identified, brought into the PRONI and there sorted, catalogued and generally made available (often for the first time) to researchers.

The late Professor W. L. Warren not only supported the project with his interest but also welcomed it to Queen's University when, after 1984, it was no longer possible to accommodate it in the Public Record Office. The Institute of Irish Studies and Queen's University of Belfast gave valuable administrative assistance and advice. On my retirement from Australia the Queen's University made me an Honorary Senior Research Fellow. Professor Peter Jupp from the School of History has been a constant source of wise advice and encouragement, while Professor R. A. Buchanan from the Institute of Irish Studies gave practical advice which enabled me to rescue the enterprise on one occasion when I failed to attract sufficient funding, always a problem with long-term projects.

The research has been greatly facilitated by the Department of Economic Development, which awarded the project an ACE scheme from 1983 to 1991 to allow secretarial staff to be trained in the use of microcomputers and word processing by recording the research data on microcomputers. Almost everybody who worked on the project in whatever capacity subsequently found suitable employment.

I am most grateful to the kind and patient librarians of the University of Sheffield, where this study commenced, the Queen's University of Belfast, and most of all, Macquarie University. Many eighteenth-century books are very difficult to obtain in Australia and nearly all the books that I have required have had to be borrowed either within Australia or sometimes from abroad. Under these difficult circumstances Macquarie librarians have invariably been resourceful and helpful. I also acknowledge the work of the archivists in the various record repositories, particularly the Public Record Office of Northern Ireland. I am grateful to the sympathetic computing staff at Macquarie University and the Queen's University of Belfast, who taught me how to make use of the computer. It was painful for me, and must have been exasperating to them, but I had to understand in order to teach my secretarial staff.

The unstinting support of so many of my colleagues when it has been most needed has shown the generous side of academic life. Many friends have encouraged me when I despaired of ever finding the money or the time to get the *History* completed. To my great regret, Professor Oliver MacDonagh, Professor F. X. Martin OSA, Professor Edward Miller, Professor G. R. Potter and Professor T. W. Moody have not lived to see the completion of the work which they so warmly encouraged. To the late Professor J. C. Beckett I owe a particular debt as, realising that I did not have easy access to the *Journals* and *Statutes*, he donated to me his copy of the Bradley edition of the *Journals*, 1614–1760, and a complete set of the *Statutes at Large*, and after his death his executors gave me some useful and valuable books from his library, including ten volumes of the *Parliamentary Register.* I owe a particular debt to those who untiringly supported my endless pleas to act as referees for my annual grant applications and by the same token I owe a debt to those, unknown to me, to whom reference was made by the grantors.

A general study of this kind owes a very great debt to the detailed scholarly work of others. I hope that the bibliography and numerous footnotes reflect that debt at least in some small degree. Readers who are interested in pursuing various topics in greater detail will be able to do so through the scholarly works cited in these references. This book has been researched throughout my entire academic career. The plan for it will be found in the contents pages of *Great Britain and Ireland,* the book of my PhD thesis. But its labour-intensive nature made it impossible until the advent of the microcomputer, which solved the previously insoluble problem of the flexible handling of such a vast and diverse amount of material. Dean Davidson, now at the University of New England, New South Wales, gave me unstinted technological support and in the early 1980s cleared up innumerable difficulties with infinite patience. When I returned to Ireland George Dunn and the Queen's University computing staff also gave me considerable assistance with an endless succession of obstacles.

To three friends I owe a particular debt; first to Professor Norman Gash, who taught me at St Andrews University and pointed me to Irish history, and who came to see the *History* launched in the House of Lords, Dr Margaret MacCurtain, who read large parts of it in manuscript, and to Dr A. T. Q. Stewart, who shared my interest over many years. As such works always do, this one owes much to my family. I came from Australia for varying periods twice a year to work on and supervise the project. My sister, Margaret Johnston, was an able deputy for me and looked after the project when I was in Australia, and did it so efficiently that many of the problems that occurred in my absence were resolved without my knowledge of their existence. My cousin, Moira Johnston, from her long experience in publishing, gave me much-needed support and advice in the final preparation of the manuscript for publication.

The Ulster Historical Foundation, although in very straightened financial circumstances, has managed with the generous support of the governments of Northern Ireland and the Republic of Ireland to make this publication possible. Both the parent *History* and this addition have always hung on a very thin financial thread, but I hope that the fact that they have proved viable will encourage others to develop and expand a very important area in Irish history as well as one which, being concerned with the complex motivation of people, is of enduring fascination.

I would once again like to thank those whose contribution I acknowledged in the preface to the original *History,* without whose assistance and loyalty it would never have been written. I now owe an additional debt to Fintan Mullan, Jonathan Hamill and the staff of the UHF, to Moira Johnston who again copy-edited, listened patiently to all my problems and made many helpful suggestions, to Wendy Dunbar, whose beautiful design of the original six-volume *History* created so much favourable comment, for also designing this one, to Paul Campbell, who typeset it and was genuinely interested in it, to Brian Smith who placed it on the internet and to John MacDermott and Jonathon Hool for their advice.

Since the publication of the *History* in 2002 I have become even more convinced of the truth of the dictum of Professor A. F. Pollard, the founder of the Institute of Historical Research, in 1936 when he reviewed the first volume of J. C. Wedgwood's *History of Parliament* in the *Times Literary Supplement* (5 December). It was a highly controversial beginning for what became a most influential project in the development of twentieth-century historiography. Pollard, comparing it with its two illustrious predecessors, the *Oxford English Dictionary* and the *Dictionary of National Biography*, commented that: 'neither great work would have appeared at all if its editors had waited for that dream of ignorance, perfection; and there is no finality in historical research.' The *History of the Irish Parliament* is – and must be – based on an acknowledgement of this fact. At the same time, the researchers have done their utmost to ensure that their scholarship is as accurate as the evidence available to them has allowed. It is my hope that future scholars will build upon their work and will regard it as a framework from which to advance. I have written and am responsible for the entire text in its final form. Now that it will be on the internet it is hoped that some revision will be possible and as our knowledge increases produce a gradual improvement which will enable us to do justice – not exalt privilege or demonology – to a section of our society, which with all its faults made an impressive contribution not only to life in Ireland, North and South, but also to the United Kingdom.

Edith Mary Johnston-Liik
September 2006

ABBREVIATIONS

GENERAL ABBREVIATIONS

appt	appointment
Arbp	Archbishop
b.	born
Bp	Bishop
B.	Baron(s), Borough
Bt	Baronet
CB	Companion of the Order of the Bath
CBEx	Chief Baron of the Exchequer
CJCP	Chief Justice Common Pleas
CJQ/KB	Chief Justice Queen's/King's Bench
CMG	Companion of the Order of St Michael and St George
d.	died
dau.	daughter
D.	Duke(s)
E.	Earl(s)
(E.)	England/English
f.	following. Final dates are not always known, especially after the Union when offices were abolished, continued or were changed in view of redundancy and the policy of economical (administrative) reform then under way in Great Britain.
GCB	Knight Grand Cross of the Order of the Bath
GCH	Knight Grand Cross of the Hanoverian Order
GCMG	Knight Grand Cross of the Order of St Michael and St George
HEIC	Honourable East India Company
HP	*History of Parliament* (in the 'List of Members' this signifies that an MP also has an entry there)
I.	Ireland/Irish
KB	Knight of the Order of the Bath
KCB	Knight Commander of the Order of the Bath
KCH	Knight Commander of the Hanoverian Order
KCMG	Knight Commander of St Michael and St George
KG	Knight of the Order of the Garter
KH	Knight of the Hanoverian Order

KP Knight of the Order of St Patrick
Kt Knight
KT Knight of the Order of the Thistle
Ld Lt Lord Lieutenant
M. Marquess
n.d.e. not duly elected (the symbol ◆◆◆◆ is used in place of a number to refer to such individuals)
pp place of profit
r. returned
RDS Royal Dublin Society
RIA Royal Irish Academy
Rt Hon. Right Honourable
(S.) Scotland/Scottish or Nova Scotia
s son
TCD Trinity College, Dublin University
V. Viscount(s)

In the Biographies on the website, information taken from the *Almanacs*, which are not necessarily reliable, is marked with an asterisk.

PRIVY COUNSELLORS

In the text, Rt Hon. before a name means that an MP was a Privy Counsellor at some time in his career.

REFERENCES AND BIBLIOGRAPHY

PRINCIPAL RECORD REPOSITORIES

PRONI – Public Record Office of Northern Ireland. All D (document), T (transcript) and MIC (microfilm) references, unless otherwise stated, refer to collections in the PRONI, e.g. G. Aynworth Pilson, *Obituaries,* Downpatrick, T684/8. (Some of the working papers relating to the history of the Irish parliament are catalogued under ENV.)

NAI – National Archives of Ireland, formerly the Public Record Office of Ireland (PROI, various references).

PRO – Public Record Office, London (viceregal correspondence, official papers, etc.; usually SP63/ or HO100/).

NLI – National Library of Ireland (MS).

BL – British Library (Add. MS).

LC – Library of Congress, Washington, Cavendish Debates.

Family histories, published, unpublished and privately printed are cited in the text.

Other repositories and private collections are specified in the text.

Reports of the NAI, NLI and the PRONI are a very useful guide to their MSS.

GENEALOGY

Apart from the basic reference books, e.g. *Complete Peerage Burke*, this is a complicated field and space prevents it from receiving the full attention that it would require. This is especially true in the case of individuals and specific families. However, the footnotes and sources give references to a variety of genealogical data and where they can be found. More complicated queries will require the resources of the Ulster Historical Foundation, Belfast, or the Genealogical Office in the National Library of Ireland.

Abstracts of Wills – P. B. Eustace (ed.), *Registry of Deeds, Dublin, Abstracts of Wills* (2 vols, Dublin, 1954).

Complete Baronetage – G. E. Cokayne (ed.), *The Complete Baronetage* (6 vols, Exeter, 1900–9).

Complete Peerage – G. E. Cokayne, Hon. Vicary Gibbs (ed.), *The Complete Peerage* (13 vols, London, 1910).

DNB – *Dictionary of National Biography.*

English Army Lists – C. Dalton, *English Army Lists and Commission Registers*, 1661–1714 (1896).

Ext. Peerage – Burke, *Extinct Peerage* (London, 1883).

George the First's Army, 1714–27, C. Dalton (ed.) (London, 1910).

IFR – H. Montgomery-Massingberd (ed.), *Burke's Irish Family Records* (London, 1976).

Ir. Gen. – *Irish Genealogist* (Irish Genealogist Research Society).

Irish Army Lists – C. Dalton (ed.), *Irish Army Lists 1661–85* (London, 1907).

Landed Gentry – J. and J. B. Burke, *Dictionary of the Landed Gentry* (London, 1853).

NDNB – *New Dictionary of National Biography.*

Peerage and Baronetage – *Burke's Peerage and Baronetage* (London, 1900; there are several editions of this work).

OFFICIAL PUBLICATIONS

Printed Records of the Parliament of Ireland 1613–1800 (Grierson edn) (Trans-Media Publishing Company, New York, 1978). This is a very comprehensive microfilm collection in 46 reels: for example, reel 46 contains minutes of evidence taken before the Select Committee on the Down Election (Dublin, 1783) and the few extant reports on other controverted elections. See D. Englefield, *Printed Records of the Parliament of Ireland.*

Commons jn. Ire. – Journals of the Irish House of Commons. Two editions have been used: the Bradley and the Grierson. They give different information, e.g. committee service is listed in Bradley but not in Grierson. Grierson is the standard edition and covers the parliament for the seventeenth and eighteenth centuries. Four editions of the *Journals* were taken from the clerks' manuscripts. The first edition was authorised by the House of Commons in 1752 and covered the years 1613 to1760 in eleven volumes. The second edition, covering the years

1613 to1780, was authorised in 1761. The printer for these editions was Abraham Bradley. Both of these editions contain lists of members chosen to serve on committees, which were the mechanism through which the House operated. The third edition was printed by Abraham Bradley and Abraham Bradley King until 1782, the year 1783–4 was printed by Isaac Jackman, and from 1785 to 1800 the printers were James King and Abraham Bradley King. This edition covered the entire period from 1613 to 1800. The fourth, and most famous, edition was authorised in 1795, when it was discovered that 'there is not one complete set of the *Journals of this House* in the Journal Office for the use of members' (*Commons jn. Ire.* (Grierson edn), vol. 16 p. 97). This committee was chaired by Sir Henry Cavendish (**0381**) and advised that 1,500 sets of the *Journals* should be printed by George Grierson. In this last edition, the format was changed to that used at Westminster. All the editions are attractive, but the 19-volume, Grierson edition, is a particularly beautiful example of the printer's art. After the Union a complex index (the other editions have simpler individual indexes) was prepared for this edition under the supervision of Speaker Foster (**0805**). (I am indebted to Dr A. P. W. Malcomson for much of this information.)

Lords jn. Ire. – *The Journal of the House of Lords in the Kingdom of Ireland 1634–1800* (8 vols, Dublin, 1779–1800).

Statutes at Large passed in the parliaments held in Ireland. This prints the public statutes. The private statutes are listed in the relevant volume of *Commons jn. Ire.* but not published. The best collection is in the Library of Trinity College, Dublin (ref. 186.38–40).

Parliamentary debates. Before the nineteenth century there was no *Hansard*. Before 1771 the British House of Commons, on which the Irish parliament modelled itself as closely as possible, repeatedly declared that direct reporting of parliamentary proceedings was considered a breach of privilege. After 1771 the prohibition became more relaxed following the case of Brass Crosby, which was part of the agitation instigated by John Wilkes. The case was complicated, but essentially involved a conflict between the Commons and the City of London over the arrest and counter arrest of a printer, J. Miller of the *London Evening Post*. The Lord Mayor, Brass Crosby MP, sitting with Aldermen Wilkes and Oliver, released Miller despite the Speaker's warrant for his arrest and took the messenger of the House into custody for assault. Amid great excitement, Brass Crosby was imprisoned in the Tower for breach of privilege by 202 to 39 votes. A writ of habeas corpus followed, querying the right of the House of Commons. The case came before Chief Justice de Grey, who upheld the right of the Commons, but thereafter restrictions were relaxed. The present situation regarding the publication of parliamentary reports etc. was enshrined in the legislation, 3 & 4 Vic., c. 9, following the 1839 case of *Stockdale v. Hansard*, which was decided for the plaintiff.

Debates. There are five sources of debates for the Irish parliament, mainly focused on the late eighteenth century and all subject to the restrictions imposed by the circumstances outlined above (see page 31, 'Principal Newspapers and Periodicals').

1. Parl. Reg. – *The Parliamentary Register, or history of the proceedings and debates of the House of Commons of Ireland* [1781–97] – a précis of the most important speeches made in parliament during those years.

2. J. Caldwell, *Debates in the Irish Parliament in the years 1763 & 1764* (2 vols, London, 1779).

3. Cavendish Debates – debates taken down verbatim by Sir Henry Cavendish (**0381**), whose hobby was Gurney shorthand (some transcribed manuscripts, some printed; e.g. J. Wright, Debates ... 1768–71 (London, 1842–3)).

4. Newspapers (see below) periodically printed versions of speeches on popular topics.

5. Various debates published or reported individually (e.g. *Report of the debates in both houses of the Parliament of Ireland on the Roman Catholic Bill ... 1792* (Dublin, 1792); the Union produced a plethora of reports on debates and pamphlets).

Anal. Hib. – *Analecta Hibernica* (an irregular publication of small groups of manuscripts by *IMC*).

Cal. HO Papers – *Calendar of Home Office Papers*: vols cited.

Cal. SP Dom. – *Calendar of State Papers, Domestic:* vols cited.

Eighteenth-Century Irish Official Papers in Great Britain, A. P. W. Malcomson (ed.) (2 vols, PRONI 1973, 1990).

HMC – *Historical Manuscripts Commission*: report cited.

IMC – *Irish Manuscripts Commission*: report cited.

Rosse MSS Calendar (introduction A. P. W. Malcomson) (PRONI Calendar).

Apart from these official reports there are collections of published Memoirs and Correspondence, as cited below and in the text.

Parliamentary Papers (papers published by the authority of the Irish or the United Kingdom parliaments; these are a great quarry of information but they are not always easy to handle. Eighteenth-century reports are often embedded in the *Journals* of one or other House of Parliament, while early nineteenth-century reports (see below, R. B. McDowell, *The Irish Administration*) can be equally applicable to the late eighteenth century. The following are some examples.

Devon Rep. – *Report from H. M. Commissioners of Inquiry into the state of the Law and Practice in respect to the Occupation of Land in Ireland – Report and Minutes of Evidence (4 vols, Dublin, 1845).*

Municipal Corporations (Ireland) – *Report of the Commission to Inquire into the Municipal Corporations in Ireland – Report and Appendices* (*HC*, 1833, 1835).

Report of the Commissioners of Irish Education Inquiry, 1791 (in *HC*, 1956–8, vol. 22, part 3); further information on the many reports on education can be obtained from the bibliographies in D. A. Akenson, *The Irish Education Experiment* (London, 1970) and K. Milne, *The Irish Charter Schools*, see below.

Report of the Commissioners of Union Compensation (1804, 1805).

Return of Members of Parliament (part 2, 1878).

Report on the State of Popery in Ireland (*Journals of the Irish House of Lords*, 1731).

R. Lascelles, *Liber munerum publicorum Hiberniae: or the Establishment of Ireland* (1152–1927) (2 vols, London, 1852).

Patentee Officers in Ireland – J. L. J. Hughes (ed.), *Patentee Officers in Ireland* (1173–1876), including high sheriffs 1661–84 and 1761–1816 (*IMC*, 1960).

WORKS OF REFERENCE

A New History of Ireland, T. W. Moody, F. X. Martin, F. J. Byrne, vols 3 (1534–1691), 4 (1691–1800), 8 (chronology) and 9 (succession lists) (vol. 4 has a good bibliography, as has R. B. McDowell, *Ireland in the Age of Imperialism and Revolution*).

Abstracts of Wills – P. B. Eustace (ed.), *Registry of Deeds, Dublin, Abstracts of Wills* (2 vols, Dublin, 1954).

Alum. Cantab. – J. and J. A. Venn (eds), *Alumni Cantabrigienses: From earliest times to 1751*, Part 1 (4 vols, Cambridge, 1922–7); Part 2 1752–1900 (6 vols, Cambridge, 1940–54).

Alum. Dub. – G. D. Burtchaell and T. U. Sadleir (eds), *Alumni Dublinenses* (2 vols, 1935).

Alum. Oxon. – J. Foster (ed.), *Alumni Oxonienses: The Members of the University of Oxford, 1500–1714* (3 vols, Oxford, 1891–2).

Annual Reg. – *The Annual Register, or a View of the History, Politics and Literature for the Year 1758* [etc.].

Bankers – *Journal of the Institute of Bankers in Ireland*, vols 2–10 (1900–10), C. MacCarthy Tennison, 'The Old Dublin Bankers' and 'The Old Provincial Bankers'.

Blackwood pedigrees – PRONI MIC/315 Blackwood pedigrees.

BNL – Belfast News Letter.

Cavan MPs – *Breifne Antiquarian Society Journal* (1920) pp. 37–47 (1921) pp. 95–111, T. S. Smyth, 'Members in the Irish Parliament for Cavan County and the Boroughs of Cavan and Belturbet'.

Cork Hist. & Arch. Soc. Jn. – *Cork Historical and Archaeological Society Journal.*

Cork MPs – *Cork Hist. & Arch. Soc. Jn.*, ser. 2, vols 2–3 (1895–6), C. M. Tennison, 'Cork Members of Parliament, 1559–1800'.

Council book of Bandon – *Cork Historical and Archaeological Journal*, vol. 14 (1908) pp. 122–7, R. Day (ed.), 'Minutes from the Council Book of the Borough of Bandon'.

Council Book of Clonakilty – *Cork Historical and Archaeological Journal*, vol. 1 (1895) p. 399, D. Townshend, 'Notes on the Council Book of Clonakilty'.

CIB – A. J. Webb, *A Compendium of Irish Biography* (Dublin, 1878).

DIB – J. S. Crone, *A Concise Dictionary of Irish Biography* (Dublin, 1937).

DJ – Dublin Journal.

D. Englefield, *The Printed Records of the Parliament of Ireland: A Survey and Bibliographical Guide* (1978).

Eton College Reg. – R. A. Austin-Leigh, *The Eton College Register* (Eton, 1921).

Fermanagh and Tyrone MPs – Earl of Belmore, *Parliamentary Memoirs of Fermanagh and Tyrone, 1613–1885* (Dublin, 1887).

Ffolliott, Biographical Notices – R. Ffolliott, *Biographical Notices, 1756–1827* (*The Hibernian Chronicle*) MIC 465/1.

FJ – Freeman's Journal.

Gentleman's & Citizen's Almanack (Dublin, 1733–1800), later referred to as *The Treble Almanac.*

Gentleman's Magazine – The Gentleman's Magazine (Exshaw's edn).

Gray's Inn – Gray's Inn Admissions (London).

Gt B. & Ire. – E. M. Johnston, *Great Britain and Ireland* (1963).

Harrow School Reg. – W. T. J. Gunn, *The Harrow School Register, 1571–1800* (London, 1934).

HC – House of Commons sessional paper.

HP [range of years] – *The History of Parliament*: B. D. Henning (ed.), *The Commons, 1660–90*; R. Sedgwick (ed.), *The Commons, 1715–54* (1970); L. Namier and J. Brooke (eds), *The Commons, 1754–90* (1964); R. Thorne (ed.), *The Commons, 1790–1820*; E. Cruickshanks, S. N. Handley & D. W. Hayton, *The Commons 1690–1715* (2003).

IHS – Irish Historical Studies (Dublin, 1938–).

IMC – The Convert Rolls, E. O'Byrne (ed.) (Dublin, 1981).

IMC King's Inns Admission Papers, 1607–1867, E. Keane, B. P. Phair & T. U. Sadleir (eds) (Dublin, 1982).

IMC Quaker Records Dublin: Abstract of Wills, P. B. Eustace and O. C. Goodbody (eds) (Dublin, 1957).

IMC Registry of Deeds: Abstracts of Wills, P. B. Eustace (ed.) (2 vols, Dublin, 1954, 1956).

Irish Pedigrees – J. O'Hart (ed.), *Irish Pedigrees* (Dublin, 1892).

Irish Privy Counsellors – A. Vicars (copy), *Index to Irish Privy Counsellors, 1711–1910* (n.d.).

E. M. Johnston-Liik, *History of the Irish Parliament 1692-1800* (Belfast, 2002).

JRSAI – Journal of the Royal Society of Antiquaries of Ireland.

Kild. Arch. Soc. Jn. – Kildare Archaeological Society Journal.

Kilkenny MPs – G. D. Burtchaell, *Genealogical Memoirs of the Members of Parliament for the County and City of Kilkenny* (Dublin, 1888).

Kilkenny School Reg. – T. B. Sadleir, *The Register of Kilkenny School 1685–1800*; *JRSAI*, vol. 54 (1924), W. E. J. Dobbs, 'A supplement to the entrance register of Kilkenny School 1684–1800'.

King's Inns Admissions – E. Keane, B. P. Phair & T. U. Sadleir (eds), *King's Inns Admission Papers, 1607–1867* (Dublin,1982).

Landed Gentry – J. & J. B. Burke, *Dictionary of the Landed Gentry* (1853).

Lincoln's Inn – Records of the Honourable Society of Lincoln's Inn (Lincoln's Inn, 1896).

A List of Governors – *JRSAI*, vol. 55 (1925), H. A. S. Upton, 'A List of Governors and Deputy Governors of Counties in Ireland in 1699'.

Louth Arch. Soc. Jn. – *Louth Archaeological Society Journal.*

Masons of Ireland – J. H. Lepper & P. Crossle (eds), *History of the Grand Lodge of Free and Accepted Masons of Ireland* (Dublin, 1925).

Middle Temple – *Middle Temple Admissions* (London, 1929).

Misc. Gen. et Herald. – J. J. Howard (ed.), *Miscellanea Genealogica et Heraldica.*

Musgrave Obits – Sir G. J. Armytage, Bt (ed.), *Sir William Musgrave 6th Baronet, A General Nomenclator and Obituary* (London, 1899).

Prerog. Wills – 'Prerogative Wills', 1811–58, a handwritten index to prerogative administrations in NAI.

Proc. RIA – *Proceedings of the Royal Irish Academy.*

PRONI *Eighteenth-century Irish official papers* 2 vols. (ed.) A. P. W. Malcomson (1973,1990).

RCBL – Miscellaneous Gravestone Inscriptions, Representative Church Body Library.

Record of Old Westminsters – G. F. Russell Baker & A. H. Stenning, *Record of Old Westminsters: A Biographical List* (London, 1928).

Records of the General Synod of Ulster 1691–1820 (3 vols, Belfast, 1890–98).

St Peter and St Kevin's Reg. – *The Register of the Parish of St Peter and St Kevin, 1669–1761* (Parish Register Society of Dublin, 1911).

St Peter's Westminster – J. L. Chester (ed.), *The Marriage, Baptismal and Burial Registers of the Collegiate Church or Abbey of St Peter, Westminster* (London, 1876).

Simms' Cards – a series of handwritten index cards containing genealogical details of some MPs sitting from 1692 to 1713, bequeathed to the project by the late Dr J. G. Simms.

Townlands and Towns, Parishes and Baronies of Ireland, General Alphabetical Index (based on 1851 census, HMSO, Dublin 1861).

Treble Almanack – see Gentleman's and Citizen's Almanack.

SELECTED PRINTED CORRESPONDENCE

Archdale – H. B. Archdale, *Memoirs of the Archdales* (Enniskillen, 1925).

Bedford Corr. – John Russell (ed.), *Correspondence of John, 4th Duke of Bedford* (3 vols, 1842–6).

Ber. Corr. – W. Beresford (ed.), *Correspondence of the Rt Hon. John Beresford* (2 vols, London, 1854).

Boulter Letters – *Letters Written by his Excellency, Hugh Boulter, DD, Lord Primate of all Ireland* (2 vols, Dublin, 1770).

Buckingham – *Courts and Cabinets of George III*, ed. by 2nd Duke of Buckingham (vols 1, 2, London, 1848) (see also *HMC Fortescue* 1, 2, 3).

Burke – T. W. Copeland and others (ed.), *Correspondence of the Rt Hon. Edmund Burke* (10 vols, Cambridge and Chicago, 1958–78).

Castlereagh Corr. – Londonderry (ed.), *Memoirs and Correspondence of Viscount Castlereagh* (vols 1, 2, 3, 4, 1859).

Charlemont – F. Hardy, *Memoirs of the Political and Private Life of James Caulfeild, Earl of Charlemont* (Dublin, 1812).

Coghill - *IMC Letters of Marmaduke Coghill 1722-1738*, D. W. Hayton (ed.) (2005).

Cornwallis Corr. – C. Ross (ed.), *Correspondence of Charles, 1st Marquis Cornwallis* (vol. 3, London, 1859); this is very inaccurate in its biographical detail.

Delany – Lady Llandover (ed.), *The Autobiography and Correspondence of Mary Granville, Mrs Delany* (6 vols, London, 1851–2).

Drennan – D. A. Chart (ed.), *The Drennan Letters* (Belfast, 1931).

Drennan – IMC – Jean Agnew (ed.), *The Drennan-McTier Letters 1776-93.*

FitzGerald – *IMC Leinster* – B. FitzGerald (ed.), *Correspondence of Emily, Duchess of Leinster* (1957).

Fitzgibbon - IMC *'A Volley of Execrations': the letters and papers of John Fitzgibbon, Earl of Clare, 1773-1802*, D. A. Fleming & A. P. W. Malcomson (eds) (2005).

Grafton – W. R. Anson (ed.), *Autobiography and Political Correspondence of Augustus Henry, 3rd Duke of Grafton* (London, 1898).

Grattan – H. Grattan (ed.), *Memoirs of the Life and Times of the Rt Hon. Henry Grattan by his son* (5 vols, 1839–46).

Harcourt Papers – W. E. Harcourt (ed.), *Harcourt Papers*, vols 9 & 10 (1888–1905, 50 copies only).

Macartney – T. Bartlett, *Macartney in Ireland, 1768–72* (PRONI, 1979).

Rutland – John, Duke of Rutland (ed.), *Correspondence between the Rt Hon. William Pitt and Charles, Duke of Rutland* (London, 1890).

Shannon's Letters – E. Hewitt (ed.), *Lord Shannon's Letters to his Son* (Belfast, 1982).

Waite – *Walton, 'The King's Business': Letters on the Administration of Ireland 1741–61* (New York, 1996; Waite MSS).

THESES

Unpublished theses and the universities where they can be found are listed in various publications and collectively in successive issues of *Irish Historical Studies* and the *Bulletin of the Institute of Historical Research*. This is a select list.

DUBLIN UNIVERSITY (Trinity College) (unpublished PhD theses)

D. Dickson, 'An Economic History of the Cork Region in the Eighteenth Century' (1977).

J. P. Starr, 'The Enforcing of Law and Order in Eighteenth-Century Ireland' (1968).

THE NATIONAL UNIVERSITY OF IRELAND (NUI) (unpublished MA theses)

M. E. Ellis (*née* Clune), 'The Third Parliament of George III, 1776–83' (1943).

M. P. Joyce, 'A Transcription and Notes towards an Edition of the Official Correspondence of Simon, Earl Harcourt, 1772–7'.

J. I. McGuire, 'Politics, Opinion and the Irish Constitution, 1688–1707' (1968).

D. O'Donovan, 'The Money Bill Dispute of 1753: a study in Anglo-Irish Relations 1750–56' (1977).

T. V. O'Neill, 'Sixth Parliament of George III, 1798–1800' (1943).

E. O'Regan, 'The Irish Parliament 1760–76'.

OXFORD UNIVERSITY (unpublished PhD thesis)

D. W. Hayton, 'Ireland and the English Ministers 1707–16: A Study in the Formulation and Working of Government Policy in the Early Eighteenth Century' (1975).

QUEEN'S UNIVERSITY, BELFAST (unpublished MA theses)

D. Lammey, 'A Study of Anglo-Irish Relations between 1772 and 1782, with particular reference to the "Free Trade" Movement' (1984).

J. L. McCracken, 'Central and Local Administration in Ireland under George II' (1948).

READING UNIVERSITY (unpublished PhD thesis)

P. J. Jupp, 'Irish Parliamentary Elections, 1800–1820' (1966).

PARLIAMENTARY LISTS

These are a series of lists usually, but not invariably, prepared for the government and giving practical parliamentary information about each sitting MP at the time they were prepared. They were ongoing and therefore often have a degree of repetition from one list to another. They were usually prepared by an anonymous Castle official. There is a short note on such lists as were then (1963) available in *Gt B. & Ire.*, pp. 331–7, and a later listing of lists in *Shannon's Letters* (see above), pp. 234–6.

1695	(1)	TCD MS 1179 ff. 37–9, Supporters and opponents of Lord Chancellor Porter.
1696	(1)	*Commons jn. Ire.* (Grierson edn), vol. 1, pp. 145–7 – the Association.
1706	(1)	BL Add. MSS 9715 ff. 150–3; PRONI MIC248 /1 – Robert Johnson MP (1101).
1706	(2)	BL Eg. MSS 917 f. 234 – Ormonde's birthday celebrations.
1707	(1)	BL Add. MSS 9715 ff. 156–7, 249–50; PRONI MIC248/1, T2827/1 – calculations.
1707	(2)	BL Add. MSS 9715 f. 34; PRONI MIC 248/1, T2827/1 – Fleece Tavern 34 MPs.
1707	(3)	BL Add. MS 9715 ff. 249–50; PRONI MIC248/1, T2827/1 – [Cox] dead & absent MPs.
1707	(4)	BL Add. MS 9715 f. 253, PRONI MIC 248/1, T2827/1 – list of absentee MPs.
1711	(1)	BL Add. MS 34777 f. 1; PRONI MIC 248/2, T2827/2 – electoral.
1711	(2)	BL Add. MS 34777 f. 70; MIC 248/2 – Fleece Tavern 31 MPs.
1711	(3)	BL Add. MS 34777 f. 72–3; PRONI 248/2.
1713	(1)	BL Add. MS 34777; PRONI 248/2 – electoral arrangements etc.
1713	(2)	BL Add. MS 34777 ff. 46–7, PRONI; MIC248/2 – Whig and Tory MPs.
1713	(3)	PRONI MIC 248/2 – Phipps Committee.
1714	(1)	*Commons jn. Ire.* (Grierson edn), vol. 3, pp. 33–4, 70 MPs' addresses in favour of Phipps.
1714–5		BL F.I.68 Blenheim MSS; PRONI T3411 – 'black' list of Tories.
1719	(1)	PRONI Castletown MSS T2825/A/8A–B – [Conolly] 72 MPs 'in employment'.
1719	(2)	PRONI T2825/A/8A–B – Conolly MSS – Tories against the repeal of the Test Act.
1755	(1)	PRONI T2812 C. O'Hara, 'Observations on the different interests in the Irish House of Commons' printed in E. Magennis, *The Irish Political System* (2000), pp. 199–209.
1769	(1)	*Irish Historical Studies* vol. XI (1958–9) pp. 18–45; NLI Clements MSS mic. p. 4086.
1771	(1)	PRO SP63 ff. 282–4 [31 government supporters voted against the Revenue Board].

1772 (1)   PRO SP63/435 ff. 51–3.

1772 (2)   PROI MS738; PRONI D572/19/4, T2833/1; *Harcourt Papers* vol. X, pp. 308–71 (1888–1905).

1773 (1)   *Proc. RIA* (1942) vol. 48C no. 4, pp. 145–232.

1773 (2)   Harcourt's Almanac List [Harcourt MSS, Stanton Harcourt, Oxfordshire].

1774 (1)   *Freeman's Journal* July–Sept. 1774 (see *Eighteenth-Century Ire.* XVIII (2004)) J. Kelly (ed.), *Review of the House of Commons, 1774* esp. pp.163-70, 'Introduction' – p. 178, Robert Stewart (**2008**) sat for Co. Down not Co. Donegal.

1775 (1)   *The Irish Parliament in 1775* (1907), W. Hunt (ed.).

1776 (1)   BL Add. MS 331188 ff. 39–98 Pelham MSS; PRONI T1255, T2876/1 [entries to 1782].

1776 (2)   NLI MS 5168; PRONI MIC 243 – Heron List 1.

1776 (3)   NLI MS 3532 – Heron List 2 [1776–83].

1777 (1)   Harcourt List – Gilbert Collection, Dublin.

1778 (1)   Senate Library of Republic of Ireland [also NLI N4736 p. 4047].

1780 (1)   PRO SP63/468, ff. 210–220, Buckinghamshire List.

1782 (1)   *Proc. RIA* (1954) vol. 56C no.1, pp. 227–86.

1783 (1)   1783 Election List [Dr T. P. O'Neill, National University of Ireland, Galway].

1783 (2)   *Newport List.*

1783 (3)   N. Kissane (compiler), *The Volunteer Convention* [PRONI 1974].

1784 (1)   Bolton List NLI MSS 15,917, 16370, Proc. RIA vol. 71C no. 5.

1784 (2)   Ashbourne List [one of the numerous fragmentary Bolton Lists F1/1].

1784 (3)   Vernon Smith List, LC Vernon Smith MSS.

1785 (1)   Rutland List [Belvoir Castle Misc. MSS 130] *Proc. RIA* vol. 71 C no. 5.

1785 (2)   PRO 30/8/320 Chatham List(s) [voting lists, working papers, interests].

1785 (3)   Northamptonshire Record Office – Stowe MSS.

1785 (4)   Stowe MSS – Huntington Library.

1787 (1)   PRONI T2955/F1/3, Proc. RIA vol. 71C no. 5 [additions to Bolton Lists].

1788 (1)   Buckinghamshire Record Office & PRONI T2627/1/1 – Hobart List.

1789 (1)   Huntington Library – Stowe MS 75 & PRONI MIC382 [Addresses 1788–9].

1789 (2)   Falkland [Rev. J. Scott] *Review of the Principal Characters in the House of Commons of Ireland* (Dublin, 1789).

1790 (1)   Falkland [Rev. J. Scott] *The Parliamentary Representation of Ireland* (Dublin, 1790).

1791 (1)   *Proc. RIA* vol. 59C no.1, PRONI D623/A/133/27 – Abercorn List.

1793 (1)   NLI MS54 ff. 19–20 – Melville List.

1794 (1)   *Dublin Evening Post* 13 March 1784 – Placemen & pensioners.

1794 (2)   Dublin Castle SPO Westmorland Papers MS 202.

1799 (1)   Falkland [Rev. J. Scott] *Review of the Principal Characters in the House of Commons of Ireland* (Dublin, 1799).

1799 (2)   PRONI D3030/1104 – Castlereagh MSS no. 1 [interests & inclinations].

1799 (3)   PRONI D3030/1099 – Castlereagh MSS no. 2 [electoral].

1800 (1)   PRONI D3030/1354, 1355 – Castlereagh MSS no. 3 [officeholders].

1800 (2)   PRONI D3030/1096 – Castlereagh MSS [peers & promises].

1800 (3)   Barrington pp. 289–99 [Union management].

DIVISION LISTS

The dividing line between these and the Parliamentary Lists, in some cases, is thin. The lists have been classified according to whether they refer to a specific division and the amount of extraneous information, particularly in the Union Lists, which have been given in both the Parliamentary and Division Lists for this reason. Sometimes only a surname is given, and when more than one person of that name or family is sitting in parliament it can be difficult to decide which MP is in question.

Many division lists were published in newspapers: these are very useful but their accuracy is often dubious. For example, the official record for the Six Month Loan Bill, 25 November 1779, was 138 for and 100 against. Only the *Freeman's Journal* tally agrees with this: but the 18 MPs in the *Freeman's Journal* 'For' column are not those in that of the *Belfast News Letter* (which is three MPs short), and 21 in the latter are not in the former. Sometimes members appear in both the 'For' and 'Against' columns. When an MP is recorded as voting out of character, unless for a good reason, it should therefore be treated with a degree of suspicion.

1709 (1)   BL Add. MS 34777 ff. 67–8 PRONI mic. 248/2 – Money Bill.

1711 (1)   BL Add. MS 34777 f. 71 – the Dublin mayoralty 29 Oct. 1711.

1713 (1)   BL Add. MS 34777 ff. 90–91 – the vote for Sir Richard Levinge as Speaker, 25 Nov. 1713 (see *Hist. Studies* vol. 4).

1713 (2)   BL Add. MS 34777 ff. 90–91 Election of Anderson Saunders (see also Hayton thesis).

1721 (1)   PRONI microfilm Surrey History Centre, Woking, 1248/5 ff. 105–6, Broderick MS – national bank, 14 Oct. 1721.

1721 (2)   PRONI Rosse Papers B/1/6 (copy from Birr Castle) – national bank, 9 Dec. 1721.

1723 (1)   Surrey History Centre, Woking, 1248/5 f. 323v – Co. Westmeath election.

1749 (1)   (combines three lists – NLI 7.R.10, *RIA* and *History of the Dublin Election in the year 1749* (London, 1753)) – Dublin city by-election, 18 Dec. 1749 (James Digges La Touche).

1753 (1)   *The Patriot Almanac* (London, 1754) – expulsion of Arthur Jones-Nevill, 23 Nov. 1753.

1753 (2)   BL Add. MS 32733 f. 511 Money Bill (NUI unpub. thesis – O'Donovan thesis).

1753 (3)   BL Add. MS 32995 f. 42, The Money Bill 17 Dec. 1753 (see also *Grattan, Memoires of the Life and Times* (London, 1839) vol. 1 pp. 423–31 – Money Bill voting list).

1757 (1)   *A Letter from a gentleman in the city to a Member of Parliament in the North of Ireland* – resolutions on pensions.

1768 (1)   PRO SP63/467 ff. 44g–f 2 May 1768 – Army augmentation.

1771 (1)   Cambridge University Library Hib. 0771.1 26 Feb. 1771, Address to Throne, compliment to Viceroy, Lord Townshend.

1771 (2)   PRONI T3224 (London broadsheet), 11 Dec. 1771 – Sir Lucius O'Brien's motion against increased expenditure.

1771 (3)   PRO SP63/434 16 Nov. 1771 – amendment to the Revenue Bill – division of Boards.

1772 (1)   PRO SP63/435 ff. 51–3, 11 Feb. 1772 – Division of the Revenue Boards.

1772 (2)   *FJ* 17–19 Mar. 1772 – Short Revenue Bill.

1773 (1)   *London Evening Post* 28–30 Dec. 1773, Absentee Tax – 25 Nov. 1773

1773 (2)   *FJ* 2–4 Dec. 1773 – an untaxed press, 1 Dec. 1773.

1774 (1)   *FJ* 5–8 Feb. – the Stamp Bill, 22 Jan. 1774.

1774 (2)   *FJ* 13–15 Feb. 1774 – Catholic Relief Bill (leases – unsuccessful).

1775 (1)   *FJ* 17–19 Oct. 1775 – Pro-American amendment to Speech from the Throne, 11 Oct. 1775.

1777 (1)   *FJ* 18–20 Nov. 1777 – postponement of Grattan's motion for retrenchment, 17 Nov 1777.

1777 (2)   *FJ* 18–20 Dec. 1777 – Trade Embargo, 16 Dec. 1777.

1778	(1)	*FJ* 7–10 Feb. – Grattan's motion for retrenchment, 6 Feb. 1778.
1779	(1)	*HC* 7 Aug. 1783 (reprint) – new taxes.
1779	(2)	*HC* 7 Aug. 1783 (reprint) – Six Months Loan Bill (see paragraph 2 above).
1780	(1)	*HC* 11 Aug. 1783 (reprint) – rights of Ireland, 19 Apr. 1780.
1780	(2)	*FJ* 4–6 May 1780 (see note on newspapers below) – Yelverton's (unsuccessful) motion for the amendment of Poynings' Law, 26 Apr. 1780.
1780	(3)	*FJ* 15–17 Aug 1780 – The Tenantry Bill, 11 Aug. 1780.
1780	(4)	*FJ* 22–24 Aug. 1780 – The Perpetual Mutiny Bill, 6 Aug. 1780.
1780	(5)	Duties on imported sugar.
1782	(1)	Dublin Corporation – bill for paving the city.
1783	(1)	*BNL* 2–5 Dec. 1783 – Flood's motion for parliamentary reform, 29 Nov. 1783.
1784	(1)	Reform Bill, 20 Mar. 1784.
1784	(2)	*FJ* 36 Apr. 1784, Protective duties against foreign woollen cloth, 2 Apr. 1784.
1784	(3)	*FJ* 13–15 Apr. 1784 – Foster's Bill against libel, 10 Apr. 1784 (partial).
1784	(4)	Address to the Duke of Rutland.
1785	(1)	PRO 30/8/320 ff. 60–61 – the Commercial Propositions, 12 Aug. 1785.
1786	(1)	*DEP* 9 Mar. 1786 – rights of Grand Juries, 6 Mar. 1786.
1786	(2)	*DEP* 7 Mar. 1786 – Forbes's motion to reform the civil list (minority), 6 Mar. 1786.
1787	(1)	*DEP* 13 Mar. 1787 – Pension Bill, 12 Mar. 1787.
1788	(1)	*DEP* 26 Feb. 1788 – Dublin Police Bill, 25 Feb. 1788 (Travers Hartley's motion).
1788	(2)	*DEP* 1 Mar. 1788 – Forbes's motion for limiting pensions, 29 Feb. 1788.
1789	(1)	*DEP* 17 Feb. 1789 – Regency Crisis, 1 Feb. 1789.
1790	(1)	Curran's motion to reduce the influence of the Crown, 1 Feb. 1790.
1790	(2)	Vote on the speakership, 2 July 1790.
1791	(1)	TCD Library IN.18.230, *Magees Weekly Packet* 19 Feb. 1791 – sale of peerages (Curran's motion on an adjournment debate).
1791	(2)	TCD Library IN.18.230, *Magees Weekly Packet* 5 Mar. 1791 – Grattan's motion against the East India Co.'s monopoly, 21 Feb. 1791.
1791	(3)	*HJ* 7 Mar. 1791 – Grattan's motion against the Dublin Police establishment, 4 Mar. 1791.
1792	(1)	National Archives (SPO) Dublin Westmorland Corr., Fane 207, 20 Feb. 1791 – Catholic Petition (partial list).

1792 (2)   Resolutions against Napper Tandy, Feb.1792.

1793 (1)   *DEP* 2 Mar. 1793 – Knox's motion for Catholic emancipation, 25 Feb. 1793.

1793 (2)   *Northern Star* 17–20 July 1793 – the Convention Bill, 17 July 1793.

1795 (1)   *Northern Star* 5–9 Mar. 1795 – a Short Money Bill, 2 Mar. 1795.

1795 (2)   *Northern Star* 4–7 and 11–14 May 1795 and *FJ* 5–7 May 1795 – Catholic emancipation, 5 May 1795.

1795 (3)   *FJ* 14 May 1795 – Parsons' motion on the reduction of military strength of the country, 13–14 May 1795 (incomplete list).

1796 (1)   *DJ* 28 Jan. 1796 – equality of trade with Great Britain, 21 Jan. 1796.

1797 (1)   *DEP* 18 May 1797 – Ponsonby's motion for parliamentary reform, 15 May 1797.

1798 (1)   PRO HO 100/75 f. 160 – Sir Laurence Parsons' motion for an inquiry into the causes of the present discontent, 5 Mar. 1798.

1799 (1)   PRONI D3030/552A – list of those voting for and against a proposed Union, 25 Jan. 1799.

1800 (1)   Hampshire Record Office, Normanton Papers 21 M 57 – Sir Laurence Parsons' amendment against Union, mentioned in the King's Speech 15 Jan. 1800.

Repeated from the Parliamentary Lists above to give voting patterns:

1800 (1)   PRONI D3030/1354, 1355 – Castlereagh MSS no. 3 (officeholders)

1800 (2)   PRONI D3030/10961 – Castlereagh MSS (peers and promises).

1800 (3)   Barrington pp. 289–99 – Union management.

ACADEMIC JOURNALS

The following is a select list: relevant articles are also to be found in journals with a wider span of interests, e.g. *EHR – English Historical Studies, TRHist. S. – Transactions of the Royal Historical Society* (a large part of the 2000 issue is devoted to papers on the Irish Act of Union), *Past & Present*. In addition, a large number of local history journals, some defunct and others irregularly produced, contain valuable information. The pressures of academic life are increasing the need to publish articles either in journals or as chapters of books. See also the journals listed under 'Works of Reference' above.

EHR – English Historical Review (London, 1886–)

Eighteenth-Century Ire. – Eighteenth-Century Ireland

Familia [the journal of the Ulster Historical Foundation]

HC – Hibernian Chronicle

Hist. Studies – Historical Studies [occasional publication of conference papers]

Ir. Econ. & Soc. Hist. – Irish Economic and Social History

Ir. Sword – The Irish Sword

JRSAI – Journal of the Royal Society of Antiquaries of Ireland

Studia Hibernica

Proceedings of the Irish Catholic Historical Society (Dublin 1955, continuing)

Proc. RIA – Procedings of the Royal Irish Academy

Ulster Folklife

PRINCIPAL NEWSPAPERS AND PERIODICALS

Odd issues of local newspapers have sometimes survived: these are often very useful, but not necessarily accurate. On the other hand, if an MP was reported dead while actually alive, he or his friends were likely to protest.

Complete or even long runs are unusual, particularly early in the eighteenth century, and these publications suffered from the restrictions on direct parliamentary reporting for most of the century (see 'Official Publications' above).

There is a more comprehensive list of these in *A New History of Ireland*, vol. 4, Moody & Vaughan (Oxford, 1985), D. Dickson, 'Bibliography', pp. 747–8.

BNL – Belfast News Letter

DEP – Dublin Evening Post

DJ – Dublin Journal

FJ – Freeman's Journal

Gentleman's Magazine (Exshaw's Dublin edn)

Hibernian Journal

Pue's Occurrences

BIBLIOGRAPHY

The bibliographies below are also select and not comprehensive. The classic bibliography (of publications up to 1985) for the period 1692–1800 is that of D. Dickson in *A New History of Ireland* (1985, vol. 4, pp. 712–95), which lists both primary and secondary sources, including a list of repositories in Ireland, Great Britain, Continental Europe and the USA. Most of the books published since 1985 have comprehensive and up-to-date bibliographies.

PUBLICATIONS UP TO AND INCLUDING 1985

J. M. BARKLEY, *Short history of the Presbyterian Church in Ireland* (Belfast, 1959).

J. M. BARKLEY, *The Eldership in Irish Presbyterianism* (1963).

J. BARRINGTON, *Rise and fall of the Irish nation* (2nd edn, London, 1830–32).

T. BARTLETT, 'The O'Haras of Annaghmore,1600–1800: survival and revival', *Irish Economic and Social History*, vol. 9 (1982).

T. BARTLETT & D. W. HAYTON (eds), *Penal era and golden age* (Belfast, 1979, reprint 2006).

J. C. BECKETT, *Protestant dissent in Ireland, 1687–1780* (London, 1948).

J. C. BECKETT, *The Anglo-Irish tradition* (1976).

G. C. BOLTON, *Passing of the Irish Act of Union* (Oxford, 1966).

I. R. CHRISTIE, *Stress and stability in late eighteenth-century Britain* (Oxford, 1984).

K. CONNELL, *The Population of Ireland* (Oxford, 1950).

S. J. CONNOLLY, *Priests and people in pre-famine Ireland 1780–1845* (Dublin, 1981).

P. J. CORISH, *The Catholic community in the seventeenth and eighteenth centuries* (Dublin, 1981).

W. H. CRAWFORD (ed.) *General Report on the Gosford Estate in Co. Armagh* (Belfast, 1976).

A. CROOKSHANK AND THE KNIGHT OF GLIN, *The painters of Ireland c. 1660–1920* (London, 1978).

L. M. CULLEN, *Anglo-Irish trade, 1660–1800* (Manchester, 1968).

L. M. CULLEN, *The emergence of modern Ireland* (London, 1981).

L. M. CULLEN & T. C. SMOUT (eds), *Comparative Aspects of Scottish and Irish Economic and Social History* (c. 1977).

T. DAVIS (ed.), *The speeches of the Rt Hon. John Philpot Curran* (Dublin & London, 1853).

B. DE BREFFNY & R. FFOLLIOTT, *The houses of Ireland* (London, 1975, 1980).

W. DERRY, *Castlereagh* (London, 1976).

T. M. DEVINE & D. DICKSON (eds), *Ireland and Scotland 1600-1850: Parallels and Contrasts in Economic and Social Development* (1983).

M. ELLIOTT, *Partners in Revolution: The United Irishmen and France* (Yale, 1982).

F. W. FETTER (ed.), *The Irish pound 1797–1825: a reprint of the report of the committee of the British House of Commons on the condition of the Irish currency* (London, 1955).

J. F. FLEETWOOD, *The history of medicine in Ireland* (Dublin, 1951, 1983).

J. A. FROUDE, *The English in Ireland in the eighteenth century* (London, 1901 edn).

N. GASH, *Aristocracy and people: Britain 1815–1865* (London, 1979).

N. GASH, *Mr Secretary Peel* (London, 1961).

N. GASH, *Politics in the age of Peel* (London, 1953).

J. M. GOLDSTROM & L. A. CLARKSON (eds), *Irish Population, Economy and Society* (1981).

D. GUINNESS & W. RYAN, *Irish houses and castles* (London, 1971).

JANE HAYTER HAMES, *Arthur O'Connor: A United Irishman* (2001).

W. HINDE, *Castlereagh* (London, 1981).

LOUIS HYMAN, *The Jews of Ireland* (IUP 1972).

B. INGLIS, *The freedom of the press in Ireland, 1784–1841* (London, 1954).

F. G. JAMES, *Ireland in the Empire* (Cambridge, MA, 1973).

E. M. JOHNSTON, *Great Britain and Ireland 1760-1800: a Study in Political Administration* (Edinburgh 1963, reprint Conn. USA 1978).

E. M. JOHNSTON, *Ireland in the eighteenth century* (Dublin, 1974).

P. J. JUPP, *Lord Grenville, 1759–1834* (Oxford, 1985).

C. S. KING, *A great Archbishop of Dublin, William King, DD 1650–1729: his autobiography, family and a selection from his correspondence* (London, 1906).

T. KING, *Carlow, the manor & town 1674–1721* (Dublin, 1997).

W. E. H. LECKY, *A history of Ireland in the eighteenth century* (London, 1871).

J. H. LEPPER & CROSSLE (eds), *History of the Grand Lodge of Free and Accepted Masons of Ireland* (Dublin, 1925).

J. LODGE, *The peerage of Ireland, revised by Mervyn Archdall* (7 vols, Dublin, 1789).

H. MCANALLY, *The Irish militia, 1793–1816: A social and military study* (London, 1949).

M. MacCURTAIN, *Tudor & Stuart Ireland* (Dublin, 1972).

M. MacDONAGH, *The Viceroy's postbag* (London, 1904).

O. MacDONAGH, *The Inspector General: life of Sir Jeremiah Fitzpatrick* (London, 1979, 1981).

R. B. MCDOWELL, *Ireland in the age of Imperialism and Revolution, 1760-1801* (Oxford, 1979).

R. B. MCDOWELL, *Irish public opinion, 1750–1800* (London, 1944).

R. B. MCDOWELL, *The Irish administration, 1800–1914* (London, 1964).

D. O. MADDEN (ed.), *The speeches of the Rt Hon. Henry Grattan* (Dublin & London, 1874).

W. A. MAGUIRE, *Living like a lord: The second Marquis of Donegall, 1769–1844* (Belfast, 1984).

W. A. MAGUIRE, *The Downshire estates in Ireland 1801–1845* (Oxford, 1972).

A. P. W. MALCOMSON, *John Foster: the politics of the Irish ascendancy* (Oxford, 1978).

A. P. W. MALCOMSON, *The pursuit of the heiress: aristocratic marriage in Ireland 1750–1820* (Belfast, 1982).

R. MANT, *History of the Church of Ireland from the reformation to the union of the churches of England and Ireland, January 1 1801* (2 vols, London, 1840).

L. MARLOW, *Sackville of Drayton* (London, 1948).

C. E. MAXWELL, *Country and town in Ireland under the Georges* (London, 1940).

C. E. MAXWELL, *A short history of Trinity College, Dublin 1551–1892* (Dublin, 1946).

C. E. MAXWELL, *Dublin under the Georges* (2nd edn, London, 1956).

T. MOLYNEUX, *Journey to the north of Ireland in 1708.*

H. MONTGOMERY HYDE, *Rise of Castlereagh* (London, 1933).

R. MUNTER, *The history of the Irish newspaper, 1685–1760* (London, 1967).

L. B. NAMIER, *England in the age of the American revolution* (London, 1930).

L. B. NAMIER, *Structure of politics at the accession of George III* (London, 1929).

J. NEWPORT, *State of the Borough Representation of Ireland in 1783 and 1800* (1832).

J. M. NORRIS, *Shelburne and Reform* (London, 1963).

M. R. O'CONNELL, *Irish politics and social conflict in the age of the American revolution* (Philadelphia, 1965).

T. PAKENHAM, *The year of liberty* (London, 1969, 1972).

E. & A. PORRITT, *The unreformed House of Commons* (2 vols, London, 1903).

J. S. REID (ed. W. D. Killen), *History of the Presbyterian Church in Ireland* (3 vols, Belfast, 1867).

P. ROEBUCK (ed.), *Public service and private fortune: The life of Lord Macartney, 1737–1806* (Belfast, 1983). This is the same book as *Macartney of Lissanoure: Essays in Biography* (Belfast, 1983).

J. G. SIMMS, *The Williamite confiscation in Ireland, 1690–1703* (London, 1956).

N. SOMERVILLE-LARGE, *Irish Eccentrics* (1975).

G. P. STEWART, *Stewart of Ballymenagh, Killymoon and Tyrcallen* (Nelson, New Zealand, 1982).

P. D. G. THOMAS, *The House of Commons in the eighteenth century* (Oxford, 1971, reprint 1992).

R. TWISS, *A tour in Ireland in 1775* (1776).

E. G. WAKEFIELD, *An account of Ireland statistical and political* (2 vols, London, 1812).

[Wakefield's estate valuations appear unduly high. It is uncertain why – he may have equated an Irish estate with an equivalent English one.]

WELLINGTON, DUKE OF (ed.), *Wellington Correspondence* (15 vols, London, 1858–72).

W. G. WOOD-MARTIN, *History of Sligo county and town from the close of the revolution of 1688 to the present time* (3 vols, Dublin, 1892).

A. YOUNG, *A tour in Ireland 1776–9* (2 vols, reprint IUP, 1970), pp. 46-54.

PUBLICATIONS SINCE 1985

(It was impossible to include books published in or after 2000 in the *History* and special attention should be given to these.)

J. AGNEW, *Belfast merchant families in the seventeenth century* (Dublin, 1996).

T. BARNARD, *A New Anatomy of Ireland: The Irish Protestants, 1649-1770* (Yale, 2003).

T. BARNARD, *The abduction of a Limerick heiress: social and political relations in mid-eighteenth century Ireland* (Dublin, 1998).

T. BARNARD, *Irish Protestants: Ascents and Descents, 1641-1770* (Dublin, 2004).

T. BARNARD, *Making the Grand Figure: Lives and Possessions in Ireland, 1641-1770* (Yale, 2004).

T. BARNARD, *A guide to the sources for the history of material culture in Ireland, 1500-2000* (Dublin, 2005).

T. BARTLETT, *The fall and rise of the Irish nation* (Dublin, 1992).

T. BARTLETT (ed.), *Life of Theobald Wolfe Tone: memoirs, journals and political writings compiled and arranged by William T. W. Tone, 1826* (Dublin, 1998).

T. BARTLETT, DAVID DICKSON, DAIRE KEOCH, KEVIN WHELAN (eds) *1798: a Bicentenary Perspective* (Dublin, 2003).

T. BARTLETT & K. JEFFERY, *A military history of Ireland* (Cambridge, 1996).

J. C. BECKETT, *The cavalier duke: A life of James Butler, 1st Duke of Ormond* (Belfast, 1990).

S. BENEDETTI, *The Milltowns: a family reunion* (National Gallery of Ireland, 1997).

M. BROWN. P. M. GEOGHAN & JAMES KELLY, *The Irish Act of Union 1800: Bicentennial Essays* (IAP, 2003).

A. N. BRUNICARDI, *John Anderson, entrepreneur* (Fermoy, 1987).

R. E. BURNS, *Irish parliamentary politics in the eighteenth century* (2 vols, Washington, DC, 1989).

P. A. BUTLER, *Three Hundred Years of Irish Watercolours and Drawings* (1990).

L. CHAMBERS, *Rebellion in Kildare, 1790–1803* (Dublin, 1998).

E. O. CIARDHA, *Ireland and the Jacobite cause, 1685-1766: A fatal attachment* (2001, rev. edn 2004).

A. CLARKE, *Prelude to restoration in Ireland* (Cambridge, 1999).

L. E. COCHRAN, *Scottish trade with Ireland* (Cambridge, 1999).

P. COLLINS, *County Monaghan sources in the PRONI* (Belfast, 1998).

S. J. CONNOLLY (ed.), *Political ideas in eighteenth-century Ireland* (Dublin, 2000).

S. J. CONNOLLY, *Religion, law and power: The making of Protestant Ireland 1660–1760* (Oxford, 1992).

W. H. CRAWFORD, *The impact of the Domestic Linen Industry in Ulster* (2005).

W. H. CRAWFORD, *The Management of a major Ulster estate in the late eighteenth century* (2001).

W. H. CRAWFORD & R. H. FOY (eds), *Townlands in Ulster* (1998).

B. COLLINS, P. OLLERENSHAW & T. PARKHILL (eds), *Industry, Trade and People in Ireland 1650-1950* (2005).

D. A. CRONIN, *A Galway gentleman in the age of improvement: Robert French of Monivea, 1716–79* (IAP, 1995).

N. J. CURTIN, *The United Irishmen, popular politics in Ulster and in Dublin, 1791–1798* (Oxford, 1994, 1998).

D. DICKSON (ed.), *The gorgeous mask: Dublin 1700–1850* (Dublin, 1987).

D. DICKSON, *Arctic Ireland: The extraordinary story of the Great Frost and Forgotten Famine of 1740-1* (Belfast, 1997, 1998).

D. DICKSON, *New foundations: Ireland 1660–1800* (Dublin, 1987, rev. edn 2000).

D. DICKSON, *Old World Colony: Cork and South Munster 1630-1830* (2005).

T. DUNNE, *Rebellions, Memoir, Memories and 1798* (Dublin, 2003).

J. EHRMAN, *The younger Pitt* (3 vols, London, 1969–96).

M. ELLIOTT, *Wolfe Tone, prophet of Irish Independence* (Yale, 1989).

P. FAGAN, *Catholics in a Protestant Country: the papist constituency in eighteenth-century Dublin* (1998).

P. FAGAN, *Dublin's turbulent priest: Cornelius Nary, 1658-1738* (RIA, 1991).

C. J. FAUSKE (ed.), *Arbp. Wm. King and the Anglican Irish Context 1688-1729* (Dublin, 2004).

E. FITZGERALD, *Lord Kildare's grand tour 1766–1769* (Cork, 2000).

A. FORD, J. McGUIRE & K. MILNE (eds), *As by law established: the Church of Ireland since the Reformation* (Dublin, 1995).

N. GARNHAM, *The courts, crime and the criminal law in Ireland, 1692–1760* (Dublin, 1996).

P. M. GEOGHEGAN, *The Act of Union: a study in high politics* (Dublin, 1999).

H. GOUGH & D. DICKSON (eds), *Ireland and the French revolution* (Dublin, 1990).

W. G. JONES, *The Wynnes of Sligo and Leitrim: the powerful family of Hazelwood and Lurganboy* (Sligo, 1994).

D. W. HAYTON, *Ruling Ireland, 1685-1742: Politics, Politicians and Parties* (2004).

D. W. HAYTON (ed.) *The Irish Parliament in the eighteenth century: the long Apprenticeship* (2001).

M. HERON, *The hidden houses of Ireland* (1999).

J. HILL, *From Patriots to Unionists: Dublin civil politics and Irish Protestant patriotism 1660–1840* (Oxford, 1997).

F. G. JAMES, *Lords of the ascendancy: The Irish House of Lords and its members, 1600–1800* (Dublin, 1995).

N. C. KAVANAUGH, *John Fitzgibbon, Earl of Clare* (Dublin, 1997).

J. KELLY, *Henry Flood: Patriots and politics in eighteenth-century Ireland* (Dublin, 1998).

J. KELLY, *Prelude to Union* (Cork, 1992).

J. KELLY, *'That damn'd thing called honour': duelling in Ireland 1570–1860* (Cork, 1995).

J. KELLY, *Sir Edward Newenham, MP 1734-1814: Defender of the Protestant Constitution* (Dublin, 2004).

T. KING, *Carlow, the manor & town 1674–1721* (Maynooth Studies in Local History, 1997).

M. LAMBE, *A Tipperary landed estate, 1750–1853* (Dublin, 1998).

B. MacDERMOTT (ed.), *The Irish Catholic petition of 1805* (Dublin, 1992).

O. MacDONAGH, *Daniel O'Connell* (2 vols, London, 1988).

R. B. McDOWELL, *Grattan, A Life* (Dublin, 2001).

R. B. McDOWELL, *Historical Essays, 1938-2001* (Dublin, 2003).

R. B. McDOWELL (ed.), *Proceedings of the Dublin Society of United Irishmen* (Dublin, 1998).

C. I. McGRATH, *The making of the eighteenth-century Irish constitution: government, parliament and the revenue, 1692–1714* (Dublin, 2000).

A. McMANUS, *The Irish Hedge School and its books 1695-1831* (2004).

P. McNALLY, *Parties, patriots & undertakers ...* (Dublin, 1997).

E. McPARLAND, *Public architecture in Ireland, 1680–1760* (2001).

E. MAGENNIS, *The Irish political system 1740–65* (Dublin, 2000).

W. A. MAGUIRE (ed.), *Kings in conflict: the revolutionary war in Ireland and its aftermath, 1689–1750* (Belfast, 1990) [illustrations of participating personalities].

A .P. W. MALCOMSON, *Archbishop Charles Agar: churchmanship and politics in Ireland, 1760–1830* (Dublin, 2002).

A. P. W. MALCOMSON, *Nathaniel Clements, Government and the governing elites in Ireland* (2005).

A. P. W. MALCOMSON, *Primate Robinson, 1709-94* (UHF, 2003).

A. P. W. MALCOMSON, *Proc. RIA,* vol. 72, sect. 3, no. 11, 'John Foster and the Speakership of the Irish House of Commons'.

A. P. W. MALCOMSON, 'Theodosia, Countess Clanwilliam', *Familia,* no. 15 (1999).

D. MANSERGH, *Grattan's Failure* (Dublin, 2005).

D. W. MILLER, *Peep O'Day boys and defenders: select documents on the disturbances in Co. Armagh, 1784–1796* (PRONI, 1990).

K. MILNE, *The Irish charter schools 1730–1830* (Dublin, 1997).

R. MITCHINSON & P. ROEBUCK (eds), *Economy and Society in Scotland and Ireland 1500-1939* (1988).

G. O'BRIEN (ed.), *Catholic Ireland in the eighteenth century: collected essays of Maureen Wall* (Dublin, 1989).

G. O'BRIEN (ed.), *Parliament, politics and people: essays in eighteenth-century Irish history* (Dublin, 1989).

J. O'BRIEN & D. GUINNESS, *Dublin: A grand tour* (1994).

J. O'BRIEN & D. GUINNESS, *Great Irish houses and castles* (London, 1992).

B. Ó DÁLAIGH, *Ennis in the 18th century: portrait of an urban community* (Dublin, 1995).

Royal Historical Society Transactions 2000 (section on 'The British–Irish Union of 1801').

J. SMYTH, *The Men of no property: Irish radicals and popular politics in the late eighteenth century* (Dublin, 1992).

A. T. Q. STEWART, *A Deeper Silence ...* (Belfast, 1998 edn).

A. T. Q. STEWART, *The shape of Irish history* (Belfast, 2001).

A. T. Q. STEWART, *The summer soldiers: The 1798 rebellion in Antrim and Down* (Belfast, 1995).

L. SWORDS, *The Irish in the French Revolution, 1789–1815* (Dublin, 1989).

W. A. THOMAS, *The stock exchanges of Ireland* (Dublin, 1986).

T. M. TRUXES, *Irish-American trade 1660–1783* (Cambridge, 1988).

T. M. TRUXES (ed.) *Letterbook of Greg & Cunningham 1756-7: Merchants of New York and Belfast* (2001).

J. WALTON, 'The King's business': letters on the administration of Ireland, 1741–61 ... (New York, 1996).

E. WASSON, *Born to rule: British political elites* (Stroud, 2000).

K. WHELAN, *The Tree of Liberty: radicalism, Catholicism and the construction of Irish identity, 1760–1830* (Cork, 1996).

THE PEERAGE

The ranks of the peerage are as follows:

1 Sovereign
2 Royal Family
3 Duke (Duchess)
4 Marquess (Marchioness)
5 Earl (Countess)
6 Viscount (Viscountess)
7 Baron (Baroness)

A duke and the four archbishops were usually called 'Your Grace', but 4, 5, 6 and 7 were called, without distinction, Lord/Lady (name of title). English/British peerages took precedence over Scottish or Irish peerages.

The eldest sons of 3, 4 and 5 were commoners but known by their father's senior subordinate title, so as the father advanced in the peerage the son advanced also, e.g. Arthur Hill (**1016**) was successively Viscount Kilwarlin (I), Viscount Fairfield (GB), Earl of Hillsborough (I & GB) and, on the death of his father, 2nd Marquess of Downshire (I). William FitzGerald (**0745**) was successively Lord William FitzGerald, Earl of Offaly (I), Marquess of Kildare (I) and, on the death of his father, 2nd Duke of Leinster (I). Until they succeeded their fathers they were commoners and as such eligible to sit in the House of Commons, but commonly called by their (successive) titles. Similarly an Irish peer, for instance Lord Hillsborough or Lord Shelburne (before they got British peerages) or the nineteenth-century Prime Ministers Lord Melbourne or Lord Palmerston, could sit in the British House of Commons because they were Irish and not British or United Kingdom peers. All the daughters of earls and the younger sons of marquesses and dukes were known as Lord or Lady _____ _____. The younger son of an earl was simply the Hon. _____ .

Peerages descended in the male line. Some Scottish and a few English medieval peerages could be inherited by women, but these were very unusual. Some eminent Irish politicians, for instance John Hely-Hutchinson (**1001**) and John Foster (**0805**), had as a special mark of distinction peerages conferred on their wives with remainder to their male heirs by them. Very rarely when a peerage was conferred it might have a special remainder to the descendants of the peer's father or to a nephew, for instance Sir Laurence Parsons (**1636**) succeeded his uncle (**0968**) as 2nd Earl of Rosse, and Warner Westenra (**2221**) succeeded his uncle (**0559**) as 2nd Lord Rossmore, but usually the peerage had to be re-created, as in the case of the Earl of Farnham, when two brothers who inherited their father's title as 2nd and 3rd Lords Farnham (**1377**, **1372**) were both created 1st Earl of Farnham and the two Lords Annaly (**0869**,

0867), who were both created 1st Baron Annaly. Immediately an MP either succeeded or was elevated to the peerage his seat in the Commons was vacated. He went to 'the other House' (House of Lords) and a by-election was held for his seat in the Commons.

Knights and baronets were not peers and could sit in the House of Commons. A knighthood could not be inherited and became extinct on the death of its holder. A baronetcy was hereditary and was inherited by the male heirs of its original holder.

Name Changes

There was no uniformity in the spelling of eighteenth-century surnames. The general rule has been to place an MP by using the surname under which he first appeared in the *Commons Journals*. This does produce anomalies, i.e. father and son spelling their surname differently, e.g. John Cleare (**0421**) and Thomas Cleere (**0422**). The taking of an additional name, e.g. MEADE (-OGLE), after the first appearance does not affect the place in the alphabetical sequence. However, an inherited additional surname, e.g. SEYMOUR-CONWAY, or a surname taken before the first appearance in parliament, e.g. BOYLE-WALSINGHAM, does and, therefore, comes after the original surname, e.g. BOYLE-WALSINGHAM after the BOYLEs. Additional surnames are usually (when first used) cross-referenced for the sake of clarity. The taking of a surname in lieu of an original surname, e.g. HULL (TONSON), after the first appearance does not affect the sequence but it is cross-referenced from TONSON. When a surname is taken in lieu before the first appearance in *Commons jn. Ire.*, e.g. FREKE (EVANS), the family name is given in brackets and there is a cross-reference from it to the adopted name. Surnames were frequently changed to meet the requirements of wills and even changed back again, as in the case of **1371** who started life as Barry Maxwell then in 1771 changed his surname to Barry, that of his maternal grandfather, and in 1779 on inheriting the title of Baron Farnham from his brother, back again to Maxwell.

Calendar

Before 2 September 1752 this can cause confusion as the year ended on 25 March so that the first three months of a year belonged to the previous year. In general it is assumed that the Julian rather than the Gregorian calendar has been used before September 1752. Some secondary sources changed the date and others did not; where this is known the date is written in the form 1725/6. This problem can be reflected in an apparent discrepancy of dates.

1

BACKGROUND

[Bold numbers refer to MPs biographies, *History of the Irish Parliament*, vols 3-6; see web site. Italic numbers refer to statutes as listed in the *History,* vol. I; see web site]

I INTRODUCTION: THE FRACTURED SOCIETY

The Irish parliament met for the first time on 18 June 1264 at Castledermott, and for the last time in the Parliament House in Dublin on 2 August 1800. From 1707 it was the only parliament in the British Empire with the medieval structure of King (represented by the Lord Lieutenant), Lords and Commons. In their introduction to *The Irish Parliament in the Middle Ages*, H. G. Richardson and G. O. Sayles wrote that: 'The kings of England brought to Ireland a two-fold gift, imperfect perhaps but of inestimable worth – parliament and the Common Law.'[1] They also pointed out that it was *gesta Dei per Francos* for the Irish, like the British parliament, was part of the European parliamentary movement of the thirteenth century. In fact the first meeting of the Irish parliament preceded that of the English parliament – if only by a few months. Thus the Irish parliament developed in parallel with the English parliament and in the eighteenth century it adjusted both to contemporary British practices and to Irish conditions. Before 1692 its meetings, like those of the English and Scottish parliaments, were erratic and peripatetic; for instance, the parliament that passed Poynings' Law 10 Henry VII Ire. c. 4, the statute which, until 1782, required all Irish legislation to have the prior approval of the Irish and English Privy Councils before it even came before the Irish parliament, was passed at a parliament meeting at Drogheda, while important meetings of the English parliament had been held at Oxford and of the Scottish parliament at St Andrews. Continuously established parliamentary politics as a method of political administration was new to both Great Britain and Ireland in the aftermath of the 1688 revolution and the 25 years which followed were a period of learning and adjustment. The wars of William III and Anne ensured that finance, the traditional motivator of parliament, would play a major part in the development of parliament in all three countries.

[1] H. G. Richardson and G. O. Sayles, *The Irish Parliament in the Middle Ages* (Philadelphia, 1964) p. 280.

Volumes 1 and 2 of the *History of the Irish Parliament* contain a series of essays and tables looking at three broad topics: who went to parliament, how they got there, and what they did there.[2] The four volumes 3,4,5,6, contain brief biographies of the 2,272 MPs[3] who went to parliament during this period; their names are listed here from page 106. Volume 2 is concerned with the constituencies – how, and under what conditions, the MPs got there. The business and interests of parliament are reflected in its statutes (see the web site: *www.historyoftheirishparliament.com*). Constraints of space would make it impossible to write a detailed sessional, let alone daily, history of the Irish parliament, but its achievements are reflected in the public statutes. These are published in 20 large folio volumes, of which 17 relate to this period. In the 110 years that separate the Battle of the Boyne from the Act of Union, the *Statutes at Large of the Kingdom of Ireland* record 1,962 public statutes passed by the Irish parliament, 982 before 1783, the session in which Poynings' Law was amended, and 980[4] afterwards. There were also a number of private statutes, which are listed in the *Journals* at the end of each session of parliament after the public statutes. These are mainly concerned with family matters such as divorce and the breaking of entails.

The seventeenth century was a period of enormous social change and disruption. Beginning with the Flight of the Earls and the Plantation of Ulster, it ended with the confiscations following William III's victories at Londonderry, the Boyne, Aughrim and finally Limerick. Although each of these added its own psychological consequences to the eighteenth century, they were preceded by much greater changes, as between 1641 and 1660 there was a major change in landholding.[5] The interregnum of the 1650s brought, in support of parliament and the Lord Protector, a great influx of speculators and adventurers of various kinds. The conquistador Bernal Diaz[6] (whose works were translated by the Irish MP Maurice Bagenal St Leger Keating (**1135**)) said of his deceased comrades 'they died in the service of God and of His Majesty, and to give light to those who sit in darkness – *and also to acquire that wealth which most men covet*'. These words, with slight adjustments, could equally be applied to the men who came to Ireland in the train of Cromwell and his armies. Wars are expensive and civil wars particularly so, as their costs both materially and otherwise have to be met within the society where they occur. Parliament had to pay its victorious troops and this was done by grants of land confiscated from their opponents. Confiscated land was used to pay war speculators and some 35,000 soldiers. Often these were quite small amounts

---

[2] These two chapters, 2 and 3, are intended to give a basic background to this *Introduction to the Internet*; they are supplements to the essays in the *History of the Irish Parliament* vols 1 and 2, not substitutes. Given the technical and introductory nature of this volume some duplication is inevitable.

[3] I originally thought that there was only one Frederick Trench whereas there were two, cousins and contemporary with each other. The internet entry has been altered accordingly.

[4] See *HIP* vol. I pp. 584-93 esp. p. 93 for a breakdown of these.

[5] S. J. Connolly, *Religion, law and power: the making of Protestant Ireland 1660-1760* (Oxford, 1992) pp. 13-14.

[6] Bernal Diaz (ed.), J. M. Cohen, *Conquest of New Spain* (Penguin, 1963); various editions paraphrase this quotation in different ways. The italics are mine.

and inevitably some recipients were glad to sell their grants and receive hard cash in these troubled times, while others collected small holdings into often scattered estates. After the death of Cromwell many of those who had come to prominence during his regime were quite happy to support the restored monarchy so long as they could retain their newly acquired possessions.[7]

Nevertheless, at the Restoration in 1660 royalists demanded a restoration of their property and some adjustments were made to meet their demands. The wily Charles II, making supportive gestures to both sides, left this problem to the wisdom of the Irish Restoration Parliament called in 1661. The situation was impossible, and its resolution in the Act of Settlement 1662 and the Act of Explanation in 1665 proved haphazard and inevitably unsatisfactory. Parliament was dissolved in 1666, and this was the last predominantly Protestant parliament which met before 1692. Land was, and remained, the basis of social, political and economic power – the principal wealth of the country. Ultimately, the uneasy result of these arrangements was that between 1641 and the Revolution in 1688 the percentage of land owned by Roman Catholics dropped steeply: while religion and landholding cannot be precisely determined, or equated, this was a very considerable change in land ownership, most of which took place during the Commonwealth and proved irreversible at the Restoration. Thus a completely new social elite emerged at the Restoration, and it was these new men who formed the majority in the eighteenth-century Irish parliament.

By 1690 the unfused society which had existed since the arrival of Henry II's Anglo-Norman barons in 1169 had reached another dimension. Before the Reformation created a religious divide, the numerical limitation of the settlers ensured that a measure of social unity had been partially acquired by the settlers 'going native'. The Elizabethan and Stuart settlements had introduced the divisive element of religion, while greater numbers and confiscations encouraged the emergence of exclusive groupings. Finally, the settlement in the aftermath of the revolutionary wars left the largest religious group, the Catholic Irish, without sufficient natural secular leaders and their accompanying infrastructure. The long duration of the Revolution Settlement favoured the development of stability in England while it prolonged uncertainty in Ireland. Furthermore, James Edward Stuart did not die until 1766 and during his lifetime the Pope adhered to his ecclesiastical nominations. On the secular side there was the presence of the Irish Brigade recruited from Ireland who served particularly, though not exclusively, in the armies of France with whom England was periodically at war throughout the century. These were ever-present practical problems and their fundamentally divisive nature consolidated the divisions in Irish society. This destruction of a natural infrastructure meant that when leadership was restored to the Catholic majority not surprisingly it had a mitre rather than a coronet, for despite the

---

[7] A. Clarke, *Prelude to Restoration in Ireland* (1999), gives a detailed interpretation of this difficult period.

recurrent efforts of a minority,[8] who realised the inherent dangers in the situation, its long continuance had solidified it. There were some attempts, particularly in the latter half of the century, to create unifying links. For instance, as the century progressed Freemasonary became very popular. This had both a vertical and a horizontal dimension as membership was open to all levels of society, from the Duke of Leinster and the Marquess of Downshire to the Ulster weavers,[9] and despite the strictures of the Catholic Church many Catholics joined this as well as other associations.

Furthermore, dynastic uncertainty aggravated the situation. Charles II was without a legitimate heir, and the aggrieved could hope that their wrongs might be rectified under his Catholic brother and heir apparent. But before this could be achieved, James II had alienated his English subjects and made Ireland a theatre of a European war, which enabled William III and his wife, James II's Protestant daughter, Mary II, to consolidate their positions. Not only was the *status quo* of Charles II's land settlement retained but it was consolidated by a further wave of confiscations. Meanwhile the uncertainty continued: William and Mary were childless and by 1700 all of Anne's large family had died.

In 1542, 33 Henry VIII, c. 1 [Ire.], declared that the King of England, previously styled Lord of Ireland, was *ipso facto* King of Ireland (interestingly, this act was brought before parliament in both Irish and English). Therefore the Act of Settlement 11 & 12 Will. III, c. 2 [Eng], passed by the English parliament in 1701, also applied to Ireland. This act settled the English crown on the Electress Sophia of Hanover, a granddaughter of James I, and her heirs being protestant. Nevertheless, no one was quite sure what would happen when Anne died. An integral part of the problem was the long uncertainty over the succession and its perceived interconnection with the finality of the land settlement. This uncertainty lasted certainly until 1746, and the threat even longer. Throughout the century nothing aroused such fear in parliament as that attainders might be reversed and estates restored to their former owners – despite the fact that as the years passed unscrambling changes in landholding would have been virtually impossible. In the 1730s Lord Clancarty, who was a British naval officer and Governor of Newfoundland from 1733 to 1735, endeavoured to persuade the British cabinet in 1736 to consider a bill to reverse his father's attainder and restore his family estates in Co. Cork, which had an income estimated at £60,000 p.a. When this became known in Ireland panic ensued and Archbishop Boulter warned Newcastle that:

> I can assure your Lordship anything of this nature will be a great blow to the Protestant interest here, and will very much shake the security Protestants think they now have of

---

[8] For the early Hanoverian period see, F. Fagan, *Dublin's turbulent priest: Cornelius Nary 1658-1738* (RIA, 1991) esp. pp.116, 120, 122; pp. 138-9 give Dr Nary and Archbishop Synge of Tuam's formulation of an oath to bridge the gap between the Catholics and the government.

[9] D. Akenson & W. H. Crawford, *James Orr, Bard of Ballycarry* (1977) p. 26.

the enjoyment of their estates ... and I think the affair of the last [utmost] importance to the Protestant interest here.[10]

Clancarty's appeal was rejected and he joined the Jacobites in France; subsequently he was implicated in the 1745 rebellion and died in exile. His was not the only, though perhaps the most prominent case. For instance, in 1755 Sir Thomas Prendergast (1725) appealed to the House of Commons for protection against the O'Shaughnessys who, since 1731, had been seeking a reversal of the estate of Gort granted to his father (1724) for 'discovering' the 1696 plot against William III. The House of Commons resolved to proceed against all such claimants 'as persons endeavouring to lessen the Protestant interest of this kingdom'.

As late as 1789 John Fitzgibbon (0749), counselling caution at the time of the Regency crisis, reiterated this fear when he reminded the House that:

> The Act by which most of us hold our estates was an Act of violence – an Act subverting the first principles of the common Law in England and Ireland. I speak of the Act of Settlement; and that gentlemen may know the extent... I will tell them that every acre of land which pays quit rent to the crown is held by title derived under the Act of Settlement. [11]

Apart from institutional holdings, such as the established Church, Dublin University and, in the north, the Irish Society, early eighteenth-century estates were fluid entities as ownership of various portions changed with inheritance, marriage, sale, purchase, or even exchange. But by the end of the century lack of fluidity and an increasing burden of debt were beginning to create problems. The maps overleaf illustrate the impact of the seventeenth-century changes.

Even after the Flight of the Earls and the Plantation of Ulster, nearly 60 per cent of the land was still in Catholic hands in 1641; by 1688 this had fallen to 22 per cent and by 1703 to 14 per cent. The Williamite confiscation added only about 8 per cent to the total confiscation. Although the confiscations following the Treaty of Limerick were restrained, they were the final instalment of a continual attrition over 150 years, and longer if a medieval component is added; for England had never really established an effective hegemony over Ireland, while the penal laws of Queen Anne's reign led to even further if gradual reductions. By 1778 Catholic proprietors were in receipt of only 1.5 per cent of the rental of Ireland – £60,000 out of a total rental estimated at £4,000,000. This was partly as a result of the gavelling clause in the penal statute, 2

---

[10] *Boulter Letters* vol. 2 pp. 118-20.
[11] *Irish Parliamentary Debates,* 20 Feb. 1789, quoted in J. A. Froude, *The English in Ireland in the eighteenth-century* (1901), vol. II pp. 552-4. Fitzgibbon is referring to the 1662 Act of Settlement, 14 and 15 Charles II Ire., c. 2. See *infra* p. 215. There is a fuller version of this quotation in *History of the Irish Parliament,* vol. I pp. 168-9.

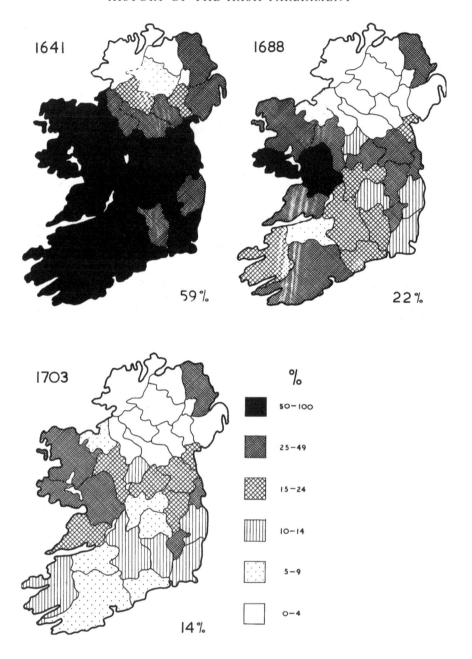

Maps by J. G. Simms showing the proportion of land owned by Catholics in Ireland according to counties in 1641, 1688 and 1703. The effect of the Cromwellian confiscation, as modified at the Restoration, is indicated by the first and second maps, and the effect of the Williamite confiscation by the second and third maps.

Source: T. W. Moody and F. X. Martin (eds), *The Course of Irish History*, 3rd edn (Cork, 1994) p. 201.
Used by permission of the family of the late J. G. Simms and with the consent of Radio Telefís Éireann.

Anne, c. 6 *(0068)*, 'an Act to prevent the further growth of popery', and was confirmed in 1709 by 8 Anne, c. 3 *(0119)*. It was also the most severe of the penal laws for the non-conforming protestant dissenting society.

Although the Commonwealth immigrants had brought with them a considerable diversity of religious opinion, the Restoration and especially the Revolution Settlement decided, not entirely for religious reasons, that despite its paucity of numbers (probably not more than 10 per cent), the established Church of Ireland would be Anglican.[12] Its position was confirmed by the penal code which affected Catholics and Dissenters in varying ways and to varying degrees. Based on religious discrimination, these laws had widespread social, political and economic consequences for Catholic landholding. But they also reflected the insecurity of the Protestants with their memories of the rebellions and uncertainties of the seventeenth century. The Restoration parliament of Charles II had been dissolved in 1666 after failing to achieve the impossible, namely to resolve the problems arising from the redistribution of land during the Commonwealth. The parliament of James II which met from 7 May to 18 July 1689 was preoccupied with the land problem as perceived by the Catholics, who had been dispossessed by the Cromwellian redistribution. But the length of the interregnum, and of the later Revolution settlement, was to make any undoing of the land settlements practically impossible.

There can be no clearer indication of the vast changes brought about by the social upheaval of the seventeenth century than the fact that every eighteenth-century Speaker came from a family which had emerged from obscurity in the seventeenth century, usually during the interregnum. The Levinges (**1230**) were a post-Restoration family originally from Derbyshire; Rochfort (**1806**), Speaker in 1695, was the son of 'Prime Iron' Rochfort, a lieutenant-colonel in Cromwell's army (executed for killing another officer in a duel); Brodrick's (**0237**) father, Sir St John Brodrick, had received large grants of land in Co. Cork under the Protectorate and also for his part in the Restoration; Conolly (**0460**) was reputed to have come from humble Irish origins and made his wealth as possibly the most successful land speculator of the post-Revolution period. Sir Ralph Gore (**0872**) was the descendant of a late sixteenth-century alderman of London who had eight sons, some of whom sought their fortune in Ireland and obtained grants of land in the north and west of Ireland in the early seventeenth century. Henry Boyle (**0210**), Gore's successor, was a descendant of Richard Boyle, Earl of Cork, the great Cork and Waterford land speculator and entrepreneur of the early seventeenth century, whose son, Lord Broghill, figured prominently during the Protectorate. John Ponsonby's (**1702**) ancestor was colonel of a regiment of horse under Cromwell and obtained two grants of land confirmed at the Act of Settlement;

---

[12] See A. Ford, J. McGuire & K. Milne (eds), *As by law established: the Church of Ireland since the Reformation* (Dublin, 1995).

the ancestors of Pery (**1671**), his successor, came to Ireland about 1650 because a Nicholas Pery had met, in London, a Miss Sexton and it was through her that Speaker Pery acquired his name and Limerick estates.[13] John Foster (**0805**), the last Speaker of the Irish House of Commons, did not date his ancestry further back than the mid-seventeenth century. Very few MPs who sat in the parliaments of William III had any previous parliamentary experience. There were probably only about six MPs who sat in both the parliaments of James II and William III.

But, while a mixture of fear and consequent hatred was undoubtedly a dominant element, in this simplistic approach there were both Catholics and Protestants concerned by the divided society created and confirmed by these sectarian measures. Then, as already noticed, after the death of James II the acknowledgment of his son as James III, *de iure* King of England by both Louis XIV and the Pope, created a problem, as did the presence of the Irish Brigade under Louis XIV and his successors and the papal recognition of 'James III's' claims to patronage over Irish Church appointments. Probably the tranquil succession of the Hanoverian dynasty encouraged some to accept the *status quo* and to strive for a way of working within it. In 1724 the parish priest of St Michans, Fr Cornelius Nary,[14] who held a doctorate of Civil and Canon Law from the University of Paris, published the *Case of the Roman Catholics of Ireland* in which he argued for the provision of an oath acceptable to both sides, and the possibility of this solution flickers throughout the intervening decades. An insurmountable problem was the longevity of 'James III' who did not die until 1766. However, the Pope did not confirm his successor, Charles Edward, in his father's *de iure* position, thereby belatedly easing the position of British and Irish Catholics. Although the Irish Brigade was not dissolved until the French Revolution and substantial amelioration was not achieved until the 1770s – with the 1776 oath *(0767)* and the acts sponsored by Luke Gardiner (**0842**) in 1778 *(0867)* and 1782 *(0980)* – a minority of MPs and churchmen were not unaware of the problem and its long-term danger throughout the century. Among these were Bishop Synge in the first half of the century and the Earl-Bishop of Derry in the second. In the middle of the century James Hamilton (**0934**), Earl of Clanbrassill, presented a petition to Lord Lieutenant Bedford for registering Catholic clergy, which contained an oath that was acceptable to many Catholics. Clanbrassill also increased the prosperity of his local town, Dundalk, giving it a 'prosperous and consequential appearance' by establishing a cambric manufacture. As the century progressed a growing minority became increasingly convinced that a house divided against itself cannot stand, particularly as the politically excluded Catholics and Dissenters became ever more wealthy and correspondingly resentful of the privileged

---

[13] I am indebted to Dr A. P. W. Malcomson for this information, which came from Lord Limerick. It is in a speech which he made in Limerick in 1995 and is published in *Georgian Limerick* (Limerick, 1996).

[14] S. J. Connolly, op. cit. p.159 – despite his abilities, Nary was not among 'James III's' ecclesiastical recommendations!

position of the Protestant ascendancy. Then, in the last decade of the century, the French Revolution and the '98 rebellion confirmed the fears of the majority and they sought security in the Union.

Land is limited, but it was the key to political power, locally as well as nationally. In 1844, when the laws affecting Catholic ownership and acquisition of land had been repealed for over 60 years, the Devon Commissioners still found their influence pervasive, commenting that: 'they interfered with almost every mode of dealing with landed property by those who professed that religion, and by creating a feeling of insecurity directly checked their industry.' They added that the political implications of the laws during their enforcement had boomeranged on the protestant landlords by restricting their choice of tenant, 'for in letting their estates they were to a great degree confined in the selection of their tenants, to those who alone could enjoy any permanent tenure under them and were exclusively entitled to the elective franchise'.[15] Until 1778, only protestants could hold a tenancy for life or lives which carried with it the vote, but until 1793 Catholics who were so qualified could not exercise the franchise.

'The laws against popery have so far operated,' remarked Lord Townshend in 1772, 'that at this day there is no popish family remaining of any great weight from landed property',[16] The 1704 Act 2 Anne, c. 6 *(0068, 0119)* contained a gavelling clause which allowed the eldest son of a Catholic if he became a Protestant to make his father a tenant for life, otherwise the inheritance was divided among the sons. However, Townshend's statement was extreme for there were some, for example the Brownes, Lords Kenmare, who had the good fortune to produce a single son and heir in succeeding generations during the penal period, and there were others whose conformity to the new regime was dubious. There were the 'reluctant conformists' – for example, De Latocnaye, visiting Galway in 1796, reported that:

> Nearly all the inhabitants in this district are Catholics, rich as well as poor; only the rich submitted, formerly to the Anglican form, in order that they might possess their goods in peace, and, now, in order that they may be eligible for election to Parliament. Thirty years ago the proprietor of a very fine estate called Oranmore, fearing that some cousin might turn Protestant in order to filch it from him, sought the bishop and offered to renounce the superstitions of the Church of Rome. 'What motives my son' said the pastor 'urge you to enter the fold of the faithful …?' 'Oranmore' replied the convert, and to all the customary questions he had but the single word – 'Oranmore' – for answer.[17]

[15] *Report from Her Majesty's Commissioners of Inquiry into the state of the Law and Practice in respect of the Occupation of Land in Ireland,* HC, 1845 (*Devon Rep.*) p. 7.
[16] *Cal. HO Papers 1770-2,* no. 1218 p. 477, Townshend to Rochford.
[17] De Latocnaye, *Frenchman's walk* (Dublin, 1797 trans. Belfast, 1917) p.146; see also *History of Irish Catholicism* (Dublin, 1971) vol. iv p. 2, J. Brady & P. J. Corish, *The Church under the Penal Code.*

The hope was that if the father was a reluctant conformist the children would conform automatically. In an overwhelmingly Catholic community this was a questionable assumption. Any career which involved taking the oath of supremacy and abjuration was barred to both Catholics and non-conformists, who were officially unable to hold any office under the crown.

The following extract from Lord Kenmare's notes on his estate in the 1750s illustrates both his discretion and the problems which, in the penal era, confronted even a fortunate Catholic landlord. Given the often scattered nature of their lands many landlords were anxious to purchase small acreages to round off their estates, and details of such purchases are to be found in estate papers. Lord Kenmare writes that:

> If ever my family should be capable of purchasing this farm [Clounmelane] would deserve it best of any in Kerry as it is surrounded on every side by our lands. It was offered to be sold me by McMahon the tenant at my coming of age but I ever avoided meddling in purchases as I scarce know the trustee I would depend on and wrangles or roguery on this head might stagger a man in the most determined resolution of (what is in all matters the most essential) his religion.[18]

Occasionally, friendly Protestants nominally held land in trust for Catholics and some families had Catholic and Protestant branches. This 'trusteeship' was illegal, so that not only did the Catholic owner have no security against fraud, but both the owner and the trustee ran the risk of being discovered by an informer.[19] Nevertheless, Catholic landlords could and did exert electoral influence through their protestant tenants.

By statute (0264) Catholics were unable to practise law and this too encouraged widespread nominal conformity. Many potential lawyers left London as Catholics and arrived in Dublin as certified members of the established church. The most famous of these was John Fitzgibbon (0248), the father of Lord Chancellor Clare (0749); while some conversions may have been genuine, membership of the established church brought with it economic and social as well as spiritual benefits. In December 1767 Lord Lieutenant Townshend wrote to Lord Shelburne pointing out that 'the lawyers of eminence here are always in Parliament', and in the last parliament of Ireland, called in 1797, it was estimated that there were fifty barristers who 'had always considered a seat in Parliament as the road to preferment'. The ascendancy (as the Protestant elite came to be called) were a litigious but a legalistic society, and the parliamentary statutes covered a very wide spectrum of every-day life; for instance, in 1721, 8 George I, c. 2 (0209) was one of a number of statutes which dealt with the process for the ejection of tenants, while 2 George I, c. 17 (0166) considered *inter alia* wages and other employment problems.

The vast majority of the population in Leinster, Munster and Connacht were

---

[18] *IMC Kenmare* p. 193.
[19] Ibid. p. xi.

Catholics. In Ulster, the fourth province, large-scale migration from Scotland in the seventeenth-century had ensured that the majority were Presbyterian. The Presbyterians owned little land outright and Presbyterian landowners, with some notable exceptions, usually conformed within a generation or two. For the Catholic landowners the situation was much more severe. No Catholic sat in parliament from 1692 to 1828. No Catholic, or protestant married to a Catholic, could vote from 1727 until 1793, and it is possible that the 1727 act *(0253)* only clarified and consolidated a widely existing tradition.[20] Nevertheless, despite their vicissitudes the remnants of the old Irish nobility did, mindful of past glories, retain a separate identity. Arthur Young, visiting Roscommon in 1776, commented on the formality of one of the leading Gaelic chieftains: 'O'Connor, the direct descendant of Roderick O'Connor, who was King of Connacht ... [whose] possessions formerly so great are reduced to £300 or £400 a year receives presents of cattle etc. upon various occasions. They consider him as the Prince of a people involved in one common ruin.'[21] Possibly these cattle were the vestiges of the traditional dues of a Gaelic chief. Some years later De Latocnaye also commented on the 'ceremonious respect' accorded to the O'Connor, adding that 'I have been told his domestics serve him kneeling' and that 'the crown of gold of the last monarch is said to be in the possession of the family, although there are those who think it has been disposed of to a jeweler.'[22]

Isolation was reduced, and identity reinforced, by the continental connection, kept alive firstly by the Catholic Church, whose clergy were educated there and many of whom remained in the Irish Colleges in France, Spain and Austria as well as in other ecclesiastical occupations and secondly by the Irish Brigade – soldiers recruited from Ireland fighting under foreign monarchs and often against Great Britain. It was and remained throughout the century a complex social mix. The ascendancy was always very conscious, and scared of the under-currents of the fractured society over which it presided. In 1778 Arthur Browne (0252), a lawyer and Fellow of Trinity College, expressed its fears, when, speaking on the anti-terrorist Whiteboy Act, 27 Geo. III, c. 15 *(1182)*, he stated that whereas: 'in other countries the land title is purchase, here it is forfeiture. The old proprietor feeds the eternal memory of his ancient claim. The property of this country resembles the thin soil of volcanic countries, lightly spread over subterraneous fires.'[23] This view was confirmed by reports of the descendants of once great families still bequeathing their former estates to their sons.[24] This is often characteristic of a people who feel that they have been deprived by military rather than economic means – a similar tradition existed among Moors expelled from Granada

[20] *IHS* (1960) vol. XII no. 45 pp. 28-37, J. G. Simms, 'Irish Catholics and the parliamentary franchise, 1692-1728', esp. p. 37.
[21] A. Young, *A tour in Ireland 1776-9*, vol. I p. 219.
[22] De Latocnaye, op. cit., p. 286.
[23] *Parl. Reg.* vol. VII p. 229.
[24] Young, op. cit. vol. I p. 300.

by the Catholic Sovereigns in 1492 and the Spanish driven out of Jamaica by the British in 1654.

Protestant dissenters mainly came in the seventeenth century and they came originally to seek a better life; indeed, for many Ulster was a stepping-stone to the land of the opportunity they were being denied – North America. Non-conforming churches were organised on congregational rather than strictly territorial, or parish, lines. The most numerous protestant dissenters belonged to the Presbyterian Church in Ireland – its title reflecting its connection with the wider reformed community in Europe and in particular with its 'established' parent church in Scotland, with which it was closely linked. Their speech, education and way of life were all Scottish. Largely concentrated in the province of Ulster, they deeply resented the dominant legal position of the Church of Ireland and attempted with some success to exercise ecclesiastical jurisdiction over their adherents on questions of faith and morals. They particularly resented Church control over wills, marriages and education. Presbyterian authority, like that of the Catholic Church, was based on moral and community pressures, not the force of law. These pressures were often strong, and the implicit dichotomy that this created between communal attitudes and the law of the land has remained one of the long-standing issues in Irish history. For instance, in 1719 Archbishop King wrote to the Archbishop of Canterbury about the basic reason for retaining the penal law against the Presbyterians, emphasising that:

> The true point between them and the gentlemen is whether the Presbyterians and lay elders in every parish shall have the greatest influence over the people, to lead them as they please, or the landlords over their tenants. This may help your Grace in some degree to see the reason why the Parliament is so unanimous against taking off the test.[25]

The fear, not without substance, was that the close-knit structure of Presbyterianism would create a state within a state.

So long as their co-religionist William III reigned, Presbyterians enjoyed a certain degree of protection, but thereafter they were deeply concerned by the penal legislation of Queen Anne, especially the 1703 statute *(0068)*. Presbyterians were seriously affected as regards marriages, wills, education and membership of municipal corporations. Even between Presbyterians, Presbyterian marriages were illegal until 1782, and interdenominational marriages until 1844, but, although excluded from municipal corporations, they retained the county franchise and the right to sit in parliament.[26]

[25] BL Add. MS 6117; C. S. King, *A great archbishop of Dublin, William King DD* (1906), p. 218; for an explanation of King's concern see J. M. Barkley, *The eldership in Irish Presbyterianism* (1963).

[26] It is for this reason that Protestant (as by law established) refers to Anglicans and protestant to all protestant denominations. Presbyterian marriages were considered invalid – in some respects as late as 1844, *Regina v. Willis* – and as wills &c. were probated in the Church courts this affected questions of legitimacy and inheritance. Marriages conducted by Catholic priests were invariably legal throughout the penal period as Catholic priests were ordained in the apostolic succession.

Although disfranchised from municipal corporations in 1703 (*0068*), the Presbyterians retained the county vote and they could occasionally, as at Lisburn in 1783, cause an electoral upset. As early as the 1690s Sir Richard Cox, while paying lip-service to toleration for 'all friends to the State', was anxious to maintain an exclusively Anglican ascendancy. People might go to heaven as they pleased but only through the portals of the Established Church might they participate in the government, practise law or enter Dublin University. To this end he moved that Presbyterians be excluded from all public offices, civil or military. Presbyterian loyalty was secured by their long-standing antipathy towards the Roman Catholic Church. In times of crisis, the government sought in various ways, mainly through a series of temporary indemnity acts, to try to surmount, without giving way to, the disadvantages hindering their utility *(0194,0277)*.

For the victors, the tapestries on the walls of the House of Lords were a reminder of the siege of Derry and the Battle of the Boyne and memories of the seventeenth century were kept alive by annual commemorative events, such as the service of thanksgiving commemorating salvation from the 1641 rebellion and the celebration of the birthday of King William III. Security, never far from their minds, was emphasised by military barracks built throughout the country *(0050)*, with corresponding pluses (security and the local economy) and minuses (various requisitions) for the community *(0281,0459,1246)*. Their distinctive mark, the Church of Ireland 'by law established', was Anglican in form and was, though subsequently disestablished in 1869, merged with the Church of England in 1800. The two hierarchies, Catholic and Anglican, were territorially similar but not identical. While both churches used the traditional diocesan system, the dioceses were variously united for purposes of ecclesiastical administration; for example, the Church of Ireland united the dioceses of Cork and Ross, and the Catholic Church the dioceses of Cloyne and Ross. As the established or official church, the Church of Ireland exercised secular judicial and administrative functions, which impinged on the everyday lives of Anglicans and non-Anglicans alike, for instance, over matters affecting family life. The parish was an important unit of civil as well as of ecclesiastical administration. Acts of parliament often assigned to the vestry responsibilities in connection with such secular duties as the oversight of rates, beggars, police and the watch. Until 1760 the parish was responsible for local roads – an unpopular task, though probably not as unpopular as the Church's role in collecting the tithes, which were levied on the entire population, and granting probate on wills.

II LOCAL GOVERNMENT

The system of local government was theoretically the same in Ireland as in England and the Irish landlord or his representative, usually his agent, participated in many similar duties. A brief look at land divisions will help to clarify the origins, often lost in antiquity, of strange place names and administrative units. By the eighteenth century the four traditional provinces had no political or administrative significance, and only a vestigial ecclesiastical one, reflected in the four archbishoprics – Armagh, Dublin, Cashel and Tuam – whose holders were respectively the Primate of all Ireland, the Primate of Ireland, the Primate of Munster and the Primate of Connacht. By the beginning of the seventeenth century the four provinces had been divided into the 32 counties of modern Ireland. In Ulster, the northern province, there were nine counties: Donegal, Londonderry, Antrim, Down, Armagh, Tyrone, Fermanagh, Cavan and Monaghan. Leinster, the most prosperous of the provinces, contained the eastern counties of Louth, Meath, Dublin, Wicklow, Wexford, Carlow, Kildare, Westmeath, Longford, King's County (Offaly), Queen's County (Leix) and Kilkenny. Munster, the southern province, comprised the south and south-west counties of Waterford, Cork, Kerry, Limerick, Tipperary and Clare. In the west, Connacht, the poorest of the provinces, claimed, with the exception of Clare, the counties lying to the west of the river Shannon – Galway, Mayo, Sligo, Leitrim and Roscommon. Each county returned two MPs. The counties were divided into a random number of baronies and parishes; for example, Co. Antrim had eight baronies and 77 parishes, Co. Galway 16 baronies and 116 parishes, Co. Cork 16 baronies and 269 parishes and Co. Kilkenny nine baronies and 127 parishes. The county, with these subdivisions, formed the basic unit of government; although some estates still had manor courts where small disputes were adjudged *(1085)*. Most legal cases were initially tried by the local JPs in the Courts of Petty Sessions who sent complicated cases to the assizes, which were presided over by justices sent on circuit from the central courts in Dublin. The focus of the county was the county town, the legal and administrative centre of local government, the meeting place of the Grand Jury and Quarter Sessions, the venue of the assize judges on circuit from the central courts in Dublin and the place of the parliamentary election for the county. The Grand Jury was composed of the leading landlords or their representatives and these included most MPs. Some of the duties of the Grand Jury are outlined in 6 George I, c.10 *(0199)*. It was a jury of indictment and also the forum of decision for the business of the county. It set the local tax or cess.

   Although the principal centre of local government in the eighteenth century was the county, and to be governor, or *Custos Rotulorum*, of your county was the ultimate recognition of your standing in it, the county was only the final tier in a series of social and administrative units. Older divisions, baronies and parishes, although they might run across county boundaries, continued to be used in the exercise of local and central government; for instance, the basic revenue, the hearth tax, was collected by centrally appointed collectors, who were assigned specific baronies, while the parish, although an ecclesiastical division, was also the grassroots unit of secular administration; some of these parish responsibilities are outlined in 10 George I, c. 3 *(0226)*. All of these units, including the counties, varied considerably in size.

Behind the counties and baronies lay older and more variable designations of place and area. The most persistent of these was the townland. It was the place name most used on an Irish estate. It is usually recorded in leases and other estate papers and interpreting them presents obvious problems, particularly as Irish estates were often made up of bits and pieces of designated townlands scattered, sometimes widely, through a number of counties and subject to different customs. Everybody in Ireland lived (or lives) in a townland. It appears in the title deeds even of town houses, while in rural areas it was the universally accepted definition of place, associated with a man's name during his lifetime and when he died recorded on his tombstone. There are about 62,000 townlands in Ireland. Approximately 5,000 of these begin with the prefix 'Bally' and other common prefixes are 'Derry', 'Kil', 'Lis' and 'Tully'. Frequently the names of townlands reflect a curious mixture of Celtic imagination and English clerical error in recording complex Irish names. Some random examples of townland names are Kilrats, Ballymorran, Tullycore, Roughan, Carron, Shilnavogie, Cushybracken, Lisbeg and Tattynuckle. To add to the confusion, in the eighteenth century spelling was not standardised as regards either personal or place names.[27]

A further complication was that at the beginning of the eighteenth century there was no fixed measurement of weights *(0095)* and measures – including land. Townlands are of a wide range of sizes, shapes and descriptions. They vary from as much as 2,000 acres, usually in mountainous regions, to under five acres, and average about 300 acres. Their variable size has frequently baffled the administrator; for instance, the census officials in 1821 listed barony, townland, ploughland and gneeve as existing definitions of areas of land, and more than 80 years later the compilers of the 1904 census embarked on the dubious exercise of trying to convert these into logically definable areas, viz. 12 gneeves = 1 ploughland; 4 ploughlands = 1 townland, and 30 townlands = 1 barony. But even this is only a cumulative arrangement of variable measurements. This lack of uniformity probably relates to the importance not of the quantity of land but of its productivity. For instance, Lord George Hill found in nineteenth-century Gweedore, Co. Donegal, that: 'the land is never let, sold or devised by the acre, but by "a cow's grass", although a cow's grass, as it varies according to the quality of the land, comprises … a rather indefinite quantity.' Nevertheless, for practical purposes all townlands in the area were divided into 'cow's grass' and then subdivided into various smaller divisions referred to as a foot, a half-foot or 'cleet'.[28] Arthur

---

[27] People did not spell names consistently – not even father and son (e.g. Cleere and Clere **0421, 0422**); Pearce/Peirce/Pierce; Taylor and Taylour and Smyth and Smith were often used interchangeably. The general rule in the biographies is to use the spelling first entered in *Commons jn. Ire.*, while keeping families together.

[28] G. P. Hill, *Facts from Gweedore* (1845) pp. 26-7.

Young, writing in the 1770s, commented that in the parish of Tooavister on the coast of Co. Kerry: 'They have a way of taking land by the ounce ... an ounce is the sixteenth part of a gineve, and is sufficient for a potato garden'.[29] The potato garden or plot was the all-important source of food in a country which depended on subsistence agriculture to feed a rapidly rising population.

III NATIONAL REVENUE AND FINANCE

Finance, national and personal, was always at the forefront of the MPs' considerations. Overwhelmingly more statutes of the Irish parliament involved revenue than any other subject, even security. From 1783 to 1800 out of a total of 981 there were 265 revenue statutes; law and order; trade, finance and commerce accounted for a further 108 and 105 statutes respectively. The revenue was divided into two parts, the hereditary and the additional. The hereditary was composed of crown rents and quit rents derived from the Tudor and Stuart confiscations following the Tyrone and the 1641 rebellions: hearth money, a general tax on hearths first raised in the reign of Charles II, certain customs duties and licences for the sale of beer ale and spirits. From the Restoration the hereditary revenue was a perpetual grant to the crown for specific purposes of government. The reigns of both William III and Anne were marked by long and expensive wars and the hereditary revenue became increasingly inadequate. After 1715 the shortfall was met by loans, and the interest and capital for these was met by a temporary grant of additional duties and occasionally by a state lottery. These required the consent of parliament and this necessity restored the financial control, endangered by the hereditary revenue, to the House of Commons. The budget was the natural ground for constitutional and administrative conflict, and this was particularly the case in the 1690s when the English and Irish governments were establishing the parameters of their post-Revolution relationship.[30]

Before 1715 the national debt had been approximately £16,000. In this year a special loan of £50,000 was raised to meet the extraordinary expenses of the 1715 rebellion. Thereafter the budget was balanced by a series of irregular borrowings. From 1715 the national debt steadily increased until by the 1790s the revenue barely serviced the debt.[31] This additional revenue required the biennial, and from 1783 the annual, consent of parliament, which jealously guarded the hold it thus acquired over the administration; for instance, in 1692 and 1769 an angry parliament threatened the government with a short Money Bill. By the late 1790s war and rebellion had reduced the country to what appeared to be irredeemable bankruptcy. Additional duties were no longer producing sufficient additional revenue and many MPs were personally similarly circumstanced.

---

[29] Young, op. cit. vol. 1, p. 347.
[30] D. W. Hayton (ed.), *The Irish Parliament in the eighteenth century: the long apprenticeship* (2001), C. I. McGrath, 'Parliamentary Additional Supply' esp. pp. 27, 38.
[31] See Johnston, *Gt B. & Ire.,* pp. 97-8.

IV LANDLORDS' FINANCES, LEASES, ESTATES AND RENT

It is the pre-eminent importance of the estate as the basic source of the MPs' wealth which has given it its place in this study and its specific reference in the biographies. The issues can best be illuminated through a study of individual estates, but many estates did not keep good records and many estate records were lost in the great land transfers of the mid-nineteenth century post-famine era. One important category of estate records is the correspondence between absentee landowners, like Lord Abercorn, and their conscientious agents. But are the records which have survived the atypical records of the better administered estates? This may well be the case, but fortunately there is a counterbalance. Historians have a valuable point of reference in what is probably the most thorough investigation of a pre-industrial society in Western Europe – the mass of evidence taken on oath from upwards of 1,100 'persons of every class and condition' and appended to the *Report from Her Majesty's Commissioners of Inquiry into the state of the Law and Practice in respect of the Occupation of Land in Ireland,* commonly called the *Devon Report.* It refers to conditions in the year 1844, but many of the customs and traditions described in the report were indisputably present in the eighteenth century, although often in an embryonic and therefore a less dangerous form, thereby illustrating the development of this problem.

There are many interpretations of what constitutes the eighteenth century in Ireland. For instance, the parliamentary century dates from 1692 to 1800 but the social and economic interpretation favours the longer view from the Restoration to the 1840s famine, and attitudes to landed estates come under this broader definition. Professor Dickson, reviewing Dr Maguire's *The Downshire estates,* has remarked that 'Irish historians have been slow to come to terms with the social institution of the landed estate and to disentangle it from the politics of tenant-right and of "landlordism". Inhibited by memories of the mid-nineteenth-century demographic disaster, few have wished to be seen to be rushing to demote the landed estate to humbler levels of demonology, where it could be examined clinically and dispassionately.'[32] Nevertheless, a balanced understanding of both aspects of landholding is essential for any real understanding of Ireland in the eighteenth century as well as for the circumstances which led to so terrible a débâcle in the nineteenth century. Yet, such disastrous famines were not unique to Ireland but were a part of both Irish and European pre-industrial societies.

The recurrent famines to which agrarian societies were subject usually were not universal and therefore could be alleviated by transferring food from one area to another, although this was not always popular with the centres providing the supplies. For instance, there was a serious shortage in Ulster in 1728/9 and in March 1728/9

[32] D. Dickson, *Studia Hibernica* (1973) p. 190; quoted in *Ir. Econ. & Soc. Hist.* (1989), Crawford, 'The significance of the landed estate in Ulster society in the seventeenth and eighteenth centuries'. Much detail for the MPs' estates has been uncovered by Dr Malcomson.

Primate Boulter in his capacity as Lord Justice wrote to the Duke of Newcastle to explain the failure of the measures he had taken to alleviate it. Money raised from an appeal for famine relief in Dublin had been used to buy corn in Munster, 'where it has been very cheap to send it to the North in order to keep the markets down'. But this scheme ran into difficulties partly because of the prevailing wind which unusually blew from the east and partly because of 'the insurrection of the mob in those parts'. The Primate added that he had sent for 2,400 quarters of rye from Copenhagen, but that this was not expected until mid-May.[33] Goods, particularly bulky or heavy goods like grain or coal, could only be transported by water, hence the importance of the wind. Weather was all important in an agricultural society. The weather was particularly changeable in the 1730s, 1740s and 1750s.

The 1740s opened not only with a European war but with severe and widespread famine and the crisis of the early 1740s was probably as disastrous as that of the mid-1840s.[34] Furthermore, the crisis of the early 1740s was followed by the political uncertainties of the 1745 rebellion. Then in the mid-1740s there was another period of scarcity in some areas. In north Tyrone, where the staple food was oatmeal porridge, one of the landlords, the absentee Lord Abercorn, requested his agents to send him a running report on the price of grain at Strabane market, and when the price rose to 19d a peck he ordered it to be sold to his tenants at subsidised prices and given to those in extreme need. While Lord Abercorn's altruism should not be denigrated, it was in the landlord's interests that his estate recover as quickly as possible. The harvest of 1746 was good, and from September 1746 to August 1747 prices at Strabane market were steady at 4d to 5d a peck. The agent reported that 'the tenants of Derrygoon ... prays a thousand blessings for your lordship for cheap meal in the greatest scarcity ever known here'.[35] Lord Abercorn was a wealthy and careful landlord with estates scattered through the three kingdoms not all of which suffered a scarcity, and consequent decline in rents, at the same time. Thus while some landlords could help their tenants over a bad patch not all had the resources to do so.

Most of the seventeenth-century migrants came without the capital necessary to develop the estates which they acquired. Consequently, at this time large grants of undeveloped land were made on the understanding that their recipients would settle them with protestant English or Scottish migrants, who would become exemplary tenants and loyal subjects. However, the Devon Commissioners found that these undertakings had been only partly fulfilled and with varying results: for instance, 'in Munster the plantation was more imperfectly carried out ... and a class of undertakers ... became the landlords of the native peasantry ... producing for that reason comparatively little change' in the population, while 'the extensive settlement of Scotch

---

[33] See *infra* p. 72, n. 78.
[34] L. M. Cullen, *The emergence of modern Ireland, 1600-1900* (1981) pp. 168-71.
[35] PRONI D.1044/677A.

and English in the counties of Ulster, has introduced habits and customs which give a different character to that province from other parts of the island'. [36]

Another consideration, which should not be overlooked, was the proximity of Scotland and the easy sea passage which encouraged infiltration, particularly into the nearby counties of Antrim and Down, especially during the Scottish scarcity of the 1690s. The Devon Commissioners considered that many of the distinctive features of Irish landholding had their origins in the consequences of the confiscations and plantations of the sixteenth and seventeenth centuries on the relatively undeveloped state of the country. Although the Scots provided the largest influx of seventeenth-century tenant migrants, the largest land transfer occurred during the interregnum and many of these Cromwellian settlers formed a 'small proprietary' whom, the Devon Commissioners noted, 'being generally resident exercised an influence on the relations of society different from that produced by the large and absent grantees of former reigns'. [37]

The rise in land values during the eighteenth century encouraged a more competent and professional approach to land surveying,[38] but even at this more sophisticated level of quantification there were three different types of measurement. The most universal measure was the Irish or plantation acre, and 5 Irish acres equalled 8 English, imperial or statute acres. The English acre was the principal unit of land measurement in two places: firstly, in a horseshoe-shaped area around Belfast, which included south Antrim, north Down, Armagh, north Cavan and east Tyrone; and secondly in west Waterford and east Cork where, for example, the great Burlington–Devonshire estates, which had once belonged to Sir Walter Raleigh, were measured in English acres. In the Ulster counties of Antrim, Down, Tyrone, Donegal and Londonderry, the variously called Scotch or Cunningham acre was widely used. It was slightly smaller than the Irish acre and slightly larger than the statute acre, as 5 Cunningham acres equalled 7 statute acres. It was not unknown for nearby estates to be measured in different types of acre. For instance, although the Cunningham acre was the most usual measurement throughout the north, the Caledon estate in south Tyrone and south Armagh was measured in Irish acres, while the nearby south Tyrone Ranfurly estate was measured in English or statute acres. In 1734 Archibald Stewart surveyed the Earl of Antrim's estates in the barony of Dunluce in north Antrim 'shewing quantities and qualities in each denomination containing Plantation, Cunningham and English measures'. [39]

It has been calculated that the pattern of landholding which was consolidated in the early eighteenth century, resulted in about 2,000 estates, usually of between 2,000

---

[36] *Devon Rep.* p. 7, see also R. Mitchinson & P. Roebuck, *Economy and society in Scotland and Ireland* pp. 81-92, Roebuck, 'The economic situation and functions of substantial landowners 1600-1815: Ulster and Lowland Scotland compared', esp. p. 90.
[37] *Devon Rep.* p. 7.
[38] See W. Greig, *General report on the Gosford Estate in Co. Armagh 1821* (PRONI, 1976). This refers to the Acheson (**0002**) estates.
[39] PRONI T2325/1/6.

and 4,000 acres. The majority of estates were not compact and often comprised parcels of land, bestowing political influence, in different counties, far beyond the county in which the landlord normally resided. A small consolidated estate, such as R. L. Edgeworth's (**0688**) in Co. Longford, could be administered by a resident landlord himself. But larger and more complicated estates were usually administered through one or more agents. Knowledge of the locality was important but it could encourage inefficiency and on occasions dishonesty.[40] The question of absenteeism was endemic from the way Irish estates were acquired. No landlord could live on all his estates at once. Nevertheless, personal supervision or at least a frequent presence was desirable. It was obviously important for the economy of the locality if he spent his money and kept up his residence there and even better if he occupied it, but perhaps the real question was whether he spent his money in Ireland or drained it abroad. This was a problem throughout the century, but it became a much greater one after the Union. At the same time the correspondence, which separation and absenteeism entailed, has in some cases given detailed information which would not otherwise be available.

Another aspect of the land problem was the way land was leased and sold. An important attempt to clarify a potentially chaotic situation was the 1707 statute, 6 Queen Anne, c. 2 *(0097)* which established the Registry of Deeds whereby land transactions were registered. Theoretically, all land belonged to the sovereign – this was tangibly reflected in the various dues, such as crown rents and quit rents, which applied to land redistributed as a result of successive confiscations. Apart from this technicality, there were two commercial ways of acquiring the ownership of land in eighteenth-century Ireland: purchase in 'fee-simple' or a lease in perpetuity, which was a halfway house, part sale, part lease. The Devon Commission referred to these leases as 'the landlords' tenure in Ireland … a species of tenure, scarcely known elsewhere, which prevails very extensively in that country, one-seventh of Ireland being said to be held under it. We allude to the tenure by lease for lives, with a covenant of perpetual renewal on payment of a fine, sometimes merely nominal upon the fall of each life.'[41]

Leases held in perpetuity separated the beneficial ownership from the possession of an estate. These leases reflected the difficulty of raising a large capital sum, representing the true value of the estate, in a poor country where land had only a limited appeal to external buyers. They overcame the market problem of raising large capital sums by an arrangement amounting to a lump sum coupled with a perpetual fixed annuity. A complex illustration of absenteeism, selling in fee simple, leasing in perpetuity, marriage and inheritance is given by the Burlington–Devonshire estates in Counties Cork and

---

[40] The way the system worked is very clearly shown in W. A. Maguire, *The Downshire estates in Ireland, 1801-1845* (1972), W. H. Crawford & B. Trainor, *Aspects of Irish social history 1750-1800* (PRONI, 1969); L.J. Proudfoot, *Urban patronage and social authority: the management of the Duke of Devonshire's towns in Ireland, 1764-1891* (Washington DC, 1995) and there are a number of other similar studies.
[41] *Devon Rep.* p. 13.

Waterford. At the beginning of the eighteenth century Charles, 3rd Earl of Cork and 2nd Earl of Burlington, sold part of the Munster estates, which had originally belonged to his grandfather, the great earl. He died in 1704 leaving his son and heir a minor. Richard Boyle, 4th Earl of Cork and 3rd Earl of Burlington, a spectacular and gifted patron of the arts, was hailed as the 'new Maecenas'. An enthusiastic collector, his zeal manifested itself early as he returned from the Grand Tour bringing 878 trunks and crates containing the start of his famous collection. He married an English heiress and lived in England; Burlington House commemorates both his name and his interests. However, his aesthetic taste was far superior to his talents for business management as in gratifying it he exhausted the income from his great estates. Moreover, his agents were dishonest and his accounts irregularly made up. In 1737 he sold in fee simple the Clonakilty estate, including the patronage of the parliamentary borough of Clonakilty, for £17,000 to his kinsman, Henry Boyle, then Speaker of the House of Commons and later 1st Earl of Shannon. At that time Lord Burlington's rents were estimated to be £80,000 in arrears, 'of which', a contemporary declared, 'he will see little or nothing, the tenants being gone off and not to be found, which proceeded from his several agents being underhand'.[42] On his death, in 1753, his still vast estates, English and Irish, passed to his sole surviving child, the Marchioness of Hartington, and to her heirs, the Dukes of Devonshire. [43]

Within the term of the lease, leases could be bought and sold and there was nothing to prevent a landlord from selling an estate leased in perpetuity. For instance, in 1738, Lord Burlington sold to Sir William Heathcote, one of his creditors, a large estate, already let in perpetuity for £3,000 p.a., around Cappoquin on the borders of Counties Cork and Waterford. Sir William, a London businessman, purchased it for £53,300 sterling or £60,000 Irish, thus securing a 5 per cent return on his capital.[44] There is no record of Sir William ever visiting his estate nor, apart from curiosity, was there any reason why he should regard it as anything other than a fixed-income investment. The owner of an estate leased in perpetuity had nothing to do with the actual management of the estate, although his 'annuity' was an extra charge upon it. The purchaser of a lease in perpetuity became the *de facto* landlord, while the grantor of the lease remained the *de iure* owner of the same estate. If a perpetuity lease was granted to an absentee, for local people there was a drain of a large sum of money out of the area. Furthermore, there is some evidence that even a comparatively wealthy county like Cork was at least temporarily affected by the drain of money created by Lord Burlington's leasing fines in the decade 1728–38, when he raised the enormous

[42] D. Dickson, Ph.D thesis (Dublin Univ.) pp. 80 *et seq.*
[43] For a study of these estates and their political implications see, Proudfoot, op. cit. The Dowager Countess of Burlington, d.1758, had a life interest in the estates (ibid. p. 68) and on her death the Duke of Devonshire received many letters congratulating him on his Burlington inheritance, see PRONI Chatsworth MSS T3158/1602, 1603, 1604.
[44] *Ir. Econ. & Soc. Hist.* I (1974) Malcomson, 'Absenteeism in eighteenth-century Ireland' p. 18.

sum of £280,000, mainly from local men who wished to buy either long or perpetuity leases.[45]

Irish leases could be measured in years or in lives or both. For most of the century leases for lives could only be held by protestants – a lease for lives usually included a term of years, 31 was common. Such leases were considered equivalent to a freehold and as such they had political as well as economic implications. A lease for lives – often for three lives – ran for the lifespan of the longest survivor plus the term of years. This caused problems, as a 'life' could move or even emigrate and no one would know when a lease ran out. A perpetuity allowed lives to be replaced as those originally named, and their successors, died. Any life, public or private, could be named and usually the lessee chose the names to be inserted. Contemporary English leases were usually for five or 21 years, but good landlord–tenant relations brought a *de facto* security of tenure, along with assistance in improving the farm and for tenants who met their obligations there were other substantial advantages. This system provided the infrastructure necessary for development and gave the landlord better control over his land, allowing him to adjust rents gradually to meet altered land values and inflation. But in Ireland during the latter part of the eighteenth and the early nineteenth centuries, inflation and rapidly rising land values compounded the problems inherent in the traditionally long Irish leases.

A major problem with Irish leases was not their brevity but their length. Theoretically a lease could last over 100 years. When a long lease fell in and another was granted, changes were abrupt and rents rose in sharp, steep steps rather than in long gradual absorbable increases.[46] Rents could vary greatly between neighbours, depending on the remaining term of the individual lease. One way round this was to 'fine it down' or compound for a lower rent by paying a lump sum, but this required the leaseholder to be a man of substance. Not surprisingly, sudden even if anticipated large rent increases caused resentment, particularly when neighbouring un-expired leases remained at a lower level. At the same time, any attempt to shorten the span of leases was construed as a threat to tenure. This could create social unrest, as did any large 'fines' required to reduce the rent demands on the new leases, and communal pressures could be strong in an alienated society. Multiple tenancies were not unknown and frequently grew illegally. These were difficult to control, partly because in some areas tenants lived in groups, or clahans, and in addition agricultural tasks were sometimes undertaken co-operatively, for example potato harvesting. At the bottom of the pyramid were tenants who held land on a casual annual basis on various terms. Thus the

---

[45] D. Dickson, Ph.D thesis (Dublin Univ.), op. cit. pp. 80 *et seq.* also Dickson, *Old World colony: Cork and South Munster 1630-1830* (2005) pp.185-6 shows Sir William's caution over the transaction.
[46] See P. Roebuck (ed.), *Plantation to Partition* (1981), Roebuck, 'Rent movements, proprietorial incomes and agricultural developments, 1730-1830' esp. p. 91; Maguire, *Downshire estates* op. cit. p. 39; *Ir. Econ. & Soc. Hist.* vol. 2 (1975), pp. 5-21, Crawford, 'Landlord Tenant relations in Ulster' esp. table on p.13; R. J. Dickson, *Ulster emigration to Colonial America* (1966); D. Dickson, Ph.D Thesis op. cit. appendix p.2.

enduring ramifications of an anachronistic leasing system prevented reform of the system of land tenure in Ireland.

After 1815 the agrarian scene was increasingly distorted by the runaway increase in population. This increase, estimated at approximately 30 per cent between 1800 and 1841, affected all levels of society.[47] Furthermore, such distortions drew force from a failure to industrialise and the agricultural slump which followed the Napoleonic wars. At this time the peculiar structure of Irish society, and the order of magnitude that these problems assumed in certain areas, gave prominence to conditions which were not in themselves unique to Ireland. Evidence of them is to be found in Scotland[48] and in similar societies in Europe and elsewhere. Not surprisingly in 1844 the Commissioners found that the homogeneity which characterised English agrarian society was unknown in Ireland. Marc Bloch, comparing England to France, thought that in France the application of Roman law to local traditions 'confirmed and reinforced the idea of perpetuity which was already implicit in the right of real property traditionally exercised by the tenant over his house and fields'.[49] A tenant, particularly in Ulster, had a right to claim for any improvement he had made during his tenancy. In this respect it is interesting to note that the concept of 'tenant right' was particularly strong in Ulster, where 'the custom of Ulster' may reflect Scottish law, which, like French, was based on Roman law. Tenant right or custom and tithing were not uniform but varied from area to area.

Landlords did not expect the marked improvements in rents and land values that came in the second half of the century, let alone their rapid escalation during the period of the French and Napoleonic wars. Little was known about inflation, long leases were customary and landlords were usually short of money. However, as the century progressed, landlords became increasingly aware of the widening gap which separated the actual from the nominal return on the land that they, or their ancestors, had leased in perpetuity. In 1776 Arthur Young found that Lord Antrim's (1317) vast estate of 173,000 acres was let for £8,000 p.a. but 'relet for £64,000 a year by tenants that have perpetuities, perhaps the cruelest instance in the world of carelessness for the interests of posterity. The present Lord's father granted those leases.'[50] By the beginning of the nineteenth century Wakefield considered that the head rent was not one-twentieth of the gross rent for the same estate. Similar reports were current throughout Ireland: for instance, Wakefield also discovered that Lord Doneraile's (1856) father (0026) let an estate of £2,000 'for ever' and lived to see it re-let at a profit rent of £18,000 p.a.; while in Co. Kerry, 'Lord Powis had the fee of a large

---

[47] Exact figures for the Irish population before 1822 are a matter of much speculation and this is particularly true of the eighteenth century.

[48] See L. M. Cullen & T. C. Smout (eds), *Comparative aspects of Scottish and Irish economic and social history*, pp. 47-64, Flinn, 'Malthus, Emigration and potatoes in the Scottish North-West, 1770-1870' esp. p. 56.

[49] M. Bloch (trans. Janet Sondheimer), *French rural history* (1978 edn) p. 129.

[50] Young, op. cit., vol. I p. 146.

estate which at present produces £30,000 per annum, but, in 1734, one of his ancestors leased it "for ever" at £1,900 per annum and a fine of £6,000.'[51] Many of these perpetuities were, like the Burlington leases, early eighteenth-century grants, which had been made in times of recession to provide the landlord with immediate money at a cost which either the locality could sustain or a foreign purchaser was willing to pay.

Inevitably, as some landlords felt inadequately recompensed for their continuing equity in the estate, they began to look for loopholes in the leases which might allow them to regain control of their estates. In 1775 there was a classic example of such a challenge in the case of *Murray v. Bateman*, which occurred about the time that Young was recording these ever-growing discrepancies. Murray, the titular owner of an estate, challenged the possession of his tenant, Bateman, who held a perpetuity lease for lives renewable but had failed to perform his contractual obligations, having been dilatory in inserting new lives and in paying the accompanying fine. Murray, the landlord, reclaimed the estate on the ground that the lease was void as the obligations specified in it had not been met. Bateman's failures were a common occurrence, and Lord Chancellor Lifford gave judgement for the defendant on the grounds of 'an old Irish equity'. The plaintiff (Murray) appealed to the British House of Lords, then the final court of appeal for Irish cases, where, according to the Irish Attorney General, John Scott (**1891**), 'the subject is not understood', and the British Lords of Appeal, dominated by the formidable Lord Chief Justice Mansfield, upheld the appeal. The appeal decision shook the whole system of landholding in Ireland to its foundations, as the majority of these tenants had sub-tenants – 'between the actual proprietor and the occupant of the land there are frequently no less than four or five progressive tenants' – each of whose leases depended on the validity of that of his superior in the 'cascade'. Furthermore, many of the estates leased in perpetuity were encumbered with family provisions such as jointures (widow's provision). Faced with potential chaos, the Irish parliament passed 19 & 20 Geo. III, c. 30 *(0897)*, commonly known as the Tenantry Bill. This statute restored the 'old Irish equity', stating that:

> Great parts of the lands in this kingdom are held under leases for lives with covenants for perpetual renewals upon payment of certain fines … and whereas … those deriving under them have frequently neglected to pay or tender such fines within the times prescribed … and whereas many such leases are settled to make provision for families and creditors, most of whom must be utterly ruined if advantage shall be taken of such neglects … in such cases [they should be relieved] against the lapse of time upon giving adequate compensation … where no fraud appears to have been intended.

The Irish parliament was sharply divided and the bill passed in both Houses by the

---

[51] E. G. Wakefield, *An account of Ireland statistical and political* (1812) vol. I p. 253.

narrowest of margins – two votes in the House of Commons and a single vote in the House of Lords.

Despite fictional representations, there was no stereotype eighteenth-century Irish landlord. As a class they varied considerably from the great nobleman, with estates scattered throughout the British Isles, for example, the Earl of Cork and Burlington or the Earl and later Marquess of Abercorn, to the country gentleman living on his single estate. Social life varied between the extreme formality of the MP for Dublin city 1767–73, Duke of Leinster's (**0745**), establishment at Carton and the scene of exhausted bacchanalia[52] which greeted Sir Jonah Barrington (**0087**), MP for Tuam 1790–7 and for Clogher 1798–1800, when he paid a surprise visit to his brother's hunting lodge. Another aspect of Irish life was represented by the Fordes of Seaforde (**0780–0783**), Co. Down, 'where the hounds circulate briskly in the morning and the bottle in the afternoon'.[53] It was a society of contrasts and contradictions. Until 1783 parliament met only every second year and the country was the MP's natural habitat. Horses were the equivalent of cars in the twentieth and twenty-first centuries. This encouraged racing and animal breeding – even if riding with their other sport, duelling,[54] led to fatal accidents (**0149, 0618**). Although racing was universally popular it could encourage 'unlawful assemblies' and it was forbidden within nine miles of Dublin Castle *(1410)*. Nevertheless there was a real interest in the environment and one of the pioneers of animal welfare was an Irish MP, Richard Martin (**1347**).

The country was very bare and for both practical and aesthetic reasons MPs were particularly anxious to encourage the growth of timber and leases often included the requirement to plant so many trees – often fruit trees. Some areas were treeless and before the enclosure movement hedge-less. Wood was the universal material, used for most of the things that metal or plastic would be used for today, for example certain types of pipes. Consequently legislation provided for quotas of trees and severe penalties for interfering with them *(0058,0134)*. There were various acts for the preservation of game, including a tariff for catching predators *(0148)*, preservation of salmon *(0170,0241)* and creation of closed seasons *(0328,0382)*. There was also a great interest in gardens and landscaping, for instance Frederick Trench's (**2108**) 'romantic' demesne at Heywood near Ballinakill,[55] and in collecting rare plants, which was an activity of Peter LaTouche (**1207**) at Bellvue, Co. Wicklow.

---

[52] D. Guinness & W. Ryan, *Irish houses and castles* (1971) pp. 187-8; J. Barrington, *Personal sketches and recollections* (1836 ed.), pp. 42 *et seq.* – Barrington's descriptions were often subject to exaggeration.

[53] W. Crawford, *Letters from an Irish land-agent* (PRONI, 1976) p. 41; various Fordes of Seaforde sat in the Irish parliament for nearly 50 years.

[54] See J. Kelly, *'That damn'd thing called honour': duelling in Ireland 1570-1860* (1995).

[55] See P. Friel, *Frederick Trench (1746-1836) and Heywood, Queen's County: the creation of a romantic demesne* (Maynooth, 2000).

V EDUCATION: THE INTELLECTUAL AND PHILISOPHICAL BACKGROUND

Education, from the hedge school to the university, was a concern at all levels of society. In 1747 the Irish parliamentarians gave the first grant for elementary education in the British Isles to the Charter Schools, although these had that proselytising element which was part of virtually all eighteenth-century support for education in the British Isles.[56] Apart from a parliamentary grant the schools were, like most eighteenth-century well-intentioned schemes, under funded and under supervised. The master and mistress controlled and profited from the labour of those they were instructing and also the school premises and equipment. They were visited by John Wesley, the evangelist, John Howard, the prison reformer, and Jeremiah Fitzpatrick, the Dublin medical doctor appointed by parliament as Inspector General of Prisons. All returned equally distressing reports: Howard in the 1770s considered that the state of the children 'was so deplorable as to disgrace Protestantism and encourage Popery in Ireland', Wesley in the 1780s endorsed Howard and added 'what are they taught? As far as I could learn, just nothing!' and he reported his findings to the Commissioners in Dublin. But the schools were a favoured project of the established Church and despite Wesley's report and Fitzpatrick's prodding nothing was achieved.[57] The idea of educating the poor was good but its implementation left much to be desired. Ideas usually cost money and supervision; both were in short supply in eighteenth-century Ireland.[58]

The best known Irish 'public' school was Kilkenny College, founded or refurbished in 1667 by the 1st Duke of Ormonde. It was attended by many MPs including the Beresford brothers (**0113, 0115**), but there were also the Royal Schools founded as part of the Plantation of Ulster; probably the most famous of these was the Royal School at Armagh where Castlereagh (**2009**) was educated. Private tutors were widely used, both for education at home and as companions, or guardians, on the Grand Tour, the completion of an aristocratic education. There were many private foundations, which produced various grades of education for a variety of academic and practical purposes, for example, the Hibernian and the Hibernian Marine Schools founded for the education of the children and orphans of soldiers and sailors from the army and the Royal or merchant navy – in the not always well-founded hope that they would encourage the pupils to join these services. There were the French schools at the Huguenot settlement of Portarlington, which included the Wellesley brothers (**2210, 2213**) among their pupils. University education was the preserve of the officially Church of Ireland Dublin University; founded in 1592, it is the oldest of the British

---

[56] 21 Geo. II, c. 3 – this was the grant to the Charter Schools and it was continued by subsequent parliaments; education and religion were not separated in the eighteenth century and denominational education has had a long history both in Ireland and Great Britain.

[57] O. MacDonagh, *The Inspector General: Sir Jeremiah Fitzpatrick and social reform, 1783-1802* (1981), pp. 86-104, 'Sir Jeremiah and the Charter Schools 1785-8'.

[58] Ibid. pp. 94-5.

universities overseas. Many MPs were educated there and throughout the eighteenth century it retained a firm parliamentary affection and support, expressed financially both academically and in its buildings. Some graduates went on to Oxford or Cambridge but their education was often followed by study at one of the Inns of Court in London, which apart from a professional training for those intending to embark on a legal career, was considered a desirable general education for a landlord, particularly one who might be called upon to act as a Justice of the Peace. For higher education, Catholics had to look to the Irish Colleges in Catholic countries on the continent, while presbyterians went mainly to the Scottish universities where they participated in and contributed to the Scottish Enlightenment.

In 1735 Archbishop Boulter considered that: 'we are not much given to buy or read books' – four years after the foundation of the well patronised Dublin Society[59] of which he was a founding vice-president! This judgment was perhaps premature as even the most casual glance at Pollard's *Dictionary of the Members of the Dublin Book Trade, 1500-1800*, paints a lively if fluctuating book trade throughout the century. In the latter part of the century, Denis Daly (**0570**), MP for Co. Galway 1768–90, and John Fitzgibbon (**0749**), MP for Dublin University 1778–83, Kilmallock 1783–9 and later Lord Chancellor, were known to possess exceptionally fine libraries. Henry Grattan (**0895**) wrote of Denis Daly that 'at Mr. Daly's we dined among his books as well as at his table – they were on it – they were lying around it…'.[60] Towards the end of the century there was also a considerable interest in Irish literature, artifacts and prehistory. For instance, Flood's (**0762**) interest in the Irish language is well known,[61] and in the Library of Trinity College there is an Irish harp donated by William Burton Conyngham (**0303**), whose cultural interests were considered second only to those of Lord Charlemont. Burton also financed James Murphy's *Arabian antiques of Spain*. Murphy was among those whom the architect Gandon employed in his alterations to the Parliament House.[62]

Apart from genuine enthusiasts, a knowledge of academic philosophies was considered part of a conventional education; for example, the 2nd Duke of Leinster (**0745**), worthy, but not very intellectual and just returned from the Grand Tour, was advised to acquire a knowledge not only of history, but also of Roman, feudal and natural law and of various authors on trade and commerce. To achieve this, he was advised to read such works as Justinian's *Institutes*, Cicero's *Offices*, and authors including the Dutchman Hugo Grotius, the German Samuel von Pufendorf, the Swiss Jean-

[59] See H. F. Berry, *A History of the Royal Dublin Society* (1915); also *The Founders of the Royal Dublin Society: with illustrations of their houses and a list of members who joined the Dublin Society between 1731 and 1800* (RDS, 2005).
[60] *Grattan*, vol. III p. 150; see T. W. Moody & W. E. Vaughan, *A New History of Ireland* (1986), chap. XIV pp. 424-70, J. C. Beckett, 'Literature in English, 1691-1800'.
[61] J. Kelly, *Henry Flood: Patriots and politics in eighteenth-century Ireland* (1998) pp. 428-36 esp. p. 436; see also *An Duanaire, 1600-1900: Poems of the dispossessed* (1981) in Irish with verse translation by Thomas Kinsella for the richness and flavour of Irish literature during the period.
[62] Guinness & Ryan, op. cit. pp. 187-8; J. Barrington, op. cit. pp. 42 *et seq.* – Barrington's descriptions were often subject to exaggeration.

Jacques Burlamaqui and the Frenchman Montesquieu.[63] Many of the Irish parliamentarians, particularly those with intellectual and political interests, would have read these authors. Nor was this reading confined to men; for instance, the Duke's (**0745**) mother and her sister, Lady Holland, were avid readers of Rousseau and Voltaire.[64] Then there were more applied political philosophies, some home-grown, some borrowed from England (late eighteenth-century patriotic radicalism) and others from international movements particularly the American and the French Revolutions.

At the beginning of the century the eminent physician Sir Patrick Dun (**0665**) had a library which became the foundation of that of the Royal College of Physicians, likewise at the end of the century the Kings Inn Library emerged from that of Mr Justice Robinson. A similar late eighteenth-century library was that of the College of Surgeons.[65] The most famous of all was that of the early eighteenth-century primate, Archbishop Marsh, which in addition to theological books, most notably from Bishop Stillingfleet's (1635-99) library, included the library and manuscripts of Elie Bouhereau (1643-1719), a Huguenot physician from La Rochelle.[66] Bouhereau was secretary to the Huguenot leader Henry de Massau, Marquis de Ruvigny and Earl of Galway, who established the colony for Huguenot veterans at Portarlington. The seventeenth-century France from which the Huguenots came had been a very troubled and disunited country and the Huguenot refugees were divided into those who found it possible to conform to the Protestantism of the Church of Ireland, and were given every government encouragement to do so, and those who found it alien to the simplicity of their traditions and joined the Presbyterians.[67] Bouhereau was a conformist Huguenot and was eventually ordained a Church of Ireland priest.

At the end of the seventeenth century Robert, 1st Viscount Molesworth (**1419**), was at the centre of an early eighteenth-century intellectual group which included Archbishop King and, rather surprisingly, the Presbyterian philosopher Francis Hutcheson. All of these men were connected with the trans-European movement known as the Republic of Letters; for instance both the French Pierre Bayle and the German Godfried Liebniz discussed King's *de origine mali* published in 1702 and William Molyneux (**1425**), who had an interest in astronomy, was a correspondent of both Flamsteed and Halley.[68] Molyneux, who was a particular friend of the philosopher

[63] S. J. Connolly (ed.), *Political Ideas in Eighteenth-Century Ireland* (2000), 'Introduction: varieties of Irish political thought', pp. 12-13.

[64] *IMC Leinster Correspondence*, vol. 1 pp. 343, 353.

[65] C. Kenny, *King's Inns and the Battle of the Books 1772: cultural controversy at a Dublin library* (2002), p. 6 n. 1, p. 7.

[66] C. E. J. Caldicott, H . Gough & J-P. Pittion (eds), *The Huguenots and Ireland: Anatomy of an emigration* (1987), pp. 37-66, 'The French Protestants and the Edict of Nantes' considers both their background and the literature deposited in Marsh's Library.

[67] Kenny, op. cit., pp. 76-7.

[68] C. J. Fauske (ed.), *Arbp. King & the Anglican Irish Context* (2004) [10 essays on various aspects of King's personality], p. 112; Pierre Bayle, *Reponse au questions d'un Provincial* (1707) and Godfried Leibniz, *Essais de Theodicee* (1710); J. G. Simms (ed.), P. H. Kelly, *William Molyneux of Dublin: a life of the seventeenth-century political writer and scientist* (1980), p. 63; Molyneux also wrote the first book on optics in English.

John Locke, held to the theory of the sanctity of property, but he had also a special interest in dioptrics and his *Dioptrica Nova* influenced George Berkeley (1685-1752) who was the Trinity College metaphysical philosopher. Later, when Berkeley was Bishop of Cloyne, Molyneux also influenced his theory of vision (*esse est percepi*). Molyneux, MP for Dublin University, was the undisputed doyen of eighteenth-century Irish constitutional theorists. His classic account,[69] *The case of Ireland's being bound by acts of parliament in England stated,* was published in April 1698, almost exactly a year before the English parliament passed a foreshadowed act aimed specifically at preventing the export of Irish woollen goods. This act was part of a general tightening-up of the Navigation Acts, the mainspring of the British imperial system. Molyneux's **(1425)** pamphlet aroused considerable debate in both England and Ireland. The English parliament's censure contained a resolution saying that it should be burned by the common hangman, but it is uncertain whether this actually happened.[70] It was acknowledged that, while Molyneux's thesis was not new – at the Restoration it had been expounded by his father-in-law, Sir Richard Domville, in an important thesis – but Molyneux had 'reduced it into form and now at last brought it forth into the world'.

Regardless of its original fate, Molyneux's book became the classic statement of what were perceived as the rights of the Irish parliament. Its reprints trace every Anglo-Irish constitutional crisis before the amendment of Poynings' Law in 1782. Early reprints appeared in 1706, at the time of the Scottish Union, for Molyneux had written that 'If ... the Parliament of England may bind Ireland; it must also be allowed that the People of Ireland ought to have their Representatives in the Parliament of England, and this I believe we should be willing enough to embrace; but this is a happiness we can hardly hope for.'[71] In 1782 this significant sentence was omitted. It was only as the eighteenth century progressed that anti-Union sentiment developed, along with that halfway house in the evolution of a national identity – colonial nationalism, or the desire for a national identity within an imperial framework. The root of the problem was that the internal conflicts of the seventeenth century had ensured an unusual degree of independence for England's transatlantic colonies, but in the eighteenth-century England emerged as a major imperial power. Consequently, imperial defence, particularly after 1763, necessitated an increasingly centralised administration. At the same time, her established dependencies, of which Ireland was the oldest, were not only reluctant to accept the enlarged and centripetal demands of the mother country but also wanted a greater degree of centrifugal independence. Thus Irish parliamentary development was marked by a growing sense of regional identity and a corresponding desire for a greater degree of autonomy.

By the end of the century the rights of property, which lay behind Molyneux's

[69] Simms (ed. Kelly), op. cit. pp. 102-119.
[70] Ibid. p. 112.
[71] Ibid. p. 106.

(1425) theory, had given way to the theory of the rights of man. This too had Irish
origins. Hutcheson, a son and grandson of the Ulster presbyterian manse, was from
1729 until his death in 1746 Professor of Moral Philosophy at the University of
Glasgow. His famous treatise, *An inquiry into the original of our ideas of beauty and
virtue*, stated: 'that action is best, which procures that greatest happiness for the greatest
numbers; and that, worst, which in like manner, occasions misery'.[72] He was a leading
figure in the Scottish Enlightment and the 'never to be forgotten' teacher of Adam
Smith. In many ways he was the philosopher of the American Revolution; his interest
lay in man and the nature of society. These views were emphasised by the American
war and lay behind the 1782 Amendment of Poynings' Law *(0966)* which gave
legislative independence to the Irish parliament. Hutcheson also held that magistrates
and rulers are the trustees and servants of the people and at all times answerable to
them and that the common interest of the whole people is the aim of all civil polity
which, if it were able to, had the right to reject an unjust ruler. Molyneux and
Hutcheson provided the two basic political philosophies of eighteenth-century Ireland
and both conflicted in the 1790s when the ideas of Paine's *Rights of Man* and the
theories of the French revolution were opposed to those of British radicalism.

Some MPs sent their children to English public schools: Eton, Harrow and
Westminster were the most popular. These school connections were often long lasting
and had far-reaching political ramifications. This was especially true of the last quarter
of the eighteenth century and of the 1790s. In 1768 Lord Kildare (0745), then on
the Grand Tour, wrote to his mother, the Duchess of Leinster, that:

> Lord Fitzwilliam, Mr. Charles Fox and Mr. Price arrived yesterday, but they propose
> going in a few days. We are about ten English at present, and eight of us were at Eton
> together. It is amazing how one picks up our old Eton acquaintances abroad. I dare say
> I have met above forty since I have been in Italy.[73]

A classic example of these connections was the famous Maidstone trial in 1798 when
Arthur O'Connor (1565), *en route* to France to negotiate with the French Directory,
was acquitted, while his co-defendant Fr James Quigley was found guilty and executed.
Grattan (0895) and the British radicals had supported O'Connor claiming despite
the evidence that O'Connor was a radical while Quigley was a revolutionary. Apart
from a very few extremists such as Lord Edward FitzGerald (0730) and Arthur
O'Connor (1565), radicalism – institutional and administrative reform – not
revolution was strongly supported by the Irish opposition dominated by the ambiguous
figure of Grattan (0895)[74] and its British allies during the 1790s. It was this mixture

[72] F. Hutcheson (ed. Wolfgang Leidhold), *An inquiry into the original of our ideas of beauty and virtue* (Indianapolis, 2004), p. xvi.
[73] See P. Friel, op. cit.
[74] See D. Mansergh, *Grattan's failure* (2005), which dissects Grattan's ambivalent position, and N. Curtin, *The United Irishmen: Popular Politics in Ulster and Dublin 1791-8* (1998 edn) which analyses the blind movement of assorted discontents which composed the United Irishmen and ensured a lack of focus to the rebellion.

within a divided society which offers an explanation for the fragmented nature of the 1798 rebellion and the reluctant acceptance of the promise of security offered to the Irish parliamentarians in the Act of Union.

The great intellectual problem[75] of the seventeenth/eighteenth centuries had been the reconciliation of reason and religion, which exercised Archbishop King in *de origine mali* (1702) in which he defended Christianity in general and Anglicanism in particular. The Huguenots did not just bring trading links, manufacturing (particularly fine linen and sugar), and banking (**1203-8**). Many of the refugees were refugees because they knew their faith and brought with them intellectual backgrounds and connections, for example Jacques Abbadie, the Huguenot Dean of Killaloe (d.1727), who had been chaplain to Marshal Schomberg, and previously minister of the French Church in Berlin, and had published in 1684 *Traité de la verité de la religion chrétienne*. This problem exercised scientists, such as Isaac Newton (1642-1727), philosophers, like René Descartes (1596-1650), and churchmen like King and Abbadie. The debate encouraged Deism, and a leading figure in this argument was the Donegal born John Toland, whose *Christianity not Mysterious* led to an acrimonious debate in the House of Commons. Here, in 1697, the orthodox majority ordered that it be burnt by the common hangman and Toland, threatened with arrest and prosecution, speedily departed from Ireland. In 1703 an MP, John Asgill (**0056**), wrote a book entitled: *An Argument proving that according to the covenant of eternal life revealed in the scriptures man may be translated from hence into that eternal life without passing through death although the human nature of Christ himself could not be thus translated til he passed through death*. This was adjudged wicked and blasphemous and the author 'to be expelled from this House and be forever hereafter incapable of being chosen, returned or sitting a Member in any succeeding Parliament of this kingdom'. The book was to be burnt by the common hangman outside both the gates of parliament and the city hall; the House ordered that 'the Sheriffs of the City of Dublin be required to see the same done accordingly'. The majority of MPs were conventionally orthodox. Nevertheless Deism became a force and produced some strange associations, such as the Hell-Fire Clubs, which were not confined to Dublin; for example Limerick not only had one but had a collective painting made of its members!

The eighteenth century was an age of clubs catering for all spectrums of society.[76] In 1684 the Philosophical Society had been established as a counterpart to the Royal Society and there was a small degree of cross membership, for instance, the Molyneux brothers William (1656–98) (**1425**)[77] and Thomas (**1424**) were both Fellows of the Royal Society as was Sir Richard Bulkeley (**0272**) and Robert, 1st Viscount Molesworth (**1419**). The Philosophical Society was a victim of the Revolution and its aftermath

---

[75] O. MacDonagh, W. E. Mandle & P. Travers (eds), *Irish culture and nationalism* (1983), pp. 14-39, E. M. Johnston, 'Problems common to both Protestant and Catholic Churches in eighteenth-century Ireland'.

[76] C. Maxwell, *Dublin under the Georges* (1946) pp. 213-4.

[77] See J. G. Simms (ed. P. H. Kelly), op. cit. pp. 34-46.

but its memory lingered. The two leading learned societies of the eighteenth century were the (Royal) Dublin Society founded in 1731 and the Royal Irish Academy in 1785; in between there was the 1744 Psysico-Historical Society, which flourished for some years in the middle of the century and whose interests were afterwards absorbed into the Academy. Another important precursor was the select committee of the Dublin Society, established in 1772 to inquire into Irish antiquities. After the foundation of the Royal Irish Academy, the Royal Dublin Society focused on practical agricultural and economic developments and the Academy on more theoretical subjects. For instance, the eighteenth century was a period of rapid climatic change,[78] weather cycles were erratic and attracted the interest of both professional and amateur scientists alike. In the middle of the century there were the notes on climate kept by the Quaker physician Dr John Rutty,[79] who was anxious to find a relationship between disease and weather patterns. There were a number of papers on it, some in the early *Proceedings* of the Royal Irish Academy, and similar interest in recording climate was shown by scientifically interested men like Richard Lovell Edgeworth (**0688**). Edgeworth, who had been involved in the foundation of the Academy, belonged to the British circle known as the Lunar Society[80] which included pioneers of the early industrial revolution like Josiah Wedgwood, Erasmus Darwin and Joseph Priestley. Intellectually, eighteenth-century Ireland was far from isolated.

At the beginning of the century like-minded people met in taverns, coffee-houses &c. Political discussion was always of enduring interest. Established meetings and venues emerged as time passed for this and other topics. In the last quarter of the eighteenth century there was an accelerated growth in political clubs; for example the Monks of the Screw met during the American war to discuss and encourage constitutional and administrative reform. Throughout the century there were always informal clubs; Dalys, much patronised by the House of Commons, was the most famous of these and there were others centred around certain coffee shops and taverns. In addition, there was the coffee house in the Parliament House, where some MPs appear to have been almost permanent fixtures, for instance, Sir John Stewart Hamilton (**0940**). Many political clubs had branches outside the capital, for example, Whig clubs, the United Irishmen, the Orange Society and the more loosely structured Defenders. Many of these clubs lacked a unity of purpose and their aims varied from revolution, reform, abolition of tithes, redistribution of land and the remedy of various local ills, often feeding on inaccurate propaganda and instinctive fears.

From the middle of the eighteenth century the population grew with ever-increasing rapidity assisted by a milder climate and fewer outbreaks of epidemic disease. The

---

[78] See D. Dickson, *Arctic Ireland: The extraordinary story of the Great Frost and Forgotten Famine of 1740-1* (1997, 1998).
[79] J. Rutty, *Chronological history of the weather and seasons and of the prevailing diseases in Dublin* (1770) – a weather diary kept over 40 years.
[80] J. Uglow, *The Lunar Men: the friends who made the future, 1730-1810* (2002); there are numerous references to Edgeworth and his friends throughout this book

country remained basically agricultural and therefore dependent on seasonal employment, while the French Revolution reduced the opportunity for finding employment on the continent. At the same time towns also grew, producing a working class for whom employment was subject to the slumps and booms of early industrialisation. Both developments were accompanied by the growth of a small but important middle-class, becoming increasingly vociferous but largely excluded from political representation. This group, literate and increasingly prosperous, from the time of the American war agitated largely for administrative reform, which they expected would give them an input into the political life of the country commensurate with their social aspirations. They were the group whom Grattan sought to attract – his indefinable 'populace'. In the 1790s there emerged a much smaller and more fanatical group attracted to the ideas promulgated by the French Revolution. Many of these groups came under the umbrella of the United Irishmen. They represented different uncoordinated movements of discontent which varied throughout the country; for instance, abolition of tythes and redistribution of clerical land were more important to the grass-roots majority in many areas, while local disputes dominated in others &c.[81] Lack of organisation and co-ordination ensured that while there was a national movement of discontent, its expression would be fragmented and local but none the less frightening in a country lacking in effective social control. The radicals wished to amend, the revolutionaries to destroy, the *status quo* and the MPs wished to preserve it and sought to do so in the Union: many ordinary people, with simpler ambitions, were caught up in this maelstrom. The divided society destroyed or nullified many of the good intentions of the MPs as enshrined in their statutes.

---

[81] See N. Curtin, op. cit. esp. p.201.

2
THE WORLD OF THE MP

I PRIVILEGE AND PATRONAGE

It would be difficult to disagree with Sir Lewis Namier's view of the reasons that attracted men to parliament:

> Men went there 'to make a figure' ... The 'figure' of their daydreams differed with their rank and profession, with age, temperament and circumstances; but so much was common to practically all – the seat in the House was not their ultimate goal but a means to ulterior aims.[1]

Membership of parliament conferred privilege (although this was diminished as the century progressed)[2] as well as prestige. At almost every point the Irish parliament modelled itself upon the Westminster parliament,[3] and the members were extremely sensitive regarding their rights and privileges. The great points of freedom of speech and freedom of access to the crown by the Speaker had long since been won, but the question of the extent of the privilege of freedom from arrest and its potential abuse remained. This freedom derived from the fact that parliament was called by the sovereign to consult with him or her on the business of the kingdom. Therefore those elected for this purpose should be free from arrest by the ordinary courts so long as their services were required, a privilege which was extended to their servants, although in 1715 the House ordered that only domestic or menial servants were protected and then only if they were not Roman Catholics.[4] In 1695 the House called upon Captain Corker to explain why he had granted protection to one John Shelley as his menial servant. Shelley was the receiver of Corker's rents and in this respect the House agreed that he was a menial servant but that when he was sued 'in *autre droit* [he] has not any protection of this House'.[5]

The privilege was an old one, dating back to the reign of Edward IV, when a statute

[1] L. B. Namier, *Structure of politics at the accession of George III* (1929) p. 2.
[2] Privilege was gradually whittled away; see *HIP* vol. III pp. 42-4.
[3] See P. D. G. Thomas, *The House of Commons in the eighteenth century* (1971, repr. 1992). The Speakership was perhaps more important in Ireland where the Speaker was *primus inter pares*, but otherwise there was little difference; in fact the Irish parliament consciously modelled itself on its British counterpart.
[4] E. & A. Porritt, *The unreformed House of Commons* (1903) vol. II p. 460.
[5] *Commons jn. Ire.* (Bradley edn) vol. II pp. 655, 657, - 6, 7. Sept. 1695.

of 1463, 3 Edward IV, c.1, 'An act whereby the lords and commons of Parliament hath privilege for certain days before and after the said Parliament' stated that for 40 days before and after the said Parliament no member 'should be impleaded, vexed nor troubled by no means'. During the reign of Henry VIII it arose in the case of George Ferrers, an MP whose arrest in 1543 brought the personal wrath of Henry VIII who summoned the Chancellor, the judges, the Speaker and some of the most prominent MPs to declare that the king was at the apex of his power in parliament and that 'whatsoever offence or injury, during that time is offered to the meanest member of the House is to be judged as done against our person and the whole court of Parliament' and that as parliament was the supreme court of the land all inferior courts must give way before it.[6] By the beginning of the eighteenth century, interpretations of this statute, 3 Edward IV, c. 1, had created a number of uncertainties between the normal jurisdiction of the state and the jurisdiction of parliament. Furthermore, as parliament began to meet more frequently this privilege became increasingly liable to abuse. An attempt was made to control and clarify it by a statute of 1707, 6 Anne, c. 8 *(0103)*, 'an act for explaining and limiting the Privileges of Parliament'. This statute confirmed the 40 days before, during adjournments, and 40 days after the prorogation or dissolution of parliament. At the same time a plaintiff was not to be debarred from prosecuting his suit by the statute of limitations; distress for rent, duty or services were excluded from privilege; and privilege did not extend to MPs in their capacity as guardians, trustees or executors, nor to crown debtors.

In 1728 a further attempt, 1 Geo. II, c. 8 *(0252)*, was made to control this by reducing the time within which MPs might be sued before and after the meeting of parliament to 14 instead of 40 days; after 14 days they might be sued, subjected to judgments &c. but not arrested during the 40 days before or after the meeting of parliament. In effect the plaintiff's action is delayed but not prevented by privilege of parliament. Freedom from imprisonment for debt was a valuable privilege[7] and, as Primate Boulter pointed out, when the bill came before the House of Lords, 'several of our Lords [who] are very much in debt and value themselves in paying nobody, were from the first very much against the bill'.

Privilege was gradually whittled away until, by 1772, 11 & 12 Geo. III, c.12 *(0709)*, 'an Act for the further preventing delays of justice by reason of privilege of parliament', admitted that the previous acts had proved insufficient and that actions or suits or processes were not to be delayed by privilege of parliament. This act was originally in force for seven years but it was subsequently extended. By this statute there was little left except freedom from arrest, which continued until the Union,[8] although as the indebtedness of the Irish parliamentarian grew, there were occasional regrets at the

---

[6] T. F. T. Plucknett (ed.), *Taswell-Langmead's Constitutional History* (11th edn 1960) p. 250, but there are many other descriptions of this famous event.

[7] See Namier, op. cit., pp. 60-1.

[8] 11 & 12 Geo. III, c. 12. See also PRONI (or Library of Congress) Cavendish Debates. On 18 May 1778 Speaker Pery pointed out that this act took away all privileges of parliament in suits and actions brought against MPs.

diminution of privilege. For example, John Beresford (**0115**) told his friend Lord
Auckland at the time of the Union debates in 1799 that: 'Lord Ormonde (**0320**) and
Lord Westmeath (**1547**) are in debt, and the traders to whom they are indebted sent
in their bills, and not being paid directly, they have procured executions. The goods
were actually advertised before the execution was laid on. This is going rather far'.[9]
The merchants, accurately gauging the effect of the Union upon their business, were
exceedingly anxious to prevent it, while necessitous parliamentarians were most likely
to vote for it.

Parliament had powers over its members and over those whom it felt had behaved
in a derogatory or disrespectful fashion towards it. These powers were usually expressed
by brief imprisonment by the Serjeant-at-Arms under the direction of the Speaker, a
fine, an apology and a reprimand by the Speaker during which, particularly in the
earlier part of the century, the defendant was usually required to kneel at the bar of
the House and express penitence. In cases of extreme annoyance a member might be
expelled[10] permanently or otherwise, depending on how seriously his offence was
judged. This was rare – there were only about eight cases in all – and none between
1717 and 1753. Reasons for expulsion varied from blasphemy in the case of John
Asgill (**0056**) in 1703, while the last case was that of Arthur Jones-Nevill (**1125**), the
Surveyor-General, who was expelled in 1753 because the House considered that he
had not obeyed its resolution regarding the repair of barracks and had thereby 'acted
in manifest contempt of the authority' of the House. This expulsion, at the height of
the Money Bill crisis in 1753, was carried by 124 to 116 votes, and the process was
really resurrected in order to attack the government.

A seat in parliament also had social significance: 'To be out of parliament is to be
out of the world and my heart is set in being in it', wrote the victorious admiral Lord
Rodney, looking for a seat in the British House of Commons, to Lord George (Sackville)
Germain (**1835**) in 1780.[11] Dublin became the focus of social as well as political life
especially during the parliamentary season, which lasted approximately eight months
in every second year from 1703 to 1781 and every year thereafter until 1800 – Dublin's
social life was the inevitable victim of the Union. During the season balls, dinners,
receptions and all manner of entertainments crowded the social calendar and
membership of parliament naturally opened many doors, even apart from those of
the Castle, which was at the centre of this social whirl. The Irish stage was smaller
than the British one, its limitations greater, but the same ambitions, modified by
harsher circumstances, inspired members of a like society and a similar way of life.
Suitable clothing, jewels, horses, carriages, including a state coach for ceremonial
occasions, &c. were all expensive necessities.

[9] *Ber. Corr.* II p. 200, Beresford to Auckland 26 Jan. 1799; for the impact of the Union on Dublin see C. E.
Maxwell, *Dublin under the Georges* (1956), pp. 92-3.
[10] See, *HIP* vol. II pp. 389 *et seq.* 'Members censured and expelled' for the names of those expelled and the
reasons for their expulsion.
[11] Namier, op.cit. (1957 edn) pp. 1-2.

Membership of Parliament conferred not only prestige but frequently professional or personal advantage on its possessor. This translated into patronage for the powerful – the prestige of gratifying one's friends – and jobs for the less well materially endowed; these varied from positions which required real ability and industry – similar to today's civil servants – to those which were largely or entirely sinecures. At the lower end of the scale of expectations Lord Annally, recommending the son of Mr Smyth (**1649**), the MP for Mullingar, remarked to Lord Nugent (father-in-law of the viceroy) that: 'his expectations cannot be very high as he is not in Parliament but there are many places in my Lord Lieutenant's gift, which are fit for a gentleman yet may not be the object of a Member of Parliament's desire'.[12] In 1769 Lord Lieutenant Townshend stressed the political importance of places in the Revenue worth £300-£400 p.a. 'requiring no particular skill or attendance on the Revenue (as may be sought by members of parliament)'.[13] At the top of the scale, the 2nd Duke of Leinster (**0745**), always very conscious of his position and the respect due to it, wrote in 1780 to Lord Lieutenant Carlisle that: 'if this Peerage [Arthur Pomeroy (**1693**)] does not come over at the top of the list when the Patents come, I must decline any intercourse in the Political line with your Ldp. or any of His Majesty's Ministers';[14] and this hostility would be extended to his friends and dependants, correspondingly affecting the voting lists. Similarly the wealthy or those possessing parliamentary boroughs sought personal advancement in the peerage, while ambitious MPs would seek a knighthood, baronetcy or a much-sought initial rung on the peerage.

Military and ecclesiastical patronage were always in demand, particularly for younger sons. In 1775 Lord Lieutenant Harcourt wrote to Lord North that: 'my private reasons for adopting Major Skeffington (**1932**) are, I will confess, founded in the exigence of the moment. He is brother to the late Lord Massareene. He is in Parliament. His two nephews (**1931**, **1935**) are in Parliament also ... If Major Skeffington is not gratified I cannot expect his own or his nephews support; and a defection of three which to us makes a difference of six voices will ... be highly prejudicial to His Majesty's government in this Kingdom'.[15] In 1787 the Earl of Mornington (Marquess Wellesley) (**2215**) wrote asking for a post as aide-de-camp 'on pay' for his brother stating that: 'my intention is.... to bring Arthur into parliament',[16] otherwise the future Duke of Wellington (**2210**) was destined for India – another career possibility. The Church also offered opportunities for employment, for example in 1768 Lord Tyrone (**0113**) had originally been against the augmentation of the army 'but it was thought prudent to alter his Way of thinking by giving his brother a good living'.[17] Irish ecclesiastical

[12] BL Add. MSS 40,179, f. 21 Lord Annally to Lord Nugent, 12 August 1782. (Sir) Skeffington Smyth was MP for Mullingar 1779-83, Belturbet 1783-90 and Galway borough 1790-7. I have not been able to trace this son who probably d.s.p. young.
[13] PRONI DOD572/1/6 Townshend to Macartney, 20 Feb. 1769; see Johnston, *Gt B. & Ire.* pp. 215, 232.
[14] BL Add. MSS 34, 417 ff. 259-60.
[15] *Harcourt Papers* X pp. 15-18, 27 Oct. 1775; see also ibid. vol. IX pp. 245-6.
[16] *HMC* XIII p. 287 31 Oct. 1787, Johnston, *Gt B. & Ire.* pp. 31, 252-3.
[17] PRONI DOD572/1/6 20 Feb. 1769, BL Add. MSS 24, 138 f. 126.

patronage and to an extent Irish patronage in general was complicated by the demands made upon it by the English administration which considered it not only valuable as patronage in itself but, in the case of ecclesiastical patronage, as a safe haven for troublesome and possibly heterodox clergy,[18] while civil patronage avoided awkward questions for the British administration. Once appointed English clergy often absorbed and expatriated the natural patronage of the Irish Church. For instance, Bishop Nicholson (who succeeded the austere Archbishop King as Bishop of Derry) on one occasion wrote of a rectory in the diocese of Derry worth £500 p.a. that: 'the benefice will make a noble provision for one of my own family'.[19] King remonstrated, but Nicholson considered that as King had no family he did not appreciate the need to make provision for one! This was unfair as the bachelor King did endeavour to make such provision as he could for his relatives – but not at the expense of the Church to whose welfare he was sincerely devoted. While the economic state of the country improved as the century progressed it is doubtful if it improved fast enough to absorb the increasing number who felt that they had demands upon the government.

II FINANCIAL INTERESTS

Finding occupations for younger sons outside the armed forces, the church or government service could prove difficult. Sometimes the agent of a large landowner, like Lord Downshire (**1016**), offered a respectable occupation, particularly if the agent was obviously the personal representative of the magnate.[20] Banking was considered a suitable occupation for a gentleman but there was a tendency to denigrate other businesses, although their fruits could be appreciated by the needy gentry. Large bank failures sent a shiver through the country and bank failures were common as nearly every recession brought a run on the banks, usually resulting in at least one failure. Irish MPs also engaged in English speculation, for example Philip Perceval wrote to Lord Perceval on 29 October 1720 that Barry (**0092**): 'with his son [in-law], Maxwell (**1374**), are sunk by South Sea from the most plentiful and affluent fortune, to the miserable circumstance of being many thousands worse than nothing. He is now obliged to sell all he has in the world ... his house in Capel Street is going with the rest'.[21] Another person who was probably deeply affected by the South Sea Bubble collapse was the vice-treasurer, John Pratt (**1721**), who in consequence of a large deficiency in the national finances landed in jail. As vice-treasurer he controlled the finances of the nation and in keeping with contemporary practice in both Great Britain and Ireland so long as he could produce the necessary money when required

[18] O. MacDonagh, W. E. Mandle & P. Travers (eds), *Irish culture and nationalism* (1983), pp. 14-39, esp. pp. 26-8, E. M. Johnston, 'Problems common to both Protestant and Catholic Churches in Eighteenth-century Ireland'.
[19] C. J. Fauske (ed.), *Arbp. Wm. King and the Anglican Irish Context 1688-1729*, pp. 61-2.
[20] The way the system worked in very clearly shown in W. A. Maguire, *The Downshire estates in Ireland, 1801-45* (1972) and W. H. Crawford & B. Trainor, *Aspects of Irish social history 1750-1800* (PRONI 1969), and there are a number of other similar studies.
[21] BL Egmont Papers, Add. MS 47029 f. 41.

he had the use of it in the interim. Pratt was unable to meet these demands, hence his downfall. Sir Henry Cavendish (**0380**), who as Teller of the Exchequer 1755-76, similarly controlled the national finances also incurred a large deficit, estimated at £50,000 but probably over £67,000. This was only discovered after his death in 1776, and although he was probably of dubious efficiency he may have been affected by the slump of the 1770s. His abler son, who was a famous shorthand writer, managed to repay a large part of it after some delay.[22] Despite these examples many family fortunes were made this way, but it was risky particularly in the early 1720s. The only bank which never closed its doors was that operated by the Huguenot family the La Touches. Six members of this family (**1203–1208**) sat in parliament. They were noted for their probity and played an important role in the foundation of the Bank of Ireland *(0934)* in 1782 which finally, if belatedly, brought a degree of financial stability to the country.

The American war resulted in an enormous strain on the national and commercial finances of the country. The financial crisis was increased by the failure of three MP bankers, Hugh Henry Mitchell (**1415**) who was declared bankrupt in 1778, Richard Underwood (**2120**) who was also declared a bankrupt in the 1778 crisis but died in March 1779, and Robert Birch (**0145**) likewise declared bankrupt but rescued by Lord Lieutenant Buckinghamshire, who made him clerk of the quit rents at £150 p.a. At the same time government was advised to extend public credit to the discount bankers Finlay & Co. as two partners of this bank sat in parliament, John Finlay (**0727**) and Richard Nevill (**1527**).[23] Transferring money overseas or even within Ireland presented a problem. Normally transfers were made by bills of exchange, which resembled a cheque or an IOU; for example, if a London merchant owed a Dublin merchant money a landlord could – at a discount – buy a bill of exchange from the Dublin merchant and present it to the London merchant for encashment. These transfers were usually handled through a discount house and much depended upon the probity of the house and merchants involved. The failure of a discount house could have far reaching consequences. Membership of parliament and its accompanying privileges protected these men from the worst consequences of their peculation and muddling.

The most spectacular bank failure was that of Burton's Bank. The bank was originally operated by Benjamin Burton (**0292**), MP for Dublin city from 1703 to 1727 and Francis Harrison. Harrison died in 1725 and Burton in 1728 and the bank failed in 1733. Winding it up proved exceedingly complicated and by 1757 four acts of parliament *(0343, 0370, 0504, 0544)* had been passed for this purpose. In the 1750s there were a number of bank failures *(0529, 0530 0531)* and in 1759 an attempt was made to exercise some control over banking *(0566)* and particularly to prevent public

[22] D. W. Hayton (ed.), *The Irish Parliament in the eighteenth century: the long apprenticeship* (2001), A. P. W. Malcomson & D. J. Jackson, ' Sir Henry Cavendish and the Proceedings of the Irish House of Commons', esp. pp. 130-2.
[23] PRO SP63/459 f. 306.

officials from acting as bankers. Public officials, such as Nathaniel Clements (**0414**),[24] controlled public money in transit and could lend it to favoured persons so long as they could produce it when required. It required considerable financial ability to balance the books at the right moment. Clements was an astute financier, but even he was in difficulties in the late 1750s when the bank – Malone (**1336**), Clements (**0414**) and Gore (**0876**), which he founded with his fellow politicians – closed. His successor as Teller of the Exchequer, Sir Henry Cavendish (**0380**), as already noted, was much less successful. Clements retained his fortune.

Following the American war there was a movement for administrative reform, known as Economical Reform. John Tunnadine (**2116**), a Master in Chancery whom Lord Lieutenant Temple found 'had converted a great sum of the lodgments entrusted to him to his own use', was, although an MP, dismissed from his employments *(1025)* and died a bankrupt in 1787.[25] In an emerging economy bankruptcies were not unusual and a number of statutes tried to resolve the situation of debtors. Small debtors were imprisoned and the statutes often gave their names and backgrounds as well as where they were jailed *(0569,0649,0659,0679)*, and under what conditions they could be released. At the beginning of the French war, in the early 1790s, there was a major recession which triggered a number of bankruptcies. Parliament was concerned and in 1793 passed a statute *(1511)* 'for the support of commercial credit' which gave temporary loans to businessmen injured by recession. It was a novel and an interesting scheme, for bankruptcies meant redundancies and unemployment meant social unrest. Another method of bolstering credit, used from time to time throughout the century, was for prominent citizens to put an advertisement in the local newspaper endorsing the credit of a specific bank.

III THE ECONOMY: COMMERCIAL ENTERPRISES AND INFRASTRUCTURE

Dublin, Cork and Belfast all developed substantial merchant communities[26] and during the century smaller towns and markets emerged elsewhere. Agrarian activity is seasonal and with the rising population in the latter part of the century there was an increasing surplus of labour. Inevitably it was drawn into the towns and cities, giving parliament an additional reason to encourage the economy. Various small ventures received parliamentary support, some by direct parliamentary grants and others were supported through parliament's grant to the Royal Dublin Society *(1008,1104,1221)*. However, all emerging economies are subject to slumps and booms and these added to the problem of unemployment which increased the growth of combinations – an early form of trade union. The authorities became justifiably worried at the potential for

[24] A. P. W. Malcomson, *Nathaniel Clements: Government and the governing elite in Ireland, 1725-75* (2005), cap. 7 'Salaries, fees and perquisites, 1728-77'.
[25] *HMC XIII Rep. App.*III p. 492, see Johnston, *Gt B. & Ire.* p. 256.
[26] See T. M. Truxes, *Letterbook of Greg & Cunningham 1756-7: Merchants of New York and Belfast* (2001) for an example.

social unrest created by large-scale unemployment in the capital especially as anti-combination acts such as the 1780 Anti-Combination Act, 19 & 20 Geo. III, c. 19 *(0886,0903)*, proved ineffective. In 1785 Robert Brooke, a former East India officer, received a large parliamentary grant *(1082,1148)* for a state-of-the-art cotton mill in Co. Kildare unfortunately named Prosperous in expectation of a success that did not materialise. The grant carried the obligation to employ in and transplant to this rural development 2,000 city workers over a period of ten years.[27] In 1786 the enterprise collapsed *(1459)*. Brooke went bankrupt[28] but on his discharge re-joined the East India Company and subsequently became a distinguished Governor of St Helena.

There were other comparatively large enterprises. The most capital-intensive attempt at establishing a viable iron smelting works in eighteenth-century Ireland was at Arigna, at the south end of Lough Allen. Here it was hoped that the combination of ore and coal might provide a suitable foundation for commercial success, and in the 1780s Mary Reilly and her sons installed a modern plant at considerable cost. In 1789 they applied to parliament for a grant to offset at least part of the cost. The investigating committee reported positively, but lack of available funds forced the Chancellor of the Exchequer to quash the committee's recommendation. In 1793 the Reillys went bankrupt.[29] At this point the Arigna enterprise was taken over by Peter La Touche (**1207**), MP for Co. Leitrim and a member of the famous Dublin banking family. La Touche was equally unsuccessful and, before he handed the enterprise over to a Mr Roper, possibly lost as much as £80,000 on it, as he later claimed that the gates of Arigna iron on his estate had cost that amount. The Arigna experiment was almost certainly doomed because of the defective mineral content of the iron ore; in addition there were probably major scientific problems caused by fuelling the furnace with coal as the country's natural timber was exhausted.

The Reillys probably felt bitter at the government's lack of support, for in May 1797 John Foster (**0805**), the Speaker of the Irish House of Commons, received a letter warning him that:

> The foundry which belonged to Mr. La Touche at Rigna (some place in Connaught) ... they have settled principles of disloyalty there, and it is almost impossible to find a man in that quarter of the country who is not a United Irishman. Mr. Reilly, who held the foundry before Mr. La Touche, is most active in this business and gives the lower orders of the people every encouragement, and that he will, when it is necessary give them a cannon. It is understood he has eight pieces concealed. I hope the foundry has supplied him with no balls, of which care should be taken the men being all disaffected.[30]

[27] L. M. Cullen & T. C. Smout, *Comparative aspects of Scottish and Irish economic and social history* (1977) pp. 102-3, Dickson, 'Aspects of the Rise and Decline'.
[28] Among Brooke's debts were £57,000 owed to the Treasury and £1,300 owed to the London-Irish House of Nesbitt and Stewart.
[29] See R. B. McDowell, *Ireland in the Age of Imperialism and Revolution*, p. 18; Parl. Reg. vol. XI, p. 130; *Report on the Arigna Ironworks* (Dublin, 1801).
[30] PRONI D207/5/66 reproduced in PRONI educational facsimiles, *United Irishmen*, no. 69.

Throughout this period Ireland remained overwhelmingly rural, dependent on pastoral and arable agriculture and, along the coast, fishing. The development of the fishing industry was a concern of the MPs, among them the Rt Hon.William Burton (Conyngham) (0303), whose enthusiasm for developing the Co. Donegal fisheries *(1106)* received the support of parliament. Apart from Dublin, Cork and rapidly growing Belfast, most towns were small. Commercial life was restricted and industrialisation had made little impact. Permission for the local landlord to hold a market could be a valuable asset, depending on its popularity and consequently the duties and tolls that it engendered. Such minerals as there were, as at Arigna, were poor in quality; for example, coal was found near Kilkenny, at Ballycastle (see 0197) in Co. Antrim and at Coalisland in Co. Tyrone. Hope of potential mineral resources was periodically revived not only by discoveries of coal and iron but also of small uneconomic discoveries of copper, tin, lead, cobalt, manganese and even silver and gold. These drew enthusiastic support from MPs. For example, at the end of the century a lead mine partly owned by Lord Henry FitzGerald (0733) was, according to Wakefield, being profitably worked at Glendalough in the first decade of the nineteenth century and so was another by Lord Leitrim (0418) near Errigal in Co. Donegal. Unfortunately most of these ventures were short lived.

Textiles *(0926,0927)* were the usual manufacture of a pre-industrial society. They provided a cottage industry, although by the end of the century a factory-based cotton industry was becoming established. Under the mercantalist system, exports, in the case of wool, were restricted by legislation *(0051)*. Internal trade was not affected. It was hoped to balance restrictions on wool by encouraging the linen manufacture, which developed in Ulster but failed, despite special encouragement *(1135,1185)*, to develop to the same extent in the rest of Ireland, although many landlords, for example Robert French of Monivea (0834),[31] tried to encourage it. For a mixture of honour and patronage MPs sought to belong to the Linen Board, which regulated and encouraged the trade. After the country recovered from the famine of the 1740s the population increased and, as has been noted, labour in agrarian societies being seasonal, there was a rising abundance of under-utilised labour. At the same time there was neither the capital to create nor the resources to sustain an industrial development such as that taking place in contemporary Britain. Nor was there the necessary infrastructure. The peasants often paid their rent by goods or labour. Many were still bound by manorial obligations, grinding their corn at the lord's mill, attending his manor court *(1085)* and paying him dues such as an inheritance tax, known as a heriot. Much trade was still done by barter and in certain areas tradesmen's tokens were used instead of specie – Edward Smyth (1946), MP for Lisburn 1743-60, issued such a token with his family crest, a unicorn, on one side and 'I owe the bearer two-pence on the other'. Ireland did not have a mint and there was a perpetual shortage

[31] D. A. Cronin, *A Galway Gentleman in the Age of Improvement: Robert French of Monivea, 1716-79* (IAP, 1995).

of specie, particularly lower denominations of the coinage. This led to a direct and often visible relationship between the metal content of a coin and its value – all sorts of coins circulated and as their value was assessed by weight, small portable scales were carried by those requiring to make a monetary exchange. The Irish pound was discounted against the pound sterling and from time to time foreign currency was revalued; this frequently created a storm, as in 1737 when over-valued Portuguese moidores were devalued. The merchants felt that they had been cheated and Cork city ordered its MPs, Hugh Dixon (**0638**) and Emanuel Pigott (**1680**), to oppose the Money Bill, deluging parliament with petitions against the devaluation.

Regulation either universally, through the mercantilist system, or locally was usual. The effectiveness of these regulations is perhaps open to question especially in view of repeated statutes on this subject. Cork was the centre of the provision trade *(0136,0165, 0232)*, which, in the South, was Ireland's principal commercial activity as linen was in the North *(0196,0225,0347,0435,0623)*. Parliament legislated repeatedly for quality control over both *(0239,0549)*. During the reign of Queen Anne weights and measures were standardised *(0095)* and throughout the century repeated efforts were made to regulate the quality of provisions, especially butter. The provision trade was particularly important in supplying the West Indian market and servicing the fleet, especially in time of war. The price of bread and grain were also regulated – grain was to be sold by weight and the assize of bread fixed on the middle price of wheat *(0381,0446,0519)*. Provisions for the capital were of special and continual concern *(0779,0835,0850,0888)*. Regulating the linen industry was complex as it involved not only the production of the web but its subsequent bleaching and potential to injure the cloth *(0400,0623)*.

One of the earliest problems confronting the MPs from both a security and a commercial necessity was the need to provide the country with an adequate communications system. Local roads were the responsibility of the parish, which was expected to exact so many days of road service from the local inhabitants *(0138,0226,0560,0693)*. This was very unpopular and the product far from adequate. By the 1730s and 1740s acts for the encouragement of toll roads were a major feature of parliamentary legislation. For instance, eight statutes *(0309-0316)* for the improvement of roads were passed in the 1731-2 session of parliament, and ten in each of the two following sessions, 1733–4 *(0333-0342)* and 1735–6 *(0357-0358,0360-0362,0364-0367,0369)*. Thereafter the many statutes were usually to finance and repair existing roads. Unlike most of Western Europe, Ireland had not benefited from the road-building proclivity of the Romans. Consequently Ireland's system of inland communications had to be developed either anew or from rudimentary bridle paths or foot tracks, often with detours to avoid intruding on a powerful landlord's estate – the Grand Jury approved local county roads. Torn by the wars of the seventeenth century, the country had by 1700 developed little more than a minimal infrastructure; and even at the end of the eighteenth century there were areas that still lacked adequate communications and to which access proved a problem at the time of the nineteenth-century famine. Nevertheless, the infrastructure which the Irish parliament established was to last, with little change, for the next 150 years.

Building an effective system of roads and canals and the direct encouragement of manufacturing industry was one of the more positive aspects of a developing national identity. Most Irish MPs were also JPs and members of the grand jury of their counties and the majority took their duties seriously. Efficient and successful JPs like Speaker Foster (**0805**) were highly respected by their contemporaries. This, and the fact that they rode to parliament, visiting their friends *en route* – Irish inns were deplorable and many colourful tales are told about them – ensured that they had an intimate knowledge of the country's communications and its needs. As grand jurors they supervised the upkeep of existing roads and the building of new ones. Before the establishment of the Post Office in 1784, these new roads were usually toll roads sanctioned by act of parliament and subject to various conditions. Throughout the eighteenth century, horseback was the quickest and most flexible method of travel; for instance, the bar rode on circuit throughout the century.

Even today Ireland's largest towns are on the coast. In 1700 the population was small, and throughout the eighteenth century there were few sizeable inland centres of population, although economic development was reflected in the great increase in the number of fairs and markets – which parliament attempted to regulate *(0478)*. By the 1730s stage-coaches were operating regular services from Dublin to Cork, Waterford, Drogheda and Kilkenny. Gradually these services extended northwards to Newry and on 13 August 1752 the first stage-coach set out from Dublin to Belfast, but a regular Dublin–Belfast service was not established until 1788. A stage-coach carried ten people inside and rather more on top. Not surprisingly, luggage was strictly limited and anything above 20 lb was likely to be surcharged as excess baggage. The coach was drawn by six horses, and the journey to Belfast, just over 100 English miles, took three days. Similarly, the service was extended westwards to Athlone, and by the end of the century there was a network of coaches throughout the country. Although at the beginning of the century the road system was by any standard 'rudimentary', by 1778 George Taylor and Andrew Skinner could produce *Maps of the Roads of Ireland*, which appeared again in a revised edition in 1783. It was intended for gentlemen and for government departments such as the Revenue Board and the Barrack Board, all of which supported the authors. Its sketch maps show the routes from one town to another and their distances, as well as points of interest along the way – including the houses of the subscribers. The postal system, naming certain towns, had been established in 1635 by a proclamation of Charles I but the unrest of the seventeenth century ensured that its development was erratic. However by 1729 there were 109 postal towns in the service, 65 of which had a twice weekly delivery and by the 1730s there was a thrice-weekly delivery in the service between Dublin and Cork. Until 1784 the service appears to have been expensive and inefficient. A statute of 1784, 23 & 24 Geo. III, c. 17 *(0999)*, established an Irish Post Office and the Post-Master General was given powers to widen and strengthen old roads and create new ones to carry the mail. These roads were paid for by a national tax, and many were not only straight but of high quality.

In a pre-industrial and early industrial society water travel and transport were always preferable, and water was the only way of transporting bulky and heavy merchandise. At the beginning of the century Ireland's ports, while varying in quality, were adequate to the demands on them. In the course of the century they were improved and a system of canals, or inland navigation, intended for the cost-effective carriage of heavy or bulky goods, was established *(0274,0492,0518)*. The most successful of these was the Newry Canal constructed between 1731 and 1741. Its success was accidental for it was built to carry coal from Coalisland on Lough Neagh to the capital; this proved uneconomic, so in the event it carried linen, with coal and other goods as back-cargo from the capital. It opened in 1742 and was among the earliest commercial canals in the British Isles. Significantly, financing of the turnpikes, and particularly canals, involved an important combination of public support and private enterprise, though this tended to be vitiated by inadequate resources spread between too many projects, temporary enthusiasms and lack of commercial viability – the trade for which they were intended did not always materialise. Nevertheless, it is difficult to see how undertakings such as the Grand and Royal canals could have been funded otherwise – these canals attempted to provide parallel water links from Dublin to the Shannon, and the Grand Canal had a branch which ran past the Kilkenny coalfields down to Waterford. Ireland felt severely the lack of viable coal supplies and attempts were also made to develop Ballycastle harbour to ship coal from a nearby outcrop to Dublin. Although turf, or peat, was the principal fuel throughout Ireland, coal was used particularly on the east coast, and supplies for the capital were always a major problem *(0145,0616,0689)*. The other cause of concern was food *(0847,1103)* and the unrest created by shortages *(0534,1019)*.

IV SOCIAL PROBLEMS: POVERTY, PRISONS, HOSPITALS AND DISPENSARIES

Irish MPs were very conscious of the insuperable social problems confronting them. They attempted to develop an infrastructure to cope with them and in some areas they presented the model for developments elsewhere. For instance, various attempts were made to control beggars – a problem which was magnified by the lack of a Poor Law. In England the great Elizabethan Poor Law of 1601, adjusted but not amended until 1834, made the poor of the parish the responsibility of the parish. In Dublin city an attempt was made to follow the English example *(0308)*. But Ireland was a rural country with a minimal infrastructure, and demands by the parish, which lacked the social homogeneity of its English counterpart, were unpopular; consequently, the poor roamed the country begging or looking for work and only too often spreading epidemic disease *(0814,1040)*. By the establishment of the Dublin Workhouse in

1703 *(0081,1224)*, followed by similar less ambitious institutions in other large towns *(0778,0856)*, MPs tried with dubious success to control the problems created by poverty and abandoned children. Provision for the latter was made in the Foundling Hospital (at first attached to the Dublin Workhouse but in 1727 separated from it) *(0271,0288,1091)* until they were of an age to be apprenticed. Many died before they reached this age. Contemporaries, though accustomed to high infant mortality, were appalled to discover that during the 12 years 1784 to 1796, 25,253 children were entered on the hospital's admission records and of these 11,253 had died. The London Foundling Hospital, founded a decade later than the Dublin one, had similar mortality in the mid-century but by its close this had fallen to 17 per cent. The Paris Foundling Hospital had a rate more comparable to the Dublin one.[32] The MPs, alerted by Sir John Blaquiere (**0162**), were deeply shocked and in 1797 the hospital was reorganised and placed under the supervision of 13 lady governesses, including the Duchess of Leinster and Lady Castlereagh, the wife of the Chief Secretary (**2009**). As well as in more public offices, resident wives, often very young, played an important supervisory role managing large and complex households, educating children on the estate and, depending on their abilities, advising and influencing their husbands.[33]

The deplorable state of the prisons and their inmates did not go unnoticed by the MPs, although there was little sustained effort at improvement on this front before the reign of George III. In 1763 there were two statutes *(0594)* and *(0617)*, the first of which absolved the innocent from fees incurred while they were in prison and the second attempted to regulate the illegal activities of jailers. These were sponsored by Henry Flood (**0762**) and Sir Hercules Langrishe (**1200**); Sir John Parnell (Sr.) (**1632**) and Henry Sheares (**1909**), the father of the two United Irishmen executed in 1798 – Sheares had previously established a charity in Cork to relieve small debtors. Many, if not most prisoners were imprisoned for debt, even very small sums. The radical MP Charles Lucas (**1276**) was also involved in prison reform until his death in 1771. In the late 1760s and 1770s Dublin's two major prisons, Newgate and the Marshalsea, were rebuilt and during the American war hulks were moored in the Liffey to hold prisoners who would previously have been transported. In fact transportation was to be a major problem in the post-war 1780s – even after Australia became a possibility, it was a very expensive one. From 1777 to 1787 there was a constant stream of reforming legislation.[34] The great fear was always the prevalence of jail fever (the jails were incredibly unhygienic) and the potential of it spreading to the outside population (e.g. through the courts).

[32] C. E. Maxwell, *Dublin under the Georges* (1956), pp.159-62; *Les Domaines de L'Histoire*, C. Delasselle, 'Les infants abandonnés a Paris au XVIIIe siècle', esp. pp. 194, 198-9.
[33] Much depended upon personality, family connections &c. but see *IMC Leinster I* for the obvious influence of the Duchess, also pp. 42, 68 on a more domestic note.
[34] *HIP* vol. 1 lists them; see *(0827,0832,0846,1016,1023,1130,1133,1206)*.

In the late 1770s a remarkable figure had appeared, Sir Jeremiah Fitzpatrick MD –
he was to be the dominant influence on prison reform until the outbreak of the
French war in the 1790s. Sir Jeremiah, a disciple of John Howard, was not an MP
but he was a singularly able and energetic advisor with a gift (partly through his
telling use of statistics) for influencing MPs, in particular Peter Holmes (**1033**), Richard
Griffith (**0904**), George Ogle (**1573**), Frederick Trench (**2108**) and Sir Edward Crofton
(**0524**). Prison reform was also supported by such influential figures as Speaker Foster
(**0805**) and Lord Chancellor Fitzgibbon (**0749**). In addition four Chief Secretaries
showed an interest: Sir John Blaquiere (**0162**), who as seen from his concern with the
Foundling Hospital had a continuing interest in social problems, William Eden (**0681**),
who had already shown interest in English prison reform before his arrival, Thomas
Orde (**1594**) and in the later 1790s Thomas Pelham (**1650**). By then, however, the
French war had transferred Sir Jeremiah to military responsibilities, and the widespread
unrest and the impending rebellion made further reform virtually impossible.[35] Irish
prison reform was also important as it resembled the structure of institutional reform
in nineteenth-century Britain; as such it was part of the baggage which Ireland brought
into the imperial parliament.[36]

Health was a major concern, as is reflected in the number of Dublin hospitals
which date from the eighteenth century. Among these was the Charitable Infirmary,
established in 1718 – it was the first 'modern' charitable hospital in Great Britain or
Ireland. Stevens followed in 1733 and Mercers in 1734, the Hospital for Incurables
a decade later. In 1745 the first maternity hospital in the British Isles was established
in Dublin. St Patrick's Hospital for the Insane (endowed by Swift) was granted a
charter in 1746 and opened in 1757, the Lock Hospital for the treatment of venereal
disease (the Aids of the eighteenth-century – 2,000 cases were estimated to have been
treated in 1792-3 alone) was opened in 1753. In 1765 parliament attempted the
ambitious scheme of creating a nationwide system of county infirmaries
(0646,0662,1080,1081). As early as 1767, 7 Geo. III, c. 15 *(0669* confirmed in
0688), authorised the Dublin Society to use part of its grant for establishing a
pharmacopoea pauperum 'for dispensing medicines to the poor of the city of Dublin
according to a plan laid down by John Wade, Chemist'. In 1792 the Belfast Dispensary
was advertising for support and in 1793 a dispensary was established in Tandragee,
Co. Armagh. By the 1780s the dispensary movement[37] had become established, and
by the close of the century Dublin and other large cities had a number of hospitals
and charitable institutions of various kinds. These received enthusiastic support from
various types of fund raising, for example designated church collections, concerts
(Handel's *Messiah* was first performed in 1742 at such a concert) or the entertainments

[35] O. MacDonagh, *The Inspector General: Sir Jeremiah Fitzpatrick and social reform, 1783-1802* (1981), pp. 109-13
(Sir John Parnell (Jnr), Chancellor of the Exchequer (**1633**)) 126.
[36] See ibid. p. 116.
[37] R. D. Cassell, *Medical Charities, Medical Politics: the Irish dispensary system and the Poor Law, 1836-1872*
(1997); although it covers the nineteenth century, chapter 1 does give some idea of earlier conditions.

in the custom-built Rotunda attached to the Lying-in Hospital. Unfortunately effective medical care had to await the discovery of antiseptics (anaethetics and antibiotics) as until then the therapeutic value of hospitals was severely limited. The MPs also concerned themselves with health and safety measures; for instance the erection of lime-kilns within the city of Dublin was prohibited as being detrimental to the health of its citizens *(0725,0813)*.

V LANDLORDS' FINANCES: LAND, MARRIAGE, INHERITANCE AND DIVORCE

At a personal level, the economic circumstances of individual landlords were as various as the class itself. De Latocnaye was probably correct when he remarked of the resident landlords that: 'nearly all the rich, I am told, spend more than their incomes, and are obliged to resort to ruinous expedients to keep up style'.[38] Family responsibilities, building and politics accounted for much if not all and more of the landlord's income. Some rebuilding was probably essential, given the wars of the seventeenth century, but possibly not on the ambitious scale so often attempted. Proximity to England and the desire for emulation was a considerable source of temptation. Furthermore, by the mid-eighteenth century a suitable residence in the capital was also considered desirable, sometimes like Leinster (Kildare) (0734) or Powerscourt House (2241) custom built. Less ambitiously, MPs bought one of the houses in Henrietta Street, Rutland (Parnell) Square, Gardiner's Mall (O'Connell Street), St Stephen's Green or Merrion Square purpose-built by speculators, such as Luke Gardiner (0842) or Nathaniel Clements (0414). Many MPs either were, or considered that they were, architects. Then houses required furniture, paintings[39] and a few family portraits by fashionable artists.[40] Added to these were personal adornments, clothes, jewellery &c. for entertainment was increasingly a feature of the eighteenth century; this could be private, charitable or public shows which could include almost anything which its sponsor thought might be profitable and that allowed the participants to see and be seen. Then encumbrances upon an estate were cumulative, not only as regards debts and mortgages but also with regard to family responsibilities. 'There are some owners of very large estates,' observed Wakefield, 'who have not a shilling income, the whole of their fortune being absorbed either by the payment of a mother's jointure, the fortunes bequeathed to brothers and sisters, or debts contracted by themselves, or left them by their predecessors'.[41]

[38] De Latocnaye, *Frenchman's walk* (Dublin, 1797, trans. Belfast, 1917) p. 20.

[39] The home market did not always appreciate its own artists, but for some indication of the talent available see *A New History of Ireland: Eighteenth-century Ireland, 1691-1800*, vol. IV pp. 471-541.

[40] S. Benedetti, *The Milltowns: a family reunion* (National Gallery of Ireland, 1997) gives some idea of the creation of a suitable collection. Russborough and the Milltown collection were largely assembled by Joseph Leeson (1212). More generally see T. Barnard, *A guide to the sources for the history of material culture in Ireland, 1500-2000* (2005).

[41] E. Wakefield, *Account of Ireland statistical and political* (1812), vol. I p.245; J. M. Goldstrom & L.A. Clarkson (eds), *Irish population, economy and society* (1981) pp. 134-54, Roebuck, 'Landlord indebtedness in Ulster in the seventeenth and eighteenth centuries'. D. W. Hayton, Ph.D. Thesis, 'Ireland and the English Ministers 1707-16' (Oxford Univ. 1975), pp. 10-11; in 1715 the Earl of Granard had an income of £2,000 p.a. and debts of £12,000 and Lords Bellew, Bellomont, Blaney, Roscommon and Granard were in receipt of government pensions.

As a class the Irish landlords were not good financial managers, though there were exceptions, notably the Stewarts (**2008, 2009**), and debts tended to pile up against mortgages on their estates, for land was the usual security for loans. The usury laws against excessive interest were in force throughout the eighteenth century and to some extent curbed the excesses of market supply and demand. At the beginning of the century, interest had been as high as 10 per cent, the official ceiling for lending decreed in 1635 by 10 Chas, 1 c. 22. This declined as the country became more stable. In 1704 the maximum chargeable interest was reduced, by 2 Anne, c. 16 *(0078)*, to 8 per cent, and in 1721, 8 Geo. I, c. 13 *(0220)* further reduced the permissible rate to 7 per cent. The final adjustment for the century was made by 5 Geo. II, c. 7 *(0301)*, which decreed that all arrangements that involved an interest charge in excess of 6 per cent 'shall be utterly void'. The official rate in England was 5 per cent but scarcity and the exchange rates militated against the Irish pound and Irish currency was devalued against the pound sterling. Landlords, bankers, merchants and insurance companies all borrowed and lent money on land, the basic security, while a reputable landlord often held small sums borrowed from local people, who felt that the landlord was safer than the bank. For example, in 1738, a widow Smith wished to lend Judge Ward (**2181**) the sum of £800,[42] and in 1783 Thomas Knox (**1188**), later 1st Earl of Ranfurly, thanking the wealthy linen draper, Thomas Greer of Dungannon, for his offer of a £200 loan, wrote that: 'I will only accept it if I can be sure of paying it back and could only do this if you will increase the amount to be lent to me to £1,000, which would cover all my requirements. Let me know if I can have £600 more in February'.[43] In 1810 the 3rd Marquess of Downshire borrowed from the Belfast merchants Hugh Crawford, John Robinson and Robert Linn, £13,000, £10,000 and £7,000 respectively and a further £10,000 from the Coleraine merchant Robert Kyle.[44]

Debts and mortgages once acquired tended to pass from generation to generation. An eighteenth-century estate was in many ways a family concern. A landlord had a duty to provide for his wife, the widows of his predecessors, his brothers and sisters and his own children. This was done by settling parts of the estate in the hands of trustees so that the income would provide jointures, or annuities for the widows, suitable dowries for the daughters and portions for the younger sons. When Joshua Dawson (**0591**) died in March 1724/5 he left his eldest son 'a very good estate' but subject to various debts, jointures and portions, while the younger sons were left £500 each of which only 5% (£5) p.a. could be used for their maintenance while they were minors – their mother's jointure was only £200 p.a. so she was not in a position to help them.[45] Once made, these settlements could only be altered by act of

---

[42] PRONI D.2092/1/5/36 May 8 1738.
[43] PRONI D.1044/677A.
[44] Maguire, op. cit. p.101, see also p. 95.
[45] *IMC Letters of Marmaduke Coghill 1722-38*, p. 22.

parliament. The further expense – and the publicity – which this involved made it an expedient of last resort. It has been estimated that during the eighteenth century half of the land of England was held under strict settlement.[46] The available evidence indicates that the situation in Ireland was more extreme, particularly as less support could be drawn from sources other than the land. Although estates could not be entailed for the following generation while the heir was a minor, on his majority he, as the interested party in the last entail, could agree to alterations being made before the estate was again tied up. Further adjustments were made when he married or remarried to absorb the dowry, ensure the jointure of the bride and make provision for any children, apart from the heir, that might be born to the marriage. About 1783 the heir (**0828**) of the French family of Co. Roscommon came of age and his father requested his permission to sell for £12,780 his Sligo estate, which then had a rent roll of £710 p.a. The son refused consent and in 1809 was receiving from it an income of £2,000 p.a. – as a result of a combination of changes in leasing policy and the rapid escalation of rents in the intervening period.[47]

The effect of these settlements was to make the landlord a tenant for life of the family estate and their intention was to ensure that the estate would pass intact to his eldest son, upon whose coming of age and marriage the various settlements would be rearranged to the same end for the next generation. Although primogeniture ensured that the estate went to the eldest male child, thereby keeping the core of the family's wealth intact, other members of the family also had a claim to provision from it. A successful politician like John Hely-Hutchinson (**1001**) or John Foster (**0805**) could hope to have their wives ennobled with a remainder to their common children, thus allowing them to continue their career in the House of Commons. In default of surviving sons, daughters could inherit the family property but not, unless there was a special remainder, any of their father's titles – this happened in the case of the 1st Marquess of Antrim (**1317**), whose earldom was remaindered to his daughters in succession and their male heirs, but this was very unusual. Therefore, it was possible for the family fortune to become separated from the family title, leaving the possessor of the title inadequate resources to sustain his dignity. For instance, the 5th Viscount Allen found himself in this position as the 'family estate went between Lady Maine (Mayne) and Lady Carysfort, daughters to a former Lord Allen'.[48] While this was a very clear-cut example, the failure to provide an obvious male heir inevitably produced problems, especially when an estate was variously divided among a number of co-heiresses. The most complicated of inheritance cases was the Rochfort (**1801**)–Loftus (**2088**) case which originated in two sides of the family claiming an estate.

---

[46] Ibid. pp. 84-5; *Transactions of the Royal Historical Society* vol. XXX (1950), H. J. Habakkuk 'Marriage settlements in the eighteenth century'. See also G. E. Mingay, *English landed society in the eighteenth century* (1963), pp. 32-6.
[47] Wakefield, op. cit. vol. 1, p. 275.
[48] *Proc. RIA* 56 C 3 p. 28.

As early as 1761 the Irish House of Commons passed by a majority of 12 – albeit in a thin House on the last day of the parliamentary session – the heads of a bill to allow Catholics to invest money in mortgages on land. Subsequently, the bill was rejected by the British Privy Council, who considered that it might endanger Protestant control over land, with consequent political implications. Nevertheless, pressure to allow Catholics to invest capital in land continued. In 1771 11 & 12 Geo. III, c. 21 *(0718)*, concessions in the length of lease and local taxes were made for reclamation of bogs, an action indicative of the growing shortage of land as well as shortage of capital for improvements. But the administration was still reluctant to allow Catholics direct investment in mortgages for, as Lord Townshend pointed out: 'It would give the Popish creditors such a control over those who are in debt as may in particular times operate very strongly'.[49] Another unsuccessful attempt to remedy this situation, sponsored by Thomas Maunsell (**1371**), was made in February 1774. Finally in 1778 Luke Gardiner (**0842**) successfully introduced a bill *(0867)* allowing Catholics to purchase and hold land on the same *de facto* terms as Protestants.

Pressure had been building from wealthy Catholic merchants, and the first of the major Catholic Relief Acts, the 1778 act, allowed the purchase of 999-year leases or virtual fee simple. During the eighteenth century money from Irish commercial ventures was still reflected in land transfers, but purchasers were finding it more and more difficult to buy estates. Restrictive practices had hindered the free flow of money for too long. Similarly, from about the middle of the century, there was a demand for small estates from the rising middle-class protestant merchants. Recognising this phenomenon, Arthur Annesley's agent vainly tried to persuade Annesley to sell his Co. Down estate in small blocks, rather than as a whole, on the grounds that nabobs, or wealthy cash purchasers, were rare, but there was an increasing number of moderately wealthy businessmen, particularly in that linen-dominated area, who were anxious to become landed gentry and were increasingly frustrated by their inability to purchase small estates.[50]

Landlords, when their finances allowed, were always anxious to round off their estates. Land was usually purchased on the basis of so many years' annual return. For example, in 1745 John Colhoun purchased for Lord Abercorn a small parcel of about 75 acres let at £22 p.a. with 15 years on the leases. He paid £535 or slightly over 24 years' purchase.[51] Sixty-five years later in 1810, Lord Downshire's agent purchased the 221-acre estate of North Tyrella, near Downpatrick, for £9,310 or 24$^{1}/_{2}$ years' purchase of a rent-roll of £381, although this purchase was encumbered with an annuity of £150 for the lifetime of a 73-year-old lady.[52] These small sales frequently

[49] W. E. H. Lecky, *A History of Ireland in the eighteenth century* vol. II, p. 193, Apr. 10 1772.
[50] W. H. Crawford, *Letters from an Irish land-agent* (1976) op. cit. p. 57.
[51] PRONI T2541/1A1/2/34.
[52] PRONI T2541/1A1/1B/53 June 16 1745; Maguire, op. cit,. p. 12.

offered opportunities for considerable chicanery. In 1800 Earl Macartney (**1302**) was considering adding to his Co. Antrim estate at Lisanoure near Ballymoney, and his agent informed him that the vendor's law agent had told him that: 'if you should give him £500 you should get the lands perhaps £1,000 cheaper than you would do otherwise' and he backed up the offer by quoting other examples of similarly fraudulent activity. As early as 1750 Nathaniel Nisbitt had told Lord Abercorn that in the Co. Donegal hinterland of Londonderry: 'the purchase of lands are greatly advanced in this country particularly small estates, as there are so many people of middle rank has got money'.[53] This indication of a growing middle class, many of whom were outside the confines of the established church, was an important feature of Irish society in the second half of the eighteenth century. Land purchases reflected the prosperity accruing from Ireland's major commercial enterprises, linen in Ulster and provisions in Munster, while land around Dublin, with the metropole's multiplicity of variously sized businesses, was always at a premium.

Land, though the basic, was not the only source of wealth. Four members of the Alexander family (**0027–0030**), East India and Londonderry merchants, and three members of the Stewart family (**2001, 2006, 2009**), from a similar commercial background, all sat in parliament. All had hastened to turn their commercial wealth into landed property. A native fortune was that of Joseph Leeson's (**1212**) whose father, 'a fanatic brewer', had made a fortune. The brewer's son built Russborough and became Earl of Milltown. Similarly, the career of Nicholas Lawless (**1209**), 1st Baron Cloncurry, illustrates the centrality of the possession of land to social advancement. His father had been a successful Dublin clothier and Nicholas Lawless was 'well versed in the commerce of money'. In 1775 he purchased the 3,683 acre estate of Abington, Co. Limerick, for £26,000. The value of an estate was usually calculated as a multiple of so many years' rental; thus, as the gross rental of the Abington estate was £982, he paid the equivalent of approximately 26 years for its purchase. However, the rental was subject to certain encumbrances, such as a jointure, or widow's annuity, of £300 p.a. and a quit rent, a due paid to the Crown, of £30 p.a. Estimating his purchase on its net rather than its gross return, he had paid nearly 40 years' purchase. Not surprisingly he considered it 'a dear bargain', particularly as he was obtaining 4 per cent from government debentures and 5 per cent from other investments. However, rents rose in the years following the American war and by 1793 Nicholas Lawless, now Lord Cloncurry, had an unencumbered income from Abington of £1,104. In addition he could calculate with satisfaction his 'other valuables, my peerage worth £10,000 [sic!], my house in Merrion Square worth £4,000, and my plate and books which cost more than £2,000'. He had been made a baronet in 1776 and for the next two parliaments had purchased his return for the borough of Lifford from Lord Erne

---

[53] PRONI T2541/1A1/2/34.

(0519).[54] During this time he earnestly pursued a peerage, which he ultimately obtained in 1790. Success of this kind reinforced a widespread faith in the value of land and parliamentary influence and Lawless's faith was almost certainly echoed by two other newly arrived peers, Lords Londonderry (2008) and Caledon (0029).

Two of the most famous land sales in the eighteenth century were of Ulster estates: the Colvill (0451, 0452, 0453) estate at Newtown(ards), Co. Down, in 1744 and, in 1776, the Hamilton–Orrery estate at Caledon, Co. Tyrone. Coincidentally, both estates were bought by merchants with Londonderry connections from capital accrued in the East India trade. The Colvill estate belonged to Robert Colvill (0453), the step-son of Brabazon Ponsonby (1696), 1st Earl of Bessborough, who administered the estate and the parliamentary borough of Newtown both during Colvill's minority and in his wild, unbalanced majority. In 1721 Colvill (0453) made a will in favour of his infant half-brother, John Ponsonby (1702), but in 1744, under the influence of his mistress, he sold the estate for £42,000 to Alexander Stewart (♦♦♦♦), a rich, ambitious Belfast flax-merchant. Stewart had inherited an estate in Co. Donegal from his older brother, but the bulk of his wealth came from his wife and cousin, Mary Cowan, daughter and heiress of both her father, Alderman Cowan of Londonderry, and more importantly her half-brother, Sir Robert Cowan, a former Governor of Bombay. Her fortune was estimated at nearly £100,000.[55] This sale was probably a considerable blow to Colvill's ambitious stepfather (1696), who in 1743 had negotiated the marriage of his son, John, with Lady Elizabeth Cavendish, daughter of the Lord Lieutenant, the 3rd Duke of Devonshire – four years earlier he had married his eldest son to her sister. When the marriage was arranged, the Newtown(ards) estate would undoubtedly have formed part of John Ponsonby's (1702) expectations. The sale was the prelude to a series of bitter and expensive legal battles between the Stewarts and the Ponsonbys over the control of the parliamentary borough of Newtown(ards), which the Ponsonbys retained, although the town was built on Stewart's estate.[56]

One of the largest estate auctions in the century, that of the Caledon estate of the Earl of Cork and Orrery, was advertised to take place at the Globe Coffee House, Essex Street, Dublin, on 1 September 1775 between 12 noon and 2 p.m. The purchaser was James Alexander (0029), a Londonderry merchant who was that most desired of purchasers, an East India 'nabob'. The sale was finalised on 18 January 1776, when the estate of 8,810 statute acres in Counties Tyrone and Armagh changed hands for

---

[54] *IHS* vol. XV (1966), Large, 'Wealth of the greater Irish landowners 1750-1815' pp. 29-30; *Proc. RIA* 71 C 5 Johnston (ed.), 'Members of the Irish Parliament, 1784-7' pp. 162, 190, 213; Cloncurry, *Personal Recollections of the Life and Times of Valentine, Lord Cloncurry* (1850) pp.2, 5-6. Lawless later bought Mornington House in Merrion Street which he rented to Lord Castlereagh at the time of the Union.
[55] *IHS* vol. XVIII (1973) pp. 317-8, A. P. W. Malcomson, 'The Newtown Act of 1748: Revision and Reconstruction'.
[56] *HMC Charlemont I*, p. iii, see also Malcomson, op. cit., pp. 313-44 and *Hist. Studies*, vol. 10, pp.43-90 'The Politics of "Natural Right": the Abercorn family and Strabane Borough'. See *infra* p. 200.

£96,500 with a down payment of £20,000 – a purchase price of nearly 30 years the value of the rental, estimated at £3,250 gross and £3,115 net.[57] Land prices were high in 1775 but the 30-year valuation took into account the fact that the estate was let at probably about 50 per cent of its potential rental and as the leases fell in a considerable increase in the rental could be expected. Furthermore, the estate was in the north and it had political value accruing from its mainly protestant tenantry, who could be given leases for lives and thereby enfranchised. Alexander's political position was further strengthened; as he sat in parliament for the prestigious seat of Londonderry and he subsequently purchased Banagher borough – speedily exchanged for Newtown(ards), much to the chagrin of the Stewarts. By 1790 he had a peerage and by 1800 an earldom. James Alexander was the ancestor of the Earls of Caledon and the Earls Alexander of Tunis and Errigal; Alexander Stewart's son Robert (**2008**) was the 1st Marquess of Londonderry and his son, Alexander's grandson, was Lord Castlereagh (**2009**).

By 1844 the Devon Commissioners found that 'estates are so generally encumbered by family settlements or otherwise' that the delay and difficulty of dividing them tended to outweigh the higher price which would almost certainly be obtained from smaller lots. Encumbered estates were not easily disposed of and, as selling the estate was the final admission of bankruptcy, it was usually desirable to sell the whole estate as speedily as possible to meet the escalating demands of creditors. The Devon Commissioners found that: 'it now rarely happens that land in Ireland is brought into the market for sales in lots of a moderate or small size'. This shortage prevented the rising commercial class from acquiring an attachment to the land and diverting their resources into its development, for while land was a 'store of value' it was also an asset which required a 'cash flow' for its maintenance and to utilise its potential. Hence the liquidity of a landlord's financial position, as well as his personality, ability and ambitions, bore a direct relation to the management of and the income from his estate. Shortage of capital for emergencies and improvements was always a major problem, both for the majority of landlords at the top and, at the bottom of the agrarian pyramid, the peasant who actually worked the land. By the end of the eighteenth century the foundations of the road to the 1849 Encumbered Estates Act had already been laid.[58]

As the land was the basic source of the landlord's income, his best hope of improving his fortunes was to expand his estates and increase their productivity. The Dublin Society, founded in 1731, was the forerunner of many local and national societies aimed at 'improvements' of various kinds. However, these invariably required money and the difficulty was to persuade a conservative tenantry, so poor that they could not

---

[57] PRONI D2433/32/2, D2433/1/100.
[58] See Lyons, *Ireland since the Famine* (1971) pp. 14-5, 35; also L. M. Cullen, *An Economic History of Ireland since 1660* p. 138; Donnelly, *Landlord and tenant in nineteenth-century Ireland* pp. 49-50.

afford to make a mistake, to adopt them. Apart from wealth acquired from family sources or through good management, where did the money for land purchases or improvements come from? Prior to the Roman Catholic Relief Act of 1778, Catholics could not hold mortgages on land and there were few Irish nabobs or wealthy heiresses. But a considerable amount of money was borrowed in England either directly or indirectly; for example, when a landlord had an estate in England as well as in Ireland he could borrow money against his English property – Irish property was not a particularly popular collateral, although it could be used. In 1779 Lord Lieutenant Buckinghamshire, concerned about the financial drain of interest payments out of Ireland, wrote to the Secretary of State Lord Weymouth to point out that: 'as the gentlemen of Ireland are not more economical than those of England, they have charged their estates with mortgages, the interest of which is, in very few instances, paid here. The interest of the national debt stands in a similar predicament'.[59]

Marriage was usually considered the best opportunity to improve the family fortune. Some attention was usually given to the personal aspects of the arrangement, as affection and respect were normally considered desirable. The chances of the couples achieving matrimonial happiness do not appear to have been markedly less than those whose marriages were established on other expectations. Lady Caroline Fox wrote to her sister, Lady Kildare: 'I own I pity those most who are parted after a long time of tenderness, friendship and affection; it is being divided from oneself, one may say.'[60] Couples conformed to the mores of their class and, particularly when both were young at the time of the marriage, they very often grew together, and there are some touching memorials to long and affectionate unions. The marriage settlement legalised the agreement made between the couple, or more often their families. Its terms usually reflected the addition made to the fortune of the bridegroom's family by the dowry of the bride. Traditionally, the bride's dowry, or an equivalent, was earmarked to provide dowries or fortunes for the younger children of the marriage and her jointure was usually assessed as an annual allowance amounting to 10 per cent of her dowry,[61] but it could be more. These complex arrangements were often the cause of family dissensions, as in the case of the settlements made in 1684 on the marriage of Sir Nicholas Browne, 2nd Viscount Kenmare, with his cousin, Helen Browne, which resulted in law suits spanning nearly a century.[62]

Marriages were essentially long, or short-term, lotteries with potential credits as well as debits. This was clearly shown in the marriage fortunes of the Hill family. In 1747, Wills Hill, 1st Earl of Hillsborough and 1st Marquess of Downshire, married Lady Margaretta FitzGerald, the daughter of the 19th Earl of Kildare. She brought

[59] PRO SP63/465, 28 May 1779 ff. 21 *et seq.*
[60] *IMC Leinster* vol. I p. 195.
[61] Maguire, op. cit., pp. 84-5.
[62] *IMC Kenmare* pp. 41-2.

her husband the unusually large dowry of £20,000 and her marriage settlement arranged for the conventional jointure of 10 per cent – £2,000 p.a. – with a portion of £10,000 each for any younger children. Lady Hillsborough died in 1766 leaving, besides a son and heir, two daughters whose fortunes, as stipulated in the marriage settlement, exactly matched their mother's dowry.[63] Two years later Lord Hillsborough married again. His second wife, Mary, *suo iure* Baroness Stawell, died in 1780, again obviating the need for a jointure as she predeceased him by 13 years and there were no children by this marriage. Two years earlier, in 1778, Lord Hillsborough had a windfall. On the death of Charles Dunbar (**0666**) he inherited the Blessington estate and parliamentary borough, which had belonged to his great-great grandfather, the seventeenth-century Primate Michael Boyle. Despite the fact that he did better on the marriage market than most of his contemporaries, when Lord Hillsborough, then 1st Marquess of Downshire, died in 1793 his debts amounted to £69,660.[64] The 2nd Marquess of Downshire (**1016**), then Lord Hillsborough, married in 1786. His bride, Mary Sandys, was one of the richest heiresses in Great Britain or Ireland. She brought her husband the Edenderry estate in King's County, the Dundrum estate in Co. Down, Easthampstead Park in Berkshire, a large sum of money invested in the funds and further expectations. These splendid additions to the family property were reflected in two settlements, one on the marriage in 1786 and another three years later, which fixed Lady Hillsborough's jointure at £5,000 p.a. and the provision for the younger children at £20,000 for one child, £15,000 each for two children and £40,000 to be divided between three or more children. The 2nd Marquess also had a windfall. He was the reluctant, but the largest, single beneficiary from the compensation given for the disfranchisement of parliamentary boroughs by the Act of Union, receiving £55,486 12s 9d (£52,500 plus £2,986 12s 9d interest). Nevertheless, when he died aged 48 in 1801 the family debt had increased to £325,212 and of this £33,837 was owed to tradesmen and other casual debtors. Subsequently the total debt was reduced to the still enormous sum of £269,726 by the £55,486 compensation which was paid after his death.[65]

If the Downshire family were lucky in marriage and the size of their families, the same could not be said of the ducal house of Leinster, which provided an illustration of the extent to which family commitments could encumber an estate. The story, though complicated, is instructive. In 1747 James, 20th Earl of Kildare (**0734**), married Lady Emily Lennox, daughter of Charles, 2nd Duke of Richmond and a great-granddaughter of Charles II. It was rumoured that Lady Emily, who was not only well connected but one of the greatest beauties of the century, brought her husband 'not a shilling'.[66] This was unlikely, as the traditional dowry of a ducal daughter appears

[63] Maguire, op. cit. p. 86.
[64] Ibid. p. 90.
[65] Ibid.
[66] See Malcomson, *The pursuit of the heiress: aristocratic marriage in Ireland 1750-1820* (PRONI, 1982), pp. 4, 9-11; this study gives considerable detail about a number of marriage arrangements.

to have been £10,000 and in his will her father bequeathed similar dowries for his younger unmarried daughters making them a first charge on his estate – a commitment which the 3rd Duke punctiliously acknowledged in 1758, when his sister, Lady Louisa, married the wealthy Thomas Conolly (0459), writing that: 'as Mr. Conolly will expect to have Lady Louisa's fortune on the day of the marriage, I must have it ready'.[67] A further reason to suspect that Lady Emily had a similar dowry to that of her sisters is the large building programme which the Earl of Kildare (0734) inherited from his father and which he continued; both Carton and Kildare (Leinster) House were built at this time. Moreover, as has been noted, Lord Kildare's sister, Lady Margaretta FitzGerald, married Lord Hillsborough in the same year, 1747, and she brought her husband the large dowry of £20,000. Possibly the rumour arose because an English viscounty was added to the FitzGerald titles at this time, most probably as a reward for Lord Kildare's support during the recent Stuart rebellion,[68] but gossip preferred the story that George II had dowered his god-daughter with English title. Subsequently, the personal qualities and family connections of the bride made their contribution to the much desired marquessate and dukedom to which Lord Kildare was successively elevated in 1761 and 1766.

Lady Emily's marriage settlement provided for the very large jointure of £3,000, later increased to £4,000, which eventually became a charge on the Leinster estates for over 40 years. Furthermore, the 1st Duke and Duchess had 23 children, six of whom died in infancy, leaving provision to be made from the estate for the remainder, ten of whom reached their majority. When the duke died in 1773 the dowager duchess had the guardianship of their younger children,[69] and she was entitled to an allowance of £400 for the education and maintenance of each of them. This appears to have been a customary allowance for minors, as it was the amount paid to Lady Holland and the duchess, then Lady Kildare, for the maintenance of their younger sisters following the death of their parents. In 1774 the dowager duchess married again and as her new husband (1571), who had been tutor to her sons, was not a wealthy man, provision had to be found for him and the two daughters of this marriage – in the event only one survived. In 1776 Lady Louisa Conolly wrote to warn her sister that their brother, the Duke of Richmond, was going to scold her for her extravagance 'as he has no notion of your not saving money for them'.[70]

William, 2nd Duke of Leinster (0745), upon whom these financial responsibilities descended was a well-meaning but not over-intelligent country gentleman, highly conscious of his position as premier peer of Ireland and, at that time, its only duke.[71]

---

[67] See Malcomson, ibid. p. 11; the Duke had to sell land to raise the money for his sister's dowry. £10,000 was also the dowry for each of the two daughters of the 3rd Duke of Devonshire on their marriages to Lord Duncannon and John Ponsonby (Chatsworth MSS).
[68] *IMC Leinster* vol. I, p. ix, he offered to raise and equip a regiment at his own expense.
[69] *IMC Leinster* vol. II, pp. 133-4; Guinness & Ryan, *Irish houses and castles,* p. 186; Malcomson, op. cit. p. 4.
[70] *IMC Leinster* vol. III, p. 195.
[71] E. M. Johnston, *Ireland in the eighteenth century* (1974) pp. 262-3.

He inherited a financial position that would have defeated better managers. He had to find jointures not only for his mother but also for his grandmother, the Dowager Lady Kildare,[72] who died in 1780, having survived her husband for 36 years. At the same time portions, dowries and maintenance had also to be provided for his younger siblings. He married a gentle and rather colourless heiress, Emilia St George,[73] and they proceeded to have a large family – eight daughters and five sons. Not surprisingly, the 2nd Duke worried about money all his life: 'He is mighty queer about money,' observed his wealthy and childless aunt, Lady Louisa Conolly, 'and his distress about it is I am sure the foundation of all that he does.' On another occasion she wrote to her sister, the Duchess Emily, 'I hope you get your money remitted but William (0745), I believe, is as ill off as his neighbours, and it's really wonderful how people go on'.[74]

Considerations of ambition and snobbery occasionally compounded the financial complexities of these arrangements. In 1777 John, Lord Crosbie (0534), married the eldest daughter of Lord George Sackville (Germain) (1835) and Lord George stipulated that 'as is usual' the bride's dowry, in this case £10,000, or an equivalent should be used to make provision for any younger children of the marriage. This arrangement did not prevent the bridegroom's family from making use of the money in the interim, and Lord Crosbie remarked to his father that it would provide his sisters with dowries equal to that of Lady Anne Talbot! Emulation was not the only peripheral consideration, as Lord Crosbie, in persuading his father to agree to the particularly large jointure of £2,000 – 20 per cent instead of 10 per cent of the bride's dowry – wrote: 'Don't you think that my marrying in this manner will mortify the narrow envious people of Kerry?' By 1784 John Crosbie (0534), now Earl of Glandore, was in such severe financial straits that he petitioned the Irish House of Lords to allow him to bring in a private bill in order to break the entail and to enable him to sell part of his estate in order to satisfy his creditors. However, in 1785 he was at least partly rescued as Lady Glandore's father (1835) died and left her £3,000 p.a.[75]

Usually marriages observed the strict hierarchical basis of eighteenth-century property-orientated society and the majority of MPs marriages took place within their own social circle. Exceptions might, however, be made in cases of well-connected poverty and respectable, if not so well-connected, wealth. For instance, Mary Granville, Mrs Pendavers, and subsequently Mrs Delany, had reluctantly consented to her family's wishes over her first marriage, which balanced her connections against her poverty and her bridegroom's wealth. Visiting Dublin in March 1731/2 Mrs Pendavers wrote to her sister that: 'Miss Burton ... is since married to Lord Netterville, – a fop and a

---

[72] *IMC Leinster* vol. 1 p. 184; his father, the 1st Duke, had also had to make provision for his mother and his grandmother, who died in 1758, aged 93.
[73] Ibid. vol. 2, pp. 160-1.
[74] Ibid. vol. 3, pp. 182, 310,
[75] *IHS* vol. 15, pp. 39-40, Large, 'Wealth of the greater Irish landowners'; Malcomson, op. cit. pp. 7, 9, 11-2.

fool, but a lord with a tolerable estate, who always wears fine clothes; she had £9,000 for her fortune, with a pretty person much in vogue'; nearly 30 years later she commented on the marriage in 1759 of the parents of the future Marquess Wellesley (**2215**) and Duke of Wellington (**2210**), remarking that: 'She [Ann Hill] has £6,000 and the family estate settled on her in case her brother has no children; Lord Mornington (**2212**) settles £1,400 jointure on her with £500 a year pin money; his estate is now £8,000 and will be £10,000 in two or three years more'.[76] These arrangements were the gossip of a small society in which everybody either knew, or knew of, everybody else.[77]

It was a cause célèbre when Emily, Dowager Duchess of Leinster, who was in effect the leader of Irish society, decided to marry her children's tutor, an obscure and penniless Scot called William Ogilvie (**1571**), for this marriage had none of the conventional ameliorating features. Gossip abounded, much of it vicious, but the ducal houses of Leinster in Ireland and Richmond in England liked Ogilvie and closed ranks behind the Duchess, although her brother, who had not at the time of the engagement met Mr Ogilvie, expressed some concern, considering that 'in the common order of things any inequality between husband and wife generally tended to make them less happy.' However, as head of the family, he decreed that they should keep any reservations 'to ourselves', and Lady Louisa Conolly remarked to her sister the Duchess that: 'You hurt your rank in the world, in my opinion that is all you do; and if you gain happiness by it, I am sure you make a good exchange'. Another sister, the shortly to be divorced Lady Sarah (Bunbury), thought that she should 'be married at Goodwood at your brother's house *dans la face de l'univers*, and not smuggle the marriage abroad, as if you were ashamed of it'.[78] The Dowager Duchess was more cautious. She was married at Toulouse and for some years afterwards she and her husband lived with their own and the younger FitzGerald children in the chateau at Aubigny which Louis XIV had given to her great-grandmother, Louise de la Keroualle, the French mistress of Charles II. The Duchess, like her sister, Lady Holland, and her brother, the 3rd Duke of Richmond, was liberal and tolerant in outlook. She was a dominant influence on her children and particularly on her most famous son, Lord Edward FitzGerald (**0730**).

One of the reasons why marriage settlements had to be made so carefully, and only finalised almost immediately before the marriage took place, was to protect the bride and her dependants from an unscrupulous husband. On her marriage a woman's property, unless it had been legally safeguarded, became her husband's, whose reciprocal duty was to provide for her and their children. The marriage settlement made this contractually binding. Under these circumstances, elopements were a serious problem for the bride and for her family, particularly if she was an heiress. They became even more so when the penurious and unscrupulous as well as the irresponsible among the

---

[76] *Delany*, ser. 1, vol. 1, p. 341; ser. 1 vol. 3, pp. 536, 539.
[77] See R. B. McDowell, op. cit., p. 28.
[78] *IMC Leinster*, vol. II, pp.126-40; vol. III, p. 94.

gentry and squireens sometimes formed clubs to recover their fortunes through abducting and forcibly marrying heiresses. Of one such club it is recorded that:

> They had emissaries and confederates in every house, who communicated information of particulars – the extent of a girl's fortune … domestic arrangements and movements. When a girl was thus pointed out the members drew lots, but more generally tossed up for her, and immediate measures were taken to secure her for the fortunate man by all the rest. No class of society was exempt from their visits.[79]

These marriages were usually performed by (Catholic or Anglican) canonically ordained but renegade priests known as couple-beggars *(0237)*. In 1745 the Irish parliament, declaring that previous laws 'have been found wholly ineffectual', passed an act, 19 Geo. II, c. 13 *(0442)*, making marriages between Protestants, or Protestants and Catholics, performed by a Catholic priest null and void and reiterated that the celebrant of such marriages was committing a capital offence; indeed, a few years earlier on 29 November 1740 Edward Sewell, a couple-beggar, had been hanged.[80]   Nevertheless, irregular marriages were sufficiently common to necessitate safeguarding against the social disruption which would occur if already existing unions were declared illegal. Thus a parallel act was passed to safeguard the civil consequences of such irregular unions. As the real problem lay with the financial necessities of the abductors and sometimes with the youth and inexperience of the heiress, the custom continued regardless of any legislative attempts to prevent it. Since 1634 parliament had repeatedly, and ineffectually, legislated against this well-established custom. Finally, in 1780, the abduction of the Kennedy sisters, two co-heiresses aged 14 and 15, brought matters to a head and indicated changing social mores, for the abductors were tried at the Kilkenny Assizes, found guilty and executed. The case was tried before John Scott **(1891)**, then the Attorney General and an assize judge, who declared that if this case was not treated with the full rigour of the law no similar family could exist in tranquillity and no heiress would be safe.[81] The decision was not popular, as the hard-riding and hard-drinking squireens, who were the main participants in this activity, enjoyed the popular admiration of the anti-establishment peasantry. This was seen in the McNaughton case. The story, which has gone down in Ulster tradition as that of 'half-hung McNaughton', began with the forcible attempt to abduct an heiress. It ended with the trial and conviction of her abductor for her murder, as during the abduction the 15-year-old heiress was killed while protecting her father, Andrew Knox **(1175)**. McNaughton, the abductor, was condemned, but at his execution the rope

---

[79] *Commons jn. Ire.* vol. III (1719), Petition of Rebecca White; *Delany,* op. cit. vol. II, pp. 348-53; see also C. E. Maxwell, *Town and country in Ireland under the Georges* (London, 1940), p. 22.
[80] S. Connolly, *Priests and people in pre-famine Ireland 1780-1845* (1981), p. 200 *et seq.*; J. Brady, *Catholics and Catholicism in the eighteenth-century press* (Maynooth, 1965), p. 62.
[81] Lecky, op. cit. vol. 1, pp. 371 *et seq.* esp. pp. 377-8n.; J. A. Froude, *The English in Ireland in the eighteenth century* (1901), vol. 1 pp. 465 *et seq.: Eighteenth-century Ireland,,* vol. 9 (1994), pp. 7-43, J. Kelly, 'The abduction of women of fortune in eighteenth-century Ireland'.

broke, whereupon, refusing the crowd's assistance to aid his escape, he declared that he would not be known as a 'half-hanged man' and the execution was duly completed.[82]

At the root of the whole problem of marriages were questions of property and inheritance, which made the legitimacy of the children of particular importance and emphasised any wrong-doing on the part of the wife (see **1807**). Divorce in the eighteenth century was rare and could only be achieved by a private act of parliament. Marriages were too complex to be easily dissolved. Apart from any ecclesiastical considerations, the social stigma was considerable, for divorce attacked the foundations of a society based on hereditary right and property. The Duchess of Leinster's sister, Lady Sarah Lennox (Bunbury), was divorced in 1776, some seven years after she had left her husband, and her sister Lady Louisa Conolly told the duchess with some relief that the bill's passage through the British parliament had coincided with the notorious bigamy trial of Elizabeth Chudleigh, Countess of Bristol *alias* Duchess of Kingston. Lady Louisa wrote that: 'this talk is lucky for us at this time as it drowns Sarah's bill of divorce which is to have the second reading tomorrow. I feel very awkward being in town while it is going on'.[83] This story had a happy ending, as after 12 years in seclusion living 'a life of penitence' she married, in 1781, Col. George Napier. Their marriage was a happy one and of their eight children the three eldest sons were generals: Sir Charles, Sir George and Sir William Napier.

Heiresses with large fortunes were comparatively rare in Ireland and the rich City of London heiress portrayed by Hogarth virtually unknown. It has been estimated that of the 151 marriages contracted by Irish peers alive in 1783, only six were definitely and a further eight possibly in this category.[84] In 1697, Lady Peyton despaired of her son Kean O'Hara finding a good wife in Sligo – 'that is to say a wife with money'[85] – although she voiced a generally held opinion when she remarked that such 'parties' were numerous in England. The desirability of marrying for money was quite openly admitted throughout the social spectrum: for example, the *Limerick Chronicle* of 17 October 1768 reported the marriage of the Rev. John Madress, Chancellor of the diocese of Ross, to Miss Baldwin, 'a most amiable lady with a large fortune'. In 1738 John, 5th Earl of Cork and Orrery, announced his marriage to a friend, declaring that 'I am the happiest man in the world! Yesterday Miss Hamilton gave me with the usual ceremony, her hand and heart. A heart filled with love and a hand with money. What a turn of fortune is here'.[86] Margaret Hamilton was one of the great Irish heiresses of the century, and her fortune included the Caledon estate which her son sold, in 1776, to James Alexander (**0029**), later 1st Earl of Caledon.

---

[82] H. Boylan, *A Dictionary* (3rd edn Dublin, 1998), p. 257.
[83] *IMC Leinster*, vol. III p.198.
[84] Large, op. cit.
[85] PRONI O'Hara MSS T2812/4/205, 263.
[86] E. C. Boyle (ed.), *The Orrery Papers* (2 vols, London, 1902), vol. 1, p. 240.

VI CONCLUSION

Perhaps the greatest memorial to the Irish MPs is Dublin itself[87] with its wide streets *(0845,0935,1138)*, street lighting *(0389)*, water supply *(0880)*, Georgian squares and classical buildings. These were not only important in themselves but where Dublin led other Irish cities followed. The Royal Dublin Society, the Royal Irish Academy and Dublin University *(1223)* all attested to its international standing in the world of learning. Out in the country the network of roads, the surviving country houses and small towns like Westport, Co. Sligo, and Castlewellan, Co. Down, reflect taste and a genuine desire to improve the country *(0664)*.

Environmental concerns were reflected in the emphasis on the planting of trees *(0643)* and various botanical interests as well as decreeing closed seasons for certain game *(0487,0624)*. Similarly attempts to resolve or at least to contain social problems such as poverty, the condition of prisons and prisoners and to provide for abandoned children were laudable if of limited success. Hospital building was encouraged *(0578)* and a surprisingly large number of Irish hospitals were established in the eighteenth century. All of these endeavours mark the beginning of the secular treatment of major social problems.

The MPs achievements were not inconsiderable, indeed they were remarkable, considering their lack of resources, but they were destroyed by their protective separateness as displayed in the religious inflexibility which marked their failure to create a united society. Indeed the combination of the seventeenth-century confiscations with the penal laws ensured that when the rights of man triumphed over the rights of property the leaders of the majority of the Irish people would be crowned with a mitre rather than a coronet and in consequence religion would continue to dominate the secular state.

[87] For various aspects of the city's development see *Two capitals: London and Dublin 1500-1840* (British Academy, 2001), e.g. public order, the effect of the Union, city government, cultural life, religion, etc.

3
LIST OF
MEMBERS

In a small hand-to-mouth project like this there is no specialisation; everyone has to participate. This section is fairly typical: I decided the format and Colin Wisdom extracted the relevant detail from the larger biographical files. David Luke and I then carefully examined each entry and balanced the assorted evidence for each case. In making the final decision I was guided by the proximity of the evidence to the birth or death concerned, for instance, newspaper notices and obituaries, and as a final resort probability – for example, a man is more likely to have gone to the university at 16 than at 26 years of age, and more likely to have died aged 60 than 110 (although there is an interesting group of MPs who reached their ninth, and even their tenth, decade).

It is rare to find two Irish genealogists in agreement. It is also difficult not to assume that the eighteenth century had a casual approach to details of birth or death: for example, the phrase 'on or about' was often used, and even appears in private members' bills. Some variations are insignificant: for instance, many people are born or die at night, so their birth or death is reported with a day's variation. Then there are curious discrepancies, like the same day in another month (e.g. 23 January and 23 June), and occasionally a complete decade is skipped, as in the case of Thomas Allan (**0031**), where there is a ten-year discrepancy between his obituary in the *Gentleman's Magazine* and the church burial records. These examples are not isolated, and may be, probably are, the result of clerical error. The notes for entries marked with an asterisk give a sample of the complexity of the evidence and the techniques used in interpreting it. The numbered code in the list of MPs explains the more usual evidence for estimated dates of birth, and occasionally of death. Both clearly show the impossibility of achieving perfection.

CODE

Dates are estimated from:

1. entry to parliament

2. university

3. Inns of Court

4. school

5. army/navy

6. office/profession

7. known date of marriage of parents or MP

8. age of siblings

9. age of children

10. other source material.

'HP' denotes that the MP has an entry in *History of Parliament*. Notes on individual entries are to be found at the end of the A to Z list, and are arranged into five categories, as follows.

(a)   The source for 1–10 above is given here or in the biographies.

(b)   Dates of death based on, or calculated from, the issue of election writs are noted. These are a rough guide, since up to 1771 the Speaker did not issue writs during the recess, therefore a writ would not be issued immediately for an MP who died between the end of one session and the beginning of the next. They are particularly useful for the long parliament of George II, 1727–60, as only death or elevation to the Bench or House of Lords could release an MP from parliament once elected and sworn. Attendance was required, and those absent when the House was called over had to offer an acceptable excuse, which was not always easy.

(c)   From 1715 to 1782 parliament was usually in session for an average of six out of eighteen months. After 1782 it met annually. From the Hanoverian succession until the 1768 Octennial Act the Irish parliament lasted for the lifetime of the sovereign, and the lack of general elections encouraged the return of MPs under age whenever a vacancy occurred in a family borough, but they generally (with some exceptions) waited until they were of age to take their seats. These MPs have been noted. The disturbed state of the country in the seventeenth century makes it more difficult to establish definite dates of birth for those born then, while dates of death present a similar problem for MPs still alive after the Union. During the reigns of William III and Anne, sessions were more variable and elections more frequent.

(d)   Another source of dates of death is wills. Wills were usually proved within months of a death but if problems arose, especially those involving litigation, the process could last for years.

(e)   Finally, the sources for the biographies of MPs quite often conflict and errors can be repeated from source to source. When this affects dates of birth or death, the more frequent, or the most probable, version is given in the text and the alternative in the notes. Such MPs are marked with an asterisk in the list.

THE MEMBERS

0001 **ACHESON**, Rt Hon. Sir Archibald [1st V. Gosford]; b. 1 Sept. 1718 d. 5 Sept. 1790; MP for TCD 1741–60, Co. Armagh 1761–8–76, Enniskillen 1776.

0002 **ACHESON**, Rt Hon. Archibald [2nd E. Gosford]; b. 1 Aug. 1776 d. 27 Mar. 1849; MP for Co. Armagh 1797–1800, [UK] 1801–7 [HP].

0003 **ACHESON**, Sir Arthur; b. 26 Jan. 1688 d. 8 Feb. 1749; MP for Mullingar 1727–49.

0004 *****ACHESON**, Rt Hon. Arthur [7th Bt [S.], 1st E. Gosford]; b. *c.* 1744/5[10] d. 14 Jan. 1807; MP for Old Leighlin 1783–90, 1790.

0005 *****ACHESON**, Sir Nicholas [4th Bt [S.]]; b. *c.* 1655–8[7] d. 1701; MP for Co. Armagh 1695–9.

0006 **ADAIR**, Robert; b. *c.* 1682[7] d. 31 July 1737; MP for Philipstown 1727–37.

0007 **ADAMS**, John; b. 1634 d. *post* 1703[6]; MP for Fore 1692–3.

0008 **ADARE** [*alias* ADAIR], Sir Robert; b. Feb. 1659 d. 9 Feb. 1745; MP for Antrim B. 1692–3.

0009 **ADDERLEY**, Thomas; b. *c.* 1713[2] d. 28 May 1791; MP for Charlemont 1752–60, Bandon-Bridge 1761–8–76, Clonakilty 1776–83–90–1.

0010 **ADDISON**, Rt Hon. Joseph; b. 1 May 1672 d. 17 June 1719; MP for Cavan B. 1709–13 [HP].

◆◆◆ **AGAR**, Charles; b. 28 May 1755 d. 15 May 1789 [n.d.e. Kilkenny city May–July 1778].

0011 **AGAR**, George [1st B. Callan]; b. 18 Apr. 1754 d. 9 Oct. 1815; MP for Callan 1776–83–90.

0012 **AGAR**, Henry; b. 1707 d. 28 Oct. 1746; MP for Gowran 1727–46.

0013 **AGAR** [AGAR-ELLIS], Hon. Henry Welbore [2nd V. Clifden and B. Mendip]; b. 22 Jan. 1761 d.

13 July 1836; MP for Co. Kilkenny 1783–9 [r. Gowran 1783] [HP].

0014 **AGAR**, James; b. 1672 d. 30 Dec. 1733; MP for Old Leighlin 1703–13, Gowran 1713–14, Callan 1715–27, St Canice 1727–33 [r. Gowran 1715].

0015 **AGAR**, James; b. 7 Sept. 1713 d. 25 Aug. 1769; MP for Gowran 1747–60, Tulsk 1768–9 [n.d.e. Callan 1761].

0016 **AGAR**, Rt Hon. James [1st B. and V. Clifden]; b. 25 Mar. 1735 d. 29 Dec. 1788; MP for Gowran 1753–60, 1776, Co. Kilkenny 1761–8–76 [r. Gowran 1768].

0017 **AGHMOOTY** [*alias* AUCHMUTY], John; b. *ante* 1640[5] d. 1726; MP for St Johnstown [Longford] 1695–9, 1703–13.

0018 *****ALCOCK**, Henry; b. 1717 d. 1784; MP for Clonmines 1761–8 [n.d.e. Waterford city 1768].

0019 **ALCOCK**, Henry; b. 1735–7[8] d. July 1812; MP for Waterford City 1783–90–7, Fethard [Wexford] 1797–9.

0020 **ALCOCK**, William; b. 5 June 1705 d. [bur. 17] Mar. 1779; MP for Fethard [Wexford] 1764–8.

0021 **ALCOCK**, William Congreve; b. 1771 d. [bur. 9] Oct. 1813; MP for Waterford city 1797–1800 [r. Enniscorthy 1797], [UK] 1801–7 Dec. 1803, Co. Wexford 1807–12 [HP].

0022 **ALDRIDGE** [ALDRIDGE-BUSBY], Robert; b. *c.* 1768[7] d. 9 July 1837; MP for Carysfort 1799–1800.

0023 **ALDWORTH**, Rt Hon. Richard; b. 1646 d. 1707; MP for TCD 1695–9.

0024 **ALDWORTH**, Richard; b. 1694 d. 25 [bur. 27] Apr. 1776; MP for Lismore 1728–60.

0025 **ALDWORTH**, Richard; b. [Jan.] 1740/1 d. 4 Apr. 1824; MP for Doneraile 1768–76.

0026 **ALDWORTH** [ALDWORTH-ST LEGER], St Leger [1st B. and V. Doneraile]; b. *c.* 1715[7] d. 15 May 1787; MP for Doneraile 1761–8–76, May–Aug. 1776.

0027 **ALEXANDER**, Hon. Du Pre [2nd E. Caledon]; b. 14 Dec. 1777 d. 8 Apr. 1839; MP for Newtown Jan.–Dec. 1800.

0028 **ALEXANDER**, Henry; b. 1763 d. 6 May 1818; MP for Newtown[ards] 1788–90, Askeaton 1790–7, Londonderry city 1797–1800, [UK] 1801–2 [HP].

0029 **ALEXANDER**, James [1st B., V., E. Caledon]; b. 1730 d. 22 Mar. 1802; MP for Londonderry city 1775–6–83–90.

0030 *****ALEXANDER**, Robert; b. 1752 d. 14 July 1827; MP for Dingle 1777–83, Newtown[ards] 1797–1800.

0031 *****ALLAN**, Thomas; b. 1725[10] d. 12 June 1798; MP for Killybegs 1768–76, Naas 1777–83.

0032 **ALLEN**, Francis; b. *ante* 1682[7] d. 9 July 1741; MP for Co. Kildare 1725–7.

0033 **ALLEN**, Rt Hon. John [1st B. and V. Allen]; b. 13 Feb. 1661 d. 8 Nov. 1726; MP for Co. Dublin 1692–3, 1703–13, 1715–17, Co. Carlow 1695–9, Co. Wicklow 1713–14.

0034 *****ALLEN**, Hon. John [3rd V. Allen]; b. [bapt. 11 June] 1713 d. 25 May 1745; MP for Carysfort 1733–42.

0035 **ALLEN**, John [4th V. Allen]; b. *ante* 1720[8] d. 10 Nov. 1753; MP for Co. Wicklow 1742–5.

0036 *****ALLEN**, Rt Hon. Joshua [2nd V. Allen]; b. [bapt. 12 May] 1685 d. 5 Dec. 1742; MP for Co. Kildare 1709–13–14, 1715–26.

0037 **ALLEN**, Hon. Richard; b. [bapt. 22 July] 1691 d. 14 Apr. 1745; MP for Athy 1715–27, Co. Kildare 1727–45.

0038 **ALLEN**, Richard; b. *post* 1728[5] d. 22 Jan. 1800; MP for Harristown 1776–83.

0039 **ALLEN**, Hon. Robert; b. [bapt. 12 May] 1687 d. 16 Dec. 1741; MP for Carysfort 1713–14, Co. Wicklow 1715–27–41.

0040 **ANDREWS**, Rt Hon. Francis; b. 1718 d. 12 June 1774; MP for Midleton 1759–60, Londonderry city 1761–8–74.

0041 **ANKETELL**, Oliver; b. 1676 d. 27 May 1760; MP for Monaghan B. 1753–60.

0042 **ANNESLEY**, Rt Hon. Arthur [6th V. Valentia [I.] and 5th E. of Anglesey [E.]]; b. *c.* 1678[2] d. 1 Apr. 1737; MP for New Ross 1703–10 [HP].

0043 **ANNESLEY**, Hon. Francis; b. 23 Jan. 1628 d. *ante* 1705; MP for Bangor 1692–3.

0044 **ANNESLEY**, Francis; b. *c.* 1653[2] d. 1707; MP for New Ross 1695–9.

0045 **ANNESLEY**, Francis; b. 14 Oct. 1663 d. 7 Aug. 1750; MP for Downpatrick 1695–9, Sept. 1703 [expelled 28 Sept. 1703], 1713–14 [HP].

0046 *****ANNESLEY**, Hon. Francis Charles [2nd V. Glerawly, 1st E. Annesley]; b. 27 Nov. 1740 d. 19 Dec. 1802; MP for Downpatrick 1761–8–70.

0047 **ANNESLEY**, Maurice; b. *post* 1653[8] d. 17 Feb. 1718; MP for Clonmines 1695–9.

0048 **ANNESLEY**, Rt Hon. Richard [2nd E. Annesley]; b. 14 Apr. 1745 d. 9 Nov. 1824; MP for Coleraine 1776–83, St Canice 1783–90, Newtown[ards] 1790–7, Blessington 1797–1800, Midleton 1800.

0049 **ANNESLEY**, William [1 B. Annesley and V. Glerawly]; b. 1709 d. 12 Sept. 1770; MP for Midleton 1741–58.

0050 **ARCHDALL**, Mervyn; b. 1725 d. 18 June 1813; MP for Co. Fermanagh 1761–8–76–83–90–7–1800, [UK] 1801–2 [HP].

0051 [MONTGOMERY] **ARCHDALL**, Nicholas; b. *ante* 1702[6] d. 19 May 1763; MP for Co. Fermanagh 1731–60.

0052 **ARCHDALL**, Richard; b. *c.* 1750[2] d. 8 Feb. 1824; MP for Ardfert 1790–7, Killybegs 1797–1800, [UK] Kilkenny city 1801–2, Dundalk 1802–6 [HP].

0053 **ARMITAGE**, Timothy; b. 1675 d. [Apr.–21 June] 1717; MP for Randalstown 1703–13.

0054 **ARMSTRONG**, John; b. 1732 d. 12 Sept. 1791; MP for Fore 1768–76, Kilmallock 1783–90–1.

0055 **ARMSTRONG**, William Henry; b. 21 June 1774 d. 21 Sept. 1835; MP for Wicklow B. 1798–1800.

0056 **ASGILL**, John; b. Mar. 1659 d. 10 Nov. 1738; MP for Enniscorthy Sept.–11 Oct. 1703 [expelled],

[E.] Bramber, Sussex 1 Apr. 1699–1700, 1702–18 Dec. 1707 [expelled] [HP].

0057 **ASHE**, Joseph; b. 1707 d. *post* 1760; MP for Trim 1735–60.

0058 **ASHE**, Richard; b. *ante* 1686[9] d. [20] Jan. 1728; MP for Trim 1713–14, 1727–8, Athboy 1721–7.

0059 *****ASHE**, Thomas; b. *ante* 1664[10] d. *ante* 17 Aug. 1721; MP for Cavan B. 1692–3, 1695–9, 1703–13.

0060 **ASHE**, Thomas; b. 1656 d. 28 Jan. 1722; MP for Swords 1695–9, Clogher 1713–14, 1715–22.

0061 **ASTON**, Tichborne; b. 1 Nov. 1716 d. 4 Mar. 1748; MP for Ardee 1741–8.

0062 **ASTON**, William; b. *ante* 1674[6] d. 23 Aug. 1744; MP for Dunleer 1721–7, Co. Louth 1727–44.

0063 **ATKINSON**, Anthony; b. 12 Apr. 1681 d. Dec. 1743; MP for St Johnstown [Longford] 1711–13, Belfast 1713–14.

0064 **AUNGIER**, Ambrose [2nd E. of Longford]; b. *c.* 1649 d. 23 Jan. 1704/5; MP for Longford B. 1697–9.

0065 **AYLMER**, Sir Fitzgerald [Bt]; b. 14 Sept. 1736 d. [*ante* 19] Feb. 1794; MP for Roscommon B. 1761–8, Old Leighlin 1768–76, Kildare B. 1776–83, Harristown 1783–90–4.

0066 **AYLMER**, John; b. *c.* 1652[5] d. 1705; MP for Naas 1692–3.

0067 **AYLWARD**, Nicholas; b. 1688 d. 5 June 1756; MP for Thomastown 1727–56.

0068 *****AYLWAY**, Robert; b. *ante* 1645[6] d. 1702; MP for Dunleer 1692–3, 1695–9.

0069 **BABINGTON**, David; b. 1753 d. 1836; MP for Ballyshannon 1797–1800.

0070 *****BADHAM**, Brettridge; b. *c.* 1678[10] d. [*ante* 18 Feb.] 1743/4; MP for Charleville 1713–14, Rathcormack 1743–4.

0071 **BAGENAL**, Beauchamp; b. 1741 d. 1 May 1802; MP for Enniscorthy 1761–8, Co. Carlow 1768–76, 1778–83.

0072 **BAGSHAW**, Samuel; b. 1 Jan. 1689 d. 20 Oct. 1762; MP for Tallow 1761–2.

0073 **BAGWELL**, John; b. *ante* 1715[7] d. [*ante* 7] Sept. 1784; MP for Tulsk 1761–8.

0074 **BAGWELL**, John; b. 1752 d. 28 Sept. 1816; MP for Co. Tipperary 1792–7–1800 [HP].

0075 **BAGWELL**, Richard; b. [*ante* 28 Mar.] 1778 d. Apr. 1826; MP for Cashel 1799–1800, [UK] Jan.–Nov. 1801 [HP].

0076 **BAGWELL**, William; b. *c.* 1728[7] d. 26 July 1756; MP for Clonmel Jan.–July 1756.

0077 *****BAGWELL**, Rt Hon. William; b. [*ante* 2] Apr. 1776[10] d. 4 Nov. 1826; MP for Rathcormack 1798–1800 [HP].

0078 **BAILEY**, William; b. *ante* 1765[7] d. 25 Sept. 1808; MP for Augher 1797–1800.

0079 **BAILIE**, James; b. 1724 d. 22 Sept. 1787; MP for Hillsborough 1777–83–7.

0080 **BALFOUR**, William; b. *ante* 1684[5] d. 19 Apr. 1739; MP for Carlingford 1705–13, Augher 1713–14, 1715–27–39.

0081 *****BALL**, Charles; b. *c.* 1755[2] d. 1822; MP for Clogher Mar.–Aug. 1800.

0082 *****BALL**, John; b. 1748 d. 24 Aug. 1813; MP for Drogheda 1796–7–1800.

0083 **BARKER**, Samuel; b. 10 Apr. 1707 d. [bur. 4] Feb. 1769; MP for Waterford city 1747–60, 1761–8.

0084 **BARRETT**, Dacres; b. [*ante* 5] Oct. 1671[1] d. 1 Jan. 1725; MP for Co. Monaghan 1692–3.

0085 *****BARRINGTON**, John; b. 1666 d. 27 Jan. 1756; MP for Ballynakill 1692–3,1703–13–14, 1727–56.

0086 **BARRINGTON**, Jonah; b. *c.* 1698[7] d. Dec. 1784; MP for Ballynakill 1747–60.

0087 **BARRINGTON**, Sir Jonah [Kt]; b. 1764 d. 8 Apr. 1834; MP for Tuam 1790–7, Clogher 1798–Jan. 1800.

0088 **BARRY**, Hon. Arthur; b. 1724 d. 23 Oct. 1770; MP for Belfast 1757–60.

0089 *****BARRY**, Hon. David John; b. 1688 d. Oct. 1744; MP for Belfast 1727–44.

0090 **BARRY**, Sir Edward [1st Bt]; b. 1696 d. 25 Mar. 1776; MP for Charleville 1744–60.

0091*****BARRY**, James; b. 1659 d. 1717; MP for Rathcormack [1689], 1692–3, 1695–9, 1713–14, Dungarvan 1703–13, 1715–17 [r. Rathcormack 1703 and 1715].

0092 **BARRY**, James; b. [15] Jan. 1660/1 d. 16 Apr. 1725; MP for Naas 1695–9, 1711–13, Kildare B. 1715–25.

0093 *****BARRY**, James; b. 1689 d. 1743; MP for Dungarvan 1713–14, 1721–7, Rathcormack 1727–43.

0094 **BARRY**, James; b. 1739 d. 25 Oct. 1793; MP for Rathcormack 1768–76.

0095 **BARRY**, Redmond; b. *ante* 17 Sept. 1696[1] d. Sept. 1750; MP for Dungarvan 1717–27, Tallow 1727–50 [r. Rathcormack 1727].

0096 *****BARRY**, Hon. Richard; b. 1665 d. 1754; MP for Enniscorthy 1692–3, 1695–9 [absent in England Aug.–Nov. 1695], Baltimore 1713–14.

0097 *****BARRY**, Robert; b. 1731 d. 1793; MP for Charleville 1761–8–76.

0098 **BARTON**, Thomas; b. 26 Jan. 1757 d. 1820; MP for Fethard [Tipperary] 1783–90–7.

0099 **BARTON**, William; b. *ante* 1665[6] d. [Aug.] 1721; MP for Co. Monaghan 1692–3, 1695–9, 1703–13.

0100 **BATEMAN**, Rowland; b. *c.* 1737[7] d. 1803; MP for Tralee 1761–8, Co. Kerry 1776–83.

0101 **BAYLY**, Sir Edward [1st Bt]; b. 20 Feb. 1683/4[1] d. 28 Sept. 1741; MP for Newry 1705–13–14.

0102 **BEAMISH**, Francis Bernard; b. 1751 d. 1805; MP for Rathcormack 1776–83.

0103 *****BEAUCHAMP**, John; b. *ante* 1661[6] d. 1745; MP for Old Leighlin 1695–9, 1713–14, 1715–27–45, Thomastown 1703–13.

0104 *****BEECHER**, Michael; b. 1673 d. [*post* 8 Mar.] 1725/6; MP for Baltimore 1713–14, 1715–26.

0105 *****BEECHER**, Thomas; b. 1640 d. 1709; MP for Baltimore 1692–3, 1695–9, 1703–9.

0106 **BELL**, Thomas; b. *ante* 1652[6] d. 16 Jan. 1717/8; MP for Antrim B. 1703–13.

0107 **BELLASIS** [*alias* BELASYSE or BELLASISE], Sir Henry [Kt]; b. 1649 d. 16 Dec. 1717; MP for Galway B. 1692–3 [HP].

0108 **BELLEW**, Thomas; b. *ante* 1668[5] d. 12 June 1746; MP for Mullingar 1713–14, 1715–27.

0109 **BELLINGHAM**, Henry; b. 1676 d. [15 Mar.] 1740/1; MP for Dundalk 1703–13–14.

0110 **BELLINGHAM**, Henry; b. *ante* 1713[6] d. 18 May 1755; MP for Co. Louth 1741–55.

0111 **BELLINGHAM**, Thomas; b. 1646 d. 15 Sept. 1721; MP for Co. Louth 1692–3, 1695–9, 1703–13.

0112 **BENNETT**, John; b. *c.* 1731[2] d. 25 Dec. 1791; MP for Castlemartyr 1775–6, 1783–7.

0113 **BERESFORD**, Rt Hon. George de la Poer [2nd E. Tyrone and 1st M. Waterford]; b. 8 Jan. 1734/5 d. 3 Dec. 1800; MP for Co. Waterford 1757–60, Coleraine 1761–3.

0114 *****BERESFORD**, Rt Hon. Henry de la Poer [Ld La Poer 1783–9, E. Tyrone 1789–1800, 2nd M. Waterford]; b. 23 May 1772 d. 16 July 1826; MP for Co. Londonderry 1790–7–1800.

0115 **BERESFORD**, Rt Hon. John; b. 14 Mar. 1738 d. 5 Nov. 1805; MP for Co. Waterford 1761–8–76–83–90–7–1800 [HP].

0116 **BERESFORD** [HORSLEY–BERESFORD], Hon. John [2nd B. Decies]; b. 20 Jan. 1774 d. 1 Mar. 1855; MP for Coleraine 1797–1800.

0117 **BERESFORD**, Hon. John Claudius; b. 23 Oct. 1766 d. 20 July 1846; MP for Swords 1790–7, Dublin City 1797–1800 [HP].

0118 **BERESFORD**, Sir Marcus [4th Bt, 1st B. Beresford, V. Tyrone and E. of Tyrone]; b. 16 July 1694 d. 4 Apr. 1763; MP for Coleraine 1715–20.

0119 *****BERESFORD**, Marcus; b. 14 Feb. 1764 d. 16 Nov. 1797; MP for Dungarvan 1783–90–7–97.

0120 **BERESFORD**, Marcus; b. 1 June 1764 d. 1803; MP for St Canice 1790–4, Swords 1798–1800.

0121 **BERESFORD**, Sir Tristram [3rd Bt]; b. 1669 d. 16 June 1701; MP for Co. Londonderry 1692–3, 1695–9.

0122 **BERMINGHAM**, Rt Hon. Thomas [15th B. Athenry, 1st E. of Louth]; b. 16 Nov. 1717 d. 11 Jan. 1799; MP for Co. Galway 1745–50.

0123 **BERNARD**, Arthur; b. 1666 d. *post* 1714; MP for Bandon-Bridge 1713–14.

0124 *****BERNARD**, Francis; b. 1663 d. 30 June 1731; MP for Clonakilty 1692–3, Bandon-Bridge 1695–9, 1703–13–14, 1715–27.

0125 **BERNARD**, Francis; b. 28 Sept. 1698 d. [bur. 21] Mar. 1783; MP for Clonakilty 1725–7–60, Bandon-Bridge 1766–8–76.

0126 *BERNARD, Francis [1st B., V. and E. of Bandon]; b. 26 Nov. 1755 d. 30 Nov. 1830; MP for Ennis 1778–83, Bandon-Bridge 1783–90.

0127 *BERNARD, James; b. 8 Dec. 1729 d. 9 July 1790; MP for Co. Cork 1781–3–90, 1790

0128 BERNARD, Stephen; b. 17 July 1701 d. 6 Sept. 1761; MP for Bandon-Bridge 1727–60.

0129 *BERRY, William; b. c. 1668[2] d. Dec. 1739; MP for Enniscorthy 1703–13, 1715–27–39, Duleek 1713–4.

0130 BETTESWORTH, Richard; b. 1689 d. 31 Mar. 1741; MP for Thomastown 1721–7, Midleton 1727–41.

0131 *BINDON, David; b. c. 1650[7] d. 1733; MP for Ennis 1715–27.

0132 BINDON, David; b. c. 1687 d. 13 July 1760; MP for Ennis 1731–60.

0133 BINDON, Samuel; b. 1680 d. 12 Aug. 1760; MP for Ennis 1715–27–60.

0134 BINGHAM, Sir Charles [7th Bt, 1st B. and E. of Lucan]; b. 22 Sept. 1735 d. 29 Mar. 1799; MP for Co. Mayo 1761–8–76 [HP].

0135 BINGHAM, Sir Henry [3rd Bt]; b. 1654 d. 5 July 1714; MP for Co. Mayo 1692–3, 1695–9,1703–13–14.

0136 *BINGHAM, Rt Hon. Henry; b. 1688 d. 5 Dec. 1743; MP for Co. Mayo 1707–13–14, Castlebar 1715–27–43.

0137 BINGHAM, Henry; b. 1715 d. 15 Apr. 1769; MP for Tuam 1750–60, 1761–8.

0138 *BINGHAM, Henry; b. [bapt. 7 Nov.] 1739 d. Dec. 1789; MP for Tuam 1761–8.

0139 BINGHAM, John; b. c. 1655[10] d. [ante 25 Mar.] 1705/6; MP for Castlebar 1692–3, Co. Mayo 1695–9, 1703–06.

0140 *BINGHAM, John; b. ante 12 Nov. 1694[1] d. 1728; MP for Castlebar 1715–27.

0141 BINGHAM, Sir John [5th Bt]; b. 1690 d. 21 Sept. 1749; MP for Co. Mayo 1727–49.

0142 BINGHAM, John; b. 1714 d. [ante 24] Oct. 1780; MP for Tuam 1739–60.

0143 BINGHAM, Sir John [6th Bt]; b. [ante 29] Nov. 1728 d. 27 Nov. 1750; MP for Co. Mayo 1749–50.

0144 *BINGHAM, John [1st B. Clanmorris]; b. 1762 d. 18 May 1821; MP for Tuam 1797–Feb. 1800.

0145 BIRCH, Robert; b. ante 1741[9] d. post 1800; MP for Belturbet 1771–6–83.

0146 BLACKWOOD, Hon. Sir Hans [4th Bt, 3rd B. Dufferin and Claneboye]; b. Oct. 1758 d. 18 Nov. 1839; MP for Killyleagh 1799–Jan. 1800.

0147 BLACKWOOD, Hon. Sir James Stevenson [3rd Bt, 2 B. Dufferin and Claneboye]; b. 8 July 1755 d. 8 Aug. 1836; MP for Killyleagh 1788–90–7–1800 [HP].

0148 BLACKWOOD, Sir John [2nd Bt]; b. 1722 d. 26 Feb. 1799; MP for Killyleagh 1761–8, 1776–83–90, 1797–9, Bangor 1768–76, 1790–7.

0149 BLACKWOOD, Robert; b. [Apr.] 1752 d. 30 Jan. 1786; MP for Killyleagh 1776–83–6.

0150 BLADEN, Rt Hon. Martin; b. 1682 d. 15 Feb. 1745/6; MP for Bandon-Bridge 1715–27 [HP].

0151 BLAIR, William; b. ante 1726[1] d. [1 Mar.] 1782; MP for Monaghan B. 1747–60.

0152 BLAKE, Joseph Henry [1st B. Wallscourt]; b. 5 Oct. 1765 d. 28 Mar. 1803; MP for Co. Galway 1792–7–1800.

0153 BLAKENEY, John; b. c. 1703[9] d. 21 Aug. 1747; MP for Athenry 1727–47.

0154 BLAKENEY, John; b. c. 1729[5] d. 25 July 1789; MP for Athenry 1763–8–76–83–9.

0155 *BLAKENEY, John; b. 12 Sept. 1756 d. 23 Aug. 1781; MP for Athenry 1776–81.

0156 BLAKENEY, Robert; b. 1679 d. 1 May 1733; MP for Athenry 1721–7–33.

0157 BLAKENEY, Robert; b. c. 1724[2] d. 30 Dec. 1762; MP for Athenry 1747–60, 1761–2.

0158 BLAKENEY, Theophilus; b. c. 1730–4[8] d. 22 Sept. 1813; MP for Athenry 1768–76, 1783–90–7–1800, Carlingford 1776–83.

0159 BLAKENEY, Sir William [1st B. Blakeney]; b. 1670 d. 20 Sept. 1761; MP for Kilmallock 1725–7–56.

0160 BLAKENEY, William; b. 1735 d. 2 Nov. 1804; MP for Athenry 1781–3, 1790–7–Apr. 1800.

0161 BLAQUIERE, James; b. 1722 d. 6 Feb. 1802; MP for Carlingford 1790–7.

0162 **BLAQUIERE**, Rt Hon. Sir John [KB, 1st Bt and B. de Blaquiere]; b. 15 May 1732 d. 27 Aug. 1812; MP for Old Leighlin 1773–6–83, Carlingford 1783–90, Charleville 1790–7, Newtown[ards] 1797–1800.

0163 *****BLENNERHASSETT**, Arthur; b. 1687 d. 3 Jan..1758; MP for Tralee 1727–43.

0164 **BLENNERHASSETT**, Arthur; b. 1719 d. [*ante* 13] June 1799; MP for Tralee 1743–60, Co. Kerry 1775–6–83.

0165 **BLENNERHASSETT**, Conway; b. 3 Oct. 1693 d. 7 June 1724; MP for Tralee 1723–4.

0166 *****BLENNERHASSETT**, John; b. 1665 d. 1709; MP for Tralee 1692–3, Dingle 1695–9, Co. Kerry 1703–9.

0167 *****BLENNERHASSETT**, John; b. 1691 d. 5 May 1775; MP for Co. Kerry 1709–13, 1715–27, 1761–8–75, Tralee 1713–14, 1727–60.

0168 **BLENNERHASSETT**, John; b. 1715 d. [May] 1763; MP for Co. Kerry 1751–60, 1762–3.

0169 **BLENNERHASSETT**, John; b. 1769 d. 6 July 1794; MP for Co. Kerry 1790–4.

0170 **BLENNERHASSETT**, Robert; b. 1652 d. [Oct.] 1712; MP for Clonmel 1692–3, 1695–9, Limerick City 1703–12.

0171 **BLIGH**, Hon. Edward; b. 19 Sept. 1769 d. 2 Nov. 1840; MP for Athboy Jan.–Aug. 1800.

0172 *****BLIGH**, John [1st B. Clifton, V. and E. of Darnley]; b. 28 Dec. 1687 d. 12 Sept. 1728; MP for Trim 1709–13, Athboy 1713–14, 1715–21.

0173 *****BLIGH**, Hon. John [3rd E. of Darnley]; b. 2 Oct. 1719 d. 31 July 1781; MP for Athboy 1739–47.

0174 **BLIGH**, Rt Hon. Thomas; b. 1654 d. 28 Aug. 1710; MP for Athboy 1692–3, Co. Meath 1695–9, 1703–10.

0175 *****BLIGH**, Thomas; b. 14 Aug. 1693 d. 17 Aug. 1775; MP for Athboy 1715–27–60, 1761–8–75.

0176 **BLIGH**, Thomas Cherburgh; b. 1761 d. 17 Sept. 1830; MP for Athboy 1783–90–7–1800 [HP].

0177 *****BLUNDELL**, Sir Francis [3rd Bt]; b. 30 Jan.1642/3 d. [*ante* 29 July] 1707; MP for King's Co. 1692–3, 1695–9, 1703–7.

0178 **BLUNDEN**, John; b. *ante* 1695[6] d. 8 Jan. 1752; MP for Kilkenny city 1727–52.

0179 **BLUNDEN**, Sir John [1st Bt]; b. *c.* 1718[2] d. Jan. 1783; MP for Kilkenny city 1761–8–76.

0180 *****BOLTON**, Cornelius; b. *c.* 1714[10] d. 16 Sept. 1779; MP for Waterford city 1768–76.

0181 **BOLTON**, Cornelius; b. 1 Oct. 1751 d. 11 Mar. 1829; MP for Waterford city 1776–83, Lanesborough 1783–90.

0182 **BOLTON**, Edward; b. 1696 d. 5 Aug. 1758; MP for Swords 1727–58.

0183 **BOLTON**, Thomas; b. 1706 d. 17 Mar. 1740/1; MP for Athenry 1733–41.

0184 **BOND**, Sir James [1st Bt]; b. 11 June 1744 d. 2 June 1820; MP for Naas 1791–7.

0185 *****BOOTH**, Samuel; b. [?]1641[5] d. [?]1701[10]; MP for Callan 1692–3, 1695–9.

0186 *****BOREMAN** [*alias* BOWERMAN], Henry; b. *ante* 1662[7] d. 1701; MP for Charleville 1692–3.

0187 **BORROWES** [*alias* BURROWES], Sir Kildare Dixon [5th Bt]; b. [bapt. 20 Jan.] 1721/2 d. 22 June 1790; MP for Co. Kildare 1745–60, 1761–8–76 [r. Randalstown 1761].

0188 **BORROWES** [*alias* BURROWES], Sir Walter Dixon [4th Bt]; b. 1691 d. 9 [bur. 14] June 1741; MP for Harristown 1721–7, Athy 1727–41.

0189 **BOTET**, Anthony; b. 1741 d. 11 May 1811; MP for Tulsk 1797–Jan. 1800.

0190 **BOURCHIER**, Charles; b. 1665 d. 18 May 1716; MP for Dungarvan 1692–3, 1695–9, Armagh City 1715–16.

0191 **BOURKE** [*alias* BURKE], Dominick; b. *ante* 1703[6] d. 8 Dec. 1747; MP for Galway B. 1735–47.

♦♦♦♦ **BOURKE** [*alias* BURKE], Gerald [Garrett]; b. *c.* 1679–81 d. 23 Apr. 1740 [n.d.e. Maryborough Oct.–Dec. 1713].

0192 **BOURKE**, Rt Hon. John [1st B. Naas, V. and E. of Mayo]; b. 1700 d. 3 Dec. 1790; MP for Naas 1727–60, 1768–76, May–Aug. 1776, Old Leighlin 1761–8.

0193 **BOURKE**, Hon. John [2nd E. of Mayo]; b. 1729 d. 21 Apr. 1792; MP for Naas 1763–8–76–83–90.

0194 **BOURKE**, Rt Hon. John [4th E. of Mayo]; b. 18 June 1766 d. 23 May 1849; MP for Naas 1790–4.

0195 *BOURKE, Theobald; b. *c.* 1683–5[3] d. June 1726; MP for Naas 1713–14, 1715–26.

♦♦♦♦ BOWEN, John. b. *c.* 1697 d. *c.* 1776 [n.d.e. Mullingar Nov. 1727–Jan. 1727/8].

0196 BOWES, Rt Hon. John [1st B. Bowes]; b. 1691 d. 22 July 1767; MP for Taghmon 1731–42.

0197 *BOYD, Hugh; b. 1765 d. 26 Nov. 1795; MP for Co. Antrim 1794–5.

0198 *BOYD, James; b. 1764 d. 29 June 1808; MP for Wexford B. 1797–9–1800.

0199 BOYD, Robert; b. 1740 d. 1814; MP for Boyle 1783–90.

0200 BOYLE, Bellingham; b. 1690 d. 13 May 1771; MP for Bandon-Bridge 1731–60, Youghal 1761–8.

0201 BOYLE, Hon. Charles; [4th E. of Orrery] b. 28 July 1674 d. 28 Aug.1731; MP for Charleville 1695–9 [HP].

0202 BOYLE, Hon. Charles [2nd V. Blessington]; b. *post* 1673[7] d. 2 June 1732; MP for Blessington 1711–13–14, 1715–18.

0203 BOYLE, Hon. Charles [styled Ld Boyle, V. Dungarvan]; b. 27 Jan. 1729 d. 16 Sept. 1759; MP for Co. Cork 1756–9.

0204 BOYLE, Hon. Charles; b. May 1734 d. 6 June 1758; MP for Lismore May–June 1758.

0205 BOYLE, Hon. Charles; b. 1774 d. 26 Nov. 1800; MP for Charleville 1797–1800.

0206 BOYLE, Hon. Hamilton [6th E. of Corke and Orrery]; b. 3 Feb. 1730 d. 17 Jan. 1764; MP for Charleville 1759–60 [HP].

0207 *BOYLE, Hon. Henry; b. *c.* 1648[8] d. 1693; MP for Youghal 1692–3.

0208 BOYLE, Rt Hon. Henry [1st B. Carleton [GB]]; b. *c.* 1668[8] d.14 Mar.1724/5; MP for Co.Cork 1692–3 [HP].

0209 BOYLE, Henry; b. *ante* [21 Sept.] 1674[1] d. 1713; MP for Youghal 1695–9.

0210 *BOYLE, Rt Hon. Henry [1st E. of Shannon]; b. 1682 d. 28 Dec. 1764; MP for Midleton 1707–13, Kilmallock 1713–14, Co. Cork 1715–27–56.

0211 BOYLE, Rt Hon. Henry [3rd E. of Shannon]; b. 8 Aug. 1771 d. 22 Apr. 1842; MP for Clonakilty 1793–7, Co. Cork 1797–1800.

0212 BOYLE, Richard; b. 1655 d. [bur. 24] Nov. 1711; MP for Old Leighlin 1695–9 [HP].

0213 BOYLE, Rt Hon. Richard [2nd E. of Shannon]; b. 30 Jan. 1728 d. 20 May 1807; MP for Dungarvan 1749–60, Co. Cork 1761–4.

0214 *BOYLE, Richard O'Brien; b. 1762 d. 13 Oct. 1788; MP for Tallow 1782–3.

0215 *BOYLE, William; b. *c.* 1678[5] d. [Oct.] 1725; MP for Charleville 1715–25.

0216 BOYLE [BOYLE-WALSINGHAM], Hon. Henry; b. *c.* 1729–30[8] d. 27 Mar. 1756; MP for Tallow 1751–6.

0217 BOYLE [BOYLE-WALSINGHAM], Hon. Robert; b. Mar. 1736 d. Oct. 1779; MP for Dungarvan 1758–60, 1761–8 [HP]

0218 BOYSE, James; ?b. *c.* 1660[10] d. May 1724; MP for Bannow 1715–24.

0219 BOYSE, Nathaniel; b. *c.* 1656[2] d. 1714; MP for Bannow 1692–3, 1695–9, 1703–13–14.

0220 BOYSE, Samuel; b. [bapt. 2 Feb.] 1696/7 d. 1 Apr. 1730; MP for Bannow 1725–7–30.

0221 BRABAZON, Hon. Anthony [8th E. of Meath]; b. Feb. 1721/2 d. 4 Jan. 1790; MP for Co. Wicklow 1745–60, Co. Dublin 1761–8–72.

0222 *BRABAZON, Rt Hon. Chambre [5th E. of Meath]; b. *c.* 1645[10] d. 1 Apr. 1715; MP for Co. Dublin 1692–3.

0223 BRABAZON, Rt Hon. Chaworth [6th E. of Meath]; b. 1686 d. 14 May 1763; MP for Co. Dublin 1713–4.

0224 BRABAZON, Hon. Edward [7th E. of Meath]; b. [bapt. 24 Nov.] 1691 d. 24 Nov. 1772; MP for Co. Dublin 1715–27–60.

0225 *BRABAZON, Hon. William; b. 1723 d. [*ante* 9] Dec. 1790; MP for Co. Wicklow 1765–8–76–83.

0226 *BRABAZON, Hon. William [9th E. of Meath]; b. 6 July 1769 d. 26 May 1797; MP for Co. Dublin 1789–90.

0227 BRADSTREET, Sir Samuel [3rd Bt]; b. Oct. 1738 d. 2 May 1791; MP for Dublin city 1776–83–4.

0228 *BRAGG, Philip; b. 1684 d. 6 June 1759; MP for Armagh City 1749–59.

0229 *BRASIER, Kilner; b. *c.* 1659–64[5] d. 1725; MP for Dundalk 1695–9, St Johnstown [Donegal] 1703–13, Kilmallock 1715–25.

0230 *BRAY, Robert; b. 1675 d. 1747; MP for Lanesborough 1715–27.

0231 *BREWSTER, Sir Francis [Kt]; b. *ante* 1642[7] d. 1705; MP for Tuam 1692–3, 1695–9, Doneraile 1703–5.

0232 BREWSTER, Francis; b. 1667 d. *post* 1713; MP for Midleton 1695–9, Dingle 1703–13.

0233 BRICE, Edward; b. 1659 d. 11 Aug. 1742; MP for Dungannon 1703–13.

0234 BRICE, Randolph [Randal]; b. 1646 d. [*ante* 15] Sept. 1697; MP for Lisburn 1692–3, 1695–7.

0235 BRIDGES, Sir Matthew [Kt]; b. 1651 d. 1703; MP for Strabane 1692–3.

0236 BRISTOW, Rt Hon. William; b. *c.* 1697–9[3] d. 18 Mar. 1758; MP for Lismore 1745–58.

0237 *BRODRICK, Rt Hon. Alan [1st B. Brodrick and V. Midleton]; b. 1656 d. [bur.29] Aug. 1728; MP for Cork City 1692–3, 1695–9, 1703–10, Co. Cork 1713–14 [HP].

0238 BRODRICK, Edward; b. [bapt. 25 Mar.] 1743/4 d. *post* 1776; Midleton 1768–76.

0239 *BRODRICK, Hon. Henry; b. 12 Dec. 1758 d. 16 June 1785; MP for Midleton 1776–83.

0240 BRODRICK, Sir St John [Kt]; b. 3 Dec. 1627 d. [bur. 23] Jan. 1710/11; MP for [Kinsale 1661–6], Co. Cork 1692–3, 1695–9.

0241 BRODRICK, St John; b. 1659 d. 12 June 1707; MP for Midleton Aug.–Sept. 1695, 1703–7.

0242 BRODRICK, Rt Hon. St John; b. *c.* 1685[4] d. 21 Feb. 1727/8; MP for Castlemartyr 1709–13, Cork city 1713–14, Co. Cork 1715–27–8 [HP].

0243 BRODRICK, Rt Hon. Thomas; b. 4 Aug. 1654 d. 3 Oct. 1730; MP for Midleton 1692–3, 1715–27, Co. Cork 1695–9, 1703–13 [HP]

0244 BRODRICK, Thomas; b. 1705 d. 1 Jan. 1769; MP for Midleton 1761–8.

0245 *BRODRICK, Hon. Thomas; b. 17 Apr. 1756 d. 13 Jan. 1795; MP for Midleton 1776–83.

0246 *BRODRICK, William; b. *c.* 1666[2] d. *post* 1733[10]; MP for Mallow 1716–27.

0247 BROOKE, Rt Hon. Sir Arthur [1st Bt]; b. 1726 d. 7 Mar. 1785; MP for Co. Fermanagh 1761–8–76–83, Maryborough 1783–5.

0248 *BROOKE, Henry; b. [bapt. 22 Jan.] 1670/1 d. 14 July 1761; MP for Dundalk 1713–14, 1715–27, Co. Fermanagh 1727–60.

0249 BROOKE, Henry Vaughan; b. 1743 d. 27 Nov. 1807; MP for Donegal B. 1777–83, Co. Donegal 1783–90–7–1800 [HP].

0250 *BROOKE, Thomas; b. *ante* 1650[9] d. 1696; MP for Antrim B. 1695–6.

0251 BROWNE, Hon. Arthur; b.1732 d. [bur. 26] July 1779; MP for Gowran 1769–76, Co. Mayo 1776–9.

0252 BROWNE, Arthur; b. 1756 d. 8 June 1805; MP for TCD 1783–90–7–1800 [re-elected pp 1795].

0253 *BROWNE, Rt Hon. Denis; b. 1763 d. 14 Aug. 1828; MP for Co. Mayo 1782–3–90–7–1800 [HP].

0254 BROWNE, [Sir] George [4th Bt] b. *c.* 1680–8[7] d. 8 May 1737; MP for Castlebar 1713–14.

0255 BROWNE, Hon. George; b. *c.* 1735–7[8] d. 22 July 1782; MP for Co. Mayo 1779–82.

0256 BROWNE, Hon. James; b. *c.* 1735–7[3] d. 22 Oct. 1790; MP for Jamestown 1768–76, Tuam 1776–83, Castlebar 1783–90.

0257 BROWNE, Hon. James Caulfeild [2nd B. Kilmaine]; b. 16 Mar. 1765 d. 22 May 1825; MP for Carlow B. Jan.–Apr. 1790.

0258 BROWNE, John [1st B. Mounteagle, V. Westport and E. of Altamont]; b. 1709 d. 4 July 1776; MP for Castlebar 1744–60.

0259 BROWNE, Sir John [7th Bt, 1st B. Kilmaine]; b. 1730 d. 7 June 1794; MP for Newtown[ards] 1776–83, Carlow B. 1783–9.

0260 BROWNE, Rt Hon. John Denis [3rd E. of Altamont, 1st M. of Sligo]; b. 11 June 1756 d. 2 Jan. 1809; MP for Jamestown 1776–80.

0261 BROWNE, William; b. 3 Jan. 1763 d. 1 Apr. 1840; MP for Portarlington 1790–7.

0262 BROWNE-KELLY, Hon. Peter [2nd E. of Altamont]; b. 1731 d. 28 Dec. 1780; MP for Co. Mayo 1761–8.

0263 **BROWNLOW** [CHAMBERLAIN], Arthur; b. 20 Mar. 1644/5 d. [27] Mar. 1710/11; MP for Co. Armagh [1689], 1692–3, 1695–9, 1703–11.

0264 **BROWNLOW**, William; b. [bapt. 31 Dec.] 1683 d. 27 Aug. 1739; MP for Co. Armagh 1711–13–14, 1715–27–39.

0265 **BROWNLOW**, Rt Hon. William; b. 10 Apr. 1726 d. 28 Oct. 1794; MP for Co. Armagh 1753–60, 1761–8–76–83–90–4 [r. Strabane 1768].

0266 **BROWNLOW**, William; b. 1755 d. 10 July 1815; MP for Co. Armagh 1795–7 [HP].

0267 **BRUCE**, Sir Stewart [1st Bt]; b. *c.* 1764–7[7] d. 19 Mar. 1841; MP for Lisburn 1798–1800.

0268 **BRUEN**, Henry; b. 1741 d. 14 Dec. 1795; MP for Jamestown 1783–90, Co. Carlow 1790–5.

0269 *****BUCKNER**, William; b. *ante* 5 Oct. 1671[1] d. 1700; MP for Dungarvan 1692–3, 1695–9.

0270 **BUCKWORTH**, Richard; b. [bapt. 18 Apr.] 1675 d. Sept. 1738; MP for Cashel 1715–27–38.

0271 **BUDGELL**, Eustace; b. 19 Aug. 1686 d. May 1737; MP for Mullingar 1715–27.

0272 **BULKELEY**, Sir Richard [2nd Bt]; b. 17 Aug. 1660 d. 7 Apr. 1710; MP for Fethard [Wexford] 1692–3, 1695–9, 1703–10.

0273 **BUNBURY**, George; b. *c.* 1750–2[3] d. 17 May 1820; MP for Thomastown 1786–90–7, Gowran 1797–1800.

0274 **BUNBURY**, Walter; b. 1664 d. July 1749; MP for Clonmines 1703–13.

0275 **BUNBURY**, William; b. [*post* 2 Mar.] 1735/6 d. 18 Apr. 1778; MP for Co. Carlow 1776–8.

0276 *****BURDETT**, Arthur; b. *c.* 1726–32[8] d. Dec. 1796; MP for Harristown 1790–7.

0277 **BURDETT**, George; b. 1735 d. 2 Feb. 1818; MP for Gowran 1783–90, 1797–1800, Thomastown 1790–7.

0278 **BURDETT**, Sir Thomas [1st Bt]; b. 14 Sept. 1668 d. 14 Apr. 1727; MP for Co. Carlow 1704–13, 1715–27, Carlow B. 1713–14.

0279 **BURGH**, Richard; b. 1725 d. [bur. 21] Sept. 1762; MP for Naas 1759–60, 1761–2.

0280 **BURGH**, Thomas; b. 1670 d. 18 Dec. 1730; MP for Naas 1713–14, 1715–27–30.

0281 **BURGH**, Thomas; b. 1696 d. 20 Sept. 1758; MP for Lanesborough 1727–58.

0282 **BURGH**, Thomas; b. [bapt. 4 Nov.] 1707 d. 23 June 1759; MP for Naas 1731–59.

0283 **BURGH**, Thomas; b. 23 Jan. 1754 d. 1832; MP for Harristown 1775–6, 1783–90, Athy 1776–83.

0284 **BURGH**, Thomas; b. May 1744 d. [bur. 17] June 1810; MP for Athy 1776–83–90, Kilbeggan 1790–7, Clogher 1797–1800, Fore Feb.–Aug. 1800.

0285 **BURGH**, William; b. 1667 d. [bur. 23] Oct. 1744; MP for Lanesborough 1713–14 [n.d.e. 1715].

0286 **BURGH**, William; b. 1741 d. 20 Dec. 1808; MP for Athy 1768–76.

0287 **BURKE**, Michael; b. 1760 d. 29 Aug. 1838; MP for Athenry 1800.

♦♦♦♦ **BURROUGHS**, Thomas; b. *ante* 1663 d. *post* 1727 [n.d.e. Carysfort Aug.–Oct. 1703].

0288 **BURROWES**, Peter; b. 8 Nov. 1753 d. 1841; MP for Enniscorthy Jan.–Aug. 1800.

0289 **BURROWES**, Thomas; b. *c.* 1742[3] d. 1830; MP for Longford B. 1800.

0290 **BURROWS** [*alias* BORROWES or BURROWES], Sir Kildare [3rd Bt]; b. *c.* 1660[10] d. [bur. 26] Sept. 1709; MP for Co. Kildare 1703–9.

0291 **BURT**, John; b. *c.* 1662–4[3] d. *post* 1699; MP for Tallow 1695–9.

0292 **BURTON**, Benjamin; b. *ante* 1665[7] d. 13 May 1728; MP for Dublin city 1703–13–14, 1715–27.

0293 **BURTON**, Rt Hon. Benjamin; b. 12 Jan. 1708/9 d. 1 Oct. 1767; MP for Knocktopher 1741–60, Co. Carlow 1761–7.

0294 **BURTON**, Benjamin; b. 12 Mar. 1736 d. [31 May–4 June] 1763; MP for Co. Sligo 1757–60, Boyle 1761–3.

0295 **BURTON**, Sir Charles [Kt, 1st Bt]; b. 1702 d. 6 June 1775; MP for Dublin city 1749–60.

0296 **BURTON**, Francis; b. 1659 d. 1 July 1714; MP for Ennis 1692–3, 1695–9, 1703–13–14.

0297 **BURTON**, Rt Hon. Francis; b. 1 Dec. 1696 d. 20 Mar. 1744; MP for Coleraine 1721–7, Co. Clare 1727–44.

0298 **BURTON**, Hon. Sir Francis Nathaniel; b. 26 Dec. 1766 d. 27 Jan. 1832; MP for Co. Clare 1790–7–1800 [HP].

0299 **BURTON**[CONYNGHAM], Francis Pierpoint [2nd B. Conyngham]; b. *c.* 1728 d. 22 May 1787; MP for Killybegs 1753–60, Co. Clare 1761–8–76.

0300 **BURTON**, Robert; b. 1695 d. Jan. 1765; MP for Co. Carlow 1727–60, Carlow B. 1761–5.

0301 **BURTON**, Samuel; b. 1687 d. 9 July 1733; MP for Sligo B. 1713–14, 1715–27, Dublin city 1727–33.

0302 *****BURTON**, Thomas; b. 1706 d. [*ante* 6] May 1773[10]; MP for Ennis 1761–8.

0303 **BURTON** [CONYNGHAM], Rt Hon. William; b. 1733 d. 31 May 1796; MP for Newtown Limavady 1761–8–76, Ennis 1776–83, 1790–6, Killybegs 1783–90 [r. Killybegs and Newtown Limavady 1776].

0304 **BURTON**, William Henry; b. 16 July 1739 d. 7 Jan. 1818; MP for Gowran 1761–8, Co. Carlow 1768–76–83–90–7–1800 [HP].

0305 *****BURY**, Charles William [1st B. Tullamore, V. and E. of Charleville]; b. 30 June 1764 d. 31 Oct. 1835; MP for Kilmallock Jan.–Apr. 1790, 1792–7.

0306 **BURY**, John; [?]b. *c.* 1650 d. 14 Sept. 1722; MP for Askeaton 1715–22.

0307 **BUSHE**, Amyas; b. *c.*1657 d. [29] Aug. 1724; MP for New Ross 1707–13, Thomastown 1713–14.

0308 *****BUSHE**, Arthur; b. *ante* 1670 d. 1731; MP for Thomastown 1695–9, 1703–13–14.

0309 **BUSHE**, Rt Hon. Charles Kendal; b. 1767 d. 10 July 1843; MP for Callan 1796–7–9, Donegal B. 1799–1800.

0310 **BUSHE**, Gervase Parker; b. [bapt. 22 Dec.] 1744 d. 13 Aug. 1793; MP for Granard 1767–8–76, Kilkenny city 1778–83, Fore 1783–90, Lanesborough 1790–3.

0311 **BUSTEED**, Jephson; b. 1678 d. *post* 1727; MP for Midleton 1713–14, Rathcormack 1715–27 [n.d.e. Doneraile 1728].

0312 **BUTLER**, Rt Hon. Brinsley [2nd B. Newtown Butler, 1st V. Lanesborough]; b. 1670 d. 6 Mar. 1735/6; MP for Kells 1703–13, Belturbet 1713–14, 1715–24.

0313 **BUTLER**, Rt Hon. Brinsley [2nd E. of Lanesborough]; b. 4 Mar. 1727/8 d. 15 Jan. 1779; MP for Co. Cavan 1751–60, 1761–8.

0314 **BUTLER**, Hon. Edmund [11th V. Mountgarret]; b. 14 July 1745 d. 15 July 1793; MP for Co. Kilkenny 1776–9.

0315 **BUTLER**, Francis; b. 1634 d. 15 Aug. 1702; MP for Belturbet [1662–6], 1692–3, 1695–9.

0316 **BUTLER**, Hon. Henry Thomas [2nd E. of Carrick]; b. 19 May 1746 d. 20 July 1813; MP for Killyleagh 1768–74.

0317 **BUTLER**, Rt Hon. Humphrey [2nd V. Lanesborough and 1st E. of Lanesborough]; b. *c.* 1700[7] d. 11 Apr. 1768; MP for Belturbet 1725–7–36.

0318 **BUTLER**, Humphrey; b. 7 Aug. 1767 d. [Oct.] 1837; MP for Donegal B. 1790–7.

0319 **BUTLER**, James; b. 1681 d. 19 Nov. 1742; MP for Clonmines 1703–13, Newcastle 1735–42.

0320 **BUTLER**[-WANDESFORD], Hon. James [19th E. of Ormonde, 12th E. of Ossory, 1st M. of Ormonde]; b. 15 July 1774 d. 18 May 1838; MP for Kilkenny city Mar.–Oct. 1796 [never took his seat], Co. Kilkenny 1796–7–1800 [HP].

0321 **BUTLER**, Hon. John; b. 1703 d. 14 Dec. 1789; MP for Newcastle 1743–60, 1761–8–76–83.

0322 **BUTLER**, John [17th E. of Ormonde and 10th E. of Ossory]; b. 10 Dec. 1740 d. 30 Dec. 1795; MP for Gowran 1776–83, Kilkenny city 1783–90–1.

0323 **BUTLER**[-WANDESFORD]; Hon. John; b. 1772 d. Apr. 1796; MP for Kilkenny city 1792–6, Co. Kilkenny Feb.–Apr. 1796.

0324 **BUTLER**, Rt Hon. Sir Pierce [4th Bt]; b. 1670 d. [17] Apr. 1732; MP for Co. Carlow 1703–13–14.

0325 **BUTLER** [BUTLER-COOPER], Hon. Pierce; b. 11 Aug. 1750 d. 5 May 1826; MP for Killyleagh 1774–6, Callan 1776–83.

0326 **BUTLER**, Sir Richard [5th Bt]; b. 1701 d. 25 Nov. 1771; MP for Co. Carlow 1730–60.

0327 **BUTLER**, Sir Richard [7th Bt]; b. 14 July 1761 d. 16 Jan. 1817; MP for Co. Carlow 1783–90, 1796–7–1800 [HP].

0328 **BUTLER**, Hon. Robert; b. [bapt. 24 Mar.] 1704/5 d. [Sept.] 1763; MP for Belturbet 1736–60, 1761–3.

0329 *BUTLER, Rt Hon. Theophilus [1st B. Newtown Butler]; b. 1669 d. 11 Mar. 1724; MP for Co. Cavan 1703–13, Belturbet 1713–14.

0330 BUTLER, Sir Thomas [3rd Bt]; b. ante 1649[6] d. Feb. 1703/4; MP for Co. Carlow 1692–3, 1695–9, 1703–4.

0331 BUTLER, Hon. Thomas; b. c. 1703[8] d. 9 Dec. 1753; MP for Belturbet 1727–53.

0332 BUTLER, Sir Thomas [6th Bt]; b. 1735 d. 7 Oct. 1772; MP for Co. Carlow 1761–8, Portarlington 1771–2.

0333 *BUTLER, Rt Hon. Walter [18th E. of Ormonde, 11th E. of Ossory and 1st M. of Ormonde]; b. 4 Feb. 1770 d. 10 Aug. 1820; MP for Co. Kilkenny 1789–90–5.

0334 *CAIRNES, Sir Alexander [1st Bt]; b. 1665 d. 30 Oct. 1732; MP for Monaghan B. 1710–13, Co. Monaghan 1713–14, 1715–27, Monaghan B. 1727–32.

0335 CAIRNES, David; b. 15 Nov. 1645 d. May 1722; MP for Londonderry city 1692–3, 1695–9.

0336 *CAIRNES, Sir Henry [2nd Bt]; b. 1673 d. 16 June 1743; MP for Monaghan B. 1733–43.

0337 CAIRNES, William; b. c. 1666–72[8] d. [bur. 9] Aug. 1707; MP for Belfast 1703–7.

0338 CALDWELL, Andrew; b. 19 Dec. 1733 d. 2 July 1808; MP for Knocktopher 1776–83, Downpatrick 1783–90.

0339 CAMPBELL, Charles; b. ante [?]1640[1] d. 28 Oct. 1725; MP for Newtown[ards] [?1661–6], 1695–9, 1703–13–14, 1715–25.

0340 *CAMPBELL, David; b. 1648 d. [ante 27 Sept.] 1698; MP for Bangor 1692–3, 1695–8.

0341 CAMPBELL, Rt Hon. Ld Frederick; b. 20 June 1729 d. 8 June 1816; MP for Thomastown 1767–8, St Canice 1768–76 [HP].

0342 CANE, Hugh; b. 1719 d. 19 Jan. 1793; MP for Tallow 1768–76–83–90–3.

0343 CANE, James; b. 1762 d. 1806; MP for Ratoath 1798–1800.

0344 *CAREW, Robert; b. 1681 d. [Sept.] 1721; MP for Dungarvan 1713–14, 1715–21.

0345 CAREW, Robert; b. c. 1715[8] d. 18 Aug. 1740; MP for Waterford city 1739–40.

0346 CAREW, Robert; b. 22 May 1747 d. 11 Apr. 1834; MP for Dungarvan 1768–76.

0347 CAREW, Robert Shapland; b. [20] [bapt. 23] June 1752 d. 29 Mar. 1829; MP for Waterford city 1776–83–90–7–1800 [HP].

0348 CAREW, Shapland; b. 1716 d. [ante 14] Oct. 1780; MP for Waterford city 1748–60, 1761–8, 1769–76.

0349 CAREW, Thomas; b. 11 Aug. 1718 d. 5 June 1793; MP for Dungarvan 1761–8.

0350 CAREY, Rt Hon. Walter; b. 17 Oct. 1685 d. 27 Apr. 1757; MP for Clogher 1731–57 [HP].

0351 CARIGUE-PONSONBY [alias CARIQUE-PONSONBY], James; b. 1738 d. Dec. 1796; MP for Tulsk 1776–83, Tralee 1783–90.

0352 CARLETON, Christopher; b. [?] 1640[6] d. 2 Jan. 1703/4; MP for Wicklow B. 1696–9, 1703–4.

0353 CARLETON, Rt Hon. Hugh [1st B. and V. Carleton]; b. 11 Sept. 1739 d. 25 Feb. 1826; MP for Tuam 1772–6, Philipstown 1776–83, Naas 1783–7.

0354 CARNCROSS, Hugh; b. [?] 1743[5] d. May 1799; MP for Newtown Limavady 1795–7.

0355 CARPENTER, George [1st B. Carpenter]; b. 10 Feb. 1657 d. 10 Feb. 1732; MP for Newtown[ards] 1703–5 [HP].

0356 *CARR, Thomas; b. 1667 d. 1720; MP for Newtown Limavady 1703–13.

0357 CARR [BUCKWORTH], William; b. 1705 d. 30 July 1753; MP for Cashel 1739–53.

0358 CARROLL, Ephraim; b. [bapt. 10 Mar.] 1753 d. 1824; MP for Fethard [Wexford] 1783–90, Bannow 1790–7–9.

0359 *CARTER, Thomas; b. [bapt. 20 Aug.] 1650 d. 19 Aug. 1726; MP for Fethard [Tipperary] 1695–9, Portarlington 1703–13, Trim 1719–27.

0360 *CARTER, Rt Hon. Thomas; b. c. 1682 d. 2 Sept. 1763; MP for Hillsborough 1727–60.

0361 CARTER, Thomas; b. 1720 d. 10 Sept. 1765; MP for Old Leighlin 1745–60.

0362 CARY, Rt Hon. Edward; b. c. 1716–21[7] d. 16 July 1797; MP for Co. Londonderry 1742–60, 1761–8–76–83–90.

0363 CARY, Henry; b. 1695 d. 14 Oct. 1756; MP for Coleraine 1727–56.

0364 **CARY-HAMILTON**, Frederick; b. *c.* 1719[2] d. 20 Nov. 1746; MP for Londonderry city 1743–6.

0365 **CASEY**, Thomas; b. 1765 d. 7 Apr. 1840; MP for Kilmallock [15 Jan.] 1800.

0366 **CAULFEILD**, Hon. Francis; b. *c.* 1730 d. 20 Oct. 1775; MP for Co. Armagh 1758–60, Charlemont 1761–8–75.

0367 **CAULFEILD**, Rt Hon. Francis William [KP, 2nd E. of Charlemont, 1st B. Charlemont [UK]]; b. 3 Jan. 1775 d. 26 Dec. 1863; MP for Co. Armagh 1797–9 [r. Charlemont 1797].

0368 **CAULFEILD**, Hon. James [3rd V. Charlemont]; b. July 1682 d. 21 Apr. 1734; MP for Charlemont 1703–5 [obliged to travel abroad], 1713–14, 1715–26.

0369 *****CAULFEILD**, Hon. John; b. 1661 d. 1707; MP for Charlemont 1703–7.

0370 **CAULFEILD**, Hon. John; b. *c.* 1688[8] d. 19 Oct. 1764; MP for Charlemont 1723–7–60.

0371 **CAULFEILD**, Rt Hon. St George; b. 16 Sept. 1697 d. 17 May 1778; MP for Tulsk 1727–51.

0372 **CAULFEILD**, Thomas; b. 1688 d. 23 Oct. 1747; MP for Tulsk 1715–27, 1741–7.

0373 **CAULFEILD**, Toby; b. 1694 d. May 1740; MP for Tulsk 1727–40.

0374 **CAULFEILD**, Toby; b. 1750 d. 11 Mar. 1772; MP for Tulsk 1771–2.

0375 **CAULFEILD**, William; b. 1665 d. 24 Aug. 1737; MP for Tulsk 1692–3, 1695–9, 1703–13–14.

0376 *****CAULFEILD**, William; b. 1698 d. 1771; MP for Tulsk 1761–8–71.

0377 *****CAULFEILD**, William; b. 1741 d. [Feb.] 1786; MP for Tulsk 1769–76–83–6.

0378 **CAUSABON**, William; b. *c.* 1688–94[7] d. *post* 1744[5]; MP for Doneraile 1715–27.

0379 **CAVENDISH**, Hon. George; b. 26 Aug. 1766 d. 13 Feb. 1849; MP for St Johnstown [Longford] 1790–7, Cavan B. 1798–1800.

0380 *****CAVENDISH**, Rt Hon. Sir Henry [1st Bt]; b. 15 Apr. 1707 d. 31 Dec. 1776; MP for Tallow 1756–60, Lismore 1761–8–76.

0381 **CAVENDISH**, Rt Hon. Sir Henry [2nd Bt]; b. 29 Sept. 1732 d. 3 Aug. 1804; MP for Lismore 1766–8, 1776–83–90, 1798–1800, Killybegs 1790–7 [HP].

0382 **CAVENDISH**, James; b. *c.* 1749[7] d. Jan. 1808; MP for Lifford 1773–6, Banagher 1776–83.

0383 **CAVENDISH**, Hon. Richard [2nd B. Waterpark]; b. 13 July 1765 d. 1 June 1830; MP for Portarlington 1790–7.

0384 **CAVENDISH-BRADSHAW**, Hon. Augustus; b. 17 Feb. 1768 d. 11 Nov. 1832; MP for Carlow B. 1790–6 [HP].

0385 **CHAIGNEAU**, David; b. *c.* 1689[9] d. 20 Jan. 1753; MP for Gowran 1715–27–53.

0386 *****CHAMBERLAYNE**, [William] Tankerville; b. [bapt. 25 June] 1752 d. 12 May 1802; MP for Clonmines 1791–3.

0387 **CHAMBRE**, Robert; b. [?] 1644[9] d. *post* 1713; MP for Ardee 1703–13.

0388 **CHAPMAN**, Sir Benjamin [1st Bt]; b. *c.* 1745[2] d. July 1810; MP for Fore 1772–6, Co. Westmeath 1776–83.

0389 **CHAPMAN**, William; b. *c.* 1750[8] d. [?]1796; MP for Athboy 1776–83.

0390 **CHATTERTON**, Sir James [1st Bt]; b. *c.* 1750–2[3] d. 9 Apr. 1806; MP for Baltimore 1781–3, Doneraile 1783–90–7.

0391 **CHETWOOD**, Benjamin; b. *c.* 1655[8] d. 1728; MP for Harristown 1713–14.

0392 **CHETWOOD**, Jonathan; b. 31 May 1757 d. 11 May 1839; MP for Downpatrick 1790–7.

0393 **CHICHESTER**, Hon. Charles; b. *c.* 1666[7] d. *post* 1699; MP for Belfast 1695–9.

0394 **CHICHESTER**, Rt Hon. George Augustus [E. of Belfast 1791–9, 2nd M. of Donegall]; b. 14 Aug. 1769 d. 5 Oct. 1844; MP for Carrickfergus 1798–9.

0395 *****CHICHESTER**, Hon. John Itchingham; b. *post* 1660[7] d. 1721; MP for Gorey 1692–3, 1695–9, 1703–13, Belfast 1715–21.

0396 **CHICHESTER**, Hon. John; b. 1700 d. 1 June 1746; MP for Belfast 1725–7, 1745–6.

0397 **CHICHESTER**, John; b. 26 Dec. 1740 d. 1783; MP for Belfast 1761–8, Carrickfergus 1768–76.

0398 **CHICHESTER**, Ld Spencer Stanley; b. 20 Apr. 1775 d. 22 Feb. 1819; MP for Belfast 1797–8 [HP].

0399 **CHINNERY**, Sir Brodrick [1st Bt]; b. [13] Feb. 1742 d. May 1808; MP for Castlemartyr 1783–90, Bandon-Bridge 1790–7–1800 [HP].

0400 **CHOPPIN**, Robert; b. [?]1638[7] d. 1695; MP for Co. Longford 1692–3.

0401 **CHRISTIAN**, Maynard; b. 13 Aug. 1668 d. [bur. 9] Aug. 1714; MP for Waterford city 1703–13–14.

0402 **CHRISTMAS**, Richard; b. 19 Apr. 1661 d. 5 June 1723; MP for Waterford city 1695–9, 1703–13.

0403 **CHRISTMAS**, Thomas; b. 22 May 1687 d. [bur. 5] Dec. 1747; MP for Waterford city 1713–14, 1715–27–47.

0404 **CHRISTMAS**, Thomas; b. 3 July 1721 d. 28 Mar. 1749; MP for Co. Waterford 1743–9.

0405 **CHRISTMAS**, William; b. 24 Sept. 1734 d. [bur. 26] Jan. 1803; MP for Kilmallock 1776–83.

0406 **CLARKE**, Michael; b. 1712 d. 30 June 1774; MP for Ballyshannon 1754–60, 1761–8–74.

0407 *****CLAYTON**, Sir Courthorpe [KB]; b. *c.* 1706[10] d. 22 Mar. 1762; MP for Mallow 1727–60, [GB] Eye, Suffolk 1749–61.

0408 **CLAYTON**, Laurence; b. 1655 d. 1727; MP for Mallow 1692–3, 1695–9, 1703–13.

0409 **CLEMENT**, William; b. 1707 d. 14 Jan. 1782; MP for TCD 1761–8, Dublin city 1771–6–82.

♦♦♦♦ **CLEMENTS**, Francis, b. *ante* 1700 d. 26 March 1749 [n.d.e. Carrickfergus Oct.–Dec. 1741].

0410 **CLEMENTS**, Henry; b. 1644 d. 2 Nov. 1696; MP for Carrickfergus 1692–3.

0411 **CLEMENTS**, Henry; b. 1704 d. May 1745; MP for Cavan B. 1729–45.

0412 **CLEMENTS**, Rt Hon. Henry Theophilus; b. 1734 d. 26 Oct. 1795; MP for Cavan B. 1769–76, 1783–90, Co. Leitrim 1776–83, 1790–5.

0413 *****CLEMENTS**, John; b. 1757 d. 10 July 1817; MP for Cavan B. 1777–83.

0414 *****CLEMENTS**, Rt Hon. Nathaniel; b. 1705 d. [*ante* 27] May 1777; MP for Duleek 1728–60, Cavan B. 1761–8, Co. Leitrim 1768–76, Carrick 1776–7.

0415 **CLEMENTS**, Rt Hon. Nathaniel [2nd E. of Leitrim]; b. 9 May 1768 d. 31 Dec. 1854; MP for Carrick 1790–7, Co. Leitrim 1797–1800 [HP].

0416 **CLEMENTS**, Robert; b. 1664 d. 29 Dec. 1722; MP for Newry 1715–22.

0417 **CLEMENTS**, Robert; b. [bapt. 30 July] 1724 d. [June–July] 1747; MP for Cavan B. 1745–7.

0418 **CLEMENTS**, Rt Hon. Robert [1st B., V. and E. of Leitrim]; b. 25 Nov. 1732 d. 27 July 1804; MP for Co. Donegal 1765–8, 1776–83, Carrick 1768–76.

0419 **CLEMENTS**, Theophilus; b. 1687 d. 1728; MP for Cavan B. 1713–14, 1715–27–8.

0420 **CLEMENTS**, William; b. 1733 d. 4 June 1770; MP for Baltimore 1761–8.

0421 **CLERE** [*alias* CLEARE], John; b. *ante* 1698[6] d. 15 Mar. 1754; MP for Fethard [Tipperary] 1727–54.

0422 *****CLERE** [*alias* CLEARE or CLEERE], Thomas; b. *ante* 1658[9] d. 6 Jan. 1705; MP for Fethard [Tipperary] 1692–3.

0423 *****CLIFFE**, John; b. 3 May 1661 d. 1728; MP for Bannow 1692–3, 1695–9, 1703–13–14, 1715–27.

0424 **CLUTTERBUCK**, Rt Hon. Thomas; b. 1697 d. 23 Nov. 1742; MP for Lisburn 1725–7–42.

0425 **COBBE**, Charles; b. 1756 d. 9 July 1798; MP for Swords 1783–90, Jan.–July 1798.

0426 **COBBE**, Thomas; b. 1733 d. 1814; MP for Swords 1759–60, 1761–8, 1776–83.

0427 **CODDINGTON**, Dixie; b. 1727 d. *c.* [Sept.] 1792; MP for Dunleer 1762–8–76.

0428 *****CODDINGTON**, Henry; b. 1734 d. 21 Sept. 1816; MP for Dunleer 1783–90, 1797–Feb. 1800.

0429 **CODDINGTON**, Nicholas; b. 1765 d. 31 Aug. 1837; MP for Dunleer 1790–7.

0430 **COGHILL**, James; b. *c.* 1677[6] d. [bur. 6] Sept. 1734; MP for Clogher 1723–7, Newcastle 1727–34.

0431 *****COGHILL**, Rt Hon. Marmaduke; b. 28 Dec. 1673 d. 9 Mar. 1738/9; MP for Armagh B. 1692–3, 1695–9, 1703–13, TCD 1713–14, 1715–27–39.

0432 *****COGHLAN**, Joseph; b. *c.* 1655[2] d. [bur. 10] Nov. 1697; MP for [TCD 1689], Limerick city 1692–3, 1695–7.

0433 **COGHLAN**, Thomas; b. 1728 d. [Feb.] 1794; MP for Banagher 1768–76, Castlebar 1776–83, Carlingford 1783–90, Augher 1790–4.

0434 ***COLCLOUGH**, Caesar; b. *c.* 1665⁷ d. [*post* 8 Mar.] 1726; MP for Taghmon 1719–26.

0435 ***COLCLOUGH**, Caesar; b. 1696 d. 15 Apr. 1766; MP for Co. Wexford 1727–60, 1761–6.

0436 ***COLCLOUGH**, Sir Vesey [?Bt]; b. 1 July 1745 d. 8 July 1794; MP for Co. Wexford 1766–8–76–83–90, Enniscorthy 1790–4.

0437 **COLE**, Rt Hon. Sir Arthur [1st B. Ranelagh]; b. 1664 d. 5 Oct. 1754; MP for Enniskillen 1692–3, Roscommon B. 1695–9.

0438 **COLE**, Sir Galbraith Lowry; b. 1 May 1772 d. 4 Oct. 1842; MP for Enniskillen 1797–1800, [UK] Co. Fermanagh 1802–23 [HP].

0439 **COLE**, John; b. [bapt. 12 Apr.] 1680 d. [*ante* Apr.] 1726; MP for Enniskillen 1703–13–14, 1715–26.

0440 ***COLE**, John [1st B. Mount Florence]; b. 13 Oct. 1709 d. 30 Nov. 1767; MP for Enniskillen 1730–60.

0441 **COLE**, Hon. John Willoughby [2nd E. of Enniskillen]; b. 23 Mar. 1768 d. 31 Mar. 1840; MP for Co. Fermanagh 1790–7–1800 [HP].

0442 ***COLE**, Sir Michael [Kt]; b. 1644 d. 11 Feb. 1710/1; MP for Enniskillen [1665–6], 1692–3, 1695–9, 1703–11.

0443 ***COLE**, Richard; b. [bapt. 8 Dec.] 1671 d. [*ante* June 1729]; MP for St Canice 1707–13, Enniskillen 1713–14, 1715–27–9.

0444 **COLE**, Hon. William Willoughby [2nd B. Mount Florence, 1st V. and E. of Enniskillen]; b. 1 Mar. 1736 d. 22 May 1803; MP for Enniskillen 1761–7.

0445 ***COLE–HAMILTON**, Hon. Arthur; b. 8 Aug. 1750 d. 1810; MP for Co. Fermanagh 1783–90, Enniskillen 1790–7–1800 [re-elected pp 1799] [HP].

0446 **COLLEY**, Henry; b. 1648 d. 1700; MP for Co. Kildare 1698–9.

0447 **COLLEY**, Henry; b. *c.* 1685⁷ d. 10 Feb. 1723/4; MP for Strabane 1723–4.

0448 **COLTHURST**, John; b. 1678 d. 15 Nov. 1756; MP for Tallow 1734–56.

0449 **COLTHURST**, Sir John Conway [1st Bt]; b. *ante* 1720⁷ d. 12 Sept. 1775; MP for Doneraile 1751–60, Youghal 1761–8, Castlemartyr 1768–75.

0450 **COLTHURST**, Sir Nicholas [3rd Bt]; b. *post* 1743⁷ d. [*ante* 23] May 1795; MP for St Johnstown [Longford] 1783–90, Clonakilty 1792–5.

0451 **COLVILL**, Hugh; b. [*ante* 27 July] 1676 d. 7 Feb. 1701; MP for Co. Antrim 1697–9.

0452 **COLVILL**, Rt Hon. Sir Robert [Kt]; b. 1625 d. 12 June 1697; MP for [Hillsborough 1661–6], Co. Antrim 1692–3, 1695–7.

0453 **COLVILL**, Robert; b. *c.* 1697–8⁷ d. 30 Mar. 1749; MP for Killybegs 1719–27, Antrim B. 1727–49.

0454 **COLVILL**, William; b. 6 Dec. 1737 d. 5 July 1820; MP for Newtown Limavady 1777–83, Killybegs 1783–90.

♦♦♦ **CONGREVE**, Ambrose; b. 1698 d. 8 Aug. 1741 [n.d.e. Co. Waterford Oct.–Dec. 1735, Waterford city 1738–9].

0455 ***CONGREVE**, John; b. 22 May 1733 d. [bur. 14] Mar. 1801; MP for Killyleagh 1761–8.

0456 ***CONGREVE**, John; b. 1764 d. 17 Mar. 1801; MP for Belfast [elected 1 Feb.] 1800.

0457 **CONNELL**, Richard; b. 1650 d. 1714; MP for St Canice 1692–3, 1695–9, 1703–13.

0458 **CONNER**, William; b. 1701 d. [bur. 9] Jan. 1766; MP for Bandon-Bridge 1761–6.

0459 **CONOLLY**, Rt Hon. Thomas; b. 1738 d. 27 Apr. 1803; MP for Co. Londonderry 1761–8–76–83–90–7–1800 [HP].

0460 **CONOLLY**, Rt Hon. William; b. 1662 d. 30 Oct. 1729; MP for Donegal B. 1692–3, 1695–9, Co. Londonderry 1703–13–14, 1715–27–9.

0461 **CONOLLY**, Rt Hon. William James; b. *ante* 15 Dec. 1706¹ d. 2 Jan. 1754; MP for Ballyshannon 1727–54 [HP].

0462 **CONWAY** [SEYMOUR-CONWAY], Rt Hon. Henry; b. [12] Aug. 1719 d. 9 July 1795; MP for Co. Antrim 1741–60, 1761–8 [HP].

0463 **CONYNGHAM**, Henry; b. [bapt. 2 July] 1664 d. 1706; MP for Killybegs 1692–3, Co. Donegal 1695–9, 1703–6.

0464 **CONYNGHAM**, Rt Hon. Henry [1st B. Mount Charles, 1st V. and E. Conyngham]; b. 1705 d. 4 Apr. 1781; MP for Killybegs 1727–53 [HP].

0465 *****CONYNGHAM**, Henry; b. *c.* 1693[2] d. [*ante* 10 Oct.] 1749; MP for Killybegs 1741–9.

0466 **CONYNGHAM**, William; b. *c.*1700[8] d. 26 Oct. 1738; MP for Killybegs 1727–38.

0467 **CONYNGHAM**, William; b. 29 Apr. 1723 d. 27 Mar. 1784; MP for Dundalk 1776–83.

0468 **COOKE**, Edward; b. [bapt. 27 June] 1755 d. 19 Mar. 1820; MP for Lifford 1789–90, Old Leighlin 1790–7–1800 [re-elected pp 1795, 1796].

0469 **COOKE**, John; b. 1657 d. [1] Oct. 1733; MP for Co. Westmeath 1707–13.

0470 **COOKE**, Sir Samuel [1st Bt]; b. *post* 1690[7] d. 9 Feb. 1758; MP for Dublin city 1749–58.

0471 **COOLEY**, Thomas; b. [bapt. 4 Dec.] 1705 d. 5 Dec. 1755; MP for Duleek 1747–55.

0472 **COOPER**, Arthur; b. *c.* 1655–60[8] d. 1710; MP for Carrick 1695–9.

0473 **COOPER**, Joshua; b. *c.* 1694–8[7] d. 4 [bur. 6] Aug. 1757; MP for Co. Sligo 1719–27–57.

0474 **COOPER**, Rt Hon. Joshua; b. 1732 d. 16 Dec. 1800; MP for Castlebar 1761–8, Co.Sligo 1768–76–83.

0475 **COOPER**, Joshua Edward; b. 5 Mar. 1762 d. 8 June 1837; MP for Co. Sligo 1790–7–1800 [HP].

0476 **COOPER**, Sir William [1st Bt]; b. 1689 d. 8 Aug. 1761; MP for Hillsborough 1733–60, 1761.

0477 **COOTE**, Rt Hon. Algernon [6th E. of Mountrath]; b. 6 June 1689 d. 27 Aug. 1744; MP for Jamestown 1715–20 [HP].

0478 **COOTE**, Charles; b. *ante* 29 Oct. 1694[1] d. 6 Oct. 1761; MP for Castlemartyr 1715–27.

0479 **COOTE**, Charles; b. 27 Aug. 1695 d. 19 Oct. 1750; MP for Granard 1723–7, Co. Cavan 1727–50.

0480 **COOTE**, Rt Hon. Sir Charles [5th B. Coote of Coloony and 1st E. of Bellomont]; b. 6 Apr. 1738 d. 20 Oct. 1800; MP for Co. Cavan 1761–6.

0481 **COOTE**, Rt Hon. Charles Henry [2nd B. Castle Coote]; b. 25 Aug. 1754 d. 22 Jan. 1823; MP for Queen's Co. 1776–83, 1797–1800, Maryborough 1783–90–7 [re-elected pp 1796] [HP].

0482 *****COOTE**, Chidley; b. *c.* 1643[2] d. 1702; MP for Kilmallock 1695–9.

0483 *****COOTE**, Hon. Chidley; b. *ante* 1677[7] d. 1719; MP for Co. Sligo 1713–14, 1715–19.

♦♦♦ **COOTE**, Sir Eyre, b. 1728 d. 2 Sept. 1784 [n.d.e. Maryborough May–Dec. 1761] [HP].

0484 **COOTE**, Sir Eyre [Kt]; b. [20] May 1759 d. 10 Dec. 1823; MP for Ballynakill 1790–7, Maryborough 1797–Jan. 1800 [HP].

0485 **COOTE**, Sir Philips [Kt]; b. [bapt. 10 Mar.] 1659 d. 1715; MP for Kilmallock 1713–14.

0486 *****COOTE**, Hon. Richard; b. Feb. 1649 d. [13 Feb.] 1703; MP for Co. Kilkenny 1692–3.

0487 **COOTE**, Hon. Thomas; b. *c.* 1663–5[3] d. 24 Apr. 1741; MP for Dublin city 1692–3, Co. Monaghan 1723–7, 1733–41.

0488 **COPE**, Henry; b. *c.* 1739[6] d. 1815; MP for Donegal B. 1779–83, Philipstown 1783–90, Tulsk 1790–7.

0489 **COPE**, Robert; b. 1679 d. 17 Mar. 1753; MP for Lisburn 1711–13, Co. Armagh 1713–14, 1727–53.

0490 **COPE**, Robert Camden; b. *c.* 1771[2] d. 5 Dec. 1818; MP for Co. Armagh 1799–1800, [UK] 1801–2 [HP].

0491 *****COPINGER**, Maurice; b. 1727 d. 6 Oct. 1802; MP for Ardfert 1758–60, 1761–8–76–83, Roscommon B. 1785–90, Aug. 1800, Belturbet 1790–7.

0492 *****CORKER**, Edward; b. *ante* 1650[7] d. 1702; MP for Ratoath 1692–3, 1695–9.

0493 **CORKER**, Edward; b. 1645[7] d. 27 Jan. 1734; MP for Rathcormack 1713–14, Midleton 1715–27, Clonmines 1727–34.

0494 **CORNWALL**, Robert; b. *c.* 1755[6] d. 1811; MP for Enniscorthy 1795–7–9.

0495 **CORRY**, Edward; b. 1723 d. 5 May 1792; MP for Newry 1774–6 [n.d.e. 1774].

0496 *****CORRY**, Edward; b. *post* 1756[8] d. *c.* 1813[10]; MP for Randalstown 1794–7.

0497 *****CORRY**, Rt Hon. Isaac; b. [15] May 1755 d. 15 May 1813; MP for Newry 1776–83–90–7–1800 [re-elected pp 1798 and 1799] [HP].

0498 **CORRY**, James; b. 1634 d. 1 May 1718; MP for Co. Fermanagh 1692–3, 1695–9, 1703–13–14, 1715–18.

0499 **CORRY**, John; b. [bapt. 8 Jan.] 1666/7 d. 11 Nov. 1726; MP for Enniskillen 1711–13, Co. Fermanagh 1719–26.

0500 **CORRY**, Leslie; b. 15 Oct. 1712 d. 20 Feb. 1741; MP for Killybegs 1739–41.

0501 **COSBY**, Dudley Alexander Sydney; b. 2 May 1672 d. 24 May 1729; MP for Queen's Co. 1703–13–14, 1715–27–9.

0502 **COSBY**, Dudley Alexander Sydney [1st B. Sydney]; b. *c.* 1730[2] d. 22 Jan. 1774; MP for Carrick 1763–8.

0503 **COTTER**, Sir James [1st Bt]; b. 1714 d. 9 June 1770; MP for Askeaton 1761–8.

0504 **COTTER**, Sir James Laurence [2nd Bt]; b. 1748 d. 9 Feb. 1829; MP for Taghmon 1771–6, Mallow 1783–90, Castlemartyr 1790–7–1800.

0505 **COTTER**, Rogerson; b. 1750 d. 19 Feb. 1830; MP for Charleville 1783–90–7–1800.

0506 **COX**, Henry; b. *ante* 8 June 1766[1] d. 2 Dec. 1821; MP for Castlemartyr 1787–90.

0507 **COX**, Richard; b. 27 Oct. 1677 d. 15 Apr. 1725; MP for Tallow 1703–13–14, Clonakilty 1717–25.

0508 ***COX**, Sir Richard [2nd Bt]; b. 23 Nov. 1702 d. 2 Feb. 1766; MP for Clonakilty 1727–60, 1761–6.

0509 **COX**, Richard; b. 15 Jan. 1744/5 d. [*ante* 8] July 1790; MP for Charleville 1776–83.

0510 **CRADOCK** [*alias* CARADOC], Sir John Francis [1st B. Howden]; b. 11 Aug. 1759 d. 26 July 1839; MP for Clogher 1785–90, Castlebar 1790–7, Midleton 1799–Apr. 1800, Thomastown May–Aug. 1800.

0511 **CRAFFORD** [*alias* CRAWFORD], William; b. *ante* 1659[7] d. [bur. 14 July] 1716; MP for Belfast 1703–13.

0512 **CRAMER** [CRAMER-COGHILL], Sir John [1st Bt]; b. 14 July 1732 d. 8 Mar. 1790; MP for Belturbet 1755–60, 1761–8–76.

0513 **CRAWFORD**, Thomas; b. *ante* 1665[6] d. *post* Aug. 1706[6]; MP for New Ross 1692–3, 1695–9, 1703–6.

0514 ***CREIGHTON**, Abraham; b. *ante* 1631[10] d. [bur. 13] Mar. 1705/6; MP for Co. Fermanagh 1692–3, Enniskillen 1695–9.

0515 **CREIGHTON**, Abraham [1st B. Erne]; b. [bapt. 31 Dec.] 1703 d. 2 June 1772; MP for Lifford 1727–60, 1761–8.

0516 **CREIGHTON**, Hon. Abraham; b. *c.* 1740[5] d. Sept. 1809; MP for Lifford 1768–76–83–90–7–1800.

0517 **CREIGHTON**, Hon. Abraham [2nd E. Erne]; b. 10 May 1765 d. 10 June 1842; MP for Lifford 1790–7.

0518 **CREIGHTON**, David; b. 1671 d. 1 June 1728; MP for Augher 1695–9, Lifford 1703–13–14, 1715–27–8.

0519 **CREIGHTON**, Rt Hon. John [2nd B., 1st V. and E. Erne]; b. 1731 d. 15 Sept. 1828; MP for Lifford 1761–8–72.

0520 **CREIGHTON**, Hon. John; b. 28 June 1772 d. 10 May 1833; MP for Lifford 1797–1800.

0521 **CROFTON**, Rt Hon. Sir Edward [2nd Bt]; b. *c.* 1662[10] d. 24 Nov. 1729; MP for Boyle 1695–9, Co. Roscommon 1703–13–14, 1715–27–9.

0522 **CROFTON**, Rt Hon. Sir Edward [3rd Bt]; b. 25 May 1687 d. 11 Nov. 1739; MP for Roscommon B. 1713–4, 1715–27–39.

0523 **CROFTON**, Sir Edward [4th Bt]; b. 12 Apr. 1713 d. 26 Mar. 1745; MP for Co. Roscommon 1735–45.

0524 **CROFTON**, Sir Edward [2nd Bt]; b. 1746 d. 30 Sept. 1797; MP for Co. Roscommon 1775–6–7, 1778–83–90–7.

0525 **CROFTON**, Hugh; b. *c.* 1708–10[7] d. 20 Oct. 1767; MP for Co. Leitrim 1743–60.

0526 **CROFTON**, Sir Hugh [2nd Bt]; b. 17 July 1763 d. 6 Jan. 1834; MP for Tulsk 1786–90.

0527 **CROFTS**, George; b. *c.* 1660[1] d. 1698; MP for Charleville Sept.–11 Oct. 1692 [expelled].

0528 ***CROKER**, John; b. [?]1690 d. 29 Aug. 1751; MP for Kilmallock 1723–7.

0529 **CROKER**, John; b. 6 Apr. 1730 d. 11 Feb. 1795; MP for Fethard [Tipperary] 1768–76.

0530 **CROMIE**, Sir Michael [Kt, 1st Bt]; b. *c.* 1744[2] d. 14 May 1824; MP for Ballyshannon 1776–83–90–7.

0531 **CROOKSHANK**, Alexander; b. 30 June 1736 d. 10 Dec. 1813; MP for Belfast 1777–83–4.

0532 **CROOKSHANK**, George; b. 26 Sept. 1770 d. 21 June 1831; MP for Belfast 1797–1800.

0533 *****CROSBIE**, James; b. *c.* 1760[3] d. 20 Sept. 1836; MP for Co. Kerry 1797–1800 [HP].

0534 **CROSBIE**, Rt Hon. John [2nd E. of Glandore]; b. 25 May 1752 d. 23 Oct. 1815; MP for Athboy 1775–6, Ardfert 1776–81.

0535 **CROSBIE**, John Gustavus; b. *ante* 1749[6] d. [6] July 1797; MP for Co. Kerry 1794–7.

0536 **CROSBIE**, Lancelot; b. *c.* 1723–5[3] d. [*ante* 15] Aug. 1780; MP for Co. Kerry 1759–60, Ardfert 1762–8–76.

0537 *****CROSBIE**, Sir Maurice [Kt, 1st B. Branden]; b. 1690 d. 13 Jan. 1762; MP for Co. Kerry 1713–4, 1715–27–58 [r. Dingle 1727].

0538 **CROSBIE**, Thomas; b. *c.* 1681–8[7] d. [4] June 1731; MP for Dingle 1713–14, 1715–27–31.

0539 *****CROSBIE**, William; b. *c.* 1662[8] d. [*ante* 16] Nov. 1743; MP for Ardfert 1713–14, 1715–27–42.

0540 *****CROSBIE**, Rt Hon. William [2nd B. Branden, 1st V. Crosbie and E. of Glandore]; b. May 1716 d. 11 May 1781; MP for Ardfert 1735–60, 1761–2.

0541 **CROSBIE**, William Arthur; b. [bapt. 23 Jan.] 1756 d. 19 Feb. 1803; MP for Trim 1781–3, 1795–7–1800 [re-elected pp 1796, 1798].

0542 **CROSBIE**, William Francis; b. *ante* 1729[7] d. 7 Jan. 1761; MP for Trim 1758–60.

0543 **CROSSE**, Silvester; b. 1671 d. 1730; MP for Callan 1703–13–14, Armagh city 1715–27, Clogher 1727–30.

0544 **CROWE**, Robert; b. 1745 d. July 1817; MP for Philipstown 1797–Jan. 1800.

0545 *****CROWE**, William; b. *c.* 1657[2] d. [*ante* 9 July] 1711; MP for Blessington 1692–3, 1703–11, TCD 1698–9.

0546 **CROWLE**, Charles John; b. 1738 d. 7 Mar. 1811; MP for Harristown 1781–3 [HP].

0547 **CUFFE**, Agmondisham; b. *c.* 1655[2] d. Dec. 1727; MP for Co. Kilkenny 1695–9.

0548 **CUFFE**, Francis; b. *c.* 1654[2] d. 26 Dec. 1694; MP for Co. Mayo 1692–3 [r. Longford B. 1692].

0549 **CUFFE**, Francis; b. *post* 1675[7] d. [bur. 13] Nov. 1717; MP for Co. Mayo 1715–17.

0550 *****CUFFE**, Gerald; b. 24 July 1669 d. *post* 1715[6]; MP for Castlebar 1703–13–14.

0551 **CUFFE**, James; b. 1707 d. 20 Mar. 1762; MP for Co. Mayo 1742–60.

0552 **CUFFE**, Rt Hon. James [1st B. Tyrawley]; b. *ante* 1747 d. 15 June 1821; MP for Co. Mayo 1768–76–83–90–7.

0553 *****CUFFE**, James; b. 1778 d. 30 July 1828; MP for Tulsk Feb.–Aug. 1800 [HP].

0554 **CUFFE**, John [1st B. Desart]; b. 1683 d. 26 June 1749; MP for Thomastown 1715–27.

0555 *****CUFFE**, Maurice; b. 1681 d. 30 Sept. 1766; MP for Kilkenny city 1715–27.

0556 *****CUFFE**, Michael; b. 1694 [bapt. 1 July 1696] d. 24 July 1744; MP for Co. Mayo 1719–27, Longford B. 1727–44.

0557 **CUFFE**, Thomas; b. 1704 d. 9 May 1742; MP for Wexford B. 1735–42.

0558 **CUFFE**, Hon. William; b. *c.* 1743[2] d. 3 Oct. 1792; MP for Kilkenny city 1783–90–2.

0559 **CUNINGHAME**, Rt Hon. Robert [1st B. Rossmore]; b. 18 Apr. 1726 d. 6 Aug. 1801; MP for Tulsk 1751–60, Armagh city 1761–8, Monaghan B. 1768–76–83–90–6, [UK] E. Grinstead 1788–9 [HP].

◆◆◆◆ **CUNNINGHAM**, Waddell, b. 1730 d. 15 Dec. 1797 [n.d.e. Carrickfergus Feb. 1784–Mar. 1785].

0560 **CURRAN**, Rt Hon. John Philpot; b. 24 July 1750 d. 14 Oct. 1817; MP for Kilbeggan 1783–90, Rathcormack 1790–7, Banagher 1800.

0561 *****CURTIS**, John; b. *c.* 1717–19[2] d. 1775; MP for Ratoath 1761–8.

0562 **CURTIS**, Robert; b. *ante* 1655[7] d. 29 July 1726; MP for Carlow B. 1695–9, Duleek 1703–13.

0563 **DALRYMPLE**, William; b. 1736 d. 23 Feb. 1807; MP for Duleek 1796–7 [HP].

0564 **DALWAY**, Alexander; b. 1669 d. [bur. 8] Feb. 1718; MP for Carrickfergus 1715–18.

0565 **DALWAY**, Marriot; b. *c.* 1725[8] d. 7 Mar. 1795; MP for Carrickfergus 1761–8.

0566 **DALWAY** [WEBB-DALWAY] Noah; b. [bapt. 24 July] 1747 d. 17 July 1820; MP for Carrickfergus 1799–1800 [HP].

0567 *****DALWAY**, Robert; b. *ante* 1649[7] d. 1699; MP for Antrim B. 1696–9.

0568 *****DALY**, Anthony; b. *c.* 1725[8] d. 1810; MP for Galway B. 1771–6–83–90.

0569 **DALY**, Charles; b. 1722 d. [*c.* 19] Nov. 1768; MP for Co. Galway 1753–60, 1761–8.

0570 *****DALY**, Rt Hon. Denis; b. 1748 d. 10 Oct. 1791; MP for Galway B. 1767–8, 1790–1, Co. Galway 1768–76–83–90.

0571 **DALY**, Rt Hon. Denis Bowes; b. 1745 d. 17 Dec. 1821; MP for Galway B. 1776–83–90, King's Co. 1790–7–1800 [HP].

0572 *****DALY**, James; b. *c.* 1715–17[3] d. 1769; MP for Athenry 1741–60, 1761–8, Galway B. 1768–9.

0573 **DALY**, Peter; b. *ante* 19 Jan. 1771[1] d. 1846; MP for Galway B. 1792–7.

0574 **DALY**, Rt Hon. St George; b. 1758 d. [bur. 22] Dec. 1829; MP for Galway B. 1797–1800 [re-elected pp 1799] [HP].

0575 **DAMER**, Rt Hon. George [2nd E. of Dorchester]; b. 28 Mar. 1746 d. 7 Mar. 1808; MP for Naas 1795–7 [HP].

0576 **DAMER**, John; b. *c.* 1729–31[3] d. Feb. 1789; MP for Portarlington 1761–8, Swords 1768–76.

0577 **DAMER**, Joseph; b. 1676 d. 1 Mar. 1737; MP for Co. Tipperary 1735–7 [HP].

0578 **DARBY**, Henry Verney Lovett; b. 1754 d. 1818; MP for Gowran Apr.–Aug. 1800.

0579 **DAVIS** [*alias* DAVYS], Edward; b. 1660 d. *post* 1699; MP for Clogher 1692–3.

0580 **DAVIS** [*alias* DAVYS], Henry; b. *c.* 1635–7[3] d. 1708; MP for [Belfast 1661–6], Carrickfergus 1692–3, 1695–9, 1703–8.

0581 *****DAVYS** [*alias* DAVIS], Arthur; b. *ante* 1670[5] d. Oct. 1733; MP for Carrickfergus 1713–4.

0582 **DAVYS** [*alias* DAVIS], Hercules; b. *c.* 1635–7[1] d. 14 Mar. 1711; MP for [Carrickfergus 1661–6], Roscommon B. 1692–3, Carrickfergus 1695–9.

0583 **DAVYS** [*alias* DAVIS], John; b. *c.* 1665[6] d. 12 Mar. 1743; MP for Coleraine 1692–3, Kildare B. 1695–9, Charlemont 1705–13, Carrickfergus 1713–14.

0584 **DAWSON**, Arthur; b. 9 Oct. 1698 d. 29 Apr. 1775; MP for Co. Londonderry 1729–42.

0585 **DAWSON**, Arthur; b. 1745 d. 6 Dec. 1822; MP for Newtown[ards] 1775–6, Carlow B. 1776–83, Midleton 1783–90–7, Banagher 1798–1800.

0586 **DAWSON**, Ephraim; b. *ante* 24 Feb. 1683/4[1] d. 27 Aug. 1746; MP for Portarlington 1713–14, Queen's Co. 1715–27–46.

0587 **DAWSON**, James; b. *ante* 1676[6] d. 19 Dec. 1737; MP for Co. Tipperary 1703–13–14.

0588 **DAWSON**, John; b. 1692 d. Mar. 1747; MP for Monaghan B. 1743–7.

0589 *****DAWSON**, Rt Hon. John [2nd V. Carlow, 1st E. of Portarlington]; b. 23 Aug. 1744 d. 30 Nov. 1798; MP for Portarlington 1766–8, Queen's Co. 1768–76–9.

0590 **DAWSON**, Hon. Joseph; b. 6 Oct. 1751 d. 9 Nov. 1787; MP for Portarlington 1773–6, 1777–83.

0591 *****DAWSON**, Joshua; b. *c.* 1660[10] d. 13 Mar. 1724/5; MP for Wicklow B. 1705–13–14.

0592 **DAWSON**, Richard; b. *c.* 1693[8] d. 29 Dec. 1766; MP for St Canice 1727–60, Monaghan B. 1761–6.

0593 **DAWSON**, Richard; b. 16 Apr. 1762 d. 3 Sept. 1807; MP for Co. Monaghan Apr.–July 1797, 1797–1800 [HP].

0594 *****DAWSON**, Thomas; b. 13 Mar. 1654/5 d. 1732; MP for Antrim B. 1695–9.

0595 **DAWSON**, Thomas [1st B. Dartrey, 1st V. and B. Cremorne]; b. 25 Feb. 1724/5 d. 1 Mar. 1813; MP for Co. Monaghan 1749–60, 1761–8.

0596 **DAWSON**, Thomas; b. [bapt. 19 Mar.] 1744/5 d. 15 Sept. 1812; MP for Co. Armagh 1776–83, Sligo B. 1783–90, Enniscorthy June–Aug. 1800.

0597 **DAWSON**, William Henry [1st B. Dawson and V. Carlow]; b. [*ante* 16 Nov.] 1712 d. 22 Aug. 1779; MP for Portarlington 1733–60, 1769–70, Queen's Co. 1761–8.

0598 **DAY**, Robert; b. 1743 d. 8 Feb. 1841; MP for Tuam 1783–90, Ardfert 1790–7–8.

0599 *DEANE, Edward; b. 1660 d. [*ante* 27 Aug.] 1717; MP for Innistiogue 1692–3, 1703–13–14, 1715–17, Co. Dublin 1695–9.

0600 DEANE, Edward; b. 1682 d. 26 Dec. 1748; MP for Newcastle 1713–14, Innistiogue 1715–27, 1728–48.

0601 DEANE, Edward; b. 1716 d. [Aug.] 1751; MP for Innistiogue 1745–51.

0602 DEANE, Jocelyn; b. [July] 1749 d. 19 Nov. 1780; MP for Baltimore 1773–6–80 [HP].

0603 DEANE, Rt Hon. Joseph; b. 1674 d. 4 May 1715; MP for Co. Dublin 1703–13–14.

0604 DEANE, Joseph; b. *post* 1687 d. *post* 1760; MP for Innistiogue 1751–60.

0605 DEANE, Joseph; b. *post* 1717 d. 1801; MP for Innistiogue 1761–8, Co. Dublin 1768–76, Co. Kilkenny 1779–83.

0606 DEANE, Sir Matthew [3rd Bt]; b. *c.* 1676–85 d. 11 Mar. 1746/7; MP for Charleville 1713–14, Co. Cork 1728–47.

0607 DEANE, Sir Matthew [4th Bt]; b. 1706 d. [bur. 10] June 1751; MP for Cork city 1739–51.

0608 DEANE, Rt Hon. Sir Robert [5th Bt]; b. 1707 d. 7 Feb. 1770; MP for Tallow 1757–60, 1761–8, Carysfort 1769–70.

0609 DEANE, Rt Hon. Sir Robert Tilson [KP, 6th Bt, 1st B. Muskerry]; b. 19 Oct. 1747 d. 25 June 1818; MP for Carysfort 1771–6, Co. Cork 1776–81.

0610 DEANE, Stephen; b. 1687 d. Mar. 1761; MP for Innistiogue 1717–27.

♦♦♦♦ DE BURGH, Henry [styled Lord Dunkellin 1743–82, 12th Earl and 1st Marquess Clanricarde] b. 8 Jan. 1742/3 d. 8 Dec. 1797 [n.d.e.. Co. Galway July–Dec. 1768].

0611 DELAFAYE, Charles; b. 1677 d. 11 Dec. 1762; MP for Belturbet 1715–27.

0612 DELAUNE, Gideon; b. *ante* 1659[5] d. [bur. 28] Feb. 1700/1; MP for Blessington 1695–9.

0613 DENNIS, Rt Hon. James [1st B. Tracton]; b. 1721 d. 15 June 1782; MP for Rathcormack 1761–8, Youghal 1768–76–7.

0614 DENNIS [SWIFT], John; b. 1763 d. 1830; MP for Clonmel Feb.–Aug. 1800.

0615 DENNY, Arthur; b. 29 Apr. 1704 d. 8 Aug. 1742; MP for Co. Kerry 1727–42.

0616 DENNY, Barry; b. 1659 d. *post* 1699; MP for Tralee 1696–9.

0617 DENNY, Sir Barry [1st Bt]; b. Mar. 1744 d. Apr. 1794; MP for Co. Kerry 1768–76, 1783–90–4.

0618 DENNY, Sir Barry [2nd Bt]; b. *c.* 1768–73[7] d. 20 Oct. 1794; MP for Co. Kerry July–Oct. 1794.

0619 DENNY, Edward; b. 10 Feb. 1651/2 d. 1712; MP for Co. Kerry 1692–3, 1695–9.

0620 *DENNY, Edward; b. *ante* 27 Aug. 1674[1] d. 1709; MP for Doneraile 1695–9.

0621 DENNY, Edward; b. 1676 d. 1727; MP for Co. Kerry 1703–13–14, Askeaton 1715–27.

0622 DENNY, Edward; b. *c.* 1745–7[8] d. 21 Feb. 1775; MP for Tralee 1768–75.

0623 DENTON, Alexander; b. 14 Aug. 1679 d. 22 Mar. 1739/40; MP for Carrickfergus 1709–13 [HP].

0624 DERING, Rt Hon. Charles; b. 1656 d. July 1719; MP for Monaghan B. 1692–3, 1695–9, Carlingford 1703–13.

0625 DESPARD, William; b. *c.* 1675 d. 1720; MP for Thomastown 1715–20.

0626 DES VOEUX, Sir Charles [1st Bt]; b. *c.* 1744 d. 24 Aug. 1814; MP for Carlow B. 1783–90, Carlingford 1790–7.

0627 DEVONSHER, Abraham; b. *ante* 1731[6] d. 22 Apr. 1783; MP for Rathcormack 1757–60, 1761–8–76.

0628 DICK, Quintin; b. 7 Feb. 1777 d. 26 Mar. 1858; MP for Dunleer Jan.–Aug. 1800 [HP].

0629 DICKSON, Thomas; b. 1741 d. 7 July 1817; MP for Ballyshannon 1790–7.

0630 DIGBY, John; b. 1691 d. 27 July 1786; MP for Kildare B. 1732–60.

0631 DIGBY, Simon; b. 1723 d. [*post* 2 Mar.] 1796; MP for Kildare B. 1769–76–83–90–6.

0632 DILKES, Michael O'Brien; b. 1698 d. Aug. 1775; MP for Castlemartyr 1728–60.

0633 DILKES, Sir Thomas [Kt]; b. 1667 d. 12 Dec. 1707; MP for Castlemartyr 1703–7.

0634 *DILLON, Sir John [Kt]; b. *ante* 1663[7] d. 21 July 1708; MP for Kells 1692–3, Co. Meath 1695–9, 1703–8.

0635 DILLON, Sir John Talbot [1st Bt]; b. 1739 d. 17 July 1805; MP for Wicklow B. 1771–6, Blessington 1776–83.

0636 DILLON, Robert; b. *ante* 1704[7] d. 11 June 1746; MP for Dungarvan 1728–46.

0637 DILLON, Robert [1st B. Clonbrock]; b. 27 Feb. 1754 d. 22 July 1795; MP for Lanesborough 1776–83–90.

0638 DIXON [*alias* DICKSON], Hugh; b. *c.* 1691–3[3] d. 14 Oct. 1738; MP for Lismore 1725–7, Cork city 1727–38.

0639 DIXON, Robert; [?]b. *c.* 1665 d. 9 Mar. 1726; MP for Randalstown 1692–3, 1713–14, 1715–26, Harristown 1703–13.

0640 *DIXON, Robert; b. 1685 d. 8 Feb. 1732; MP for Kildare B. 1727–31.

0641 DOBBS, Arthur; b. 2 Apr. 1689 d. 28 Mar. 1765; MP for Carrickfergus 1727–60.

0642 *DOBBS, Conway Richard; b. 22 July 1727 d. 11 Apr. 1811; MP for Carrickfergus 1768–76–83–90.

0643 DOBBS, Francis; b. 27 Apr. 1750 d. 1811; MP for Charlemont 1798–1800.

0644 DOBSON, Robert; b. *ante* 1730[7] d. [Nov.] 1788; MP for Monaghan B. 1777–83.

0645 *DODINGTON, Rt Hon. George; b. *c.* 1658[10] d. 28 Mar. 1720; MP for Charlemont 1707–13 [HP].

♦♦♦ DODSWORTH, Edward; b. *ante* 1692 d. 1730 [n.d.e. Maryborough Oct.–Dec. 1713].

0646 DOMINICK, Christopher; b. *c.* 1644[2] d. [*post* 3 Nov.] 1692; MP for Ardfert 1692.

0647 [POCKLINGTON] DOMVILE, Charles; b. 1740 d. 19 Apr. 1810; MP for Co. Dublin Apr.–June 1768.

0648 DOMVILE , Rt Hon. Sir Compton [2nd Bt]; b. 1696 d. 13 [bur. 16] Mar. 1768; MP for Co. Dublin 1727–60, 1761–8.

0649 DOMVILE, Sir Thomas [1st Bt]; b. *c.* 1655[4] d. 15 Apr. 1721; MP for Mullingar 1692–3.

0650 DOMVILE, William; b. 1686 d. [Nov.] 1763; MP for Co. Dublin 1717–27.

♦♦♦♦ DONNELLAN, James; b. 1678 d. 25 Feb. 1732/3 [n.d.e. Co. Roscommon Nov.–Dec. 1713].

0651 DONNELLAN, John; b. [bapt. 25 Sept.] 1704 d. 20 Apr. 1741; MP for Ardee 1727–41.

0652 DONNELLAN, Nehemiah; b. 1649 d. 25 Dec. 1705; MP for Galway B. 1692–3.

0653 DONNELLAN, Nehemiah; b. 1698 d. [May] 1770; MP for Co. Tipperary 1737–60.

0654 DONNELLAN [DONNELLAN-NIXON], Nehemiah; b. 1722 d. 9 Mar. 1784; MP for Clogher 1757–60.

0655 DOPPING, Rt Hon. Samuel; b. 1671 d. 17 Sept 1720; MP for Armagh city 1695–9, 1703–13–14, TCD 1715–20 [r. Armagh city 1715].

0656 DOUGLAS, Rt Hon. Sylvester [1st B. Glenbervie]; b. 24 May 1743 d. 2 May 1823; MP for St Canice 1794–6 [HP].

0657 *DOWNES, Robert; b. [bapt. 18 May] 1708 d. 24 June 1754; MP for Kildare B. 1735–54.

0658 DOWNES, Rt Hon. William [1st B. Downes]; b. 1751 d. 3 Mar. 1826; MP for Donegal B. 1790–2.

0659 DOYLE, Sir John [1st Bt]; b. 1756 d. 8 Aug. 1834; MP for Mullingar 1783–90–7–9 [re-elected pp 1795] [HP].

0660 DOYNE, Philip; b. 1685 d. 23 Jan. 1754; MP for Clonmines 1715–27, Fethard [Wexford] 1733–54.

0661 DOYNE, Rt Hon. Robert; b. 1651 d. 28 Feb. [bur. 2 Mar.] 1732/3; MP for New Ross 1692–3.

0662 DOYNE, Robert; b. 2 June 1705 d. 2 Jan. 1768; MP for Wexford B. 1743–60, Donegal B. 1761–8.

0663 DOYNE, Robert; b. 11 Nov. 1738 d. 1790; MP for Carlow B. 1765–8.

0664 DUIGENAN, Rt Hon. Patrick; b. 1735 d. 11 Apr. 1816; MP for Old Leighlin 1791–7, Armagh City 1797–1800 [HP].

0665 DUN, Sir Patrick [Kt]; b. Jan. 1641/2 d. 24 May 1713; MP for Killyleagh 1692–3, Mullingar 1695–9, 1703–13.

0666 DUNBAR, Charles; b. [bapt. 11] July 1717 d. 13 Oct. 1778; MP for Blessington 1771–6–8.

0667 *DUNBAR, David; b. *c.* 1687[5] d. 8 Mar. 1752; MP for Blessington 1719–27.

0668 *DUNBAR, George; b. *ante* 10 Mar. 1730/1[10] d. Apr. 1803; MP for Gowran 1761–8, 1783–90–7, Thomastown 1769–76, 1797–1800.

0669 *DUNBAR, John; b. 1651 d. 1724; MP for Old Leighlin 1692–3.

0670 DUNKIN, Roscarrick; b. *ante* 1680[6] d. 6 Nov. 1714; MP for Knocktopher 1713–14.

0671 DUNN, James; b. 1700 d. 7 Apr. 1773; MP for Dublin city 1758–60.

0672 DUNN, John; b. *c.* 1752 d. 1827; MP for Randalstown 1783–90–7.

0673 DUNNE, Edward; b. 14 Oct. 1763 d. 12 Nov. 1844; MP for Maryborough [Feb.–Aug.] 1800.

0674 DUNSCOMB, Noblett; b. 1699 d. May 1745; MP for Lismore 1727–45.

0675 DUQUERY, Henry; b. *c.* 1749–51[3] d. 9 June 1804; MP for Armagh city Jan.–Apr. 1790, Rathcormack 1790–7.

0676 EARBERRY [*alias* EARBERY or ERBERY], Mathias; b. *c.* 1731–3[3] d. [*ante* 5] Oct. 1779; MP for Lanesborough 1768–76.

0677 ECCLES, Hugh; b. *c.*1660[7] d. [bur. 16] Oct. 1716; MP for Carysfort 1698–9, 1703–13–14, 1715–16.

0678 ECHLIN, Charles; b. 1682 d. Mar. 1754; MP for Dungannon 1727–54.

0679 *ECHLIN, Robert; b. 1674 d. 20 Dec. 1706; MP for Newtown[ards] 1692–3, Newry 1695–9, 1703–6.

0680 ECHLIN, Robert; b. 1657 d. 1724; MP for Monaghan B. 1695–9, Co. Monaghan 1703–13 [HP].

0681 EDEN, Rt Hon. William [1st B. Auckland]; b. 3 Apr. 1744 d. 28 May 1814; MP for Dungannon 1781–3 [HP].

0682 *EDGEWORTH, Ambrose; b. *post* 1656[8] d. [*ante* 9 July] 1711; MP for St Johnstown [Longford] 1703–11.

0683 EDGEWORTH, Francis; b. 1657 d. 7 June 1709; MP for Longford B. 1703–9.

0684 EDGEWORTH, Henry; b. *post* 1658[8] d. 1720; MP for Mullingar 1703–13, Co. Longford 1713–14, St Johnstown [Longford] 1715–20.

0685 EDGEWORTH, Henry; b. 1697 d. Aug. 1751; MP for St Johnstown [Longford] 1721–7–51.

0686 EDGEWORTH, Sir John [Kt]; b. 1638 d. 26 Jan. 1700/1; MP for St Johnstown [Longford] [1661–6], 1692–3, 1695–9 [r. Clonmines 1661].

0687 EDGEWORTH, Richard; b. 16 May 1701 d. 4 Aug. 1770; MP for Longford B. 1737–60.

0688 EDGEWORTH, Richard Lovell; b. 31 May 1744 d. 13 June 1817; MP for St Johnstown [Longford] 1798–1800.

0689 EDGEWORTH, Robert; b. *post* 1657[8] d. 8 July 1730; MP for St Johnstown [Longford] 1713–14, 1715–27.

0690 EDMONSTONE, Archibald; b. 1680 d. 25 Dec. 1767; MP for Carrickfergus 1715–27.

0691 EDWARDS, Cadwallader; b. *ante* 1657[7] d. *post* 1727; MP for Wexford B. 1703–13, 1715–27.

0692 EDWARDS, Richard; b. 1659 d. 17 Nov. 1722; MP for Carysfort 1692–3, Co. Wicklow 1695–9, 1703–13, Wicklow B. 1715–22.

0693 EGAN, Darby; b. *c.* 1660–2[3] d. 23 Oct. 1736; MP for Kilkenny city 1713–14 [n.d.e. 1715].

0694 EGAN, John; b. 1755 d. May 1810; MP for Ballynakill 1789–90, Tallow 1791–7–1800.

0695 ELLIOT, Rt Hon. William; b. 12 Mar. 1766 d. 29 Oct. 1818; MP for St Canice 1796–7, 1798–1800 [r. Carlow B. 1797] [HP].

0696 ELWOOD, John; b. 1673 d. 20 Apr. 1740; MP for TCD 1713–14, 1728–40.

0697 ENGLISH, William Alexander; b. *ante* 1724[7] d. [bur. 10] May 1794; MP for Taghmon 1776–83 [n.d.e. Enniscorthy 1783].

0698 ERLE, Rt Hon. Thomas; b. 1650 d. 23 July 1720; MP for Cork city 1703–13 [HP].

0699 EUSTACE, Charles; b. [bapt. 2 Feb.] 1739 d. 10 June 1801; MP for Clonmines 1794–7, Fethard [Wexford] 1797–1800.

0700 EUSTACE, Henry; b. *c.* 1767–72[5] d. 5 Oct. 1844; MP for Clonmines Jan.–Aug. 1800.

0701 **EUSTACE**, Sir Maurice [Kt]; b. 1637/8[3] d. 13 Apr. 1703; MP for [Knocktopher 1664–6], Harristown 1692–3, Aug.–Dec. 1695 [expelled].

0702 **EVANS**, Eyre; b. 1695 d. ?1773; MP for Co. Limerick 1721–7–60.

0703 **EVANS**, Rt Hon. George; b. 1655 d. May 1720; MP for Co. Limerick 1692–3, Askeaton 1695–9, Charleville 1703–13, 1715–20.

0704 ***EVANS**, Rt Hon. George [1st B. Carbery]; b. c. 1680[10] d. 28 Aug. 1749; MP for Co. Limerick 1707–13–14 [HP].

0705 ***EVANS**, George; b. c. 1716–19[7] d. 1764; MP for Queen's Co. 1747–60.

0706 **EVANS**, George; b. July 1772 d. 19 June 1829; MP for Baltimore 1797–1800.

0707 **EVANS**, Thomas; b. c. 1697[7] d. 17 Sept. 1753; MP for Castlemartyr 1737–53.

0708 **EVANS**, William; b. 16 May 1747 d. Feb. 1796; MP for Baltimore 1777–83.

0709 ***EVERARD**, Sir Redmond [4th Bt, 1st V. Everard]; b. [ante 28] July 1690 d. 13 Apr. 1742; MP for Kilkenny city 1711–13, Fethard [Tipperary] 1713–14.

0710 **EYRE**, Edward; b. 1666 d. 5 Nov. 1739; MP for Castlebar 1695–9, Galway B. 1703–13, 1716–27.

0711 ***EYRE**, George; b. 1680 d. [ante 9 July] 1711; MP for Banagher 1703–11.

0712 ***EYRE**, John; b. 1659 d. [ante 28] July 1709; MP for Co. Galway 1692–3, 1695–9, 1703–9.

0713 **EYRE**, John; b. c. 1682–6[8] d. Oct. 1745; MP for Co. Galway 1713–14, 1727–45, Armagh city 1716–27.

0714 **EYRE**, John [1st B. Eyre]; b. 1720 d. 30 Sept. 1781; MP for Galway B. 1748–60, 1761–8.

0715 **EYRE**, Samuel; b. 1651 d. 10 Aug. 1728; MP for Galway B. 1713–14.

0716 **EYRE**, Thomas; b. 1708 d. 22 Feb. 1772; MP for Thomastown 1761–8, Fore 1768–72.

0717 **FALKINER**, Daniel; b. 1683 d. 20 Jan. 1759; MP for Baltinglass 1727–59.

0718 **FALKINER**, Sir Frederick John [1st Bt]; b. 8 Apr. 1768 d. 14 Sept. 1824; MP for Athy 1791–7, Co. Dublin 1797–1800 [HP].

0719 ***FALKINER**, Sir Riggs [1st Bt]; b. c. 1708–16[7] d. 24 Apr. 1797; MP for Clonakilty 1768–76, Castlemartyr 1776–83.

0720 ***FANE**, Rt Hon. Charles [1st B. Loughguyre and V. Fane]; b. Jan. 1675/6 d. 4 July 1744; MP for Killybegs 1715–18.

0721 **FARRELL**, Fergus; b. 1652 d. c. 1697; MP for Lanesborough Sept.–Oct. 1692 [expelled].

0722 **FEILDING**, Rt Hon. Sir Charles [Kt]; b. [?]1645 d. 24 Apr. 1722; MP for Limerick city 1692–3, Duleek 1695–9.

0723 **FENN**, John; b. ante 1653[9] d. post 1693; MP for Wexford B. 1692–3.

0724 **FERGUSON**, Sir Andrew [1st Bt]; b. 7 Oct. 1761 d. 17 July 1808; MP for Londonderry city 1798–1800.

0725 ***FETHERSTON**, Sir Ralph [1st Bt]; b. ante 1731[7] d. [late] May 1780; MP for Co. Longford 1765–8, St Johnstown [Longford] 1768–76–80.

0726 **FETHERSTONE** [alias FETHERSTONHAUGH], Sir Thomas [2nd Bt]; b. 1759 d. 19 July 1819; MP for St Johnstown [Longford] 1783–90, Co. Longford 1796–7–1800 [HP].

0727 **FINLAY**, John; b. 1737 d. 24 Jan. 1823; MP for Kilmallock 1777–83, Co. Dublin Feb.–Apr. 1790, 1791–7.

0728 ***FITZGERALD**, Rt Hon. Ld Charles James [1st B. Lecale]; b. 30 June 1756 d. 16 Feb. 1810; MP for Co. Kildare 1776–83–90, Cavan B. 1790–7, Ardfert 1798–1800 [HP].

0729 ***FITZGERALD**, Edward; b. 1738 d. 8 Mar. 1814; MP for Co. Clare 1776–83–90, Castlebar 1790–7.

0730 ***FITZGERALD**, Ld Edward; b. 15 Oct. 1763 d. 3 June 1798; MP for Athy 1783–90, Co. Kildare 1790–7.

0731 ***FITZGERALD**, Garret [Gerald]; b. ante 21 Dec. 1740 d. [Aug.] 1775; MP for Kildare B. 1761–8, Harristown 1768–75.

0732 ***FITZGERALD**, George; b. 14 Feb. 1671 d. 1698; MP for Co. Kildare 1692–3, 1695–8.

0733 **FITZGERALD**, Rt Hon. Ld Henry; b. 30 July 1761 d. 8 July 1829; MP for Kildare B. 1783–90, Dublin City 1790–7 [r. Athy 1790] [HP].

0734 *FITZGERALD, Rt Hon. James [styled Ld Offaly 1722–44, 20th E. of Kildare, E. of Offaly, 1st M. of Kildare and 1st D. of Leinster]; b. 29 May 1722 d. 19 Nov. 1773; MP for Athy 1741–4.

0735 FITZGERALD, Rt Hon. James; b. 1742 d. 20 Jan. 1835; MP for Fore 1776–83, Tulsk 1783–90–7, Kildare B. 1797–1800 [HP].

0736 *FITZGERALD, John; b. c. 1646–8[3] d. Mar. 1728; MP for Castlemartyr 1727–8.

0737 FITZGERALD, John [Kt of Kerry]; b. 1706 d. 10 June 1741; MP for Dingle 1728–41.

0738 FITZGERALD, Maurice [Kt of Kerry]; b. c. 1734–40[7] d. 24 June 1779; MP for Dingle 1761–8–76.

0739 FITZGERALD, Rt Hon. Maurice [Kt of Kerry]; b. 29 Dec. 1772 d. 7 Mar. 1849; MP for Co. Kerry 1795–7–1800 [re-elected pp 1800] [HP].

0740 *FITZGERALD, Richard; b. ante 1733[9] d. [ante 27] Feb. 1776; MP for Boyle 1763–8–76.

0741 FITZGERALD, Rt Hon. Robert; b. 1637 d. 31 Jan. 1697/8; MP for Co. Kildare [1661–6], 1692–3, 1695–8.

0742 FITZGERALD, Robert; b. 1654 d. 23 Sept. 1718; MP for Youghal 1692–3, 1695–9, Castlemartyr 1703–13.

0743 FITZGERALD, Robert; b. 1671 d. 21 Jan. 1724/5; MP for Charleville 1703–13.

0744 *FITZGERALD, Robert [Kt of Kerry]; b. 1716 d. 5 Dec. 1781; MP for Dingle 1741–60, 1761–8–76–81.

0745 *FITZGERALD, Rt Hon. William Robert [2nd D. of Leinster]; b. 12 Mar. 1749 d. 20 Oct. 1804; MP for Dublin city 1767–8–73.

0746 FITZGERALD-VILLIERS, Rt Hon. Edward; b. c. 1652–6[7] d. Jan. 1692/3; MP for Co. Waterford 1692–3.

0747 FITZGERALD-VILLIERS, Hon. James; b. [ante 9 Mar.] 1708/9 d. 12 Dec. 1732; MP for Co. Waterford 1730–2.

0748 FITZGIBBON, John; b. 1708 d. 11 Apr. 1780; MP for Newcastle 1761–8, Jamestown 1768–76.

0749 *FITZGIBBON, Rt Hon. John [1st B. and V. FitzGibbon, 1st E. of Clare]; b. 1748 d. 28 Jan. 1802; MP for TCD 1778–83, Kilmallock 1783–9.

0750 FITZHERBERT, Rt Hon. Alleyne [1st B. St Helens]; b. 1 Mar. 1753 d. 19 Feb. 1839; MP for Carysfort 1788–90.

0751 FITZHERBERT, William; b. 1681 d. 5 Apr. 1742; MP for Kilbeggan 1713–14, Rathcormack 1728–42.

0752 FITZMAURICE [PETTY], Rt Hon. John [1st B. Dunkerron, V. Fitzmaurice and E. of Shelburne]; b. 1706 d. 14 May 1761; MP for Co. Kerry 1743–51 [HP].

0753 FITZMAURICE, Rt Hon. Thomas [20th B. Kerry and Lixnaw, 1st V. Clanmaurice and E. of Kerry]; b. 1668 d. 16 Mar. 1741/2; MP for Co. Kerry 1692–3, 1695–7.

0754 FITZMAURICE, Hon. Thomas; b. July 1742 d. 28 Oct. 1793; MP for Co. Kerry 1763–8 [HP].

0755 FITZMAURICE, Hon. William; b. [ante 24 Nov.] 1671 d. [post 9 Nov.] 1711; MP for Dingle 1692–3, 1695–9, 1703–13.

0756 FITZPATRICK, Rt Hon. Richard [1st B. Gowran]; b. c. 1662[10] d. 9 June 1727; MP for Harristown 1703–13, Queen's Co. 1713–14.

♦♦♦♦ FITZPATRICK [alias FITZGERALD], Richard; b. ante 1700 d. 1767 [n.d.e. Youghal 9–27 Oct. 1721].

0757 FITZPATRICK, Richard; b. 1706 d. 17 July 1767; MP for Galway B. 1761–7.

0758 FITZPATRICK, Rt Hon. Richard; b. 24 Jan. 1747/8 d. 25 Apr. 1813; MP for Maryborough 1782–3 [HP].

0759 FLETCHER, William; b. 1750 d. 20 Mar. 1823; MP for Tralee 1795–7 [re-elected pp 1795].

0760 FLOOD, Francis; b. c. 1660[5] d. 1730; MP for Callan 1703–7, June 1705 [expelled], 1713–14, 1715–27.

0761 FLOOD, Sir Frederick [1st Bt]; b. 1739 d. 1 Feb. 1824; MP for Enniscorthy 1776–83, Ardfert 1783–90, Carlow B. 1796–7 [HP].

0762 FLOOD, Rt Hon. Henry; b. 1732 d. 2 Dec. 1791; MP for Co. Kilkenny 1759–60, Callan 1762–8–76, Enniskillen 1777–83, Kilbeggan 1783–90 [HP].

0763 *FLOOD, Jocelyn; b. [bapt. 15 July] 1746 d. 19 May 1767; MP for Callan 1765–7.

0764 *FLOOD, John; b. 1736 d. [*post* 30 June] 1807; MP for Callan 1767–8–76, Innistiogue 1777–83.

0765 FLOOD, Rt Hon. Warden; b. 1694 d. 15 Apr. 1764; MP for Callan 1727–60.

0766 *FLOOD, Warden; b. 1735 d. Mar. 1797; MP for Longford B. 1769–76, Carysfort 1776–83, Baltinglass 1783–90, Taghmon 1790–7.

0767 FLOWER, Rt Hon. William [1st B. Castle Durrow]; b. [11] Mar. 1685/6 d. 29 Apr. 1746; MP for Co. Kilkenny 1715–27, Portarlington 1727–33.

0768 FOLLIOTT, Francis; b. 1667 d. 1701; MP for Ballyshannon 1692–3, 1695–9.

0769 FOLLIOTT, Hon. Henry [3rd B. Folliott]; b. 1662 d. 17 Oct. 1716; MP for Ballyshannon 1695–7.

0770 FOLLIOTT, John; b. 1660 d. 1697; MP for Ballyshannon 1692–3.

0771 FOLLIOTT, John; b. [bapt. 25 Jan.] 1690/1 d. 26 Feb. 1762; MP for Longford B. 1721–7, Granard 1727–60, Sligo B. 1761–2.

0772 *FOLLIOTT, John; b. 1696 d. 12 Jan. 1765; MP for Donegal B. 1730–60, Kinsale 1761–5.

0773 FOORD, William; b. *ante* 4 Nov. 1694[1] d. [bur. 4] Mar. 1732/3; MP for Limerick city 1715–27.

0774 FORBES, Arthur; b. *ante* 1749[7] d. 14 Oct. 1788; MP for Ratoath 1783–8.

0775 FORBES, Rt Hon. George [4th E. of Granard]; b. 15 Mar. 1709/10 d. 16 Oct. 1769; MP for Mullingar 1749–60, 1761–5.

0776 FORBES, Rt Hon. George [5th E. of Granard]; b. 2 Apr. 1740 d. 15 Apr. 1780; MP for St Johnstown [Longford] 1762–8.

0777 FORBES, Hon. John; b. 17 July 1714 d. 10 Mar. 1796; MP for St Johnstown [Longford] 1751–60, Mullingar 1761–8.

0778 FORBES, John; b. 1750 d. 3 June 1797; MP for Ratoath 1776–83, Drogheda 1783–90–6.

0779 FORDE, Edward; b. 1642 d. 17 May 1705; MP for Monaghan B. 1692–3, Ratoath 1703–5.

0780 FORDE, Mathew; b. *ante* 1647[7] d. Jan. 1709; MP for Co. Wexford 1695–9, 1703–9.

0781 *FORDE, Mathew; b. 1675 d. 1729; MP for Downpatrick 1703–13–14.

0782 FORDE, Mathew; b. [bapt. 10 Oct.] 1699 d. 1780; MP for Bangor 1751–60.

0783 FORDE, Mathew; b. 1726 d. 6 Aug. 1795; MP for Downpatrick 1761–8–76.

0784 *FORDE, Robert; b. *c.* 1749–55[7] d. 1795; MP for Thomastown 1776–83.

0785 FORSTER, Rt Hon. John; b. 1668 d. 2 July 1720; MP for Dublin City 1703–13–14.

0786 *FORSTER, Richard; b. *c.* 1634[2] d. 1711; MP for Swords 1692–3.

0787 FORTESCUE, Chichester; b. 5 June 1718 d. 16 July 1757; MP for Trim 1747–57.

0788 FORTESCUE, Sir Chichester [Kt]; b. 7 June 1750 d. 22 Mar. 1820; MP for Trim 1797–1800.

0789 FORTESCUE, Chichester; b. 12 Aug. 1777 d. 25 Nov. 1826; MP for Hillsborough Jan.–Aug. 1800.

0790 FORTESCUE, Faithful; b. *c.* 1697–9[3] d. 22 Mar. 1741; MP for Co. Louth 1727–41.

0791 FORTESCUE, Faithful William; b. 4 Apr. 1773 d. 1824; MP for Monaghan B. Jan.–Aug. 1800.

0792 *FORTESCUE, Rt Hon. James; b. 15 May 1725 d. [*ante* 28] May 1782; MP for Dundalk 1757–60, Co. Louth 1761–8–76–82.

0793 FORTESCUE, Thomas; b. 1683 d. 23 Jan. 1769; MP for Dundalk 1727–60.

0794 *FORTESCUE, Thomas; b. 1 May 1744 d. [*ante* 11] Dec. 1779; MP for Trim 1768–76–9.

0795 FORTESCUE, Thomas James; b. 15 Feb. 1760 d. [*ante* 21] July 1795; MP for Co. Louth 1782–3–90–5.

0796 FORTESCUE, William; b. 29 July 1733 d. 1816; MP for Monaghan B. 1798–1800.

0797 FORTESCUE, William Charles [2nd V. Clermont]; b. 12 Oct. 1764 d. 24 June 1829; MP for Co. Louth 1796–7–1800 [HP].

0798 FORTESCUE, Rt. Hon. William Henry [1st B., V. and E. of Clermont]; b. 5 Aug. 1722 d. 30 Sept. 1806; MP for Co. Louth 1745–60, Monaghan B. 1761–8–70.

0799 FORTH, James; b. 1677 d. 5 June 1731; MP for King's Co. 1713–4, Philipstown 1715–27.

0800 **FORTICK**, Sir William [Kt]; b. *ante* 18 June 1755[1] d. May [bur. 1 June] 1789; MP for Augher 1776–83.

0801 *****FORWARD**, John; b. 1640 d. 1709; MP for St Johnstown [Donegal] 1692–3.

0802 *****FORWARD**, William; b. 1696 d. 22 Jan. 1770; MP for St Johnstown [Donegal] 1715–27, 1727–60, 1761–8.

0803 **FORWARD** [FORWARD-HOWARD], Rt Hon. William [3rd E. of Wicklow]; b. Jan. 1761 d. 27 Sept. 1818; MP for St Johnstown [Donegal] 1783–90–7–1800 [re-elected pp 1800].

0804 **FOSTER**, Rt Hon. Anthony; b. 1705 d. [*ante* 29] Apr. 1779; MP for Dunleer 1738–60, Co. Louth 1761–6.

0805 *****FOSTER**, Rt Hon. John [1st B. Oriel]; b. [28] Sept. 1740 d. 23 Aug. 1828; MP for Dunleer 1761–8, Co. Louth 1768–76–83–90–7–1800 [HP].

0806 *****FOSTER**, Hon. John; b. 1769 d. Feb. 1792; MP for Dunleer 1790–2.

0807 **FOSTER**, John Thomas; b. 1748 d. 10 Oct. 1796; MP for Dunleer 1776–83, Ennis 1783–90.

0808 **FOSTER**, John William; b. 1745 d. [Jan.] 1809; MP for Dunleer 1783–90.

0809 **FOSTER** [SKEFFINGTON], Rt Hon. Thomas Henry [2nd V. Ferrard]; b. [*ante* 10 Jan] 1772 d. 18 Jan. 1843; MP for Dunleer 1792–7–1800 [re-elected pp 1798] [HP].

0810 *****FOULKE** [*alias* FOULKES], Robert; b. 1663 d. [bur. 12] July 1741; MP for Rathcormack 1692–3, 1695–9, Midleton 1703–13.

0811 **FOWNES**, Sir William [Kt, 1st Bt]; b. *ante* 1672[6] d. 3 Apr. 1735; MP for Wicklow B. 1704–13.

0812 **FOWNES**, Rt Hon. Sir William [2nd Bt]; b. 1709 d. 5 June 1778; MP for Dingle 1749–60, Knocktopher 1761–8–76, Wicklow B. 1776–8.

0813 *****FOX**, Henry; b. *c.* 1657[2] d. 1726; MP for Lanesborough 1703–13.

0814 **FOX**, Luke; b. 1757 d. 26 Aug. 1819; MP for Fethard [Wexford] 1793–7, Clonmines 1797–9, Mullingar 1799–1800 [re-elected pp 1795].

0815 **FOX**, Patrick; b. *ante* 1669[5] d. 1734; MP for Kilbeggan 1703–13, Fore 1715–27.

0816 **FRANKS**, Matthew; b. 1768 d. 25 Mar. 1853; MP for Ardfert 22 Sept. 1800 [as he was returned after Aug. he did not have an opportunity to take his seat].

0817 *****FRASIER**, Alexander; b. *ante* 5 Oct. 1671[1] d. [bur. 26] Sept. 1709; MP for St Johnstown [Longford] 1692–3.

0818 **FREEMAN**, Samuel; b. 1655 d. [bur. 11] Jan. 1731/2; MP for Ballynakill 1715–27.

0819 **FREKE**, George; b. *ante* 21 Sept. 1682[1] d. [Sept.] 1730; MP for Clonakilty 1703–13–14, 1715–27, Bandon-Bridge 1727–30.

0820 **FREKE** [EVANS], Sir John [1st Bt]; b. 1744 d. 20 Mar. 1777; MP for Baltimore 1768–76–7.

0821 *****FREKE**, Sir John [2nd Bt, 6th B. Carbery]; b. 11 Nov. 1765 d. 12 May 1845; MP for Donegal B. 1783–90, Baltimore 1790–7–1800.

0822 **FREKE**, Sir John Redmond [3rd Bt]; b. *ante* 6 May 1707[8] d. 13 Apr. 1764; MP for Baltimore 1728–60, Cork city 1761–4.

0823 *****FREKE**, Percy; b. *c.* 1643–5[3] d. [*ante* 1 July] 1707; MP for Clonakilty 1692–3, 1695–9, Baltimore 1703–7.

0824 **FREKE**, Sir Percy [2nd Bt]; b. 1700 d. 10 Apr. 1728; MP for Baltimore 1721–7–8.

0825 *****FREKE**, Sir Ralph [1st Bt]; b. 2 June 1675 d. 1717; MP for Clonakilty 1703–13–14, 1715–17.

0826 **FREMANTLE**, Stephen Francis William; b. *ante* 2 July 1769[1] d. [Sept.] 1794; MP for Fore 1790–4.

0827 **FRENCH**, Arthur; b. 1690 d. June 1761; MP for Tulsk Jan.–Aug. 1714, Co. Roscommon 1721–7, Boyle 1727–60.

0828 *****FRENCH**, Arthur; b. [bapt. 6 Apr.] 1765 d. 24 Nov. 1820; MP for Co. Roscommon 1783–90–7–1800 [HP].

0829 **FRENCH**, Humphrey; b. [8] May 1680 d. 13 [bur. 16] Oct. 1736; MP for Dublin city 1733–6.

0830 **FRENCH**, John; b. 1662 d. 1734; MP for Carrick 1695–9, 1713–14, Co. Galway 1703–13, Tulsk 1715–27.

0831 **FRENCH**, John; b. 9 Nov. 1723 d. [20] Oct. 1775; MP for Co. Roscommon 1745–60, 1761–8–75.

0832 **FRENCH**, Patrick; b. 1681 d. 3 June 1744; MP for Co. Galway 1713–14, Blessington 1727–44.

0833 **FRENCH**, Robert; b. 1690 d. 29 May 1772; MP for Jamestown 1727–45.

0834 **FRENCH**, Robert; b. 1716 d. 30 Jan. 1779; MP for Co. Galway 1753–60, Carrick 1761–8, Galway B. 1768–76.

0835 **GAHAN**, Sir Daniel [Kt]; b. [*ante* 5 Oct.] 1671 d. 1713; MP for Portarlington 1692–3, Rathcormack 1703–13.

0836 *****GAHAN**, Daniel; b. *c.* 1721–7[6] d. [*post* 1 June] 1799; MP for Fethard [Tipperary] 1785–90–7, Wicklow B. 1797–9.

0837 *****GALBRAITH**, Sir James [1st Bt]; b. *c.* 1759[6] d. 30 Apr. 1827; MP for Augher 1798–1800.

0838 *****GAMBLE**, Robert; b. 1735 d. *c.* 1799[10]; MP for Newcastle 1776–83.

0839 **GAMBLE**, William; b. *ante* 1714[9] d. [*ante* 13] Mar. 1779; MP for Ballyshannon 1769–76.

0840 **GARDINER**, Rt Hon. Charles; b. 21 Feb. 1720 d. 20 Nov. 1769; MP for Taghmon 1742–60.

0841 **GARDINER**, Rt Hon. Luke; b. *ante* 1690[7] d. 25 Sept. 1755; MP for Tralee 1725–7, Thomastown 1727–55.

0842 *****GARDINER**, Rt Hon. Luke [1st B. and V. Mountjoy]; b. 7 Feb. 1745 d. 5 June 1798; MP for Co. Dublin 1773–6–83–9.

0843 **GARDINER**, Richard; b. *ante* 27 Aug. 1674[1] d. 26 Oct. 1700; MP for Lanesborough 1695–9.

0844 **GARDINER**, William; b. 23 Apr. 1748 d. 7 Feb. 1805; MP for Thomastown Apr.–Aug. 1800.

0845 *****GEERING**, Richard; b. *ante* 21 Sept. 1682[1] d. 1742; MP for Ballyshannon 1703–13, Jamestown 1721–7.

0846 **GETHIN**, Percy; b. 1650 d. 1723; MP for Sligo B. 1692–3, 1695–9, 1703–13.

0847 **GIFFARD**, Duke; b. *c.* 1660 d. [bur. 13] June 1707; MP for Philipstown 1692–3, 1695–9.

0848 **GILBERT**, Bartholomew William; b. 1712 d. 1761; MP for Maryborough 1755–60.

0849 *****GILBERT**, St Leger; b. *ante* 1668[10] d. Oct. 1737; MP for Maryborough 1692–3, 1695–9, 1703–13, Old Leighlin 1713–14, 1715–27.

0850 **GILBERT**, William; b. [bapt. 17] Sept. 1737 d. 4 Jan. 1764; MP for Maryborough 1761–4.

0851 **GISBORNE**, James; b. *c.* 1720–5[8] d. 20 Feb. 1778; MP for Tallow 1763–8, Lismore 1768–76–8.

0852 *****GLEADOWE**, Edward; b. *ante* 1741[8] d. 1814; MP for Ardfert 1781–3.

0853 **GLEADOWE-NEWCOMEN**, Sir William [1st Bt]; b. 1741 d. 21 Aug. 1807; MP for Co. Longford Jan.–Apr. 1790, 1790–7–1800 [HP].

0854 *****GLOVER**, George; b. *ante* 1736[6] d. [*c.* 28] Feb. 1770; MP for Belturbet 1768–70.

0855 *****GODFREY**, Sir William [1st Bt]; b. 1739 d. 20 Jan. 1817; MP for Tralee 1783–90, Belfast 1792–7.

0856 **GODLEY**, John; b. 1732 d. 5 Aug. 1806; MP for Baltinglass 1777–83.

0857 **GORE**, Sir Arthur [2nd Bt]; b. [*ante* 21 Sept.] 1682[8] d. 10 Feb. 1741/2; MP for Ballynakill 1703–13, Donegal B. 1713–14, Co. Mayo 1715–27–42.

0858 *****GORE**, Arthur; b. *ante* 1685 d. [*ante* 5 Oct.] 1730; MP for Ennis 1727–31.

0859 *****GORE**, Rt Hon. Sir Arthur [3rd Bt, 1st B. Saunders, V. Sudley and E. of Arran]; b. 1703 d. 17 Apr. 1773; MP for Donegal B. 1727–58.

0860 *****GORE**, Arthur; b. 1711 d. [bur. 15] Apr. 1758; MP for Co. Longford 1739–58.

0861 *****GORE**, Rt Hon. Arthur Saunders [2nd E. of Arran]; b. 25 July 1734 d. 8 Oct. 1809; MP for Donegal B. 1759–60, 1768–73, Co. Wexford 1761–8.

0862 *****GORE**, Hon. Arthur Saunders [3rd E. of Arran]; b. 20 July 1761 d. 20 Jan. 1837; MP for Baltimore 1783–90, Co. Donegal 16 Dec. 1800 [HP].

0863 **GORE**, Francis; b. *ante* 1664[9] d. [*ante* 23 Apr.] 1724; MP for Ennis 1695–9, 1713–14, Co. Clare 1715–24.

0864 *****GORE**, Frederick; b. *c.* 1690[5] d. [bur. 5] Mar. 1764; MP for Tulsk 1747–60.

0865 **GORE**, George; b. 1675 d. 13 Jan. 1753; MP for Longford B. 1709–13–14, 1715–20.

0866 **GORE**, Henry; b. 1698 d. 1787; MP for Killybegs 1749–60.

0867 **GORE**, Henry [1st B. Annaly]; b. 8 Mar. 1727/8 d. 5 June 1793; MP for Co. Longford 1758–60, 1768–76–83–9, Lanesborough 1761–8.

0868 **GORE**, John; b. *c.* 1642 d. 1700; MP for Ennis 1692–3.

0869 **GORE**, Rt Hon. John [1st B. Annaly]; b. 2 Mar. 1718 d. 3 Apr. 1784; MP for Jamestown 1747–60, Co. Longford 1761–4.

0870 **GORE**, John; b. *post* 1735[7] d. 1814; MP for Co. Leitrim 1784–90.

0871 *****GORE**, Paul Annesley; b. *post* 1703[7] d. 1780; MP for Co. Mayo 1751–60, Co. Sligo 1765–8.

0872 **GORE**, Rt Hon. Sir Ralph [4th Bt]; b. 1675 d. 23 Feb. 1732/3; MP for Donegal B. 1703–13, Co. Donegal 1713–14, 1715–27, Clogher 1727–33.

0873 **GORE**, Sir Ralph; b. *c.* 1722–6[7] d. [*ante* 5] Mar. 1778; MP for Kilkenny city 1748–60, 1776–8.

0874 *****GORE**, Hon. Richard; b. *c.* 1735–40[8] d. [bur. 30] Dec. 1807; MP for Castlebar 1761–8, Donegal B. 1769–76.

0875 *****GORE**, William; b. *ante* 1670[7] d. [*ante* 10] Feb. 1729/30; MP for Donegal B. 1695–9, Co. Leitrim 1703–13–4, 1715–27–30.

0876 **GORE**, William; b. 1703[4] d. 18 Feb. 1748; MP for Kilkenny city 1727–48.

0877 *****GORE**, William; b. 1709 d. [*ante* 21] Sept. 1769; MP for Co. Leitrim 1730–60, 1768–9.

0878 **GORE**, William; b. 11 Aug. 1744 d. 2 Apr. 1815; MP for Co. Leitrim 1769–76.

0879 **GORE**, William; b. 1767 d. 1 Sept. 1832; MP for Carrick 1798–1800 [re-elected pp 1800].

0880 *****GORE** [*alias* GORE-ST GEORGE], Sir St George [5th Bt]; b. 25 June 1722 d. 25 Sept. 1746; MP for Co. Donegal 1741–6.

0881 **GORE-ST GEORGE**, Sir Ralph [6th Bt, 1st B. Gore, V. Bellisle and E. of Ross]; b. 23 Nov. 1725 d. Sept. 1802; MP for Co. Donegal 1747–60, 1761–4.

0882 **GORGES**, Hamilton; b. 1711 d. 8 Apr. 1786; MP for Coleraine 1757–60, Swords 1761–8.

0883 **GORGES**, Hamilton; b. 1737 d. 14 June 1802; MP for Co. Meath 1792–7–1800 [HP].

0884 **GORGES**, Richard; b. 22 Mar. 1662 d. 12 Apr. 1728; MP for Charlemont 1692–3, Bandon-Bridge 1703–13, Ratoath 1713–14, 1715–27.

0885 **GORGES**, Richard; b. 1709 d. [Mar.] 1778; MP for Augher 1739–60, Enniskillen 1761–8.

0886 **GORGES** [GORGES-MEREDYTH], Sir Richard [1st Bt]; b. 7 May 1735 d. Sept. 1821; MP for Enniskillen Feb.–May 1768, 1768–76, Naas 1787–90.

0887 **GORGES**, Robert; b. *ante* 1624[2] d. [bur. 10] Nov. 1699; MP for [Bandon-Bridge 1661–6], Ratoath 1692–3.

0888 **GOULD** [*alias* GOOLD], Thomas; b. 1765 d. 16 July 1846; MP for Kilbeggan Jan.–Aug. 1800.

0889 **GRACE**, Richard; b. 1761 d. 9 Jan. 1801; MP for Baltimore 1790–7.

0890 **GRADON** [*alias* GRAYDEN or GRAYDON], Alexander; b. *c.* 1666 d. [bur. 13] May 1739; MP for Naas 1703–13, Harristown 1713–14, 1715–27.

0891 **GRADY**, Henry Dean; b. 1765 d. 8 Sept. 1847; MP for Limerick city 1797–1800 [HP].

0892 *****GRAHAM**, John; b. *ante* 1659[7] d. 1717; MP for Drogheda 1710–13–14, 1715–17.

0893 *****GRAHAM**, John; b. 1729 d. 17 Apr. 1777; MP for Drogheda 1749–60, 1761–8.

0894 *****GRAHAM**, Rt Hon. William; b. [*ante* 28 Nov.] 1706 d. 17 Mar. 1749; MP for Drogheda 1727–48.

0895 **GRATTAN**, Rt Hon. Henry; b. June [bapt. 3 July] 1746 d. 4 June 1820; MP for Charlemont 1775–6–83–90, Dublin city 1790–7, Wicklow B. Jan.–Aug. 1800 [HP].

0896 *****GRATTAN**, James; b. 1711 d. 12 June 1766; MP for Dublin city 1761–6.

0897 **GRAYDON**, John; b. 1693 d. [bur. 16] July 1774; MP for Harristown 1727–60.

0898 **GRAYDON**, Robert; b. *ante* 5 Oct. 1671[1] d. 1725; MP for Harristown 1692–3, 1695–9.

0899 **GRAYDON**, Robert; b. *c.* 1744[2] d. 1800; MP for Harristown 1768–76, Kildare B. 1790–7.

0900 **GREEN**, Samuel; b. 1657 d. [*ante* 20 May] 1710; MP for Cashel 1692–3, 1695–9, 1703–10.

0901 **GREENE**, Godfrey; b. 6 May 1742 d. 16 Apr. 1798; MP for Dungarvan 1777–83–90.

0902 **GREGORY**, Rt Hon. William; b. 1762 d. 13 Apr. 1840; MP for Portarlington Jan.–Aug. 1800.

0903 **GREVILLE**, William Fulk; b. 8 Nov. 1751 d. 1837; MP for Granard 1797–8.

0904 **GRIFFITH**, Richard; b. 10 June 1752 d. 30 June 1820; MP for Askeaton 1783–90.

0905 ***GROGAN**, Cornelius; b. 1733 d. 27 June 1798; MP for Enniscorthy 1768–76.

0906 ***GROGAN**, John; b. 1717 d. [*ante* 6] Jan. 1784; MP for Enniscorthy 1761–8.

♦♦♦♦ **HACKETT**, John, b. *ante* 1676 d. 6 Nov. 1760 [n.d.e. Mullingar 1727–8].

0907 ***HALL**, John; b. [bapt. 16 Dec.] 1729 d. 1788; MP for Jamestown 1781–3.

0908 **HALL**, Roger; b. [bapt. 3 Apr.] 1716 d. 1797; MP for Longford B. 1756–60, Newry 1761–8, Co. Down 1768–76.

0909 **HALTRIDGE**, John; b. 1670 d. 4 Feb. 1725; MP for Killyleagh 1703–13–14, 1715–25.

0910 ***HAMERTON**, Robert; b. *c.* 1678[10] d. 26 Jan. 1733; MP for Clonmel 1703–13–14, 1715–27, 1728–33.

0911 ***HAMILL**, Hugh; b. *c.* 1649[6] d. [*ante* 5 May] 1709; MP for Lifford 1692–3, 1695–9, 1703–9.

0912 **HAMILTON**, Alexander; b. *post* 1685[7] d. Aug. 1768; MP for Killyleagh 1739–60.

0913 ***HAMILTON**, Alexander; b. 1765 d. 4 Mar. 1809; MP for Ratoath 1789–90, Carrickfergus 1790–7, Belfast 1798–1800.

0914 **HAMILTON**, Charles; b. *c.* 1640 d. 25 July 1710; MP for Co. Donegal [1661–6] 1692–3, Killybegs 1695–9, 1703–10.

0915 **HAMILTON**, Charles; b. *c.* 1700[5] d. 16 May 1753; MP for Ratoath 1727–53.

0916 **HAMILTON**, Hon. Charles; b. [bapt. 13 Nov.] 1704 d. 11 Sept. 1786; MP for Strabane 1727–60 [HP].

0917 **HAMILTON**, Claude; b. *c.* 1741 d. Jan. 1782; MP for Strabane 1769–76.

0918 ***HAMILTON**, Sir Francis [3rd Bt]; b. *c.* 1640[2] d. 4 Feb. 1713/14; MP for Co. Cavan [1661–6], 1692–3, 1695–9, 1703–13–14.

0919 **HAMILTON**, Rt Hon. Frederick; b. *c.* 1663–8[5] d. 10 Dec. 1715; MP for Co. Donegal 1707–13–14, Oct.–Dec. 1715.

0920 **HAMILTON**, Frederick; b. 1650 d. July 1732; MP for Coleraine 1713–14, 1715–27.

0921 **HAMILTON**, Hon. George; b. *c.*1697[2] d. 3 May 1775; MP for St Johnstown [Donegal] 1727–60 [HP].

0922 **HAMILTON**, George; b. 1732 d. 14 Nov. 1793; MP for Belfast 1768–76.

0923 ***HAMILTON**, George; b. 1734 d. July 1796; MP Augher 1776–83.

0924 **HAMILTON**, Rt Hon. Gustavus [1st B. Hamilton and V. Boyne]; b. 1642 d. 16 Sept. 1723; MP for Co. Donegal 1692–3, 1695–9, 1703–13, Strabane 1713–14.

0925 **HAMILTON**, Hon. Gustavus; b. *c.* 1685–7[3] d. 26 Feb. 1735; MP for Co. Donegal 1716–27–35.

0926 **HAMILTON**, Hans; b. *ante* 27 Aug. 1674[1] d. [bur. 18] Feb. 1728; MP for Killyleagh 1695–9, Newry 1707–13–14, 1715–27, Dundalk 1727–8.

0927 **HAMILTON**, Sir Hans [2nd Bt]; b. 1673 d. 1731; MP for Co. Armagh 1703–13, Carlingford 1713–14.

0928 **HAMILTON**, Hans; b. [bapt. 19 July] 1758 d. Dec.1822; MP for Co. Dublin 1797–1800 [HP].

0929 **HAMILTON**, Hon. Henry; b. [bapt. 3 Mar.] 1693 d. 3 June 1743; MP for St Johnstown [Donegal] 1725–7, Co. Donegal 1730–43.

0930 **HAMILTON**, Sir Henry [1 Bt]; b. 1710 d. 26 June 1782; MP for Londonderry city 1747–60, 1761–8, Killybegs 1768–76–82.

0931 ***HAMILTON**, Sir James [Kt]; b. 1644 d. 18 Jan. 1705/6; MP for [?Strabane 1666], Co. Down 1692–3, Bangor 1695–9, 1703–6.

0932 **HAMILTON**, James; b. 1651 d. May 1700; MP for Downpatrick 1692–3, Co. Down 1695–9.

0933 ***HAMILTON**, Rt Hon. James [6th E. of Abercorn]; b. 1661 d. 28 Nov. 1734; MP for Co. Tyrone 1692–3, 1695–9.

0934 ***HAMILTON**, Rt Hon. James [1st B. Claneboye, V. Limerick and E. of Clanbrassill]; b. *c.* 1691[10] d. 17 Mar. 1758; MP for Dundalk 1715–19 [HP].

0935 **HAMILTON**, James; b. [bapt. 27 Nov.] 1685 d. [*ante* 9] Nov. 1771; MP for Newry 1723–7, Carlow B. 1727–60.

0936 **HAMILTON**, Rt Hon. James [2nd E. of Clanbrassill]; b. 23 Aug. 1730 d. 6 Feb. 1798; MP for Midleton 1755–8 [HP].

0937 **HAMILTON**, John; b. *ante* 1662[6] d. *ante* 25 Mar. 1714/5; MP for Donegal B. 1692–3, St Johnstown [Donegal] 1713–14.

0938 **HAMILTON**, John; b. 1656 d. Jan. 1712/3; MP for Dungannon 1692–3, 1695–9, Augher 1703–13.

0939 **HAMILTON**, John; b. [bapt. 27 Nov.] 1685 d. Mar. 1757; MP for Carlow B. 1725–7, Dundalk 1728–57 [HP].

0940 **HAMILTON**, Sir John Stewart [1st Bt]; b. *c.* 1740[10] d. Apr. 1802; MP for Strabane 1763–8–76–83–90–7.

0941 ***HAMILTON**, John William; b. *c.* 1745 d. 14 Jan. 1781; MP for Castlebar 1775–6, St Canice 1776–81.

0942 **HAMILTON**, Richard; b. 1689 d. [*post* 11 June] 1727; MP for Lifford 1719–27.

0943 **HAMILTON**, Richard [4th V Boyne]; b. 24 Mar. 1723/4 d. 31 July 1789; MP for Navan 1755–60.

0944 **HAMILTON**, Robert; b. 1704 d. [14] Oct. 1768; MP for Bangor 1761–8.

0945 **HAMILTON**, Rt Hon. Sackville; b. 14 Mar. 1731/2 d. 29 Jan. 1818; MP for St Johnstown [Longford] 1780–3, Clogher 1783–90–5, Armagh city 1796–7.

0946 **HAMILTON**, William; b. 1708 d. 31 July 1762; MP for Strabane 1733–60, 1761–2.

0947 **HAMILTON**, William; b. 1693 d. 15 Aug. 1760; MP for Londonderry city 1759–60, 1760.

0948 **HAMILTON**, Rt Hon. William Gerard; b. 28 Jan. 1727/8 d. 16 July 1796; MP for Killybegs 1761–8 [HP].

0949 **HANDCOCK**, Gustavus; b. 13 Aug. 1693 d. 4 Sept 1751; MP for Athlone 1723–7, 1732–51.

0950 **HANDCOCK**, John; b. *ante* 1755[7] d. Oct. 1786; MP for Philipstown 1776–83.

0951 **HANDCOCK**, John Gustavus; b. 1720 d. 26 Feb. 1766; MP for Ballyshannon 1761–6.

0952 **HANDCOCK**, Richard [2nd B. Castlemaine]; b. 14 May 1767 d. 18 Apr. 1840; MP for Athlone May–Aug. 1800.

0953 **HANDCOCK**, Robert; b. 1712 d. 24 Nov. 1758; MP for Athlone 1751–8.

0954 ***HANDCOCK**, Thomas; b. 28 May 1654 d. 1726; MP for Lanesborough 1692–3, 1695–9.

0955 ***HANDCOCK**, William; b. *ante* 1631[7] d. [*ante* 1 July] 1707; MP for [Co. Westmeath 1661–6], Athlone 1692–3, 1695–9, Co. Westmeath 1703–7.

0956 **HANDCOCK**, William; b. 11 Sept. 1654 d. Sept. 1701; MP for Boyle 1692–3, Dublin city 1695–9.

0957 ***HANDCOCK**, William; b. 1676 d. [*ante* 29 Aug.] 1723; MP for Athlone 1703–13–14, Co. Westmeath 1721–3.

0958 **HANDCOCK**, William; b. 1704 d. 13 Aug. 1741; MP for Fore 1727–41.

0959 **HANDCOCK**, William; b. 1737 d. [Apr.] 1794; MP for Athlone 1759–60, 1761–8–76–83.

0960 **HANDCOCK**, Rt Hon. William [1st B. and V. Castlemaine]; b. 28 Aug. 1761 d. 7 Jan. 1839; MP for Athlone 1783–90–7–1800 [HP].

0961 **HANMER**, Rt Hon. Sir John [3rd Bt]; b. *c.* 1625–30[4] d. Aug. 1701; MP for Carlingford 1695–9 [HP].

0962 **HARDINGE**, Sir Richard [1st Bt]; b. 10 Nov. 1756 d. 5 Nov. 1826; MP for Knocktopher 1796–7, Midleton 1797–9 [re-elected pp 1798].

0963 **HARDMAN**, Edward; b. Sept. 1741 d. 10 Feb. 1814; MP for Drogheda 1798–1800 [HP].

0964 **HARDY**, Francis; b. 1751 d. 26 July 1812; MP for Mullingar 1783–90–7–1800.

0965 **HARE**, Hon. Richard [styled V. Ennismore 1822–7]; b. 20 Mar. 1773 d. 24 Sept. 1827; MP for Athy 1797–1800 [HP].

0966 **HARE**, William [1st B., V. Ennismore and Listowel, E. of Listowel]; b. Sept. 1751 d. 13 July 1837; MP for Cork city 1796–7, Athy 1797–1800.

0967 **HARMAN**, Caleb Barnes; b. *ante* 10 Jan. 1772[1] d. 3 Jan. 1796; MP for Co. Longford 1793–6.

0968 **HARMAN** [PARSONS], Laurence Harman [1st B., V. Oxmantown and E. of Rosse]; b. 26 July 1749 d. 20 Apr. 1807; MP for Co. Longford 1775–6–83–90–2.

0969 **HARMAN**, Robert; b. 1699 d. 4 Sept. 1765; MP for Kildare B. 1755–60, Co. Longford 1761–5.

0970 **HARMAN**, Wentworth; b. *ante* 1655[7] d. 3 May 1714; MP for Co. Longford 1695–9, Granard 1703–13.

0971 **HARMAN**, Wentworth; b. *c.* 1676–83[7] d. 3 Nov. 1757; MP for Lanesborough 1713–4, 1715–27.

0972 **HARRISON**, Edward; b. 1644 d. 12 Oct. 1700; MP for Lisburn 1692–3, 1695–9.

0973 *HARRISON**, Francis; b. 1677 d. 27 June 1725; MP for Knocktopher 1703–13, Lisburn 1713–14, Co. Carlow 1715–25.

0974 **HARRISON**, James; b. 1655 d. 25 July 1727; MP for Co. Tipperary 1707–13.

0975 **HARRISON**, John; b. *ante* 1747[9] d. 1801; MP for Doneraile 1788–90.

0976 **HARRISON**, Jones; b. 1768 d. 1 Sept. 1844; MP for Kildare B. 1796–7.

0977 *HARRISON**, Michael; b. 1669 d. Apr. [*ante* 5 May] 1709; MP for Lisburn 1703–9.

0978 **HARRISON**, William; b. *ante* 5 Oct. 1671[1] d. 3 June 1736; MP for Thomastown 1692–3, Bannow 1730–6.

0979 **HARTLEY**, Travers; b. 1723 d. 28 Mar. 1796; MP for Dublin city 1782–3–90.

0980 *HARTPOLE**, George; b. 21 Sept. 1710 d. 4 Dec. 1763 [writ not issued until 23 Jan. 1766]; MP for Portarlington 1761–3.

0981 *HARTSTONGE**, Sir Henry [3rd Bt]; b. *c.* 1725[10] d. 25 Mar. 1797; MP for Co. Limerick 1776–83–90.

0982 *HARTSTONGE**, Price [Pryce]; b. 1692 d. [*ante* 9] Feb. 1743/4; MP for Charleville 1727–44.

0983 *HARTSTONGE**, Standish; b. 1656 d. 31 May 1705; MP for Kilkenny city 1695–9, 1703–5.

0984 **HARTSTONGE**, Sir Standish [2nd Bt]; b. *c.* 1672[9] d. 20 July 1751; MP for Kilmallock 1695–9, Ratoath 1703–13, St Canice 1713–14, 1715–27.

0985 *HARVEY**, John; b. *ante* 1654[7] d. [?]1749[10]; MP for Wexford B. 1695–9.

0986 **HARWARD**, William; b. 1694 d. 8 July 1770; MP for Doneraile 1743–60, Lanesborough 1761–8–70.

0987 **HATCH**, John; b. 1722 d. [*ante* 26] Sept. 1797; MP for Swords 1769–76, 1783–90.

0988 **HATTON**, George; b. 1761 d. 1831; MP for Lisburn 1791–7–1800 [re-elected pp 1796] [HP].

0989 *HATTON**, Henry; b. *ante* 1679[7] d. 1735; MP for Wexford B. 1727–35.

0990 **HATTON**, Henry; b. 1760 d. 9 Nov. 1793; MP for Donegal B. 1783–90, Fethard [Wexford] 1793.

0991 **HAWLEY**, Hon. Henry; b. 1657 d. 17 July 1724; MP for Kinsale 1703–13–14, 1715–24.

0992 *HAYDOCK**, Josiah; b. *ante* 1638[9] d. June 1693; MP for Kilkenny city 1692–3.

0993 *HAYES**, John; b. *post* 1633[8] d. *c.* 1706[10]; MP for Thomastown 1692–3, Doneraile 1695–9 [HP].

0994 **HAYES**, Sir Samuel [1st Bt]; b. 1737 d. 21 July 1807; MP for Augher 1783–90.

0995 **HAYES**, Samuel; b. 1743 d. 28 Nov. 1795; MP for Wicklow B. 1783–90, Maryborough 1790–5.

0996 **HAYMAN**, John; b. 1664 d. 21 Aug. 1731; MP for Youghal 1703–13.

0997 *HEATLEY**, Conway; b. *c.* 1755[2] d. *c.* 1820[10]; MP for Enniscorthy 1783–90.

0998 **HELLEN**, Robert; b. 1725 d [*ante* 6] Aug. 1793; MP for Bannow 1768–76, Fethard [Wexford] 1776–9.

0999 **HELY-HUTCHINSON**, Hon. Christopher; b. 5 Apr. 1767 d. 26 Aug. 1826; MP for Taghmon 1795–6 [HP].

1000 **HELY-HUTCHINSON**, Hon. Francis; b. 26 Oct. 1759 d. 16 Dec. 1827; MP for TCD 1790–7, Naas 1797–1800 [re-elected pp 1800].

1001 **HELY-HUTCHINSON**, Rt Hon. John; b. 1723 d. 4 Sept. 1794; MP for Lanesborough 1759–60, Cork city 1761–8–76–83–90, Taghmon 1790–4.

1002 **HELY-HUTCHINSON**, Hon. John [1st B. Hutchinson, 2nd E. of Donoughmore]; b. 15 May 1757 d. 29 June 1832; MP for Lanesborough 1776–83, Taghmon 1789–90, Cork city 1790–7–1800 [HP].

1003 **HELY-HUTCHINSON**, Rt Hon. Richard [2nd B., 1st V. and E. of Donoughmore], b. 29 Jan. 1756 d. 22 Aug. 1825; MP for Sligo B. 1778–83, Taghmon 1783–8.

1004 **HENNIKER**, Hon. Sir Brydges Trecothic [1st Bt] b. 10 Nov. 1767 d. 3 July 1816; MP for Kildare B. 1797–1800.

1005 **HENRY**, Hugh; b. *c.* 1680[6] d. Dec. 1743; MP for Antrim B. 1713–14, 1715–27–43.

1006 *****HENRY**, Joseph; b. *c.* 1683 d. [*ante* 27 Aug] 1717; MP for Newtown Limavady 1715–17.

1007 **HENRY**, Joseph; b. 1727 d. 7 Nov. 1796; MP for Longford B. 1761–8, Kildare B. 1769–76.

1008 *****HERBERT**, Edward; b. 1727 d. 2 Mar. 1770; MP for Innistiogue 1749–60, Tralee 1761–8–70.

1009 **HERBERT**, Richard Townsend; b. 1755 d. 18 Dec. 1832; MP for Co. Kerry 1783–90, Clogher 1790–7, Granard Jan.–Aug. 1800.

1010 **HERON**, Rt Hon. Sir Richard [1st Bt]; b. 1726 d. 18 Jan. 1805; MP for Lisburn 1777–83.

1011 **HEWETSON**, Christopher; b. *ante* 1664[7] d. *c.* 1753 [will proved Mar. 1754], MP for Thomastown 1695–9.

1012 **HEWITT**, Hon. Joseph; b. 1754 d. 1 Apr. 1794; MP for Belfast 1784–90–1.

1013 **HICKMAN**, Robert; b. 1693 d. Aug. 1756; MP for Co. Clare 1745–56.

1014 *****HILL**, Arthur; b. 24 Mar. 1682/3 d. 6 Apr. 1704; MP for Carlingford 1703–4.

1015 **HILL** [HILL–TREVOR], Rt Hon. Arthur [1st B. Hill and V. Dungannon]; b. *c.* 1694[2] d. 30 Jan. 1771; MP for Hillsborough 1715–27, Co. Down 1727–60, 1761–6.

1016 **HILL**, Rt Hon. Arthur [2nd M. of Downshire]; b. 23 Feb. 1753 d. 7 Sept. 1801; MP for Co. Down 1776–83–90–3 [HP].

1017 **HILL**, Rt Hon. Sir George FitzGerald [2nd Bt]; b. 1 June 1763 d. 8 Mar. 1839; MP for Coleraine 1791–5, Londonderry city 1795–7–8 [HP].

1018 *****HILL**, Sir Hugh [1st Bt]; b. 1 Jan. 1727/8 d. 10 Feb. 1795; MP for Londonderry city 1768–76–83–90–5.

1019 **HILL**, Rt Hon. Michael; b. 7 Aug. 1672 d. [15 June–7 Aug.] 1699; MP for Hillsborough 1695–9.

1020 *****HILL**, Rowley; b. 1672 d. 24 Apr. 1739; MP for Ratoath 1734–9 [n.d.e. 1728].

1021 *****HILL**, Rt Hon. Trevor [1st B. Hill and V. Hillsborough]; b. 1693 d. 5 May 1742; MP for Hillsborough 1713–4, Co. Down 1715–17 [HP].

1022 **HOARE**, Bartholomew; b. 1754 d. 13 Dec. 1816; MP for Dingle 1795–7 [re-elected pp 1795].

1023 *****HOARE**, Edward; b. *c.* 1678[10] d. 20 July 1765; MP for Cork city 1710–13–14, 1715–27.

1024 **HOARE**, Sir Edward [2nd Bt]; b. 14 Mar. 1744/5 d. 30 Apr. 1814; MP for Carlow B. 1768–76, Banagher 1790–7, 1798–1800.

1025 *****HOARE**, Sir Joseph [1st Bt]; b. 25 Dec. 1713 d. 24 Dec. 1801; MP for Askeaton 1761–8–76–83–90–7–1800.

1026 **HOBART**, Rt Hon. Robert [4th E. of Buckinghamshire]; b. 6 May 1760 d. 4 Feb. 1816; MP for Portarlington 1784–90, Armagh city 1790–7 [HP].

1027 *****HOBSON**, John; b. *ante* 1739[7] d. Mar. 1803; MP for Innistiogue 1761–8.

1028 *****HOBSON**, John; b. 1763 d. Mar. 1803; MP for Tallow 1783–90, Castlemartyr 1792–7, Clonakilty 1797–1800 [re-elected pp 1799].

1029 *****HOEY**, William; b. *ante* 1644[1] d. [*ante* 27 Sept.] 1698; MP for [Naas 1665–6], Carysfort 1695–8.

1030 **HOEY**, William; b. 1699 d. 22 Aug. 1746; MP for Co. Wicklow 1725–7–46.

♦♦♦♦ **HOLMES**, Galbraith; b. 1706 d. Nov. 1763, [n.d.e. Banagher 1734–5].

1031 **HOLMES**, George; b. 1676 d. 29 Apr. 1734; MP for Banagher 1727–34.

1032 **HOLMES**, Peter; b. 1675 d. 8 Feb. 1731/2; MP for Banagher 1713–14, Athlone 1727–32.

1033 **HOLMES**, Peter; b. 1731 d. Dec. 1802; MP for Banagher 1761–8–76–83–90, Kilmallock 1790–7, Doneraile 1798–1800.

♦♦♦♦ **HOLMES**, Robert, b. 1706 d. 22 Jan. 1759 [n.d.e. Banagher Nov.–Dec. 1735].

1034 **HOPKINS**, Rt Hon. Edward; b. 1675 d. 17 Jan. 1735/6; MP for TCD 1721–7 [HP]

1035 **HOPKINS**, Sir Francis [1st Bt]; b. 2 Aug. 1756 d. 19 Sept. 1814; MP for Kilbeggan 1797–1800.

1036 **HORE**, Walter; b. *post* 1701[7] d. Feb. 1762; MP for Taghmon 1746–60.

1037 **HORE**, Walter; b. 1738 d. 26 Feb. 1795; MP for Taghmon 1761–8.

1038 **HORE**, William; b. c. 1679[2] d. 13 Apr. 1741; MP for Co. Wexford 1709–13.

1039 *****HORE**, William; b. c. 1699–1701[3] d. [ante 10] Mar. 1745/6; MP for Taghmon 1727–46.

1040 *****HOUGHTON**, George; b. c. 1670–2[8] d. [ante 5 Oct.] 1733; MP for Clonmines 1713–14, 1715–27, Fethard [Wexford] 1727–33.

♦♦♦♦ **HOWARD**, Hon. Charles [9th Earl of Suffolk (E)]; b. 1675 d. 28 Sept. 1733 [n.d.e. Carlow B. Sept.–Oct. 1703].

1041 **HOWARD**, Ld Frederick; b. Sept. 1684 d. 16 Mar. 1726/7; MP for Duleek 1716–27.

1042 **HOWARD**, Hugh; b. 1731 d. 27 Oct. 1799; MP for St Johnstown [Donegal] 1769–76–83, Athboy 1783–90–7–9.

1043 **HOWARD**, Hon. Hugh; b. 27 Jan. 1761 d. 3 Nov. 1840; MP for St Johnstown [Donegal] Jan.–Apr. 1790, 1790–7–1800 [re-elected pp 1796, 1799].

1044 **HOWARD**, Rt Hon. Ralph [1st B. Clonmore and V. Wicklow]; b. 29 Aug. 1727 d. 26 June 1789; MP for Co. Wicklow 1761–8–76.

1045 **HOWARD**, Robert, b. c. 1733[8] d. post 1783; MP for St Johnstown [Donegal] 1776–83.

1046 **HOWARD**, Hon. Robert [2nd V. Wicklow and 1st E. of Wicklow]; b. 7 Aug. 1757 d. 23 Oct. 1815; MP for St Johnstown [Donegal] 1783–9.

1047 **HOWARD**, William; b. c. 1680 d. 30 Dec. 1727; MP for Dublin city Oct.–Dec. 1727.

1048 **HUGHES**, Samuel; b. c. 1643[10] d. 1694; MP for Cashel 1692–3.

1049 **HULL**, Sir Richard [Kt]; b. 1641 d. 1693; MP for Castlemartyr 1692–3.

1050 **HULL**, Richard; b. ante 25 Sept. 1708[1] d. 21 June 1759; MP for Carysfort 1728–59.

1051 **HULL** [TONSON], William [1st B. Riversdale]; b. 3 May 1724 d. 4 Dec. 1787; MP for Tuam 1768–76, Rathcormack 1776–83.

1052 **HUME**, Rt Hon. Sir Gustavus [3rd Bt]; b. c. 1670[10] d. 31 Oct. 1731; MP for Co. Fermanagh 1713–14, 1715–27–31.

1053 **HUME**, William; b. 1742 d. 8 Oct. 1798; MP for Co. Wicklow 1790–7–8.

1054 *****HUME**, William Hoare; b. 3 Feb 1772 d. 5 Nov. 1815; MP for Co. Wicklow 1799–1800 [HP].

1055 *****HUNT**, Edward; b. c. 1738–40[4] d. c. 1802[10]; MP for Bangor 1778–83–90.

1056 **HUNT**, Raphael; b. ante 5 Oct. 1671[1] d. 1705; MP for Athy 1692–3.

1057 **HUNT**, Sir Vere [1st Bt]; b. 1761 d. 11 Aug. 1818; MP for Askeaton 1798–1800.

1058 **HUSSEY**, Dudley; b. c. 1741–3[3] d. 17 [bur. 19] Nov. 1785; MP for Taghmon 1783–5.

1059 **HUSSEY** [HUSSEY-BURGH], Rt Hon. Walter; b. 23 Aug. 1742 d. 29 Sept. 1783; MP for Athy 1769–76, TCD 1776–82.

1060 **HUTCHINSON**, Sir Francis [1st Bt]; b. 1726 d. 18 Dec. 1807; MP for Jamestown 1783–90.

1061 **HYDE**, Arthur; b. ante 1674[7] d. 6 Oct. 1720; MP for Tralee 1703–13, Midleton 1713–14, Youghal 1715–20.

1062 **HYDE**, Arthur; b. 1697 d. 16 Dec. 1772; MP for Youghal 1721–7, Co. Cork 1747–60.

1063 *****HYDE**, Arthur; b. 1720 d. 31 Dec. 1801; MP for Youghal 1758–60.

1064 *****HYDE**, John; b. 1738 d. post 10 Apr. 1799[10]; MP for Co. Carlow 1767–8, Co. Cork 1768–76.

1065 **INGOLDSBY**, Rt Hon. Sir Henry [1st Bt]; b. 1622 d. Mar. 1701; MP for Co. Clare [1661–6, 1689], 1695–9.

1066 **INGOLDSBY**, Henry; b. ante 25 Nov. 1692[1] d. [31] July 1731; MP for Limerick city 1713–14, 1727–31.

1067 **INGOLDSBY**, Rt Hon. Richard; b. ante 1651[5] d. 29 Jan. 1712; MP for Limerick city 1703–12.

1068 **IRVINE**, Henry; b. 1773 d. post 23 Feb. 1811[6]; MP for Tulsk 1797–1800.

1069 **IRVINE**, William; b. 15 July 1734 d. May 1814; MP for Ratoath 1769–76, 1790–7.

1070 *****IVERS** [alias IEVERS], John; b. c. 1650[10] d. [bur. 4] Dec. 1729; MP for Co. Clare 1715–27.

1071 **IVEY** [alias IVIE], Joseph; b. ante 5 Oct. 1671 d. [bur. 2] Sept. 1710; MP for Co. Waterford 1692–3.

1072 *****IVORY**, Sir John [Kt]; b. 1654 d. 24 Feb. 1694/5; MP for Co. Wexford 1692–3.

1073 *IRWIN [alias ERWIN or IRVINE], Christopher; b. c. 1642[10] d. 9 May 1714; MP for Co. Fermanagh 1695–9, 1703–13.

1074 *JACKSON, Sir George [1st Bt [UK]]; b. 1770 d. 1846; MP for Coleraine 1789–Apr. 1790, 1790–6, Randalstown 1797–1800.

1075 JACKSON, George; b. 1761 d. 1805; MP for Co. Mayo 1797–1800 [HP].

1076 JACKSON, Rt Hon. Richard; b. c. 1729[2] d. [23] Oct. 1789; MP for Coleraine 1751–60, 1761–8–76–83–9.

1077 JACKSON, Samuel; b. ante 27 Aug. 1674[1] d. 19 Jan. 1706; MP for Coleraine 1695–9.

1078 JACKSON, Thomas; b. 1680 d. 24 Mar. 1751; MP for Coleraine 1728–51.

1079 *JACKSON, William; b. 1660 d. 1712; MP for Co. Londonderry 1697–9.

1080 *JACOB, Matthew; b. ante 1655[10] d. 1740; MP for Fethard [Tipperary] 1695–9, 1703–13.

1081 *JACOB, Matthew; b. c. 1691–3[3] d. [ante 17] Jan. 1764; MP for Fethard [Tipperary] 1727–60.

1082 JEFFEREYES [alias JEFFEREYS or JEFFREYS], James St John; b. 1734 d. 14 Sept. 1780; MP for Midleton 1758–60, 1761–8–76, Randalstown 1776–80.

1083 JEFFREYS [alias JEFFEREYS], Sir James [Kt]; b. ante 1650[9] d. Nov. 1719; MP for Lismore 1703–13–4.

1084 JEPHSON, Anthony; b. c. 1688–9[8] d. 28 Dec 1755; MP for Mallow 1713–14, 1715–27–55.

1085 JEPHSON, Anthony; b. post 1748[7] d. [bur. 22] June 1794; MP for Mallow 1781–3.

1086 JEPHSON, Denham; b. c. 1721[2] d. 6 Apr. 1781; MP for Mallow 1756–60, 1761–8–76–81.

1087 *JEPHSON, Denham; b. 1748 d. 9 May 1813; MP for Mallow 1768–76–83–90–7–1800 [HP].

1088 JEPHSON, John; b. c. 1638[8] d. Sept. 1693; MP for Mallow 1692–3.

1089 *JEPHSON, John; b. 1652 d. [ante 6] Feb. 1723/4; MP for Blessington 1703–13–14, 1715–24.

1090 JEPHSON, Sir Richard Mountney [1st Bt]; b. 1 May 1765 d. 1825; MP for Charlemont 1794–7–8.

1091 JEPHSON, Robert; b. 1737 d. 31 May 1803; MP for St Johnstown [Donegal] 1773–6, Old Leighlin 1777–83, Granard 1783–90.

1092 *JEPHSON, William; b. 1665 d. Dec. 1698; MP for Mallow 1695–8.

1093 *JEPHSON, William; b. ante 1686[5] d. Apr. 1716; MP for Mallow 1713–14, 1715–16.

1094 JEPHSON, William; b. c. 1722–9[8] d. June 1779; MP for Mallow 1761–8.

1095 JERVIS, Sir Humphrey [Kt]; b. ante 1650[6] d. 1708; MP for Lanesborough 1692–3.

1096 JOCELYN, Hon. George; b. [bapt. 21 July] 1762 d. 11 Mar. 1798; MP for Dundalk 1783–90–7–8 [re-elected pp 1796].

1097 JOCELYN, Hon. John; b. [bapt. 30 July] 1768 d. 21 Jan. 1828; MP for Dundalk 1797–1800.

1098 JOCELYN, Rt Hon. Robert [1st B. Newport and V. Jocelyn]; b. c. 1688[3] d. 3 Dec. 1756; MP for Granard 1725–7, Newtown[ards] 1727–39.

1099 *JOCELYN, Rt Hon. Robert [2nd V. Jocelyn and 1st E. of Roden]; b. [31] July 1721 d. 21 June 1797; MP for Old Leighlin 1745–56.

1100 JOCELYN, Rt Hon. Robert [2nd E. of Roden]; b. 26 Oct. 1756 d. 29 June 1820; MP for Dundalk 1783–90–7.

1101 JOHNSON, Robert; b. c. 1657[2] d. 1730; MP for Trim 1697–9, Athboy 1703–5.

1102 *JOHNSON, Robert; b. c. 1681–4[5] d. [ante 12 Sept.] 1721; MP for Athboy 1705–13, Harristown 1715–21.

1103 JOHNSON, Robert; b. 1745 d. 1833; MP for Hillsborough 1788–90–7–1800, Philipstown Jan.–Aug. 1800.

1104 JOHNSON, William; b. 1761 d. 1845; MP for Roscommon B. 1799–1800.

1105 JOHNSTON, Arthur; b. 1721 d. 30 Dec. 1814; MP for Killyleagh 1769–76.

1106 JOHNSTON, Baptist; b. post 1694[8] d. 14 Apr. 1753; MP for Monaghan B. 1747–53.

1107 *JOHNSTON, George; b. c. 1692–4[3] d. [ante 18] Mar. 1730; MP for Portarlington 1727–30.

1108 JOHNSTON [JOHNSTON-WALSH], Sir John Allen [1st Bt]; b. [bapt. 19 Sept.] 1744 d. Dec. 1831; MP for Baltinglass 1784–90.

1109 *JOHNSTON, Richard; b. *c.* 1641[10] d. 1706; MP for Clogher 1695–9.

1110 *JOHNSTON, Sir Richard [1st Bt]; b. 1 Aug. 1743 d. 22 Apr. 1795; MP for Kilbeggan 1776–83, Blessington 1783–90–5.

1111 JONES, Edmond; b. *ante* 27 Aug. 1674[1] d. *c.* 1700; MP for Carlow B. 1695–9.

1112 *JONES, Edward; b. *c.* 1637[6] d. [Aug.–21 Oct.] 1695; MP for Old Leighlin 1692–3, 1695.

1113 JONES, Edward; b. 1674 d. Apr. 1735; MP for New Ross 1713–14, Wexford B. 1715–27–35.

1114 JONES, Nicholas; b. *ante* 1643[6] d. [bur. 28] Oct. 1695; MP for Naas 1692–3.

1115 JONES, Richard; b. 1662 d. 2 Feb. 1729; MP for Donegal B. 1703–13.

1116 JONES, Richard; b. 1723 d. May 1790; MP for Killybegs 1761–8, Newtown Limavady 1768–76.

1117 JONES, Theophilus; b. 2 Sept. 1666 d. 14 Mar. 1741/2; MP for Sligo B. 1692–3, Co. Leitrim 1695–9, 1703–13–14, 1715–27–42.

1118 JONES, Rt Hon. Theophilus; b. 1729 d. 8 Dec. 1811; MP for Co. Leitrim 1761–8, 1776–83, 1790–7–1800, Coleraine 1769–76, Monaghan B. 1783–90 [HP].

1119 JONES, Thomas; b. 1680 d. [14] July 1716; MP for Kildare B. 1703–13–14.

1120 *JONES, Thomas; b. [?]1658 d. [?]22 July 1733; MP for Trim 1713–14.

1121 JONES, Walter; b. 29 Dec. 1754 d. 1839; MP for Coleraine 1798–1800 [HP].

1122 *JONES, William; b. *c.*1657–9[3] d. [*ante* 29 Aug.] 1723; MP for Athlone 1703–13–14, 1715–23.

1123 JONES, William Todd; b. [22] Dec. 1757 d. 17 Feb. 1818; MP for Lisburn 1783–90.

1124 JONES-AGNEW, Edward; b. 1767 d. 1833; MP for Co. Antrim 1792–7.

1125 JONES-NEVILL, Arthur; b. *c.* 1712[2] d. 24 Sept. 1771; MP for Co. Wexford 1751–3 [expelled 23 Nov. 1753], Wexford B. 1761–8–71.

1126 *KAVANAGH, Bryan; b. 1763 d. [?*ante* Aug.] 1797[10]; MP for Kilkenny city 1796–7.

1127 KAVANAGH, Thomas; b. 10 Mar. 1767 d. 20 Jan. 1837; MP for Kilkenny city 1797–9 [HP].

1128 KEANE, Sir John [1st Bt]; b. 21 May 1757 d. 19 Apr. 1829; MP for Bangor 1791–7, Youghal 1797–1800 [HP].

1129 *KEARNEY, James; b. 1729 d. 1810; MP for Kinsale 1768–76–83–90–7.

1130 KEARNEY, James; b. *ante* 1753[7] d. 1 June 1812; MP for Thomastown 1797–1800.

1131 *KEATING, John; b. *ante* 1674[10] d. [*ante* 27 Aug.] 1717; MP for Trim 1715–17.

1132 KEATING, Maurice; b. 1664 d. 4 May 1727; MP for Athy 1695–9, 1703–13–14, 1715–27.

1133 KEATING, Maurice; b. Feb. 1690 d. 17 Nov. 1769; MP for Kildare B. 1725–7, 1768–9, Co. Kildare 1727–60, Naas 1761–8.

1134 KEATING, Maurice; b. 1715 d. 30 May 1777; MP for Harristown 1776–7.

1135 KEATING, Maurice Bagenal St Leger; b. *c.* 1758–62[5] d. 1835; MP for Co. Kildare 1790–7–1800 [HP].

1136 KEATING, Michael; b. *ante* 1741[7] d. [bur. 29] Sept. 1781; MP for Harristown 1776–81.

1137 *KEIGHTLEY, Rt Hon. Thomas; b. *c.* 1650[10] d. 19 Jan. 1718/9; MP for Innistiogue 1695–9, Co. Kildare 1703–13–14.

1138 KELLER, William; b. *ante* 28 Jan. 1772[1] d. Oct. 1801; MP for Donegal B. 1793–7.

1139 KELLY, Dennis; b. *ante* 1684[9] d. [*post* Mar.–*ante* Dec.] 1757; MP for Fore 1713–14.

1140 *KELLY, John; b. 1774 d. *c.* 1813[10]; MP for Lanesborough 1800.

1141 KELLY, Joseph; b. 1673 d. 21 May 1713; MP for Doneraile 1705–13.

1142 KELLY, Joseph; b. [*ante* 9] May 1719 d. 8 May 1749; MP for Blessington 1748–9.

1143 *KELLY, Rt Hon. Thomas; b. 1724 d. [bur. 7] June 1809; MP for Portarlington 1783–4.

1144 KEMMIS, Henry; b. 19 Sept. 1776 d. 18 Mar. 1857; MP for Tralee 1798–1800.

1145 KENNEDY, David; b. *ante* 1689[6] d. *post* 1713; MP for Roscommon B. 1711–13.

1146 *KENNEDY, John; b. *ante* 1692[1] d. 25 Mar. 1724; MP for St Johnstown [Longford] 1713–14.

1147 **KER**, David; b. 1747 d. 12 Dec. 1811; MP for Blessington 1796–7.

1148 *****KILPATRICK**, John; b. *c.* 1755[2] d. Dec. 1779; MP for Granard 1776–9.

1149 **KING**, Charles; b. 1737 d. [*ante* 12] Nov. 1799; MP for Swords 1776–83, Belturbet 1797–9.

1150 **KING**, Rt Hon. Sir Edward [5th Bt, 1st B.,V. and E. of Kingston]; b. 29 Mar. 1726 d. 13 Nov. 1797; MP for Boyle 1749–60, Co. Sligo 1761–4.

1151 **KING**, Edward; b. *c.* 1754–6[3] d. Nov. 1793; MP for Carrick 1781–83–90–3.

1152 *****KING**, George; b. [bapt. 23 Apr.] 1689[10] d. July 1722; MP for Co. Limerick 1713–14, Kilmallock 1715–22.

1153 **KING**, Hon. George [3rd E. of Kingston]; b. 28 Apr. 1771 d. 18 Oct. 1839; MP for Co. Roscommon 1797–9.

1154 **KING**, Gilbert; b. 15 June 1658 d. [bur. 16] June 1721; MP for Jamestown 1709–13–14, 1715–21.

1155 **KING**, Gilbert; b. *c.* 1707–12[7] d. 23 Aug. 1788; MP for Jamestown 1737–60.

1156 *****KING**, Sir Gilbert [1st Bt]; b. [bapt. 3 July] 1739 d. 8 Aug. 1818; MP for Jamestown 1797–1800.

1157 **KING**, Rt Hon. Sir Henry [3rd Bt]; b. 1680 d. 1 Jan. 1740/1; MP for Boyle 1707–13–14, 1715–27, Co. Roscommon 1727–40/1.

1158 **KING**, Rt Hon. Henry; b. 18 Feb. 1733 d. 23 Feb. 1820/1; MP for Boyle 1761–8–76–83–90–7–1800 [re-elected pp 1800].

1159 **KING**, Sir John [2nd Bt]; b. 1673 d. 19 Mar. 1720/1; MP for Boyle 1695–9, 1703–13–14, Co. Roscommon 1715–20.

1160 **KING**, John; b. 1680 d. [bur. 19] Jan. 1737; MP for Jamestown 1703–13–14, 1721–7, 1727–37.

1161 **KING**, John; b. 1760 d. 1821; MP for Jamestown 1797–1800.

1162 **KING**, John; b. *ante* 29 Mar. 1779[1] d. 12 Sept. 1810; MP for Clogher Mar.–Aug. 1800.

1163 *****KING**, Nathaniel; b. [bapt. 4 Sept.] 1670 d. 1 Oct. 1696; MP for Wicklow B. 1692–3, 1695–6.

1164 **KING**, Rt Hon. Sir Robert [1st Bt]; b. *c.* 1625[2] d. [16 Feb.–3 Mar.] 1706/7; MP for [Ballyshannon 1661–6], Co. Roscommon 1692–3, 1695–9, Boyle 1703–7.

1165 *****KING**, Robert; b. *ante* 4 Oct. 1677[1] d. Sept. [bur. 1 Oct.] 1711; MP for Lifford 1698–9, 1709–11.

1166 **KING**, Sir Robert [4th Bt, 1st B. Kingsborough]; b. [bapt. 18 Feb.] 1723/4 d. 22 May 1755; MP for Boyle 1744–8.

1167 **KING**, Hon. Robert [2nd E. of Kingston]; b. 1754 d. 10 Apr. 1799; MP for Boyle 1776–83, Co. Cork 1783–90, 1791–7, July–Nov. 1797.

1168 **KING**, Hon. Robert Edward [1st B. Erris and V. Lorton]; b. 12 Aug. 1773 d. 20 Nov. 1854; MP for Jamestown 1796–7, Boyle 1798–1800 [re-elected pp 1800].

1169 *****KING**, Sir William [Kt]; b. *ante* 1635[1] d. 4 Sept. 1706; MP for Co. Limerick [1661–6], 1692–3, 1695–9.

1170 **KINGSMAN**, William Long; b. 1748 d. 9 Aug. 1793; MP for Granard 1780–3.

1171 *****KIRWAN**, Edward; b. *ante* 17 Oct. 1748[1] d. 1807; MP for Castlebar 1768–76.

1172 **KNAPP**, Edmond; b. 1659 d. 3 Mar. 1747; MP for Cork city 1715–27.

1173 **KNATCHBULL**, Sir Edward [7th Bt]; b. 12 Dec. 1704 d. [23] Nov. 1789; MP for Armagh city 1727–60.

1174 **KNOTT**, William; b. 1766 d. Mar. 1822; MP for Duleek 1790–6, Taghmon 1797–1800.

1175 **KNOX**, Andrew; b. 1709 d. 1774; MP for Co. Donegal 1743–60, 1761–8.

1176 **KNOX**, Andrew; b. 1766 d. 1840; MP for Strabane 1798–1800.

1177 **KNOX**, Hon. Charles; b. 10 Feb. 1770 d. 30 Jan. 1825; MP for Dungannon 1797–9.

1178 **KNOX**, Francis; b. 1754 d. 12 Apr. 1821; MP for Philipstown 1797–1800.

1179 **KNOX**, George; b. *ante* 1695[6] d. Apr. 1741; MP for Co. Donegal 1735–41.

1180 **KNOX**, Rt Hon. George; b. 14 Jan. 1765 d. 13 June 1827; MP for Dungannon 1790–7, TCD 1797–1800 [HP].

1181 KNOX [KNOX-GORE], James; b. 25 Mar. 1775 d. 21 Oct. 1818; MP for Taghmon 1797–1800.

1182 *KNOX, John; b. 1728 d. [ante 1 Aug.] 1775; MP for Donegal B. 1761–8, Castlebar 1768–74.

1183 *KNOX, John; b. 1740 d. 2 May 1791[10]; MP for Dungannon 1769–76.

1184 *KNOX, Hon. John; b. 1758 d. Nov. 1800; MP for Killybegs 1777–83, Dungannon 1790–4.

1185 *KNOX, Rt Hon. Thomas; b. c. 1640[10] d. 11 May 1728; MP for Newtown[ards] 1692–3, Dungannon 1695–9, 1703–13–14, 1715–27.

1186 KNOX, Thomas; b. 1694 d. 25 Mar. 1769; MP for Dungannon 1731–60, 1761–8–9.

1187 *KNOX, Thomas [1st B. Welles and V. Northland]; b. 29 Apr. 1729 d. 5 Nov. 1818; MP for Dungannon 1755–60, 1761–8–76–81.

1188 KNOX, Hon. Thomas [2nd V. Northland and 1st E. of Ranfurly]; b. 5 Aug. 1754 d. 26 Apr. 1840; MP for Carlingford 1776–83, Dungannon 1783–90, Co. Tyrone 1790–7 [HP].

1189 LAKE, Gerard [1st B. and V. Lake]; b. 27 July 1744 d. 20 Feb. 1808; MP for Armagh B. 1799–1800 [HP].

1190 LAMBART, Charles; b. c. 1671–4[7] d. 1 Sept. 1753; MP for Kilbeggan 1695–9, 1703–13, 1715–27–53, Cavan B. 1713–14.

1191 LAMBART, Charles; b. Oct. 1703 d. Dec. 1740; MP for Kilbeggan 1727–40.

1192 LAMBART, Charles; b. [bapt. 15 Sept.] 1746 d. Mar. 1785; MP for Kilbeggan 1768–76–83.

1193 LAMBART, Gustavus; b. c. 1704–5[8] d. 23 June 1782; MP for Kilbeggan 1741–60, 1761–8–76.

1194 LAMBART, Gustavus; b. 16 Sept. 1772 d. 22 Sept. 1850; MP for Kilbeggan 1797–1800.

1195 LAMBART, Hamilton; b. 1712[8] d. 1789; MP for Kilbeggan 1753–60.

1196 LAMBART, Hon. Oliver; b. c. 1631–9[7] d. 13 Dec. 1700; MP for Kilbeggan [1661–6], 1692–3, 1695–9.

1197 LAMBERT, Patrick; b. ante 1660[6] d. post 1693; MP for Taghmon 1692–3.

1198 LANGFORD, Sir Arthur [2nd Bt]; b. c. 1652[2] d. 29 Mar. 1716; MP for Duleek 1692–3, Coleraine 1695–9, 1703–13, Co. Antrim 1715–16.

1199 LANGFORD, Sir Henry [3rd Bt]; b. c. 1655–7[3] d. 1725; MP for St Johnstown [Donegal] 1695–9.

1200 *LANGRISHE, Rt Hon. Sir Hercules [1st Bt]; b. 1729 d. 1 Feb. 1811; MP for Knocktopher 1761–8–76–83–90–7–1800.

1201 LANGRISHE, Sir Robert [2nd Bt]; b. [bapt. 25 Oct.] 1756 d. 25 May 1835; MP for Knocktopher 1783–90–6.

1202 LANGSTON, Francis; b. ante 1660[5] d. 6 Apr. 1723; MP for Baltimore 1709–13.

1203 LA TOUCHE, Rt Hon. David; b. 29 Aug. 1729 d. 1 Aug. 1817; MP for Dundalk 1761–8, Longford B. 1768–76–83, Belturbet 1783–90, Newcastle 1790–7–1800.

1204 *LA TOUCHE, David; b. 9 May 1768 d. 15 Mar. 1816; MP for Newcastle 1790–7, 1798–1800 [HP].

♦♦♦♦ LA TOUCHE, James Digges, b. 1707 d. 20 June 1763 [n.d.e. Dublin city Nov.–Dec. 1749].

1205 LA TOUCHE, John; b. 21 Aug. 1732 d. 3 Feb. 1810; MP for Newcastle 1783–90, Newtown[ards] 1790–6, Harristown Feb.–July 1797, Co. Kildare 1797–1800 [HP].

1206 LA TOUCHE, John; b. [ante Apr.] 1775 d. 30 Jan. 1820; MP for Newtown[ards] 1796–7, Harristown 1797–1800.

1207 LA TOUCHE, Peter; b. 1733 d. Nov. 1828; MP for Co. Leitrim 1783–90, 1796–7.

1208 LA TOUCHE, Robert; b. Oct. 1773 d. 19 May 1844; MP for Harristown 1794–7–1800 [HP].

1209 LAWLESS, Sir Nicholas [1st Bt, 1st B. Cloncurry]; b. 3 Dec. 1733 d. 28 Aug. 1799; MP for Lifford 1776–83–9.

1210 *LECKY, William; b. 1748 d. 16 May 1825; MP for Londonderry city 1790–7.

1211 LEE, Edward; b. 1761 d. Sept. 1837; MP for Dungarvan 1798–1800 [HP].

1212 LEESON, Rt Hon. Joseph [1st B., V. Russborough and E. of Milltown]; b. 11 Mar. 1711 d. 22 Oct. 1783; MP for Rathcormack 1743–56.

1213 *LEESON, Hon. Joseph [2nd E. of Milltown]; b. 1730 d. 27 Nov. 1801; MP for Thomastown 1757–60.

1214 **LE HUNT**, Richard; b. 1685 d. June 1747; MP for Enniscorthy 1713–14, 1715–27–47.

1215 **LE HUNT**, Richard; b. 1728 d. [1] Feb. 1783; MP for Wexford B. 1768–76–83.

1216 **LE HUNT**, Thomas; b. *c.* 1699[2] d. 21 Feb. 1775; MP for Wexford B. 1735–60, 1761–8, Newtown[ards] 1768–75.

1217 **LEIGH**, Francis; b. 1706 d. 2 Dec. 1778; MP for Drogheda 1741–60, 1761–8–76.

1218 **LEIGH**, Francis; b. [bapt. 18 Jan.] 1758 d. 1839; MP for Wexford B. 1785–90–7, 1800 [HP].

1219 ***LEIGH**, John; b. *c.* 1665[2] d. 1733; MP for Drogheda Aug.–17 Sept. 1717 [expelled].

1220 **LEIGH**, John; b. *c.* 1703–6[7] d. 16 Aug. 1758; MP for New Ross 1727–58.

1221 **LEIGH**, John; b. 1732 d. 1810; MP for Enniskillen 1776–83.

1222 **LEIGH**, Robert; b. 1729 d. 1802; MP for New Ross 1759–60, 1761–8–76–83–90–7–1800 [HP].

1223 **LENOX**, James; b. 1652 d. 4 Aug. 1723; MP for Londonderry city 1703–13.

1224 **LESLIE**, Charles Powell; b. 20 Jan. 1738/9 d. 24 July 1800; MP for Hillsborough 1771–6, Co. Monaghan 1783–90–7–1800.

1225 **LESLIE**, Sir Edward [1st Bt]; b. 1744 d. 21 Nov. 1818; MP for Old Leighlin 1787–90.

1226 **LESLIE**, William; b. *ante* 1660[7] d. 27 Dec. 1698; MP for Coleraine 1692–3.

1227 **LESLIE–CORRY**, Edmond; b. 23 Nov. 1690 d. [bur. 28] Nov. 1764; MP for Newtown Limavady 1742–60, 1761–4.

1228 **LESTRANGE**, Henry; b. *ante* 26 Nov. 1714[1] d. 12 May 1774; MP for Banagher 1735–60.

1229 **LESTRANGE**, Thomas; b. 1645 d. 1732; MP for Banagher [1666] 1692–3, 1695–9, 1703–13, 1715–27.

1230 **LEVINGE**, Rt Hon. Sir Richard [1st Bt]; b. 2 May 1656 d. 13 July 1724; MP for Blessington 1692–3, Longford B. 1698–9, 1703–13, Kilkenny city 1713–14 [HP].

1231 **LEVINGE**, Sir Richard [2nd Bt]; b. 1685 d. 24 Feb. 1747/8; MP for Co. Westmeath 1723–7, Blessington 1727–48.

1232 **LEVINGE**, Richard; b. 1724 d. [*ante* 17] Apr. 1783; MP for Duleek 1768–76.

1233 **LIDDELL**, Rt Hon. Richard; b. *c.* 1694[2] d. 22 June 1746; MP for Jamestown 1745–6 [HP].

1234 ***LIGHTBOURNE**, Stafford; b. 1662 d. [*ante* 1 May] 1697; MP for Trim 1692–3, 1695–7.

1235 **LIGHTON**, Sir Thomas [1st Bt]; b. *ante* 1756[7] d. 27 Apr. 1805; MP for Tuam 1790–7, Carlingford 1798–1800.

1236 **LILL**, Godfrey; b. 1719 d. Sept. 1783; MP for Fore 1761–8, Baltinglass 1768–74.

1237 **LINDSAY**, Robert; b. 1679 d. 1742; MP for Co. Tyrone 1729–33.

1238 **LINDSAY**, Robert; b. 11 Apr. 1747 d. 8 Jan. 1832; MP for Dundalk 1781–3.

1239 **LINDSAY**, Thomas; b. *ante* 1736[7] d. 1814; MP for Castlebar 1798–1800.

1240 **LINDSAY**, Thomas; b. [bapt. 15 Apr.] 1759 d. 1811; MP for Castlebar 1797–1800 [re-elected pp 1798].

1241 **LLOYD**, Andrew; b. *ante* 25 Nov. 1692[1] d. *post* 1714; MP for Charlemont 1713–14.

1242 **LLOYD**, John; b. *c.* 1737–9[3] d. 1822; MP for King's Co. 1768–76–83–90, Innistiogue 1790–7.

1243 **LLOYD**, Thomas; b. 1716 d. 1805; MP for Tralee 1777–83.

1244 **LLOYD**, Trevor; b. 1701 d. 12 Dec. 1747; MP for King's Co. 1741–7.

1245 **LOCKE**, Richard; b. *ante* 1653[7] d. 1720; MP for Athy 1692–3, 1695–9, Kildare B. 1703–13–14.

1246 **LOFTUS**, Arthur; b. 12 Dec. 1724 d. May 1781; MP for Fethard [Wexford] 1768–76, Clonmines 1776–81.

1247 **LOFTUS**, Dudley; b. 1619 d. June 1695; MP for [Naas 1642–8, Bannow 1661–6], Fethard [Wexford] 1692–3.

1248 **LOFTUS**, Sir Edward [1st Bt]; b. *c.* 1742[2] d. [17] May 1818; MP for Jamestown 1761–8.

1249 **LOFTUS**, Henry; b. 31 Dec. 1636 d. 1716; MP for Clonmines 1692–3, 1695–9.

1250 **LOFTUS**, Rt Hon. Henry [4th V. Ely and 1st E. of Ely]; b. 18 Nov. 1709 d. 8 May 1783; MP for Bannow 1747–60, 1761–8, Co. Wexford 1768–9.

1251 **LOFTUS**, Henry; b.1725 d. Dec. 1792; MP for Clonmines 1768–76, Bannow 1776–83–90.

1252 **LOFTUS**, Rt Hon. John [2nd M. of Ely]; b. 15 Feb. 1770 d. 26 Sept. 1845; MP for Co. Wexford 1791–7–1800 [re-elected pp 1800] [HP].

1253 **LOFTUS**, Sir Nicholas [Kt]; b. 1635 d. 5 Apr. 1708; MP for Fethard [Wexford] [1661–6], 1695–9.

1254 **LOFTUS**, Rt Hon. Nicholas [1st B. and V. Loftus]; b. 1687 d. 31 Dec. 1763; MP for Fethard [Wexford] 1710–13, Clonmines 1713–14, Co. Wexford 1715–27–51.

1255 **LOFTUS** [*alias* LOFTUS-HUME], Rt Hon. Nicholas [2nd V. Loftus, 1st E. of Ely]; b. 1714 d. 31 Oct. 1766; MP for Bannow 1737–60, Fethard [Wexford] 1761–3.

1256 **LOFTUS-HUME** [*alias* HUME-LOFTUS], Hon. Nicholas [2nd E. of Ely]; b. 11 Sept. 1738 d. 12 Nov. 1769; MP for Fethard [Wexford] 1759–60, 1761–7.

1257 **LOFTUS**, Thomas; b. 1705 d. 15 Jan. 1768; MP for Clonmines 1727–60.

1258 **LOFTUS**, Thomas; b. 1750 d. 28 Jan. 1792; MP for Clonmines 1781–3–90, Fethard [Wexford] 1790–2.

1259 **LOFTUS**, William; b. 1752 d. 15 June 1831; MP for Fethard [Wexford] 1796–7, Bannow 1797–1800 [HP].

1260 **LONGFIELD**, John; b. 5 July 1741 d. 18 Dec. 1815; MP for Mallow 1790–7–1800 [HP].

1261 **LONGFIELD**, John; b. May 1767 d. 18 Oct. 1842; MP for Philipstown 1795–7, Ballynakill 1797–1800.

1262 **LONGFIELD**, Mountifort; b. 22 Aug. 1746 d. 8 June 1819; MP for Enniscorthy 1776–83, 1783–90–7, Cork city 1797–1800 [re-elected pp 1800] [HP].

1263 **LONGFIELD**, Rt Hon. Richard [1st B. and V. Longueville]; b. 9 Oct. 1734 d. 23 May 1811; MP for Charleville 1761–8, Clonakilty 1768–76, Cork City 1776–83, 1790–6, Baltimore 1783–90.

1264 **LONGFIELD**, Robert; b. [*ante* 13] Aug. 1756 d. [*c.* 13] Aug. 1778; MP for Donegal B. 1777–8.

1265 **LOVETT**, John; b. *ante* 3 Oct. 1677[1] d. 1710; MP for Philipstown 1698–9.

1266 ***LOWE**, Samuel; b. *c.* 1714[2] d. [*ante* 22 Oct.] 1765; MP for Clogher 1761–5.

1267 **LOWRY**, Robert; b. 3 Feb. 1702/3 d. 21 Aug. 1764; MP for Strabane 1761–4.

1268 **LOWRY**[-CORRY], Galbraith; b. 11 July 1706 d. 28 Dec. 1769; MP for Co. Tyrone 1748–60, 1761–8.

1269 **LOWRY-CORRY**, Armar [1st B., V. and E. Belmore]; b. 7 Apr. 1740 d. 2 Feb. 1802; MP for Co. Tyrone 1768–76–81.

1270 **LOWRY-CORRY**, Hon. Somerset [2nd E. Belmore]; b. 11 July 1774 d. 18 Apr. 1841; MP for Co. Tyrone 1797–1800 [HP].

1271 ***LOWTHER**, George; b. *ante* 6 June 1684[1] d. [*ante* 13] June 1716; MP for Ratoath 1705–13–14, 1715–16.

1272 **LOWTHER**, George; b. 1739 d. 18 Aug. 1784; MP for Ratoath 1761–8, Ardee 1768–76, Newtown[ards] 1783–4.

1273 **LOWTHER**, Gorges; b. 5 Nov. 1713 d. 21 Feb. 1792; MP for Ratoath 1739–60, Co. Meath 1761–8–76–83–90–2.

1274 **LOWTHER**, Gorges; b. [*ante* 2 July] 1769 d. 1854; MP for Ratoath 1790–7–8.

1275 **LOWTHER-CROFTON**, Sir Marcus [1st Bt]; b. *c.* 1716[2] d. 17 Jan. 1784; MP for Ratoath 1753–60, 1769–76, Roscommon B. 1761–8.

1276 **LUCAS**, Charles, b. 26 Sept. 1713 d. 4 Nov. 1771; MP for Dublin city 1761–8–71.

1277 **LUCAS**, Edward; b. 1723 d. Aug. 1775; MP for Co. Monaghan 1761–8–75.

♦♦♦ **LUCAS**, Francis, b. 1646 d. 29 Mar. 1705 [n.d.e. Co. Monaghan Aug.–Sept. 1795].

1278 **LUCAS**, Francis; b. 1669 d. May 1746; MP for Monaghan B. 1713–14, 1715–27–46.

1279 **LUDFORD**, John; b. 18 May 1707 d. 1775; MP for Belfast 1761–8.

1280 **LUDLOW**, Peter; b. *c.* 1684–6[2] d. 14 [bur. 19] June 1750; MP for Dunleer 1713–14, Co. Meath 1719–27–50.

1281 **LUDLOW**, Stephen; b. *ante* 1648[7] d. [bur. 24] Feb. 1720/1; MP for Boyle 1692–3, Charlemont 1695–9, Dunleer 1703–13, 1715–21, Co. Louth 1713–14.

1282 **LUM**, Elnathan; b. *ante* 1668[7] d. 23 May 1708; MP for Carlingford 1692–3, 1695–9.

1283 **LUTHER**, Henry; b. [11] Feb. 1667 d. 19 Mar. 1713/4; MP for Youghal 1703–13–14.

1284 **LUTTRELL**, Henry; b. 1768 d. 19 Dec. 1851; MP for Clonmines 1799–1800.

1285 **LUTTRELL**, Rt Hon. Henry Lawes [styled V. Luttrell 1785–7, 2nd E. of Carhampton]; b. 7 Aug. 1737 d. 25 Apr. 1821; MP for Old Leighlin 1783–7 [HP].

1286 **LYNCH-BLOSSE**, Sir Henry [7th Bt]; b. 14 Oct. 1749 d. 1788; MP for Tuam 1776–83.

1287 **LYNDON**, Edward; b. 1671 d. 1727; MP for Armagh B. 1692–3, Carrickfergus 1703–13, 1719–27.

1288 **LYNDON**, John; b. 1699 d. 23 Aug. 1741; MP for Carrickfergus 1727–41.

1289 **LYONS**, Colley; b. *c.* 1678–86[7] d. 26 June 1741; MP for King's Co. 1727–41.

1290 **LYONS**, Henry; b. *c.* 1716–18[3] d. 2 July 1783; MP for King's Co. 1748–60, 1761–8.

1291 **LYONS**, John; b. *c.* 1667 d. ?1726 or 1732; MP for Athy 1713–14.

1292 **LYSAGHT**, Hon. James; b. *c.* 1739–41[3] d. 16 Jan. 1801; MP for Charleville 1768–76, Castlemartyr 1776–83.

1293 **LYSAGHT**, John [1st B. Lisle]; b. 1702 d. 8 June 1781; MP for Charleville 1727–58.

1294 **LYSAGHT**, Hon. John [2nd B. Lisle]; b. 1729 d. 9 Jan. 1798; MP for Castlemartyr 1753–60, Co. Cork 1765–8.

1295 **LYSAGHT**, Hon. Joseph; b. *c.* 1736[2] d. 8 Aug. 1799; MP for Youghal 1768–76, Cashel 1797–9.

1296 **LYSAGHT**, Hon. Nicholas; b. *c.* 1742[2] d. 27 Feb. 1782; MP for Tallow 1768–76–82.

1297 **LYTTLETON**, Hon. George Fulke [2nd B. Lyttleton]; b. 27 Oct. 1763 d. 12 Nov. 1828; MP for Granard 1797–1800 [HP].

1298 **MACARELL**, John; b. *c.* 1695[6] d. 26 May 1757; MP for Carlingford 1741–57.

1299 **MACARTNEY**, Francis; b. *post* 1715[7] d. [Jan.] 1759; MP for Blessington 1749–59.

1300 **MACARTNEY**, George; b. 7 Feb. 1671/2 d. 17 Oct. 1757; MP for Belfast 1692–3, 1715–27–57, Newtown Limavady 1703–13, Donegal B. 1713–14.

1301 **MACARTNEY**, George; b. *ante* 1700[1] d. [*ante* 11 Aug.] 1724; MP for Belfast 1721–4.

1302 **MACARTNEY**, Rt Hon. Sir George [1st B., V. and E. Macartney]; b. 3 May 1737 d. 31 Mar. 1806; MP for Armagh B. 1768–76 [HP].

1303 **MACARTNEY**, James; b. *c.* 1651–3 d. 16 Dec. 1727; MP for Belfast 1692–3, 1695–9.

1304 **MACARTNEY**, James; b. 1692 d. 24 Mar. 1770; MP for Longford B. 1713–14, 1715–27, Granard 1727–60.

1305 **MACARTNEY**, Sir John [1st Bt]; b. 9 Mar. 1746/7 d. 29 May 1812; MP for Fore 1792–7, Naas 1798–1800.

1306 *__MACARTNEY__, William; b. 1714 d. 27 June 1793; MP for Belfast 1747–60.

1307 **McAULEY**, Alexander; b. *c.* 1702–4[3] d. 11 July 1766; MP for Thomastown 1761–6.

1308 *__McCAUSLAND__, John; b. 21 Sept. 1704[1] d. [*ante* 23 Sept.] 1729; MP for Strabane 1725–7–9.

1309 **McCAUSLAND**, John; b. *ante* 1719[6] d. Nov. 1804; MP for Co. Donegal 1768–76.

1310 **McCAUSLAND**, Oliver; b. *ante* 1655 d. [*ante* 29 Aug*] 1723; MP for Strabane 1692–3, 1695–9, 1703–13–14, 1715–23.

1311 *__McCAUSLAND__, Oliver; b. *c.* 1706 d. [Oct.] 1733; MP for Strabane 1729–33.

1312 **McCLEAN**, Joseph; b. *ante* 3 Feb. 1779[1] d. *post* 1 Apr. 1801; MP for Bannow 1800.

1313 **McCLELLAND**, James; b. 1768 d. 27 May 1831; MP for Randalstown 1798–1800.

1314 **McCLINTOCK**, John; b. 1 Jan. 1742/3 d. 23 Feb. 1799; MP for Enniskillen 1783–90, Belturbet 1790–7.

1315 **MACDONNELL**, Charles; b. 1736 d. 23 Apr. 1773; MP for Co. Clare 1765–8, Ennis 1768–73.

1316 **MACDONNELL**, Charles; b. 21 Aug. 1761 d. 7 Sept. 1803; MP for Taghmon 1796–7, Rathcormack 1797–1800 [HP].

1317 *MACDONNELL, Rt Hon. William Randall [6th E. of Antrim, styled 1st V. Dunluce, E. of Antrim [spec. rem.], 1st M. of Antrim]; b. 4 Nov. 1749 d. 28 July 1791; MP for Co. Antrim 1768–75.

1318 McMANUS, James; b. 1695 d. 21 Oct. 1761; MP for Athy Apr.–Oct. 1761.

1319 *McMULLAN, John [William]; b. c. 1680 d. [bur. 10] Nov. 1716; MP for Antrim B. 1715–16.

1320 *MACNAGHTEN, Edmund Alexander; b. 2 Aug. 1762 d. 15 Mar. 1832; MP for Co. Antrim 1797–1800 [HP].

1321 *McNAMARA, Francis; b. 1750 d. 1815; MP for Ardee 1776–83, Co. Clare 1790–7, Killybegs 1798–1800.

♦♦♦ MAGAN, Arthur, b. 1721 d. (ante 12 Sept.) 1777 [n.d.e. Newtown Limavady Nov.–Dec. 1765].

1322 *MAGENIS, Richard; b. 1737 d. [ante 30] June 1807; MP for Bangor 1783–90, Fore 1794–7, Carlingford 1798–1800.

1323 *MAGENIS, Richard; b. 1763 d. 6 Mar. 1831; MP for Enniskillen 1790–7 [HP].

1324 MAGILL [HAWKINS], John; b. 1675 d. 5 Sept. 1713; MP for Co. Down 1703–13.

1325 MAGILL [JOHNSTON], Sir John [1st Bt]; b. ante 1639[6] d. 18 Jan. 1699/1700; MP for Hillsborough 1692–3, Downpatrick 1695–9.

1326 MAGILL, John; b. ante 1723[7] d. 13 May 1775; MP for Rathcormack 1745–60, Castlemartyr 1761–8.

1327 *MAGILL [HAWKINS], Robert; b. 27 Jan. 1703/4 d. 10 Apr. 1745; MP for Co. Down 1724–7–45.

1328 MAHON, James; b. 20 Apr. 1774 d. Mar. 1837; MP for Philipstown Jan.–Aug. 1800.

1329 *MAHON, John; b. 1663 d. [ante 5 May] 1709; MP for Jamestown 1692–3, 1695–9, 1703–9.

1330 MAHON, Maurice [1st B. Hartland]; b. 21 June 1738 d. 4 Jan. 1819; MP for Co. Roscommon 1782–3.

1331 *MAHON, Nicholas; b. c. 1679–81[3] d. [ante 7 Oct.] 1735; MP for Co. Roscommon 1730–5.

1332 *MAHON, Sir Ross [1st Bt] b. 1763 d. 10 Aug. 1835; MP for Granard 1798–1800.

1333 MAHON, Hon. Stephen; b. 6 Feb. 1768 d. 27 Aug. 1828; MP for Knocktopher 1800 [HP].

1334 MAHON, Thomas; b. 1701 d. 13 Jan. 1782; MP for Roscommon B. 1740–60, Co. Roscommon 1761–8–76–82.

1335 MAHON, Hon. Thomas [2nd B. Hartland]; b. 2 Aug. 1766 d. 8 Dec. 1835; MP for Co. Roscommon 1799–1800 [HP].

1336 MALONE, Rt Hon. Anthony; b. 5 Dec. 1700 d. 8 May 1776; MP for Co. Westmeath 1727–60, 1768–76, Castlemartyr 1761–8 [HP].

1337 MALONE, Edmond; b. 1713 d. 24 Jan. 1758; MP for Ardfert 1743–58.

1338 MALONE, Edmond; b. 16 Apr. 1702 d. 22 Apr. 1774; MP for Askeaton 1753–60, Granard 1761–7.

1339 MALONE, Richard; b. 13 Nov. 1706 d. 26 July 1759; MP for Fore 1741–59.

1340 *MALONE, Richard; b. c. 1738–40 d. [ante 26] July 1783; MP for Granard 1769–76.

1341 MALONE, Richard [1st B. Sunderlin]; b. 1737 d. 14 Apr. 1816; MP for Banagher 1783–5.

1342 *MANLEY, Isaac; b. ante 19 Feb. 1681/2[5] d. 30 Dec. 1735; MP for Downpatrick 1705–13, Newtown Limavady 1715–27–35.

1343 MARLAY, Anthony; b. 1710 d. 30 July 1760; MP for Lanesborough 1731–60.

1344 MARLAY, Rt Hon. Thomas; b. c. 1678[2] d. 5 July 1756; MP for Newtown Limavady 1717–27, Lanesborough 1727–30.

1345 *MARSH, Epaphroditus; b. Jan. 1636/7 d. [ante 29] July 1719; MP for Fethard [Tipperary] 1703–13, 1715–19, Armagh B. 1713–14.

1346 MARSHALL, Robert; b. 1697 d. 4 Sept. 1774; MP for Clonmel 1727–54.

1347 MARTIN, Richard; b. Feb. 1754 d. 6 Jan. 1834; MP for Jamestown 1776–83, Lanesborough 1798–1800, Co. Galway Aug. 1800 [HP].

1348 *MARTIN, William; b. c. 1680[10] d. 5 Feb. 1736/7; MP for Gowran 1725–7.

1349 MASON, Aland; b. 2 Sept. 1714 d. 26 Mar. 1759; MP for Co. Waterford 1749–59.

1350 *MASON, Sir John [Kt]; b. 1667 d. 1720; MP for Co. Waterford 1695–9, 1703–13–14.

1351 MASON, John; b. post 1681[7] d. [bur. 7 Mar.] 1738; MP for Waterford city 1715–27–38.

1352 *MASON, Rt Hon. John Monck; b. 1725 d. 2 Apr. 1809; MP for Blessington 1761–8, 1769–76, St Canice 1776–83–90–7–1800.

1353 MASSEY, Sir Edward [Kt]; b. *c.* 1646 d. *post* 1699; MP for Ballynakill 1695–9.

1354 MASSY, Eyre [1st B. Clarina]; b. 24 May 1719 d. 17 May 1804; MP for Swords 1790–7.

1355 MASSY, Hugh [1st B. Massy]; b. 1700 d. 30 Jan. 1788; MP for Co. Limerick 1759–60, 1761–8–76, Old Leighlin May–July 1776.

1356 MASSY, Hon. Hugh [2nd B. Massy]; b. 14 Apr. 1733 d. 20 Apr. 1790; MP for Askeaton 1776–83, Co. Limerick 1783–8.

1357 MASSY, Sir Hugh Dillon [1st Bt]; b. *c.* 1740[2] d. 29 Apr. 1807; MP for Co. Clare 1783–90.

1358 MASSY, Sir Hugh Dillon [2 Bt]; b. 9 Nov. 1767 d. 28 Mar. 1842; MP for Co. Clare 1797–1800 [HP].

1359 MASSY, Hon. John; b. 1 Oct. 1737 d. 6 Aug. 1815; MP for Co. Limerick 1790–7.

1360 *MATHEW, Francis [1st B., V. and E. of Landaff]; b. Sept. 1738 d. 30 July 1806; MP for Co. Tipperary 1768–76–83.

1361 *MATHEW, Hon. Francis James [2nd E. of Landaff]; b. 2 Jan. 1768 d. 12 Mar. 1833; MP for Callan Mar.–Nov. 1796, Co. Tipperary 1796–7–1800 [HP].

1362 MATHEW, George; b. *post* 1675[7] d. 21 Jan. 1738; MP for Co. Tipperary 1713–14, 1728–38.

1363 *MATHEW, Hon. Montagu; b. 18 Aug. 1773 d. 20 Mar. 1819; MP for Ballynakill 1797–1800 [HP].

♦♦♦♦ MATTHEW, Thomas, b. 1721 d. Oct. 1777 [n.d.e. Co. Tipperary 1761–2].

1364 *MATTHEWS, Joseph; b. 1738[2] d. 1796; MP for Innistiogue 1768–76.

1365 MAUDE, Anthony; b. 1638 d. 20 Feb. 1702; MP for Cashel 1695–9.

1366 MAUDE, Sir Cornwallis [3rd Bt, 1st B. de Montalt and V. Hawarden]; b. [19] Sept. 1729 d. 23 Aug. 1803; MP for Roscommon B. 1783–5.

1367 MAUDE, Sir Robert [1st Bt]; b. 1677 d. 4 Aug. 1750; MP for Gowran 1703–13, St Canice 1713–14, 1715–27, Bangor 1727–50.

1368 MAUDE, Rt Hon. Sir Thomas [2nd Bt, 1st B. de Montalt]; b. 1726 d. 17 May 1777; MP for Co. Tipperary 1761–8–76.

1369 MAUNSELL, Richard; b. 1684 d. 11 Sept. 1767; MP for Limerick city 1741–60.

1370 MAUNSELL, Thomas; b. [bapt. 12 Mar.] 1725/6 d. July 1814; MP for Thomastown 1768–76, Granard 1776–83.

1371 MAUNSELL, Thomas; b. *c.* 1705[7] d. [*ante* 5] May 1778[10]; MP for Kilmallock 1769–76.

1372 MAXWELL [BARRY [1771] MAXWELL [1779]], Rt Hon. Barry [3rd B., 1st V. and E. of Farnham]; b. 1723 d. 7 Oct. 1800; MP for Co. Cavan 1756–60, 1768–76–9, Armagh B. 1761–8.

1373 MAXWELL, Rt Hon. Henry; b. 1669 d. 12 Feb. 1729/30; MP for Bangor 1698–9, 1703–13, Killybegs 1713–4, Donegal B. 1715–27–30.

1374 MAXWELL, John [1st B. Farnham]; b. 1687 d. 6 Aug. 1759; MP for Co. Cavan 1727–56.

1375 MAXWELL [MAXWELL-BARRY], Rt Hon. John [5th B. Farnham]; b. 18 Jan. 1767 d. 20 Sept. 1838; MP for Doneraile 1792–7, Newtown Limavady 1798–1800 [HP].

1376 MAXWELL [BARRY-MAXWELL], Hon. John James [2nd E. of Farnham]; b. 5 Feb. 1759 d. 23 July 1823; MP for Co. Cavan 1780–3, 1793–7–1800.

1377 MAXWELL, Rt Hon. Robert [2nd B., 1st V. and E. of Farnham]; b. *c.* 1720 d. 16 Nov. 1779; MP for Lisburn 1743–59 [HP].

1378 MAY, Edward; b. *ante* 1653[9] d. 1710; MP for Gowran 1695–9.

1379 MAY, Edward; b. [bapt. 23 Jan.] 1672/3 d. [bur. 30] Dec. 1729; MP for Co. Waterford 1715–27–9.

1380 MAY, Sir [James] Edward [2nd Bt]; b. [bapt.5 Oct.] 1751 d. 23 July 1814; MP for Belfast 1800 [HP].

1381 MAY, Humphrey; b. [*ante* 27] Aug. 1674[1] d. 11 Sept. 1722; MP for St Johnstown [Donegal] 1695–9, Charlemont 1715–22.

1382 *MAY, James; b. *c.* 1697–1701 d. [*ante* 7 Oct] 1734; MP for Co. Waterford 1725–7, 1733–4.

1383 *MAY, Sir James [1st Bt]; b. 6 Nov. 1723 d. 8 Nov. 1811; MP for Co. Waterford 1759–60, 1761–8–76–83–90–7.

1384 **MAYNARD**, Samuel; b. 1656 d. 1712; MP for Tallow 1692–3, 1695–9, 1703–12.

1385 **MAYNARD**, William; b. 1690 d. 3 Apr. 1734; MP for Tallow 1713–14, 1715–27–34.

1386 **MAYNE**, Rt Hon. Sir William [1st Bt and B. Newhaven]; b. 1722 d. 23 May 1794; MP for Carysfort 1761–8–76 [HP].

1387 **MEADE**, Sir John [1st Bt]; b. 1642 d. 12 Jan. 1706/7; MP for [TCD 1689], Co. Tipperary 1692–3, 1695–9, 1703–7.

1388 *****MEADE**, Sir John [4th Bt, 1st B. Gillford, V. and E. of Clanwilliam]; b. 21 Apr. 1744 d. 7 Oct. 1800; MP for Banagher 1764–6.

1389 **MEADE**, Sir Richard [3rd Bt]; b. 1697 d. 27 Apr. 1744; MP for Kinsale 1725–7–44.

1390 *****MEADE** [MEADE-OGLE], William; b. [ante 14 Oct.] 1729 d. 28 June 1811; MP for Drogheda 1768–76–83, 1790–7.

1391 **MEADE–OGLE**, Henry; b. 1762 d. 18 Feb. 1823; MP for Drogheda 1783–90 [HP].

1392 **MEDLYCOTT**, Thomas; b. 22 May 1662 d. [July] 1738; MP for Kildare B. 1692–3, 1695–9, Clonmel 1703–13, Ballynakill 1713–14, Downpatrick 1715–27, Newtown Limavady 1728–38 [HP].

1393 **MEEKE**, William; b. 3 Jan. 1758 d. 15 July 1830; MP for Callan 1790–7 [HP].

1394 *****MELVILLE** [alias MELVYN], Charles; b. ante 5 Oct. 1671[1] d. post 1713; MP for St Johnstown [Donegal] 1692–3, 1703–13, Killybegs 1695–9, Mullingar 1713–14.

1395 **MEREDYTH**, Arthur; b. [6] Mar. 1639 d. 4 May 1732; MP for Navan 1690–3, 1695–9, 1703–13, 1715–27.

1396 **MEREDYTH**, Arthur Francis; b. 1726 d.[ante Feb.] 1775; MP for Co. Meath 1751–60.

1397 **MEREDYTH**, Rt Hon. Sir Charles [Kt]; b. c. 1627–9[3] d. [11] Nov. 1700; MP for [?Old Leighlin 1661–6], Gowran 1692–3.

1398 *****MEREDYTH**, Charles; b. ante 1639[8] d. [ante 23] June 1710; MP for Co. Meath 1692–3, Kells 1695–9, 1703–10.

1399 **MEREDYTH**, Henry; b. 1675 d. 12 Dec. 1715; MP for Kells 1710–13, Navan 1713–14.

1400 **MEREDYTH**, Henry; b. post 1708[8] d. 10 Dec. 1789; MP for Armagh B. 1776–83–9.

1401 *****MEREDYTH**, Richard; b. 1657 d. [bur. 8] Oct. 1743; MP for Athy 1703–13.

1402 **MEREDYTH**, Rt Hon. Thomas; b. 1665 d. 17 June 1719; MP for Navan 1703–13, Lismore 1715–19 [HP].

1403 **MEREDYTH**, Thomas; b. c. 1680–2[3] d. 14 Jan. 1731/2; MP for Wexford B. 1713–14, New Ross 1715–27, Navan 1727–32.

1404 **MERVYN**, Audley; b. ante 1663[3] d. 17 June 1717; MP for Strabane 1695–9, Co. Tyrone 1703–13–14, 1715–17.

1405 **MERVYN**, Audley; b. c. 1687[3] d. 1746; MP for Co. Tyrone 1717–27.

1406 *****MERVYN**, Henry; b. ante 1640 d. c. Jan.–Feb. 1698/9; MP for [Augher 1661–6], Co. Tyrone 1692–3, 1695–9.

1407 **MERVYN**, Henry; b. c. 1684–90[7] d. 11 Jan. 1748; MP for Augher 1713–14, 1715–27, Co. Tyrone 1727–48.

1408 *****METGE**, John; b. post 1741[8] d. 1824; MP for Ratoath 1784–90, Banagher 1790–7, Tallow 1797–1800 [HP].

1409 **METGE**, Peter; b. c. 1741[2] d. 1809; MP for Ardee 1776–83, Ratoath 1783–4.

1410 **MILLER**, George; b. [bapt. 9 Sept.] 1763 d. 1808; MP for Castlebar Jan.–Aug. 1800.

1411 *****MILLER**, Robert; b. ante 1689[7] d. [ante 7 Sept.] 1725; MP for Donegal B. 1716–25.

1412 *****MINCHIN**, Humphrey; b. Dec. 1660 d. [bur. 5] July 1734; MP for Co. Tipperary 1715–27.

1413 **MINCHIN-WALCOTT**, John; b. 1701 d. 2 Oct. 1753; MP for Askeaton 1747–53.

1414 **MITCHELL**, Henry; b. ante 1716[6] d. 2 Aug. 1768; MP for Castlebar 1747–60, Bannow 1761–8.

1415 **MITCHELL**, Hugh Henry; b. ante 31 Mar. 1745[1] d. [ante 27 Apr.] 1830; MP for Ballyshannon 1766–8, Enniskillen 1771–6.

1416 *****MITCHELL**, Sir Michael [Kt]; b. ante 5 Oct. 1671[1] d. c. 1699; MP for Dublin city 1692–3.

1417 **MOLESWORTH**, Hon. Bysse; b. c. 1697[8] d. 23 [bur. 27] Nov. 1779; MP for Swords 1727–60.

1418 **MOLESWORTH**, Rt Hon. Richard [3rd V. Molesworth]; b. 1680 d. 12 Oct. 1758; MP for Swords 1715–26.

1419 **MOLESWORTH**, Rt Hon. Robert [1st B. and V. Molesworth]; b. 6 Sept. 1656 d. 22 May 1725; MP for Co. Dublin 1695–9, Swords 1703–13–14 [HP].

1420 **MOLESWORTH**, Hon. William; b. 1681 d. 5 Mar. 1770; MP for Philipstown 1717–27–60.

1421 **MOLYNEUX**, Rt Hon. Sir Capel [3rd Bt]; b. 1717 d. [*ante* 24] Aug. 1797; MP for Clogher 1761–8, 1776–83, TCD 1768–76.

1422 **MOLYNEUX**, George William; b. *c.* 1751^2 d. 27 July 1806; MP for Granard 1783–90.

1423 **MOLYNEUX**, Rt Hon. Samuel; b. 16 July 1689 d. 13 Apr. 1728; MP for TCD 1727–8 [HP].

1424 **MOLYNEUX**, Sir Thomas [1st Bt]; b. 14 Apr. 1661 d. 19 Oct. 1733; MP for Ratoath 1695–9.

1425 **MOLYNEUX**, William; b. 17 Apr. 1656 d. 11 Oct. 1698; MP for TCD 1692–3, 1695–8.

1426 **MONCK**, Charles; b. [bapt. 19 May] 1678 d. 28 Dec. 1751; MP for Newcastle 1711–13, 1715–27, Innistiogue 1713–14.

1427 **MONCK**, Charles Stanley [1st B. and V. Monck]; b. 1754 d. 9 June 1802; MP for Gorey 1790–7.

1428 **MONCK**, George; b. 1672 d. 28 July 1726; MP for Philipstown 1703–13.

1429 *****MONCK**, George Paul; b. 1733 d. 7 Oct. 1803; MP for Coleraine 1763–8.

1430 **MONCK**, Henry; b. 1708 d. 17 Dec. 1787; MP for Duleek 1755–60, 1761–8.

1431 **MONCK**, Thomas; b. 1723 d. Oct. 1772; MP for Old Leighlin 1768–72.

1432 **MONCK**, William Domville Stanley; b. 1763 d. Aug. 1840; MP for Coleraine 1795–7, Gorey 1797–9.

1433 **MONSELL**, William Thomas; b. 21 Dec. 1754 d. 1836; MP for Dunleer 1776–83, Dingle 1798–1800.

1434 **MONTGOMERY**, Alexander; b. 1667 d. 25 Mar. 1722; MP for Co. Monaghan 1713–14, 1715–22.

1435 **MONTGOMERY**, Alexander; b. 1686 d. 19 Dec. 1729; MP for Donegal B. 1725–7, Co. Donegal 1727–9.

1436 **MONTGOMERY**, Alexander; b. *c.* 1721–2^3 d. Aug. 1785; MP for Co. Monaghan 1743–60, 1768–76–83.

1437 *****MONTGOMERY**, Alexander; b. 1720 d. 29 Sept. 1800; MP for Co. Donegal 1768–76–83–90–7–1800.

1438 **MONTGOMERY** [LESLIE], George; b. *c.* 1726–8^3 d. Mar. 1787; MP for Strabane 1765–8, Co. Cavan 1768–76–83–7.

1439 **MONTGOMERY**, Hon. Hugh [4th E. of Mount Alexander]; b. *c.* 1678–82^7 d. 27 Feb. 1745; MP for Antrim B. 1703–13.

1440 **MONTGOMERY**, John; b. 20 Sept. 1657 d. Feb. 1697/8; MP for Lifford 1692–3, 1695–8.

1441 **MONTGOMERY**, John; b. *c.* 1701 d. Aug. 1733; MP for Co. Monaghan 1727–33.

1442 **MONTGOMERY**, John; b. *c.* 1719^2 d. Nov. 1741; MP for Co. Monaghan [Oct.] 1741.

1443 **MONTGOMERY**, John; b. 7 Sept. 1747 d. Apr. 1797; MP for Co. Monaghan 1783–90–7.

1444 **MONTGOMERY** [MONTGOMERY-MOORE], Nathaniel; b. 1757 d. 4 Dec. 1834; MP for Co. Tyrone 1781–3–90, Strabane 1797–1800.

1445 **MONTGOMERY**, Thomas: b. *c.* 1700^5 d. Apr. 1761; MP for Lifford 1729–60.

1446 **MONTGOMERY**, William; b. [?]1700 d. [?]Aug. 1783; MP for Augher 1761–8.

1447 **MONTGOMERY**, William; b. 1721 d. Nov. 1799; MP for Hillsborough 1761–8–76–83–90–7–9.

1448 *****MONTGOMERY**, Sir William [1st Bt]; b. 9 Nov. 1717 d. 25 Dec. 1788; MP for Ballynakill 1768–76–83–8.

1449 *****MOORE**, Acheson; b. 1691 d. 14 Mar. 1770; MP for Bangor 1716–27–60.

1450 **MOORE**, Rt Hon. Arthur; b. 1765 d. 6 Jan. 1846; MP for Tralee 1798–1800 [HP].

1451 **MOORE**, Brabazon; b. 27 Aug. 1674^1 d. 13 Aug. 1721; MP for Ardee 1695–9.

1452 *****MOORE**, Hon. Capel; b. [bapt. 26 Oct.] 1693 d. *post* Feb. 1755; MP for Bangor 1713–14.

1453 *MOORE, Hon. Charles; b. [bapt. 1 Dec.] 1676 d. 21 May 1714; MP for Drogheda 1692–3, 1695–9, 1703–13.

1454 MOORE, Rt Hon. Charles [6th E. and 1st M. of Drogheda]; b. 29 June 1730 d. 22 Dec. 1822; MP for St Canice 1757–8 [HP].

1455 *MOORE, Hon. Colvill; b. c. 1734–40[8] d. [ante 13] June 1799; MP for Clonmel 1761–8–76.

1456 MOORE, Rt Hon. Edward [5th E. of Drogheda]; b. 1701 d. 28 Oct. 1758; MP for Dunleer 1725–7.

♦♦♦ MOORE, Hon. Edward [styled V. Moore 1770–82, 7th E. and 2nd M. of Drogheda]; b. 23 Aug. 1770 d. 6 Feb. 1837 [n.d.e. Queen's Co. 1790–1].

1457 MOORE, Sir Emanuel [3rd Bt]; b. 1685 d. 1733; MP for Downpatrick 1715–27.

1458 MOORE, Guy; b. 1691 d. 21 June 1735; MP for Fethard [Tipperary] 1715–27.

1459 *MOORE [MOORE-COOTE], Guy; b. post 1717[7] d. 1799; MP for Clonmel 1757–60, 1761–8–76–83.

1460 *MOORE, Henry William; b. 26 Dec. 1725 d. [May] 1762; MP for Charlemont 1761–2.

1461 MOORE, Rt Hon. John [1st B. Moore]; b. ante 1676[7] d. 8 Sept. 1725; MP for Philipstown 1703–13, King's Co. 1713–14.

1462 MOORE, John; b. May 1675 d. 1 May 1752; MP for Charlemont 1727–52.

1463 MOORE, John; b. 21 Dec. 1726 d. 24 Sept. 1809; MP for Ballynakill 1768–76, 1777–83.

1464 MOORE, John; b. 1756 d. 21 May 1834; MP for Ballynakill 1783–90, Lisburn 1791–7, Newry 1799–1800.

1465 MOORE, Hon. John; b. 19 June 1772 d. Feb. 1803; MP for Clonmel 1792–7.

1466 MOORE, Lorenzo; b. c. 1741[2] d. 1804; MP for Dungannon 1783–90, Ardfert 1798–1800.

1467 MOORE, Hon. Ponsonby; b. 29 June 1730 d. 9 Aug. 1819; MP for Lismore 1759–60.

1468 MOORE, Richard; b. ante 5 Oct. 1671[1] d. 1699; MP for Clonmel 1692–3, 1695–9.

1469 MOORE, Richard; b. 1716 d. 30 July 1771; MP for Kells 1757–60, 1761–8.

1470 MOORE, Hon. Richard; b. 15 Dec. 1725 d. 22 Sept. 1761; MP for Clonmel 1761.

1471 MOORE, Hon. Robert; b. [bapt. 11 Apr.] 1688 d. [5] Oct. 1762; MP for Belfast 1713–14, Co. Louth 1715–27.

1472 MOORE, Roger; b. c. 1644–6[8] d. 27 Jan. 1704/5; MP for Mullingar 1692–3, 1695–9.

1473 *MOORE, Stephen; b. 1653 d. 1703; MP for Co. Tipperary 1692–3, 1695–9.

1474 MOORE, Stephen; b. 1689 d. 1750; MP for Clonmel 1713–14, 1715–27.

1475 *MOORE, Stephen; b. ante 1686[6] d. June 1737[10]; MP for Fethard [Tipperary] 1719–27.

1476 MOORE, Stephen [1st B. Kilworth, 1st V. Mountcashell]; b. 1696 d. 26 Feb. 1766; MP for Co. Tipperary 1738–60.

1477 *MOORE, Stephen; b. c. 1722 d. 11 Feb. 1781; MP for Fethard [Tipperary] 1761–8, Clonmel 1776–81.

1478 MOORE, Rt Hon. Stephen [2nd V. and 1st E. Mountcashell]; b. 25 July 1730 d. 21 May 1790; MP for Lismore 1761–6.

1479 *MOORE, Stephen; b. 1749 d. 1829; MP for Clonmel 1783–90, Lanesborough 1790–7, Kells 1797–1800.

1480 MOORE, Hon. Stephen [2nd E. Mountcashell]; b. 19 Mar. 1770 d. 27 Oct. 1822; MP for Clonmel Apr.–May 1790.

1481 MOORE, Stephen; b. 4 Sept. 1769 d. 1 Sept. 1838; MP for Clonmel 1797–1800.

1482 MOORE, Thomas; b. 1744 d. [1] May 1781; MP for Kells 1768–76–81.

1483 MOORE, Sir William [2nd Bt]; b. 1663 d. 28 Aug. 1693; MP for Bandon-Bridge 1692–3.

1484 MOORE, Hon. William; b. c. 1685[7] d. 1 Apr. 1732; MP for Ardee 1715–27.

1485 MOORE, Hon. William; b. c. 1732–3[8] d. 21 Nov. 1810; MP for Clogher 1765–8–76, Clonmel 1781–3–90–7, St Johnstown [Longford] 1798–9.

1486 MORGAN, Hugh; b. 1664 d. 1721; MP for Co. Sligo 1692–3, 1695–9, 1703–13, Fethard [Wexford] 1713–14.

1487 MORGAN, Marcus Anthony; b. 1703 d. 3 Oct. 1752; MP for Athy 1727–52.

1488 **MORGELL**, Crosbie; b. *c.* 1747[6] d. 12 Nov. 1794; MP for Tralee 1790–4.

1489 **MORRES**, Sir Haydock Evans [2nd Bt]; b. 1743 d. 18 Dec. 1776; MP for Kilkenny city 1768–76, May–Dec. 1776.

1490 **MORRES**, Hervey [1st B. and V. Mountmorres]; b. 1707 d. 6 Apr. 1766; MP for St Canice 1734–56.

1491 ***MORRES** [DE MONTMORENCY], Rt Hon. Lodge Evans [1st B. Frankfort and V. Frankfort De Montmorency]; b. 14 Jan. 1746/7 d. 21 Sept. 1822; MP for Innistiogue 1768–76, Bandon-Bridge 1776–83–90–6, Ennis 1796–7, 1801–18, Dingle 1797–1800 [re-elected pp 1795].

1492 **MORRES**, Redmond; b. 1712 d. 4 July 1784; MP for Thomastown 1755–60, Newtown[ards] 1761–8, Dublin city 1773–6.

1493 **MORRES**, Sir William Evans [1st Bt]; b. 1710 d. 11 Oct. 1774; MP for Kilkenny city 1752–60, 1761–8, Newtown[ards] 1769–74.

1494 **MORRES** [DE MONTMORENCY], Sir William Evans Ryves [3rd Bt]; b. 7 Nov. 1763 d. 14 Apr. 1829; MP for Newtown[ards] 1785–90.

1495 **MORRIS**, Abraham; b. [bapt. 9 Apr.] 1752 d. 13 Feb. 1822; MP for Co. Cork 1791–7.

1496 **MORRIS**, Jonas; b. ? d. Dec. 1734; MP for Cork city 1731–4.

1497 **MORRIS**, Richard; b. *ante* 5 Oct. 1671[1] d. [bur. 26] Feb. 1705/6; MP for Newcastle 1692–3.

1498 ***MORRIS**, Samuel; b. *ante* 1667 d. [*ante* 29 Aug.] 1723; MP for Castlemartyr 1695–9, Tralee 1703–13–14, 1715–23.

1499 **MORRISON** [*alias* MORYSON], Henry; b. *ante* 1670[5] d. 16 Oct. 1720; MP for Dundalk 1719–20.

1500 **MOSSOM**, Eland; b. [bapt. 11 Aug.] 1708 d. 30 Apr. 1774; MP for St Canice 1759–60, 1761–8–74.

1501 **MOSSOM**, Eland; b. 1749 d. [bur. 28] June 1808; MP for Kilkenny city 1777–83.

1502 **MOUTRAY**, James; b. *ante* 1661[6] d. 1719; MP for Augher 1692–3, 1703–13.

1503 **MOUTRAY**, James; b. 1722 d. 21 May 1777; MP for Augher 1761–8–76.

1504 **MULLINS**, Frederick William; b. *ante* 1625 d. 3 Nov. 1712; MP for Dingle 1692–3, Tralee 1695–9.

1505 **MULLINS**, Hon. William Townsend [2nd B. Ventry]; b. 25 Sept. 1761 d. 5 Oct. 1827; MP for Dingle Feb.–Aug. 1800.

1506 **MURRAY**, Alexander; b. 1725 d. [*ante* 20] Apr. 1799; MP for Newtown Limavady 1776–83.

1507 **MURRAY**, John; b. 1707 d. July 1743; MP for Co. Monaghan 1741–3.

1508 **MUSCHAMP**, Denny; b. *c.* 1637[2] d. 1699; MP for [Swords 1665–6], Blessington 1695–9.

1509 **MUSGRAVE**, Sir Richard [1st Bt]; b. 1746 d. 6 Apr. 1818; MP for Lismore 1778–83–90–7–1800.

1510 **MUSSENDEN**, Daniel; b. *c.* 1745[2] d. 22 Dec. 1829; MP for Killyleagh Mar.–Aug. 1800.

1511 ***NAPPER** [*alias* NAPER or NAPIER], James; b. *c.* 1622–3[8] d. [*ante* 1 July] 1719; MP for Athboy 1695–9, Trim 1703–13, Co. Meath 1715–18.

1512 **NAPPER** [NAPPER-DUTTON] [*alias* NAPER or NAPIER], James Lenox; b. [*ante* 15 Nov.] 1712 d. [8] Sept. 1776; MP for Co. Meath 1733–60.

1513 ***NAPPER** [*alias* NAPER or NAPIER], Rt Hon. Robert; b. *c.* 1664–9[8] d. Nov. 1739; MP for Athboy 1727–39.

1514 **NAPPER** [*alias* NAPER or NAPIER], William; b. 1661 d. 1708; MP for Trim 1695–9, 1703–8.

1515 **NAPPER** [*alias* NAPER or NAPIER], William; b. [?]1716 d. *post* 1760; MP for Athboy 1748–60.

1516 ***NEAVE**, William; b. *c.* 1662–4[3] d. [Dec.] 1713; MP for Tulsk 1692–3, 1695–9, 1703–13, Nov.–Dec. 1713.

1517 **NEEDHAM** [*alias* NEDHAM], George; b. *c.* 1738[2] d. 12 Dec. 1767; MP for Newry 1761–7.

1518 **NEEDHAM** [*alias* NEDHAM], Robert; b. *ante* 1683[9] d. [May] 1753; MP for Newry 1727–53.

1519 **NEEDHAM** [*alias* NEDHAM], Robert; b. 1704 d. 13 Aug. 1762; MP for Newry 1753–60 [HP].

1520 **NEEDHAM** [*alias* NEDHAM], William; b. *c.* 1741[2] d. 27 Apr. 1806; MP for Newry 1767–8–76 [HP].

1521 **NEEDHAM** [*alias* NEDHAM], William; b. 18 Mar. 1770 d. 13 Feb. 1844; MP for Athenry Apr.–Aug. 1800.

1522 **NESBITT**, Alexander; b. 1707 d. 1778; MP for Newtown Limavady 1736–60.

1523 **NESBITT**, Cosby; b. 1718 d. 1791; MP for Cavan B. 1750–60, 1761–8.

1524 **NESBITT**, Thomas; b. *c.* 1672–9[7] d. [10 Apr.] 1750; MP for Cavan B. 1715–27–50.

1525 **NESBITT**, Thomas; b. *c.* 1744–5[7] d. Dec. 1820; MP for Cavan B. 1768–76–83–90–7–1800.

1526 **NEVILL**, Richard; b. 1654 d. 1720; MP for Naas 1695–9.

1527 *****NEVILL**, Richard; b. 1743 d. [Jan.] 1822; MP for Wexford B. 1771–6–83–90–7–1800 [HP].

1528 **NEWBURGH**, Brockhill; b. *c.* 1658–60[8] d. 11 Jan. 1740/1; MP for Co. Cavan 1715–27.

1529 **NEWCOMEN**, Sir Arthur [7th Bt]; b. 1701 d. 25 Nov. 1759; MP for Co. Longford 1735–59.

1530 *****NEWCOMEN**, Brabazon; b. 1688 d. [*ante* 7] June 1766; MP for Kilbeggan 1713–14, 1715–27.

1531 *****NEWCOMEN**, Charles; b. 1707 d. [*ante* 17 Oct.] 1772; MP for St Johnstown [Longford] 1761–8–72.

1532 **NEWCOMEN**, Sir Robert [6th Bt]; b. 1664 d. 6 Mar. 1734/5; MP for Co. Longford 1692–3, 1695–9, 1703–13–14, 1715–27–35.

1533 **NEWCOMEN**, Thomas; b. 1693 d. May 1782; MP for St Johnstown [Longford] 1727–60.

1534 *****NEWCOMEN**, Sir Thomas [8th Bt]; b. 1740 d. 27 Apr. 1789; MP for Co. Longford 1759–60, Longford B. 1761–8.

1535 *****NEWENHAM**, Sir Edward [Kt]; b. 14 May 1730 d. [bur. 27] Sept. 1814; MP for Enniscorthy 1769–76, Co. Dublin 1776–83–90–7.

1536 **NEWENHAM**, John; b. *ante* 22 Oct. 1740[1] d. 1787; MP for Fore 1761–8.

1537 **NEWENHAM**, Thomas Worth; b. 13 May 1729 d. [Oct.] 1766; MP for Cork city 1751–60.

1538 **NEWENHAM**, Thomas Worth; b. 2 Mar. 1762 d. 16 Oct. 1831; MP for Clonmel 1797–1800.

1539 *****NEWTON**, John; b. 1680 d. 1714; MP for Londonderry city 1713–14.

1540 **NICHOLLS**, Henry; b. *ante* 1640[1] d. 1695; MP for [?New Ross 1661–6], Waterford city 1692–3.

1541 *****NICHOLLS**, John; b. *ante* 1632 d. [*ante* 28 Mar.] 1696; MP for Longford B. 1692–3, 1695–6.

1542 **NICHOLSON**, Edward; b. [bapt. 31 Dec.] 1712 d. [*ante* 20] Jan. 1780; MP for Old Leighlin 1761–8.

1543 **NORMAN**, Charles; b. 1666 d. 1731; MP for Londonderry city 1703–13–14, 1715–27.

1544 **NORMAN**, Robert; b. [bapt. 8 Jan.] 1684/5 d. 4 Nov. 1743; MP for Londonderry city 1733–43.

1545 **NORTH**, Francis; b. 1683 d. 6 Mar. 1737/8; MP for Dunleer 1727–38.

1546 **NUGENT**, Sir George [1st Bt]; b. 10 June 1757 d. 11 Mar. 1849; MP for Charleville 1800 [HP].

1547 *****NUGENT**, Rt Hon. George Frederick [7th E. of Westmeath]; b. 18 Nov. 1760 d. 30 Dec. 1814; MP for Fore 1780–3–90–2.

1548 **NUGENT**, James; b. *ante* 5 Oct. 1671[1] d. 11 Feb. 1748/9; MP for Fore 1692–3.

1549 *****NUGENT**, Hon. Richard; b. 1742 d. 6 Aug. 1761; MP for Fore 1759–60.

1550 *****NUGENT**, Walter; b. [bapt. 4 Oct.] 1667 d. [*ante* 6 Dec.] 1727; MP for Fore Sept.–Dec. 1727.

1551 **NUTLEY**, Richard; b. 1673 d. 1729; MP for Lisburn 1703–11.

1552 **O'BRIEN**, Rt Hon. Sir Donough [1st Bt]; b. 1642 d. 17 Nov. 1717; MP for Co. Clare 1692–3, 1695–9, 1703–13–14.

1553 **O'BRIEN**, Sir Edward [2nd Bt]; b. 7 Apr. 1705 d. 29 Nov. 1765; MP for Co. Clare 1727–60, 1761–5 [HP].

1554 **O'BRIEN**, Edward; b. [bapt. 4 May] 1737 d. [bur. 5] Dec. 1787; MP for Ennis 1773–6.

1555 **O'BRIEN**, Sir Edward [4th Bt]; b. 17 Apr. 1773 d. 13 Mar. 1837; MP for Ennis 1795–7–1800 [HP].

1556 **O'BRIEN**, Hon. James; b. 1696 d. [bur. 6] Dec. 1769; MP for Charleville 1725–7, Youghal 1727–60.

1557 **O'BRIEN**, Lucius; b. *c.* 1674[3] d. 6 Jan. 1716/7; MP for Co. Clare 1703–13–14.

1558 **O'BRIEN**, Rt Hon. Sir Lucius Henry [3rd Bt]; b. 2 Sept. 1731 d. 15 Jan. 1795; MP for Ennis 1761–8, 1790–5, Co. Clare 1768–76, 1778–83, Tuam 1783–90.

1559 O'BRIEN [*alias* O'BRYAN], Rt Hon.
Murrough [5th E. of Inchiquin and 1st M. of
Thomond]; b. 1726 d. 10 Feb. 1808; MP for Co.
Clare 1757–60, Harristown 1761–8 [HP].

1560 O'CALLAGHAN [*alias* CALLAGHAN],
Cornelius; b. *c.* 1680–2 d. 3 Jan. 1741/2; MP for
Fethard [Tipperary] 1713–14.

1561 O'CALLAGHAN, Cornelius; b. 1712 d. 1781;
MP for Fethard [Tipperary] 1761–8, Newtown[ards]
1775–6.

1562 O'CALLAGHAN, Cornelius [1st B. Lismore];
b. 7 Jan. 1741/2 d. 12 July 1797; MP for Fethard
[Tipperary] 1768–76–83–5.

1563 O'CALLAGHAN, Robert; b. 10 July 1710 d.
Jan. 1761; MP for Fethard [Tipperary] 1755–60.

1564 O'CALLAGHAN, Hon. Sir Robert William; b.
Oct. 1777 d. 9 June 1840; MP for Bandon-Bridge
1797–1800.

1565 O'CONNOR [*alias* CONNER], Arthur; b. 4
July 1763 d. 23 Apr. 1852; MP for Philipstown
1790–5.

1566 ODELL, John; b. *c.* 1641 d. Apr. 1700; MP for
Askeaton 1692–3.

1567 ODELL, William; b. 1752 d. 8 June 1831; MP
for Co. Limerick 1797–1800 [HP].

1568 O'DONELL, James Moore; b. 1764 d. 24
Sept. 1801; MP for Ratoath 1797–1800.

1569 O'DONNELL, Hugh; b. 1760 d. [*ante* 10]
Sept. 1799; MP for Donegal B. 1797–9.

1570 O'FLAHERTY, John Bourke; b. *c.* 1756–61[7] d.
1800–1; MP for Callan 1783–90.

1571 OGILVIE, William; b. 1740 d. 18 Nov. 1832;
MP for Gorey 1781–3, Ballyshannon 1783–90.

1572 OGLE, George; b. [bapt. 18 May] 1704 d. 20
Oct. 1746; MP for Bannow 1727–46.

1573 OGLE, Rt Hon. George; b. 14 Oct. 1742 d. 10
Aug. 1814; MP for Co. Wexford 1769–76–83–90–7,
Dublin city 1798–1800 [HP].

1574 OGLE, Samuel; b. [25] Mar. 1659 d. 10 Mar.
1717/8; MP for Belfast 1707–13 [HP].

1575 O'HARA, Charles; b.1715 d. 3 Feb. 1776; MP
for Ballynakill 1761–8, Armagh B. 1769–76.

1576 O'HARA, Charles; b. 26 Apr. 1746 d. 19 Sept.
1822; MP for Dungannon 1776–83, Co. Sligo
1783–90–7–1800 [HP].

1577 O'HARA, Henry; b. *c.* 1695 d. 15 Dec. 1745;
MP for Randalstown 1727–45.

1578 O'KEEFE, Cornelius; b. 1735 d. 3 [bur. 8]
Apr. 1780; MP for Fore 1776–80.

1579 OLIVER, Charles; b. 1646 d. 13 Apr. 1706;
MP for Midleton 1695–9, Co. Limerick 1703–6.

1580 OLIVER, Charles Silver; b. *c.* 1765–70 d. 10
Oct. 1817; MP for Kilmallock 1798–9 [HP].

1581 OLIVER, Philip; b. *c.* 1720 d. Dec. 1768; MP
for Kilmallock 1745–60.

1582 OLIVER [OLIVER-GASCOIGNE], Richard
Philip; b. 1763 d. 14 Apr. 1843; MP for Co.
Limerick 1788–90.

1583 OLIVER, Robert; b. 1674 d. Mar. 1739; MP
for Kilmallock 1703–13, 1727–39, Castlemartyr
1713–14, Co. Limerick 1715–27.

1584 OLIVER, Robert; b. 1709 d. 6 May 1745; MP
for Kilmallock 1739–45.

1585 OLIVER, Rt Hon. Silver; b. [bapt. 17 July]
1736 d. 17 Nov. 1798; MP for Kilmallock 1757–60,
1761–8, Co. Limerick 1768–76–83.

1586 OLIVER, Silver; b. [bapt. 17 Mar.] 1770 d.
1834; MP for Kilmallock 1797–9.

1587 O'NEILL, Rt Hon. Charles; b. *ante* 15 June
1676[1] d. [Aug.] 1716; MP for Randalstown 1697–9,
1713–14, Bangor 1707–13.

1588 O'NEILL, Charles; b. *ante* 1702 d. 6 Aug.
1769; MP for Randalstown 1727–60, 1761–8–9.

1589 O'NEILL, Charles; b. *c.* 1729–31 d. [*ante* 28]
May 1793; MP for Clonakilty 1784–90–3.

1590 O'NEILL, Clotworthy; b. *c.* 1680[3] d. 24 July
1744; MP for Randalstown 1745/6–9.

1591 O'NEILL, Henry; b. *c.* 1674[3] d. [16 Mar.–11
May] 1697; MP for Randalstown 1695–7.

1592 O'NEILL, Rt Hon. John [1st B. and V.
O'Neill]; b. 16 Jan. 1739/40 d. 18 June 1798; MP
for Randalstown 1761–8–76–83, Co. Antrim 1783–
90–3.

1593 O'NEILL, St John; b. 6 May 1741 d. 1790;
MP for Randalstown 1771–6.

1594 **ORDE** [ORDE-POWLETT], Rt Hon. Thomas [1st B. Bolton [GB]]; b. 30 Aug. 1746 d. 30 July 1807; MP for Rathcormack 1784–90 [HP].

1595 **ORMSBY**, Arthur; b. 1677 d. [bur. 28] Mar. 1732; MP for Athenry 1725–7.

1596 **ORMSBY**, Arthur; b. 29 Feb. 1743/4 d. 17 Feb. 1809; MP for Athy 1790–7.

1597 **ORMSBY**, Sir Charles Montague [1st Bt]; b. 23 Apr. 1767 d. 3 Mar. 1818; MP for Duleek 1790–7–1800 [re-elected pp 1800] [HP].

1598 **ORMSBY**, Edward; b. 1676 d. 1744; MP for Co. Galway 1709–13, 1715–27, Carrick Jan.–Aug. 1714.

1599 **ORMSBY**, Francis; b. *c.* 1684–94 d. 20 May 1751; MP for Sligo B. 1727–51.

1600 **ORMSBY**, Gilbert; b. *ante* 1655 d. *post* 1713; MP for Tuam 1692–3, 1695–9, 1703–13.

1601 **ORMSBY**, John; b. *c.* 1658–60 d. [*ante* 5 Nov.] 1711; MP for Kilmallock 1692–3,1703–11, Charleville 1695–9.

1602 **ORMSBY**, John; b. 1654 d. 16 June 1721; MP for Athenry 1695–9, 1703–13–14, 1715–21.

1603 **ORMSBY**, Joseph Mason; b. 1761 d. 1820; MP for Gorey 1799–1800.

1604 **ORMSBY**, Robert; b. 1667 d. 28 Dec. 1727; MP for Kilmallock 1692–3.

1605 **ORMSBY**, Robert; b. *c.* 1647–9[3] d. 1714; MP for Castlebar 1692–3, Galway B. 1695–9.

1606 **ORMSBY**, William; b. 1656 d. 1738; MP for Co. Sligo 1713–14, 1715–27.

1607 **ORMSBY**, William; b. 1718 d. 1781; MP for Sligo B. 1757–60, 1761–8–76.

1608 **OSBORNE**, Charles; b. 1759 d. 5 Sept. 1817; MP for Carysfort 1790–7–1800 [re-elected pp 1798].

1609 **OSBORNE**, Francis; b. [*ante* 5] Oct. 1671 d. 1703; MP for Navan 1692–3, 1695–9.

1610 **OSBORNE**, Sir Henry [11th Bt]; b. *c.* 1760–2 d. 27 Oct. 1837; MP for Carysfort 1797–9, Enniskillen Feb.–Aug. 1800.

1611 **OSBORNE**, John; b. *c.* 1641–3 d. 5 Nov. 1692; MP for Co. Meath 1692.

1612 **OSBORNE**, Sir John [7th Bt] b. 1697 d. 11 Apr. 1743; MP for Lismore 1719–27, Co. Waterford 1727–43.

1613 **OSBORNE**, John Proby; b. 1755 d. [bur. 18] Dec.1787; MP for Carysfort 1783–7.

1614 **OSBORNE**, Sir Thomas [9th Bt]; b. 1753 d. 15 May 1821; MP for Carysfort 1776–83–90–7.

1615 **OSBORNE**, Rt Hon. Sir William [8th Bt]; b. *c.* 1722 d. [bur. 27] Oct. 1783; MP for Carysfort 1761–8, Aug.–Oct. 1783, Dungarvan 1768–76–83.

1616 **PACEY**, John; b. *ante* 1671 d. [bur. 29] Aug. 1727; MP for Callan B. 1705–13.

1617 **PAKENHAM**, Edward; b. *c.* 1680–2 d. [*ante* 12 Sept.] 1721; MP for Co. Westmeath 1713–14, 1715–21.

1618 **PAKENHAM**, Hon. Sir Edward Michael; b. 19 Mar. 1778 d. 8 Jan. 1815; MP for Longford B. 1799–1800.

1619 **PAKENHAM**, Rt Hon. Edward Michael [2nd B. Longford]; b. 1 Apr. 1743 d. 6 June 1792; MP for Co. Longford 1765–6.

1620 **PAKENHAM**, Hon. Robert; b. *c.* 1744–5[8] d. 7 July 1775; MP for Co.Longford 1768–75.

1621 **PAKENHAM**, Sir Thomas [Kt]; b. 1651 d. 1706; MP for Augher 1695–9.

1622 **PAKENHAM**, Thomas [1st B. Longford]; b. May 1713 d. 30 Apr. 1766; MP for Longford B. 1745–56.

1623 **PAKENHAM**, Hon. Sir Thomas; b. 29 Sept. 1757 d. 2 Feb. 1836; MP for Longford B. 1783–90, 1797–1800, Kells 1790–7.

1624 **PALLISER**, Thomas; b. 1661 d. Nov. 1756; MP for Fethard [Wexford] 1703–13–14, 1715–27.

1625 **PALMER**, Sir Roger [1st Bt]; b. 1729 d. 25 [bur. 27] Jan. 1790; MP for Jamestown 1761–8, Portarlington 1768–76–83.

1626 **PALMER**, William; b. 1657 d. 22 Sept. 1726; MP for Castlebar 1695–9, 1703–13.

1627 **PALMES**, Rt Hon. Francis; b. *ante* 1663[5] d. 4 Jan. 1718/9; MP for Youghal 1715–19 [HP].

♦♦♦♦ **PARKER**, Rt Hon. Gervais; b. *c.* 1679 d. 19 June 1750 [n.d.e. Kinsale 22 Oct.–25 Nov. 1731].

1628 **PARKER**, Matthew; b. [bapt. 11 Oct.] 1718 d. 27 July 1781; MP for Clonakilty 1766–8.

1629 **PARKINSON**, Robert; b. 1694 d. 14 Feb. 1761; MP for Ardee 1727–60.

1630 **PARNELL**, Rt Hon. Sir Henry Brooke [4th Bt, 1st B. Congleton [UK]]; b. 3 July 1776 d. 8 June 1842; MP for Maryborough 1797–1800 [HP].

1631 **PARNELL**, John; b. [bapt. 21 Dec.] 1680 d. 2 July 1727; MP for Granard 1713–14, 1715–22.

1632 **PARNELL**, Sir John [1st Bt]; b. 1717 d. 14 Apr. 1782; MP for Maryborough 1761–8–76–82.

1633 **PARNELL**, Rt Hon. Sir John [2nd Bt]; b. 25 Dec. 1744 d. 5 Dec. 1801; MP for Bangor 1767–8, Innistiogue 1777–83, Queen's Co. 1783–90–7–1800 [HP].

1634 **PARRY**, Rt Hon. Benjamin; b. 1672 d. 20 [bur. 24] Jan. 1735/6; MP for Killybegs 1703–13, Newtown Limavady 1713–14, Tallow 1715–27, Dungarvan 1727–36.

1635 **PARSONS**, Sir Laurence [3rd Bt]; b. 1708 d. 24 Oct. 1756; MP for King's Co. 1741–56.

1636 **PARSONS**, Rt Hon. Sir Laurence [5th Bt, 2 B. Oxmantown and E. of Rosse]; b. 21 May 1758 d. 24 Feb. 1841; MP for TCD 1782–3–90, King's Co. 1791–7–1800 [HP].

1637 **PARSONS**, Wentworth; b. 25 Oct. 1745 d. [15] Oct. 1794; MP for Co. Longford 1766–8.

1638 **PARSONS**, Sir William [2nd Bt]; b. 8 June 1661 d. 17 Mar. 1740/1; MP for King's Co. 1692–3, 1695–9, 1703–13, 1715–27–41.

1639 **PARSONS**, Sir William [4th Bt]; b. [bapt. 6] May 1722 d. 1 May 1791; MP for King's Co. 1757–60, 1761–8–76–83–90–1.

1640 **PATERSON**, Rt Hon. Marcus; b. 1712 d. 12 Mar. 1787; MP for Ballynakill 1756–60–61–8, Lisburn 1768–70.

1641 **PAUL**, Christmas; b. *c.* 1710–17 d. 13 Mar. 1747/8; MP for Waterford city 1741–8.

1642 **PAUL**, Jeffrey; b. *ante* 19 July 1690 d. [*ante* 15 Sept.] 1721; MP for New Ross 1711–13, Co. Carlow 1713–14, Baltinglass 1715–21.

1643 **PAUL**, Jeffrey; b. *ante* 1687 d. 6 Feb. 1730; MP for Co. Carlow 1725–7–30.

1644 **PAUL**, Robert; b. *c.* 1742–4 d. 1821; MP for Lismore 1791–6.

1645 **PEARCE** [*alias* PEIRCE], Edward; b. *ante* 1660 d. *post* 1715; MP for Athenry 1692–3.

1646 **PEARCE** [*alias* PIERCE], Sir Edward Lovett [Kt]; b. *c.* 1699 d. 7 Dec. 1733; MP for Ratoath 1728–33.

1647 **PEARCE** [*alias* PEIRCE or PIERCE], Rt Hon. Thomas; b. *c.* 1667 d. 16 Jan. 1739; MP for Coleraine 1703–13, Limerick city 1727–39 [HP].

1648 **PEARSON**, Nathaniel; b. *ante* 1701 d. 12 May 1749; MP for Dublin city 1737–49.

1649 **PEARSON**, Thomas; b. 1678 d. 28 June 1736; MP for Killybegs 1710–13–14, 1715–27, Ballyshannon 1727–36.

1650 **PELHAM**, Rt Hon. Thomas [2nd E. of Chichester]; b. 28 Apr. 1756 d. 4 July 1826; MP for Carrick 1783–90, Clogher 1795–7, Armagh B. 1797–9 [HP].

1651 **PENNEFATHER**, Kingsmill; b. [bapt. 10 Jan.] 1670 d. 1 Feb. 1734/5; MP for Cashel 1703–13–14, Co. Tipperary 1715–27–35.

1652 **PENNEFATHER**, Kingsmill; b. 1727 d. 2 May 1771; MP for Cashel 1753–60, 1761–8–71.

1653 **PENNEFATHER**, Matthew; b. [bapt. 15] June 1675 d. 28 Nov. 1733; MP for Cashel 1710–13–14, 1715–27–33.

1654 **PENNEFATHER**, Richard; b. 1701 d. *c.* 7 Oct. 1777; MP for Cashel 1734–60, 1761–8–76–7.

1655 **PENNEFATHER**, Richard; b. [*ante* 26 Oct.] 1756 d. 16 May 1831; MP for Cashel 1777–83–90–7–1800 [HP].

1656 **PENNEFATHER**, William; b. 1733 d. Nov. 1819; MP for Cashel 1771–6–83.

1657 **PENNEFATHER**, William; b. *c.* 1760–2 d. 8 [bur. 10] Apr. 1803; MP for Cashel 1783–90–7.

1658 **PEPPARD**, James; b. *ante* 1664[9] d. [*ante* 7 Sept.] 1725; MP for Swords 1703–13, Philipstown 1713–14, Granard 1715–25.

1659 **PEPPARD**, Robert; b. *ante* 1640 d. [*ante* 27 Sept.] 1698; MP for Philipstown 1695–8.

1660 **PEPPER**, John; b. *ante* 1668 d. 22 Oct. 1725; MP for Gowran 1715–25 [HP].

1661 **PEPPER**, Thomas; b. 1733 d. [Dec.] 1800; MP for Kells 1761–8–76.

1662 **PEPPER**, Thomas; b. 12 Oct. 1774 d. 9 Oct. 1857; MP for Longford B. 1794–7, Kells Jan.–Aug. 1800.

1663 **PERCEVAL**, John; b. *c.* 1630 d. [June] 1719; MP for Granard 1692–3, 1695–9, 1703–13, Trim 1715–19.

1664 **PERCEVAL**, Rt Hon. Sir John [5th Bt, 1st B., V. Perceval and E. of Egmont]; b. 12 July 1683 d. 1 May 1748; MP for Co. Cork 1703–13–14 [HP].

1665 **PERCEVAL**, Rt Hon. John [2nd E. of Egmont]; b. 24 Feb. 1710/11 d. 20 Dec. 1770; MP for Dingle 1731–48 [HP].

1666 **PERCEVAL**, Philip; b. 13 Nov. 1686 d. 26 Apr. 1748; MP for Askeaton 1713–14.

1667 **PERCEVAL**, Robert; b. *ante* 21 Sept. 1696[1] d. 1777; MP for Trim 1717–27, 1761–8, Fore 1727–60.

1668 **PERCEVAL**, Thomas; b. *ante* 5 Oct. 1671[1] d. 1703; MP for Dundalk 1692–3, 1695–9.

1669 **PERCY**, Henry; b. 1674 d. [*ante* 7 Sept.] 1725; MP for Wicklow B. 1713–14, Co. Wicklow 1715–25.

1670 **PERY**, Rt Hon. Edmond Henry [2nd B. Glentworth, 1st V. Limerick and E. of Limerick]; b. 8 Jan. 1758 d. 7 Dec. 1844; MP for Limerick city 1786–90–4.

1671 **PERY**, Rt Hon. Edmond Sexton [1st V. Pery]; b. 8 Apr. 1719 d. 24 Feb. 1806; MP for Wicklow B. 1751–61, Limerick city 1761–8–76–83–5.

1672 **PETTY**, Rt Hon. Henry [1st B. Shelburne, V. Dunkerron and E. of Shelburne]; b. 22 Oct. 1675 d. 17 Apr. 1751; MP for Midleton 1692–3, Co. Waterford 1695–9 [HP].

1673 **PETTY** [FITZMAURICE], Rt Hon. William [2nd E. of Shelburne and 1st M. of Lansdowne]; b. 2 May 1737 d. 7 May 1805; MP for Co. Kerry Apr.–Oct. 1761 [HP].

1674 **PEYTON**, George; b. 1632 d. 15 Mar. 1698/9; MP for Co. Westmeath 1695–9.

1675 **PHILIPS**, Ambrose; b. 1675 d. 18 June 1749; MP for Armagh B. 1727–49.

1676 **PHILIPS**, Chichester; b. *ante* 1664 d. 1728; MP for Askeaton 1696–9, 1703–13.

1677 **PHILIPS**, George; b. 1630 d. 1697; MP for [Newtown Limavady 1661–6], Co. Londonderry 1692–3, 1695–7.

1678 **PHILIPS**, Thomas; b. *ante* 5 Oct. 1671[1] d. 1731; MP for Clonmines 1692–3.

1679 **PHILIPS**, William; b. *ante* 1677 d. 12 Dec. 1734; MP for Doneraile 1703–13.

1680 **PIGOTT**, Emanuel; b. 1684 d. 30 June 1762; MP for Cork city 1735–60.

1681 **PIGOTT**, John; b. 1715 d. 12 Dec. 1763; MP for Banagher 1761–3.

1682 **PIGOTT**, Robert; b. [*ante* 21 Sept.] 1682 d. 28 Mar. 1730; MP for Maryborough 1703–13–14, 1715–27–30.

1683 **PIGOTT**, Thomas; b. 13 Oct. 1734 d. 12 Oct. 1793; MP for Taghmon 1776–83, Midleton 1783–90–3.

1684 **PLUNKET**, Hon. Charles Patrick; b. 1686 d. [*ante* 23 Sept.] 1729; MP for Banagher 1711–13–14, 1715–27–9.

1685 **PLUNKET**, Sir Walter [Kt]; b. [bapt. 3 Sept.] 1622 d. 6 June 1702; MP for [Gorey 1661–6], Granard 1692–3, 1695–9.

1686 **PLUNKET**, Rt Hon. William Conyngham [1st B. Plunket]; b. 1 July 1764 d. 5 Jan. 1854; MP for Charlemont 1798–1800 [HP].

1687 **PLUNKET** [STOWELL-PLUNKET], Plunket; b. 1685 d. 29 Dec. 1748; MP for Swords 1713–14, 1715–27.

1688 **POCKRICH**, Richard; b. *c.* 1666 d. 1719; MP for Monaghan B. 1713–14.

1689 **POLE**, Periam; b. *ante* 1657 d. Oct. 1704; MP for Maryborough 1692–3.

1690 **POLE**, Rt Hon. William; b. *ante* 1727 d. Dec. 1781; MP for Queen's Co. 1761–8–76.

1691 **POLLARD**, Dillon; b. *c.* 1671 d. 1740; MP for Co. Westmeath 1692–3.

1692 **POLLARD**, Walter; b. *ante* 1641 d. 1718; MP for Fore 1695–9, 1703–13.

1693 **POMEROY**, Arthur [1st B. and V. Harberton]; b. 16 Jan. 1722/3 d. 11 Apr. 1798; MP for Co. Kildare 1761–8–76–83.

1694 **POMEROY**, Hon. Henry [2nd V. Harberton]; b. 8 Dec. 1749 d. 29 Nov. 1829; MP for Strabane 1776–83–90–7.

1695 **POMEROY**, Rt Hon. John; b. 1724 d. 10 June 1790; MP for Carrick 1755–60, Trim 1761–8–76–83–90, May–June 1790.

1696 **PONSONBY**, Rt Hon. Brabazon [V. Duncannon and 1st E. of Bessborough], b. 1679 d. 3 July 1758; MP for Newtown[ards] 1705–13–14, Co. Kildare 1715–24.

1697 **PONSONBY**, Chambre Brabazon; b. *c.* 1720 d. 20 Feb.1762; MP for Newtown[ards] 1750–60.

1698 **PONSONBY** [PONSONBY-BARKER], Chambre Brabazon; b. 12 June 1762 d. 13 Dec. 1834; MP for Dungarvan 1790–7.

1699 **PONSONBY**, Rt Hon. George; b. 4 Mar. 1755 d. 8 July 1817; MP for Wicklow B. 1778–83, Innistiogue 1783–90–7, Galway B. 1797–1800 [HP].

1700 **PONSONBY**, Hon. George; b. 1773 d. 5 June 1863; MP for Lismore 1796–7–8 [HP].

1701 **PONSONBY**, Hon. Henry; b. 1685 d. 11 May 1745; MP for Fethard [Wexford] 1715–27, Innistiogue 1727–45.

1702 **PONSONBY**, Rt Hon. John; b. 29 Mar. 1713 d. 16 Aug. 1787; MP for Newtown[ards] 1739–60, 1783–7, Co. Kilkenny 1761–8–76–83.

1703 **PONSONBY**, Hon. Sir John Brabazon [2nd B. and 1st V. Ponsonby]; b. 1770 d. 21 Feb. 1855; MP for Tallow 1793–7, Dungarvan 1797–1800 [r. Banagher 1797] [HP].

1704 **PONSONBY**, Richard; b. *ante* 29 Oct. 1710[1] d. 29 Nov. 1763; MP for Kinsale 1731–60.

1705 **PONSONBY**, Hon. Richard; b. 2 July 1722 d. 1800; MP for Knocktopher 1747–60, Newtown[ards] 1761–8.

1706 **PONSONBY**, Rt Hon. William [1st B. Bessborough and V. Duncannon]; b. 1659 d. 17 Nov. 1724; MP for Co. Kilkenny 1692–3, 1695–9, 1703–13–14, 1715–21.

1707 **PONSONBY**, Rt Hon. William [2nd E. of Bessborough]; b. [*ante* 28 Nov.] 1704 d. 11 Mar. 1793; MP for Newtown[ards] 1725–7, Co. Kilkenny 1727–59 [HP].

1708 **PONSONBY**, Hon. Sir William; b. 13 Oct. 1772 d. 18 June 1815; MP for Bandon-Bridge 1796–7, Fethard [Tipperary] 1797–1800 [HP].

1709 **PONSONBY**, Rt Hon. William Brabazon [1st B. Ponsonby [UK]]; b. 15 Sept. 1744 d. 5 Nov. 1806; MP for Cork city 1764–8–76, Bandon-Bridge 1776–83, Co. Kilkenny 1783–90–7–1800 [HP].

1710 **POOLEY**, Robert; b. *c.* 1644[8] d. *post* 1699; MP for Castlemartyr 1692–3, 1695–9.

1711 **POOLEY**, Thomas; b. 1640 d. [bur. 13] Feb. 1722/3; MP for Newcastle 1695–9.

1712 **POPHAM**, Stephen; b. 5 July 1745 d. 13 June 1795; MP for Castlebar 1776–83.

1713 **PORTER**, Frederick; b. *ante* 5 Oct. 1671 d. *post* 1699; MP for Newry 1692–3, 1695–9.

1714 **PORTER**, William; b. 30 Mar. 1633 d. 1716; MP for Newtown Limavady 1695–9.

1715 **PORTLOCK**, Benjamin; b. *c.* 1666 d. 6 Sept. 1740; MP for Innistiogue 1703–13.

1716 **POULTENEY** [*alias* PULTENAY], John; b. *ante* 1668 d. 2 May 1726; MP for Wexford B. 1692–3 [HP].

1717 **POWER**, Richard; b. *c.* 1724 d. 2 Feb. 1794; MP for Monaghan B. 1767–8, Tuam 1768–72.

1718 **POWER**, Richard; b. *c.* 1747 d. 18 Mar. 1814; MP for Co. Waterford 1797–1800 [HP].

1719 **POWER**, Roger; b. *ante* 1672 d. [*ante* 5 May] 1709; MP for Dungarvan 1703–9.

1720 **PRATT**, James: b. *c.* 1745 d. *c.* 1804; MP for Navan 1781–3.

1721 **PRATT**, John; b. 1670 d. 24 Mar. 1741; MP for Dingle 1713–14, 1715–27.

1722 **PRATT**, Mervyn; b. [bapt. 27 Apr.] 1667 d. 1751; MP for Co. Cavan 1715–27.

1723 **PRENDERGAST** [PRENDERGAST-SMYTH], John [1st B. Kiltarton and V. Gort]; b. 1742 d. 23 May 1817; MP for Carlow B. 1776–83, Limerick city 1785–90–7.

1724 **PRENDERGAST**, Sir Thomas [1st Bt]; b. *c.* 1660 d. 11 Sept. 1709; MP for Monaghan B. 1703–9.

1725 **PRENDERGAST**, Rt Hon. Sir Thomas [2nd Bt]; b. *c.* 1700 d. 23 Sept. 1760; MP for Clonmel 1733–60 [HP].

1726 **PRENDERGAST**, Thomas; b. 1764 d. 1804; MP for Clonakilty 1796–7–1800.

1727 **PRESTON**, John; b. 23 Apr. 1677 d. 23 Sept. 1732; MP for Co. Meath 1709–13–14, 1715–27–32.

1728 **PRESTON**, John; b. 25 Jan. 1699/1700 d. 27 Dec. 1753; MP for Navan 1732–53.

1729 **PRESTON**, John; b. *c.* 1731–4 d. 19 Jan. 1781; MP for Navan 1761–8, 1769–76–81.

1730 **PRESTON**, Rt Hon. John [1st B. Tara]; b. 4 Nov. 1764 d. 18 July 1821; MP for Navan 1783–90–7–1800.

1731 **PRESTON**, Joseph; b. *c.* 1732–40 d. 1819; MP for Navan 1761–8–76–83–90–7–1800.

1732 **PRESTON**, Nathaniel; b. *c.* 1678 d. [Nov.] 1760; MP for Navan 1713–14, 1715–27–60.

1733 **PRICE**, Cromwell; b. 1696 d. 4 Nov. 1776; MP for Downpatrick 1727–60.

1734 **PRICE**, Cromwell; b. 1752 d. 23 Mar. 1798; MP for Kinsale 1783–90, Monaghan B. 1791–7, Fore 7–23 Mar. 1798.

1735 **PRICE**, Francis; b. June 1728 d. 7 Mar. 1794; MP for Lisburn 1759–60, 1761–8–76.

1736 **PRICE**, John; b. *ante* 1662 d. [23] Sept. 1704; MP for Co. Wicklow 1692–3, 1695–9, Wicklow B. 1703–4.

1737 **PRICE**, Nicholas; b. *c.* 1665[7] d. 29 Sept. 1734; MP for Downpatrick 1692–3, Co. Down 1695–9, 1703–13–14.

1738 **PRICE**, Nicholas; b. 1700 d. [16–22] Dec. 1742; MP for Lisburn 1736–42.

1739 **PRIOR**, Thomas; b. 1773 d. 1832; MP for Bannow Mar.–Aug. 1800.

1740 **PRITTIE**, Hon. Francis Aldborough; b. 4 June 1779 d. 8 Mar. 1853; MP for Doneraile Jan.–Aug. 1800 [HP].

1741 **PRITTIE**, Henry; b. 1708 d. 11 Apr. 1768; MP for Co. Tipperary 1761–8.

1742 **PRITTIE**, Henry [1st B. Dunalley]; b. 3 Oct. 1743 d. 3 Jan. 1801; MP for Banagher 1767–8, Gowran 1769–76, Co. Tipperary 1776–83–90.

1743 **PRITTIE**, Hon. Henry Sadleir [2 B. Dunalley]; b. 3 Mar. 1775 d. 19 Oct. 1854; MP for Carlow B. 1797–1800 [HP].

1744 **PURCELL**, Theobald; b. *ante* 1667 d. *post* 1713; MP for Ardfert 1695–9.

1745 **PURDON**, Bartholomew; b. 1675 d. 17 July 1737; MP for Mallow Jan.–June 1699, 1703–13, Doneraile 1713–14, Castlemartyr 1715–27–37.

1746 **PURDON**, George; b. [bapt. 25] July 1688 d. July 1740; MP for Co. Clare 1725–7.

1747 **PURDON**, Henry; b. *c.* 1687–9[3] d. 9 Dec. 1737; MP for Charleville 1721–7.

1748 **PURDON**, Simon; b. 1655 d. 4 Nov. 1720; MP for Ennis 1703–13.

1749 **PUREFOY**, Peter; b. *c.* 1640[6] d. *c.* 1693[10]; MP for Philipstown 1692–3.

1750 **PUREFOY**, William; b. 1660 d. 26 Oct. 1737; MP for King's Co. 1707–13, 1715–27, Philipstown 1713–14.

1751 **PUTLAND**, George; b. 1745 d. 1811; MP for Ratoath 1776–83.

1752 **PYNE**, Henry; b. [*ante* 13 May] 1688 d. 28 Feb. 1712/3; MP for Dungarvan 1709–13.

1753 **QUIN**, Sir Valentine Richard [1st Bt, 1st B. and V. Adare, V. Mount-Earl and E. of Dunraven]; b. 30 July 1752 d. 24 Aug. 1824; MP for Kilmallock 1800 [sworn 15 January 1800].

1754 **QUIN**, Windham; b. 1717 d. May 1789; MP for Kilmallock 1768–76.

1755 **RADCLIFFE**, Thomas; b. 1715 d. 24 Jan. 1776; MP for St Canice 1774–6.

1756 **RAM**, Abel; b. 1669 d. 14 Sept. 1740; MP for Gorey 1692–3, 1695–9, 1703–13, 1715–27–40.

1757 **RAM**, Abel; b. [bapt. 4 Feb.] 1705/6 d. [*ante* 20] Aug. 1778; MP for Gorey 1727–60, 1761–8–76.

1758 **RAM**, Abel; b. [bapt. 31 Jan.] 1754 d. 1830; MP for Duleek 1783–90, Co. Wexford 1797–1800 [HP].

1759 **RAM**, Andrew; b. *ante* 1657 d. [*ante* 27 Sept.] 1698; MP for Duleek 1692–3, 1695–8.

1760 **RAM**, Andrew; b. 1711 d. Aug. 1793; MP for Co. Wexford 1755–60, Duleek 1761–8, 1769–76–83–90.

1761 **RAM**, George; b. 1676 d. [*ante* 22 Oct.] 1725; MP for Gorey 1713–14, 1715–25.

1762 **RAM**, Humphreys; b. *c.* 1707–9 d. 2 Feb. 1781; MP for Gorey 1741–60, 1776–81.

1763 **RAM**, Stephen; b. *c.* 1671–5 d. 16 Oct. 1746; MP for Gorey 1725–7, Duleek 1728–46.

1764 **RAM**, Stephen; b. 1744 d. 8 Mar. 1821; MP for Gorey 1764–8–76–83–90.

1765 **RAWDON**, Rt Hon. Sir Arthur [2nd Bt]; b. 17 Oct. 1662 d. 17 Oct. 1695; MP for Co. Down 1692–3, Aug.–Oct. 1695.

1766 **RAWDON** [RAWDON-HASTINGS], Rt Hon. Francis [1st Viscount Loudoun, 2nd E. of Moira, 1st B. Rawdon, 1st M. of Hastings]; b. 7 Dec. 1754 d. 28 Nov. 1826; MP for Randalstown 1781–3.

1767 **RAWDON**, Sir John [3rd Bt]; b. 1690 d. 2 Feb. 1723/4; MP for Co. Down 1717–23/4.

1768 **RAWSON**, George; b. *ante* 1746 d. 8 Jan. 1796; MP for Armagh B. 1777–83–90–6.

1769 **READE**, George Harrison; b. 1762 d. 28 Oct. 1833; MP for Fethard [Wexford] 1799–1800 [re-elected pp 1800].

1770 **READING**, Daniel; b. *ante* 1642 d. [*ante* Mar.] 1706/7; MP for Newcastle 1692–3, 1703–7.

1771 **READING**, Daniel; b. *ante* 1664 d. [*ante* 17] Feb. 1725/6; MP for Newcastle 1707–13–14, 1715–26.

1772 **READING**, John; b. 1665 d. [*post* 14 June] 1699; MP for Swords 1692–3, 1695–9.

1773 **REILLY**, John; b. 1745 d. 26 July 1804; MP for Blessington 1779–83–90–7–1800.

1774 **REILLY**, William Edmond; b. [*ante* 3 Feb.] 1779 d. Apr. 1849; MP for Hillsborough Jan.–Aug. 1800.

1775 **REYNELL**, Edmund; b. *ante* 1673 d. 3 Feb. 1697/8; MP for Jamestown 1695–8.

1776 **REYNELL**, Sir Richard [2nd Bt]; b. [8] Dec. 1673 d. June 1723; MP for Wicklow B. 1692–3.

1777 **REYNOLDS**, John; b. 1670 d. 1699; MP for Co. Leitrim 1692–3, 1695–9.

1778 **RICASEY** [*alias* RICHASIES or RICKASEY], Charles; b. 1667 d. July 1742; MP for Baltinglass 1696–9, 1703–13–14.

1779 **RICHARDS**, Fitzherbert; b. 1729 d. 1811; MP for Lisburn 1776–83.

1780 **RICHARDSON**, Archibald; b. *ante* 1660 d. *post* 1693; MP for Augher 1692–3.

1781 **RICHARDSON**, Edward; b. *ante* 5 Oct. 1671 d. 5 Dec. 1729; MP for Baltimore 1692–3, 1695–9.

1782 **RICHARDSON**, John; b. 1741 d. 1801; MP for Newtown Limavady 1783–90–5.

1783 **RICHARDSON**, St George; b. *post* 1711 d. [bur. 9] Sept. 1777; MP for Augher 1755–60.

1784 **RICHARDSON**, William; b. 1656 d. 1 June 1727; MP for Co. Armagh 1692–3, 1715–27, Hillsborough 1703–13.

1785 **RICHARDSON**, William; b. [?]*c.* 1690 d. 26 May 1755; MP for Augher 1737–55.

1786 **RICHARDSON**, William; b. 1710 d. 22 Feb. 1758; MP for Co. Armagh 1739–58.

1787 **RICHARDSON**, William; b. 1749 d. 23 Mar. 1822; MP for Co. Armagh 1783–90–7 [HP].

1788 **RICHARDSON**, Sir William [1st Bt]; b. *post* 1749 d. 29 Oct. 1830; MP for Augher 1783–90, Ballyshannon 1798–1800.

1789 **RIGBY**, Rt Hon. Richard; b. Feb. 1722 d. early Apr. 1788; MP for Old Leighlin 1757–60 [HP].

1790 **RIGGS**, Edward; b. *c.* 1620 d. 1706; MP for Bandon-Bridge 1692–3, 1695–9.

1791 **RIGGS**, Edward; b. *ante* 11 July 1686 d. 13 Nov. 1741; MP for Baltimore 1707–13, Bangor 1716–27, Newtown Limavady 1739–41.

1792 **RILEY** [*alias* REILLY], Edward; b. *ante* 1654 d. [bur. 21] Nov. 1723; MP for Charlemont 1695–9.

1793 **ROBARTES**, Rt Hon. Francis; b. [bapt. 6 Jan.] 1649/50 d. 3 Feb. 1717/8; MP for Kildare B. 1692–3 [HP].

1794 **ROBERTS**, Robert; b. *c.* 1680 d. 4 Jan. 1758; MP for Dungarvan 1736–58.

1795 **ROBINSON**, Sir William [Kt]; b. [bapt. 18 May] 1644 d. 22 Oct. 1712; MP for Knocktopher 1692–3, Wicklow B. 1695–9, TCD 1703–12.

1796 **ROCHE**, Sir Boyle [Kt, 1st Bt]; b. Oct. 1736 d. 5 June 1807; MP for Tralee 1775–6, 1790–7, Gowran 1777–83, Portarlington 1784–90, Old Leighlin 1797–1800.

1797 **ROCHE**, George; b. *c.* 1677–9 d. 18 Dec. 1740; MP for Limerick city 1713–14, 1715–27.

1798 **ROCHFORT**, Arthur; b. 7 Nov. 1711 d. 22 Apr. 1774; MP for Co. Westmeath 1738–60.

1799 **ROCHFORT**, George; b. 17 Jan. 1683 d. 8 July 1730; MP for Co. Westmeath 1707–13–14, 1727–30.

1800 **ROCHFORT**, Hon. George [2nd E. of Belvidere]; b. 12 Oct. 1738 d. 14 Dec. 1815; MP for Philipstown 1759–60, Co. Westmeath 1761–8–75.

1801 **ROCHFORT**, George; b. 24 Apr. 1713 d. 1786; MP for Co.Westmeath 1775–6.

1802 **ROCHFORT**, Gustavus Hume; b. *c.* 1750 d. 30 Jan. 1824; MP for Co. Westmeath 1798–1800 [HP].

1803 **ROCHFORT**, John; b. Aug. 1692 d. 30 Jan. 1771; MP for Ballyshannon 1713–14, 1715–27, Mullingar 1727–60.

1804 **ROCHFORT**, John Staunton; b. 1763 d. 5 May 1844; MP for Coleraine 1796–7, Fore 1798–1800.

1805 **ROCHFORT** [ROCHFORT-MERVYN], Hon. Richard; b. 12 Dec. 1740 d. 26 Jan. 1776; MP for Co. Westmeath 1761–8, Philipstown 1768–76.

1806 **ROCHFORT**, Rt Hon. Robert; b. 9 Dec. 1652 d. 10 Oct. 1727; MP for Co. Westmeath 1692–3, 1695–9, 1703–7.

1807 **ROCHFORT**, Rt Hon. Robert [1st B., V. Belfield and E. of Belvidere]; b. 26 Mar. 1708 d. 13 Nov. 1774; MP for Co. Westmeath 1731–8.

1808 **ROCHFORT**, Hon. Robert; b. 1743 d. 17 Oct. 1797; MP for Philipstown 1761–8, Augher 1768–76, Co. Westmeath 1776–83–90–7, July–Oct. 1797.

1809 **ROGERS**, George; b. 1650 d. 11 May 1710; MP for Lismore 1692–3, 1695–9.

1810 **ROGERS**, Robert; b. *post* 1650 d. 1717; MP for Cork City 1692–3, 1695–9.

1811 **ROGERSON**, Sir John [Kt]; b. 1648 d. 1724; MP for Clogher 1692–3, Dublin city 1695–9.

1812 **ROGERSON**, Rt Hon. John; b. 1676 d. 24 Aug. 1741; MP for Granard 1713–14, Dublin city 1715–27.

1813 **ROSE**, Henry; b. 1675 d. 12 Jan. 1742/3; MP for Ardfert 1703–13–14, 1715–27–34.

1814 **ROSS**, Robert; b. *c.* 1679[7] d. 29 Nov. 1750; MP for Killyleagh 1715–27, Newry 1727–50.

1815 **ROSS**, Robert; b. *c.* 1701–2 d. 5 Feb. 1769; MP for Carlingford 1723–7–60, 1761–8.

1816 **ROSS**, Rt Hon. Robert; b. [bapt. 24 Feb.] 1728/9 d. 24 Feb. 1799; MP for Carlingford 1768–76, Newry 1776–83–90–7–9.

1817 **ROTH**, George; b. 1729 d. 19 Jan. 1786; MP for Thomastown 1783–6.

1818 **ROWLEY**, Clotworthy; b. 1731 d. 25 Mar. 1805; MP for Downpatrick 1771–6–83–90–7–1800 [HP].

1819 **ROWLEY**, Hercules; b. 1679 d. 19 Sept. 1742; MP for Co. Londonderry 1703–13–14, 1715–27–42.

1820 **ROWLEY**, Hon. Hercules [2nd V. Langford]; b. 29 Oct. 1737 d. 24 Mar. 1796; MP for Co. Antrim 1783–90–1.

1821 **ROWLEY**, Rt Hon. Hercules Langford; b. 1708 d. 25 Mar. 1794; MP for Co. Londonderry 1743–60, Co. Meath 1761–8–76–83–90–4.

1822 **ROWLEY**, Hugh; b. *ante* 1640 d. 1701; MP for Newtown Limavady 1692–3.

1823 **ROWLEY**, Sir Josias [1st Bt]; b. 1765 d. 10 Jan. 1842; MP for Downpatrick 1797–1800 [HP].

1824 **ROWLEY**, Samuel Campbell; b. 19 Jan. 1774 d. 28 Jan. 1846; MP for Kinsale 1797–1800 [HP].

1825 **ROWLEY**, William; b. 1764 d. 25 Feb. 1812; MP for Kinsale 1790–7–1800 [re-elected pp 1799] [HP].

1826 **RUGGE**, Henry; b. 1683 d. Dec. 1762; MP for Youghal 1719–27.

1827 **RUSSELL**, Hon. Francis [styled M. of Tavistock [E.] 1739–67]; b. 27 Sept. 1739 d. 22 Mar. 1767; MP for Armagh B. 1759–60 [HP].

1828 **RUSSELL**, Sir William [4th Bt]; b. *ante* 1669 d. Sept. 1709; MP for Carlow B. 1692–3.

1829 **RUTLEDGE**, Robert; b. 1766 d. 25 May 1833; MP for Taghmon Mar.–July 1797, Duleek 1797–1800.

1830 **RUXTON**, Charles; b. 1726 d. 1806; MP for Ardee 1761–8, 1783–90, 1797–9.

1831 **RUXTON**, John; b. 1721 d. 7 Mar. 1785; MP for Ardee 1751–60, 1761–8–76, 1783–5.

1832 **RUXTON**, William; b. 1697 d. 15 Feb. 1750/1; MP for Ardee 1748–51.

1833 **RUXTON**, William; b. *c.* 1742–9[8] d. 1821; MP for Ardee 1785–90, 1797–1800.

1834 **RUXTON**, William Parkinson; b. 1766 d. 11 Oct. 1847; MP for Ardee 1790–7, 1799–1800.

1835 **SACKVILLE** [GERMAIN], Rt Hon. Ld George [1st V. Sackville]; b. 26 Jan. 1716 d. 26 Aug. 1785; MP for Portarlington 1733–60 [HP].

1836 **ST GEORGE**, Arthur; b. 1629 d. Aug. 1701; MP for Athlone [1661–6], 1692–3, 1695–9.

1837 **ST GEORGE**, Rt Hon. Sir George [2nd Bt, 1st B. St George]; b. 1651 d. 4 Aug. 1735; MP for Co. Roscommon 1692–3, 1695–9, 1703–13–14.

1838 **ST GEORGE**, Sir George [Kt]; b. *ante* 1640 d. [Dec.] 1713; MP for [Co. Leitrim 1661] Co. Galway 1695–9, Carrick 1703–11.

1839 **ST GEORGE**, George; b. 2 July 1682 d. 23 Dec. 1762; MP for Athlone 1723–7–60.

1840 **ST GEORGE**, Henry; b. 30 July 1676 d. Oct. 1723; MP for Clogher 1703–13, Athlone 1715–23 [r. Clogher 1715].

1841 **ST GEORGE**, Henry; b. 18 Apr. 1716 d. July 1763; MP for Athlone 1761–3.

1842 **ST GEORGE**, Rt Hon. Sir Oliver [1st Bt]; b. *ante* 1640[1] d. Oct. 1695; MP for Co. Galway [1661–6], 1692–3.

1843 **ST GEORGE**, Rt Hon. Oliver; b. 1661 d. 15 Apr. 1731; MP for Carrick 1703–13, Dungannon 1713–14, 1715–27–31.

1844 **ST GEORGE**, Richard; b. 28 Aug. 1670 d. Jan. 1755; MP for Galway B. 1695–9, Carrick 1715–27–55.

1845 **ST GEORGE**, Rt Hon. Richard; b. 1657 d. 28 Sept. 1726; MP for Clogher 1703–13–14, 1715–26.

1846 **ST GEORGE**, Sir Richard [1st Bt]; b. 1718 d. 25 Feb. 1789; MP for Athlone 1763–8–76–83–9.

1847 **ST GEORGE**, Richard; b. 5 Oct. 1757 d. 10 Mar. 1790; MP for Charleville 1783–90.

1848 **ST GEORGE**, Sir Richard Bligh [2nd Bt]; b. 5 June 1765 d. 29 Dec. 1851; MP for Athlone 1789–90–7–1800.

1849 **ST GEORGE** [USSHER-ST GEORGE], St George [1st B. St George]; b. *c.* 1715 d. 2 Jan. 1775; MP for Carrick 1741–60, 1761–3.

1850 **ST GEORGE**, Thomas; b. Oct. 1738 d. 1 Apr. 1785; MP for Clogher 1776–83–5.

1851 **ST LAWRENCE**, Rt Hon. William [14th B. Howth]; b. 11 Jan. 1687/8 d. 4 Apr. 1748; MP for Ratoath 1716–27.

1852 **ST LEGER**, Rt Hon. Arthur [1st B. Kilmayden and V. Doneraile]; b. 1657 d. 7 July 1727; MP for Doneraile 1692–3.

1853 **ST LEGER**, Hon. Arthur [2nd V. Doneraile]; b. 1695 d. 13 Mar. 1733/4; MP for Doneraile 1715–27.

1854 **ST LEGER**, Hon. Barry Boyle; b. 23 Nov. 1768 d. *post* Jan. 1800; MP for Doneraile 1798–9.

1855 **ST LEGER**, Rt Hon. Hayes [4th V. Doneraile]; b. [1] Jan. 1701/2 d. 16 Apr. 1767; MP for Doneraile 1728–51.

1856 **ST LEGER**, Hon. Hayes [2nd V. Doneraile]; b. 9 Mar. 1755 d. 8 Nov. 1819; MP for Doneraile 1776–83–8.

1857 **ST LEGER**, John; b. *ante* 1634 d. 31 Mar. 1696; MP for [Co. Cork 1665–6], Doneraile 1692–3, Tralee 1695–6.

1858 **ST LEGER**, Sir John [Kt]; b. 1674 d. 14 May 1743; MP for Doneraile 1713–14.

1859 **ST LEGER**, John; b. 10 Apr. 1726 d. [bur. 20] Mar. 1769; MP for Doneraile 1761–8, Athy 1768–9.

1860 **ST LEGER**, Hon. Richard; b. 12 July 1756 d. 30 Dec. 1840; MP for Doneraile 1777–83.

1861 **SALE**, John; b. *ante* 1679 d. 7 July 1732; MP for Carysfort 1715–27–32.

1862 **SAMPSON**, Michael; b. *ante* 1679 d. [*ante* 8 Oct.] 1719; MP for Lifford 1711–13–14, 1715–19.

1863 **SANDES**, William; b. *ante* 18 Aug. 1676[1] d. 1721; MP for Co. Kerry 1697–9.

1864 **SANDFORD**, Blayney; b. 1666 d. 1710; MP for Knocktopher 1695–9.

1865 **SANDFORD**, Edward; b. *c.* 1696 d. 5 Oct. 1781; MP for Roscommon B. 1759–60, Harristown 1761–8.

1866 **SANDFORD**, George [3rd B. Mount Sandford]; b. 10 May 1756 d. 25 Sept. 1846; MP for Roscommon B. 1783–90–7, 1798–9.

1867 **SANDFORD**, Henry; b. *ante* 5 Oct. 1671[1] d. 9 Sept. 1733; MP for Roscommon B. 1692–3, 1695–9, 1703–13–14, 1715–27–33.

1868 **SANDFORD**, Henry; b. 30 Dec. 1719 d. 1796; MP for Co. Roscommon 1741–60, Kildare B. 1761–8, Carrick 1768–76.

1869 **SANDFORD**, Henry Moore [1st B. Mount Sandford]; b. 28 July 1751 d. 20 June 1814; MP Roscommon B. 1776–83, 1791–7–1800.

1870 **SANDFORD**, Robert; b. 1692 d. 24 Mar. 1777; MP for Boyle 1715–27, Newcastle 1727–60.

1871 **SANDFORD**, Robert; b. 13 June 1722 d. 14 July 1793; MP for Athy 1753–60, 1761–8, Roscommon B. 1768–76–83.

1872 **SANDFORD**, William; b. [bapt. 3 Sept.] 1704 d. [*ante* 16 Oct.] 1759; MP for Roscommon B. 1733–59.

1873 **SANDYS** [*alias* SANDES], Lancelot; b. *ante* 1671 d. [Mar./Apr.] 1728; MP for Portarlington 1723–7.

1874 **SANDYS**, Robert; b. *ante* 1661[6] d. Oct. 1703; MP for Roscommon B. Aug.–Oct. 1703.

1875 **SANKEY**, Nicholas; b. 1657 d. [4] Nov. 1722; MP for Lanesborough 1703–13.

1876 **SANKEY**, Richard; b. *ante* 1657 d. 1693; MP for Fethard [Tipperary] 1692–3.

1877 **SANKEY**, William; b. *c.* 1745–7 d. 25 Nov. 1813; MP for Philipstown 1790–7.

1878 **SAUNDERS**, Anderson; b. *c.* 1653 d. Feb. [bur. 1 Mar.] 1717/8; MP for Taghmon 1692–3, 1695–9, 1703–13–14, 1715–18.

1879 **SAUNDERS**, Anderson; b. 1716 d. 1783; MP for Enniscorthy 1740–60.

1880 **SAUNDERS**, Morley; b. 1671 d. 1737; MP for Enniscorthy 1703–13–14.

1881 **SAUNDERS**, Richard; b. 1679 d. 28 July 1730; MP for Taghmon 1703–13, 1715–27–30, Wexford B. 1713–14.

1882 **SAUNDERS**, Robert; b. *c.* 1652–4 d. 1708; MP for Cavan B. 1692–3, 1695–9, 1703–8.

1883 **SAUNDERSON** [*alias* SANDERSON], Francis; b. 15 Sept. 1754 d. 1827; MP for Co. Cavan 1788–90–7–1800 [HP].

1884 **SAUNDERSON** [*alias* SANDERSON], James; b. *ante* 1706 d. 7 May 1767; MP for Enniskillen 1727–60.

1885 **SAUNDERSON** [*alias* SANDERSON], Robert; b. 1653 d. 28 Mar. 1724; MP for Co. Cavan 1692–3, 1695–6, 1713–14 [expelled 1696 for refusing to sign the Association].

1886 **SAURIN**, Rt Hon. William; b. 1757 d. 11 Jan. 1839; MP for Blessington Jan.–Aug. 1800.

1887 **SAVAGE**, Francis; b. 16 Dec. 1769 d. 19 Sept. 1823; MP for Co. Down 1794–7–1800 [HP].

1888 **SAVAGE**, James; b. 1765 d. 18 May 1803; MP for Callan 1799–1800.

1889 **SAVAGE**, Rt Hon. Philip; b. Feb. 1644 d. [bur. 13] July 1717; MP for Co. Wexford 1692–3, 1695–9, 1703–13–14.

1890 **SAVILLE**, George; b. 1682 d. *post* 1714; MP for Taghmon 1713–14.

1891 **SCOTT**, Rt Hon. John [1st B. Earlsfort, V. Clonmell and E. of Clonmell]; b. 8 June 1739 d. 23 May 1798; MP for Mullingar 1769–76–83, Portarlington 1783–4.

1892 **SCOTT**, Robert; b. 1718 d. 22 Dec. 1773; MP for Newry 1751–60, 1768–73, Sligo B. 1762–8.

1893 **SCOTT**, William; b. 1705 d. 17 Apr. 1776; MP for Londonderry city 1739–59.

1894 **SEDGWICK**, Zaccheus; b. *ante* Aug. 1671 d. [bur. 20] Aug. 1695; MP for Carlingford 1692–3, 1695.

1895 **SEYMOUR**, John; b. *ante* 1641 d. 1701; MP for Enniscorthy 1692–3, 1695–9.

1896 **SEYMOUR-CONWAY** [INGRAM-SEYMOUR-CONWAY], Rt Hon. Francis [2nd M. of Hertford]; b. 12 Feb. 1742/3 d. 17 June 1822; MP for Lisburn 1761–8, Co. Antrim 1768–76 [HP].

1897 **SEYMOUR-CONWAY**, Hon. Sir Henry [KB]; b. 15 Dec. 1746 d. 5 Feb. 1830; MP for Co. Down 1766–8, Co. Antrim 1776–83 [HP].

1898 **SEYMOUR-CONWAY**, Popham; b. *c.* 1674–6 d. 18 June 1699; MP for Lisburn 1697–9.

1899 **SEYMOUR-CONWAY**, Hon. Robert; b. 20 Dec. 1748 d. 23 Nov. 1831; MP for Lisburn 1771–6 [HP].

1900 **SHAEN**, Sir Arthur [2nd Bt]; b. *post* 1650 d. 24 June 1725; MP for Lismore 1692–3, 1695–9, 1703–13–14, 1715–25.

1901 **SHAEN**, Sir James [1st Bt]; b. *ante* 1629 d. 13 Dec. 1695; MP for [Clonmel 1661–6], Baltinglass 1692–3, Aug.–Dec. 1695.

1902 **SHARKEY**, Richard Fortescue; b. 1756 d. [?]1827; MP for Dungannon 1799–1800.

1903 **SHARMAN**, William; b. *c.* 1695 d. 1775; MP for Randalstown 1749–60.

1904 **SHARMAN**, William; b. 1730 d. 21 Jan. 1803; MP for Lisburn 1783–90.

1905 **SHAW**, Robert; b. *c.* 1682–4³ d. [6] Nov. 1737; MP for Galway B. 1715–27.

1906 **SHAW**, Sir Robert [1st Bt]; b. 29 Jan. 1774 d. 10 Mar. 1849; MP for Bannow 1799–1800, St Johnstown [Longford] Jan.–Aug. 1800 [HP].

1907 **SHAW**, William; b. *c.* 1659–65 d. 1720; MP for Hillsborough 1692–3, 1695–9.

1908 **SHAW**, William; b. 1662 d. *c.* 1713; MP for Dundalk 1692–3.

1909 **SHEARES**, Henry; b. [bapt. 20 Oct.] 1728 d. 1 Dec. 1775; MP for Clonakilty 1761–8.

1910 **SHEE**, Sir George [1st Bt]; b. Jan. 1754 d. 3 Feb. 1825; MP for Knocktopher 1797–1800 [re-elected pp 1800].

1911 **SHEIL**, James; b. *c.* 1723 d. *c.* 1782; MP for Dundalk 1771–6.

1912 **SHEPPARD**, Anthony; b. 1668 d. 14 June 1738; MP for Co.Longford 1703–13, 1715–27–38.

1913 **SHEPPARD**, Anthony; b. 1701 d. 5 Apr. 1737; MP for Newcastle 1726–7, Longford B. 1727–37.

1914 **SHERIDAN**, Charles Francis; b. June 1750 d. 24 June 1806; MP for Belturbet 1776–83, Rathcormack 1783–90.

1915 **SHERIDAN**, Richard; b. 1750 d. 12 Dec. 1793; MP for Charlemont 1790–3.

1916 **SHERLOCK**, William; b. [bapt. 13 May] 1770 d. 1820; MP for Kilbeggan 1790–7.

1917 **SHIRLEY**, Washington [2nd E. Ferrers]; b. 22 June 1677 d. 14 Apr. 1729; MP for Fore 1713–14.

1918 **SHORT**, John; b. [?]1682 d. 1723; MP for Portarlington 1716–23.

1919 **SIBTHORPE**, Robert; b. 1724 d. [*ante* 5] Mar. 1791; MP for Granard 1761–8, Dunleer 1769–76.

1920 **SIBTHORPE**, Stephen; b. *c.* 1696 d. [*ante* 10] Apr. 1773; MP for Co. Louth 1767–8.

1921 **SILVER**, John; b. *c.* 1665 d. 1724; MP for Rathcormack 1703–13.

1922 **SINGLETON**, Edward; b. *ante* 1653 d. 1710; MP for Drogheda 1692–3, 1695–9, 1703–10.

1923 **SINGLETON**, Edward; b. *c.* 1674 d. [*ante* 8 Mar.] 1725/6; MP for Drogheda 1717–26.

1924 **SINGLETON**, Rt Hon. Henry; b. 1682 d. 9 [bur. 28] Nov. 1759; MP for Drogheda 1713–14, 1715–27–40 [r. Dunleer 1727].

1925 **SINGLETON**, Mark; b. 1762 d. 17 July 1840; MP for Carysfort 1800 [HP].

1926 **SINGLETON** [FOWKE], Sydenham; b. *ante* 1732⁷ d. 1801; MP for Drogheda 1776–83.

1927 **SKEFFINGTON**, Hon. Arthur; b. 1715 d. 8 Apr. 1747; MP for Co. Antrim 1741–7.

1928 **SKEFFINGTON**, Hon. Chichester [4th E. of Massereene]; b. 1751 d. 25 Feb. 1816; MP for Antrim B. 1776–83–90, 1791–7.

1929 **SKEFFINGTON**, Hon. Clotworthy [3rd V. Massereene]; b. 1661 d. 14 Mar. 1713/4; MP for Co. Antrim 1692–3.

1930 **SKEFFINGTON**, Hon. Clotworthy [4th V. Massereene]; b. *c.* 1681 d. 11 Feb. 1738/9; MP for Co. Antrim 1703–13–14.

1931 **SKEFFINGTON**, Hon. Henry [3rd E. of Massereene]; b. 1744 d. 12 June 1811; MP for Belfast 1768–76–83–90–7, Antrim B. 1797–1800.

1932 **SKEFFINGTON**, Hon. Hugh; b. 1725 d. [bur. 19] Apr. 1803; MP for Co. Antrim 1747–60, 1761–8, Antrim B. 1769–76.

1933 **SKEFFINGTON**, Hon. Hungerford; b. 1725 d. 18 Sept. 1768; MP for Antrim B. 1749–60, 1761–8, July–Sept. 1768.

1934 **SKEFFINGTON**, Hon. John; b. 1696 d. 12 Nov. 1741; MP for Antrim B. 1717–27, Co. Antrim 1727–41.

1935 **SKEFFINGTON**, Hon. William John; b. 1747 d. 1811; MP for Antrim B. 1768–76–83–90–7–1800.

1936 **SLATTERY**, Joseph; b. *c.* 1681[3] d. 13 Nov. 1726; MP for Blessington 1724–6.

1937 **SLOANE**, James; b. 1655 d. 5 Nov. 1704; MP for Killyleagh 1692–3, 1695–9 [HP].

1938 **SMITH**, Rt Hon. Sir Michael [1st Bt]; b. 7 Sept. 1740 d. 17 Dec. 1808; MP for Randalstown 1783–90, 1791–3.

1939 **SMITH**, Robert; b. Apr. 1670 d. Apr. 1695; MP for Kilkenny city 1692–3 [HP].

1940 **SMITH**, Roger; b. *ante* 1656 d. *post* 1703; MP for Carrick 1692–3, Sligo B. 1695–9.

1941 **SMITH** [*alias* SMYTH], Thomas; b. *post* 1644 d. 27 [bur. 30] Oct. 1712; MP for Killybegs 1692–3, Fore 1695–9, 1703–12.

1942 **SMITH**, William; b. *ante* 12 Jan. 1740/1 d. Jan. 1805; MP for Athy 1762–8.

1943 **SMITH** [CUSACK-SMITH], Sir William [2nd Bt]; b. 23 Jan. 1766 d. 21 Aug. 1836; MP for Lanesborough 1794–7, Donegal B. 1797–1800 [re-elected pp 1796].

1944 **SMYTH**, Boyle; b. *ante* 25 Nov. 1692 d. 25 Aug. 1730; MP for Youghal 1713–14.

1945 **SMYTH**, Charles; b. 1698 d. 18 Aug. 1784; MP for Limerick city 1731–60, 1761–8–76.

1946 **SMYTH**, Edward; b. 1705 d. 2 Feb. 1788; MP for Lisburn 1743–60.

1947 **SMYTH**, George; b. 1705 d. 15 Feb. 1772; MP for Blessington 1759–60, 1761–8, June–Nov. 1768.

1948 **SMYTH**, James; b. *c.* 1712–20 d. 22 June 1771; MP for Antrim B. 1744–60, 1761–8, Dundalk 1769–71.

1949 **SMYTH**, Rt Hon. Sir Skeffington Edward [1st Bt]; b. May 1745 d. 9 Sept. 1797; MP for Mullingar 1779–83, Belturbet 1783–90, Galway B. 1790–7.

1950 **SMYTH**, Sir Thomas [2nd Bt]; b. *post* 1657 d. 20 June 1732; MP for Kilkenny city 1703–13, Duleek 1713–14.

1951 **SMYTH**, Thomas; b. *c.* 1732 d. 14 Jan. 1785; MP for Ballyshannon 1775–6, Limerick city 1776–83–5.

1952 **SMYTH**, William; b. 1685 d. 30 Mar. 1742; MP for Fore 1715–27.

1953 **SMYTH**, William; b. 1744 d. May 1827; MP for Co. Westmeath 1784–90–7–1800 [HP].

1954 **SNEYD**, Edward; b. *c.* 1719 d. 15 Feb. 1781; MP for Carrick 1777–81.

1955 **SNEYD**, Nathaniel; b. 1767 d. 31 July 1833; MP for Carrick 1794–7–1800, Co. Cavan Jan.–Aug. 1800 [HP].

1956 **SOMERVILLE**, James; b. *c.* 1664 d. 6 July 1705; MP for Dundalk 1703–5.

1957 **SOMERVILLE**, Sir James [1st Bt]; b. *ante* 1693 d. 16 Aug. 1748; MP for Dublin city 1729–48.

1958 **SOMERVILLE**, James; b. [bapt. 22 Oct.] 1722 d. [*ante* 5] Sept. 1797; MP for Carlow B. 1769–76, Newtown[ards] 1776–83.

1959 **SOMERVILLE**, Sir Marcus [4th Bt]; b. 1772 d. 11 July 1831; MP for Co. Meath Aug. 1800 [HP].

1960 **SOUTH**, John; b. *c.* 1668–70 d. 29 Apr. 1711; MP for Newcastle 1703–11.

1961 **SOUTHWELL**, Bowen; b. [bapt. 23 Mar.] 1712/3 d. 1796; MP for Downpatrick 1755–60.

1962 **SOUTHWELL**, Rt Hon. Edward; b. 4 Sept. 1671 d. 4 Dec. 1730; MP for Kinsale 1692–3, 1695–9, 1713–14, 1715–27–30, TCD 1703–13 [HP].

1963 **SOUTHWELL**, Rt Hon. Edward; b. 16 June 1705 d. 16 Mar. 1755; MP for Downpatrick 1727–55 [HP].

1964 **SOUTHWELL**, Edward [20th B. de Clifford [E.]]; b. 6 June 1738 d. 1 Nov. 1777; MP for Kinsale 1761–8 [HP].

1965 **SOUTHWELL**, Hon. Henry; b. [bapt. 6 Oct.] 1700 d. 20 Oct. 1758; MP for Co. Limerick 1729–58.

1966 **SOUTHWELL**, Richard; b. *c.* 1667 d. 17 Sept. 1729; MP for Co. Limerick 1727–9.

1967 **SOUTHWELL**, Hon. Robert Henry; b. Oct. 1745 d. 1817; MP for Downpatrick 1776–83.

1968 **SOUTHWELL**, Rt Hon. Sir Thomas [2 Bt, 1st B. Southwell]; b. 1665 d. 4 Aug. 1720; MP for Co. Limerick 1695–9, 1703–13, 1715–17.

1969 **SOUTHWELL**, Rt Hon. Thomas [2nd B. Southwell]; b. 7 Jan. 1697/8 d. 21 Nov. 1766; MP for Co. Limerick 1717–20.

1970 **SOUTHWELL**, Hon. Thomas Arthur [2nd V. Southwell]; b. 16 Apr. 1742 d. 14 Feb. 1796; MP for Co. Limerick 1767–8.

1971 **SOUTHWELL**, Hon. Thomas George [3rd B. and 1st V. Southwell]; b. 4 May 1721 d. 29 Aug. 1780; MP for Enniscorthy 1747–60, Co. Limerick 1761–6.

1972 **SOUTHWELL**, William; b. *ante* 21 Sept. 1682 d. 23 Jan. 1719/20; MP for Kinsale 1703–13, Castlemartyr 1713–14, Baltimore 1715–20.

1973 **SPENCER**, Brent; b. *ante* 1683 d. 16 Feb. 1735/6; MP for Lisburn 1709–13–14, 1715–27–36.

1974 **SPRIGGE**, William; b. 9 July 1633 d. *post* 1699; MP for Banagher 1692–3, 1695–9.

1975 **SPRIGGE**, William; b. 1678 d. 15 Aug. 1735; MP for Tralee 1723–7, Banagher 1729–35.

1976 **SPRING**, Francis; b. *ante* 1660 d. [*ante* 9 July] 1711; MP for Naas 1703–11.

1977 **STAFFORD** [ECHLIN], Edmond Francis; b. *c.* 1660–2 d. 13 Jan. 1723/4; MP for Randalstown 1692–3, 1695–9, 1703–13, Lisburn 1715–24.

1978 **STANLEY**, Sir Edmund [Kt]; b. [bapt. 7 Dec.] 1760 d. 28 Apr. 1843; MP for Augher 1790–7, Lanesborough 1797–1800.

1979 **STANLEY**, Rt Hon. Sir John [1st Bt]; b. 1663 d. 30 Nov. 1744; MP for Gorey 1713–14.

1980 **STANLEY**, Stephen; b. 1659 d. [7 Sept.] 1725; MP for Co. Waterford 1715–25.

1981 **STANNARD**, Eaton; b. 1685 d. 10 Feb. 1755; MP for Midleton 1727–55.

1982 **STANNUS**, James; b. 1686 d. [7 Sept.–3 Oct.] 1721; MP for Carlingford 1713–14, 1715–21.

1983 **STANNUS**, Thomas; b. 1734 d. 17 May 1813; MP for Portarlington 1798–1800.

1984 **STANNUS**, William; b. 1695 d. [*ante* 26] Oct. 1732; MP for Carlingford 1721–7, Portarlington 1730–2.

1985 **STAPLES**, Rt Hon. John; b. 1 Mar. 1734 d. 22 Dec. 1820; MP for Newtown Limavady 1765–8, 1783–90–6, Clogher 1768–76, Ballyshannon 1776–83, Co. Antrim 1796–7–1800 [HP].

1986 **STAPLES**, Sir Robert [4th Bt]; b. [bapt. 9 May] 1643 d. 21 Nov. 1714; MP for Dungannon 1692–3, Clogher 1696–9.

1987 **STAPLES**, Sir Thomas [9th Bt]; b. 31 July 1775 d. 14 May 1865; MP for Knocktopher Mar.–Apr. 1800.

1988 **STAUNTON**, John; b. 1667 d. 5 Sept. 1735; MP for Galway B. 1703–13–14, 1727–35.

1989 **STAUNTON**, Thomas; b. *post* 1667 d. 5 Mar. 1731/2; MP for Galway B. 1727–32.

1990 **STAUNTON**, Thomas; b. [bapt. 13 Mar.] 1706/7 d. 1 Oct. 1784; MP for Galway B. 1732–60 [HP].

1991 **STAWELL**, Jonas; b. 1658 d. 1716; MP for Kinsale 1692–3.

1992 **STAWELL**, Jonas; b. 1700 d. 1772; MP for Kinsale 1745–60.

1993 **STEELE**, Sir Richard [1st Bt]; b. 1701 d. [bur. 20] Feb. 1785; MP for Mullingar 1765–8–76.

1994 **STEPNEY**, Joseph; b. *c.* 1651–3 d. 1725; MP for Gowran 1695–9.

1995 **STEVENSON**, Hans; b. *ante* 1678 d. 1713; MP for Killyleagh 1703–13.

1996 **STEVENSON**, James; b. *ante* 25 Nov. 1692 d. 14 Nov. 1738; MP for Killyleagh 1713–14, 1727–38, Randalstown 1715–27.

1997 **STEVENSON**, James; b. 1699 d. 1769; MP for Killyleagh 1725–7–60.

◆◆◆ **STEWART**, Alexander; b. 1697 d. 22 Apr. 1781 [n.d.e. Londonderry city 18 Mar.–8 May 1760].

1998 **STEWART**, Sir Annesley [6th Bt]; b. 1725 d. Mar. 1801; MP for Charlemont 1763–8–76–83–90–7.

1999 **STEWART**, Hon. Charles; b. 1681 d. 5 Feb. 1740/1; MP for Co. Tyrone 1715–27 [HP].

2000 **STEWART**, Charles; b. *c.* 1742–50 d. 23 Feb. 1793; MP for Co. Cavan 1783–90–3.

2001 **STEWART** [VANE-TEMPEST-STEWART], Rt Hon. Sir Charles William [3rd M. of Londonderry]; b. 18 May 1778 d. 6 Mar. 1854; MP for Thomastown Mar.–May 1800, Co. Londonderry 29 May 1800 [HP].

2002 **STEWART**, Henry; b. 10 May 1749 d. Sept. 1840; MP for Longford B. 1783–90, 1791–7–9.

2003 **STEWART**, Hon. James; b. [25] Oct. 1687 d. 9 Mar. 1747/8; MP for Co. Tyrone 1733–48.

2004 **STEWART**, James; b. 1742 d. 18 Jan. 1821; MP for Co. Tyrone 1768–76–83–90–7–1800 [HP].

2005 **STEWART**, Sir James [7th Bt]; b. 1756 d. 20 May 1827; MP for Enniskillen 1783–90 [HP].

2006 **STEWART**, Rt Hon. Sir John [1st Bt]; b. 1757 d. 22 June 1825; MP for Augher 1794–7, Bangor 1797–1800 [re-elected pp 1795, 1798] [HP].

2007 **STEWART**, Hon. Richard; b. 1677 d. 4 Aug. 1728; MP for Co. Tyrone 1703–13–14, 1727–8, Strabane 1715–27.

2008 **STEWART**, Rt Hon. Robert [1st B. Londonderry, V. Castlereagh, E. and M. of Londonderry]; b. 27 Sept. 1739 d. 6 Apr. 1821; MP for Co. Down 1771–6–83.

2009 **STEWART**, Rt Hon. Robert [V. Castlereagh, 2nd M. of Londonderry]; b. 18 June 1769 d. 12 Aug. 1822; MP for Co. Down 1790–7–1800 [HP].

2010 **STEWART**, William; b. 1625 d. 1706; MP for Charlemont 1692–3.

2011 **STEWART** [*alias* STEUART], Rt Hon. William; b. 1652 d. 4 June 1726; MP for Co. Waterford 1703–13–14.

2012 **STEWART**, William; b. 1710 d. 9 May 1797; MP for Co. Tyrone 1748–60, 1761–8.

2013 **STEWART**, William; b. 1710 d. [*ante* 18] Aug. 1778; MP for Co. Cavan 1766–8, Newcastle 1768–76.

2014 **STONE**, Richard; b. 27 Aug. 1674[1] d. 20 [bur. 22] Sept. 1727; MP for Newtown Limavady 1695–9.

2015 **STOPFORD**, Hon. Edward; b. 1732 d. 24 Oct. 1794; MP for Duleek 1776–83.

2016 **STOPFORD**, James; b. 1668 d. 9 July 1721; MP for Wexford B. 1703–13, Co. Wexford 1713–14, 1715–21.

2017 **STOPFORD**, James [1st B. Courtown, V. Stopford and E. of Courtown]; b. 1699 d. 12 Jan. 1770; MP for Co. Wexford 1721–7, Fethard [Wexford] 1727–58.

2018 **STOPFORD**, Rt Hon. James [2nd E. of Courtown]; b. 28 May 1731 d. 30 Mar. 1810; MP for Taghmon 1761–8 [HP].

2019 **STOPFORD**, Robert; b. *c.* 1664 d. [bur. 6] Aug. 1699; MP for Innistiogue 1692–3, 1695–9.

2020 **STOYTE**, Francis; b. *c.* 1695 d. 6 Feb. 1732/3; MP for Hillsborough 1727–33.

2021 **STOYTE**, John; b. *c.* 1660–3 d. [*ante* 23 Sept.] 1729; MP for Dublin city 1728–9.

2022 **STRATFORD**, Hon. Benjamin O'Neale [4th E. of Aldborough]; b. 1746 d. 11 July 1833; MP for Baltinglass 1777–83, 1790–7–1800.

2023 **STRATFORD**, Edward; b. 28 Jan. 1663/4 d. 23 Feb. 1739/40; MP for Carysfort 1695–9, Baltinglass 1703–13–14, 1715–27, Harristown 1727–40.

2024 **STRATFORD**, Hon. Edward [styled V. Amiens Feb.–June 1777, 2nd E. of Aldborough]; b. 1734 d. 2 Jan. 1801; MP for Baltinglass 1759–60, 1761–8, 1775–7 [HP].

2025 **STRATFORD**, John [1st B. Baltinglass, V. Aldborough, V. Amiens and E. of Aldborough]; b. 10 Aug. 1697 d. 29 June 1777; MP for Baltinglass 1721–7–60, 1761–3.

2026 **STRATFORD**, Hon. John [3rd E. of Aldborough]; b. *c.* 1740 d. 7 Mar. 1823; MP for Baltinglass 1763–8–76, 1790–7–1800, Co. Wicklow 1776–83–90.

2027 **STRATFORD**, Robert; b. *c.* 1632–41[8] d. 26 Oct. 1699; MP for Co. Wicklow 1692–3.

2028 **STRATON**, John; b. *c.* 1725–7 d. 1803; MP for Dundalk 1799–1800.

2029 **STUART** [*alias* STEWART], Charles; b. 1677 d. [8 Apr.–18 June] 1740; MP for Tuam 1713–14.

2030 **STUBBER**, Robert; b. 1747 d. 1820; MP for Taghmon 1786–90.

2031 **SUXBURY**, Anthony; b. *ante* 5 Oct. 1671 d. *c.* 1702; MP for Waterford city 1692–3, 1695–9.

2032 **SWAN**, Edward Bellingham; b. 1734 d. 21 Sept. 1788; MP for Lanesborough 1771–6, Thomastown 1776–83, Banagher 1785–8.

2033 **SWIFT**, Adam; b. *ante* 1643 d. May 1704; MP for Newry 1703–4.

2034 **SYNGE**, Francis; b. 15 Apr. 1761 d. 1831; MP for Swords 1797–1800.

2035 **TALBOT** [CROSBIE], John; b. *c.* 1778 d. 26 Jan. 1818; MP for Ardfert Feb.–Aug. 1800.

2036 **TALBOT**, William; b. 1715 d. [*ante* 10] May 1787; MP for St Johnstown [Donegal] 1761–8–76.

2037 **TALBOT**, William; b. [*ante* 26] Mar. 1776 d. 19 May 1851; MP for Kilkenny city 1799–1800 [HP].

2038 **TAYLOR**, Berkeley; b. *ante* 1683[9] d. 25 June 1736; MP for Askeaton 1723–7–36.

2039 **TAYLOR** [*alias* TAYLOUR] [ROWLEY], Hon. Clotworthy [1st B. Langford]; b. 31 Oct. 1763 d. 13 Sept. 1825; MP for Trim 1791–5, Co. Meath 1795–7–1800.

2040 **TAYLOR**, Edward; b. *post* 1694 d. [Dec.] 1760; MP for Askeaton 1727–60.

2041 **TAYLOR**, Sir John; b. 29 Sept. 1771 d. 8 Dec. 1843; MP for St Johnstown [Longford] 1790–7, Fethard [Tipperary] 1797–1800.

2042 **TAYLOR**, Robert; b. *ante* 1660 d. [*ante* 28] Mar. 1696; MP for Askeaton 1692–3, 1695–6.

2043 **TAYLOR**, Robert; b. *c.* 1682 d. [*ante* 29 Aug.] 1723; MP for Askeaton 1703–13–14, Tralee 1715–23.

2044 **TAYLOR** [*alias* TAYLOUR], Rt Hon. Sir Thomas [1st Bt]; b. 25 July 1662 d. 8 Aug. 1736; MP for Kells 1692–3, 1695–9, 1713–14, 1715–27–36, Belturbet 1703–13.

2045 **TAYLOR** [*alias* TAYLOUR], Rt Hon. Sir Thomas [2nd Bt]; b. 20 Nov. 1686 d. 19 Sept. 1757; MP for Kells 1713–14, 1715–27–57.

2046 **TAYLOR** [*alias* TAYLOUR], Rt Hon. Thomas [3rd Bt, 1st B. and V. Headfort and E. of Bective]; b. 20 Oct. 1724 d. 14 Feb. 1795; MP for Kells 1747–60.

2047 **TAYLOR**, William; b. Feb. 1693 d. 15 May 1746; MP for Askeaton 1737–46.

2048 **TAYLOUR**, Hon. Hercules Langford; b. 9 Sept. 1759 d. [*ante* 11] May 1790; MP for Kells 1781–3–90, Apr.–May 1790.

2049 **TAYLOUR**, James; b. 20 Jan. 1700/1 d. May 1747; MP for Kells 1737–47.

2050 **TAYLOUR**, Hon. Robert; b. 26 Nov. 1760 d. 23 Apr. 1839; MP for Kells 1791–7–1800.

2051 **TAYLOUR**, Hon. Sir Thomas [2nd E. of Bective and 1st M. of Headfort]; b. 18 Nov. 1757 d. 24 Oct. 1829; MP for Kells 1776–83–90, Longford B. 1790–4, Co. Meath 1794–5.

2052 **TENCH**, John; b. 1655 d. *post* 1713; MP for Co. Carlow 1692–3, Newcastle 1695–9, Old Leighlin 1703–13.

2053 **TENISON**, Henry; b. 1667 d. 22 Sept. 1709; MP for Co. Monaghan 1695–9, Co. Louth 1703–9.

2054 **TENISON**, Richard; b. 1684 d. 22 Nov. 1725; MP for Dunleer 1715–25.

2055 **TENISON**, Thomas; b. 1707 d. 27 Mar. 1779; MP for Dunleer 1728–60, Apr.–Dec. 1761.

2056 **TENISON**, Thomas; b. 1730 d. [*ante* 24] Dec. 1788; MP for Co. Monaghan 1775–6–83.

2057 **TENISON**, Thomas; b. 1761 d. 1835; MP for Boyle 1792–7.

2058 **TENISON**, William; b. *c.* 1706 d. [*ante* 3 May] 1728; MP for Dunleer 1727–8.

2059 **THEAKER**, Thomas; b. *ante* 1692 d. 24 Aug. 1751; MP for Wicklow B. 1735–51.

2060 **THOMPSON**, Richard; b. *ante* 1663[9] d. 1719; MP for Baltinglass 1692–3, 1695–9, Carysfort 1703–13.

2061 **TICHBORNE**, Rt Hon. Sir Henry [Kt, 1st Bt and 1st B. Ferrard]; b. 1662 d. 3 Nov. 1731; MP for Ardee 1692–3, Co. Louth 1695–9, 1710–13.

2062 **TICHBORNE**, Sir William [Kt]; b. *ante* 1640 d. 12 Mar. 1693/4; MP for [Swords 1661–6], Co. Louth 1692–3.

2063 **TICHBORNE**, Hon. William; b. *c.* 1686 d. [27 Aug.–8 Sept.] 1717; MP for Philipstown 1715–Aug./Sept. 1717.

2064 **TIGHE**, Edward; b. 1740 d. 1801; MP for Belturbet 1763–8, Wicklow B. 1768–76, 1783–90–7, Athboy 1776–83.

2065 **TIGHE**, Henry; b. 29 Aug. 1771 d. 1836; MP for Innistiogue Apr.–July 1797, 1797–1800.

2066 **TIGHE**, Rt Hon. Richard; b. 1678 d. 27 July 1736; MP for Belturbet 1703–13, Newtown 1715–27, Augher 1727–36.

2067 **TIGHE**, Richard Stearne; b. 1717 d. 24 Dec. 1761; MP for Athy 5–24 Dec. 1761.

2068 **TIGHE**, Richard William; b. 1744 d. 1828; MP for Wicklow B. 1767–8.

2069 **TIGHE**, Robert; b. *c.* 1719 d. 1799; MP for Roscommon B. 1769–76, Carrick 1777–83.

2070 **TIGHE**, Robert; b. *post* 1740 d. 1828; MP for Carrick Feb.–Aug. 1800.

2071 **TIGHE**, William; b. 21 Dec. 1710 d. [early] Sept. 1766; MP for Clonmines 1734–60, Wicklow B. 1761–6.

2072 **TIGHE**, William; b. 1738 d. 7 May 1782; MP for Athboy 1761–8–76.

2073 **TIGHE**, William; b. 5 May 1766 d. 19 Mar. 1816; MP for Banagher 1789–90, Wicklow B. 1790–7, Innistiogue 1797–1800 [HP].

2074 **TIPPING**, Thomas; b. *post* 1708 d. 8 Mar. 1776; MP for Co. Louth 1755–60, Kilbeggan 1761–8.

2075 **TISDALL**, James; b. 1649 d. 2 May 1714; MP for Ardee 1692–3, 1695–9, 1703–13–14.

2076 **TISDALL**, James; b. 1694 d. 1 Oct. 1757; MP for Dundalk 1721–7.

2077 **TISDALL**, Michael; b. [bapt. 29 Nov.] 1672 d. 7 Dec. 1726; MP for Ardee 1713–14, 1715–26.

2078 **TISDALL**, Rt Hon. Philip; b. [1] Mar. 1703 d. 11 Sept. 1777; MP for TCD 1739–60, 1761–8–76, Armagh B. 1776–7.

2079 **TISDALL**, Richard; b. *c.* 1677–9 d. Oct. 1742; MP for Dundalk B. 1707–13, Co. Louth 1713–14, 1715–27.

2080 **TOLER**, Daniel; b. 1740 d. June 1796; MP for Co. Tipperary 1783–90–6.

2081 **TOLER**, Rt Hon. John [1st B. Norbury, V. Glandine and E. of Norbury]; b. 3 Dec. [?]1741 d. 27 July 1831; MP for Tralee 1776–83, Philipstown 1783–90, Gorey 1790–7–1800 [re-elected pp 1798].

2082 **TOMKINS**, George; b. *ante* 1680 d. Sept. 1739; MP for Londonderry city 1715–27–39.

2083 **TONSON**, Richard; b. 6 Jan. 1692/3 d. 24 June 1773; MP for Baltimore 1727–60, 1761–8–73.

2084 **TOPHAM**, James; b. [bapt. 27 July] 1677 d. [bur. 14] Nov. 1724; MP for Strabane 1703–13, St Johnstown [Donegal] 1713–14, 1715–24.

2085 **TOPHAM**, Sir John [Kt]; b. *ante* 1642 d. 3 Apr. 1698; MP for Newtown Limavady 1692–3.

2086 **TOTTENHAM**, Charles; b. 1685 d. 20 Sept. 1758; MP for New Ross 1727–58.

2087 **TOTTENHAM**, Charles; b. 1716 d. 10 Sept. 1795; MP for Fethard [Wexford] 1755–60, 1790–5, New Ross 1761–8, Bannow 1768–76, Clonmines 1776–83–90.

2088 **TOTTENHAM** [LOFTUS], Rt Hon. Sir Charles [2nd Bt, 1st B. and V. Loftus, E. and M. of Ely] b. 23 Jan. 1737/8 d. 22 Mar. 1806; MP for Clonmines 1761–8–76, Fethard [Wexford] 1776–83, Wexford B. 1783–5.

2089 **TOTTENHAM**, Charles; b. 19 Apr. 1743 d. 13 June 1823; MP for New Ross 1768–76–83–90–7–1800.

2090 **TOTTENHAM**, Sir John [1st Bt]; b. 6 July 1714 d. 2 Jan. 1787; MP for New Ross 1759–60, Fethard [Wexford] 1767–8–76.

2091 **TOTTENHAM**, Nicholas Loftus; b. 1745 d. 11 Mar. 1823; MP for Bannow 1776–83–90, Clonmines 1790–7.

2092 **TOTTENHAM**, Ponsonby; b. 1746 d. 13 Dec. 1818; MP for Fethard [Wexford] 1779–83–90, Bannow 1790–7, Clonmines 1797–1800 [HP].

2093 **TOWNLEY**, Blayney; b. 1666 d. 3 Sept. 1722; MP for Dunleer 1692–3, 1695–9, 1703–13–14, Carlingford 1715–22.

2094 **TOWNLEY-BALFOUR**, Blayney; b. 1705 d. [*ante* 26] Aug. 1788; MP for Carlingford Jan.–Oct. 1760, 1761–8–76.

2095 **TOWNLEY-BALFOUR**, Blayney; b. 28 May 1769 d. 22 Dec. 1856; MP for Belturbet Jan.–Aug. 1800.

2096 **TOWNLEY-BALFOUR**, William Charles; b. *c.* 1725–33 d. 21 Nov. 1759; MP for Carlingford 1757–9.

2097 **TOWNLY** [*alias* TOWNLEY] [TOWNLEY-BALFOUR], Henry; b. 19 Dec. 1693 d. 20 July 1741; MP for Carlingford 1727–41.

2098 **TOWNSEND**, Bryan; b. *ante* 1660 d. 1726; MP for Clonakilty 1695–9.

2099 **TOWNSEND**, John; b. 1737 d. 4 Aug. 1810; MP for Dingle 1783–90–7, Castlemartyr 1797–1800 [re-elected pp. 1796, 1800].

2100 **TOWNSEND**, Richard; b. *ante* 1731 d. 12 Dec. 1783; MP for Co. Cork 1759–60, 1761–8–76–83.

2101 **TOWNSEND**, Richard Boyle; b. 1756 d. 26 Nov. 1827; MP for Dingle 1782–3–90–5.

2102 **TOWNSEND**, Thomas; b. 7 Oct. 1768 d. *c.* 1835[10]; MP for Belturbet 1797–1800.

2103 **TRANT**, Dominick; b. 1738 d. 18 June 1790; MP for St Canice 1781–3.

2104 **TRENCH**, Hon. Charles; b. Dec. 1772 d. 1839; MP for Newtown Limavady 1799–1800.

2105 **TRENCH**, Eyre Power; b. 1749 d. 27 June 1808; MP for Newtown Limavady 1798–9.

2106 **TRENCH**, Francis; b. 29 July 1757 d. Nov. 1829; MP for Ballynakill Mar.–Aug. 1800.

2107 **TRENCH**, Frederick; b. 1681 d. 3 Oct. 1752; MP for Co. Galway 1715–27, 1727–52.

2108 **TRENCH**, Michael [Frederick]; b. May 1730 d. April 1836; MP for Maryborough 1785–90.

2108a **TRENCH**, Frederick [1st B. Ashtown]; b. 17 Sept. 1755 d. 1 May 1840; MP for Portarlington 1798–1800; UK Jan.–12 Feb. 1801 [HP].

2109 **TRENCH**, Richard; b. 1708 d. 1770; MP for Banagher 1735–60, Co. Galway 1761–8.

2110 **TRENCH** [LE POER-TRENCH], Rt Hon. Richard [2nd E. of Clancarty] b. 18 May 1767 d. 24 Nov. 1837; MP for Newtown Limavady 1796–7, Co. Galway 1797–1800 [HP].

2111 **TRENCH**, William Power Keating [1st B. Kilconnel, V. Dunlo and E. of Clancarty]; b. 1741 d. 27 Apr. 1805; MP for Co. Galway 1768–76–83–90–7.

2112 **TREVOR** [HILL-TREVOR], Hon. Arthur; b. 24 Dec. 1738 d. 19 June 1770; MP for Hillsborough 1761–8–70.

2113 **TREVOR**, Rt Hon. Sir John [Kt]; b. 1627 d. 20 May 1717; MP for Newry 1692–3, Aug.–Dec. 1695 [expelled from the House for neglecting to attend] [HP].

2114 **TROTTER**, Stephen; b. [bapt. 27] Jan. 1713/4 d. [bur. 31] Mar. 1764; MP for Carysfort 1743–60, Gorey 1761–4.

2115 **TROTTER**, Thomas; b. Feb.–Mar. [bapt. 9 Mar.] 1683/4 d. Oct. 1745; MP for Duleek 1715–27, Old Leighlin 1727–45 [r. Duleek 1727].

2116 **TUNNADINE**, John; b. [bapt. 19 Dec.] 1726 d. [bur. 15] May 1787; MP for Askeaton 1768–76, Longford B. 1776–83.

2117 **TYDD**, Sir John [1st Bt]; b. *c.* 1742 d. 11 May 1803; MP for Maryborough 1778–83, Ardfert 1783–90, Ballynakill 1790–7, Clogher 1797–8, Fore 1798–1800 [re-elected pp 1798].

2118 **TYNTE** [WORTH], Rt Hon. James; b. 1682 d. 8 Apr. 1758; MP for Rathcormack 1716–27, Youghal 1727–58.

2119 **TYRRELL**, Duke; b. 1717 d. 1796; MP for Philipstown 1761–8, 1769–76.

2120 **UNDERWOOD**, Richard; b. *ante* 9 Mar. 1749/50 d. 12 Mar. 1779; MP for Tralee 1771–6, Mullingar 1776–9.

2121 **UNIACKE**, James; b. 1736 d. 31 May 1803; MP for Youghal 1776–83–90–7.

2122 **UNIACKE**, Robert; b. 1753 d. 9 Oct.1802; MP for Youghal 1777–83–90–7–1800 [re-elected pp 1800].

2123 **UNIACKE-FITZGERALD**, Robert; b. 17 Mar. 1750/1 d. 20 Dec. 1814; MP for Co. Cork 1797–1800 [HP].

2124 **UPTON**, Arthur; b. 31 May 1623 d. 1706; MP for [Carrickfergus 1661–6], Antrim B. 1692–3, Co. Antrim 1695–9.

2125 **UPTON**, Rt Hon. Arthur; b. 9 Jan. 1715 d. 27 Sept. 1768; MP for Carrickfergus 1741–60, 1761–8.

2126 **UPTON**, Clotworthy; b. 6 Jan. 1664/5 d. 6 June 1725; MP for Newtown[ards] 1695–9, Co. Antrim 1703–13–14, 1715–25.

2127 **UPTON**, John; b. 19 Apr. 1671 d. 26 Apr. 1740; MP for Co. Antrim 1725–7–40.

2128 **UPTON**, Thomas; b. 4 Aug. 1677 d. 10 Nov. 1733; MP for Antrim B. 1713–14, Co. Antrim 1716–27, Londonderry city 1727–33.

2129 **USSHER**, Beverley; b. *c.* 1700 d. Sept. 1757; MP for Co. Waterford 1735–57.

2130 **USSHER**, Charles; b. 1694 d. 28 Dec. 1769; MP for Blessington 1745–60, 1761–8–69.

2131 **USSHER**, John; b. *c.* 1682 d. [*ante* 7 Oct.] 1741; MP for Carrick 1715–27–41.

2132 **USSHER**, John; b. 1703 d. 3 Jan. 1748/9; MP for Dungarvan 1747–9.

2133 **USSHER**, John; b. 1730 d. Oct. 1796; MP for Innistiogue 1783–90.

2134 **USSHER**, William; b. [bapt. 19 Nov.] 1675 d. 1719; MP for Newtown Limavady Jan.–Aug. 1714.

2135 **VANDELEUR**, Crofton; b. [bapt. 19 Nov.] 1735 d. [bur. 17] Aug. 1794; MP for Ennis 1768–76.

2136 **VANDELEUR**, Rt Hon. John Ormsby; b. [Nov.–Dec.] 1765 d. [bur. 18] Nov. 1828; MP for Carlow B. 1790–7, Ennis 1798–1800 [re-elected pp 1800] [HP].

2137 **VANDELEUR**, John Ormsby; b. [bapt. 17 Apr.] 1767 d. 3 Nov. 1822; MP for Granard 1790–7.

2138 **VANDELEUR**, Thomas Pakenham; b. [bapt. 9 Feb.] 1768 d. 1 Nov. 1803; MP for Granard 1790–7.

2139 **VAN HOMRIGH**, Bartholomew; b. *ante* 1665 d. 29 Dec.1703; MP for Londonderry city 1692–3, 1695–9.

2140 **VAUGHAN**, Hon. Sir John [KB]; b. *c.* 1731 d. 30 June 1795; MP for St Johnstown [Longford] 1776–83 [HP].

2141 **VEREKER**, Rt Hon. Charles [2nd V. Gort]; b. 1768 d. 11 Nov. 1842; MP for Limerick city 1794–7–1800 [HP].

2142 **VERNER**, James; b. 1 Mar. 1745/6 d. 1823; MP for Dungannon 1794–7–1800.

2143 **VERNON**, Sir Richard [3rd Bt]; b. 22 June 1678 d. 1 Oct. 1725; MP for Monaghan B. 1703–13.

2144 **VESEY**, Agmondisham; b. 21 Jan. 1676/7 d. 24 Mar. 1738/9; MP for Tuam 1703–13–14, 1715–27–39.

2145 **VESEY**, Rt Hon. Agmondisham; b. 1708 d. 1785; MP for Harristown 1740–60, Kinsale 1765–8–76–83.

2146 **VESEY**, George; b. [24] Jan. 1760 d. 30 May 1841; MP for Tuam Feb.–Aug. 1800.

2147 **VESEY**, Hon. John [2nd V. de Vesci]; b. 15 Feb. 1771 d. 19 Oct. 1855; MP for Maryborough 1796–7.

2148 **VESEY**, Sir John Denny [2nd Bt, 1st B. Knapton]; b. 1709 d. 25 June 1761; MP for Newtown[ards] 1727–50.

2149 **VESEY**, William; b. 26 Sept. 1687 d. 6 Apr. 1750; MP for Tuam 1715–27–50.

2150 **VILLIERS**, Edward; b. *ante* 1740 d. 1783; MP for Kilmallock 1761–8.

2151 **VINCENT**, Richard; b. 1672 d. 14 May 1762; MP for Clogher 1733–60.

2152 **VOWELL**, Richard; b. *ante* 1752 d. *post* 1800; MP for Gorey 1783–90.

2153 **WADE**, John; b. 1661 d. 9 Oct. 1735; MP for Athboy 1703–13–14, Trim 1728–35.

2154 **WAITE**, Rt Hon. Thomas; b. 11 Nov. 1718 d. 2 Feb. 1780; MP for St Canice 1761–8.

2155 **WAKELEY**, John; b. 1656 d. 1713; MP for Kilbeggan 1692–3.

2156 **WALL**, William; b. *ante* 1690 d. 9 Sept. 1755; MP for Maryborough 1713–14, 1715–27–55.

2157 **WALL**, William; b. *c.* 1689 d. 2 May 1747; MP for Knocktopher 1715–27–47.

2158 **WALLER**, James; b. *post* 1632 d. 1702; MP for Tralee 1692–3, Kinsale 1695–9.

2159 **WALLER**, John; b. *ante* 1690 d. Dec. 1742; MP for Doneraile 1727–42.

2160 **WALLER**, John; b. 1762 d. 14 Nov. 1836; MP for Co. Limerick 1790–7–1800 [HP].

2161 **WALLER**, Sir Robert [1st Bt]; b. *c.* 1736 d. [bur. 27] July 1780; MP for Dundalk 1761–8–76–80.

2162 **WALLIS**, Charles; b. *c.* 1641–3 d. *post* 1728; MP for Duleek 1698–9, 1703–13.

2163 **WALPOLE**, Rt Hon. Sir Edward [KB]; b. 1706 d. 12 Jan. 1784; MP for Ballyshannon 1737–60 [HP].

2164 **WALSH**, David; b. 1740 d. 1802; MP for Fethard [Tipperary] 1776–83, Ballynakill 1800.

2165 **WALSH**, Hunt; b. 1720 d. 28 Feb. 1795; MP for Maryborough 1764–8–76.

2166 **WALTON**, Samuel; b. *ante* 1674 d. [?]*post* 1713; MP for Sligo B. 1703–13.

2167 **WANDESFORD**, Rt Hon. Sir Christopher [2nd Bt, 1st B. Wandesford and V. Castlecomer]; b. 19 Aug. 1656 d. 13 Sept. 1707; MP for St Canice 1692–3, 1695–9, 1703–7 [HP].

2168 **WANDESFORD**, Rt Hon. Christopher [2nd V. Castlecomer]; b. [2] Mar. 1683/4 d. 23 June 1719; MP for St Canice July–11 Oct. 1707 [HP].

2169 **WARBURTON**, George; b. *c.* 1639–49 d. 14 Nov. 1709; MP for Gowran 1692–3, Portarlington 1695–9.

2170 **WARBURTON**, George; b. 1713 d. 9 Mar. 1753; MP for Co. Galway 1750–3.

2171 **WARBURTON**, John; b. *c.* 1645–8 d. 1703; MP for Belturbet 1692–3, 1695–9.

2172 **WARBURTON**, John; b. *c.* 1727–9 d. June 1806; MP for Queen's Co. 1779–83–90, 1791–7.

2173 **WARBURTON**, Richard; b. 1664 d. [*ante* 16] Jan. 1715/6; MP for Portarlington 1692–3, 1695–9, 1703–13–14, 1715–16.

2174 **WARBURTON**, Richard; b. 1636 d. Feb. 1716/7; MP for Ballyshannon 1697–9, 1703–13.

2175 **WARBURTON**, Richard; b. 1674 d. 23 Jan. 1746/7; MP for Portarlington 1715–27, Ballynakill 1727–47.

2176 **WARBURTON**, Richard; b. 6 Dec. 1696 d. 23 Oct. 1771; MP for Queen's Co. 1729–60.

2177 **WARD**, Bernard [1st B. and V. Bangor]; b. Aug. 1719 d. 20 May 1781; MP for Co. Down 1745–60, 1761–8–70.

2178 **WARD**, Bernard Smyth; b. [bapt. 16 Mar.] 1742/3 d. [*ante* 12] May 1770; MP for Enniskillen 1769–70.

2179 **WARD**, Hon. Edward; b. 30 Apr. 1753 d. Nov. 1812; MP for Bangor 1776–83, Co. Down 1783–90.

2180 **WARD**, Michael; b. 1683 d. 21 Feb. 1759; MP for Co. Down 1713–14, 1715–27, Bangor 3–29 Nov. 1727.

2181 **WARD**, Hon. Nicholas [2nd V. Bangor]; b. 20 Nov. 1750 d. 11 Sept. 1827; MP for Bangor 1771–6.

2182 **WARD**, Robert; b. 1684 d. *post* 1730; MP for Bangor 1713–14.

2183 **WARD**, Robert; b. *ante* 22 Oct. 1740[1] d. *ante* 8 Dec. 1767; MP for Bangor 1761–7.

2184 **WARD**, Rt Hon. Robert; b. 14 July 1754 d. Mar. 1831; MP for Wicklow B. 1777–83, Killyleagh 1790–7, Bangor 1797–1800 [HP].

2185 **WARING**, Samuel; b. Aug. 1660 d. 15 Dec. 1739; MP for Hillsborough 1703–13–14, 1715–27.

2186 **WARNEFORD**, Robert; b. *ante* 27 Aug. 1674 d. 8 Aug. 1707; MP for Queen's Co. 1695–9.

2187 **WARREN**, Sir Augustus Louis Carre [2nd Bt]; b. 1754 d. 30 Jan. 1821; MP for Cork City 1784–90.

2188 **WARREN**, Ebenezer; b. 1658 d. [*ante* 18] Sept. 1721; MP for Kilkenny city 1695–9, 1715–21.

2189 **WARREN**, Edward; b. 20 Feb. 1680/1 d. 25 Apr. 1743; MP for Kilkenny city 1721–7.

2190 **WARREN**, Nathaniel; b. 1737 d. 15 Jan. 1796; MP for Dublin city 1784–90, Callan 1790–6.

2191 **WARREN**, Richard; b. *ante* 1692[8] d. 6 Feb. 1734/5; MP for Kildare B. 1716–27–35.

2192 **WARREN**, Thomas; b. 1756 d. *c.* 1820; MP for Charleville 1776–83, Castlebar 1783–90.

2193 **WEAVER**, Daniel; b. [?]*c.* 1656 d. *post* 1693; MP for Ballynakill 1692–3.

2194 **WEAVER**, John; b. *ante* 1632 d. *c.* 1716; MP for [King's Co. 1661–6], Queen's Co. 1692–3, Maryborough 1695–9 [declared n.d.e. Maryborough 1703 although never duly returned].

2195 **WEAVER**, John; b. 1654 d. *post* 1727; MP for Queen's Co. 1692–3, 1695–9, 1703–13, Ballynakill 1715–27.

2196 **WEBBER**, Edward; b. *c.* 1672[8] d. 12 Nov. 1730; MP for Cork city 1727–30.

2197 **WEBSTER**, Rt Hon. Edward; b. *ante* 1691[6] d. 1755; MP for Carysfort 1717–27.

2198 **WELCH**, Patrick; b. *ante* 1728 d. Apr. 1802; MP for Thomastown 1783–90, Gowran 1790–7.

2199 **WELCH**, Patrick; b. *c.* 1749–53 d. 1816; MP for Callan B. 1797–1800.

2200 **WELDON**, Stewart; b. 6 July 1750 d. 2 Jan. 1829; MP for Ennis 1783–90.

2201 **WELDON**, Walter; b. *ante* 1662 d. 16 May 1729; MP for Carlow 1692–3, 1703–13–14, 1715–27, Ballynakill 1695–9.

2202 **WELDON**, Walter; b. 1 July 1724 d. 23 Aug. 1773; MP for Athy 1745–60.

2203 **WEMYS**, Francis; b. *ante* 1673 d. 1738; MP for Harristown 1695–9.

2204 **WEMYS**, Sir Henry [Kt]; b. *ante* 1643 d. 1722; MP for Callan 1692–3, 1695–9, Co.Kilkenny 1703–13–14.

2205 **WEMYS**, Henry; b. 1703 d. 12 Oct. 1750; MP for Callan 1727–50.

2206 **WEMYS**, James; b. *c.* 1709 d. 20 Apr. 1765; MP for Callan 1751–60, 1762–5.

2207 **WEMYS**, James; b. [?*ante*] 1755 d. 8 Aug. 1820; MP for Kilkenny city 1793–7–1800.

2208 **WEMYS**, Patrick; b. 1679 d. 25 Sept. 1747; MP for Gowran 1703–13–14, Co. Kilkenny 1721–7–47.

2209 **WEMYS**, Patrick; b. 1707 d. 20 Jan. 1762; MP for Co. Kilkenny 1747–60, Callan 2–20 Jan. 1762.

2210 **WESLEY** [*alias* WELLESLEY], Rt Hon. Sir Arthur [1st B., M. Douro, V., E. and D. of Wellington] b. [bapt. 30 Apr.] 1769 d. 14 Sept. 1852; MP for Trim 1790–7 [HP].

2211 **WESLEY**, Garret [Gerald]; b. *c.* 1665 d. 23 Sept. 1728; MP for Trim 1692–3, 1727–8, Athboy 1695–9, Co. Meath 1711–13–14.

2212 **WESLEY** [*alias* WELLESLEY], Rt Hon. Garret [2nd B. Mornington, 1st V. Wesley, E. of Mornington]; b. 19 July 1735 d. 22 May 1781; MP for Trim 1757–8.

2213 **WESLEY** [*alias* WELLESLEY], Rt Hon. Sir Henry [1st B. Cowley]; b. 20 Jan. 1773 d. 27 Apr. 1847; MP for Trim Feb.–Apr. 1795 [HP].

2214 **WESLEY** [COLLEY], Richard [1st B. Mornington]; b. *c.* 1690 d. 31 Jan. 1758; MP for Trim 1729–46.

2215 **WESLEY** [*alias* WELLESLEY], Rt Hon. Richard Colley [2nd E. of Mornington and 1st M. Wellesley] b. 20 June 1760 d. 26 Sept. 1842; MP for Trim 1780–1 [HP].

2216 **WESLEY** [*alias* WELLESLEY] [WELLESLEY-POLE], Rt Hon. William [1st B. Maryborough, 3rd E. of Mornington]; b. 20 May 1763 d. 22 Feb. 1845; MP for Trim 1783–90.

2217 **WESTBY**, Nicholas; b. 28 Mar. 1750/1 d. 30 Nov. 1800; MP for Tulsk 1772–6, Co. Wicklow 1783–90–7–1800.

2218 **WESTENRA**, Henry; b. 12 Jan. 1741/2 d. [Mar.] 1801; MP for Monaghan B. 1771–6, 1796–7–1800.

2219 **WESTENRA**, Peter; b. *ante* 1662[10] d. 1693; MP for Athboy 1692–3.

2220 **WESTENRA**, Warner; b. [bapt. 17 Mar.] 1705/6 d. [bur. 20] Mar. 1772; MP for Maryborough 1730–60.

2221 **WESTENRA**, Warner William [2nd B. Rossmore]; b. 14 Oct. 1765 d. 10 Aug. 1842; MP for Co. Monaghan Aug. 1800 [HP].

2222 **WESTGARTH**, William; b. *ante* 21 Sept. 1682[1] d. [Aug.–Dec.] 1710; MP for Roscommon B. 1703–10.

2223 **WESTON**, Rt Hon. Edward; b. 1703 d. 15 July 1770; MP for Cavan B. 1747–60.

2224 **WHALEY**, Richard; b. *ante* 1663[7] d. 1725; MP for Athenry 1692–3, 1695–9, 1703–13–14, 1715–25.

2225 **WHALEY**, Richard Chapel; b. 1700 d. 14 Feb. 1769; MP for Co. Wicklow 1747–60.

2226 **WHALEY**, Thomas; b. 15 Dec. 1766 d. 2 Nov. 1800; MP for Newcastle 1785–90, Enniscorthy 1798–1800.

2227 **WHITE** [*alias* WHYTE], Francis; b. 1661 d. *post* 1700; MP for Co. Cavan 1697–9.

2228 **WHITNEY**, Boleyn; b. 1686 d. 18 Apr. 1758; MP for Philipstown 1737–58.

2229 **WHITSHED**, James; b. *c.* 1687 d. Jan. 1734/5; MP for Wicklow B. 1723–7–35.

2230 **WHITSHED**, James; b. *c.* 1716 d. 20 Feb. 1789; MP for Wicklow B. 1747–60 [HP].

2231 **WHITSHED**, Samuel Warter; b. 1685 d. Mar. 1745/6; MP for Wicklow B. 1715–27–46.

2232 **WHITSHED**, Thomas; b. 1645 d. [Mar.–Apr.] 1697; MP for Carysfort 1692–3.

2233 **WHITSHED**, Rt Hon. William; b. 1679 d. 26 Aug. 1727; MP for Co.Wicklow 1703–13–14.

2234 **WHITSHED**, William; b. [bapt. 24 Aug.] 1719 d. 20 Feb. 1771; MP for Wicklow B. 1761–8–71.

2235 **WILLIAMSON**, Rt Hon. Sir Joseph [Kt]; b. 25 July [bapt. 4 Aug.] 1633 d. 3 Oct. 1701; MP for Co. Clare 1692–3, Limerick city 1695–9 [HP].

2236 **WILLOUGHBY** [WILLOUGHBY-MONTGOMERY], Hugh; b. *ante* 1687 d. 26 July 1748; MP for Monaghan B. 1715–27, Co. Monaghan 1728–48.

2237 **WILLSON**, James; b. 1734 d. Mar. 1812; MP for Taghmon 1768–76, Co. Antrim 1776–83.

2238 **WILSON**, Ezekiel Davys; b. 1738 d. Jan. 1821; MP for Carrickfergus 1785–90–7–1800.

2239 **WILSON**, William; b. 1687 d. 2 Apr. 1741; MP for Limerick city 1739–41.

2240 **WINGFIELD**, Edward; b. 1659 d. 7 Jan. 1727/8; MP for Co. Sligo 1692–3, 1695–9, 1703–13.

2241 **WINGFIELD**, Rt Hon. Richard [1st B. Wingfield and V. Powerscourt]; b. [19] Aug. 1697 d. 21 Oct. 1751; MP for Boyle 1727–44.

2242 **WINGFIELD**, Hon. Richard [3rd V. Powerscourt]; b. Dec. 1730 d. 8 Aug. 1788; MP for Co. Wicklow 1761–4.

2243 **WOLFE**, Rt Hon. Arthur [1st B. and V. Kilwarden]; b. 19 Jan. 1738/9 d. 23 July 1803; MP for Coleraine 1783–90, Jamestown 1790–7, Dublin city 1797–8.

2244 **WOLFE**, John; b. 18 May 1753 d. 18 Apr. 1816; MP for Co. Kildare 1783–90, Killybegs 1790–7, Carlow B. 1798–1800.

2245 **WOLFE**, Hon. John [2nd B. and V. Kilwarden]; b. 11 Nov. 1769 d. 22 May 1830; MP for Ardee 1790–7.

2246 **WOLSELEY**, Richard; b. *c.* 1655 d. 1724; MP for Carlow B. 1703–13, 1715–24.

2247 **WOLSELEY**, Sir Richard [1st Bt]; b. Feb. 1695/6 d. 8 Apr. 1769; MP for Carlow B. 1727–60, 1761–8.

2248 **WOLSELEY**, Robert; b. 1649 d. *c.* 1701; MP for Taghmon 1695–9.

2249 **WOLSELEY**, Rt Hon. William; b. 1640 d. [bur. 17] Dec. 1697; MP for Longford B. 1692–3, 1695–7.

2250 **WOOD**, Attiwell; b. 1728 d. 28 Mar. 1784; MP for Castlemartyr 1768–76, Clonakilty 1776–83–4.

2251 **WOOD**, Henry; b. 1758 d. *post* 1796; MP for Jamestown 1790–6.

2252 **WOOD**, John; b. *c.* 1664 d. 1730; MP for Co. Westmeath 1715–27.

2253 **WOODWARD**, Benjamin Blake; b. 1769 d. 1841; MP for Midleton 1794–7–1800.

2254 **WORTH**, Edward; b. 1672 d. 13 Nov. 1741; MP for Knocktopher 1695–9, 1703–13–14, 1715–27–41.

2255 **WORTH**, Edward; b. 1678 d. 23 Feb.–Mar. 1731/2; MP for New Ross 1715–27.

2256 **WYBRANTS**, Daniel; b. *c.* 1650 d. 1739; MP for Wexford B. 1695–9.

2257 **WYCHE**, Rt Hon. Sir Cyril [Kt]; b. *c.* 1632 d. 28 Dec. 1707; MP for TCD 1692–3 [HP].

2258 **WYNNE**, James; b. *ante* 1665 d. 11 Sept. 1709; MP for Co. Leitrim 1692–3.

2259 **WYNNE**, James; b. *c.* 1713–15 d. 25 Dec. 1748; MP for Co. Sligo 1737–48.

2260 **WYNNE**, John; b. *c.* 1688–91 d. 9 Feb. 1746/7; MP for Castlebar 1727–47.

2261 **WYNNE**, John; b. 1720 d. [*ante* 24] Jan. 1778; MP for Sligo B. 1751–60, 1768–76, 1777–8, Co. Leitrim 1761–8.

2262 **WYNNE**, Rt Hon. Owen; b. 1665 d. 28 Feb. 1736/7; MP for Carrick 1692–3, Ballyshannon 1713–14, 1715–27, Co. Sligo 1727–37.

2263 **WYNNE**, Owen; b. 1687 d. 1 June 1756; MP for Sligo B. 1713–14, 1715–27–56.

2264 **WYNNE**, Rt Hon. Owen; b. 1723 d. 18 Mar. 1789; MP for Co. Sligo 1749–60, 1761–8–76, Sligo B. 1776–83–9.

2265 **WYNNE**, Owen; b. 1755 d. 12 Dec. 1841; MP for Co. Sligo 1778–83–90, Sligo B. 1790–7, 1798–1800 [HP].

2266 **WYNNE**, Robert; b. 4 May 1761 d. 31 May 1838; MP for Sligo B. 1789–90–7–9.

2267 **WYNNE**, William; b. *c.* 1764 d. 1855; MP for Sligo B. 1799–1800.

2268 **YELVERTON**, Rt Hon. Barry [1st B. Yelverton, B. and V. Avonmore]; b. 28 May 1736 d. 19 Aug. 1805; MP for Donegal B. 1774–6, Carrickfergus 1776–83, 1783.

2269 **YELVERTON**, Hon. Walter Aglionby; b. 23 Jan. 1772 d. 3 June 1834; MP for Tuam 1797–1800 [re-elected pp 1800].

2270 **YOUNG**, Andrew; b. *ante* 5 Oct. 1671 d. 5 [bur. 7] Oct. 1718; MP for Ardfert 1692–3, 1695–9, 1703–13.

2271 **ZUYLESTEIN**, Hon. William Henry [2nd E. of Rochford]; b. 1681 d. 27 July 1710; MP for Kilkenny city 1705–10 [HP].

NOTES ON LIST OF MEMBERS

0004 His estimated year of birth, from *Complete Peerage* vol. VI p. 31, is 1742. His obituary in *BNL* (23 Jan. 1807) says that he was 'above 60 years of age', so he was certainly born before 1747, but he entered TCD in 1762, which would suggest a date of birth *c.* 1744/5.

0005 *Burke's Peerage* (1900) says he married in 1686.

0018 Year of death from *Prerog. Wills.*

0019 PRONI T808 p. 3172. Date of death from Abstract of Will in Groves MS.

0030 *Ir. Gen.* vol. 1 no. 8 (1940) p. 237, L. A. Wilson, 'A List of Irish Stockholders, 1779' says that he was aged 27 in 1779.

0031 For year of birth see *IHS* vol. X (1956–7) pp. 279–334, E. M. Johnston, 'The Career and Correspondence of Thomas Allan, 1725–98'. Frequently sources give dates a decade out: this is one such example.

0034 Sitting under age. He was sworn on 15 Oct. 1733.

0036 *Complete Peerage* vol. I p. 110 says that he was born on 17 Sept. 1685. *Gentleman's Magazine* Dec. 1742 reports his death on 4 Dec.

0046 Pilson Obituaries says that he died on 20 Dec. 1802 aged 60.

0059 IMC *King's Inns Admissions* (Dublin, 1982) records his son's entrance to King's Inns on 18 Apr. 1721, with 'father deceased'.

0068 Date of death from *Prerog. Wills.*

0070 McCracken thesis p. 232, estimated year of birth. PRONI T797/43 Welply's *Prerogative Will Abstracts and Marriage Registers* gives date of death and *Gentleman's Magazine* July 1744 reports his death.

0077 *DJ* 30 Mar.–2 Apr. 1776 announces his birth.

0081 Date of death from *Prerog. Wills.*

0082 Rev. W. B. Wright, *Ball Family Records* (York, 1908) pp. 98–102 says that he was born in 1744. RCBL M56 says that he died in his 66th year.

0085 *Memoirs of the Archdales* p. 74 says that he was born in 1652 and died aged 104.

0089 The previous session ended on 9 Feb. 1744. The new one began on 8 Oct. 1745. Writ issued on 22 Oct. 1745. McCracken thesis p. 234 and *IFR* p. 73 say that he died in 1744.

0091 The previous session ended on 20 June 1716. The new one began on 27 Aug. 1717. Writ issued on that date.

0093 The previous session ended on 15 Feb. 1742. The new one began on 4 Oct. 1743. Writ issued on that date.

0096 Lodge, vol. 1 p. 302 says that his parents married in 1666 and that he is a second son; this would make him born *c.* 1668 but TCD entrance date makes him born 1665.

0097 Date of death from *Prerog. Wills.*

0103 The previous session ended on 9 Feb. 1744. The new one began on 8 Oct. 1745. Writ issued on that date.

0104 A replacement writ has not been located but the session ended on 8 Mar. 1726 and parliament was dissolved on 11 June 1727.

0105 The previous session ended on 30 Oct. 1707. The new one began on 5 May 1709. Writ issued on that date.

0114 Returned under age, Apr. 1790. No date of swearing but the first session of the new parliament began on 2 July 1790.

0119 Returned under age, 20 Aug. 1783. No date of swearing but the first session of the new parliament began on 14 Oct. 1783.

0124 Burke, *Commoners* (1836) vol. 4 p. 32 says that he was born in 1663 and died in 1721. Council Book of Clonakilty p. 399 also says that he was born in 1663.

0126 *Cornwallis Corr.* vol. 3 p. 245 says that he was born on 30 Nov. 1755.

0127 Council Book of Bandon says that he died on 7 July 1790, as does Ffolliott, Biographical Notices. *DJ* 13–15 Apr. 1790 announces his death at Castle Bernard and 8–10 July 'at his lodgings in Dame Street'.

0129 The session began on 9 Oct. 1739 and ended on 31 Mar. 1740. Writ issued on 24 Dec. 1739. *George the First's Army*, vol. 2 p. 136 says that he died in 1717.

0131 Year of death from *Prerog. Wills.*

0136 Sitting under age. He was sworn on 8 Aug. 1707.

0138 *Peerage and Baronetage* p. 341 says that he died in 1790.

0140 The sources confuse this and the following MP (0141).

0144 *Memorials of the Dead* vol. 7 p. 417 says that he died on 10 May 1821 aged 56.

0155 Returned under age. No date of swearing but the first session of the new parliament began on 18 June 1776.

0163 *Commons jn. Ire.*, especially in the early part of this period, often refers to Mr Hassett rather than Blennerhassett.

0166 A List of Governors, pp. 38, 47 calls him Sir John.

0167 An MP for 66 years and for many years father of the House.

0172 *Peerage and Baronetage* p. 360 says that he was born on 28 Dec. 1687. *St Peter's Westminster* p. 323 says that he died in his 41st year.

0173 Returned under age, 20 Dec. 1739, but not sworn until 6 Oct. 1741. *HP* 1715–54 says that he was born on 1 Oct. 1719.

0175 *JRSAI* vol. 63 (1933) p. 164, H.G. Leask, 'Rathmore Church, Co. Meath' says that he was born in 1695. *Memorials of the Dead* v. III p. 115 says that he died aged 80.

0177 The previous session ended on 16 June 1705. The new one began on 1 July 1707. Writ issued on 9 July 1707.

0180 *Ir. Gen.* vol 4 no. 2 (1987), pp. 186–200, J. C. Walton, 'The Boltons of Co. Waterford' estimated his date of birth.

0185 Year of death from *St Peter and St Kevin's Reg.* p. 166 but identification of the MP is not definite. *HMC Ormonde* new series, vol. VIII p. 42 quotes a letter of 10 Sept. 1701 that says: 'Mr Booth, Seneschal of the Duke of Ormonde's Manors, is dead.'

0186 Estimated year of birth from *Complete Baronetage*, vol. II p. 269. RCBL, Dunlavin Parish Register, p. 251/1/1 says that he was buried on 26 Sept. 1709.

0197 *BNL* and *DJ* report his death in late November 1795; *Memorials of the Dead* vol. 2 p. 410 says that he died on 23 Feb. 1795.

0198 Re-elected on accepting a place of profit.

0207 Sources confuse this MP and 0209. *English Army Lists* vol. III pp. 13, 24 says that he died in 1694.

0210 *Shannon's Letters* p. xiii says that he was born in 1684. Burns, p. 238 says that he was born in 1682, which agrees

with his age at entry into university. Geoffrey H. White (ed.), *Complete Peerage* (London, 1945) vol. 10 p. 657 says that he was born in 1686.

0214 Sitting under age. He was sworn on 16 Apr. 1782.

0215 The previous session ended on 10 Feb. 1724. The new one began on 7 Sept. 1725. Writ issued on 24 Sept. 1725.

0222 Estimated year of birth from H. A. Doubleday and Lord Howard de Walden (eds), *Complete Peerage* (London, 1932) vol. 8 p. 615.

0225 *Alum. Dub.* says that he entered TCD in 1740 aged 14. He died at Bath and was buried on 3 Jan. 1791 in St Catherine's Church, Dublin.

0226 Returned under age. The session ended on 25 May 1789; the writ on which he came in was issued some time after that and before the beginning of the new session, on 21 Jan. 1790.

0228 *BNL* 15 June 1759 says that he died on 6 June.

0229 The previous session ended on 10 Feb. 1724. The new one began on 7 Sept. 1725. Writ issued on that date.

0230 Year of death from *Prerog. Wills.*

0231 The previous session ended on 4 Mar. 1704. Writ issued at the beginning of the new session, on 10 Feb. 1705.

0237 *Peerage of England, Scotland and Ireland* p. 239 says that he died on 29 Aug. 1728.

0239 Returned under age, *c.* 26 May 1776. No date of swearing but the session began on 18 June 1776.

0245 Returned under age, *c.* 26 May 1776. No date of swearing but the session began on 18 June 1776.

0246 Estimated year of death from Cork MPs.

0248 He is called Brookes in the 1713–14 parliament. *DJ* 14–18 July 1761 says that he died on 15 July.

0250 Parliament was in recess from 14 Dec. 1695 to 28 Mar. 1696. Writ issued 28 Mar. 1696.

0253 Returned under age. No date of swearing but the writ was issued on 22 July 1782 and the last session of the 1776 parliament ended five days later.

0260 Returned under age. No date of swearing but the session began on 18 June 1776.

0269 Date of death from *Prerog. Wills.*

0276 The session began on 13 Oct. 1796 and ended on 3 July 1797. Writ issued on 16 Jan. 1797.

0302 *DJ* 4–6 May 1773 says that he was killed in a carriage accident.

0305 *DJ* 3–7 July 1764 says that he was born on 2 July.

0308 Year of death from *Abstracts of Wills.*

0329 The session began on 21 Sept. 1703 and ended on 4 Mar. 1704. Writ issued on 22 Feb. 1704.

0333 Sitting under age. He was sworn on 19 Jan. 1792. *DJ* 5 May 1795 says that he died in London 'last week'.

0334 *Pue's Occurrences* 7 Nov. 1732 says that he died on 6 Nov.

0336 *Memorials of the Dead* vol. 12 p. 198 says that he died on 5 June 1743.

0340 The previous session ended on 3 Dec. 1697. The new one began on 27 Sept. 1698. Writ issued on that date.

0344 The session began on 12 Sept. 1721. Writ issued on 6 Oct. 1721.

0356 Date of death from *Prerog. Wills*.

0359 The three generations of Thomas Carters are confusing (particularly **0359**, for whom definite dates are not known). For their various offices (which are difficult to reconcile) see *Patentee Officers in Ireland*.

0360 Information from P. Aronsson Esq. says that he was born in 1682.

0369 The previous session ended on 16 June 1705. The new one began on 1 July 1707. Writ issued on that date.

0376 The previous session ended on 26 Dec. 1769. The new one began on 26 Feb. 1771. Writ issued on 28 Feb. 1771.

0377 The previous session ended on 7 Sept. 1785. The new one began on 19 Jan. 1786. Writ issued on 16 Feb. 1786.

0380 *Alum. Oxon.* vol. I p. 231 says that he died on 31 Mar. 1776. *Peerage and Baronetage* p. 1671 says that he died on 31 May 1776. *Dublin Hibernian Chronicle* says that he died before 21 Dec., and *Waterford Chronicle* says that he died on 31 Dec. 1776. In fact he died on 31 Dec. 1776: see *DJ* 31 Dec. 1776 – 2 Jan. 1777.

0386 RCBL P344/11/8 Registry of Monuments, St Anne's Parish Church, Dublin, says that he died aged 51.

0395 The previous session ended on 2 Nov. 1719. The new one began on 12 Sept. 1721. Writ issued on that date.

0407 *HP* 1715–54 gives an estimated date of birth.

0413 The writ on which he came in was issued on 3 Nov. 1777. No date of return or swearing.

0414 He was buried in St Michan's Church on 29 May 1777.

0422 A List of Governors says that he died on 6 Jan. 1705.

0423 Date of death from *Prerog. Wills*.

0428 *BNL* 27 Sept. 1816 says that he died in his 82nd year.

0431 Returned under age, 21 Oct. 1692. No date of swearing but the only session of the 1692 parliament ended on 3 Nov. 1692. *BNL* 13 Mar. 1738/9 reports his death in his 66th year.

0432 On 23 Nov. 1697 a writ issued for Limerick city in the room of Joseph Coghlan, deceased. The session ended on 3 Dec. 1697 and the new one began on 27 Sept. 1698 but no replacement for Coghlan has been located from Nov. 1697 to the end of the parliament on 26 Jan. 1699.

0434 The previous session ended on 8 Mar. 1726. The parliament was dissolved on 11 June 1727. No writ has been located.

0436 Returned under age, 26 May 1766. No date of swearing but the session ended on 7 June 1766.

0442 Earl of Belmore, *History of Two Ulster Manors* (Dublin, 1903) pp. 113, 165 says that John Corry (*see* **0499**)) replaced Cole in 1703 whose election was declared void for failure to attend the House. *HMC Ormonde* vol. VIII pp. 175, 221–2, 226 also says that Cole was replaced by Corry for Enniskillen in 1705 because the former was expelled for failure to attend. On 2 Nov. 1703 the Commons ordered the Speaker to issue his writ to replace Cole unless he appeared before them within a fortnight. Five other MPs were also given time limits within which to report for service. The Speaker on 12 Nov. reported that he had received a letter from Cole seeking to be excused from attendance because of ill health, '… which was read but not admitted as an excuse by the House'. There is no record of a writ issuing to replace Cole from this to the end of the session in Mar. 1704. The Commons were reluctant to accept sickness as a valid reason for absenteeism because of its precedent-setting potential, but, if future conduct is any guide, they were also unwilling to expel, or allow a member to resign on a plea of illness, mental or physical. There is no mention of Cole in *The Censured and Expelled* (see 'Members censured and expelled') section of *Commons jn. Ire.*, and the return at the beginning of the 1707 session says Corry '… loco Michael Cole defuncti'. This is curious since Cole did not die until 1711. An explanation is perhaps to be found in the *Commons jn. Ire.* returns for the sessions of the 1703 parliament. These seem to have been corrected retrospectively and there may have been some confusion about when Corry replaced Cole. However, the failure to locate the writ of replacement, even after Cole's death, possibly indicates his expulsion from the House before that time.

0443 The previous session ended on 6 May 1728. The new one began on 23 Sept. 1729. Writ issued on 17 Mar. 1730. Kilkenny MPs says that he died in June 1729.

0445 *Cornwallis Corr.* vol. 3 p. 45 says that he died on 25 Apr. 1822.

0455 Date of death from *Prerog. Wills*.

0456 Date of death suspect.

0465 The previous session ended on 9 Apr. 1748. The new one began on 10 Oct. 1749. Writ issued on that date.

0482 Date of death from *Prerog. Wills*.

0483 Ibid.

0486 *Irish Army Lists* pp. 100, 136 gives a Thomas Coote died in Mar. 1703.

0491 RCBL, P344/11/8, Registry of Monuments, St Anne's Parish Church, Dublin, says that he died aged 63.

0492 Sources confuse this MP and **0493**.

0496 PRONI T1345 Pedigrees of the Russell, Corry and Montgomery Families says that he died before 1813.

0497 *Cornwallis Corr.* vol. 3 p. 39 says that he was born in 1755. According to sources, his father did not marry until Sept. 1752. Family tree in A. P. W. Malcomson, *Isaac Corry* (PRONI 1974) pp. 32–3 gives 1753; *BNL* 21 May 1813 says that he died on 16 May.

0508 *BNL* 14 Feb. 1766 says that he died on 2 Feb. as does *DJ* 4–8 Feb. 1766 and Ffolliott, Biographical Notices, which also says that he died aged 65.

0514 J. H. Steele, *Genealogy of the Earls of Erne* (Edinburgh, 1910) p. 33 says that his father died in 1631.

0528 *BNL* 4 Sept. 1750 says that he died on 28 Aug.

0533 *Harrow School Reg.* Part 2 p. 59 says that he died on 30 Sept. 1836.

0537 *Peerage of England, Scotland and Ireland* p. 155 says that he died on 20 Jan. 1762.

0539 The previous session ended on 15 Feb. 1742. The new one began on 4 Oct. 1743. Writ issued on 16 Nov. 1743.

0540 Returned under age. No date of swearing but the session began on 7 Oct. 1735 and ended on 30 Mar. 1736.

0545 The previous session ended on 28 Aug. 1710. The new one began on 9 July 1711. Writ issued on that date.

0550 *Ext. Peerage* p. 149 says that he was born in 1669.

0553 PROI, MFCI, Reel 35 Parish Registers of Ballinrobe, Co. Mayo, says that he died on 30 July and was buried on 17 Aug. 1828.

0556 *JRSAI* vol. 54 (1924) pp. 55–67, T. U. Sadleir, 'The Register of Kilkenny School (1685–1800)' says that he was aged 14 in May 1709. McCracken thesis p. 277 says that he was born in 1694. *Dublin Courant* 28 July 1744 says that he died on 17 July.

0561 Date of death from *Prerog. Wills*.

0567 Ibid.

0568 Ibid.

0570 Returned under age, 27 Oct. 1767. No date of swearing but the session began on 20 Oct. 1767.

0572 The previous session ended on 26 Dec. 1769. The new one began on 26 Feb. 1771. Writ issued on that date.

0581 Date of death from *Prerog. Wills*.

0589 *Eton College Reg.* vol. 3 p. 151 says that he died on 25 Nov. 1798.

0591 Estimated date of birth from *IFR* p. 236.

0594 Date of death from *Prerog. Wills*.

0599 The previous session ended on 20 June 1716. The new one began on 27 Aug. 1717. Writ issued on that date.

0620 Date of death from *Prerog. Wills*.

0634 PRONI T559 vol. 18 p. 144 Extract Pedigrees (mainly from wills proven in the Prerogative Court of Ireland, 16th–18th centuries, compiled by Sir Bernard Burke, Ulster King at Arms), says that he died in 1709.

0640 *Kild. Arch. Soc. Jn.* vol. 13 (1946–63) p. 373, Sir E. F. Tickell, 'The Eustace Family and their Lands in County Kildare' says that he was born in 1674. *Alum. Dub.* says that he entered Dublin University 3 May 1701: under normal circumstances this would be late if born 1674, but he may have been delayed by the war.

0642 Sources confuse this MP's date of death with **0643**.

0645 Estimated date of birth from *HP* 1715–54.

0657 *HMC Stopford-Sackville* vol. I p. 214, a letter dated 25 June 1754 reports his death 'last night'. *BNL* 2 July 1754 says that he died on 25 June.

0667 *Gentleman's Magazine* Apr. 1752 reports the death of Colonel Dunbar.

0668 He declined to serve on a committee on 10 Mar. 1791, taking advantage of the provision enabling MPs 60 years old and over to be excused.

0679 Returned under age, 26 Sept. 1692. No date of swearing but the session began on 5 Oct. 1692.

0682 The previous session ended on 28 Aug. 1710. The new one began on 9 July 1711. Writ issued on that date.

0704 Estimated year of birth from *Complete Peerage* (1913) vol. 3 p. 9.

0705 Date of death from *Prerog. Wills*.

0709 *Irish Pedigrees* vol. II p. 188 says that he died *c.* 1746.

0711 The previous session ended on 28 Aug. 1710. The new one began on 9 July 1711. Writ issued on that date.

0712 The session began on 5 May and ended on 30 Aug. 1709. Writ issued on 28 July 1709.

0719 *Cork Hist. & Arch. Soc. Jn.* 1st Series, vol. 1 (1892) pp. 221–4, vol. II (1893) pp. 8 *et seq.*, vol. III (1894) p. 56, C. M. Tenison, 'The Private Bankers of Cork and the South of Ireland'. Vol. I (1892) p. 224 says that he died in 1799.

0720 *Alum. Oxon.* vol. I p. 482 says that he died on 7 July 1744.

0725 *DJ* 1–3 June 1780 notes his death. Writ issued on 3 June 1780.

0728 Returned under age. No date of swearing but the session began on 18 June 1776.

0729 NAI MFCI, Reel 5, Vestry Books of Kilnasoolagh Parish, Co. Clare, says that he died aged 78.

0730 Returned under age. No date of swearing but the session began on 14 Oct. 1783.

0731 *DJ* 17–19 Aug. 1775 says he died 'at Paris'. A replacement writ has not been located. The session began on 10 Oct. 1775 and ended on 4 Apr. 1776. The parliament was dissolved on Apr. 5 1776.

0732 Kildare MPs says that he died in 1698 but a writ has not been located during the last session of the parliament from 27 Sept. 1698 to 26 Jan. 1699, so he probably died late in the year.

0734 Returned under age, 17 Oct. 1741. No date of swearing but the session began on 6 Oct. 1741. BL Add. MS 51426, f. 214, in a letter of [9] June 1765 he says: 'I am this day forty-three …'.

0736 The session began on 28 Nov. 1727 and ended on 6 May 1728. Writ issued on 2 Apr. 1728.

0740 The session began on 10 Oct. 1775 and ended on 4 Apr. 1776. Writ issued on 27 Feb. 1776.

0744 *Memorials of the Dead* vol. IV p. 41 says that he died aged 90.

0745 Returned under age, 28 Nov. 1767, but from 1776 to 1779 he was on a Grand Tour. *Peerage and Baronetage* (1900) gives his date of birth as 13 March 1749; *IMC Leinster* vol. III p. xi gives his birthday as 2 Mar. 1749; *DJ* 15–17 Mar. 1768 carries a report of his birthday celebrations held on 14 Mar.

0763 Returned under age, 2 Nov. 1765. No date of swearing but the session began on 22 Oct. 1765 and ended on 7 June 1766.

0764 Date of death from *Prerog. Wills.*

0766 The session began on 13 Oct. 1796 and ended on 3 July 1797. Writ issued on 31 Mar. 1797.

0772 For some unknown reason, *Commons jn. Ire.* (Bradley ed.) vol. V p. 789 records that John Wynne was sworn as the new member for Donegal Borough on 2 Apr. 1730.

0781 Blackwood pedigrees, /9/61 says that he was born *c.* 1675.

0784 Date of death from *Prerog. Wills.*

0786 Ibid.

0792 The session began on 9 Oct. 1781 and ended on 27 July 1782. Writ issued on 28 May 1782.

0794 Writ issued on 10 June 1780. *DJ* 11–14 Dec. reports his death 'at his house in Merrion Square'.

0801 Year of death from *Prerog. Wills.*

0802 Returned under age, 3 Nov. 1715. No date of swearing but the session began on 12 Nov. 1715.

0805 Returned under age 29 Apr. 1761 but the session did not begin until 22 Oct. 1761.

0806 *DJ* 1–3 Mar. 1792 announces the death.

0810 In the 1709 and 1710 sessions he is called Foulkes in *Commons jn. Ire.* (Bradley edn).

0813 Year of death from *Prerog. Wills.*

0817 *English Army Lists* vol. III p. 372 reports an Alexander Frasier killed at Schollenborg in 1704. The name was quite common and this is probably not the MP.

0821 Returned under age. No date of swearing but the writ was issued on 11 Dec. 1783. The session ended on 14 May 1784.

0823 A List of Governors says that he was born *post* 1673; Council Book of Clonakilty says that he was born *c.* 1645 and died *ante* 1 July 1706.

0825 The previous session ended on 20 June 1716. The new one began on 27 Aug. 1717. Writ issued on 29 Aug. 1717. *Cork Hist. & Arch. Soc. Jn.* vol. 16 (1910) p.153 'Mrs Elizabeth Freke, her Diary 1671–1714' says that he died in 1718.

0828 This MP is said to have been baptised on 6 Apr. 1765, but this is probably incorrect and may be a misprint for 1763, for if 1765 is anywhere near his date of birth, he was considerably under 21 when returned for Co. Roscommon in 1783 (a date of swearing has not been located). He married in October 1784.

0836 The session ended on 1 June 1799. The writ was issued sometime between that and the beginning of the new session on 15 Jan. 1800.

0837 *Ir. Gen.* vol. 2, no. 6 (1948) p. 176, E. S. Gray, 'Some Notes of the High Sheriffs of Co. Donegal' says that he died in 1828.

0838 He is listed as Collector of Killybegs in *Gentleman's and Citizen's Almanack* until 1798.

0842 RCBL, p. 80/1/1a Parish Registers of St Thomas, Dublin, says that he died aged 52.

0845 Date of death from *Prerog. Wills.*

0849 He was named and his estates confiscated in 1689, so presumably he was over 21 years of age.

0854 *DJ* 1–3 Mar. 1770 says that he died 'yesterday'.

0855 *Peerage and Baronetage* (1903) p. 648 says that he died on 21 Jan. 1817; Ffolliott, Biographical Notices says that he died on 19 Jan. aged 79.

0858 *Complete Baronetage* vol. III p. 316 says that he was born in or about 1685. The previous session ended on 15 Apr. 1730. The new one began on 5 Oct. 1731. Writ issued on that date.

0859 *DJ* 22–4 Apr. 1773 says that he died on 21 Apr.

0860 *Gentleman's Magazine* Mar. 1758 says that he died in Mar. The session ended on 29 Apr. 1758. The writ for his replacement was issued on 3 Apr. He was buried on 15 Apr. 1758.

0861 *Gentleman's Magazine* Sept. 1746 p. 485 says that he was born in 1731.

0863 The previous session ended on 10 Feb. 1724. The new one began on 7 Sept. 1725. Writ issued on that date.

0870 Date of death from *Prerog. Wills.*

0873 PRONI T3435/1/7 p. 86 The Cavendish MSS – Proceedings of the Irish House of Commons, says the House was informed of his death on 5 Mar. 1778.

0875 The session began on 23 Sept. 1729 and ended on 15 Apr. 1730. Writ issued on 10 Feb. 1730.

0877 *DJ* 21–3 Sept. 1769 reports his death.

0880 Returned under age, 26 Oct. 1741. No date of swearing but the session began on 6 Oct. 1741.

0892 The previous session ended on 20 June 1716. The new one began on 27 Aug. 1717. Writ issued on that date.

0893 Sitting under age. He was sworn on 7 Nov. 1749.

0894 Blackwood pedigrees, /4/14 says that he was born in 1705.

0897 *Commons jn. Ire.* (Bradley edn) vol. 3 p. 339. Estimated year of birth comes from the evidence he volunteered during the report of the committee to consider the petition of Eustace Sherlock against Maurice and John Annesley.

0900 The previous session ended on 30 Aug. 1709. The new one began on 19 May 1710. Writ issued on 20 May 1710.

0905 Pakenham, p. 215 says that he died aged 65. This means his father married when aged 16. *DNB* suggests that he was born [?]1738.

0906 Year of death from a will in PRONI T559 vol. 22 p. 226.

0907 Year of death from *Prerog. Wills.*

0910 Estimated year of birth from Michael O'Donnell Esq.

0911 The previous session ended on 30 Oct. 1707. The new one began on 5 May 1709. Writ issued on that date.

0913 *Cornwallis Corr.*, vol. 3 p. 46 says that he was born in 1765. *Record of Old Westminsters*, 2 vols, p. 416 says that he died in 1808.

0918 *Memorials of the Dead* vol. 4 pp. 203–4 says that he died aged 58. Lodge vol. 6 p. 27 says that he was MP for Co. Cavan 1661–6.

0923 PRONI /7 Pilson Obituaries says that he died aged 60.

0931 Ibid., p. 81 says that he died in 1707.

0933 *Complete Baronetage* vol. III p. 305 says that he was born in 1661. He married in January 1684.

0934 Estimated year of birth from *HP* 1715–54.

0941 Estimated year of birth from *Complete Baronetage* vol. 5 p. 401.

0954 Date of death from *Prerog. Wills.*

0955 The previous session ended on 16 June 1705. The new one began on 1 July 1707. Writ issued on that date.

0957 The previous session ended on 18 Jan. 1722. The new one began on 29 Aug. 1723. Writ issued on that date.

0973 PRONI D3000/27/2 Falkiner Genealogical Notes says he was born in 1677.

0977 Information from Dr Jean Agnew of the Ulster Historical Foundation says that he was baptised on 15 July 1671, but *Alum. Dub.* says that he entered TCD 9 July 1683 aged 14. The previous session ended on 30 Oct. 1707. The new one began on 5 May 1709. Writ issued on that date.

0980 *Musgrave Obits* vol. III p. 161 says that he died on 13 Dec. 1763. This is unlikely since the session ended on 12 May 1764. The new session began on 22 Oct. 1765 and ended on 7 June 1766. The replacement writ was issued on 23 Jan. 1766.

0981 Estimated date of birth from *Complete Baronetage* vol. 4 p. 214.

0982 The session began on 4 Oct. 1743 and ended on 9 Feb. 1744. Writ issued on that date.

0983 *Ir. Gen.* vol. 2 no. 5 (1947) p. 142, L. E. O'Hanlon, 'Testamentary Records' says that his will was proved on 12 May 1705.

0985 PRONI D3000/22 estimated year of death from Harvey Family Bible.

0989 The previous session ended on 29 Apr. 1734. The new one began on 7 Oct. 1735. Writ issued on that date.

0992 A writ was issued in Oct. 1692 and Robert Stopford replaced one of the MPs elected in Sept. Robert Smith, the third man, did not die until 1720 so it seems likely that Stopford replaced Haydock.

0993 Estimated year of death from Dr David Hayton.

0997 He is listed in the 'Barristers' section of the *Treble Almanack* until 1822.

1002 Returned under age, 11 May 1776. No date of swearing but the session began on 18 June 1776; PRONI T3459 Donoughmore Papers, pp. 14–22 says that he died on 6 July 1832.

1006 The previous session ended on 20 June 1716. The new one began on 27 Aug. 1717. Writ issued on that date.

1014 Returned under age, 13 Sept. 1703. No date of swearing but the session began on 21 Sept. 1703.

1018 PRONI T618/328 Crossle Papers says that he died on 10 Feb. 1795.

1020 PRONI T618/329 Crossle Papers says that he died on 10 Feb. 1739.

1021 Returned under age, 14 Nov. 1713. No date of swearing but the session began on 25 Nov. 1713.

1023 Estimated year of birth from Simms' Cards.

1025 Ffolliott, Biographical Notices says that he died in his 88th year.

1027 He is listed as a member of the Dublin Society in the *Treble Almanack* from 1764 to 1803. Some sources confuse this MP with **1028**.

1028 Returned under age, 20 Aug. 1783. No date of swearing but the session began on 14 Oct. 1783.

1029 The previous session ended on 3 Dec. 1697. The new one began on 27 Sept. 1698. Writ issued on that date.

1039 The session began on 8 Oct. 1745 and ended on 11 Apr. 1746. Writ issued on 10 Mar. 1745/6.

1040 The previous session ended on 10 Mar. 1732. The new one began on 4 Oct. 1733. Writ issued on 5 Oct. 1733.

1051 Estimated date of birth from *Complete Baronetage* vol. 4 p. 207.

1054 Ibid., vol. 3 p. 188 says that he died on 15 Nov. 1815 aged 42.

1055 He is listed in the 'Attornies' section of *Gentleman's and Citizen's Almanack* until 1802.

1063 *BNL* says Col. Hyde died on 31 Dec 1801; *IFR* p. 618 says that he died on 22 Dec. 1772 [*sic*].

1064 Estimated date of death from *Shannon's Letters* p. 187.

1070 Estimated year of birth from *IFR* p. 620.

1072 *Irish Army Lists* p. 150 says that he died in 1694.

1073 Estimated year of birth from PRONI T1203/1/5, Pedigree of the D'Arcy Irvine Family of Co. Fermanagh.

1074 Sitting under age. He was sworn on 21 Jan. 1790.

1079 Year of death from *Prerog. Wills*.

1080 Ibid.

1081 *Ir. Gen.* vol. 5, no. 1 (1974) pp. 72–86, W. G. Skehan, 'Extracts from the Minutes of the Corporation of Fethard, Co. Tipperary' says that he died on 6 Dec. 1764. This could be 6 Dec. 1763 as *DJ* 17–21 Jan. 1764 announces his death.

1087 Returned under age, 6 July 1768. No date of swearing but parliament did not meet until 17 Oct. 1769.

1089 The session began on 29 Aug. 1723 and ended on 10 Feb. 1723/4. Writ issued on 6 Feb. 1723/4.

1092 The session began on 27 Sept. 1698 and the writ issued on 29 Dec. 1698.

1093 The session began on 12 Nov. 1715 and ended on 20 June 1716. Writ issued on 3 May 1716.

1099 *Alum. Oxon.* (1888) vol. 2 p. 754 says that he died on 29 June 1797. *Ir. Gen.* vol. 5, no. 1 (1974) pp. 72–86, W. G. Skehan, 'Extracts from the Minutes of the Corporation of Fethard, Co. Tipperary' says that he died on 22 June. *FJ* 24 June 1797 reports his death the day before in his 76th year.

1102 The previous session ended on 2 Nov. 1719. The new one began on 12 Sept. 1721. Writ issued on that date.

1107 The session began on 23 Sept. 1729 and ended on 15 Apr. 1730. Writ issued on 18 Mar. 1730.

1109 Estimated year of birth from PRONI D3000/10/5/1–29 Genealogical Papers, Pedigrees of the Johnston Family. Year of death from *Prerog. Wills*.

1110 PRONI/6 Pilson Obituaries says that he died on 23 Apr. 1795.

1112 The session began on 27 Aug. 1695 and ended on 3 Dec. 1697. Writ issued on 21 Oct. 1695.

1122 The previous session ended on 18 Jan. 1722. The new one began on 29 Aug. 1723. Writ issued on that date.

1126 He is listed in the 'Judges and Barristers' section of the *Treble Almanack* until 1797.

1129 Various sources confuse this MP with **1130**.

1131 *The Records of the Honourable Society of Lincoln's Inn* p. 276 gives a John, son of Edmund Keating of Dublin, entered Lincoln's Inn 22 May 1657, but no more definite identification. The previous session ended on 20 June 1716. The new one began on 27 Aug. 1717. Writ issued on that date.

1137 Estimated year of birth from *DNB*.

1140 He is listed in the 'Judges and Barristers' section of the *Treble Almanack* until 1813.

1143 *Irish Privy Counsellors* says that he died in 1812.

1146 *Ir. Gen.* vol. 2, no. 1 (1943) p. 14, E. S. Gray, 'Some Notes on the High Sheriffs of Co. Longford, 1701–1800' quotes a will with date of death.

1148 *DJ* 17–19 Feb. 1780 states that the by-election was on 9 Feb. 1780.

1152 *St Peter and St Kevin's Reg.* p. 120 has a George, son of William King baptised on this date but no more definite identification.

1156 *Ir. Gen.* vol. 2, no. 9 (1951) p. 273, E. S. Gray, 'Further Notes on the High Sheriffs of Co. Sligo' says that he was born in 1746 and his parents married in 1744.

1163 Parliament was in recess from 22 Sept. to 1 Oct. 1696. Writ issued on the latter date.

1165 The session began on 9 July and ended on 9 Nov. 1711. The writ was issued on 4 Oct. 1711.

1166 Returned under age, 6 Mar. 1744. However, he was not sworn until 8 Apr. 1746.

1169 *Irish Army Lists* pp. 4, 81, 90 says that he died on 4 Sept. 1706.

1171 Year of death from *Prerog. Wills.*

1182 Writ issued August 1775, see *DJ* 24–6 Aug. 1775.

1183 Estimated date of death from Ellis thesis, vol. 2 p. 151.

1184 Returned under age, Nov. 1777. No date of swearing but the session began on 14 Oct. 1777.

1185 Estimated year of birth from Dr Jean Agnew of the Ulster Historical Foundation. *Alum. Dub.* gives a Thomas Knox matriculated 1671 aged about 17.

1187 *BNL* 1 May 1750 says that he came of age on 24 Apr.

1200 *Cornwallis Corr.* vol. 3 p. 32 says that he was born in 1738. *JRSAI* 5th series, vol. VII (1897) pp. 434–6, R. Langrishe, 'A Refutation' says that he was 21 in 1750.

1204 *HP* 1790–1820, Professor Jupp gives his date of birth as 5 May 1769.

1210 PRONI D1946/Box 7 Lecky Family Papers says that his father died in May 1748 aged 39 and that he died in his 77th year.

1213 *BNL* 15 Dec. 1801 says that he died in his 73rd year.

1219 Year of death from *Prerog. Wills.*

1234 The session began on 27 Aug. 1695 and ended on 3 Dec. 1697. Writ issued on 1 May 1697.

1266 The previous session ended on 12 May 1764. The new one began on 22 Oct. 1765. Writ issued on that date.

1271 The session began on 12 Nov. 1715 and ended on 20 June 1716. Writ issued on 13 June 1716.

1291 Estimated year of birth from Kildare MPs. *St Peter and St Kevin's Reg*, p. 347 gives one John Lyons buried in 1726 and another in 1732.

1300 Returned under age.

1306 *BNL* 28 June–2 July 1793 says that he died on 25 June.

1308 The previous session ended on 6 May 1728. The new one began on 23 Sept. 1729. Writ issued on that date.

1310 The previous session ended on 18 Jan. 1722. The new one began on 29 Aug. 1723. Writ issued on that date.

1311 The session began on 4 Oct. 1733 and ended on 29 Apr. 1734. Writ issued on 14 Oct. 1733. Burke, *Landed Gentry of Ireland* (1904) p. 364 says that he died in 1756.

1317 Returned under age, 19 July 1768. No date of swearing but the session began on 17 Oct. 1769.

1319 The session began on 27 Aug. 1717. Writ issued on 31 Aug. 1717.

1320 *Cornwallis Corr.* vol. 3 p. 43 says that he was born on 3 Aug. 1762.

1321 Year of death from *Prerog. Wills.*

1322 Date of death from a will in Magenis family and PRONI T185/9, Miscellaneous wills.

1323 *Masons of Ireland* vol. I p. 219 states that he was born in 1764.

1327 Returned under age, 12 Mar. 1724 but was not sworn until 14 Oct. 1725.

1329 The previous session ended on 30 Oct. 1707. The new one began on 5 May 1709. Writ issued on that date.

1331 The previous session ended on 29 Apr. 1734. The new one began on 7 Oct. 1735. Writ issued on that date.

1332 PROI, MFCI Reel 29, Parish Registers of Ahascragh, Co. Galway, say that he was buried on 15 Aug. 1835 aged 75 i.e. b. 1760, but *Alum. Dub.* says he entered TCD in 1780 aged 16.

1340 and **1341** are confusing. They are cousins, both nephews of Anthony Malone (**1336**).

1342 His predecessor in Downpatrick, Francis Annesley (*see* **0043**), was expelled on 28 Sept. 1703 and although the session continued to 4 Mar. 1704 an election writ was not issued until the beginning of the following session, on 10 Feb. 1705.

1345 The session began on 26 June and ended on 2 Nov. 1719. Writ issued on 29 July 1719.

1348 Sources are confused. *Alum. Dub.* gives one William Martin entered TCD in 1697 aged 17 and another, a BA in 1720. *Prerog. Wills* has the proven will of a William Martin dated 1752. On balance this is probably the William buried on 7 Feb. 1737 according to *St Peter and St Kevin's Reg.* p. 351.

1350 *Patentee Officers in Ireland* gives Sir John, Searcher of Waterford Passage and Ross, 1671. *Alum. Dub.* gives a John entered TCD 1685 aged 18. Date of death from a will in T559, vol. 28 p. 25.

1352 *Ir. Gen.* vol. 5 no. 3 (1976) p. 344, H. F. Morris, 'Ramsey's Waterford Chronicle, 1776' says that he was born in 1726. But he entered TCD in 1741 and the Middle Temple in 1745. *BNL* 7 Apr. 1809 says that he died aged 81, i.e. b. 1728 or 1727/8.

1360 *Complete Peerage* vol. 7 p. 419 says that he was born in 1738 or 1744. *Annual Reg.* (1806) p. 544 and *Cornwallis Corr.* vol. 3 p. 125 say that he was born in 1738.

1361 *DJ* 2–5 Jan. 1768 says that he was born on 3 Jan. 1768; *Harrow School Reg.* p. 104 says that he died on 21 Mar. 1833.

1363 *Harrow School Reg.* p. 104 says that he died on 19 Mar. 1819.

1364 Year of death from *Prerog. Wills.*

1382 The previous session ended on 29 Apr. 1734. The new one began on 7 Oct. 1735. Writ issued on that date.

1383 *Ir. Gen.* vol. 6, no.. 2 (1981) p. 155, H. F. Morris, 'The Waterford Herald, 1792' says that he was born in 1729. *BNL* 15 Nov. 1811 says that he died aged 91; Ffolliott, Biographical Notices says that he celebrated his 89th birthday on 6 Nov. 1811. He entered TCD in June 1742, which suggests he was b. 1722 rather than 1720, but most probably 1723.

1388 Returned under age, 13 Jan. 1764. No date of swearing but the session began on 11 Oct. 1763.

1390 *BNL* 9 July 1811 says that he died in his 80th year.

1394 The Clerk of the Commons seems to have had particular difficulty with this member's surname. In 1692 he is called Melville, in 1695 Melvyn; he starts as Melvyn in 1703 but reverts to Melville by 1709 and remains so throughout the parliament. In 1713 he has become Melvyn once more. He is called Melville in *Parliamentary Lists* from 1695 to 1714, with the exception of the 1696 list.

1398 The session began on 19 May and ended on 28 Aug. 1710. Writ issued on 23 June 1710.

1401 *Peerage and Baronetage* (1903) p. 1040 says that he was born in 1657 and died in 1737. J. H. Bernard (ed.), *The Register of St Patrick's, Dublin, 1677–1800* (Dublin, 1907) pp. 45, 95 records a Richard Meredyth buried on 8 Nov. 1743; in a footnote it remarks that according to a family pedigree, Sir Richard was buried in the family vault in 1737 but there is no notice of this in the Register.

1406 Fermanagh and Tyrone MPs p. 241 says that he was dead by 9 Feb. 1698.

1408 Year of death from *Prerog. Wills, 1811–58.*

1411 The previous session ended on 10 Feb. 1724. The new one began on 7 Sept. 1725. Writ issued on that date.

1412 Burke, *Landed Gentry* p. 406 says that he was MP for Okehampton: this is a mistake for his grandson, also Humphrey Minchin.

1416 PRONI T559, vol. 28 pp. 280, 290, date of death from a will.

1429 *Annual Reg.* (1804) p. 503 says that he died aged 73.

1437 *FJ* 17 Oct. 1797 says that he is between 80 and 90 years old.

1441 G. S. Montgomery, *A Family History of the Montgomerys of Ballyleck* (Belfast, 1897) pp. 3–35 says that he died in 1732.

1446 Our information about this MP is uncertain. *DJ* 19–21 Aug. 1783 notes the death of William Montgomery, Esq. at Dunleary in his 82nd year. The Montgomery Pedigree, Ulster Historical Foundation, says that his father died in 1725. He probably purchased his seat.

1452 Returned under age, 13 Nov. 1713. No date of swearing but the session began on 25 Nov. 1713.

1453 If his date of baptism is anywhere near his date of birth he was returned under age, 19 Sept. 1692; there is no date of swearing but the session began on 5 Oct. 1692. He was also returned under age to the 1695 parliament, 5 Aug. 1695.

1455 Year of death from *Prerog. Wills.*

1459 Ibid.

1460 Date of death from *Prerog. Wills.*

1468 Year of death from abstract of will in Canon W. P. Burke MS, Mount Melleray Abbey, Cappoquin, Co. Waterford. Information courtesy of Michael O'Donnell Esq. says that his will was proved in 1699.

1473 Year of death from *Prerog. Wills.*

1475 The information on this MP is uncertain. *Gentleman's Magazine* reports the death of a Stephen Moore in June 1737.

1477 Date of death from *Prerog. Wills.*

1480 Returned under age. Writ issued on 9 Apr. 1790. No date of return or swearing but the writ to replace him was issued on 24 July 1790.

1498 RCBL P45/1/2 Parish Registers of St Peter's, Dublin says that he died aged 76. The previous session ended on 18 Jan. 1722. The new one began on 29 Aug. 1723. Writ issued on that date.

1508 Year of death from *Prerog. Wills.*

1511 The session began on 26 June and ended on 2 Nov. 1719. Writ issued on 1 July 1719. *IFR* p. 874 says that he died in 1718.

1513 C. Dalton (ed.) *The Blenheim Roll* (1899) p. 18 and *George the First's Army* vol. I p. 328 say that he died on 10 Nov. 1739.

1516 The session began on 25 Nov. and ended on 24 Dec. 1713. Writ issued on 21 Dec. 1713.

1527 *Cornwallis Corr.* vol. 3 p. 45 says that he was born in 1745. *Kild. Arch. Soc. Jn.* vol. 3 (1899–1902) p. 463, N. J. Synott, 'Notes on Furness or Great Forenaghts', agrees, but *JRSAI* (1924) T. U. Sadlier, 'Kilkenny School Register' pp. 152–9, says that he entered Kilkenny College in 1751 aged 8, and *Alum. Dub.* that he entered TCD in 1759.

1530 *DJ* 7–10 June 1766 says that he died aged 78.

1531 The previous session ended on 2 June 1772, and in a report of his daughter's wedding in *DJ* 17–20 Oct. 1772 he is described as 'the late Charles Newcomen'. The writ for the by-election was not issued until March 1773.

1534 Sitting under age. He was sworn on 4 Feb. 1760.

1535 RCBL P45/1/2, Parish Registers of St Peter's, Dublin, says that he died aged 84.

1539 *Prerog. Wills* gives the will, proved in 1714, of Major General John Newton. See also *IMC, Registry of Deeds*, vol. I, no. 90.

1541 Parliament was in recess from 14 Dec. 1695 to 28 Mar. 1696. Writ issued on the latter date.

1547 Sitting under age. He was sworn on 19 Apr. 1780.

1549 Sitting under age. He was sworn on 4 Mar. 1760.

1550 The session began on 28 Nov. 1727 and ended on 6 May 1728. Writ issued on 6 Dec. 1727.

1552 *JRSAI* 5th series, vol. I (Dublin, 1892) pp. 75, 77, P. D. Vigors, 'Alphabetical List of Free Burgesses of New Ross … 1685–1839' says that he died on 18 Nov. 1717 aged 76.

1556 *DJ* 12–14 Dec. 1769 says he died 'a few days ago at his house in College Green'.

1558 PRONI/329 Crossle Papers says that he died on 22 Jan. 1795 probably as a result of a duel.

1562 *Complete Peerage* vol. 8 p. 81 says that he was MP for Fethard from 1761.

1564 Returned under age, 25 July 1797. No date of swearing but the session began on 9 Jan. 1798.

1570 Year of death from *Prerog. Wills*.

1575 R. J. S. Hoffman, *Edmund Burke* (Philadelphia, 1956) p. 7 estimates his year of birth *c.* 1715. He married in 1742.

1577 Estimated year of birth from D. Hogg Esq. and B. O'Hara Esq.

1589 The session began on 10 Jan. and ended on 16 Aug. 1793. Writ issued on 28 May 1793.

1591 Parliament was in recess from 16 Mar. to 11 May 1697. Writ issued on the last date.

1601 Year of death from *Prerog. Wills*. A writ has not been located but the last session of the 1703 parliament ended on 9 Nov. 1711.

1608 *Cornwallis Corr.* vol. 3 p. 43 says that he died on 2 Sept. 1817.

1609 Year of death from *Prerog. Wills*.

1617 The previous session ended on 2 Nov. 1719. The new one began on 12 Sept. 1721. Writ issued on that date.

1624 *JRSAI* vol. 42 (1912) pp. 37–40, W. O. Cavanagh, 'Castletown Carne and its owners' says that his obituary in *The London Magazine* reports his death aged 107.

1625 NAI MFCI, Reel 32, Parish Registers of Killala, Co. Mayo, says that he was buried on 27 Jan. 1789 but since this appears in the midst of the Jan. 1790 entries, it is probably a transcription error. *Prerog. Wills* gives a will proved in 1794.

1642 The previous session ended on 2 Nov. 1719. The new one began on 12 Sept. 1721. Writ issued on 15 Sept. 1721.

1644 He is listed in the 'Judges and Barristers' section of the *Treble Almanack* until 1821.

1646 *Irish Georgian Society* vol. 18 (1974), p. 10, M. Craig, 'Sir Edward Lovett Pearce' estimates his date of birth as 1699 but P. Aronsson, Esq. points out that he was possibly appointed a captain in his father's regiment in 1707/8. His parents were married in 1690 so he may have been b. 1691.

1654 *DJ* Oct. 9–11 1777 says he died 'at Newpark' (Co. Tipperary); *BNL* 10–14 Oct. 1777 'a few days ago'.

1657 He is listed in the 'Revenue' section of the *Treble Almanack* until 1803.

1658 The previous session ended on 10 Feb. 1724. The new one began on 7 Sept. 1725. Writ issued on that date.

1659 Information from P. F. Meehan, Esq. says that his father died in 1640. The previous session ended on 3 Dec. 1697. The new one began on 27 Sept. 1698. Writ issued on that date.

1662 Sitting under age. He was sworn on 22 Jan. 1795.

1663 The session began on 26 June and ended on 2 Nov. 1719. Writ issued on 1 July 1719.

1664 Returned under age, 25 Aug. 1703. No date of swearing but the session began on 21 Sept. 1703. *Record of Old Westminsters* p. 733 says that he was born on 22 July 1683.

1665 Sitting under age. He was sworn on 3 Nov. 1731.

1668 Year of death from *Prerog. Wills*.

1669 The previous session ended on 10 Feb. 1724. The new one began on 7 Sept. 1725. Writ issued on that date.

1672 Returned under age, 22 Oct. 1692. No date of swearing but the session ended on 3 Nov. 1692. Again returned under age for the following parliament, 6 Aug. 1695. No date of swearing but the session began on 27 Aug. 1695.

1676 Year of death from *Prerog. Wills*.

1677 *JRSAI* vol. 41 (1911) pp. 161, 171, 173, E. M. F.-G. Boyle, 'Record of the Town of Limavady, 1609– 1804' says that he died in 1697. *DNB* says that he was born *c.* 1599, but he entered Christ's College, Cambridge in 1645 aged 15 years!

1678 Year of death from *Prerog. Wills*.

1679 *DNB* says that his first play was published in London in 1698.

1684 The previous session ended on 6 May 1728. The new one began on 23 Sept. 1729. Writ issued on that date.

1691 Year of death from *Prerog. Wills*.

1705 *Prerog. Wills* gives the will of 'Richard of the Kingdom of Ireland' proved in 1800 but no definite identification.

1718 *HP* 1790–1820, Professor Jupp's estimate of his year of birth.

1719 The previous session ended on 30 Oct. 1707. The new one began on 5 May 1709. Writ issued on that date.

1720 The information on this MP is slender. He came in by purchase and sat for about 18 months. Year of death from *Prerog. Wills*.

1724 J. S. Crone (ed.), *A Concise Dictionary of Irish Biography* (Dublin, 1928) p. 271, estimate of year of birth.

1725 Ibid. p. 211 says that he was born *c.* 1698; he entered Clare College, Cambridge in 1719 and the Inner Temple in 1721, so he may have been born a year or so later.

1726 Year of death from *Prerog. Wills*.

1730 Returned under age, 6 Aug. 1783. No date of swearing but the session began on 14 Oct. 1783.

1731 Year of death from *Prerog. Wills*.

1735 *BNL* 23 Mar. 1794 reports that he died 'a few days ago in London'.

1745 He was returned to the 1695 parliament after 29 Dec. 1698, when the writ was issued.

1749 NAI, M5131. Estimated year of death from 'Extracts from the Parish Registers of Tuam' and some genealogical notes.

1755 *DJ* 23–5 Jan. 1776 reports his death.

1757 *DJ* 20–22 Aug. 1778 reports his death.

1759 The previous session ended on 3 Dec. 1697. The new one began on 27 Sept. 1698. Writ issued on that date.

1761 The session began on 7 Sept. 1725 and ended on 8 Mar. 1726. Writ issued on 22 Oct. 1725.

1764 Returned under age, 14 May 1764. No date of swearing but the session began on 22 Oct. 1765.

1771 The session began on 7 Sept. 1725 and ended on 8 Mar. 1726. Writ issued on 17 Feb. 1726.

1776 Returned under age, 23 Sept. 1692. No date of swearing but the session began on 5 Oct. 1692.

1778 Date of death from *Prerog. Wills*.

1781 Ibid.

1782 Estimated year of birth from *Peerage and Baronetage* (1956) p. 325.

1789 Ibid. 8–11 Apr. 1788 says that he died 'last week'; *DJ* 9 Apr. by a letter from London 'a few days ago'.

1790 PRONI /27/1 Year of death from PRONI D/3000/ 27/1 Falkiner Genealogical Notes, which quote a will proved on 6 Nov. 1706.

1792 See *Memorials of the Dead* vol. 11 p. 211 for the estimated year of birth. The information on this MP is sometimes conflicting.

1795 *Irish Sword* vol. 13 (1977–9) pp. 289–98, R. Loeber, 'Biographical Dictionary of Engineers of Ireland, 1600– 1730' says that he was born *c.* 1643 and also that he was aged 30 when he married in 1677.

1800 Returned under age, 27 Apr. 1758, but not sworn until 5 Dec. 1759.

1802 Date of death from *Prerog. Wills*.

1804 *Irish Builder* 1 Dec. 1886, 'St Audoen's Church', says that he died on 6 May 1844 aged 81.

1805 Returned under age, 19 May 1761. No date of swearing but the session began on 22 Oct. 1761.

1808 Returned under age, 2 May 1761. No date of swearing but the session began on 22 Oct. 1761.

1811 Year of death from *Prerog. Wills*.

1822 Ibid.

1827 Sitting under age. He was sworn on 29 Oct. 1759.

1828 *English Army Lists* vol. 3 p. 23 says that he died in 1709.

1835 Sitting under age. He was sworn on 12 Nov. 1733.

1838 *Misc. Gen. et Herald.*, vol. 3, new series (1880), p. 80 says that he was MP for Co. Leitrim in 1661. *Irish Army Lists* pp. 26, 32 says that he was knighted in 1660 and was a cornet in 1659. In Mar. 1686 Clarendon commented that he 'has served ever since the King's restoration'.

1840 The session began on 29 Aug. 1723 and ended on 10 Feb. 1724. Writ issued on 29 Oct. 1723.

1853 Returned under age, 19 Oct. 1715. No date of swearing but the session began on 12 Nov. 1715.

1854 Writ issued on 15 Jan. 1800 on his appointment as Escheator of Ulster with no mention of his decease.

1855 *Peerage of England, Scotland and Ireland* p. 292 says that he died on 25 Apr. 1767.

1862 The session began on 26 June and ended on 2 Nov. 1719. Writ issued on 8 Oct. 1719.

1863 *Kild. Arch. Soc. Jn.* vol. 5 (1906–8) p. 254, 'Autobiography of Pole Cosby, of Stradbally, Queen's Co., 1703–1737(?)' says that he died at Easter 1728.

1865 Date of death from *Prerog. Wills.*

1869 RCBL P344/11/8 Registry of Monuments St Anne's Parish Church, Dublin, records his death on 20 Dec. 1814 aged 62. *Cornwallis Corr.* vol. 3 p. 255 says that he died on 29 Dec. 1824: this is almost certainly erroneous. *Misc. Gen. et Herald,* vol. 1 (1874) p. 310 says that he died on 29 Dec. 1814.

1882 Year of death from *Prerog. Wills.*

1895 The information on this MP is slender. Year of death from *Prerog. Wills.*

1896 Returned under age, 18 Apr. 1761. No date of swearing but the session began on 22 Oct. 1761.

1897 Returned under age, 14 Mar. 1766. No date of swearing but the session began on 22 Oct. 1765.

1904 PRONI D1759/3A/1 says that he died aged 74.

1907 PRONI D3469/28, A–B Roche Estate Papers gives estimated year of birth.

1909 PROI, MFCI Reel 29 Parish Registers of Innishannon, Co. Cork, says that he was baptised on 8 Jan. 1730, but *Alum. Dub.* records that he entered TCD 3 Apr. 1744 aged 16 years.

1911 He is listed in the 'Judges and Barristers' section of the *Gentleman's and Citizen's Almanack* until 1782.

1918 The previous session ended on 18 Jan. 1722. The new one began on 29 Aug. 1723. Writ issued on that date.

1919 He is listed in the 'Judges and Barristers' section of the *Almanacks* until 1793. *DJ* 5–8 Mar. 1791 gives a Robert Sibthorpe Esq. dying at Island Bridge; *DJ* 11–13 May 1780 gives the death of his wife.

1920 Malcomson, *John Foster* p. 120: a letter of 23 Sept. 1766 says that he is 70 years of age; *DJ* 10–13 Apr. 1773 reports his death.

1922 Year of death from *Prerog. Wills.*

1923 The last session of the parliament ended on 8 Mar. 1726. A writ has not been located.

1924 RCBL P277/1/2, the Parish Registers of St Mary's, Dublin, says that he was buried on 28 Nov. 1759.

1927 *Peerage of England, Scotland and Ireland* p. 85 says that he died on 1 Apr. 1747. A week's variation is often the result of ambiguities in newspaper reporting.

1935 Year of death from *Prerog. Wills.*

1937 Blackwood pedigrees says that he was born in 1635, but his brother Sir Hans Sloane was born in 1660.

1946 *DJ* 7–9 Feb. 1788 reports that he died at Lisburn aged 83.

1951 J. Ferrar, *History of Limerick* (Limerick, 1787) p. 92 says that he died on 15 Jan. 1785 at Bordeaux.

1956 The information on this MP is slender. In 1707 he was described as 'ever perverse while he lived to vote'.

1958 *DJ* 5 Sept. 1797 reports his death.

1969 Returned under age, 26 Sept. 1717 but not sworn until 17 Aug. 1719. *BNL* 2 Dec. 1766 says that he died on 22 Nov. 1766.

1975 *Gentleman's Magazine* Aug. 1735 says that he died on 5 Aug.

1976 The previous session ended on 28 Aug. 1710. The new one began on 9 July 1711. Writ issued on that date.

1978 *Gentleman's Magazine* Aug. 1843 says that he died aged 82.

1980 The previous session ended on 10 Feb. 1724. The new one began on 7 Sept. 1725. Writ issued on that date. *Complete Baronetage* vol. IV p. 179 says that he was an MP 1717–25. *Commons jn. Ire.* returned 1715.

1982 The session began on 12 Sept. 1721 and ended on 18 Jan. 1722. Writ issued on 3 Oct. 1721.

1983 *BNL* 28 May 1813 says that he died in his 80th year.

1984 The previous session ended on 10 Mar. 1732. The new one began on 4 Oct. 1733. Writ issued on 26 Oct. 1733.

1991 Year of death from *Prerog. Wills.*

1994 Ibid.

1995 Ibid.

1996 Date of death from *Prerog. Wills.*

2009 *BNL* 30 Apr.–4 May 1790 says that Robert Stewart was objected to on account of being under age, but as the poll lasted 69 days, closing 20 July 1790, he attained his majority during it.

2013 *DJ* 18–20 Aug. 1778 says he died 'suddenly'.

2014 The information on this MP is slender.

2015 Ffolliott, Biographical Notices says that he died on 24 Oct. 1794.

2019 Robert Stopford replaced Josias Haydock for Kilkenny City (*see* **0992**), deceased, in Oct. 1692, but there is no record of his abandoning Innistiogue. However, the only session of the 1692 parliament was so short that the sorting of seats may not have been completed before it ended.

2021 The previous session ended on 6 May 1728. The new one began on 23 Sept. 1729. Writ issued on that date.

2024 *Ir. Gen.* vol. 5 no. 4 (1977) p. 485, H. F. Morris, 'Ramsey's Waterford Chronicle, 1777' says that he died in 1802.

2025 *Complete Peerage* vol. I p. 98 says that he was born in 1698.

2028 Year of death from *Prerog. Wills*.

2029 PRONI T1075/29 date of death based on a will in Canon Leslie's notes.

2030 Year of death from *Prerog. Wills*.

2031 The information on this MP is slender. Estimated year of death from Simms' Cards.

2037 PRONI T/3166/1B Hartnell Notes says that he died in 1857. *DJ* 26–8 Mar. 1776 announces his birth.

2039 *JRSAI* vol. 34 (1904) p. 132, T. W. Westropp, 'Notes on Askeaton' says that his will was dated 1761 and proved 1765.

2041 Returned under age, Apr. 1790. No date of swearing but the session began on 2 July 1790.

2042 Parliament was in recess from 14 Dec. 1695 to 28 Mar. 1696. Writ issued on the last date.

2043 The previous session ended on 18 Jan. 1722. The new one began on 29 Aug. 1723. Writ issued on that date.

2044 Cavan MPs says that he was born on 25 July 1662.

2048 *DJ* 11–13 May 1790 announces his death.

2051 Returned under age, May 1776. No date of swearing but the session began on 18 June 1776.

2053 *Louth Arch. Soc. Jn.* vol. 5 (1922) p. 105, 'Extracts from Isaac Butler's Journal' says that he died on 22 Sept. 1709 aged 42.

2058 The session began on 28 Nov. 1727 and ended on 6 May 1728. Writ issued on 3 May 1728. PRONI T2934/1 Pedigree of the Tenison Family of Thomastown, Co. Louth and Loughbawn, Co. Monaghan says that he died on 6 May 1728. This cannot be correct but he could have died a week earlier, i.e. 'on or about', to use a customary phrase.

2060 Year of death from *Prerog. Wills*.

2064 The return given in *Commons jn. Ire.* at the beginning of the 1797 parliament says that Edward and William Tighe (**2073**) are the MPs for Wicklow Borough. Edward Tighe was among those who voted for Ponsonby's parliamentary reform motion and may not have not sought election in 1797. At the beginning of the 1799 session Daniel Gahan (**0836**) and William Henry Armstrong (**0055**) represented the borough, the latter having replaced William Tighe who elected to sit for Innistiogue. Year of death from *Prerog. Wills*.

2065 PRONI D2685/14/1 p. 96 W. G. S. Tighe, 'The Tighe Story' (unpublished family history, 1959) says that he was born in 1768, but *Alum. Dub.* says that he entered TCD 21 Apr. 1789 aged 18 years.

2067 Kilkenny MPs says that he died on 29 Dec. 1761.

2070 Year of death from *Prerog. Wills*.

2073 *IFR* p. 1102 says that he was born in 1776.

2081 RCBL P277/5/4 Parish Registers of St Mary's, Dublin, says that he died aged 91. *Alum Dub.* says that he entered TCD 2 Dec. 1756, presumably aged *c.* 16.

2083 *DJ* 26–9 June 1773 says that he died in his 81st year. The Parliamentary Lists describe him in 1772 as 'too old to attend' parliament, and in 1773 as 'very old'.

2093 PRONI T2842/2 Ardee Corporation Minutes says that he died before 3 Sept. 1722.

2102 He is listed in the 'Barristers' section of the *Treble Almanack* until 1835.

2105 Ffolliott, Biographical Notices says that he died aged 60.

2108 *Cornwallis Corr.* vol. 3 p. 304 says that he was born on 3 Sept. 1755. *St Peter and St Kevin's Reg.* records his baptism on 23 Oct. 1755. See also **2108a**.

2108a There were three branches of the Trench family, Ashdown (**2108**), Heywood (**2108a**) and Clancarty (**2111**). I originally thought there were two.

2109 Year of death from *Prerog. Wills* which calls him Richard Power Trench.

2115 The session began on 8 Oct. 1745 and ended on 11 Apr. 1746. Writ issued on 1 Nov. 1745.

2119 Year of death from *Abstracts of Wills*.

2129 Estimated year of birth from *IFR* p. 1156. The previous session ended on 8 May 1756. The new one began on 11 Oct. 1757. Writ issued on that date.

2131 Estimated year of birth from *IFR* p. 1157. Previous session ended on 31 Mar. 1740. The new one began on 6 Oct. 1741. Writ issued on 7 Oct. 1741.

2136 RCBL P277/5/3 Parish Registers of St Mary's, Dublin, says that he died aged 66.

2140 *HP* 1754–90 estimates year of birth and *HP* 1790–1820 date of death.

2143 *Alum. Oxon.* vol. 2 p. 1543 says that he died on 7 Feb. 1726 in France.

2148 Returned under age, 8 Nov. 1727. No date of swearing but the session began on 28 Nov. 1727.

2150 Year of death from *Prerog. Wills.*

2155 Ibid.

2156 *King's Inns Admissions* says that he died on 9 Oct. 1755.

2158 Year of death from *Prerog. Wills.*

2164 Ibid.

2171 Ibid.

2173 The session began on 12 Nov. 1715 and ended on 20 June 1716. Writ issued on 16 Jan. 1716.

2176 *DJ* 27–31 Oct. 1771 reports his death aged 85.

2183 The session began on 20 Oct. 1767 and ended on 27 May 1768. Writ issued on 8 Dec. 1767.

2188 The session began on 12 Sept. 1721 and ended on 18 Jan. 1722. Writ issued on 18 Sept. 1721.

2192 Returned under age, May 1776. No date of swearing but the session began on 18 June 1776. He is listed in the 'Judges and Barristers' section of the *Treble Almanack* until 1820.

2194 Estimated year of death from P. F. Meehan, Esq.

2205 *Irish Builder* 1 Apr. 1888, 'St Audoen's Church' says that he died on 12 Nov. 1750.

2214 Estimated year of birth from H. A. Doubleday and Geoffrey H. White (eds), *Complete Peerage* (1913) vol. III p. 235.

2215 Returned under age, June 1780. No date of swearing but the session began on 12 Oct. 1779 and ended on 2 Sept. 1780.

2216 Returned under age, 7 Aug. 1783. No date of swearing but the session began on 14 Oct. 1783; PRONI Crossle Papers /328 says that he was born on 28 May 1763.

2218 *Kild. Arch. Soc. Jn.* vol. 5 (1906–8) p. 436, 'Autobiography of Pole Cosby, of Stradbally, Queen's Co., 1703–1737(?)' says that he was born in December 1741.

2219 He and his father were naturalised by Act of Parliament in 1662.

2222 Date of death from *Prerog. Wills.*

2223 *DJ* 21–4 July 1770 says that he died on 16 July aged 68.

2224 The previous session ended on 10 Feb. 1724. The new one began on 7 Sept. 1725. Writ issued on that date.

2231 *Commons jn. Ire.* up to 1727 calls this MP Samuel Whitshed. In the list of the returns at the opening of the 1727 parliament he is called Samuel-Walter Whitshed, and it is not until the beginning of the following session that he becomes Samuel Warter Whitshed. He probably took the additional surname of Warter sometime after the opening of the 1725 session and the beginning of the new parliament. He is called Colonel Whitshed throughout the text of *Commons jn. Ire.*

2240 *Peerage of England, Scotland and Ireland* p. 264 says that he died on 7 June 1729.

2244 R. T. Wolfe, *The Wolfes of Forenaghts* (Guildford, n.d.) p. 14 says that he was born on 9 Feb. 1754. Malcomson, *John Foster*, Table 3, also says that he was born in 1754. But in fact he was born on 18 May 1753 and entered TCD on 1 Nov. 1769.

2245 Returned under age, Apr. 1790. No date of swearing but the session began on 2 July 1790.

2248 This year of death is from *Camden Miscellany* (London, 1990) vol. 39, appendix, p. 413, even though a new session began on 27 Sept. 1698 when presumably a writ would have been issued for Taghmon. This MP is confused with the Colonel Robert whose will was proved in 1702. They belonged to the same family but to different generations. The latter, according to *Irish Army Lists* p. 27, was an elder brother of **2249**.

2252 Year of death from *Prerog. Wills.*

2257 *Alum. Oxon.* vol. 2 p. 1691 says that he died on 29 Dec. 1707.

2262 *Pue's Occurrences* 5 Mar. 1737 says that he died on 2 Mar. *English Army Lists* vol. IV pp. 14, 60 says that he died in 1732.

2264 *IFR* p. 1227 says that a younger brother was born in 1720.

2270 The information on this MP is slender.

2271 He succeeded as 2nd Earl of Rochford in 1709 but it appears that the Irish House of Commons was unaware of this, as the writ to replace 'Viscount Tunbridge, deceased', was not issued until 9 July 1711.

4

THE MAJOR CONCERNS
OF PARLIAMENT IN ANY SESSION

I NOTE ON THE CLASSIFICATION OF THE STATUTES

'The chief function of parliament,' declared the Victorian constitutional historian Frederic William Maitland, 'is to make statutes.' Bagehot, a commentator of an earlier generation, gave at least equal prominence to its role as the critic of executive government and a brake on its arbitrary power.[1] Parliament's function was to be not only the grand jury of the nation but also the grand inquisitor of executive government, and to remedy the nation's grievances. Many would have considered that parliament did not make, but rather defined, the common law, which had existed from time immemorial. However, in a less esoteric context it is difficult to disagree with Dr Taylor when he declares parliament's omnicompetence: 'the fact is that the very essence of Parliament is its power to make statute law.' In the 110 years that separate the Battle of the Boyne from the Act of Union, the *Statutes at Large of the Kingdom of Ireland* record the 1,962 public statutes passed by the Irish parliament, 982 before 1783, the session in which Poynings' Law was amended, and 980 afterwards.[2] There were also a number of private statutes, which are listed in the *Journals* at the end of each session of parliament after the public statutes.[3] These are mainly connected with family matters such as divorce and the breaking of entails.

The public statutes are published in 20 large volumes, of which 17 relate to this period. They give a unique insight into the business of the kingdom and the concerns of parliament. Their value emerges only as they are analysed and, to avoid confronting the reader with an amorphous mass of apparently impenetrable formality, in this introduction legislation will be considered, with examples, under a number of broadly defined categories that often overlap; for instance, should bills concerned with the post be classified under communications or Revenue? I have classified them as the latter, because that appeared to be the chief concern of the statutes. Similarly, there is obvious overlap between law and order, local government and security.

[1] Quoted and discussed in E. Taylor, *The House of Commons at Work* (9th edn, London, 1979) p. 87.
[2] See Thomas, *House of Commons* p. 61. There was a similar escalation in legislation in the British parliament during this period, and although the reasons may have differed there was probably a similar rise in parliamentary interest and activity.
[3] Unfortunately there is no complete list of the private bills. The best collection is in the library of TCD (186.s.38–40).

The content of a statute was often far-ranging and not always confined to its specified title: 'tacks' were not unusual. For instance, the English Revenue Bill, 10 & 11 Will. III, c. 10, had a 'tack' which provided for the appointment of commissioners of inquiry into the administration of forfeited estates in Ireland. A statute could be quite simple and straightforward but often it had disconnected bits and pieces added to it. Both the text and the tables attempt to answer the question, 'what was the business of parliament between 1692 and 1800?' Sometimes it is difficult not to conclude that regulation and taxation were prominent, if often ineffectual, considerations, as successive efforts were made to prohibit or control undesirable activities and to balance the budget. A statute[4] was often repeated, sometimes because, as with the famous penal statute of 1703, 2 Anne, c. 6, confirmed in 1709, 8 Anne, c. 3, they wanted to see how it operated. The statutes are treated below under the following classification (the small letter(s) indicating the classification in the two tables given as appendices, 'Dates and classification 1692–1782' and 'Number of classified statutes 1783–1800').

1   THE CONSTITUTIONAL POSITION [c]

2   COMMUNICATIONS [cm]
    2.1   Roads
    2.2   Inland navigation – rivers and canals

3   EDUCATION [ed]
    3.1   Tudor and Stuart educational policy
    3.2   Early charity and charter schools
    3.3   Vocational schools
    3.4   Hedge schools
    3.5   Catholic and Nonconformist academies
    3.6   The Erasmus Smith and other benefactions

4   EMPLOYMENT [em]
    4.1   Domestic employment
    4.2   Urban employment

5   ENVIRONMENT [ev]
    5.1   Afforestation
    5.2   Fish and game
    5.3   Farming practices

6   STATUTE EXTENSION – HOTCHPOTCH [h]

[4]Dates are cited as in the *Statutes at Large (Ireland)* – Julian calendar until 1752 and Gregorian thereafter. Under the Julian calendar the year began on 25 March. Dates in the Julian calendar are sometimes, but not in this section, given in the form '12 March 1726/7'.

II THE MAJOR CONCERNS OF PARLIAMENT IN ANY SESSION

TABLE I. DATES AND CLASSIFICATION 1692–1782

	1692	1695	1697	1698	1703	1705	1707	1709	1710	1712	1715	1717	1719	1721	1723	1725
Constitution	0001c	0007c	0031c 0034c	0062c	0067c 0070c						0151c 0153c	0176c				
Communications									0138cm		0161cm					
Education							0114ed									
Employment							0108em				0166em	0181em				
Environment				0054ev 0058ev		0090ev			0134ev	0148ev	0170ev			0215ev		0241ev
Law & Order	0004j	0006j 0010j 0011j 0014j 0015j 0022j 0023j 0024j 0025j 0029j	0036j 0038j 0039j 0042j 0044j	0047j 0055j 0060j	0074j 0075j 0080j	0091j 0092j 0094j	0099j 0100j 0102j 0105j 0106j 0110j	0121j 0122j 0123j 0124j 0125j	0133j 0135j 0139j 0140j		0157j* 0160j 0169j 0171j 0172j	0183j 0186j	0190j 0195j 0201j 0206j		0234j	0242j
Hotchpotch												0182h		0213h	0227h	0240h
Land		0012l 0016l 0026l	0040l 0041l	0053l 0056l			0097l 0098l	0126l	0137l	0143l 0144l	0155l	0178l		0209l 0211l 0212l 0222l		

TABLE I (CONTINUED)

	1727	1729	1731	1733	1735	1737	1739	1741	1743	1745	1747	1749	1751	1753	1755–6	1757
Constitution	0251c									0430c			0485c			
Communications	0247cm	0274cm	0305cm	0333cm	0357cm	0387cm	0402cm		0429cm	0448cm	0463cm	0479cm	0499cm	0508cm	0527cm	0550cm
	0257cm	0289cm	0309cm	0334cm	0358cm	0388cm	0403cm			0449cm					0528cm	
	0270cm	0290cm	0310cm	0335cm	0360cm		0404cm						0500cm			
			0311cm	0336cm	0361cm		0405cm						0501cm			
			0312cm	0337cm	0362cm								0502cm			
			0313cm	0338cm	0364cm								0503cm			
			0314cm	0339cm	0365cm											
			0315cm	0340cm	0366cm											
			0316cm	0341cm	0367cm											
				0342cm	0369cm											
Education										0434ed	0453ed	0467ed	0486ed		0512ed	0539ed
Employment	0268em	0285em	0307em											0490em	0520em	
Environment				0325ev	0350ev	0382ev				0443ev			0487ev			
Law & Order	0258j	0275j	0304j	0331j	0346j	0376j	0394j		0420j	0439j	0456j	0480j	0496j		0514j	0547j
	0269j	0286j			0363j	0378j			0422j		0462j				0525se	
		0291j				0386j										
Hotchpotch	0261h	0276h	0300h	0324h	0349h	0383h	0393h	0411h	0424h	0444h	0457h	0471h	0488h		0516h	0541h
															0518h	
Land		0278l	0298l	0329l	0348l		0398l	0413l	0426l		0461l		0495l		0517l	
			0302l													
			0303l													

TABLE I (CONTINUED)

	1759	1761	1763	1765	1767	1770	1772	1771–2	1773–4	1775–6	1777–8	1779–80	1781–2
Constitution													0965c 0966c
Communications	0560cm	0585cm	0595cm 0600cm 0619cm 0620cm 0621cm 0625cm 0626cm	0639cm 0640cm 0651cm 0652cm 0653cm 0654cm	0664cm 0665cm 0667cm 0680cm		0693cm	0701cm 0717cm 0721cm 0723cm 0728cm 0732cm	0744cm 0758cm 0760cm 0761cm 0762cm 0763cm 0764cm 0765cm 0766cm 0768cm 0771cm	0785cm 0791cm 0792cm 0807cm 0815cm 0816cm	0828cm 0834cm 0840cm 0841cm 0849cm 0855cm 0857cm 0858cm	0889cm 0899cm 0910cm 0911cm 0912cm 0913cm 0914cm 0915cm 0916cm 0917cm	0957cm 0982cm
Education	0558ed	0576ed	0593ed	0632ed	0673ed			0700ed	0741ed 0772ed	0797ed	0824ed	0876ed	0932ed 0945ed 0946ed
Employment								0730em				0886em	0951em
Environment			0612ev 0624ev	0643ev	0677ev		0690ev			0805ev	0837ev 0853ev		0971ev
Law & Order	0569j	0573j 0586j	0594j 0608j 0617j	0634j 0647j 0649j	0659j 0679j		0692j	0702j 0729j 0731j	0736j 0748j 0776j 0777j	0800j 0808j	0827j 0829j 0832j 0846j	0893j 0904j 0905j 0907j	0929j 0950j 0952j 0959j 0960j 0967j 0968j 0969j 0977j 0979j
Hotchpotch		0587h	0605h 0609h		0674h		0685h 0686h	0716h	0773h 0774h	0810h 0811h	0854h	0881h 0882h	0958h
Land		0528l	0618l	0636l 0644l	0682l			0707l 0718l	0757l 0769l	0806l		0897l	

TABLE I (CONTINUED)

	1692	1695	1697	1698	1703	1705	1707	1709	1710	1712	1715	1717	1719	1721	1723	1725
Local Government		0017lg				0087lg				0149lg			0199lg	0217lg	0226lg	0238lg
Manufacturing & Mining						0084m	0104m	0128m	0132m		0162m	0179m	0196m		0225m	
						0085m									0228m	
						0093m										
Parliament							0103p				0168p					
Religion	0002rl	0008rl	0030rl	0052rl	0065rl	0083rl	0101rl	0119rl	0141rl		0159rl	0187rl	0194rl	0218rl	0229rl	0243rl
		0009rl	0032rl	0059rl	0068rl		0116rl	0129rl			0163rl	0188rl	0198rl	0219rl	0230rl	0244rl
		0013rl	0045rl		0069rl						0164rl	0189rl	0200rl		0231rl	
		0018rl			0071rl						0173rl		0202rl			
		0021rl			0072rl								0203rl			
					0073rl											
					0076rl											
Revenue	0003rv	0005rv	0033rv	0049rv	0063rv	0082rv	0096rv	0117rv	0130rv	0142rv	0150rv	0174rv	0193rv	0208rv	0224rv	0235rv
		0019rv	0035rv	0051rv	0064rv			0118rv	0131rv		0152rv	0175rv	0197rv			0236rv
		0020rv	0037rv		0066rv						0156rv					
		0027rv									0167rv					
Security				0050se			0109se				0158se	0180se	0192se	0216se		
				0061se												

TABLE I (CONTINUED)

	1727	1729	1731	1733	1735	1737	1739	1741	1743	1745	1747	1749	1751	1753	1755–6	1757
Local Government		0280lg, 0287lg					0399lg					0476lg, 0477lg			0522lg, 0523lg	
Manufacturing & Mining	0255m			0326m, 0327m, 0330m	0347m	0374m	0400m	0415m	0419m	0435m		0469m, 0472m		0507m		0534m, 0542m, 0549m
Parliament	0252p, 0253p	0279p				0375p				0440p, 0441p	0460p					
Religion	0246rl, 0249rl, 0256rl, 0259rl, 0262rl, 0263rl, 0264rl, 0266rl, 0267rl	0277rl, 0282rl, 0283rl	0299rl	0321rl, 0322rl, 0323rl	0355rl, 0356rl, 0359rl, 0368rl	0380rl, 0385rl	0395rl, 0396rl	0409rl, 0410rl	0425rl	0437rl, 0445rl, 0447rl	0455rl, 0458rl	0470rl, 0475rl, 0483rl	0489rl		0510rl, 0515rl, 0526rl, 0532rl	0536rl, 0537rl, 0543rl
Revenue	0245rv, 0248rv, 0250rv	0272rv, 0273rv	0295rv, 0296rv, 0297rv	0318rv, 0319rv, 0320rv	0344rv, 0345rv	0371rv, 0372rv, 0373rv	0390rv, 0391rv, 0392rv	0406rv, 0407rv, 0408rv	0417rv, 0418rv, 0423rv	0431rv, 0432rv, 0433rv	0451rv, 0452rv, 0454rv	0464rv, 0465rv, 0466rv, 0468rv	0483rv, 0484rv, 0491rv, 0492rv	0506rv	0509rv, 0511rv	0533rv, 0538rv
Security		0281se				0377se				0436se, 0438se	0459se		0494se		0513se	

TABLE I (CONTINUED)

	1759	1761	1763	1765	1767	1770	1772	1771–2	1773–4	1775–6	1777–8	1779–80	1781–2
Local Government	0559lg 0565lg 0568lg		0596lg 0597lg	0641lg 0648lg	0658lg			0712lg	0750lg 0751lg		0856lg 0861lg 0862lg 0865lg	0885lg 0908lg	
Manufacturing & Mining	0557m	0579m	0601m 0603m 0623m	0629m 0635m 0638m	0669m		0688m		0753m	0783m 0786m	0825m 0839m 0851m	0887m 0891m 0896m 0900m	0926m 0927m 0941m 0953m
Parliament			0602p		0657p		0694p 0696p	0709p	0747p	0790p 0795p 0809p	0844p		0928p 0939p 0981p
Religion	0555rl 0563rl	0574rl 0583rl	0592rl 0614rl 0615rl	0637rl	0663rl 0670rl 0671rl 0675rl		0687rl	0713rl 0714rl 0719rl 0724rl 0726rl	0742rl 0745rl 0755rl 0759rl 0767rl	0784rl 0793rl 0796rl [0818rl]	0823rl 0843rl 0867rl	0873rl 0895rl 0906rl	0925rl 0942rl 0943rl 0944rl 0949rl 0970rl 0975rl 0980rl
Revenue	0553rv 0554rv 0562rv	0571rv 0572rv 0575rv 0577rv	0590rv 0591rv 0610rv 0611rv	0627rv 0628rv 0631rv 0642rv	0655rv 0656rv 0681rv 0660se 0668se	0683rv 0684rv	0697rv	0698rv 0699rv 0703rv 0704rv	0733rv 0734rv 0735rv 0737rv 0738rv 0739rv 0740rv	0780rv 0781rv 0782rv 0787rv 0788rv 0789rv 0794rv 0802se	0819rv 0820rv 0821rv 0822rv 0826rv 0859rv 0831se	0868rv 0869rv 0870rv 0872rv 0874rv 0875rv 0877rv 0878rv 0879rv 0902rv 0883se	0919rv 0920rv 0921rv 0922rv 0923rv 0924rv 0933rv 0938rv 0948rv 0961se 0962se 0976se

0818 16 GIII c.1 is an indemnity Act and the sole statute for 1776

TABLE I (CONTINUED)

	1692	1695	1697	1698	1703	1705	1707	1709	1710	1712	1715	1717	1719	1721	1723	1725
Social				0057so	0081so	0086so	0111so 0112so	0120so		0146so 0147so						0237so
Trade, Finance & Commerce		0028t	0043t	0048t	0077t 0078t 0079t	0088t 0089t 0095t	0107t 0113t	0127t	0136t	0145t	0165t	0177t 0185t	0191t	0210t 0214t 0220t 0221t	0232t 0233t	0239t
Urban Amenities			0046u				0115u				0154u	0184u	0204u 0205u 0207u	0223u		
TOTAL STATUTES	4	25	17	16	19	14	21	13	12	8	24	16	18	16	11	10

TABLE I (CONTINUED)

	1727	1729	1731	1733	1735	1737	1739	1741	1743	1745	1747	1749	1751	1753	1755-6	1757
Social	0271so	0288so 0294so	0306so 0308so		0353so 0354so		0397so			0442so 0450so		0473so 0474so 0481so	0493so 0498so 0505so			
Trade, Finance & Commerce	0254t 0260t 0265t		0301t 0317t	0328t 0332t 0343t	0352t 0370t	0379t 0381t 0384t	0401t	0412t 0414t	0421t 0427t 0428t	0446t		0478t	0497t 0504t		0519t 0524t 0529t 0530t 0531t	0540t 0544t 0545t 0546t 0547t
Urban Amenities		0284u 0292u 0293u				0389u		0416u							0521u	0535u 0551u 0552u
TOTAL STATUTES	27	23	23	26	27	19	16	11	13	21	13	19	23	3	24	20

TABLE I (CONTINUED)

	1759	1761	1763	1765	1767	1770	1772	1771–2	1773–4	1775–6	1777–8	1779–80	1781–2
Social	0561so	0578so 0584so	0607so	0646so	0662so			0708so 0720so 0727so	0749so 0756so 0775so 0778so	0804so 0814so 0817so	0830so 0833so	0898so	0931so 0956so 0963so
Trade, Finance & Commerce	0556t 0566t		0599t 0613t 0616t 0622t	0630t 0633t 0645t	0672t 0676t		0691t 0695t	0705t 0722t	0743t 0746t 0770t 0779t	0798t 0812t	0838t 0848t 0860t 0863t 0866t	0871t 0884t 0890t 0892t 0903t 0918t	0934t 0937t 0940t 0954t 0955t 0964t 0972t 0973t 0974t
Urban Amenities	0564u 0567u 0570u	0580u 0581u 0588u 0589u	0598u 0604u 0606u	0650u	0661u 0666u 0678u		0689u	0706u 0710u 0711u 0715u 0725u	0752u 0754u	0799u 0801u 0803u 0813u	0835u 0842u 0845u 0847u 0850u 0852u 0864u	0880u 0888u 0894u 0901u 0909u	0930u 0935u 0936u 0947u 0978u
TOTAL STATUTES	18	19	37	28	28	2	13	35	45	39	49	51	64

TABLE II. NUMBER OF CLASSIFIED STATUTES 1783–1800

	1783–4	1785	1786	1787	1788	1789	1790	1791	1792	1793	1794	1795	1796	1797	1798	1799	1800	Total
Constitutional	2											1	2		1		4	10
Communications		4	5	5	6	6	9	4	8	6		8	4	3	7	3	8	86
Education	1	4	3	1	1		1	1				1					1	14
Employment														1	1			2
Environment	3		2	2				1	1					1		1		11
Hotchpotch	1	1			1	1	1	1	1		1		1				1	10
Law & Order	10	5	5	8	8	1	2	7	2	7	3	3	9	6	20	5	7	108
Land	1	3			1	1		1	2	1		1	1	1			4	17
Local Government	3	2	3	1			2	4	1	2	1	3	4	1	2	3	1	33
Manufacturing & Mining	5	6	6	5	4	2	3	6	4	3	3	1	5	5	4	3	5	70
Parliament	3	1	2		1	1	1	1		1		2		1	3		1	18
Religion	2	6	2	2	3	3	4	2	7	4	1	3	1	3	2	2	9	56
Revenue	12	15	14	16	14	21	14	9	9	10	8	10	11	22	25	27	28	265
Security	1	1	2	1	1	2	1	1	1	10	4	5	8	6	9	11	10	74
Social	4	9	3	5	5	2	5	6	2	3	1	3	4	3	4	2	7	60
Trade, Finance & Commerce	9	9	9	13	5	2	5	4	3	5	1	6	6	8	4	8	8	105
Urban Amenities	2	1	5	1	2	1	3	2	1	4	3	1	4	3	1	2	6	42
Total Statutes	59	65	61	60	50	42	48	51	41	56	26	48	60	63	83	67	100	981

5
LIST OF CONSTITUENCIES

There were 150 double-member constituencies: 32 counties, eight county boroughs (marked with an asterisk in the alphabetical list of constitutencies below), the university, and 109 boroughs.

An MP's constituency service has been divided into parliaments, e.g.:

0029 ALEXANDER, James [1st B., V., E. Caledon]; b. 1730 d. 22 Mar. 1802; MP for Londonderry city 1775–6–83–90.

The future Earl of Caledon, James Alexander, therefore sat in three parliaments: 1768–1776, 1776–1783 and 1783–1790.

An MP's service is dated, where possible, from the date of his return to parliament, not the date of his swearing in parliament and, although there was inevitably a delay in issuing a writ to replace an MP – and in lists published in *Commons jn. Ire.* he may still be said to be sitting – we have taken the termination of his service from the date of death or of appointment to debarring legal office, for instance to the Bench or of advancement to the peerage.

ALPHABETICAL LIST OF CONSTITUENCIES

1   Antrim B.
2   Antrim Co.
3   Ardee – Co. Louth
4   Ardfert – Co. Kerry
5   Armagh B.
6   Armagh Co.
7   Askeaton – Co. Limerick
8   Athboy – Co. Meath
9   Athenry – Co. Galway
10 Athlone – Co. Westmeath
11 Athy – Co. Kildare
12 Augher – Co. Tyrone
13 Ballynakill – Queen's County
14 Ballyshannon – Co. Donegal
15 Baltimore – Co. Cork
16 Baltinglass – Co. Wicklow
17 Banagher – King's County
18 Bandon-Bridge (also known as Bandon) – Co. Cork
19 Bangor – Co. Down
20 Bannow – Co. Wexford
21 Belfast – Co. Antrim
22 Belturbet – Co. Cavan
23 Blessington – Co. Wicklow
24 Boyle – Co. Roscommon
25 Callan – Co. Kilkenny
26 Carlingford – Co. Louth
27 Carlow B.
28 Carlow Co.
29 Carrick – Co. Leitrim
30 Carrickfergus* – Co. Antrim
31 Carysfort – Co. Wicklow
32 Cashel – Co. Tipperary
33 Castlebar – Co. Mayo
34 Castlemartyr – Co. Cork
35 Cavan B.
36 Cavan Co.

37	Charlemont – Co. Armagh		87	King's County
38	Charleville – Co. Cork		88	Kinsale – Co. Cork
39	Clare Co.		89	Knocktopher – Co. Kilkenny
40	Clogher – Co. Tyrone		90	Lanesborough – Co. Longford
41	Clonakilty – Co. Cork		91	Leitrim Co.
42	Clonmel – Co. Tipperary		92	Lifford – Co. Donegal
43	Clonmines – Co. Wexford		93	Limerick city*
44	Coleraine – Co. Londonderry		94	Limerick Co.
45	Cork city*		95	Lisburn – Co. Antrim
46	Cork Co.		96	Lismore – Co. Waterford
47	Dingle – Co. Kerry		97	Londonderry city
48	Donegal B.		98	Londonderry Co.
49	Donegal Co.		99	Longford B.
50	Doneraile – Co. Cork		100	Longford Co.
51	Down Co.		101	Louth Co.
52	Downpatrick – Co. Down		102	Mallow – Co. Cork
53	Drogheda* – Co. Louth		103	Maryborough – Queen's County
54	Dublin City*		104	Mayo Co.
55	Dublin Co.		105	Meath Co.
56	Duleek – Co. Meath		106	Midleton – Co. Cork
57	Dundalk – Co. Louth		107	Monaghan B.
58	Dungannon – Co. Tyrone		108	Monaghan Co.
59	Dungarvan – Co. Waterford		109	Mullingar – Co. Westmeath
60	Dunleer – Co. Louth		110	Naas – Co. Kildare
61	Ennis – Co. Clare		111	Navan – Co. Meath
62	Enniscorthy – Co. Wexford		112	Newcastle – Co. Dublin
63	Enniskillen – Co. Fermanagh		113	New Ross – Co. Wexford
64	Fermanagh Co.		114	Newry – Co. Down
65	Fethard – Co. Tipperary		115	Newtown (also known as Newtownards) – Co. Down
66	Fethard – Co. Wexford			
67	Fore – Co. Westmeath		116	Newtown Limavady – Co. Londonderry
68	Galway B.*		117	Old Leighlin – Co. Carlow
69	Galway Co.		118	Philipstown – King's County
70	Gorey – Co. Wexford		119	Portarlington – Queen's County
71	Gowran – Co. Kilkenny		120	Queen's County
72	Granard – Co. Longford		121	Randalstown – Co. Antrim
73	Harristown – Co. Kildare		122	Rathcormack – Co. Cork
74	Hillsborough – Co. Down		123	Ratoath – Co. Meath
75	Innistiogue – Co. Kilkenny		124	Roscommon B.
76	Jamestown – Co. Leitrim		125	Roscommon Co.
77	Kells – Co. Meath		126	St Canice – Co. Kilkenny
78	Kerry Co.		127	St Johnstown – Co. Donegal
79	Kilbeggan – Co. Westmeath		128	St Johnstown – Co. Longford
80	Kildare B.		129	Sligo B.
81	Kildare Co.		130	Sligo Co.
82	Kilkenny city*		131	Strabane – Co. Tyrone
83	Kilkenny Co.		132	Swords – Co. Dublin
84	Killybegs – Co. Donegal		133	Taghmon – Co. Wexford
85	Killyleagh – Co. Down		134	Tallow – Co. Waterford
86	Kilmallock – Co. Limerick		135	Thomastown – Co. Kilkenny

136 Tipperary Co.
137 Tralee – Co. Kerry
138 Trim – Co. Meath
139 Trinity College Dublin (TCD) –
Co. Dublin
140 Tuam – Co. Galway
141 Tulsk – Co. Roscommon
142 Tyrone Co.

143 Waterford city*
144 Waterford Co.
145 Westmeath Co.
146 Wexford B.
147 Wexford Co.
148 Wicklow B.
149 Wicklow Co.
150 Youghal – Co. Cork

6

ELECTIONS
AND THE ELECTORATE[1]

'Ireland before the accession of James I,' stated Lord Chancellor Clare in 1800, 'never had anything like a regular government or Parliamentary constitution.'[2] In its final form the Irish parliament, although medieval in origin, was essentially a seventeenth-century creation. It was not until the reign of James I that the 32 counties assumed their final shape, while the majority of the Irish boroughs were Stuart creations. The House of Commons was drawn from 150 double-member constituencies, and the 64 seats for the 32 counties amounted to 21 per cent of the total seats.

As each constituency returned two members, each elector had two votes. He could, however, use only one vote if he wished, and thus he 'plumped' for the candidate he voted for. Some landlords – for instance Lord Fitzwilliam, who inherited the great Wentworth interest in Co. Wicklow – required their dependants' first vote but allowed them to exercise their second vote as they pleased, but this was far from universal.

As in the parliament of Great Britain, the majority of the Irish MPs represented the parliamentary boroughs. Only 55 of the Irish boroughs were enfranchised prior to 1603; to these James I added 46, Charles I one and Charles II 15, thus making a total of 117 borough constituencies. Attendance in parliament was not particularly popular before the eighteenth century, and many of these boroughs were enfranchised on the rather cynical advice of Sir Arthur Chichester, Lord Deputy 1604–16, who in 1612 remarked that:

> In making of the borough-towns, I find more and more difficulties and uncertainties. Some return that they are but tenants at will and pleasure to certain gentlemen who have the fee farm or by lease for a few years, so as they are doubtful to name themselves for burgesses without the landlord's consent, and the landlord is of the Church of Rome and will return none but recusants, of which kind of men we have no need and shall have less use. Some other towns have few others to return than recusants, and others none but soldiers, so as my advice in that point is that you bring direction and

---

[1] In this section I have made considerable use of work that I did for *Great Britain and Ireland: a Study in Political Administration* (first published 1963, reprinted by the Greenwood Press, Westport, CT, 1978; *Gt B. & Ire.*).
[2] The Lord Chancellor's (John Fitzgibbon, Earl of Clare (**0749**)) Speech, 10 Feb. 1800, p. 11.

authority to make such towns boroughs only as we think fit and behoveful for the service, and to omit such as are named if they be like to be against us, and to enable others by charter if we can find them answerable to our expectation, albeit they be not in the list sent thither.[3]

By the Act of Union in 1800, Irish representation was reduced by two-thirds, mainly by disfranchising a large number of these boroughs which had failed to live up to expectations and develop into viable towns, becoming 'close' as a result. The Irish parliament represented the landed proprietors of the country, who controlled the majority of the borough constituencies virtually absolutely. It was this that gave the epithet 'a borough parliament'[4] its peculiarly derogatory application. In fact they were property to such a degree that it was necessary to compensate their patrons to the amount of £1,260,000 to obtain consent to the Act of Union. In September 1799 Castlereagh, who had hoped that compensation would not be necessary, was obliged to admit that:

> There are two modes of making compensation; the one by Representation, the other by money. The latter seems almost exclusively applicable to Boroughs where the interest is so distinctly understood to be property by the parties, that all interested will acquiesce in the equitable application of money.[5]

The Commissioners appointed under the Act *(1900)* – Richard Annesley (**0048**), Sackville Hamilton (**0945**), Patrick Duigenan (**0664**), Clotworthy Rowley (**1818**) and Robert French – took their task very seriously and appear to have achieved this equitable distribution. The Act of Union changed the weighting of Irish representation from the boroughs to the counties, thereby making the 1793 Catholic Enfranchisement Act ultimately effective. It is very difficult to calculate the effect of Catholic enfranchisement on the electorate either in the one general election before the Union or immediately thereafter.

I THE COUNTY CONSTITUENCIES

To represent the county was the endorsement of one's family's standing and prestige in it. Thus the county constituencies were the object of great rivalry and considerable ambition among the Irish gentry. After 1793 the Place Act, 33 Geo. III, c.41 *(1500)*, allowed MPs to apply for one of the escheatorships in order to seek re-election for

---

[3] *HMC Hastings*, IV, p. 6 (see 'Abbreviations: Principal Record Repositories, Official Publications, Parliamentary and Division Lists' for further details). This letter was written to Sir John Davis, who was then Attorney General for Ireland. *Municipal Corporations (Ireland)*, app. III, pp. 1115–77. The report on Londonderry city discusses the 'plantation boroughs' at some length; see pp. 1115–20. Much of Chichester's concern was with the establishment of the plantation.

[4] Bartlett & Hayton, *Penal Era and Golden Age*, pp. 137 *et seq.*, A. P. W. Malcomson, 'The parliamentary traffic of this country'.

[5] PRONI D607/484, 488, *Castlereagh Corr.* vol. 3 p. 63, 23 Sept. 1799.

another constituency. Clothworthy Taylor (**2039**), MP for Trim, applied for the escheatorship of Munster in 1795, to be immediately elected for Co. Meath; James Butler-Wandesford (**0320**), MP for Kilkenny city, applied for the escheatorship of Ulster in May 1796 and was immediately re-elected for Kilkenny city. This placed both MPs in a favourable position for re-election for their counties in the general election of 1797. In May 1800 Charles Stewart (**2001**) similarly exchanged Thomastown for Co. Londonderry. Stewart's move was prompted by the imminent disfranchisement of Thomastown. All county MPs continued to sit after the Union in the united parliament.

Frequently, MPs preferred to stand for the county, where the election was usually disputed and expensive, than to be cheaply and automatically returned for their 'close' borough. For instance, Sir Lucius O'Brien (**1558**), member for Co. Clare from 1768 to 1783, told Lord Charlemont 'that in the year 1768, an opposed election … cost me £2,000', although Sir Lucius could have returned himself unopposed for the Borough of Ennis, in which he controlled at least one seat at this time. In 1783 O'Brien, like Stewart in Co. Down, lost his election for the county. Nevertheless, glancing through the returns for the counties gives an overall picture of the leading interests in them. Returns were consistent if expensive.

Another feature of county elections was double returns. In the general election of 1768, nine MPs who were returned for county constituencies were also returned for 11 boroughs; and 11 other MPs found that they were representing two boroughs each, thus making a total of 17 members returned for 36 seats. On the same occasion Nathaniel Clements (**0414**), the Deputy Vice-Treasurer, felt sufficiently nervous about his election for Co. Leitrim to have himself also nominated for two 'close' boroughs, Cavan and Roscommon; at least one of these returns was probably with a view to keeping the seat 'open' until the final returns were known. Apart from genuinely doubtful results in the county elections, some of the double returns, especially those from such boroughs as Cavan and Roscommon, or Gorey and Duleek, can only have been made with a view to keeping these 'safe' seats open. 'The Number of double Returns,' wrote Portland to Northington in September 1783, 'makes me hope that seats may be found for my Friends.'[6] In 1797 Cromwell Price (**1734**), a neighbour and long-time supporter, wrote to the Marquess of Downshire:

> I am griev'd to think that I have no chance of coming into Parliament under your protection, particularly as I Cannot think of giving any Sum whatever for a Seat, I had flatter'd myself that as so many of your Seats were fill'd with double returns & all the old establish'd Members in … that I might have some hope of success.[7]

---

[6] BL Add. MS 38,716, f. 109, 18 Sept. 1783, Secret & Confidential.
[7] PRONI D607/1330, 2 Dec. 1797. Cromwell Price was previously MP for Kinsale and for Monaghan (purchased) 1790–7; a Co. Down landlord, he had been a supporter of the Downshire interest since 1783. He died a few months later, in March 1798.

His chances must have revived, as he was returned for the Downshire borough of Fore in place of Robert Ross (**1816**), who had successfully been returned for the more open, but more prestigious borough of Newry. Ross lived in the Newry area.

Sir Lewis Namier has commented on a similar practice in Great Britain: 'to stand simultaneously for two places,' he remarks, 'was a method of hedging used at general elections by those who, whilst contesting doubtful seats, were able to reinsure by having themselves at the same time returned for pocket boroughs.' In Ireland this precaution was doubly necessary as until 1793 there was no Irish equivalent to the Chiltern Hundreds. Nothing but death, elevation to the Bench or the peerage, an MP taking Holy Orders, or expulsion from the House could release a seat, although at the beginning of the century, in 1705, James Caulfeild (**0368**), later 3rd Viscount Charlemont, was allowed to vacate the borough of Charlemont in order to travel abroad. But this obviously caused some debate, as the House passed a standing order, 21 March 1704/5, that writs might not be issued at the request of members excusing them from service. After 1715 the uncertain, but predictably long, life of parliament, which from 1715 to the Octennial Act of 1767 *(0657)* depended on the lifespan of the sovereign, encouraged a careful distribution of seats at a general election. From 1768 to 1793 there was a general election only every eight years, which was a long time for a would-be MP to wait.

The 1705 standing order appears to have been rigidly applied, as on 10 December 1743 the Provost and burgesses of Sligo town petitioned the House of Commons to issue a writ to replace Francis Ormsby (**1599**), MP for Sligo borough, who 'hath for want of health not been able to attend his duty in parliament since the year 1731, and that there is not the least probability of his ever recovering his health'. The Speaker (**0210**) then read out a letter from Ormsby supporting the borough officials' request. The House reacted by passing a motion, by 86 to 62 votes, that Ormsby be ordered to attend in his place. On the day appointed, 23 January 1744, the Speaker read out a further letter from Ormsby, excusing himself due to incapacity, and again requesting that the corporation of Sligo be allowed to replace him. The House divided 79 for and 106 against issuing a new writ, but agreed to excuse Ormsby, who did not die until 1751, for not attending.[8]

However, until a member had actually taken his seat he appears to have escaped the worst rigours of the House's discipline. For example, at the time of the disputed election for Armagh in 1753, Thomas Adderley (**0009**) wrote to Lord Charlemont that 'Mr [Hon. George] Hamilton (**0921**) arrived here the 7th from London, on purpose to serve his nephew, Mr [Arthur] Brownlow. This gentleman has been a member since 1727, but did not take his seat before this session.'[9]

Failure to find a seat at a general election could result in a long period in the political wilderness. The only parliament called by George II lasted 33 years, 1727–60; the

---

[8] *Commons jn. Ire.* (Bradley edn), vol. VII pp. 474, 496; ibid. (Grierson edn), vol. IV pp. 423, 433.
[9] *HMC Charlemont I*, p. 189. Hamilton was a son of the 6th Earl of Abercorn and an English MP.

only parliament of George I lasted for the 12 years of his reign. Quite possibly this, as well as the even division of interests in many of the counties, encouraged the comparatively numerous election petitions despite their increasing inconvenience, unpopularity and expense. During this period there were 313 petitions: county elections accounted for 97 and there were a further 43 from the eight county boroughs with the addition of Londonderry, probably the most significant of the non-county boroughs, and the notoriously corrupt potwalloping borough of Swords. The remaining 170 came from the other boroughs.[10] Considering that there were only 12 general elections, this represents not only an inclination to disputatious litigiousness but a real anxiety to be in parliament. The county franchise was based on the Act of 1542, 33 Henry VIII. Like the English Act of 1430, 8 Henry VI, the 1542 Act gave the franchise to the freeholders whose land was worth over 40 shillings per annum. From the early eighteenth century[11] until 1793, the franchise was withheld from Roman Catholics and those married to Roman Catholics, and many election petitions centred on this point.

The number of contests at county elections was unconnected with the size of the electorates, which before 1793, with the exception of Co. Down, were all below 4,000. During the debates over the Catholic Enfranchisement bill in 1793 *(1480)*, Sir Laurence Parsons (**1636**), concerned over the calibre rather than the religion of the voter, declared that:

> If they had all been Protestants for fifty generations back, I would not consent to the overwhelming of the constitution by such a torrent. In some counties where there are but 2,200 electors now, you will, if this bill passes, have 10,000; in others 20,000 in others 30,000; and I am well informed in the county of Cork alone you will have 50,000; that is half of what I have stated the whole elective body to be of all the counties in England.[12]

The total county electorate in Ireland was probably between 40,000 and 45,000. There was only one post-Catholic enfranchisement election, that of 1797, and the act had little immediate impact.

Contested elections depended not on the size of the electorate but on the division of interests within the county: for instance, despite its large electorate, the 1768 and 1776 elections for Co. Down were uncontested. Many northern voters were Presbyterian and less submissive than those in the other provinces. In 1783, however, the famous struggle between the Hill and Stewart families began, and subsequently

---

[10] Malcomson, *op. cit.*; the figures were provided by Mrs Geraldine Wylie who assisted Dr Malcomson with his research. These figures are notoriously difficult to stabilise, as petitions were withdrawn or lapsed, for instance during the long prorogation, 1769–71, following the augmentation crisis.

[11] See Porritt & Porritt, *The Unreformed House of Commons*, vol. 2 pp. 218–21; *IHS* vol. 12, 1960–1, J. G. Simms, 'Irish Catholics and the parliamentary franchise, 1792–1828'. The exact date at which Roman Catholics were disfranchised is uncertain.

[12] Parsons' speech, which is long and interesting, is quoted in Lecky, vol. III pp. 153–64.

the election for Down was fiercely contested by their representatives. The Stewart determination to be recognised was matched by the Hills' determination to control the county. Robert Stewart had been defeated in 1783 and, from the report of the committee which considered his appeal, it appears to have been a fairly murky affair arranged by the Hills and the Wards. The committee members always had to consider that their own elections might be challenged in the future, and the Stewarts were far from popular. The showdown came in 1790, when Robert Stewart, now Lord Londonderry, challenged the Marquess of Downshire's monopoly of the county representation. As a Presbyterian, Lord Londonderry commanded the Presbyterian vote, which was substantial in Co. Down. The ensuing election campaign was probably the most expensive contest in the history of the Irish parliament: reputedly it cost Lord Londonderry £60,000, a suspiciously high figure, and the Marquess of Downshire over £30,000 – a total of over £90,000 on one county election.[13] The election lasted over two months and resulted in the heirs of both families being returned.

The effect of this quarrel on the franchise was unaltered by the Union, which left untouched the electorates of constituencies not expressly disfranchised by the act, and in 1816 T. H. B. Oldfield found that Co. Down 'contains 30,000 freeholders, who elect the friends of the Marquess of Downshire without a contest. To ensure this object the Marquess' estate has been divided, sub-divided and again divided until it has become a warren of freeholders, and the scheme has completely succeeded.'[14] This subdivision was effected by the creation of fictitious freeholders. The county electorate was, as in England, the 40-shilling freeholder, who until 1793 had to be a Protestant. A fictitious freeholder was one who possessed the title deeds to a freehold, which he swore had an annual value of 40 shillings, a qualification fixed in the middle ages, but was in fact the dependent tenant of the landlord. The Dowager Marchioness, during the minority of her son the 3rd Marquess, had 'indulged her passion for politics' and her desire to settle old scores with the Stewarts, whom she considered to be at least in part responsible for her husband's suicide. The 3rd Marquess was born in 1788 and his father died in 1801, so there was a long minority before he came of age in 1809. In 1812, to his mother's displeasure, the 3rd Marquess made a pact with the Stewarts on the sensible grounds that 'The genius of electioneering is a ruinous genius, come when it will.'[15]

Prior to 1793 the electors in Co. Down numbered c. 6,000; in Counties Tyrone, Antrim and Cork 3,000–4,000; in Armagh, Donegal, Fermanagh, Londonderry and Wexford 2,000–3,000; in Kilkenny, Clare, Leitrim, Limerick, Mayo, Cavan, Dublin, Meath, Queen's County, Westmeath, Tipperary, Kerry, Roscommon and Kildare and Monaghan 1,000–2,000, and in Carlow, Louth, Wicklow, King's County, Longford,

---

[13] PRONI D607/484, 488, *Castlereagh Corr.* vol. 1 p. 7; *Shannon's Letters*, p. 8.
[14] T. H. B. Oldfield, *The Representative History of Great Britain and Ireland* (1816), vol .VI pp. 224–8; Wakefield, vol. I, calculated that the estate was worth £15,000 p.a. but divided into very minute portions.
[15] Maguire, *The Downshire Estates*, p. 22.

Waterford, Galway and Sligo under 1,000.[16] Contested elections were largely due to the distribution of land inside the counties, where the territorial divisions frequently created a number of approximately equal interests, and consequently few landlords had sufficient electoral influence to carry the county unaided. For most of the century, the Duke of Leinster 'governs the county of Kildare and has three boroughs in it'. Until 1783 the Boyle interest, managed by the Shannon branch of the family, carried Co. Cork and even thereafter one seat for the county.

Cork was the largest and probably the most prosperous county in Ireland. Here Lord Shannon's (**0213**) territorial power and his personal astuteness were enhanced by the traditional prestige attached to the Boyle family, the descendants of the seventeenth-century 'great' Earl of Cork.[17] The largest share of the Cork inheritance had passed through his mother, Lady Charlotte Boyle, to the 5th Duke of Devonshire, and Lord Shannon (**0213**) administered the Devonshire interest: had the absentee Duke of Devonshire been more politically active, the Boyle interest might have presented a greater challenge at the end of the century. Cork was a complex county, and in the 1783 election the Shannon interest suffered a reverse. On this occasion the election lasted 36 days, and 'The great contest was between Lord Kingsborough (**1167**) and Mr Towns[h]end (**2100**); or in fact between the independent and the Shannon parties, the latter was rendered as contemptible on this occasion as it was ever before conspicuous … During the contest there were 22 duels fought.'[18] The Bishop of Cloyne told the Earl of Buckinghamshire that 'The dignity of the Shannon family is shorn of its beams by the loss of a general influence over so great a county.'[19] On one occasion Lord Townshend pointed out to Hely-Hutchinson (**1001**) that 'Amongst other qualifications for public station the gladiatorial is one of the most essential in your country.'[20] By this time duelling was in decline in Great Britain,[21] although it continued with certain notorious examples into the nineteenth-century.

Occasionally the exercise of 'real' interest was totally unconnected with the landlord's residence – either on the estate from which it was derived or even the county in which it was exercised. For instance, the Abercorn interest in Co. Tyrone was exercised in this way for most of the century. The absentee Earl of Bessborough (**1707**) delegated his interest in Kilkenny (always overshadowed by the sleeping Butler interest) to his brother, John Ponsonby (**1702**); the respective interests of the Earls of Hertford and

---

[16] See 'The Structure of the Electorate in the Parliament of Ireland in the late Eighteenth Century' for details.
[17] This family astuteness is illustrated by the skill with which his father, Speaker Boyle (**0210**), quietly achieved everything that he could legitimately expect, while always managing to ensure that his contemporaries underestimated him: see Johnston, *Ireland in the Eighteenth Century*, p. 117; for the 2nd Earl of Shannon, see Froude, vol. II, p. 160 – he showed considerable astuteness in negotiating the terms of his support with the Townshend administration in 1772.
[18] *BNL*, 7–10 Oct. 1783.
[19] *HMC Lothian*, pp. 419–20.
[20] *HMC Donoughmore*, p. 282; Porritt & Porritt, vol. 2 pp. 409–15. See Kelly, *'That Damn'd thing Called Honour'*, e.g. pp. 141–2.
[21] Thomas, *The House of Commons*, pp. 6–7.

Donegall were likewise exercised arbitrarily by their nominees, while the Duke of Devonshire delegated his great interest in Counties Cork and Waterford to Lord Shannon and his closer relatives the Ponsonbys. The Marquess of Rockingham, who was also Earl Malton in the peerage of Ireland, had extensive estates in Co. Wicklow; on the eve of the 1761 election he wrote to Lord Charlemont, illustrating the position and influence of the absentee proprietors on the returns for the county, that he: 'wished him [Lord Bessborough] to give me some insight into the personal character and inclinations of those who might offer for the county; as in truth, not having been able to take a trip to my estate in Ireland, I had not the advantage of being personally acquainted with any gentleman in the county'. This correspondence reflects the 'real' interest of the great absentee landlords at elections – an interest that was not only represented but vocal in the Irish parliament, while its possessor was frequently to be found in one or other House of the concurrent British parliament. By requiring MPs to be re-elected every eight years, the Octennial Act *(0657)* tightened and strengthened this type of permanent authority, which undoubtedly contributed to the British administration's acquiescence in that ostensibly popular measure. Their powerful interest, led by Rockingham, was behind the lobby against the 1773 absentee tax.[22]

In some counties residence joined with family connections and estates to create a dominant influence. It was said of the Rt Hon. Owen Wynne (**2264**), member for Co. Sligo, that 'He has the best real interest in this county in which is a great independent yeomanry. Heaslewood, his seat, is nigh Sligo and he lives much among them', while the other member, the Rt Hon. Joshua Cooper (**0474**), 'has a large estate' and 'is connected in the county interest with Owen Wynne'.[23] Representatives of these families sat undisturbed in successive parliaments until 1783, when a three-way division of interest emerged with the O'Haras, an old Irish family. Charles O'Hara was returned in 1783 and in 1790 Owen Wynne (**2265**) was defeated in the county, although members of his family had represented it for nearly 50 years. Thereafter, Wynne represented Sligo town, where he had a controlling interest and, as Sligo was not disfranchised in 1800, after the Union Wynne either arranged its disposal or sat for it himself. Owen Wynne lacked the abilities of his father and he does not appear to have been as dominant a personality as some of his ancestors. Personality counted, especially in the counties. Throughout the 1790s the O'Haras shared the representation with the Coopers.

A strongly defined family unity has always been a feature of Irish society, and the structure of politics in the eighteenth century undoubtedly strengthened this loyalty. In Co. Roscommon, for instance, Thomas Mahon (**1334**) 'came in by his own interest which is very great all his relations marrying through one another';[24] when he died during the course of the 1776–83 parliament, his son (**1330**) was returned in his

---

[22] *IHS*, vol. 8 (1953), J. E. Tyler, 'A letter from the Marquis of Rockingham to Sir William Mayne on the proposed absentee tax of 1773'; see also *Gt B. & Ire.*, pp. 269, 280.

[23] Parliamentary Lists; *Proc. RIA*, 48C4 (1942), M. Bodkin, 'Notes on the Irish Parliament in 1773', p. 212; W. Hunt (ed.), *The Irish Parliament in 1775* (Dublin, 1907), p. 14.

[24] Parliamentary Lists; Bodkin, op. cit., p. 211.

place. In 1768 Co. Leitrim was represented by the Clements family and their relations the Gores. Nathaniel Clements (**0414**) was returned for the county with William Gore (**0877**), who 'has a large estate in this county, but no place of residence in it and a number of poor freeholders, Mr Clements joining with him brought him in'.[25]

In Co. Meath, Hercules Langford Rowley (**1821**) had built up a considerable influence through marriages. He himself had only one small estate in that county, although he had extensive ones in Antrim and Dublin as well as property valued at £700 per annum in England. However, he married one of his daughters to Lord Longford (**1619**) and the other to the Earl of Bective (**2046**), both of whom had considerable influence in Meath, and in consequence 'He will always be returned.'[26] He sat for the county from 1761 until his death in 1794. Another county in which marriage consolidated an interest was Londonderry, where Edward Cary (**0362**) added to the great real interest arising from his own estates by his marriage to the Earl of Tyrone's (**0118**) sister, thus uniting his own with the strong Beresford interest in that county. The Beresfords held large estates, on advantageous leases, from the Irish Society. The other great Londonderry interest was that of the Conollys and, though he visited his northern estates, Thomas Conolly (**0459**) lived mainly in his smaller estate at Castletown, near Celbridge, Co. Kildare.

In Counties Antrim, Armagh and Fermanagh a political alliance between two great landed families could secure them one member each. In Co. Antrim, if the Earls of Antrim and Hertford joined their interests, 'the county is a mere borough',[27] and the election for the county in 1768 was uncontested – those nominated on this occasion were Lords Dunluce and Beauchamp, the respective heirs of the McDonnell and Conway families. Nevertheless, this was the only time that family circumstances and political influence were able to unite in a county election. In the Co. Armagh election of 1768, three candidates – William Brownlow (**0265**), Sir Archibald Acheson (**0001**) and Arthur Cope – advertised their intention of standing for the county, but shortly before the poll was opened Cope withdrew: 'Finding the major part of the Freeholders unable to oppose the authority of landlords, has forced him this day to submit the necessity of the times and decline polling.'[28] Acheson and Brownlow were returned unopposed. In Co. Fermanagh a similar interest was enjoyed by the Brookes and the Archdalls.

In some counties a group of minor 'interests' would band together to oppose the major ones, as happened in the 1768 election for King's County: on this occasion John Lloyd (**1242**) was returned for the county and 'came in by independent interest. Sir William Parsons (**1639**) joined Armstrong in hopes to throw him out, but the people fearing to be rid by this united interest elected Lloyd.' The 'real' interest in the

---

[25] Bodkin, op. cit., p. 201. This was the Rt Hon. Nathaniel Clements; his wife was Hannah Gore.
[26] Ibid., p. 207.
[27] Ibid., p. 175. For Co. Antrim see 'The Structure of the Electorate in the Parliament of Ireland'.
[28] *BNL*, 26 July 1768.

county was held by Parsons, the other member, who 'has a very good interest and a good Estate in this Co.'. However, Lloyd, 'a very independent and worthy character', also 'had a good Estate' and he continued to represent the county until 1790. Invariably, members returned for the counties had an initial support from their personal landed possessions, although their success might ultimately depend on a combination of external circumstances, personality, influences and interests.

Occasionally a quarrel among the major interests in a county provided one of the lesser influences with a temporary triumph. In the 1768 election for Co. Longford, the Hon. Robert Pakenham (**1620**), brother to Lord Longford, was unexpectedly returned as 'He carried his election by Deane Harnican playing Sir Thomas Newcomen (**1534**) foul, for his brother Lord Longford has but an indifferent interest in this county.'[29] Another unexpected return was made for Co. Carlow, where the chief interests 'were those of the Butlers and the Burtons', but the notorious duellist Beauchamp Bagenal (**0071**) consolidated his own interest, and contrived his return, by fighting a representative of the Butler family and frightening the Burtons into joining their interest to his instead of the Butlers'.

The 1768 election in County Tipperary is of particular interest; here Francis Mathew (**1360**) 'came in by the papist interest', and from this statement three factors in the system of Irish county representation are immediately obvious: a considerable number of estates in Tipperary must have been owned by Roman Catholics (which was in itself unusual); there must have been a considerable number of protestant freeholders on these estates; and the control of the unfranchised landlords over their freeholders was politically absolute. Something similar probably happened in Co. Westmeath, where the same election brought an unexpected result when the 'real' interest of the Earl of Belvidere was successfully challenged by Anthony Malone (**1336**), one of the foremost lawyers and most highly respected men in Ireland and a known Catholic sympathiser. His success was due to 377 freeholders voting exclusively for him, and at the final poll the numbers stood thus: Lord Belfield (**1800**), heir to the Earl of Belvidere, 475; Col. Richard Rochfort-Mervyn (**1805**), son of Lord Belvidere, 387; Rt Hon. Anthony Malone, 469. This return demonstrated that it remained possible for a great 'real' interest to be temporarily challenged, and challenged successfully, by a combination of some 'real' interest with a great personal prestige.

The political prestige and the power of patronage attached to a great office were often personified in the holder, and inseparably attached to his 'real' and personal influence. The loss of office, therefore, meant not only the loss of the actual patronage accompanying it, but also of an intangible though none the less genuine authority, which was the attribute of political success. Thus John Ponsonby's (**1702**) interest in Co. Kilkenny 'was very great while he was a commissioner of the Revenue, but now he has lost that by setting himself among an association of divers persons combined to the offence of Government, who to make themselves great have made him nothing'.

[29] Parliamentary List 1773 (1); *Proc. RIA* (1942) vol. 48 C no. 4 p. 85.

Although Ponsonby was not actually removed from office until April 1770, his position was in jeopardy from the rejection of the Augmentation Bill in 1768. In the ensuing general election Ponsonby made elaborate arrangements to secure his own return and the continuance of his parliamentary influence. He was returned for no fewer than three constituencies: Co. Kilkenny, Gowran and Newtown(ards). Even after his dismissal the Ponsonby family had sufficient 'real' interest for him to remain the leader of a formidable group in the House of Commons and to secure the return of many of his friends in 1768 and to subsequent parliaments.

After the fall of the 'undertakers' in 1770, it was Lord Townshend's intention to ensure that all government patronage flowed directly from the Castle to its recipient without passing through the hands of an intermediary, thereby encouraging people to look to the Castle as the source of patronage rather than to the local political magnate. Subsequent viceroys, however, gradually relaxed this ideal, for in 1777 Lord Hillsborough wrote to the viceroy that:

> Your Excellency knows by your Norfolk and Norwich affairs how useful and indeed necessary to one's importance in one's county the favour and countenance of Government are; I should therefore hope that in what relates to the county of Downe you will permit me from time to time to lay my wishes before you, and to receive them with as much indulgence as circumstances and engagements may allow.[30]

In 1791 the Marquess of Abercorn, who had extensive electoral influence in Donegal and Tyrone, instructed Thomas Knox (**1188**), his political 'other self' in Ireland, that 'We must insist upon every article of patronage of the two counties.'[31]

Nevertheless, there was in some counties an *ex officio* type of interest; possibly the best example was discernible in the composition of the Co. Dublin electorate. Before the 1783 election, Luke Gardiner (**0842**), who represented the county in successive parliaments, remarked to Lord Buckinghamshire that 'The General Election approaches and the Archbishop of Dublin has a very strong interest in this county.'[32] Apart from the clerical interest, there was also a very strong Revenue influence in the county. 'The Commissioners of the Revenue,' reported the *Belfast News Letter* in 1784, 'have a very great share of influence in this county on account of the many revenue officers they oblige to obtain freeholds.' The opposition movement for parliamentary reform in the 1780s included the disfranchisement of Revenue officers in its programme, but, although this obtained in Great Britain, it remained – however much discussed – unfulfilled in Ireland. For instance, in 1782 Richard Martin (**1347**), MP for Jamestown, said that:

> He would not assert that his Majesty's present commissioners of revenue had ever made use of any direct influence over the minds of revenue officers; but this, he

---

[30] *HMC Lothian*, p. 134; see also *Gt B. & Ire.*, p. 136 n. 1.
[31] PRONI J2541/181/2.
[32] See *HMC Lothian*, p. 417.

observed, was owing to their nature and not to their want of power ... he would venture to assert, that his Hon. Friend behind him [Mr Beresford (**0115**)] had more weight with the lower class of them, holding revenue employments in the county of Galway, where he himself resided, that [than] he or the two members who had the honour to represent the country, joined with him had; and that this would be found to be the case throughout the thirty-two counties of Ireland ... the idea at present was so prevalent among the voters, that any man who voted against a government candidate, might be either dismissed from his employment or that his future preferment might be retarded ... this influenced in a great measure the suffrage of electors.[33]

Martin was a supporter of Flood (**0762**), and afterwards MP for Lanesborough from 1798 to 1800 and for Co. Galway in 1800. The question was revived in a more pointed manner after the Regency Crisis, as in April 1789 the opposition introduced a bill to disfranchise Revenue officials 'for the avowed Purpose of preventing the Crown or its Ministers from exercising Influence in the Election of Members of Parliament'; in reply government took the line that 'It was not thought advisable to adopt a law that should lessen the Number of protestant Electors for Representatives in Parliament.'[34] On this occasion: 'It was explained to be particularly levelled against the Earl of Tyrone (**0113**) and his brother Mr Beresford (**0115**) whose zeal for His Majesty's Service on the late Regency Questions had made them very obnoxious to the Opposition, and whose influence in the County of Waterford was supposed to be assisted by the Revenue Officers.' This attack aroused considerable interest, as the viceroy noted that 'The House of Commons has not for years been so full.' Influence by patronage, place and pension was the keystone of administration in Ireland, and under these circumstances the aim of disfranchising Revenue officials was a Utopian ideal rather than a practical possibility.

Counties such as Cork, Kildare, Fermanagh, Armagh and Antrim were frequently uncontested owing to the division of interests within them, but the even distribution of influence in most counties ensured that each general election would produce a contest. Before 1768 general elections were rare, and information about them is correspondingly limited. As we have seen, there was no equivalent to the Chiltern Hundreds in Ireland. A member who no longer wished to attend simply absented himself, although he might be called upon to explain his absence to the House, which might or might not accept his excuse. From 1793 (*1500*), however, the office of escheator of any of the four provinces – Ulster, Munster, Leinster and Connaught – allowed its holder to vacate his seat. For the first five years these offices, worth 30 shillings a year, were granted to all applicants. Nevertheless, they were at the disposal of the Castle, and in the final two years of the Irish parliament the administration tried to tighten its control and exercised this right with discrimination, partly to

[33] *Parl. Reg.*, vol. 1, 1781–2, p. 443.
[34] See *HMC Fortescue* I, pp. 457–8.

reorganise the House in order to pass the Act of Union *(1900)* and partly to prohibit exorbitant sales of vacated seats to members of the opposition. In this they had mixed success, and in the end gave up the unequal struggle.

Apart from encouraging a proclivity for duelling, Irish elections had their own peculiar flavour, as reflected in the endless legislation to improve their conduct. 'I have always considered county elections,' wrote Richard Levinge (**1232**) to the Earl of Charlemont in 1774, 'as one of the most troublesome and expensive hobby horses that any man ever kept for the amusement of his youth or old age.' Some justification for this statement is reflected in Lord Townshend's dispatch of 10 May 1768, in which he remarked to Lord Shelbourne that:

> From the day in which the Royal assent was given to the Octennial Bill, the gentlemen have been almost totally employed in soliciting votes and interest. Many of the counties and boroughs are strongly contested, and considerable sums of money have been already lavished, to the great encouragement of idleness and riot among the common people and to the great injury of the private fortunes of the candidates.[35]

Before the next election in 1776 Lord Harcourt wrote to Charles Jenkinson:

> There are many disputed Elections, in some Places the Contest will be no less warm than expensive, which makes Gentlemen extremely impatient to get their Elections over. The Time of a General Election is a Time of Riot and disorder in England, in this Kingdom it is still more so, which is very sufficient to justify my Anxiety and wishes on the Occasion.

The report of the 1768 committee 'to take into consideration what may be further necessary to regulate the elections of members to serve in Parliament' was not solely, or even mainly, concerned with defects in the franchise. Its resolutions also give an interesting picture of the abuses that were a feature of Irish county elections. 'It is the opinion of this Committee,' the report stated, 'that the great expense and dissipation caused by the continuance of the poll at elections for many days, and sometimes for weeks, tends to corrupt the morals of the people, and to lessen the freedom of elections.' The closing and the adjournment of the poll was the decision of the Sheriff, who was the returning officer for the counties.

The implications of closing the poll are best shown by an illustration. In the general election of 1768 the poll for Co. Tyrone was held at Omagh, the county town, where on 29 July the voting stood at: Armar Lowry-Corry (**1269**), 818; Thomas Knox (**1187**), 801; James Stewart (**2004**), 792; Claude Hamilton (**0917**), 756. Before the poll reopened on 2 August, the following incident occurred:

> This morning on the opening of the poll to elect knights for the county of Tyrone, counsel on behalf of Mr Knox, one of the candidates, moved that the sheriff should

---

[35] Cal. H. O. Papers 1766–9, no. 871.

declare the poll on the former proceedings, and that he should return the writ, alleging that the writ was returnable on the first day of August; but the greater part of the principal gentlemen of the county who attended to give their votes, having demanded a continuance of the poll, the sheriff being of opinion he ought to receive their suffrages, Mr Knox and Mr. Hamilton immediately withdrew from the court; whereupon the usual proclamations were made for the attendance of such persons as were inclined to give their voices to those gentlemen, and none appearing, the poll continued until this evening when it stood thus: for Mr Corry 1168, for Mr Stewart 1127, for Mr Knox 905, for Mr Hamilton 827. Mr. Corry and Mr Stewart proposed to continue the poll for the ensuing day when it is expected there will be such a considerable majority as will demonstrate, as well by the quality of the voters as their numbers, how the prinicipal interest of the county inclined upon this occasion.[36]

On 2 August the poll was duly closed, and the final numbers were: Armar Lowry Corry, 1,257; James Stewart, 1,215; Thomas Knox, 905; Claude Hamilton, 827 – 'upon which,' the reporter concludes, 'Mr Corry and Mr Stewart were declared by the Sheriff duly elected'. Tyrone was a large county, and on this occasion the influence of the Earl of Abercorn was not fully exerted; the election, therefore, was fought out by relatively equal interests.

The integrity of the Sheriff in his position as returning officer was not invariably above question, and the House of Commons resolved that 'An oath should be prescribed for the returning officer and his deputy or deputies to take the poll impartially, without favour to any candidate.' The resolutions of the 1768 committee were embodied in a bill that was transmitted to England but not returned. However, in 1775 most of these resolutions were again embodied in the heads of a bill, which after passing through all the necessary stages became law *(0795)*. In 1774 a number of motions on electoral matters were laid before the Irish House of Commons, including one which, reiterating the first resolution of the committee of 1768, stated 'that it appears to this House that the Poll at several Elections for members to serve in Parliament has been protracted to a Fortnight and sometimes to three Weeks and longer'. This complaint was endorsed by Flood **(0762)**, who, in 1784, remarked upon the enormous abuses in the last election (1783): 'In some counties in this kingdom, the poll continued for weeks.'[37]

The Commons, in 1774, also considered 'that idleness dissipation and riot have been the consequence of such long continuance of the poll at such elections', and two other motions stressed the significance of riots at elections: one stated 'that the poll at several county elections for members to serve in Parliament broke up in riots at the last general election', and the other 'that such riots afford a pretence to sheriffs to make improper returns of members to serve in Parliament'. The picture of 'idleness, dissipation and riot' is completed in 1775 by a clause in 15 & 16 Geo. III, c. 16 *(0795)*, entitled 'An Act for better regulating the election of members to serve in

---

[36] *BNL*, 9 Aug. 1768.
[37] *Parl. Reg.*, vol. 3 p. 80.

Parliament', which was aimed at the punishment of those who were guilty of 'having wilfully defaced, obliterated, torn or altered, or destroyed the whole or any part of the poll book of a Returning Officer, or of having forcibly or fraudulently secreted the same'. To the major crimes of riot, destruction and theft were added the minor sins of impersonation and perjury. The case of Anthony Broderick, 'pilloried for wilful and corrupt perjury' following the 1768 election, was not unique.[38]

Under these circumstances it is not surprising that in comparison with the number of elections contested, the number of petitions complaining of 'undue elections' was considerable. When parliament met in 1769 there were 15 petitions complaining of the 1768 election returns,[39] including seven petitions against the returns for the counties, namely Galway, Roscommon, Longford, Cavan, Limerick, Louth, and the triple return for Waterford against which no petition was actually lodged. The Roscommon election had ended in a riot, and the House decided by 94 to 49 votes that the said riot 'was stirred up and raised by the friends of Edward Crofton (**0524**) or his agent'.[40] In Co. Galway the poll had also been closed by a riot; the return was successfully petitioned against by William Power Keating Trench (**2111**), who alleged that one of the candidates, Lord Dunkellin, had by expending £1,900 acquired a 'large and leading interest'[41] in the last election and 'that many who would otherwise have given their second voices to Mr Trench, were by undue influence, by corruption, by menaces, and when these failed, even by stripes compelled to vote for Lord Dunkellin'.[42] According to the evidence of a Mr Dennis Kelly, the 'large and leading interest' so acquired amounted to 23 votes.

At the close of the poll in Co. Cavan on 2 August 1768 the numbers had stood thus: Mr Maxwell (**1372**), 727; Mr Montgomery (**1438**), 648; Mervyn Pratt, 570; Col. Newburgh, 402. The poll finally closed on 11 August with the results: Maxwell 927, Montgomery 739, Pratt 668, Newburgh 451. When the new parliament met in 1769, Mervyn Pratt petitioned against the return of George Montgomery on grounds of bribery, corruption and undue influence. This petition, however, was not finally determined owing to the premature prorogation of parliament in December 1769. Subsequently Montgomery remained undisturbed, and he continued to represent the county until his death in 1787. Sir James Nugent complained of an undue election in Co. Longford, and the House of Commons ordered the High Sheriff and the Clerk of the Peace for the county to 'attend the House with the Poll Book and the Book of Registry of the Freeholders, and to explain where the Poll Book had been since the election'.[43]

---

[38] *BNL*, 16 August 1768.

[39] In 1776, 18 elections were controverted: eight counties and ten boroughs.

[40] *Commons jn. Ire.*, vol. 14 p. 726.

[41] Ibid., pp. 728–9. Lord Dunkellin alleged that this money was paid to Charles Daly to defray 'the expenses attending the poll during the election'.

[42] Ibid., p. 706.

[43] *Commons jn. Ire.*, vol. 14 p. 707.

In disputed elections numerous witnesses had to be produced by both parties for cross-examination by the Committee of Privileges and Elections, before which such petitions were heard. This committee then prepared a report on the election which was heard by the House when the final settlement of the election was under consideration. In 1777 'several inhabitants of the county of Clare' petitioned the House to make some provision for the expenses of witnesses called to attend the Committee of Privileges and Elections for this purpose, and on 22 November 1777 the House passed by a division of 51 to 38 a resolution making provision for the expenses of such witnesses. Witnesses were allowed 4d per mile while they were going to or coming from Dublin, and 4s per day while they were in the capital. These expenses were to be paid by the person 'who has summoned or shall summon such witness'. Thus the minimum approximate cost of bringing a witness from Londonderry was £7 4s, from Cork £7 10s 8d, from Galway £6 12s and from Tralee £8 8s. These calculations allow for ten days to be spent in Dublin, and the distances are calculated as 151, 161, 133 and 187 English miles respectively. An example of the expense involved in an election petition is provided by the controverted election for Antrim town in 1776, when Samuel Heron, the Skeffington agent, expended £756 9s 5d, of which £166 1s 6d was paid in witnesses' expenses.

The numerous election petitions were frequently, particularly before the 1771 O'Brien–Lucas Act *(0696)*, simply an extension of the election, for the House of Commons represented the same influences and interests as were found in the counties, with the important addition that in the House of Commons political and family ramifications could be exploited to the full. Lord Charlemont, who had suffered from his brother's **(0366)** narrow rejection in 1753, bitterly commented that:

> While disputed elections were decided by the House, their influence was sure in spite of justice to secure the seat for their friend. The wrongs they [the 'undertakers'] committed in this line were innumerable, and to the last degree atrocious. The representation of Ireland was, in effect, in their hands; every candidate must be their suitor, no matter who had the majority of votes. If their dependant was routed in the country, he 'petitioned, and his success was infallible'.[44]

In 1769 the Earl of Tyrone **(0113)** wished to be elevated to the rank of marquess. Lord Townshend wrote to Lord Weymouth to state his case, enclosing Lord Tyrone's letter, which said that:

> In consequence of the position he took up re the augmentation the whole artillery of those persons who might think they had a right to assist their friends, or to punish him for the part he had acted had been levelled as he foresaw against his two friends who had been elected for the borough of Swords.

---

[44] *HMC Charlemont* I, p. 88 n. 1; also pp. 214–15.

II THE COUNTY BOROUGHS

The eight county boroughs were, as their name suggests, small areas surrounding and including a town or city, whose area and privileges were defined in their charter. All these boroughs were medieval in origin and they all displayed a mixture of the characteristics of county and borough constituencies. Being essentially small counties, their similarity to the county constituencies is immediately obvious. At elections the Sheriff was the Returning Officer, while the 40-shilling freeholders formed a substantial section of the electorate. As in the counties, fictitious freeholders were created to uphold the landed interest, and, inevitably, the landlord exercised considerable influence. The borough side of the electorate varied, as it depended on the corporations and their by-laws.

With the exception of Dublin, where it was generally acquired through the guilds, freedom could usually be obtained in five different ways, although the method or methods used differed from borough to borough and often the apparent legal methods by which the freedom of a specific borough might be obtained differed from the actual method sanctioned by the corporation and upheld by restrictive by-laws, or simply by custom. The five methods were: (a) birth, (b) marriage, (c) an apprenticeship of seven years to a freeman, (d) nomination by the mayor of one or two freemen during his year of office, and (e) grace or nomination of the corporation (the most common method). The first two could apply to all or some of the children of a freeman or citizen.

Although the structure of the county boroughs made it inevitable that they should be open to the electoral abuses seen in both the county and freeman constituencies, they also had independent characteristics, which were strengthened where there was a conflict between the interests in the county and the corporation. They were, therefore, the most independent of the Irish borough constituencies, and as such a short individual description will be given of each. After the 1768 election the returns from four of them – Carrickfergus, Drogheda, Galway and Waterford – were controverted, and the petition against the return for Waterford was successful.

The electorates were comparatively large, ranging, in 1784, from 500 to 4,000; four of the eight county boroughs had an electorate of over 1,000. The denominational exclusiveness of the county franchise was intensified in the boroughs. Before 1793 no Roman Catholic could possess either the municipal or the parliamentary franchise. The Presbyterians, who composed the overwhelming majority of the Dissenters, were technically eligible for the franchise, but by the Test clause in the 1704 Act 'to prevent the further growth of popery' (0068) they were excluded from the membership of municipal corporations. All municipal corporations were by law exclusively Anglican, and this continued through the self-elected nature of these corporations long after its legal basis had been removed; as late as 1833 the denominational exclusiveness of the vast majority of these corporations was a source of continual comment by the

Commissioners for the Inquiry into Municipal Corporations. In addition to the freeholders, the electorate in the county boroughs also included the members of the corporation and the freemen of the city. In 1747 the passing of the act, 21 Geo. 11, c. 10, commonly called the Newtown Act *(0460)*, made the residence of burgesses and freemen unnecessary; thus the way was left open for the creation of large numbers of honorary freemen, who confined their interest in municipal affairs to ensuring that a suitable candidate was chosen to represent the borough in parliament. Many of the large electorates were merely an indication of a struggle between conflicting interests to gain control of the constituency; as a result the majority of the freemen were usually honorary and absentee, while the majority of the freeholders were fictitious. Frequently a dominant interest was acquired by creating sufficient freemen in the corporation to overwhelm the freeholders in the county.

In 1835 the commissioners made the following comments:

> In many corporations (we may instance those of Galway, Limerick, Cork and Drogheda), the creation of non-resident freemen has prevailed to an extent apparently only limited by the necessity of providing a sufficient number in the interest of the corporation to bear down the resident freehold constituency. As members of the corporation for general municipal purposes the non-resident freemen do not appear to have interfered.[45]

The MPs for the county boroughs were always either national figures or connected with their constituency. They were expected to benefit the town. For instance, the most prominent MP for Cork city during this period was John Hely-Hutchinson (**1001**), Secretary of State and Provost of Dublin University. In 1768 the electors of Cork city, with a view to government patronage and commercial advantages, chose as one of their representatives William Brabazon Ponsonby (**1709**), John Ponsonby's eldest son. By so doing, 'The citizens of Cork imagined to secure themselves great benefits by his interests.' In August 1782 Chief Secretary Fitzpatrick (**0758**) wrote to him that 'I flatter myself your constituents at Cork will see that their interests have been attended to, and that your influence with the administration here has been so far successfully exerted in their favour as to procure a recommendation of the proposed means to the other side of the water, which was everything they [the administration] had it in their power to do.' Drogheda tended to choose local citizens, often from the Meade, Ogle or Leigh families. One of its most illustrious MPs was John Forbes (**0778**), the son of an alderman, who introduced the 1793 Place Bill *(1500)*; at the end of the century the Drogheda MPs were considered to be influenced by Speaker Foster (**0805**).

Dublin city had an electorate of 3,000 to 4,000, which made it one of the largest in the country, and its return was controlled by the guilds. In 1768 the return for Dublin was interesting, as the representatives were the Marquess of Kildare (**0745**) and the

---

[45] *Municipal Corporations (Ireland), General Report.*

political reformer, Dr Charles Lucas (**1276**), who had been called the Irish Wilkes. Later, in 1790, they were to combine another member of the FitzGerald family (**0733**) with Grattan (**0895**). Kilkenny appears to have specialised in the use of by-laws and the creation of absentee freemen, the usual means by which the political control of a corporation was acquired and maintained. It was interesting because of its connection with the Butler family, whose interest slept for most of the century. After the attainder of the 2nd Duke, the representatives of the family were Catholic until towards the end of the century, when they converted and reasserted their influence and part of their titles.

In Galway town before the 1783 election, 295 freemen were created to consolidate the Daly interest in the corporation, which perhaps was concerned about the latest spate of electoral legislation. Including this sudden influx, the electorate in that year numbered approximately 569. Subsequently the Daly interest was unsuccessfully challenged by the Blake family. Limerick city was under the influence of the Smith and Pery families. Speaker Pery (**1671**) made considerable improvements in and around Limerick; Newtown Pery records his interest. One of the more interesting returns at the 1783 election was that of the Belfast merchant Waddell Cunningham (♦♦♦♦) for Carrickfergus. This caused consternation among the establishment. Cunningham had American connections and was considered a violent Patriot, but it took two years to unseat him and during this time as the sitting MP he was entitled to vote and to all the privileges of the House. The more open electorate of Carrickfergus made it a safety valve for the 'close' borough of nearby Belfast, although the Donegall family had a considerable influence here also.

Waterford's MPs gave a practical support to the community which returned the Carews, father and son (**0347, 0348**), successively from 1768 until the Union. Shapland Carew (**0348**) was 'bred a lawyer but does not practise. He has a good estate here and recommends himself to the people by asserting the right of freedom for many persons here … He also ingratiated himself into their favour by giving £100 towards building a market-house for their wool'; the other MP, Cornelius Bolton (**0181**), strengthened his interest as he: 'constantly resides among the people and spends his money in Waterford which will always secure him a seat'. Nevertheless, Bolton lost the 1783 election, largely because his opponents, Henry Alcock (**0019**) and Shapland Carew had introduced a number of freemen from Wexford. But the merchants, although outvoted, subscribed to purchase a seat for him (Lanesborough).

Tact, tradition, prestige, patronage, residence, property and personality all played a part in creating and sustaining interest in this type of constituency. Of all the Irish borough constituencies, the county boroughs were the most difficult to acquire control in, and constant, unremitting care was required to maintain an influence in them.

III THE BOROUGHS

The overwhelming majority of the members of the Irish House of Commons sat for the 109 parliamentary boroughs (i.e. 150 minus 32 counties, eight county boroughs and Dublin University[46]). Most of these corporations had been enfranchised by the Stuarts, especially by James I as part of the plan for his new plantations. Many of them were stillborn, while others, once great, had declined. The Stuart boroughs usually followed a pattern of a Chief Magistrate, 12 burgesses (variously named) and a vaguely defined commonalty which often had never existed, or vanished before the eighteenth century began or in the course of it. The situation was more fluid in the first half of the eighteenth century; by the end of the century it had solidified into the situation described in 'The Structure of the Electorate in the Parliament of Ireland' and shown in the following tables. Each borough has been tabulated to indicate its general type, patron and such electoral details as could be ascertained. This is an area which requires caution as new research adds more depth and detail to general classification.

By the end of the eighteenth century many municipal corporations were divorced from the towns they were created to serve and represent, for three main reasons:

1. the denominational restrictions operating against both Roman Catholics and Dissenters, which automatically excluded the majority of the population in nearly all Irish towns from any participation in municipal affairs;
2. the 'Newtown Act' of 1747 *(0460)*, which, by making residence unnecessary for burgesses and freemen, led to most of the corporations being composed of absentees;
3. the fact that the majority of corporation vacancies were filled by co-opting members elected by the remaining burgesses, ensuring continuity of interest.

All these circumstances simplified the emergence of a 'patron' or 'proprietor' with virtually absolute political control, and led to a situation in which 'The influence thus acquired became regarded as the property of its possessor and was transmitted as part of the family inheritance to his descendants.' Indeed, wills were often presented to the Union Commissioners along with municipal charters.

There remained, however, a small number of boroughs in which the right to vote was dependent on residence or property within the borough. Many of these boroughs either had been enfranchised without a corporation or through time their corporation had become extinct. With the exception of a few large cities and towns, municipal life, apart from markets, was virtually non-existent in Ireland even during the latter part of the eighteenth century; the majority of corporations existed solely to return members to parliament at the dictates of their 'patron'. In 'The Structure of the Electorate in the Parliament of Ireland' each borough as it stood in 1784 has been tabulated to indicate its general type, patron and such electoral details as could be

[46] Dublin University was enfranchised as an academic corporation, and was in a category of its own.

ascertained. Therefore, the remainder of this section is devoted to commenting, by specific examples, on the different groups into which these boroughs have been divided. For the purposes of this survey the remaining boroughs have been divided into two main types, namely those having a franchise based on property or residence, and those in which the right to vote is inherent in the corporation and unrelated to residence and property. But it is important to remember that no two boroughs were identical, and deductions from a particular example are of general rather than precise application. Sometimes definition is complicated by the fact that a borough was enfranchised as one type but developed as another. Some potwalloping boroughs, including Baltimore, Tallow, Dungarvan, Lismore, and probably Knocktopher (whose origins are unclear) and Downpatrick, were enfranchised as corporation boroughs with freemen, but in the course of time they evolved a potwalloping franchise.

There were 12 potwalloping[47] and six manor boroughs, where the franchise was held by the protestant five-pound householder and freeholder respectively. The two types of borough had many features in common, especially the predominant position of the lord of the manor or the proprietor of the soil. In 16 of the 18 boroughs in this group, the seneschal of the manor, or nearby manor, acted as the returning officer at parliamentary elections. Thus it was relatively simple for the proprietor to exercise and perpetuate his control; the tenant in town or manor was as closely bound to his landlord as the fictitious freeholder in the counties. Although these boroughs were opened to the Catholic five-pound householder by the Acts of 1793 *(1480)* and 1795 *(1570)*, before 1800 this enfranchisement created no visible change in their nature: only four potwalloping boroughs (Newry, Downpatrick, Lisburn and Dungarvan) and one manor borough (Mallow) survived the Act of Union.

In the potwalloping boroughs the franchise was vested in the five-pound, and until 1793 protestant, householder, who before 1782 had been resident in the borough for at least six months; after 1782 a year's residence was necessary. In addition, the householder had to swear that his house was worth £5 per annum in his own estimation, an oath that seldom caused much difficulty. In three of these boroughs (Rathcormack, Dungarvan and Lismore) the freeholders of the manor, which surrounded the borough, also possessed the franchise. With the exception of Swords and Knocktopher, the seneschal of the nearby manor was the returning officer at parliamentary elections. In Swords and Knocktopher the portreeve acted as the returning officer: in Knocktopher he was the only municipal officer 'and his only duty was to return members to Parliament'.[48] It seems probable that no corporation ever existed in Antrim, Lisburn, Randalstown and Rathcormack, and they appear to have been enfranchised solely for parliamentary purposes. In 1833 no trace could be found of any charters of enfranchisement for Swords, Downpatrick and Knocktopher. However, this is not surprising, as municipal documents in Ireland were often carelessly kept, ruined by

---

[47] The 12 potwalloping boroughs were Antrim, Lisburn, Randalstown, Rathcormack, Newry, Swords, Downpatrick, Baltimore, Tallow, Lismore, Dungarvan and Knocktopher.
[48] *Municipal Corporations (Ireland)*, app. I, p. 554.

damp, eaten by mice, rats, etc., or even wantonly destroyed. For instance, in 1784 it was stated about Baltimore, Co. Cork, 'that there was formerly a charter to this borough, which the late Sir John Freke (**0820**) destroyed';[49] nevertheless, in 1833 the commissioners stated that two charters were still extant, a valid one of James I and an invalid one of James II (although, as Baltimore is described as an 'ancient borough', there may have been other and earlier charters).

The three Co. Antrim boroughs (Antrim town, Lisburn and Randalstown) were usually under the complete control of Lord Massereene, Lord Hertford and John O'Neill, the respective proprietors of the soil, and lords of the nearby manors. Nevertheless, the only one in which there was not at some time a dispute was Randalstown. Lord Hertford lost control of Lisburn in the 'Volunteer' election of 1783 but subsequently recovered it, while from 1776 to 1791 the Skeffington interest in Antrim was repeatedly challenged by Skeffington Thompson.[50] Baltimore was similarly controlled by the Freke family, although from about 1767 to 1773 their influence appears to have been temporarily shaken by Richard Tonson (**2083**), who was reported to have 'cajoled the late Sir John Freke out of it';[51] however, Tonson died in 1773 and the Freke family reasserted their full patronage.

In the third quarter of the century Baltimore, Rathcormack and Newry provided instances of boroughs that were receiving inadequate attention from their patrons, but in each case the patron could and did reassert his complete control without difficulty. In Rathcormack Abraham Devonsher (**0627**) 'came in here by constantly residing and entertaining and drinking with the people', although James Barry (**0094**) 'had the natural interest here but his father being idle and negligent and he not much better the interest is almost gone'.[52] About 1774 James Barry sold 'the Rathcormack estate and borough' to William Hull Tonson (**1051**), Richard Tonson's illegitimate son, and Tonson swiftly and completely reasserted the influence of the lord of the manor of Rathcormack over the borough. No borough influence could be indefinitely left to look after itself, although boroughs attached to a manor rather than a corporation had the best chance of being recovered.

Newry was the largest of the potwalloping boroughs and to some extent an open one, although the interest of the Nedham (Needham) family was periodically exerted and appears to have been dominant in 1832. However, in 1769 William Nedham (**1520**) 'was fonder of diversion than business', and Robert Scott (**1892**), 'by living here and pleasing the people ... established an interest for himself', which he astutely strengthened by building 'a number of houses in the town'.[53] In 1776 Isaac Corry (**0497**), 'son of a merchant (**0495**) at Newry, who was at the time of the last election

[49] *BNL*, 13–16 Jan. 1784.
[50] *IHS*, vol. 17 (1970), A. P. W. Malcomson, 'Election politics in the Borough of Antrim, 1750–1800', esp. pp. 37–42; see also *Gt B. & Ire.*, pp. 179–88.
[51] Parliamentary List 1773 (1).
[52] PLI 1773 (1); *Proc. RIA* (1942) vol. 48 C no. 4, p. 187.
[53] Parliamentary List 1773 (1).

agent to Mr Needham',[54] represented the borough with Robert Ross (**1816**). In 1791 it was stated that 'Mr Needham … takes no part in elections', and this may well have accounted for Robert Ross's remark to the Marquess of Downshire (**1016**) in 1796: 'It is a great misfortune that Newry is an open borough.'[55]

In Knocktopher, where the portreeve, and not the seneschal of the manor, made the return, there was an agreement between the Langrishes and the Ponsonbys whereby Sir Hercules Langrishe (**1200**) nominated one member and John Ponsonby, on paying £500, could nominate the other: this agreement appears to have been terminated by the death of John Ponsonby in 1787. Dungarvan, Lismore and Tallow were the property of the Duke of Devonshire, and as the manors shared a common seneschal, the boroughs shared a returning officer. The Duke of Devonshire, who was closely related to the Ponsonbys, did not look after his interest very carefully and, as the Earl of Tyrone, the head of the Beresford family, possessed property in Dungarvan, he attempted for many years to exert his influence in the borough, with varying degrees of success. Lord Tyrone's brother (**0115**) was First Commissioner of the Revenue, and in 1790 it was alleged that 'All the artificers of the new Customs House had before been exported in the potatoe boats of Dungarvan to storm that borough.'[56]

The most notorious borough in the Irish parliament was the potwalloping borough of Swords. Before the 1790 election, General Massy and John Beresford were alleged to have attempted to control Swords through the competitive enfranchisement of soldiers and Revenue officers respectively. The Molesworth, Bolton, Cobbe and Hatch families had previously tried individually and conjointly to control it, but in reality Swords had no patron, and a contemporary opinion was that 'Elections in this town afford scenes of the greatest corruption.' Swords and the very few similar potwalloping boroughs, where the electorate was large and uncontrolled, were described as:

> the very worst species of Representation – potwalloping Boroughs and open elections by the mob, where neither property, nor family connexions, nor the good opinion of the neighbourhood, nor any other good species of influence, would weigh against adventurers from Dublin or London with large purses, or backed by any temporary clamour.[57]

The Journals of the Irish House of Commons in the eighteenth century contain numerous records of controverted elections for Swords.

The towns that exercised the potwalloping franchise were usually small, and some of them were little more than villages. While the electorate was confined to the protestant householder or freeholder it was invariably small; for instance, in Knocktopher there was one qualified voter in the year 1783–4. In the general election

[54] Parliamentary List 1791 (1).
[55] PRONI DOD 607/638, 8 March 1796.
[56] *Dublin Evening Post*, 10 Oct. 1789 *et. seq.*
[57] *Castlereagh Corr.*, vol. 3, p. 60; this letter is unsigned. See also Porritt & Porritt, vol. 2 pp. 350–3.

of 1783 there were seven voters in Rathcormack and 11 in Baltimore, although in the latter borough 23 voted either in the by-election following Richard Tonson's (**2083**) death in 1773 or in the general election of 1776. Of the four boroughs that continued to send representatives to the Imperial parliament after the Union, Dungarvan had an electorate prior to 1793 of 120, Downpatrick of 250, Lisburn of 400, and Newry of 600–700. The dominant position of the lord of the manor and the connection of the electorate with the ownership of the town made this type of borough one of the easiest to exercise control over, or in which to regain a lapsed interest.

The six manor boroughs – Doneraile, Mallow, Granard, Athboy, Ratoath and Mullingar – were similar; they usually began as small towns, which became absorbed into the surrounding manor whose seneschal either was from the beginning or through course of time became the returning officer. The franchise was vested in the protestant freeholders of the manor, and the control of the lord of the manor over the borough was as inevitable as it was absolute. The electorates were invariably small, especially during this period when the franchise was confined to protestants. In Mullingar about 12 possessed the right to vote, in Athboy, 30, and in Granard, 50. Only Mallow remained enfranchised after the Union. Four of these boroughs – Mallow, Granard, Athboy, and probably Ratoath (for which the 1833 Commissioners could discover no charter) – were enfranchised with the apparent intention of creating corporations, but these either were never created or had become extinct at a very remote date. Four boroughs were enfranchised by the Stuarts (Mallow by James I and Doneraile, Granard and Mullingar by Charles II), while Athboy and Ratoath were medieval in origin. These boroughs were the simplest to buy, sell or bequeath, and little attention was required to enable the patron to maintain his interest. For instance, William Chapman (**0389**), who was returned for Athboy in 1776, 'got by stealth into this borough' due to 'the inattention of the late Lord Darnley but it being a manor and the voters his Lordship's tenants it is improbable he can succeed again',[58] and he did not represent Athboy in the parliament of 1783–90.

By far the largest class of Irish constituencies is composed of 91 boroughs (i.e. the 109 boroughs excluding the potwalloping and manor ones), which returned 182 members to the Irish House of Commons. With the possible exception of Londonderry, each of these boroughs had its definite patron or patrons. The franchise was exclusively protestant until 1793, and afterwards usually so. As a result of an Act of 1704 (*0068*) which incorporated the English Test Act, the corporations were exclusively Anglican, and in the overwhelming majority of the municipal corporations which enfranchised freemen, freedom was acquired through grace especial, which amounted to nomination by the mayor or corporation. Vacancies in the corporations were almost invariably filled by the existing members, who co-opted such burgesses as they required, and once nominated, except for resignation or expulsion, burgesses held office for life. During the seventeenth and eighteenth centuries, two distinct types of corporation

[58] Parliamentary List 1782 (1).

borough gradually emerged: those which included freemen in their parliamentary franchise and those in which there were either no freemen at all, or else no freemen possessing the franchise.[59]

In 36 parliamentary boroughs freemen were admitted to the franchise. Technically the freedom of a borough, like a county borough, could be acquired in five ways: by grace especial, by nomination of the mayor, portreeve or sovereign during his year of office, and by 'right', namely birth, marriage or apprenticeship. In some corporations freedom by grace was the sole method granted in the charter of incorporation, and in others it was the only method deduced from a narrow interpretation of the municipal charter, while yet another group had, through restrictive by-laws, excluded all other methods in defiance of the provisions laid down in their governing charter – this was what happened at Youghal, where:

> On the 17th January 1774, a by-law was passed, whereby … all other bye-laws and regulations recognising any right to freedom were repealed; and a bye-law of the 28th September, 1719 was re-enacted whereby it was declared 'that no person whatsoever on any pretence whatever should have any right to claim to be free of the corporation but such and such only, as the members of the D'Oyer Hundred, with the consent of the mayor and bailiffs, or members of the common council legally assembled should think fit'. From then admittance has been by grace; alone and as a result the corporation has degenerated into a select body consisting of a few families in the town and the non-resident friends of the Patron.[60]

Boroughs in which the admission to the freedom was solely by grace included Clonakilty, Dingle, Athy, Kildare, Dundalk, Dunleer, Kells and Cashel, and there were many others. In some boroughs freedom was obtained through other methods: in Bandon-Bridge it could be claimed by right of birth, the eldest sons of freemen being entitled, while in Londonderry city all who had served an apprenticeship to a freeman, and all the sons with the husbands of all the daughters of any member of the common council, excluding only the sheriffs, were eligible for the freedom of the city. In both Bandon-Bridge and Londonderry freemen were also admitted by grace. With the enacting of the 'Newtown Act' in 1747 *(0460)*, residence became inessential for burgesses and freemen, and subsequently absenteeism was the rule rather than the exception. One consequence of this famous act was that the freemen of the borough of Kinsale in Co. Cork resided in the province of Ulster, where the patron, Lord de Clifford, who was also patron of the potwalloping borough of Downpatrick in Co. Down, had his estates. The borough of Dingle in Co. Kerry had 150 freemen, only two of them resided in the town, and not more than ten in the county. Richard Townsend, the

[59] *Municipal Corporations (Ireland), General Report* gives a short, clear study of the general nature of these corporations: see pp. 1–25, especially pp. 8–9. This short report is followed by long and detailed appendices, which have preserved a picture, already fading in 1833, of the eighteenth-century parliamentary boroughs. The report shows throughout the painstaking care and accuracy of the commissioners.
[60] *Municipal Corporations (Ireland)*, app. I, p. 109.

patron, came from Co. Cork.

In Maryborough in this period there were approximately 350 freemen, but this comparatively large electorate was an indication of conflicting interests struggling to gain control of the borough rather than of an independent electorate.[61] By 1783 this very complicated quarrel had become simplified into an issue between two families, the Parnells and the Cootes, and:

> in that year the Parnell and Coote families entered into an arrangement that they should each return one member, and that there should be no more admissions; accordingly no freeman was admitted or burgess elected in this corporation subsequently to 1783, until 1830. In that year the idea was entertained of reviving it.[62]

These 'arrangements' were not unusual, and often they were written legal or quasi-legal documents: for instance, the Clements and Nesbitt families had such an arrangement for Cavan (see 'Constituencies and Members Returned' on the internet) and the Fosters had one for Dunleer. In many other boroughs, such as Carlingford, Athenry and Longford, freemen were gradually declining in numbers, as those who died were not replaced.

In some freemen boroughs, the lord of the manor had a special influence. For instance, the charter enfranchising the borough of Clonakilty 'constituted Sir Richard Boyle, Knight, his heirs and assigns, Lord of the town of Cloughnakilty, giving him the power of appointment of several of the officers, and the direction to a certain extent of the affairs of the corporation'. The descendant and heir of Sir Richard Boyle was, at this time, the Earl of Shannon, and he nominated the Provost from three burgesses elected by the corporation and freemen. The charter that enfranchised the town of Blessington in Co. Wicklow stated that the election of members of parliament to represent the borough should take place in the hall of Blessington House: it is hardly surprising that it was described as 'a corrupt and venal borough the absolute command of Lord Hillsborough' (the owner of Blessington House).

Freemen boroughs were bought, sold and bequeathed with comparative ease. Dingle was inherited by Richard Townsend on 'the death of his relations, Maurice Fitzgerald, Esq., the Knight of Kerry (**0738**), and his cousin, Mr Robert Fitzgerald (**0744**)'. Lord Hillsborough had inherited Blessington 'by Mr Dunbar's (**0666**) death', and control was unaffected by the change in patron. In the middle of the eighteenth century Lord Belvidere purchased the political control of Philipstown; his control was absolute, until the borough was disfranchised at the Union, and 'No person could be elected to any office without his approbation and consent.' He who controlled the corporation controlled the borough, and Thomas Adderley (**0009**) wrote to his stepson Lord

---

[61] *IHS*, 1954, H. F. Kearney, 'A handlist of the voters of Maryborough, 1760'. This list was prepared in readiness for the 1761 election.
[62] *Municipal Corporations (Ireland)*, app. I, p. 205.

Charlemont that 'I would beg leave to recommend it to you that you will not allow (your brother excepted) on any account any person to be elected one of your burgesses except a dependent tenant; by this means you probably will secure it against every attempt which can be made to turn you out of it.'[63] When a municipal corporation was sold, the former corporation resigned and the new owner appointed a new corporation. Control of the corporation was therefore all-important, and the patronage of a borough could be challenged and even overthrown, as happened in St Johnstown, Co. Donegal, and nearly happened in Strabane[64] and a number of other boroughs. In St Johnstown the Earl of Abercorn was the proprietor of the soil, and the borough had originally belonged to the Earls of Abercorn, but Ralph Howard (**1044**), later Lord Clonmore and subsequently Viscount Wicklow, acquired political control of the borough through his wife, whose family had obtained it in the following manner:

> It is said that long before the Union, the ancestor of the present Marquess of Abercorn was the patron of the borough and nominated the members of the corporation and the two members sent by them to the Irish House of Commons; but that an individual, named Forward, gained over a majority of the burgesses, and having, upon one occasion, secured the return of members to the House of Commons, became thenceforth the owner of its patronage; and that from his family it passed by marriage into that of the present Earl of Wicklow ... Since the Union the corporation has been suffered to expire, and it is understood to be now wholly extinct.[65]

Most of these hostile takeovers occurred in the first half of the century. In the second half boroughs were simply bought and sold: Lord Abercorn, Lord Caledon, Lord Belmore and Lord Londonderry[66] all bought boroughs in the 1780s and 1790s, as did a number of others. Arranging the purchase of Augher, the Marquess of Abercorn wrote:

> If £12,000 is to be the price be it so ... you will draw up a note of hand for me to sign, I will sign it or direct my Banker which you please. The Burgesses will be James Hamilton father and son, Andrew Hamilton, Revd Thomas Pemberton and such as James Hamilton shall fix upon as being the readiest, at hand ... It is certainly a very important consideration but there can be no scarcity. It is of course to be attended to that they should be persons that would be ready at the shortest notice.[67]

---

[63] *HMC Charlemont I*, p. 182.

[64] *Historical Studies*, vol. 10 (1976), A. P. W. Malcomson, 'The politics of "natural right": the Abercorn family and Strabane borough 1692-1800', pp. 43–90.

[65] *Municipal Corporations (Ireland)*, app. II, pp. 1285–6.

[66] They bought Augher, Banagher (exchanged for Newtownards), Belturbet and Newtown Limavady, respectively.

[67] Abercorn MSS, Letter Book for 1790 in the archives of the Duke of Abercorn at Barons Court, Co. Tyrone, N. Ireland, 1st Marquess of Abercorn to Thomas Knox, MP for Co. Tyrone, 11 April 1790, 17 April 1790. There is a photostat copy of this book in PRONI T1230/2. The Abercorn MSS are now in the PRONI.

It was a complete business deal.[68]

The safest way to secure a borough was to elect the members of your family, reliable friends or dependants. Athlone, Cashel and Longford are examples of corporations composed of the patron's family and immediate relations. Cashel was controlled by the Pennefather family, and in 1833 the members of the corporation had the following relation to the patron and head of the family: two were sons, three sons-in-law, one brother and one grandson, four nephews, three cousins, one cousin by marriage and one nephew by marriage. In the ecclesiastical borough of Irishtown or St Canice the patron was the Bishop of Ossory, and its entire corporation was almost invariably composed of clergymen from the diocese, who were naturally under the influence of their bishop. At the Union the then Bishop of Ossory endeavoured to claim the compensation for the disfranchisement of the borough on the grounds that all his predecessors, by insisting that the MPs returned for this borough should support the government of the day, had been rewarded with preferment to higher and more lucrative sees. This claim was disallowed although it had a degree of veracity. In 1779 one of his predecessors, Dr William Newcome, 'a very learned man' and later Bishop of Waterford, wrote to John Hely-Hutchinson giving this picture of borough management:

> Now I have … supported an interest in this borough at a great expense, for a year before the last General Election; absolutely preserved the borough by making forty new freemen in the midst of the greatest obloquy and newspaper abuse (for our majority on the poll was only 19), and returned two members recommended by Government, after a well contested opposition, headed by Mr Ponsonby, in favour of Mr Mossom (**1500**), a popular candidate, and a native of this place.[69]

The elections were held in the palace yard of the Bishop of Ossory, and other corporate meetings in his hall.[70]

The 55 corporation boroughs without freemen returned 110 members, more than one-third of the entire House of Commons. Some of these boroughs had been enfranchised by charters that excluded freemen, and in others freemen had declined to the point when they became non-existent, apart from those who were created freemen in order that they might immediately qualify for co-option as burgesses. A case can be made that each borough had individual characteristics and required individual treatment, for the real issue was maintenance of control over the corporation. But there was also a sense in which all these boroughs were from a parliamentary point of view exactly alike, and during the debates on Flood's Reform Bill in November

---

[68] One of the best and clearest descriptions of what actually happened when the patronage of a borough passed into new hands is given by the Commissioners for Municipal Corporations in their description of the borough of Limavady, which Lord Londonderry purchased from Thomas Conolly (**0459**) in 1792.

[69] *Rep. of the Commissioners of Union Compensation* (1804), pp. 32–4, *Further Proceedings of the Commissioners – St Canice*. A number of the Mossom family are buried in the cathedral.

[70] *BNL* 16–20 Jan. 1784.

1783 John Monck Mason (**1352**) underlined this inevitable similarity:

> With respect to those which these people call rotten boroughs, where the right of
> suffrage is vested in a few persons only, the depopulation of the places can have no
> effect upon the representatives: Belfast is as much a rotten borough as Harristown;
> the number of inhabitants is nothing to the purpose, for those inhabitants could
> have no right to poll, and the members for such boroughs are returned at this day by
> the self-same number of voters that they were at the time the charters were granted.[71]

Nevertheless, it is interesting to glance briefly at the type and nature of some of these
boroughs. The electorate was usually confined to 13 burgesses and occasionally to 12,
although, as in the case of Coleraine, the corporation could be more complicated.
The question of whether the returning officer, usually the mayor or his equivalent,
could exercise his vote, except as a casting vote, appears to have been ambiguous and
probably varied from corporation to corporation, while the frequent presence of the
patron in the capacity of mayor or sovereign gives weight to the probability that the
mayor was usually able to exercise this power. Catholic enfranchisement in 1793 *(1480)*
could and did have little effect, as in boroughs that were not completely disfranchised by
the Union, including Belfast, the franchise remained unaltered until the passing of the
first Reform Bill in 1832. However, most of the 'close' or 'rotten' boroughs were
disfranchised by the Act of Union, including Harristown with 'but one tree inhabiting',
and Clonmines, Fethard and Bannow, Co. Wexford, which shared the same corporation
but returned six MPs, which 'must be a burlesque on all representation'.[72] On 23
September 1783 Lord Northington wrote to Lord North that:

> A parliamentary Reform is the grand Subject of Discussion intended to be proposed
> by the Delegates of the Volunteer Corps, but they are not as yet decided in what
> shape to introduce it. There can be little room for apprehension with regard to the
> fate of this question, when the present constitution of the House of Commons in
> this Country is referred to.[73]

It is idle to speculate, but if the 'ascendancy' had widened the franchise in 1784 and
thus placed the House of Commons on a broader base, a national body might in the
course of time have been welded together, and an Irish nation inclusive of all classes
and creeds might gradually have emerged. But this is a Utopian idea, because it would
have meant the renunciation of the special position and privileges of the 'ascendancy'
in an age which was not utilitarian. It would also have produced the complete collapse
of government by further divorcing the legislature from the executive, for while
governments were increasingly recognising the importance of people, parliament still
represented the property of the nation.

[71] *Parl. Reg.*, vol. 3, 1781–97, p. 44.
[72] *BNL* 15–20 Jan. 1784.
[73] BL Add. MS 38,716, f. 90.

7

ELECTORAL LEGISLATION

I THE DEVELOPMENT OF ELECTORAL LEGISLATION 1692–1800

Ireland never had a qualification act requiring MPs to have a property qualification, despite attempts to pass such an act in 1711, 1713 and 1719. In 1719 the bill passed all its stages but did not come back from England. In 1768 a similar bill, sponsored by the radical MP Charles Lucas (**1276**), met a similar fate. There were further unsuccessful attempts to introduce a property qualification in 1783, 1784, 1785, 1790, 1791 and 1793. These bills proposed a property qualification of £500 p.a. for county MPs, and £300 for borough MPs, eldest sons of peers and sons of persons qualified to serve as county MPs; the Chief Secretary would be exempted. However, even so moderate a measure met with hostility from impecunious MPs and from the government, which saw its influence over needy MPs diminishing.

As in England, the county franchise depended on land, but landholding was complicated by suddenly changing ownership, the policy of religious exclusiveness and the poverty of the country. The most severe of the penal laws regarding the non-conforming secular society was that of 1703/4, 2 Anne, c. 6 *(0068)*, 'an Act to prevent the further growth of popery', confirmed in 1709 by 8 Anne, c. 3 *(0119)*. These acts contained a gavelling clause which not only prevented Catholics from amassing land but led to partible inheritance, while the oaths required of officeholders ensured that only members of the Established Church would be able to participate in government.

Until 1782 Catholics could only hold land for years, which, apart from other restrictions, did not carry political rights – not even the 999-year leases made possible by the 1778 Relief Act *(0867)* – but protestants, conforming or dissenting, could hold land for lives, and, if valued at 40s in the holder's estimation, this brought with it the county franchise. The homogeneity that was so marked a feature of English society[1] was almost totally lacking in Ireland. In Ireland there was a Protestant government, fractured by its dependent nature, and an overwhelmingly Catholic people in three of the four provinces, while in the fourth, Ulster, protestantism itself was seriously divided between conforming Protestants (members of the established Church of Ireland) and Presbyterians, known as Dissenters. In eighteenth-century Ireland the word 'Protestant' referred exclusively to the former, and membership of the Established Church brought

[1] See Christie, op. cit, esp. chaps 3 & 4.

social, political and educational privilege along with a dominant position in state and society.

It is extremely difficult to deduce accurate denominational figures for the population of Ireland in the eighteenth century. 'The papists of Ireland,' wrote Lord Harcourt, 'are four, if not five, to one of the inhabitants';[2] Lord Charlemont stated that the Anglicans were one in ten of the population[3] and the Presbyterians were certainly as numerous, but the entire protestant population cannot have been more than a quarter, and probably fluctuated between a quarter and one-fifth of the whole. Under these circumstances genuine freeholders were, inevitably, few, and the county electorates correspondingly narrow. The scarcity of the genuine freeholder, combined with the even territorial interests in the majority of the counties, led to the creation of a class of fictitious freeholders, who, despite the frequent legislation aimed at their annihilation, continued to increase with the rising tide of political interest. This class was a constant feature in county politics, and petitions were levelled against it after nearly every general election and frequently also after by-elections.

A further complication was that the protestant population was centred in the north of Ireland, mainly in the counties directly associated with or, as in the case of Counties Antrim and Down, adjoining the seventeenth-century plantation of Ulster. They were largely Presbyterian, although the real increase in Irish Presbyterianism came not with the plantation but with the migration at the end of the seventeenth century, as a result of famine in Scotland.[4] This concentration is reflected in the comparatively large electorates of the Ulster counties, with the exception of Cavan and Monaghan.

The two principal branches of protestantism viewed each other with a mutual and enduring animosity. The Earl of Cork and Orrery probably summed up the views of the Protestant establishment when, writing in the middle of the century, he explained that:

> I held both Presbyterians and Roman Catholics in the utmost abhorrence ... I esteemed Presbyterians ... as cunning, designing, canting, ignorant hypocrits, and for Roman Catholics, I thought every one of them held a knife at my throat.[5]

There is little doubt that, all things being equal, many of the Church of Ireland would have preferred the hierarchical structure of Catholicism to the democratic–congregational structure of Presbyterianism, which had the potential to create a state

---

[2] *Harcourt Papers*, IX, p. 175 (see Abbreviations: Principal Record Repositories, Official Publications, Parliamentary and Division Lists for further details).
[3] *HMC Charlemont* I, p. 43.
[4] *Ethnologia Europaea* vol. VII, 1975, pp. 1–22, A. Gailey, 'The Scots element in North Irish popular culture', esp. the maps on pp. 6–7 showing the cumulative areas of Presbyterianism 1611–1720; 44 congregations were added to the Synod of Ulster *c.* 1691–1715; these all sat under the Scottish Assembly as there was no General Assembly of the Presbyterian Church in Ireland until the nineteenth century.
[5] Emily, Countess of Cork and Orrery, *Orrery Papers* (1903) vol. II p. 354.

within a state. In 1719 Archbishop King told the Archbishop of Canterbury that the 'true point ... is whether the Presbyterians and lay elders shall have the greatest influence over the people ... or the landlords over their tenants'.[6] The Church of Ireland 'as by law established' was confirmed in its exclusive position by a series of laws collectively known as the penal code, and described by a contemporary as 'the shell in which Protestant power was hatched'. In the 1690s Sir Richard Cox declared that he had no objection to people going to heaven by the route of their choice, but he wished 'for the security of the established church to exclude from office, or any share in the government, all those who would not conform to the church established by law'.[7] Collectively these laws affected all aspects of family, educational and ecclesiastical life for both Catholics and Presbyterians.[8] Politically, Catholics were excluded from sitting in parliament by an English Act of 1692, and no Roman Catholic appears to have sought election between the Revolution and the Union, but there was always a very small group of Presbyterians sitting in parliament: the most eminent of these were the Uptons (**2124, 2126, 2127, 2128**) of Templepatrick, successively MPs for Co. Antrim at the beginning of the century, and Robert Stewart (**2008**), MP for Co. Down (1771–83) and 1st Marquess of Londonderry; another group were merchants like Travers Hartley (**0979**), MP for Dublin city (1782–90). The Presbyterians, recalcitrant tenants and voters, retained the county franchise throughout the century. The most notorious of the penal laws, 2 Anne, c. 6 *(0068)*, in addition to the singularly harsh restrictions placed on the Catholics, declared that 'No person shall take benefit of this act as a protestant within the intent and meaning hereof, that shall not conform to the Church of Ireland as by law established.' A test was imposed making the taking of the sacrament of the Lord's Supper according to the rites of the Anglican Church a condition of holding any office, civil or military, under the Crown. This was modified by a series of Indemnity Acts, often to cover emergencies, such as the 1715 and 1745 rebellions and the various French threats that occurred during the Anglo-French wars of the century. In Londonderry ten out of 12 aldermen and 14 out of 24 burgesses were turned out of their respective offices by the 1703/4 act. In 1707 there was a by-election in Belfast following the death of William Cairnes (**0337**), an English MP

[6]BL Add. Ms 6117.

[7]Quoted in *IHS* vol. II no. 7 (1941) pp. 280–302, J. C. Beckett, 'The government of the church of Ireland under William III and Anne', p. 282. Cox was unable to do this under the tolerant and Calvinist William III.

[8]Probably the most influential studies of the penal laws and their effects were those of Maureen Wall, whose series of essays have been collected and edited by G. O'Brien under the title *Catholic Ireland in the Eighteenth Century*. The most comprehensive study of the Catholic question from 1690 to 1830 is Bartlett, *The Fall and Rise of the Irish Nation*. Two shorter studies of the penal period are Corish, *The Catholic Community in the Seventeenth and Eighteenth Centuries* and P. J. Corish (ed.), *A History of Irish Catholicism* (1971), vol. IV. See also H. Fenning, *The Undoing of the Friars of Ireland* (Louvain, 1972); further social insights can be gained from J. Brady, *Catholics and Catholicism in the Eighteenth-Century Press* (Maynooth, 1965). For the Presbyterians: Reid, *History of the Presbyterian Church in Ireland*; Barkley, *A Short History of the Presbyterian Church in Ireland*.

Samuel Ogle (**1574**) was returned and the return was contested by Alexander Cairnes (**0334**). It transpired that only four of the 13 burgesses had been present at the election, the rest not having taken the test.[9]

The point at which the Catholics were actually disfranchised is difficult to ascertain. The 1716 Act *(0168)* states that no Catholic is to vote unless he has taken the oaths of allegiance and abjuration at least six months before the election, and the latter oath would have been unacceptable to Catholics. But in the eighteenth century there was often a difference between passing a statute and ensuring its performance: certainly the problem of Catholics or crypto-Catholics voting was recurrent. Until the enfranchisement of the Catholics in 1793, typical accusations were that the challenged voter had not conformed within the specified time; had lapsed; had not been seen in church; his family were Roman Catholic; his wife was a Roman Catholic who had not conformed on marriage; and after 1746 *(0440)* proof of a Protestant marriage was required if demanded. Local pressures may have encouraged the Sheriff, despite the various inducements offered to any reporting non-compliance, to ignore this prohibition as, in 1727, 1 Geo. II, c. 9 *(0253)*, clause 7 states that:

> and for the better preventing papists from voting in elections be it further enacted ... that no papist shall be entitled or admitted to vote at the election of any member to serve in Parliament as knight, citizen burgess or at the election of any magistrate for any city or other town corporate; any law statute or usage to the contrary notwithstanding.

Unquestionably Catholics had legally lost the franchise by 1727.[10]

The Sheriff was the returning officer for the counties. As such he could not return himself, and if an election (e.g. through the death of the member or of the sovereign) was thought to be imminent, one way of incapacitating an opponent was to have him chosen Sheriff. The Sheriff was responsible for keeping the poll book in which the voters were registered, for controlling his assistants and for the general conduct of the election. However, the Sheriff, who held office for a year, was usually a county figure, even if that county was not the location of his major property, and inevitably he had local involvements. Throughout the century the Commons regarded the role of the Sheriff at elections with some suspicion. As early as 1697 the House brought forward the heads of a bill to prevent 'charge and expense in election of Members to serve in Parliament, and for regulating elections and to prevent irregular proceedings of sheriffs

---

[9]Reid, op. cit. vol. II pp. 511 and 528–9. Alexander Cairnes, a merchant and banker in London and Dublin, was created a baronet (in both Great Britain and Ireland) in 1708 and returned for Monaghan Borough in 1710–13 and 1715–27. He sat for Co. Monaghan 1713–14 and from 1727 until his death in 1732. Ogle was a Commissioner of the Revenue 1699 to 1714, when he was removed; he was supported in Belfast by James Macartney (**1303**).

[10]*IHS* (1960) vol. XII no. 45 pp. 28–37, J. G. Simms, 'Irish Catholics and the parliamentary franchise, 1692–1728', esp. p. 37.

and other officers, in electing and returning such Members'.[11] They requested that it might be 'put … in form and transmitted into England', and the Lords Justices agreed. Nevertheless, there is no further record of the heads of this bill, so presumably it was not returned. For his conduct at the 1695 election the Sheriff of Co. Cavan received a reprimand 'on his knees at the bar of the House, from Mr Speaker, for his undue management of himself at the said election of Cavan'.[12] After the 1713 election a resolution of the House defined the role of the returning officer, resolving that:

> No sheriff of a county, Mayor, Provost, Portrieve, sovereign or other chief magistrate of any city, town, borough or corporation, nor Seneschal of a manor, hath right to vote in any election (except where the votes of the other electors are equal) any usage or custom to the contrary notwithstanding; unless where by expressed words of the charter, they have other or greater power, or where there hath been usage to the contrary time out of mind, in boroughs by perscription.[13]

In some of the medieval boroughs, for instance Youghal, the mayor had three votes and the recorder, bailiff and aldermen two each.[14]

The 1715 act *(0168)* also attempted to regulate the role of the sheriff, particularly at county elections where, as well as making the return, he named the place where the election was to be held and declared the poll open and closed. If he was not impartial, candidates could arrive and find the election over or called in an obscure part of the county. It was therefore decreed that elections were to be open and not in any way clandestine, and they were to be held where the assize last met, usually the county town. Elections lasted several days, and in some cases for a month or even months. This statute states that, without the consent of the candidates, adjournments are to be no longer than from day to day, except at weekends. Furthermore, within four days of receiving the writ the Sheriff was officially to inform the returning officers for the boroughs within the county, who were to proceed to hold elections within 21 days. At least four days beforehand they were to declare their intention to hold the election in some public place. No fee or gratuity was to be offered or accepted by a returning officer, who was the only person able to the make the return to the Sheriff.

The Irish parliament was continually tinkering with or ostensibly[15] perfecting electoral machinery. There was no land tax, and a constant problem throughout the century was the satisfactory definition of those eligible to vote. Many controverted elections turned on the eligibility of the voters. An act of 1715, 2 Geo. I, c. 19 *(0168)*, 'for the more effectual preventing fraudulent conveyances in order to multiply votes for

---

[11] *Commons jn. Ire.* (Bradley edn) vol. II p. 872.
[12] Ibid., p. 844.
[13] Ibid., p. 986, 18 Dec. 1713.
[14] Porritt & Porritt, vol. II, p. 210.
[15] Often one gets the feeling that their desire was for future rather than present virtue, for instance in both 29 Geo. III, c. 29, and 30 Geo. III, c. 17, the period for non-registration is extended.

electing members to serve in parliament; and for preventing irregular proceedings of sheriffs and other officers in electing and returning such members', stated that a voting freeholder must be in possession and enjoyment of his freehold for at least six months prior to an election, unless such lands were acquired by marriage or inheritance within that time. Furthermore, every freeholder before being admitted to the poll would have, if required by a candidate or any other qualified voter, to take the oath as follows:

> You shall swear that you are a freeholder in the county of ___ and have freehold lands
> or hereditaments lying or being at ___ in the county of ___ of the clear annual value
> of forty shillings above all charges payable out of the same; and that you believe the
> same may be so let to a responsible tenant; and such freehold estate hath not been
> made or granted to you fraudulently, or on purpose to qualify you to give your vote;
> and that the place of your abode is at ___ in the county of ___ and that you have not
> been polled before at this election.

The oath was administered by the Sheriff or his representative, who wrote 'jurat' against those sworn. A penalty of £40 was to be paid to anyone making a successful prosecution for the inadequate performance of this act, and the poll book was to be kept carefully with the county records. For a successful conviction there was a penalty of £100, half of which went to the king and half to the informer. This statute also touched on another of the other great election problems, direct or indirect bribery, for it enacted that no candidate: 'shall by himself, his friends or agents, or any employed on his behalf ... directly or indirectly give, present or allow, to any person or persons, having voice or vote in such elections, any money, meat, drink entertainment, or provision, or make any present gift, reward or entertainment ... in order to be elected'. This was always more a pious hope than a reality. The reality was to keep bribery and corruption within reasonable limits.

In 1727 Lord Newtown Butler remarked that 'We can hardly expect poor people can refuse £50, or more for a vote, which is the case in some places amongst us.'[16] Electorates were small, and where they were evenly divided bribes of this size could occur. Even apart from this, electors and their friends expected certain attentions at the time of an election. In 1740 Lord Orrery's agent told him that 'Without much application, good words and kind promises, few people have success in elections.'[17] For example, this translated into the £760 3s 6d that Agmondisham Vesey (2145) distributed to the publicans of Kinsale when he secured his election for that town in 1765.[18] A list of the voters of Maryborough, a large electorate, in 1760 repeatedly

[16]PRONI T659/8 Newtown Butler to Charles Delafaye, 30 Sept. 1727, quoted in Bartlett & Hayton, p. 149, Malcomson, 'The parliamentary traffic of this country'.
[17]Hull Univ. Lib. MS Eng. 218/4F/7, quoted in D. Dickson, 'An Economic History of the Cork Region in the Eighteenth Century' (unpub. PhD thesis, TCD) pp. 126–7; see also *IHS* (1946–7) pp. 109–30, J. L. McCracken, 'Irish parliamentary elections', esp. pp. 119–20.
[18]See Dickson, op. cit., pp. 126–7; Johnston, *Gt B. & Ire.*, p. 141.

comments beside a number of voters that 'whoever gives his wife most money will get him', and this proved to be the case for some of the 50 so noted.[19] Dr Malcomson writes of John Foster (**0805**) and James Fortescue (**0792**) that in the 1768 election for Co. Louth: 'Between 19 and 20 July 1768 one of the five pubs reserved for the entertainment, accommodation and intoxication of their supporters, served 295 breakfasts, 492 dinners, and 39 suppers. The expenses in all five pubs came to £1,350 and the total expenses of the election to £3,000.'[20] Furthermore, it was a small electorate – only 1,401 votes were cast – and there had been a by-election the year before. The Irish MPs were for the most part poor, and they would not have expended this money had it not been considered necessary. Size was not always relevant, but the balance of interests was paramount in any constituency.

The 1727 act, 1 Geo. II, c. 9 *(0253)*, carried the registration process further by distinguishing between freeholders. A freeholder whose freehold was under £10 could not vote unless he had been registered for six months prior to the election. The poll book recorded his name, the nature of his freehold (lives etc.),[21] grantor and grantee, lessor or lessee, quantity of land, consideration, rent and date of deed. The clerk was paid 6d for making the entry. Further legislation in 1745, 19 Geo. II, c. 11 *(0440)*, made a renewed effort to remedy grievances in the conduct of elections, declaring that 'Elections of members to serve in parliament are grown burdensome and grievous to candidates, and ruinous to their estates, by many evil and dilatory practices, which have been allowed at such elections by Sheriffs and their returning officers'; at this point it refers to 1 Geo. II, c. 9 *(0253)*. This act arranged for the public registration of freeholds of £2 and under £10, every such freehold to be registered at the Quarter Sessions and six months before an election, and the elector to state on oath that he had such a freehold. The Clerk of the Peace was to keep a register and on the last day of the Quarter Sessions to deliver a true copy to the Treasurer of the county. Freemen voters in boroughs had to be already freemen *before* the parliamentary vacancy occurred; before 1771 if a vacancy recurred during a recess, quite a long time could elapse before the writ for the election was issued. Finally, anyone injuring or destroying a poll book or falsely swearing against the true intent of this act would suffer such penalties as persons convicted of wilful and corrupt perjury. The effect of this and subsequent legislation appears to have been limited. In 1768 Sir James Nugent complained of an undue election for Co. Longford, and the House of Commons ordered the Clerk of the Peace for the county to attend the House with the poll book

---

[19] *IHS* vol. 9 no. 33 (March 1954) pp. 67–82, H. F. Kearney, 'A handlist of the voters of Maryborough': at least 50 (of *c.* 400) electors were specifically noted as being directly venal either themselves or through their wives.
[20] Malcomson, *John Foster*, p. 125; the results were: John Foster 437 votes, James Fortescue 397, Blainey Balfour 325, Faithful Fortescue 242.
[21] A lease for lives counted as a freehold.

and the book of registry of freeholders and to explain where the poll book had been since the election.[22]

Parliament then turned its attention to municipal corporations returning members to parliament. In 1745, 19 Geo. II, c. 12 *(0441)*, 'An act for the better regulation of corporations', pointed out that irregularities had 'of late illegally intruded into' elections to municipal corporations of mayors, bailiffs, portreeves etc. 'whereby great mischiefs have already ensued and more are likely to ensue if not timely prevented'. The statute goes on to underline the various legal methods, in particular *mandamus* and *quo warranto*, by which such iniquities can be remedied. Mayors and their equivalents often had considerable control over the election of burgesses, who held the franchise for the borough. But the important act, with severe long-term consequences, came two years later in the form of 19 Geo. II, c. 11 *(0440)*, 'An act to amend and make more effectual an act intituled an act for better regulating elections of members to serve in parliament and for the more effectual quieting of corporations, and securing the right of persons who have been or shall be elected into the offices of aldermen and Burgesses within any corporation of this kingdom'. The effect of this act was to divorce the corporation from the municipality that it was designed to serve. Burgesses did not need to reside within the corporation. It was the follow-through, and in many places the logical consequence, of the 1703/4 *(0068)* penal restrictions.

There are two interpretations of this act. One says that it simply did as it said, and confirmed a situation already in existence, as was indicated by the final verdict in the long-running legal cases that surrounded it: 'The judicial decision when it came at last in 1758, showed that the act had done no more than clarify the previous legal position.'[23] The other, not entirely incompatible, theory considers that it was a political manoeuvre by the Ponsonby family against the newly arrived Stewarts. The story has already been told in relation to the sale of the Colvill estate but the transfer had a political aspect which was at least equally important certainly to the politically ambitious Brabazon Ponsonby (**1696**) who had married Sarah, widow of Hugh Colvill (**0451**). Her son, Robert Colvill (**0453**), was unstable and for most of his life Ponsonby managed his affairs on the assumption that Colvill's principal estate, a large estate in and around Newtown(ards) and Comber, Co. Down, would come to his younger son and Colvill's half-brother, John Ponsonby (**1702**). It would have been a great inheritance, for not only was the estate intrinsically valuable, but it was filled with protestant (albeit Presbyterian) tenants and therefore politically valuable as well, as was shown in 1790 when Robert Stewart, later Lord Castlereagh, was returned for Co. Down largely on the Presbyterian vote. Ponsonby could do little about the county vote either then or in the future, but attached to the estate was a parliamentary borough. In 1739 the ambitious Brabazon Ponsonby (**1696**) arranged the marriage of his eldest son, William (**1707**), to Lady Caroline Cavendish. Four years later, in 1743, his younger son John married her sister, Lady Elizabeth Cavendish, and

---

[22] *Commons jn. Ire.* (Grierson edn) vol. XIV p. 707.
[23] *IHS* vol. XVIII no. 71 (1973) pp. 313–44, A. P. W. Malcomson, 'The Newtown Act of 1748: revision and reconstruction'; see *supra* p. 53.

doubtless on this occasion his political at least as well as his financial expectations were not overlooked.

But in 1744, Robert Colvill's (**0453**) mistress persuaded him to sell the Newtown(ards)), estate to Alexander Stewart who when he bought the Colvill estate, assumed that the parliamentary borough went with it. Stewart appears to have driven a hard bargain, as Colvill asked an additional £500 for the control of the borough; whether Colvill could deliver this, given that the borough had been managed by Brabazon Ponsonby, is another question. In any case Stewart refused, believing that as he owned the ground on which the borough stood he would automatically acquire it. He had some grounds for this view as only seven years before, in 1737, Speaker Boyle (**0210**) had purchased an estate which included the borough of Clonakilty from his kinsman Lord Burlington, and with it had come the patronage of the borough, but Boyle had managed the estate and the borough for many years and Burlington was an absentee. Managerially Boyle was in the same position as Brabazon Ponsonby in regard to Newtown(ards). Stewart probably reasoned that as the owner of the soil, if the burgesses were resident, he must – if not immediately, in the fullness of time – control the borough. Furthermore, an act of 1542, 33 Henry VIII, c. 1, stated that:

> Every citizen and burgess, for every parliament hereafter within this realm of Ireland to be held, shall be a resident and dwelling within the counties, cities and towns, chosen and elected by the greater number of the inhabitants of the said counties, cities and towns, being present at the said election by virtue of the King's writ to that intent addressed.

However, there was a national complication (which did not apply to Newtown(ards)): the paucity (or even non-existence) of Protestant inhabitants qualified under the 1703/4 act *(0068)* in most parliamentary boroughs. This had led to the appointment of non-resident friends of the patron, and it was this practice that the act confirmed. What gives credence to Lord Charlemont's view that it was a vendetta against Stewart,[24] a Presbyterian, a newcomer and an upstart merchant, is the timing, the long drawn-out litigation that paralleled it and the lobbying of the Primate, an enthusiastic Ponsonby supporter, for the return of the bill. On 18 January 1747/8 the Primate wrote to Lord George Sackville as follows:

> You may know the previous transactions from Lord Duncannon [Ponsonby] as his family is principally concerned. Mr Stewart bought an estate, but refused to pay a consideration for the borough, upon an opinion that he could get it for nothing. He has proceeding [*sic*] by moving in the court of King's Bench for informations against the burgesses upon their non-observance of their charter, which directs they should be chosen out of the town; which all the charters in Ireland respectively do, but are not, never have been, nor in the present circumstances of Ireland can be adhered to,

---

[24] *HMC Charlemont* I, p. 111.

as the low state of the towns cannot supply inhabitants fit for the purpose. The persons who have the influence of the boroughs are all justly alarmed lest some enterprising men should bring them all into question, as they are all open to it, and have therefore brought in this quieting clause ... I am strongly for it for many prudential reasons; and one among the rest is, that if the influence over the corporations should be taken out of the hands of gentlemen and thrown at large among the lower inhabitants (which they must do as the law is at present), the consequence must be (setting apart the influence gained to the Papists in the south) the whole province of Ulster will be under the direction of the Presbyterians; so that the only strength of the established church is really in this extraordinary corporation interest, and if that comes to be distributed equally according to numbers we should have but a small share.[25]

Interestingly, the Primate does not query the *legality* of such residence, but its *prudence*. Surprisingly, although conscious of the act of Henry VIII, he appears to have been unaware of the restrictions of the 1703/4 penal act *(0068)*, which excluded not only Catholics but also Presbyterians from municipal corporations. However, the real loss was the divorce between the town's municipal life and its parliamentary representation. It also crystallised a situation which a degree of fluidity might have allowed to be effectively modified later in the century.

Alexander Stewart lived all his life in Newtown(ards) and was buried there. His son Robert, 1st Marquess of Londonderry, also lived there until he began to build nearby Mount Stewart in the 1780s. Ironically, Robert's son, also Robert, 2nd Marquess of Londonderry but usually known as Lord Castlereagh (**2009**), was born in Newtown(ards) and as Chief Secretary arranged the destruction of the majority of the parliamentary boroughs, including Newtown(ards), in the Act of Union. The so-called 'Newtown Act' act had serious consequences for the development of Irish municipal life, for no landlord was going to improve a town from whose administration he was divorced, while absentee burgesses had little interest in its development. The ultimate consequence of the 1703/4 *(0068)* and 1747 acts *(0460)* was the ossification of the Irish electoral system, which was largely borough-oriented.

The parliament that George II called at his accession in 1727 was dissolved only by his death in 1760. Considerable excitement was generated by the general election called in 1761, following the accession of George III. Acts of 1763 *(0602)* and 1771 *(0696)* resulted from the conduct of this and the 1768 election, which was itself the result of a major electoral change: the Octennial Act *(0657)*, which prevented any parliament from lasting longer than eight years. The acts of 1763 and 1771 returned to the theme of the conduct of elections. Early in the reign of George II, in 1729, the House had resolved 'that in case any member has procured himself to be elected ... by

---

[25]Malcomson, *Eighteenth-Century Irish Official Papers,* vol. I, p. 36, Primate Stone to Lord George Sackville 18 Jan. 1747/8.

bribery or any other corrupt practice, this House will proceed with the utmost severity against such person'.[26] Thirty-four years later, in 1763 at the beginning of the reign of George III, a statute was passed, 3 Geo. III, c. 13 *(0602)*, entitled 'an act for the more effectually preventing bribery and corruption in the elections of members to serve in parliament and magistrates of cities, boroughs and towns corporate'. It declared that the previous laws had been ineffective, and enacted that all electors at the request of the candidates or any two electors should take a prescribed oath that they had not benefited in any way from their vote and that they had not polled previously at that election – multiple voting and impersonation were fairly common practices at Irish elections. A Justice of the Peace was to be specially appointed to administer the oath, while any returning officer admitting any elector from whom this oath had been demanded but not administered would, along with the voter, forfeit £100 with costs. The returning officer was also to take an oath, immediately after he read the writ, that neither he nor his family had benefited or would benefit from making this election return, and 'that I will return such person or persons, as shall appear to me to have the majority of legal votes'.

Finally, the statute turned to the problem of protracted elections: 'Where the right of voting is vested in the protestant inhabitants in general of such boroughs … elections in some such boroughs have been protracted to an unreasonable length of time to the great detriment of both candidates and electors.' A voter in these boroughs was to take an oath (or make an affirmation) stating that he had been an inhabitant of the borough or manor, paid the regular taxes levied on a householder, that he had not taken up residence since the electoral vacancy, was not a Catholic, married to a Catholic nor educating his children in the popish religion. The returning officer was to administer this oath at the request of any of the candidates or their agent, and there were severe penalties for perjury. No person guilty of perjury was to vote at any subsequent parliamentary election. However, the extent to which this was effective is dubious. For example, following the 1768 election for Co. Roscommon, 'Anthony Broderick was tried at Roscommon and is to be pilloried for wilful and corrupt perjury at the late election for that county where he voted for two of the candidates.'[27] The election had ended in a riot which the House of Commons later decided 'was stirred up and raised by the friends of Edward Crofton or his agent'.[28] Crofton **(0524)** was one of the candidates, and on this occasion was declared not duly elected.

In 1768 the Irish House of Commons resolved itself into a committee of the whole House 'to take into consideration what may be further necessary to regulate the elections of Members to serve in Parliament'.[29] Three of the four resolutions in the report of

---

[26] *Commons jn. Ire.* (Bradley edn), vol. V p. 648.

[27] *BNL*, 16 Aug. 1768: presumably, as he had two votes anyway, he had voted for each of them twice.

[28] *Commons jn. Ire.* (Grierson edn) vol. XIV p. 726.

[29] Ibid., vol. XIV pp. 490–2: this report was presented to the House by Robert French (**0834**).

this committee were aimed against fictitious freeholders, and they give some insight into their economic status. Resolution two stated 'that it is the opinion of this Committee, that the permitting of persons to vote as freeholders from rent-charges of forty shillings yearly value, arising out of lands, is an inlet to corruption, and such freeholders are of no real advantage to the public'. Resolution three continued 'that if freeholders of a less yearly value than £10 had some public object upon their freeholds by which it might be known where their freeholds lie, the same would tend to prevent fraud, imposition and the danger of perjury'. Resolution four suggested 'that if such freeholders had each a tenement, occupied by himself or a tenant, with one or more glass windows, and a chimney of lime and stone, or lime and brick, the same would answer the ends aforesaid, and tend to the welfare of poor protestants, and the improvement of the kingdom'. The House disagreed with resolution three and divided evenly on resolution four, which was finally carried by the casting vote of the Speaker. This verdict is an interesting demonstration of the attitude of the House on an issue involving theoretical principle and practical expediency in relation to electoral issues.

At the same time, complaints were made to the Committee on Privileges and Elections that riots were frequently organised to make the Sheriff close the polls, or give him a pretext for doing so. There is no shortage of examples of this throughout the century; for instance, a contemporary pamphleteer alleged that at the famous Dublin by-election of 1749 there were fears that 'the aldermen would occasion some riot, and whilst they had the majority, oblige the sheriffs to close their books'.[30] The 1768 fears were recollected in 1774; the *Journals* recorded that at the last general election (1768) the poll at several county elections was broken up by riot and, indeed, the Co. Galway poll had been closed by a riot, following which William Power Keating Trench (**2111**) successfully petitioned against the return of Lord Dunkellin (♦♦♦♦) – the representative of the de Burghs, one of the oldest families in Ireland – on the grounds that he had by expending £1,900 acquired a 'large and leading interest' in the last election and 'that many who would otherwise have given their second voices to Mr Trench were by undue influence, by corruption, by menaces, and when these failed even by stripes compelled to vote for Lord Dunkellin'. According to the evidence of a Mr Dennis Kelly, the 'large and leading interest' so acquired amounted to 23 votes.[31]

Previously if an MP died during the parliamentary recess a writ for an election to fill the vacancy could not be issued until parliament reassembled, but, in 1771, 11 Geo. III, c. 10 *(0694)*, gave the Speaker permission to issue the writ should the House be adjourned or prorogued for more than 20 days. The notice of the death of the member was to be inserted in the *Dublin Gazette* and 14 days after the notice appeared the Speaker was forthwith to issue his warrant, 'provided always that no petition shall have been preferred or other question depending in the House of Commons' regarding

[30]Quoted in Porritt & Porritt, vol. II p. 214.
[31]*Commons jn. Ire.* (Grierson edn) vol. XIV pp. 706, 728–9.

the validity of the deceased's election. Before this seats could be vacant for up to 18 months, which allowed more than adequate time for arranging the registration of voters before the election should this be necessary.

The same session of parliament, in 11 Geo. III, c. 12 *(0696)*, looked at what had long been a vexatious process and often one of dubious equity – the conduct of controverted elections. These had often been re-runs of the original election in the House of Commons where the complaining party felt that he could count on the votes of his friends. The bill, which was complicated and detailed, was modelled on the British Election Act of 1770, commonly known as Grenville's Act. It was sponsored by Sir Lucius O'Brien (**1558**), MP for Co. Clare, and Dr Charles Lucas (**1276**), MP for Dublin city. It stated that no petition was to be considered until a fortnight after the commencement of the parliamentary session. A day and an hour to hear the petition were to be appointed and notified to the sitting member(s) and petitioner(s) by the Speaker in writing. These could subsequently be altered by the House.

At the time appointed the serjeant-at-arms was to go with the mace to notify all members in the vicinity and require their immediate attendance. On the serjeant's return the House was to be counted for a quorum of 60, of whom at least 37 had to be eligible to serve on the committee. If these were not present the House was to be adjourned from day to day. When the quorum was present the doors of the House were to be locked and the petitioners or their agents ordered to attend at the bar of the House. The names of the eligible members present (those over 60 years of age could be excused, as could those who had already served on an election committee that session) were to be written on equally sized pieces of paper, similarly rolled or folded, and placed in six glass jars or boxes standing on the table. The clerk or assistant clerk then in public view drew out of the glasses alternately, handing them to the Speaker, who read them to the House, until 37 names had been drawn. Excuses had to be verified on oath and accepted by the House of Commons; excuses depending on illness or accident did not excuse the member from future service. The petitioners or their agents and the sitting member might each add one additional name, these persons could not be struck off the committee, but if they did not wish to serve then additional name(s) would be drawn – these, like the original names, could be struck off. A sitting MP was the man whose name was on the original return, and he was assumed to be the MP, with the right to vote etc., until such time as the House decided that he was not duly elected. Many not-duly-elected MPs sat for months or even years. MPs in this category who were not subsequently returned for other seats are marked ♦♦♦ in the text, and are included in the biographies.

Once these 39 committee members had been chosen, the doors of the Commons could be opened and the petitioners or their agents and the sitting members then withdrew to strike off alternately until the number was reduced to 13 plus the two nominated members. The select committee comprised these 15 members, who 'shall be sworn [in the House] at the table well and truly to try the matter of the petition referred to them, and a true judgment to give according to the evidence'. They were to elect a chairman from among those chosen by lot, and if the committee were equally divided over the choice of chairman, then the member first chosen by the House of Commons would have a casting vote. When they had heard all the evidence the committee was to deliberate in private. Their decision was to be by majority and, if necessary, the chairman had a casting vote. If there were more than two petitioners the same procedure was to be followed in regard to the others. Finally the committee was to report back to the House, which almost invariably agreed to its decision.

The committee had the power to send for papers and examine witnesses. Sundays and seven special holidays excepted, the committee was not to be adjourned for longer than 24 hours unless the House of Commons granted it leave. The chairman was to report those absent without leave, who would be taken into custody by the serjeant-at-arms for neglect of duty 'and otherwise punished or censured at the direction of the House'. If more than two members were absent the committee was to adjourn, and if membership of the committee by death or other permanent absence was reduced to fewer than 13, the committee would be dissolved. However, should the committee resolve otherwise they were to report it to the House for its decision. Any witness who refused to appear, prevaricated or otherwise misbehaved would be reported to the House. One such was Joseph Redford, Esq. of Antrim who 'absented himself, and closed his doors and windows, in order to prevent his being served with a summons for his attendance at the said committee'.[32] Attendance at election committees was exceedingly unpopular. It was also very expensive. In 1777 'several inhabitants of the county of Clare' petitioned the House to make some provision for the expenses of witnesses called to attend the Committee of Privileges and Elections, and on 22 November 1777 the House passed by 51 to 38 a resolution giving an allowance of 4d per mile while they were going to or coming from Dublin and 4s per day while they were in the capital.[33] These expenses were to be paid by the person who summoned the witness, and added considerably to the expense of contesting or defending an election, particularly as there were, in addition, the legal fees for counsel etc. For example, in the controverted election for Antrim borough in 1776 the Skeffington agent expended £756 9s 5d, of which £166 1s 6d was spent in witnesses' expenses.[34]

Although certain irregularities continued, the O'Brien–Lucas Act (0696) did much to sort out the chaos that had often prevailed when decisions had been made by the whole House. Nevertheless, those sitting on these committees were aware that they could find their own elections controverted at some future date, and this had to be borne in mind. Election committees were unpopular, and getting the attendance necessary to put in place the mechanism laid down in the 1771 act, 13 & 14 Geo. III,

[32]Ibid., vol. XVIII p. 360: this was a committee on a controverted election for Antrim Borough in 1776.
[33]Ibid., vol. IX p. 360.
[34]PRONI D562/LIV; see Johnston, *Gt B. & Ire.*, p. 143.

c. 15 *(0747)*, was difficult. An act to amend the 1771 act attempted to remedy this problem. On the day appointed to consider controverted elections, the House was to be called over and the absentees noted by the clerk directed to attend the House at the next sitting when, unless they could offer an acceptable excuse, they, for neglect of duty, would either be taken into custody by the serjeant-at-arms or otherwise censured as the House saw fit. As there had been doubts as to whether the chairman of the select committee appointed to try the petition had a vote except a casting vote, it was declared that he had both an ordinary and a casting vote. The select committee was dissolved when the membership permanently fell to fewer than eleven. When the committee fell to eleven any member absenting himself had to have his excuse verified on oath and accepted by the House of Commons. No member could be added to the original committee chosen by lot; thus the petitioner and the sitting member lost the right each to add a member to the committee. Where a committee had come to a decision, such determination would be entered in the *Journals* and would be the conclusive evidence of the legality or illegality of any such return. No provision had been made for a member of the committee to report to the House in the absence of the chairman. Now the remaining members were to choose one of their number to report his absence to the House, and should he be absent at the next meeting the committee was to elect another chairman in his place.

As the 1776 election approached, further efforts were made to improve electoral procedure by 15 & 16 Geo. III, c. 16 *(0795)*, 'an act for better regulating the elections of members to serve in parliament', which commented on the ongoing problem that 'the idleness and dissipation, caused by the length of time frequently spent in the poll at elections are productive of many evils, and are of dangerous tendence to the freedom of elections'. When the electorate exceeded 400 the Sheriff was to appoint a deputy who would take the poll under him either in the same courthouse or a convenient place nearby. Before the poll was taken the Sheriff and every other returning officer and their deputies had to take an oath in open court that they would 'honestly and impartially without favour to any candidate take the poll at this election' and that they would accept no bribes; for the deputy the phrase was added 'that I will make a fair and true return of the poll to be by me taken to the returning officer ... as often as I shall thereunto be required by him'. The deputy was each day to close his poll book and deliver it immediately to the returning officer, who would then total the votes cast for each candidate that day. The poll was to be adjourned from day to day except from Saturday to Monday. Disturbance or riot would not be an excuse for the returning officer to close the poll; instead he was to adjourn the poll:

> as the occasion may require ... till such disturbances shall have ceased ... [and] every person who shall be convicted of having violently and outrageously disturbed the ... poll or of having wilfully effaced, obliterated, torn, altered or destroyed the whole or any part of the poll book ... or fraudulently taken or secreted the same, or any part

thereof, or the writ or precept for holding such election, he shall be judged guilty of felony and be transported for seven years to one of His Majesty's plantations abroad.

After the writ had been issued, no candidate or his agent was to offer any gift, entertainment etc., and any candidate so doing would be disabled from standing and debarred from parliament as though he had never been elected. Nor was any officer to return more than the number required on the return: this was probably a reaction to the election for 1768, in which John Beresford (**0115**) stood for Co. Waterford, where his brother, Lord Tyrone (**0113**), had 'great real and personal interest'.[35] Beresford had taken the precaution of joining his interest to that of both the opposing candidates, Sir James May (**1383**) and John Congreve (**0455**), with the result that the Sheriff returned his name coupled with those of both May and Congreve. The House of Commons then decided that the majority in the county was for May, and ordered Congreve's name to be erased from the return. Obviously the House was exceedingly annoyed at this method of hedging on the part of the returning officer, as the new act stated that:

> No Sheriff or other returning officer or officers shall upon any pretence whatsoever return more than the number of persons he shall by his writ or precept be required to return; and that in case of an equality of voices for any two or more candidates upon the close of the poll he shall be at liberty to give his casting voice, whether otherwise legally qualified to vote or not at such election.

Furthermore, any returning officer found guilty of returning more than the required members was to be fined £2,000 and to be forever disqualified from voting for any member to serve in parliament.[36] Sheriffs usually belonged to the county they served, and were naturally anxious to keep on good terms with as many of the political factions within it as possible.

Definition of freeholders was taken further by the 1775–6 act *(0795)*. It declared that freeholders with rent-charges of £2 were 'an inlet to corruption and … such freeholders are of no real advantage to the public'. Therefore, an elector whose freehold consisted of rent-charges had to have a rent-charge of £20 regardless of any law to the contrary, and had to take an oath that he had received a year's rent of £20 clear of any charges and that he had not refunded any part of the £20. An elector whose freehold did not consist of rent-charges had to take an oath that he had a freehold consisting of lands or tenements 'of clear annual value of forty shillings', that he had been in possession of it for at least six months prior to the election, and that he did not acquire this in any fraudulent manner, and also that he had not been polled before. These oaths were to replace those prescribed in 21 Geo. II, c. 10 *(0460)*. Freeholders requiring to be registered had to have been registered as prescribed before they were re-eligible. If the freehold, rent-charge etc. came through marriage, presentation to a

---

[35] *Proc. RIA* (1942) p. 216, M. Bodkin (ed.), 'Notes on the Irish Parliament in 1773'.
[36] 15 & 16 Geo. III, c. 16.

benefice, promotion to office, etc. the period for qualification was reduced to six months. If required, the elector had to add to the oath that he was not a Catholic, married to a Catholic nor had he educated any of his children in the Catholic religion, and that he 'verily believed' that he was 21. Should he be a convert he was required to add that since his conformity he had not married a Catholic. The oath was conclusive and the returning officer was not to make any further scrutiny, but false oaths were punishable as perjury. In effect this meant that the freeholder was the judge of the value of his freehold.

By 1781 another election was visible, and the constitutional conflicts leading up to the constitution of 1782 ensured a highly charged political atmosphere. A further attempt to tighten procedures at controverted elections was made in 21 & 22 Geo. III, c. 10 *(0928)*. This act[37] was introduced by John Fitzgibbon (0749), the future Lord Chancellor, who had acted as counsel on a number of these committees. In 21 & 22 Geo. III, c. 21 *(0939)*, an attempt was made to resolve the problem created by the multiplication of freemen in boroughs where freemen were enfranchised. The act declared that it had been found that the existing laws were not sufficiently effective, and that 'the rights of legal voters have been grievously injured and infringed upon: and whereas it has been found by experience that the registering of votes has been highly ineffectual in preventing such illegal and corrupt practices ...' As in preceding statutes, voters were to be registered at the Quarter Sessions of the county where the borough lay and be subject to oath. However greater detail was now required about the place of the voter's abode and the neighbours, who might vouch for him. The voter had to be a Protestant, not married to a Catholic since his conversion and not educating his children as Catholics.

These sworn affadavits were to be alphabetically indexed, and for this the Clerk of the Peace was to receive 6d. On giving 24 hours' notice, registered voters could inspect the books on payment of 1s. Those inspecting the records could not have pen or ink with them, but a copy of the book could be obtained on paying 2d for four full entries or 1d for every ten names in the index. On the last day of the Quarter Sessions the Clerk of the Peace was to give the church wardens of the parish an identical copy of his register. This the church wardens were to preserve unaltered from one Quarter Session to another. Upon receiving a writ for election, the Clerk of the Peace was to deliver his book to the church wardens, who would attend on the returning officer in the court where the poll was to be taken, and any person concerned therein could inspect the poll book. If the Clerk of the Peace was found to have tampered with the book he would be fined £20 for each alteration, 'crazing, tearing out or designedly making the same or any part thereof illegible; or designedly or through neglect suffering any person to do so'. The Clerk of the Peace on receipt of 6d would issue the voter

---

[37] *Commons jn. Ire.* Introduced on 30 Oct. 1781, it received the Royal Assent on 12 Feb. 1782. Fitzgibbon was one of the legal team in the 1777 Co. Roscommon and Co. Mayo elections, and probably for a number of others whose records have not survived.

with a certificate 'signed by the court and counter-signed by himself' which, when proved, would be sufficient evidence of the voter's registration should anything untoward happen to the poll book. Only registered voters of 12 months' standing were eligible to vote. The voter then had to swear a further oath that he was a genuine inhabitant and had not taken up residence for electoral purposes, and if required further swear that he was 21 and not married to a Catholic etc. Any person violating this act would be guilty of wilful and corrupt perjury and would be forever incapable of voting at an election. This act referred to eligible Protestant voters whose vote depended upon residency, and not to eligible Protestant burgesses who were not compelled to live within the borough. Voters for municipal officers were also required to register. This act did not apply to the 1783 election, and in that year the Daly family were reputed to have admitted 295 freemen to Galway Corporation in order to secure their hold over the borough.[38]

Following the 1783 election, in 1783–4, 23 & 24 Geo. III, c. 13 *(0995)*, returned to the old question of 'preventing bribery and corruption in elections for members to serve in parliament'. This act had a despairing sound, as the preamble repeated 3 Geo. III, c. 13 clause 8 *(0602)*, which stated that any person, his family, employee etc. receiving any present or reward for their vote or abstention should forfeit the sum of £500 and be forever disabled from voting at an election as if he were dead. The 1783–4 Act stated that 'whereas the discovery of such secret transaction is often prevented, from an apprehension of subjecting the parties discovering to the penalties and disabilities of the said act', if anyone accused but not yet convicted could within the space of a year discover any other person so offending and ensure his conviction, the original defendant would be given immunity.

In 1785, 25 Geo. III, c. 52 *(1093)*, 'an act for the more effectual registration of freeholders' did for the counties what the 1781–2 statute had done for the towns. It was concerned with the safe custody of the poll book and its availability for inspection on giving due notice at any time and also at elections. Copies were available for a fee: 2d for every four full entries and 1d for every six names in the index. Voters were to be issued with certificates of registration, and there were severe penalties for any county treasurer who tampered with the copy of the poll book delivered to him by the Clerk of the Peace, namely a fine of £100 and dismissal from office, while 'if any person shall steal, secrete or destroy, or maliciously alter or deface the said registry book, or affadavit(s) … required by this act to be kept by the Clerk of the Peace of any county &c. … the person who shall be convicted of having so offended, shall suffer three years imprisonment', and those forging certificates would suffer a year's imprisonment for each offence. In 1786, 26 Geo. III, c. 22 *(1128)*, suspended this act until after January 1791, allegedly because of the large number of unregistered freeholders. Thus the act did not apply to the 1790 election.

[38] *BNL*, 13–16 Jan. 1784.

There is no doubt that in the increased political tempo of the 1780s the question of fictitious freeholders had become notorious, especially as the failure of the parliamentary reform movement in the mid-1780s had emphasised the defects in the representative system. Flood, the persistent leader of the movement for representative reform, declared bitterly in 1785 that:

> It is well known that gentlemen in different counties agree to make freeholders on this condition, 'I will make forty or fifty freeholders in your county if you will make the same in mine, and they shall go to you on condition that yours come to me'. Thus they travel about; and a band of itinerant freeholders dispose the representation of the country; while mock electors are brought from North to South, and from South to North, an army of fictitious freeholders produced as true.[39]

This situation was possible because, as Flood remarked in an earlier debate, 'by the laws now submitting, a 40s freeholder may vote everywhere';[40] the freeholder was not confined by law to the county in which he normally resided and as 'elections carried on from day to day for a very long period'[41] it was practicable as well as legal for a freeholder to vote in more than one county, even when the dates of polling coincided, which was not always the case. This curious anomaly in the county electorates was exacerbated by the shortage of qualified freeholders and the even balance of the electoral interests in many counties. The creation of artificial interest by means of fictitious freeholders increased throughout the century, particularly in its final decade when the landlords' scope was greatly augmented by the enfranchisement of the Catholic freeholders.

The complete subserviency of the fictitious freeholder – the consequence of his real status – to his landlord secured the efficiency of this peculiar system. Fictitious freeholders had the legal possession, in the form of the title deeds and rent-charges, of their freeholds, but not the actual ownership. They were, in fact, the actual tenants of a landlord, who had made them freeholders solely for his political purposes, and the nominal owners of freeholds they had often never seen. The power of his landlord over this type of freeholder was naturally absolute, and Lord Charlemont, one of the most liberal and enlightened Irishmen of his day, has left in his *Memoirs* his considered opinion concerning the duty of a tenant freeholder to his landlord at a county election:

> I will briefly mention my sentiments and conduct respecting my tenantry in election matters. In the general election of 17(83)2[42] I had espoused the interest of Sir Capel Molyneux (1421) against Mr Dawson (0596), merely because the latter had little or no estate in the county, and was a person whose principles were utterly unknown to

---

[39] *Parliamentary Register*, vol. V p. 151.
[40] Ibid., vol. III p. 80.
[41] Ibid., vol. V p. 151.
[42] The election was in fact that of 1776 – not, as the editor supposed, 1783.

me. My tenantry, as had indeed been always the case, gave their votes according to my known inclinations, all except five, who, carried away by the opinion of the day voted for Mr Dawson. A few months after the election one of these came to me to ask a favour; I desired to know of him whether he thought his request grounded upon right, or whether what he asked was in his opinion merely a matter of favour; and upon his replying that it was certainly the latter, I asked him whether he thought himself entitled to any particular degree of favour from me. He answered, with much confusion, that he well knew he was not. 'And now, my friend', said I, 'lest you should imagine that I in any sort resent your behaviour at the late election, what you desire shall be granted; and I am glad of this opportunity of stating to you, and through you to all my tenants, my opinion with regard to the influence a landlord ought to have over the votes of his tenantry. Every freeholder has an absolute right to give his vote as to him shall seem best … He is to act to the best of his judgment, and to vote for that candidate whom he shall think most likely to serve the country. But if he should happen to have a landlord who has in every respect performed his duty towards him and towards the public, and whose … public principles and conduct have uniformly been such as to merit his esteem, the recommendation of that landlord ought to have the greatest weight with him, both because he may be assured that a man of the above mentioned description could never recommend an improper person, and because he ought to suppose that the landlord from his situation in life, and his consequent opportunities of knowing men and characters, is more likely to form a proper judgment of the fitness of a candidate than the tenant possibly can. This is all the influence I shall ever desire, and so much, and no more, I shall always expect; my influence will thus depend upon the good opinion of my tenantry, and when I deservedly lose the one, I ought, most unquestionably to lose the other.' The poor man burst into tears, declared he would give the world to recall the past transaction, and that while he breathed he never more would vote against my wish, and he has been as good as his word.[43]

The vast majority of Irish landowners were by no means so tolerant, though Lord Fitzwilliam allowed his voters to use their *second* vote as they wished. On the other hand, the tenant had some security in the longevity of his lease, which if it was three lives and 31 years could last for a century and could be bought, sold or bequeathed. The tenant usually named the lives: he could name his infant son who could live to be 80, and after his death there was a further 31 years. A lease for lives was dependent on the *last* surviving life, and a lease could be extended by mutual consent, for instance adding lives as those named died. Nevertheless, tenants seldom disobeyed the directions of their landlord.

In 1786, 26 Geo. III, c. 23 *(1129)*, 'an act for amending the several laws relative to the registering of Freeholders', repealed and consolidated the various statutes of the reign of George II that had laid down the policy of registration. Freeholders of a yearly value of £10 but under £100 had to register and to state the barony in which their freehold lay,

---

[43] *HMC Charlemont* I, p. 150.

'and in case of his omitting to do so the registry of his freehold shall be deemed null and void'. Registrations could now be made at an adjourned Quarter Sessions to be held on the first Tuesday of every month if it was not a market day. The usual time allowance, six instead of 12 months, was made for marriage, inheritance, clerical benefices, enfranchised offices, etc. If a freeholder of over £100 p.a. took the oath, he had to declare that he had a freehold of £100 at least. This statute was not to apply to any election before 1 January 1788. In 1788, 28 Geo. III, c. 33 *(1260)*, allowed £10 freeholders not registered before the passing of this act not to be precluded from voting at any election before 25 March 1789, and before that date it was not necessary to insert into the oath £100 in place of £10. In 1789, 29 Geo. III, c. 29 *(1306)*, further extended the period of registration to 25 March 1790, and finally, in 1790, 30 Geo. III, c. 17 *(1336)*, extended the period of non-registration to 25 March 1792. It is difficult not to conclude that MPs preferred the theory of electoral virtue to its practice.

Controverted elections remained a problem, and following the 1790 election, in 1791, 31 Geo. III, c. 36 *(1403)*, 'an act to amend and consolidate the several acts relating to the trials of controverted elections or returns of members to serve in parliament', attempted to consolidate the various statutes of 1771, 1773–4, 1777–8 and 1781–2. All of these were repealed and their substance re-enacted. The rule decreeing the lapse of 14 days for presenting the petition was retained, with the addition that within 14 days following the presentation of the petition the petitioner was to enter into a recognisance of £200, supported by two sureties of £100 each. If this recognisance was not met, the Speaker would inform the House and the petition be dismissed unless the House wished to enlarge the time stated. But until the recognisance was made, the petition could not be heard. This was to prevent 'frivolous and vexatious' petitions, which were a frequent subject of complaint. Should the hearing of the petition be delayed, this recognisance was to be renewed within 14 days every session until the Select Committee to hear it met. A petition could not be withdrawn, except by permission of the House or by the death of one of the parties. If the petitioner, his agent or representative did not appear on the day appointed and if the House had not previously consented to the withdrawal of the petition, the petitioners' recognisances would be forfeited and the Speaker would certify such recognisance to the Court of the Exchequer.

The remainder of the act tightened up the procedures laid down in the 1771 act about the selection of the committee and its conduct. Petitions were to be heard in order, and the adjournment of one had a knock-on effect for the rest. When the names were placed in the glasses they were to be shaken. Those above the age of 60, if they wished, were excused, but if they did not claim this privilege then they had to continue to be available for the session. If there were more than two parties before the House complaining of the election on different grounds, the second petitioner would strike off the names from the same 37 until 15 were reached. The senior member of the committee (the first name out of the glass) was to report in the absence of the chairman, and in reporting its decision to the House the committee was to declare if it found the petition 'frivolous or vexatious'. If the election was shown to be corrupt, the petitioner was to recover costs from the 'sitting' member. Costs and expenses were to be ascertained by the Speaker. Finally, evidence to the select committee was to be given on oath.

The Irish legal system, like the English, depended largely on sworn evidence: 'that great bond of society,' declared R. L. Edgeworth (**0688**), 'which rests on religion'.[44] Edgeworth took his duties as a magistrate seriously, and endeavoured to explain to witnesses the perils of perjury. In addition to perjury, maintenance was not unknown. Another MP, the popular Sir William Richardson (**1788**) of Augher Castle, resorted to trial by combat: sturdy disputants who appealed to him in his magisterial capacity were dispatched to his back yard and told to fight it out.[45] Arthur Young in the 1770s commented on a 'circumstance, which has the effect of screening all sorts of offenders, is men of fortune protecting them, and making an interest for their acquittal, which is attended by a variety of evil consequences'.[46] John Hotham, Bishop of Clogher, writing about the time of Young's visit in the late 1770s declared: 'I believe there is no country in the world where real justice is so seldom done by the determination of a jury.'[47] Undoubtedly it was this system that, reflecting the instability of society, lay behind the repeated injunctions concerning oaths in electoral legislation.

In 1793 the British government, worried about the French Revolution and the imminent outbreak of war, compelled a reluctant Irish parliament to concede the franchise to Catholics otherwise qualified in 33 Geo. III, c. 21 *(1480)*, 'an act for the relief of His Majesty's Popish or Roman Catholic Subjects of Ireland'. This was in line with British policy already adopted regarding Quebec and other predominantly Catholic dependencies acquired as a result of the wars of the century. However, in Ireland the political situation had remained ossified in its late seventeenth-century mould, and although times had changed in the course of the century the majority of the Irish parliament remained frozen in its fear of the numerical strength of the Catholics, and 'ill confiding in the paucity of their numbers, had been long accustomed

---

[44]R. L. Edgeworth, *Memoires of Richard Lovell Edgeworth begun by himself and concluded by his daughter, Maria Edgeworth* (London, 1821), p. 275. Interestingly, perjury was a crime for which only the Irish were transported to New South Wales in the early days of the colony – see L. L. Robson, *The Convict Settlers of Australia* (MUP, 1965), p. 58.

[45]William Carleton, *Life of William Carleton: being his Autobiography and Letters* (1896), p. 42; W. Carleton, *Traits and Stories of the Irish Peasantry* (1843), p. 3. 'The geography of an Irish oath – Would not law and lawyers soon become obsolete, if nothing but truth was *sworn*?' Carleton, like Maria Edgeworth, wrote for an English audience but there is usually a substratum of truth in his comments.

[46]Young, vol. II, p. 154.

[47]*HMC Stopford-Sackville* I, p. 248.

to look up to England for support, and were ever fearful of offending that kingdom, from whose powerful interference, in case of emergency, they hoped for protection.'[48] Henry Dundas, the Home Secretary, who was responsible for Ireland, had little comprehension of the country or its problems. Instead of trying to manage MPs into compliance he frightened them into submission, and the result was an ungracious and botched acquiescence. The real problem was the insecurity that still persisted over the land question and the fear engendered by protestants' numerical inferiority.

Fitzgibbon (0740) reiterated this fear when he reminded the House that:

> the only security by which they hold their property, the only security they have for their present constitution in Church and State, is the connexion of the Irish crown with, and its dependence upon the crown of England.[49]

Four years later, Sir Laurence Parsons (1636), one of the ablest Irish MPs, highlighted Protestant fears when he pointed out during the debate on the Enfranchisement Act *(1480)* that:

> In England the lands are mostly let from year to year … but leases for lives are seldom granted. Consequently the rabble of the people there cannot obtain freehold property … Here the tenures are quite different; almost all the lands of the country are let for lives, so that almost every peasant has a freehold tenure, and, if not disqualified by religion a vote. See then the effect of this upon the present question … You give them all at once the elective franchise, by which they will in nearly every county in three provinces out of four, be the majority of electors, controlling you, overwhelming you, resisting and irrestible … I would not trust so much to any body of men in this country in such circumstances; not to the Protestants to whom I belong; not to the dissenters whom I respect.[50]

Parsons was not averse to enfranchising the Catholic community, considering that 'To give some participation of franchise to the Roman Catholics is no longer a matter of choice, but of most urgent and irresistible policy', but he wished it to be restricted to Catholics of substance. Some MPs thought that the landlords were all-powerful with the small tenants and that they would continue to return the county representatives. Parsons thought that this was short-term thinking and reminded them of the recent Catholic Convention and the part that the Catholic congregations had played in selecting the representatives for that body, pointing out that 'The power of the landlords might do much but the power of religion might do more. How much might these people be wrought upon by their priests … How easily might they be

---

[48] *HMC Charlemont* I, p. 47.
[49] *Parl. Reg.*, vol. IX pp. 128–35, 20 Feb. 1789, esp. pp. 129–31, see *supra* p. 5.
[50] Quoted in Lecky, vol. III, pp. 154–7.

persuaded that their temporal as well as their eternal felicity depended upon their uniting together in the exercise of their franchise.'[51]

Grudgingly and reluctantly, the act, 33 Geo. III, c. 21 *(1480)*, was wrung from the Irish parliament. Some saw it as a prelude to Union and others felt that they had committed political suicide; there was an element of truth in both views. Nevertheless, the 1793 Catholic Enfranchisement Act was the keystone of what has been called the Catholic Revolution: all the remaining restrictions on Catholic ownership of property were removed, while Dublin University and the professions were opened to their children, and only a very few legal positions and the viceroyalty itself were excluded. In order to register his vote a Catholic had to take the oath of loyalty prescribed in 1774. The enfranchisement act was quickly followed by another protecting the rights of the newly enfranchised Catholics: 33 Geo. III, c. 38 *(1497)*, 'an act for giving relief in proceedings upon writs of *mandamus* for the admission of freemen into corporations', ensured that anyone who should be admitted and was refused could recoup his expenses from the official who refused him. Lists of freemen and burgesses were to be made available on the payment of 1s for every 72 words. In 1794, 'an act for ascertaining the fees payable by such Roman Catholics as qualify' laid down that those taking the oath should receive a certificate from the official concerned, to whom they should pay 1s and no more. An officer refusing to administer the oath was subject to a fine of £20.

Two years later the Election Act of 1795, 35 Geo. III, c. 29 *(1570)*, codified and consolidated existing electoral legislation. The 1795 Act was concerned with both the nature of the freeholder's franchise and the conduct of elections. It divided the qualified freeholders into three categories: firstly, the 40-shilling freeholder – this was confined to the resident owner, residence being established by dwelling, tilling or grazing on the freehold; secondly, the freeholder whose property was worth between £20 and £50 – for this type of freeholder residence was not essential, although both the 40-shilling and the 20-pound freeholder were required to have registered within eight years of an election; thirdly, the freeholder of £50 and upwards, who could vote without either residence or registration. Thus, although all freeholders were equal at the polls, they took different oaths at registration: the rent-charge freeholder took the oath that he had £20 p.a. at least, and the freeholders for £2 (who had to be resident), £20 or £50; the £10 householder in the boroughs also had to be resident.

The remainder of the act was concerned with the conduct of elections. Cockades were not to be given to electors, and any voter caught impersonating another was liable to be pilloried on three successive market days and imprisoned for six months in the county jail. Poll books could be inspected as before by those without pen or ink. There were strict penalties for not looking after the poll books or not delivering them as required.

[51]Lecky, vol. III, pp. 155–7. For the Catholic Convention see Dickson, *New Foundations*, p. 177; McDowell, *Ire. in Age of Imp. & Rev.*, pp. 408–9; Bartlett, op. cit., pp. 149–52.

In 1797 further details of the act were spelt out in 37 Geo. III, c. 47 *(1696)*, in particular regarding the oath for the £20 and £50 freeholders. Freeholders were to be registered for a year before an election; exceptions were made in cases where the franchise depended on a marriage or the succession to a benefice. In county boroughs or cities where two sheriffs presided, the senior of the two had the casting vote. If a candidate was under 21 on the day of election, the election was null and void.

The Sheriff's duties were defined. The election was to be held where the last Assize Court was held. Ten to 20 days after he received the writ he was to affix a signed notice on the door of the courthouse of the day for holding the election. He was to inform the officers of the boroughs within the county, who were to do likewise. Elections were not to be adjourned (except for Sunday) or moved to another place without the consent of the candidates. He was to continue the poll until all freeholders had been polled. The poll was to be kept open seven hours a day except with the consent of the candidates. Votes were to be counted each day. The returning officers were to take the usual oaths of impartiality in making the return, and promise that they would not receive bribes or any other favours. Riot was not an excuse for closing the poll, and:

> Every person who shall by due course of law be convicted of having violently, riotously or outrageously disturbed the court, or otherwise misbehaved, so as forcibly to interrupt the proceeding of the poll, or having wilfully effaced, obliterated, torn, altered or destroyed the whole or any part of the poll book … shall be adjudged guilty of felony, and be transported for seven years to some part of His Majesty's dominions out of Europe … or be imprisoned for … not more than seven years at the discretion of the judge or judges.

Only the number required on the writ were to be returned, on a penalty of £2,000. The returning officer was to have a casting vote if necessary. No fees or gratuities were to be taken for making out the writ, otherwise it was void. The Sheriff was to deliver the poll book within 20 days of the election, verified on oath, to the Clerk of the Peace.

A Sheriff expecting a contest was to arrange for polling in each barony; the cost, jointly borne by the candidates, was to be paid to the Sheriff on demand. The official conducting the election in boroughs where more than 200 polled at the last election could on demand provide one polling station for every 100 voters who polled at a former election. Candidates were similarly made jointly responsible for expenses in connection with the erection of these polling booths and the employment of clerks to serve in them, but they were forbidden to pay a fee or reward to a returning officer or to employ counsel for the purpose of challenging any voter's franchise.

The reason for this injunction was probably the vast expense incurred by the candidates in employing legal counsel to look after their interests at the poll. Usually candidates for the county grouped the county interest into two blocks, and in a bitterly

divided county the leading one from each pair might expect to be elected, although
this could indicate a setback for *the* leading interest. This happened to Lord Shannon
in the 1783 election for Co. Cork, and in a more spectacular fashion to Lord Downshire
in 1790. Since they bought the Colvill estate in 1744, the Stewarts had been determined
to establish themselves as one of the leading interests in the county. Both Alexander
Stewart and his son Robert Stewart (**2008**) lost elections, Alexander Stewart was
declared not duly elected for Londonderry city in 1760 and Robert, the sitting MP
for Co. Down in 1783, was none the less defeated by an alliance of the Hills and the
Wards – a defeat that aroused considerable popular indignation.[52] Subsequently the
Stewarts made an alliance with the Wards of Castle Ward, and in 1790 the contest
was resumed. This time Stewart's son, another Robert, barely 21,[53] confronted Lord
Hillsborough (**1016**), the sitting MP and heir of the Marquess of Downshire. The
Belfast News Letter gave a daily account of the progress of the election, including a the
list of counsel supporting the two principal contestants: Counsellors Caldbeck,
Johnston, Downs, Stewart, Dawson, Knox and Sheridan attended for Lord
Hillsborough and Counsellors Chamberlaine, Dunn, Fletcher, Saurin and Hawthorn
for Messrs Ward and Stewart. Lord Hillsborough and Robert Stewart were returned
after a poll lasting 69 days.

   The statute then turned to the candidates. No candidate, his friends or agent were
to give any voter 'any money, meat, drink, or entertainment, or provisions, cockades,
ribbands or any other mark of distinction'. A candidate so doing would be disqualified.
A candidate could employ only one clerk and one agent for each barony or half-
barony, and no candidate for a borough was to employ more than one agent or one
clerk for every 100 voters at the previous election. No agent or clerk was to be paid
more than 5 guineas the first day and 2 guineas thereafter, and the penalty for every
offence against this law was £1,000. Those who created fictitious freeholders 'in a
fraudulent or collusive manner … on purpose or with the intent to qualify him or
them so to give his or their vote or votes' would (each person involved, donor,
conveyencer, etc.) forfeit the sum of £100 to anyone who could successfully convict
them. No voter was to be under the age of 21. Any voter claiming qualification under
a rent charge must have a rent-charge of at least £20, unless he was actually in possession
and living on his freehold at the time of his registration. The act gave a sample of a
poll book ruled in eight vertical columns labelled: (1) Freeholder's name; (2) Place of
abode; (3) Place and nature of freehold; (4) Parish &c. where the freehold is situated;
(5) barony or half-barony where the freehold is situated; (6) Value; (7) Date of registry;
(8) Affidavit or affirmation where and when made. In the course of the election the
clerk was to enter the names in alphabetical order for each barony or half-barony.
There was, of course, no question of a secret ballot in either Great Britain or Ireland
before 1872.

[52] *BNL*, 5–9 Sept. 1783; *HMC Charlemont* I, p. 119.
[53] He was born on 18 June 1769; the election began on 11 April 1790 and ended on 20 July 1790.

This succession of statutes leaves a strong impression that electoral virtue was recognised as desirable, but its achievement interfered with too many vested interests. Once the Irish parliamentarians had accepted the enfranchisement of the Catholics, despite the strict registration laws, they turned to creating Catholic fictitious freeholders. Lord Cloncurry declared that the immediate effect of the act was stimulating 'to an extraordinary degree the progress of corruption'.[54] Shortly after the general election of 1797, a Co. Down landlord, John Auchinlich, wrote to the Marquess of Downshire (in 1790 Lord Hillsborough) that 'It is now in my power to serve you: almost all my tenants were Catholicks I have now made them freeholders and you may rely upon it that everything in my power shall be done to support your interest.'[55] Over thirty years later this wholesale creation of fictitious voters was to turn in the hands of its creators and provide O'Connell with the tool to overturn the system they sought to protect.

In 1798, Gilbert Roycroft of Deansfort, Co. Roscommon, and Richard Tyler Sr, Richard Tyler Jr and Edward Jones, all of Roscommon, were disqualified by name under 38 Geo. III (1773) 'for ever hereafter from voting at any election for any member or members to serve in parliament in this kingdom'. They had incurred the wrath of the select committee appointed to try the controverted election for Co. Roscommon, and through them of the House of Commons, because they:

> did as far as lay within their power, endeavour to obstruct the beneficial effects of the laws for securing the freedom of elections … by contumaciously withstanding every process to compel them to give evidence before the select committee of the House of Commons appointed to try the merits of the late election for the county of Roscommon … and if any sheriff or other returning officer … shall accept at any such election the vote of any of the said persons … such sheriff … shall forfeit the sum of five hundred pounds …

The remainder of the Act was concerned with the conduct of elections for the county of Roscommon.

Shortly before the 1797 election, Dr Alexander Halliday of Belfast wrote to Lord Charlemont in 1796 commenting on: 'the apathy with respect to elections which was pervading these two counties … nothing but the power of the landlords and their agents can goad the people on to register their votes and they trot on sullenly to the courts grunting … like a herd of swine'. The only general election held between Catholic enfranchisement and the Union, that of 1797, was apathetic. It was the last general election of the parliament of Ireland, and it was held against a background of simmering rebellion. Only 18 changes were made in the 64 county seats. Of these, 11 represented the leading interests in their respective counties before 1793, and at least a further four (John La Touche (1205), Co. Kildare; Edmund Alexander Macnaghten

[54]Valentine Lawless, Lord Cloncurry, *Personal Recollections* (1849) p. 35.
[55]PRONI D607/1276, 18 Oct. 1797.

(1320), Co. Antrim; Frederick Falkiner (0718), Co. Dublin; George Jackson (1075), Co. Mayo) had strong personal connections with their counties. The disturbed state of the country was probably partly responsible for this very static return, which, nevertheless, emphasises the immediate futility of Catholic enfranchisement against the entrenched authority of the Anglican ascendancy: an authority whose force had always been apparent before 1793 in the more heavily enfranchised counties of Ulster.

In 1800 an act (which actually came on to the Statute Book before the Act of Union, 40 Geo. III, c. 38 *(1900)*), 40 Geo. III, c. 29 *(1891)*, 'an act to regulate the mode by which the Lords Spiritual and Temporal and the Commons to serve in the United Kingdom on the part of Ireland shall be summoned and returned to the said parliament' defined Irish representation in the new parliament of the United Kingdom. The House of Lords was to be represented by 28 peers chosen for life from among their number. Their actual representation was, of course, rather more than this as a number of Irish peers also had English or British peerages and a further number acquired British peerages at the Union. The archbishops sat in rotation and the bishops were divided into six groups which were to rotate three sitting in each session.[56] The Commons were reduced from 300 to 100. The franchise in all cases remained unchanged, and all the counties returned two MPs as before, but an important feature of the new arrangement was that instead of a preponderance of borough MPs there was now a preponderance of county representatives; these were the most open constituencies but also the most vunerable to the creation of fictitious freeholders. Eleven counties had only county representation: Cavan, Donegal, Kildare, King's County, Leitrim, Longford, Mayo, Meath, Monaghan, Roscommon and Wicklow. The surviving boroughs each returned one member, with the exception of Dublin and Cork cities, which each returned two, and Dublin University lost one member. Co. Cork retained eight MPs out of a former 26; Antrim and Dublin five each, Down, Londonderry, Louth, Tipperary, Waterford and Wexford four each, and Armagh, Carlow, Clare, Fermanagh, Galway, Kerry, Kilkenny, Limerick, Queen's County, Sligo, Tyrone and Westmeath three each. Boroughs were selected on a mixture of population and wealth as estimated by their contribution to the exchequer in Hearth Money and Window Tax, but population differences were considered by allowing 2s for each exempted house (i.e. a house with only one hearth). Wakefield gives the following table for the boroughs that continued to be represented after the Union; it gives an idea of the economy and population of the major towns at this time.

[56]One of the four archbishops to sit in each session: Armagh, Dublin, Cashel (created an English peer at the Union) and Tuam. Three bishops to sit in each session: Session 1, Meath, Kildare, Derry; Session 2, Raphoe, Limerick & Ardfert & Aghadoe, Dromore; Session 3, Elphin, Down & Connor, Waterford & Lismore; Session 4, Leighlin & Ferns, Cloyne, Cork & Ross; Session 5, Killala & Kilfenora, Kilmore, Clogher; Session 6, Ossory, Killala & Anchonry, Clonfert & Kilmacduagh. Once established this rotation was to continue automatically.

II BOROUGHS REPRESENTED AFTER THE UNION[57]

Town	Tax value rank	Population rank
Waterford	1	1
Limerick	2	4
Belfast	3	3
Drogheda	4	2
Newry	5	6
Kilkenny	6	5
Londonderry	7	14
Galway	8	10
Clonmel	9	8
Wexford	10	9
Youghal	11	10
Bandon-Bridge	12	12
Armagh	13	19
Dundalk	14	15
Kinsale	15	16
Lisburn	16	22
Sligo	17	13
Carlow	18	21
Ennis	19	34
Dungarvan	20	7
Downpatrick	21	24
Coleraine	22	20
Mallow	23	27
Athlone	24	25
New Ross	25	17
Tralee	26	23
Cashel	27	18
Dungannon	18	44
Portarlington	29	57
Enniskillen	30	47
Carrickfergus	31	38

[57]Wakefield, vol. II, p. 300; see also Porritt & Porritt, vol. II.

8
OVERVIEW: THE STRUCTURE OF
THE ELECTORATE IN THE
PARLIAMENT OF IRELAND IN THE
LATE EIGHTEENTH CENTURY

The summary of the electorate gives a very generalised view, for all eighteenth-century figures are 'soft' and can only be approximate.

All constituencies returned two members.

All electors had two votes, but could use only one ('plump') if they wished.

In the tables below:

figures after county names show percentages of Catholic households in 1732[1];

square brackets after percentages are estimates of the total population in 1784[2];

figures preceded by c. are guesses at the electorate, extrapolated from the electoral returns;

square brackets after the electorate represent estimates of the county electorate 1800 to 1832 taken from the *History of Parliament 1790–1820* (indicating the effects of the 1793 Catholic Enfranchisement Act);

boroughs disfranchised by the Act of Union are shown in italics.

THE CONSTITUENCIES:

32 counties	64
8 county boroughs	16
109 boroughs	218
Dublin University (TCD)	2
TOTAL	300

The representation system is considered in greater detail in the chapter on Elections and the Electorate.

County boroughs were medieval in origin and they incorporated both county (a defined area around the town/city) and corporation characteristics.

Boroughs: the medieval boroughs, such as Youghal, were enfranchised on very varied terms. In addition there were 12 potwalloping and six manor boroughs, but the majority of the boroughs were corporation boroughs and, although in some the franchise was extended to freemen, the normal pattern was for a mayor (sovereign, portreeve or burgomaster) elected from the burgesses annually and 12 burgesses (making 13 in all and stated as 13 or 12 depending on whether the mayor was counted electorally or as a burgess). The mayor was the returning officer and held a casting vote. By the end of the century this pattern was more theoretical than actual.

CO. ANTRIM 19%, [110,920 + Carrickfergus 3,225]   *c.* 3,500,[3] [*c.* 8,000 (1815)]

CONSTITUENCY	TYPE	PATRON	ELECTORATE
Antrim[4]	Potwalloping	E. of Massereene	250–300
Belfast	Corporation	E. of Donegall	13 burgesses, 5 resident (unchanged 1800–32)
Lisburn	Potwalloping	E. of Hertford	350–400 electors (1808 – *c.* 75)
Randalstown	Potwalloping	John O'Neil	80–200 electors
CARRICKFERGUS	County borough	E. of Donegall (1 seat) Open (1 seat)	900 freemen and freeholders (1812 – *c.* 800)

CO. ARMAGH 33%, [84,000]   *c.* 2,400,[5] [*c.* 6,000 (1815)]

CONSTITUENCY	TYPE	PATRON	ELECTORATE
Armagh	Corporation	Primate	13 burgesses (unchanged 1800–32)
Charlemont	Corporation	E. of Charlemont	13 burgesses

CO. CARLOW 80%, [34,176]   *c.* 550–650,[6] [*c.* 4,000 (1815)]

CONSTITUENCY	TYPE	PATRON	ELECTORATE
Carlow	Corporation	William Burton; sold 2 seats 1795 (£13,000)[7] to Charles Bury (Charleville)	13 burgesses (unchanged 1800–32)
Old Leighlin	Corporation	Bishop of Ferns	13 burgesses

CO. CAVAN 76%, [68,000]   *c.* 1,850,[8] [*c.* 4,000 (1815)]

CONSTITUENCY	TYPE	PATRON	ELECTORATE
Belturbet	Corporation	E. of Lanesborough; sold 1 seat to David La Touche; sold 2 seats *c.* 1783 to E. of Belmore[9]	12 burgesses (very few resident)
Cavan	Corporation[10]	Thomas Nesbitt (1 seat) Robert Clements (1 seat)	13 burgesses

CO. CLARE 93%, [66,000]   *c.* 1,000,[11] [*c.* 7,000 (1801), *c.* 6,000 (1815), *c.* 10,000 (1818)]

CONSTITUENCY	TYPE	PATRON	ELECTORATE
Ennis	Corporation	Sir Lucius O'Brien (1 seat) Pierpont Burton-Conyngham (1 seat)	12 burgesses (unchanged 1800–32)

CO. CORK 89%, [250,000 + Cork city 100,000]   *c.* 3,000,[12] [*c.* 20,500 (1818)]

CONSTITUENCY	TYPE	PATRON	ELECTORATE
Baltimore	Potwalloping	Sir John Freke	23 voted in 1774[13]
Bandon-Bridge	Corporation	Francis Bernard (Bandon)	13 burgesses, 50 freemen 13 burgesses 1800–32
Castlemartyr	Corporation	E. of Shannon	13 burgesses
Charleville	Corporation	E. of Shannon (1) E. of Cork (1)	6 burgesses at present alive[14]
Clonakilty	Corporation	E. of Shannon	Burgesses and freemen: 7 voted (1783)
Cork city 68%	County borough	Open	1200–1500 freemen and freeholders (1,895 in 1818)
Doneraile	Manor	Lord Doneraile	Freeholders of manor
Kinsale	Corporation	Lord de Clifford	Burgesses and freemen resident in Ulster (176 in 1831)
Mallow	Manor	Denham Jephson	Freeholders of manor (524 in 1831)
Midleton	Corporation	Lord Midleton	6 burgesses
Rathcormack	Potwalloping	William Hull (Tonson) (Riversdale)	7 voted in 1783
Youghal	Corporation	E. of Shannon	Burgesses and freemen (263 in 1831)

CO. DONEGAL 43%, [66,720]   *c.* 2,500,[15] [*c.* 6,000 (1815)]

CONSTITUENCY	TYPE	PATRON	ELECTORATE
Ballyshannon	Corporation	Conolly family; sold[16] 2 seats in 1797 to E. of Belmore	13 burgesses, one resident
Donegal	Corporation	E. of Arran	13 burgesses, one resident
Killybegs	Corporation	E. of Conyngham and heirs	13 burgesses, all non-resident
Lifford	Corporation	Lord Erne	13 burgesses, one resident
St Johnstown	Corporation	E. of Abercorn (2 seats) William Forward and heiress – Countess of Wicklow[17] (2 seats)	13 burgesses, all non-resident

CO. DOWN 27%, [135,835][18]   *c.* 6,000,[19] [*c.* 13,000 (1811), *c.* 15,000 (1815)]

CONSTITUENCY	TYPE	PATRON	ELECTORATE
Bangor[20]	Corporation	Sir James Hamilton and heiresses (2 seats) Lord Bangor (1 seat) E. of Carrick (1 seat)	12 burgesses
Downpatrick	Potwalloping	Lord de Clifford	250 electors (393 voted in 1818)
Hillsborough	Corporation	E. of Hillsborough (Downshire)	13 burgesses
Killyleagh	Corporation	Stevenson family (pre-1769) (2 seats) Sir John Blackwood[21] (2 seats)	13 burgesses
Newry[22]	Potwalloping	William Needham (1 seat) Open (1 seat)	600–700 electors (*c.* 500 post-1800)
Newtown(ards)	Corporation	Colvill family (mid-1740s) (2 seats); John Ponsonby[23] (2 seats) – heir exchanged Banagher with Lord Caledon *c.* 1787	13 burgesses

CO. DUBLIN 77%, [56,800 + Dublin city *c.* 300,000]   *c.* 1,200–1,500,[24] [*c.* 2,000 (1815)]

CONSTITUENCY	TYPE	PATRON	ELECTORATE
Dublin city[25] 32%	County borough	Open	3,000–4,000 freemen and freeholders (3,000 in 1806)
Dublin University TCD	Corporation	Provost (2 seats) post-1776 ?Open (2 seats)	70 Scholars and 22 Fellows (unchanged 1800–32)
Newcastle[26]	Corporation	E. of Lanesborough; sold 2 seats 1776–9 (£7,000–8,000) to David La Touche	12 burgesses
Swords[27]	Potwalloping	Open	160 electors

CO. FERMANAGH 42%, [30,000]   *c.* 3,000,[28] [*c.* 7,000 (1815)]

CONSTITUENCY	TYPE	PATRON	ELECTORATE
Enniskillen	Corporation	E. of Enniskillen	12–14 burgesses (unchanged 1800–32)

CO. GALWAY 95%, [166,249 + Galway town 12,600]   *c.* 700, [*c.* 13,000 (1815)]

CONSTITUENCY	TYPE	PATRON	ELECTORATE
Athenry	Corporation	John Blakeney	13 burgesses and 2 freemen
Galway	County borough	Denis Daly (1 seat) Denis Bowes Daly (1 seat)	569 freemen and freeholders (including 295 admitted in 1783)[29] (560 in 1812); 847 voted in 1818
Tuam	Corporation	Bingham family[30] (Clanmorris)	13 burgesses

CO. KERRY 92%, [75,000]   *c.* 1,000, [*c.* 5,000 (1815)]

CONSTITUENCY	TYPE	PATRON	ELECTORATE
Ardfert	Corporation	E. of Glandore	12 burgesses and 6 freemen
Dingle	Corporation	Maurice FitzGerald heirs – Townshend family	150 freemen, 2 resident
Tralee	Corporation	Sir Barry Denny	13 burgesses (unchanged 1800–32)

CO. KILDARE 92%, [49,968]   [?]*c.* 300–1,500,[31] [*c.* 2,000 (1815)]

CONSTITUENCY	TYPE	PATRON	ELECTORATE
Athy	Corporation	Duke of Leinster	'A few' burgesses and freemen
Harristown	Corporation	Duke of Leinster; sold 2 seats 1793 (£14,000–16,000) to John La Touche	13 burgesses – uninhabited
Kildare	Corporation	Duke of Leinster	13 burgesses plus 'a few' freemen
Naas	Corporation	John Bourke (E. of Mayo)	'A few' burgesses and freemen

CO. KILKENNY 91%, [86,574 + Kilkenny city 13,865]   *c.* 1,050,[32] [2,300 (1815)]

CONSTITUENCY	TYPE	PATRON	ELECTORATE
Callan	Corporation	James Agar (Callan)	Freemen
Gowran	Corporation	James Agar and heir (Clifden)	*c.* 13 burgesses
Innistiogue	Corporation	Col. Ponsonby (1692) [33] (2 seats); Sir William Fownes and heirs (2 seats)	13 burgesses
Kilkenny city[34]	County borough	Duke of Ormonde (1692–1715) Sir Haydock Morres (1 seat) Sir John Blunden (1 seat) From 1783, Cuffe and Butler families (2 seats)	1,400–1,800 freemen and freeholders (865 in 1831)
Knocktopher	Potwalloping	Sir Hercules Langrishe (1 seat) John Ponsonby (1 seat) After 1783, Langrishe (2 seats)	Potwallopers and freemen 1 elector in 1783–4
St Canice or Irishtown	Corporation	Bishop of Ossory	13 burgesses and freemen
Thomastown	Corporation	James Agar (Clifden)	[?]13 Burgesses

KING'S COUNTY 84%, [48,000]   *c.* 900–1,500,[35] [*c.* 3,000 (1815)]

CONSTITUENCY	TYPE	PATRON	ELECTORATE
Banagher[36]	Corporation	Misses Plunket (2 seats); sold (2 seats) to Peter Holmes; sold (2 seats) 1787 (£10,500) to James Alexander; exchanged (2 seats) for Newtown(ards) 1788 with G. Ponsonby	13 burgesses and 'a few freemen'
Philipstown[37]	Corporation	E. of Belvidere	13 burgesses and 'a few freemen'

CO. LEITRIM 85%, [35,280]   *c.* 1,076,[38] [*c.* 7,000 (1815)]

CONSTITUENCY	TYPE	PATRON	ELECTORATE
Carrick	Corporation	Nathaniel Clements (E. of Leitrim)	13 burgesses, all non-resident[39]
Jamestown	Corporation	King family	13 burgesses, one resident

CO. LIMERICK 88%, [120,000 + 40,000 Limerick city]   *c.* 1,500,[40] [*c.* 1,500 (1815)]

CONSTITUENCY	TYPE	PATRON	ELECTORATE
Askeaton	Corporation	Edward Taylor[41] – heirs E. of Carrick (1 seat); Hugh Massy (1 seat)	13 burgesses
Kilmallock	Corporation	Silver Oliver	13 burgesses
Limerick	County borough	Smyth and Pery families	800 freemen and freeholders (*c.* 1,000 in 1818)

CO. LONDONDERRY 24%, [99,000]   [?]*c.* 2,252–2,432,[42] [*c.* 8,500 (1815)]

CONSTITUENCY	TYPE	PATRON	ELECTORATE
Coleraine	Corporation	Richard Jackson (1 seat), died 1789; E. of Tyrone (1 seat), sold *c.* 1793 (£7,000) to E. of Tyrone (M. of Waterford) (2 seats – bought from Richard Jackson's heir)	Mayor, 12 aldermen and 24 non-resident burgesses (52 in 1831)
Limavady	Corporation	E. of Conyngham and heir, Thomas Conolly; sold[43] 1792 to Lord Londonderry	13 burgesses
Londonderry	Corporation	Open	700–750 freemen electors (*c.* 1,000 in 1812)

CO. LONGFORD 82%, [40,000]   *c.* 700,[44] [*c.* 3,100 (1813)]

CONSTITUENCY	TYPE	PATRON	ELECTORATE
Granard	Manor	Mrs Macartney and heirs	Freeholders
Lanesborough	Corporation	Robert Dillon (of Clonbrock)	Burgesses and freemen (very few)
Longford	Corporation	E. of Longford	Burgesses and freemen (very few)
St Johnstown	Corporation	E. of Granard	Burgesses, all non-resident

CO. LOUTH 85%, [46,446]   [?]*c.* 400,[45] [*c.* 600 (1815)]

CONSTITUENCY	TYPE	PATRON	ELECTORATE
Ardee	Corporation	John Ruxton and heirs	24 burgesses and 80 freemen
Carlingford	Corporation	Ross Moore (1 seat); Col. Robert Ross (1 seat), sold *c.* 1790s to M. of Downshire	13 burgesses and 'some' freemen
Drogheda	County borough	Francis Leigh (?1 seat) Open (1 seat)	500 freemen and freeholders (650 in 1815)
Dundalk[46]	Corporation	E. of Clanbrassill 1798 Countess of Roden	16 burgesses and 700 freemen (*c.* 30 post-1800)
Dunleer[47]	Corporation	Lord Dartmouth until 1698 Tenison family until 1735 Foster family (1 seat) Dixie Coddington (1779 1 seat)	13 burgesses and 30 freemen

CO. MAYO 94%, [120,084]   *c.* 1,000,[48] [*c.* 12,000 (1802), *c.* 11,000 (1814)]

CONSTITUENCY	TYPE	PATRON	ELECTORATE
Castlebar	Corporation	Sir Charles Bingham (E. of Lucan)	13 burgesses, all non-resident

CO. MEATH 90%, [94,600]   *c.* 1,200,[49] [*c.* 4,300 (1815)]

CONSTITUENCY	TYPE	PATRON	ELECTORATE
Athboy	Manor	E. of Darnley	30 freeholders (1783)
Duleek	Corporation	Abel Ram; sold 2 seats *c.* 1789 (£10,000) to Henry Bruen[50]	13 burgesses (probably fewer)
Kells	Corporation	E. of Bective (M. of Headfort)	A few freemen and burgesses
Navan	Corporation	E. of Ludlow (1 seat) John Preston (Lord Tara) (1 seat)	13 burgesses and 60–70 freemen; only 9 voted in 1783
Ratoath	Manor	Gorges Lowther (2)	Freeholders
Trim	Corporation	E. of Mornington (Wellesley)	13 burgesses and 300 freemen

CO. MONAGHAN 64%, [99,225]   [?]*c.* 1,500,[51] [*c.* 3,500 (1807)]

CONSTITUENCY	TYPE	PATRON	ELECTORATE
Monaghan	Corporation	Sir Alexander Cairnes and heirs; E. of Clermont (1 seat) and heirs; Lady Blayney (1 seat) and heirs	13 burgesses, all non-resident

QUEEN'S COUNTY 84%, [70,000]   *c.* 1,400,[52] [*c.* 6,500 (1815), 4,037 polled (1818)]

CONSTITUENCY	TYPE	PATRON	ELECTORATE
Ballynakill	Corporation	E. of Drogheda	12 burgesses, 2 resident
Maryborough[53]	Corporation	Sir John Parnell (1 seat) Dean Coote (1 seat)	Mayor, 2 bailiffs, 12 burgesses and *c.* 350 freemen
Portarlington	Corporation	Lord Carlow (E. of Portarlington)	13 burgesses and 50 freemen[54] (12 in 1815, 15 in 1831)

CO. ROSCOMMON 90%, [40,000]   [?]*c.* 1,500–1,600,[55] [*c.* 6,000 (1815)]

CONSTITUENCY	TYPE	PATRON	ELECTORATE
Boyle	Corporation	E. of Kingston	13 burgesses, mostly non-resident
Roscommon	Corporation	Henry Sandford (Mt Sandford)	13 burgesses
Tulsk	Corporation	Sir George Caulfeild and heirs	13 burgesses, all non-resident

CO. SLIGO 81%, [36,900]   *c.* 1,000,[56] [*c.* 2,000 (1815)]

CONSTITUENCY	TYPE	PATRON	ELECTORATE
Sligo	Corporation	Owen Wynne	13 burgesses (unaltered 1800–32)

CO. TIPPERARY 91%, [119,706]   *c.* 1,500,[57] [*c.* 18,000 (post-1800)]

CONSTITUENCY	TYPE	PATRON	ELECTORATE
Cashel	Corporation	Richard Pennefather	Mayor, 17 aldermen and 70–80 freemen (25 in 1829)
Clonmel	Corporation	Moore family (Mountcashell)[58]	Mayor, 19 burgesses and 72 freemen (*c.* 90 post-1800)
Fethard	Corporation	Cornelius O'Callaghan (Lismore) (1 seat) Mr William Barton (1 seat)	13 burgesses and 900 freemen[59]

CO. TYRONE 52%, [112,612]   *c.* 3,500 [20,000 (post-1800), 10,000 (1812)]

CONSTITUENCY	TYPE	PATRON	ELECTORATE
Augher	Corporation	Sir Archibald Erskine and heirs; James Moutray (1 seat) William Richardson (1 seat)[60] M. of Abercorn purchased 2 seats 1790 (£11,500)	13 burgesses
Clogher	Corporation	Bishop of Clogher[61] (2)	13 burgesses, clergy
Dungannon	Corporation	Thomas Knox (Ld. Welles) (2)	13 burgesses (unaltered 1800–32)
Strabane	Corporation	E. of Abercorn[62]	13 burgesses

CO. WATERFORD 93%, [52,000 + Waterford city 40,000]   *c.* 700,[63] [*c.* 3,300 (1815)]

CONSTITUENCY	TYPE	PATRON	ELECTORATE
Dungarvan[64]	[?]Potwalloping	D. of Devonshire (1 seat) [65] E. of Tyrone and others (1 seat)	120 freeholders and householders
Lismore	[?]Manor	D. of Devonshire	Freeholders and householders
Tallow	[?]Potwalloping	D. of Devonshire	Resident householders (96 in 1783)
Waterford city[66]	County borough	Alcock, Bolton, Carew and Christmas families	Resident freemen and freeholders (*c.* 1,000 post-1800)

CO. WESTMEATH 86%, [70,350]   *c.* 1,120,[67] 2,700(1806), [*c.* 3,000 (1815)]

CONSTITUENCY	TYPE	PATRON	ELECTORATE
Athlone[68]	Corporation	Sir Richard St George (1 seat) Dean Handcock (1 seat)	Burgesses and 400–500 freemen (71 in 1832)
Fore	Corporation	E. of Westmeath	13 burgesses
Kilbeggan	Corporation	Charles Lambart	13 burgesses
Mullingar[69]	Manor	E. of Granard	Freeholders (12 voted in 1783)

CO. WEXFORD 83%, [77,628]   [?]c. 2,500,[70] [c. 7,500 (1818)]

CONSTITUENCY	TYPE	PATRON	ELECTORATE
Bannow	Corporation	E. (M.) of Ely	13 burgesses, 1 resident*
Clonmines	Corporation	E. (M.) of Ely	13 burgesses, 1 resident*
Enniscorthy	Corporation	Sir Vesey Colclough	13 burgesses, 1 resident
Fethard	Corporation	E. (M.) of Ely	13 burgesses, 1 resident*
Gorey	Corporation	Abel Ram	13 burgesses
New Ross	Corporation	Charles Tottenham (1 seat) Robert Leigh (1 seat)	13 burgesses and freemen (38 in 1831)
Taghmon[71]	Corporation	Hore family; sold *ante* 1795 to Henry Bruen	13 Burgesses + 20 Freemen
Wexford[72]	Corporation	Richard Nevill (1 seat) Richard Le Hunt (1 seat)	Mayor, 2 bailiffs, 24 burgesses and 600–800 freemen (*c.* 150 post-1800)

* Bannow, Clonmines and Fethard shared the same 13 burgesses.

CO. WICKLOW 67%, [56,532]   c. 900,[73] [c. 3,000 (1803), c. 1,500 (1815)]

CONSTITUENCY	TYPE	PATRON	ELECTORATE
Baltinglass	Corporation	E. of Aldborough	12 burgesses plus 20 freemen
Blessington	Corporation	Charles Dunbar and heirs (Hillsborough/ M. of Downshire)	12 burgesses plus 6 freemen
Carysfort	Corporation	V. Allen[74] and heir Lord Carysfort	13 burgesses, all non-resident
Wicklow	Corporation	William Tighe	13 burgesses

CONTROL OF BOROUGH REPRESENTATION *c.* 1783

Individuals controlling the return of more than two MPs	Individuals controlling the return of two MPs	Individuals controlling the return of one MP	Seats that were open or not controlled by a single interest
4 bishops (on behalf of government): 8 MPs 11 peers: 51 MPs 3 commoners: 11 MPs	25 peers: 50 MPs 33 commoners: 66 MPs	6 peers: 6 MPs [?]26–31 commoners: 26–31 MPs	13

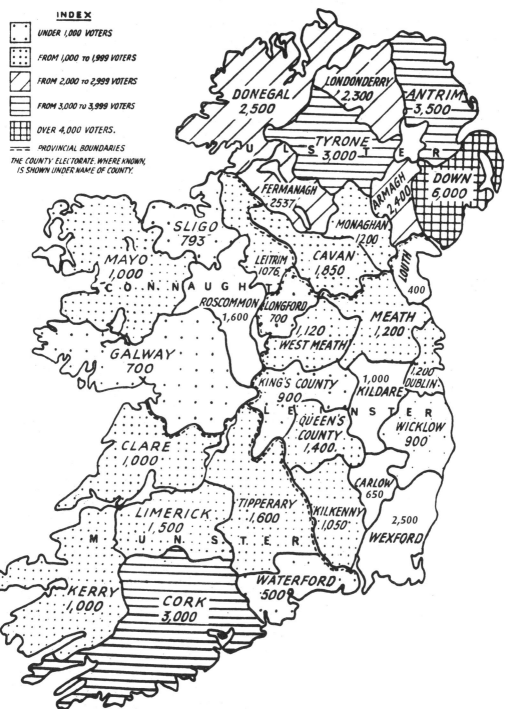

Map illustrating the electorate prior to 1793

Based on a map in Edith Mary Johnston, *Great Britain and Ireland 1760–1800*

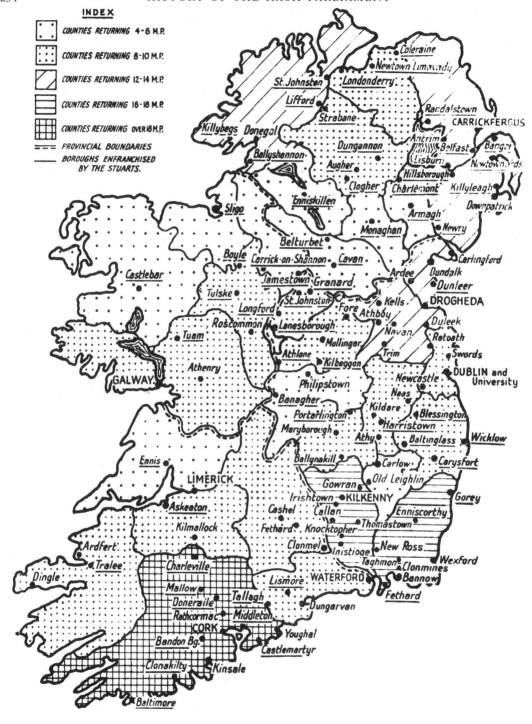

Map illustrating the representation prior to 1800

Courtesy of Edith Mary Johnston, *Great Britain and Ireland 1760–1800*

NOTES

[1] S. J. Connolly, *Religion, Law and Power* (Oxford, 1992), p. 146: Ulster 38%, Leinster 79%, Munster 89%, Connacht 91% – Ireland 73%. The percentages probably remained fairly constant throughout the century.

[2] This estimates the population of Ireland in 1784 as 3,047,085. It is almost certainly an underestimate, although the Hearth Money returns for 1785 suggest 2,845,932 – the returns for 1791 estimate 4,206,612! Gervase Parker Bushe, a Commissioner of the Revenue, thought that in 1788 the population was *c.* 4,040,000. For the most recent estimates see *Proc. RIA*, vol. 82 C6, D. Dickson, C. Ó Gráda and S. Daultry, 'Hearth tax, household size and population change 1671–1821'; also *Jn. Econ. Hist.*, vol. XLI (1981), Daultry, Dickson and Ó Gráda, pp.601–28, esp. 602 n. 3, 'Eighteenth-century Irish population: New perspectives from old sources'. They estimate the population at *c.* 5,250,000 in 1800. After the famine of the early 1740s reduced the population to *c.* 2,100,000 it rose rapidly, with only small checks until the great famine of the 1840s.

[3] *BNL*, 13–16 Jan. 1784, but the actual numbers of votes cast in earlier elections suggest either a smaller electorate or a degree of 'plumping' (i.e. voting for one instead of two candidates). 2,079 votes were cast in 1761 – H. (Seymour-)Conway 663, H. Skeffington 659, J. O'Neill 406, C. O'Hara 351. The 1768 election was uncontested. 4,626 votes were cast in 1776 – H. (Seymour-)Conway 1,246, James Willson 1,234, H. Skeffington 1,125, M. Dalway 1,021. The 1783 election was uncontested. In 1790, 7,013 votes were cast from a gross poll of 3,507 – J. O'Neill 1,939, H. Rowley 1,867, J. Leslie 1,708, E. Macnaghten 1,499. The by-elections following the elevation of O'Neill to the peerage in 1793 and the death of Hugh Boyd in 1795 were uncontested, and 4,483 votes were cast in the 1797 general election – J. Staples 1,984, E. Macnaghten 1,518 and J. Agnew 981.

[4] See *IHS*, vol. XVII no.65 (1970), A. P. W. Malcomson, 'Election politics in the borough of Antrim'. In the 1776, 1783 and 1790 elections the Skeffingtons were challenged by a local and independent influence led by Skeffington Thompson, possibly a local leaseholder and linen draper, but they retained their authority, despite his petitions against the return of their candidates. The vunerability of the constituency was heightened by the absence of Lord Massereene, whose disinterest was acknowledged by the equal division of the compensation for the disfranchisement of the borough at the Union between him and his three brothers.

[5] *BNL*, 23 Mar. 1753: this by-election following the death of Robert Cope at the height of the Money Bill dispute was among the most significant of the century. Lord Charlemont's brother narrowly lost to William Brownlow, the Primate's nominee. 2,123 votes were cast in 1783: William Brownlow 1,010, Thomas Dawson 567, Mr Richardson 546 (*BNL*, 3 Sept. 1783, 16 Jan. 1784). *ibid.* In the 1790 election the total was 2,259: Brownlow and Richardson each polled 820 votes and Mr Moore 619

(*BNL*, 6 May 1790, see also 11–14 May 1790).

[6] See 'Carlow MPs'. Despite its small electorate this constituency was frequently contested: 1,001 votes were cast in the 1776 election (William Burton 417, William Bunbury 351, William Warren 246); 1,196 in 1783 (W. Burton 508, Sir Richard Butler 351, John Rochfort 337 (Rochfort's total included 107 single (plumped) votes); 3,999 in 1797 (following Catholic enfranchisement) (William Burton 1,072, Sir R. Butler 1,069, Sir Philip Newtown 936, Walter Kavanagh 922).

[7] PRONI T2541/IA5/1/16: the asking price may have been as high as £16,000; see also *HP* [1790–1820], vol. 2, p. 360.

[8] *BNL*, 13–16 Jan. 1784, 23 May 1761. 1761 election (total votes cast, 2,238): Lord Newtown Butler 612, Charles Coote 600, George Montgomery 549, Barry Maxwell 477. 1768 election (total votes cast, 2,347): Barry Maxwell 926, George Montgomery 739, Mr Pratt 687, Col. Newburgh 451 (*BNL*, 12 Aug. 1768).

[9] *BNL*, 13–16 Jan. 1784. This borough was twice sold by the Lanesborough family: firstly to David La Touche for £11,000; when it came back to the Lanesborough family, as part of the dowry of Elizabeth La Touche, Countess of Lanesborough, it was subsequently sold to Armar Lowry-Corry, 1st Earl of Belmore.

[10] *Rep. Municipal Corporations (Ireland)*, app. II, p. 990. In 1733 the Commissioners found that this borough had been divided in 1722 by written agreement between the Clements and Nesbitt families, who duly shared its compensation when it was disfranchised in 1800.

[11] This was often a bitterly divided county both before and after the Union: see *HP* [1790–1820], vol. 2, pp. 632–4; *DJ*, 22–26 July 1768. In the 1768 election a total of 1,052 *accepted* votes were cast for three candidates: F. P. Burton 413 (+ rejected 24), Sir Lucius O'Brien 361 (+ rejected 32), M. O'Brien 278 (+ rejected 17). *DJ*, 25–28 May 1776: in the 1776 election, 716 votes had been cast on 20 May and the poll stood thus: Edward FitzGerald 249, Sir Lucius O'Brien 194, Hugh Dillon Massy 183, Nicholas Westby 90. Westby then dropped out, and the final poll on 25 May gave a total of 1,328 votes – Edward FitzGerald 601, Hugh Dillon Massy 365 and Sir Lucius O'Brien 362. O'Brien successfully petitioned against the return of Massy. In 1783 Sir Lucius O'Brien was defeated and, having sold his seat for Ennis, had to purchase one for Tuam.

[12] Given its size and importance, the relatively few contested elections for Co. Cork indicate the arrangement of the interests therein. The most spectacular election contest was that of 1783, when the poll lasted 36 days.

[13] *BNL*, 13–16 Jan. 1784 says that only 11 voted in 1783, but *The Volunteer Journal or Independent Gazetteer*, 11 Aug. 1783, reported that 66 votes were cast for the four candidates.

[14] *BNL*, 13–16 Jan. 1784 declares that there were only 5 'in being'. The patron was originally the Earl of Cork but he was thought to have sold the patronage to Lord Shannon. The borough originally belonged to Lord Cork, but Lord Shannon 'managed' it and at the Union they divided the

compensation between them; see *Proceedings of Union Compensation Commissioners – Boroughs*, p. 25.

[15] *DJ*, 13–18 June 1776. In the 1776 election the gross poll was 1,980 and the votes cast 3,543: Robert Clements 1,124, Alexander Montgomery 882, John Hamilton 828, John McCausland 395, John Cowan 314.

[16] The amount of this sale is unknown.

[17] This borough originally belonged to the Earls of Abercorn but through a corporation *coup* early in the century they lost it to a neighbouring landowner, William Forward-Howard of Castle Forward, and his daughter and heiress became Countess of Wicklow. Despite their anxiety to do so, the Abercorns could never recover it. The Abercorns had vast estates in Counties Tyrone and Donegal but they also had large property in Great Britain, and although their correspondence reveals them as careful landlords their absenteeism made them vulnerable to this type of *coup*.

[18] *BNL*, 13–16 Jan. 1784. This calculation was based on 27,367 houses allowing five per house. It was thought that the electorate would shortly increase 'very considerably'.

[19] The 1790 election for this county, fought out between the Hill (Downshire) and Stewart (Londonderry) families, was possibly the most famous during this period – it lasted 36 days.

[20] Judge Michael Ward and 6th Viscount Ikerrin (died 1719) married coheiresses of James Hamilton of Bangor. The Ward family later became Lords Bangor and the Butlers (Lords Ikerrin) Earls of Carrick, hence the division of the borough.

[21] Sir John Blackwood m. (1751) Dorcas (cr. Baroness Dufferin), daughter and heir of James Stevenson (died 1769) of Killyleagh; the borough was part of her inheritance.

[22] *DJ*, 18–21 May 1776 – a comparatively large and relatively open constituency, its elections tended to be hard fought. In 1776, 1,729 votes were cast: Isaac Corry 480, Robert Ross 448, Sir Richard Johnston 419 and Mr Benson 382. The last two were convinced that they had polled a majority of legal votes. Ross d. 1799 and Corry and John Moore were returned until 1800.

[23] Until 1744 this borough belonged to the Colvill family, but when the estate was sold to Alexander Stewart in 1744 he refused to pay an addition for the borough, which was then acquired by Robert Colvill's half-brother, John Ponsonby. The transfer of this borough was the background to the Newtown Act, 21 Geo. II, c. 10.

[24] *HP* [1790–1820], vol. 2, p. 648. Dublin was one of the smallest counties in Ireland, but it was proximate to the capital and had a substantial number of well-to-do residents. Professor Jupp estimates its electorate at 800–900 in 1800: I think that this may be on the low side; in the general elections of 1768, 1776 and 1790, 1,679 (840), 1,769 (885) and 2,321 (1,161) votes were cast: allowing for plumpers, absentees, etc., the electorate was probably nearer 1,500.

[25] Elections for Dublin city were nearly always scenes of riot and excitement. In 1761, 4,831 votes were cast: Ald.

Hunt 673, James Grattan 1,569, Sir Charles Burton 1,210, Charles Lucas 1,302, J. La Touche 77 (*DJ*, 5–9 May 1761). *ibid*. 28 Nov.–1 Dec. 1767. At the by-election in 1767 following the death of James Grattan, 3,277 votes were cast: 1,708 for the Marquess of Kildare and 1,569 for John La Touche; in 1768 the Marquess and Dr Lucas were returned uncontested (*DJ*, 23–6 July 1768). In 1782, following the death of Dr Clement, 2,670 votes were cast – 1,472 for Travers Hartley and 1,202 for Alderman Warren (*DJ*, 26–28 Feb. 1782).

[26] *IHS*, XVIII (1973), A. P.W. Malcomson, 'The Newtown Act of 1748: Revision and reconstruction', p. 340. *BNL*, 13–16 Jan. 1784, says John La Touche, but it was the memorial of David La Touche and the will of the late David La Touche that were submitted to the Union Compensation Commissioners: see *Proceedings of Union Compensation Commissioners – Boroughs*, p. 12, 23 Oct. 1800.

[27] Though considered open, this was the most notoriously corrupt borough in the Irish parliament. In the 1761 election Col. Thomas Cobbe and Hamilton Gorges each polled 56 votes and John Hatch and Adams Williams each polled 35, making a total of 182 (*DJ*, 21–25 Apr. 1761). In 1776 John Hatch polled 83, Charles King 83, John Hatch 76 and Stephen Popham 73 – total 315 votes (*BNL*, 18–21 May 1776).

[28] 2,498 votes were cast for three candidates (*DJ*, 18–20 June 1776); *BNL*, 13–16 Jan. 1784, states that there was a poll of 2,537 in 1783; *FJ*, 6 Aug. 1797 gives 1,931 votes cast for four candidates.

[29] *BNL*, 13–16 Jan. 1784 – the influence of the two Dalys had recently, probably because of the new electors, become such as to give them patronage over this town, which was otherwise independent.

[30] The Bingham family had two branches: the Binghams of Castlebar, Earls of Lucan and the Binghams of Newbrook, Barons Clanmorris. In 1797 Walter Yelverton, the son of Chief Baron Yelverton, had purchased a seat from Lord Clanmorris and he was awarded £1,000 of the £15,000 compensation for the borough; the rest went to Lord Clanmorris.

[31] Co. Kildare was under the influence of the Duke of Leinster; and there do not appear to have been many contested elections. In 1776, 1,062 votes were cast: the Duke of Leinster's brother, Lord Charles FitzGerald (393) and the Duke's protégé, Arthur Pomeroy (332) were returned; the unsuccessful candidates were Sir Kildare Dixon Burrows (225) and Thomas Whelan (112). See *DJ*, 25–28 May 1776.

[32] *BNL*, 13–16 January 1784. In 1768 1,576 votes were cast. All the leading interests were represented – Ponsonby 494, Agar 438, Butler 331, Flood 313 (*DJ*, 19–21 July 1768). In 1776, 833 votes were cast – Ponsonby 300, Butler 285, Flood 248.

[33] *Analecta Hibernica*, Longford to Ellis, Dublin, 10 Oct. 1692: 'Col. Ponsonby who had so overuling an interest in Innistiogue, that he could dispose of the elections in that borough as he pleased.'

[34] Originally the stronghold of the Butler family, Dukes of Ormonde – the town is dominated by their imposing castle. After the 2nd Duke was attainted in 1715 the Palatinate of Tipperary was abolished but his brother was allowed to purchase his estates. In 1766 these passed to another branch of the family, who about 1783 resumed what remained of the family's political influence; the earldom of Ormonde was revived in 1791.

[35] *BNL*, 16–20 Jan. 1784, states that there were 900 electors. Certainly the poll appears to have been very small: see *BNL*, 15 Nov. 1757; Sir William Parsons and Simon Digby each polled 232 votes. In 1761 there were three candidates who polled 1,346 votes between them: Sir William Parsons 522, Henry Lyons 441 and Henry L'Estrange 383 (see *DJ*, 19–23 May 1761. There were, however, a number of interests, as five candidates stood for the 1768 election when Sir William Parsons and John Lloyd were returned. In 1776 2,158 votes were cast, which suggests an electorate of *c.* 1,500.

[36] BL Add. MSS 19,829 Banagher Borough Book 1693–1748, lists 13 burgesses and freemen but it is difficult to ascertain the number of the latter as the list continues over half a century and only notes deaths. The burgesses (quorum five) had the right to nominate three of their number for the office of sovereign and the common council (which also comprised the freemen) then nominated one. In 1788 Alexander exchanged this borough for Newtown(ards) with W. B. Ponsonby.

[37] See *HMC Molesworth*, pp. 217, 227, 237, 247, 412; in the late seventeenth and the early eighteenth century this borough belonged to Robert, Viscount Molesworth. Compensation for its disfranchisement at the Union was paid in accordance with trusts (established in favour of his son, daughter and grandson) under the will of the late Robert, Earl of Belvidere, to whom the borough belonged in the latter part of the eighteenth century.

[38] *BNL*, 16–20 Jan. 1784.

[39] *Ibid.* The charter allowed for freemen but by 1784 none were extant.

[40] *Ibid.*; also *BNL*, 14–18 June 1776: 1,783 votes were cast for three candidates, Silver Oliver (880), Sir Henry Hartstonge (530), Hugh Massy Jr (373).

[41] Edward Taylor of Askeaton and Ballynort, Co. Limerick left 2 daughters: coheiress Catherine married (1760) Hugh, 2nd Baron Massy; Sarah married (1774) Henry Thomas, 2nd E. of Carrick, hence the division of the borough.

[42] *BNL*, 7–11 June 1776. 3,341 votes were cast in 1776: Thos. Conolly 1,488, Edward Cary 1,009, Mr Richardson 837, Mr Leckey 7.

[43] The price of this sale is unknown.

[44] *BNL*, 16–20 January 1784. In the 1768 election 1,183 votes were cast: Col. Gore 401, Robert Pakenham 283, Sir James Nugent 281, Sir Thomas Newcomen [?]218 (*DJ*, 2–4 Aug. 1768).

[45] I have not been able to ascertain figures for this county but the electorate was probably very small, as its post-1800 electorate indicates. In the 1767 by-election 639 votes were

cast: 312 £10 householders and 327 40-shilling freeholders. See Malcomson, *Foster*, pp. 293–4, 308. From 1785 it was the Speaker's constituency.

[46] See *Louth Arch. Soc. Jn.*, vol. XVII no.1 (1969), A. P. W. Malcomson, 'The struggle for control of Dundalk borough, 1782–92'. The Hamiltons, later Viscounts Limerick (1719) and Earls of Clanbrassill (1756), purchased the surrounding estate in 1699 and in 1798 it passed to their heiress Anne, Countess of Roden. In the beginning their control of the borough was unclear, as in 1707 there was a hard-fought by-election followed by a petition, but from 1707 until 1782 the Hamiltons' control appears to have been undisturbed. In 1782 the Clanbrassill agent, Thomas Read, attacked Clanbrassill's control: he was able to do so largely because of Clanbrassill's personality – he was described as 'a strange proud man' – and his indebtedness. Clanbrassill had mortgaged his Dundalk estate and by 1780 he was £6,000 in arrears on the interest on this mortgage, thereby leading to the appointment of a stranger as a receiver of rents and the alienation of his tenantry; furthermore he had little money to defend an attack on his borough. Read attempted to swamp the electorate by the creation of freemen; Clanbrassill declared that the number of freemen could not exceed 500. In the end the legal struggle went to the House of Lords, which decided in Clanbrassill's favour.

[47] See *Louth Arch. Soc. Jn.* xvii no.3 (1971) pp.156–63, A. P. W. Malcomson, 'The Foster family and the Borough of Dunleer 1683–1800'. The borough was originally enfranchised in 1683 as part of Lord Dartmouth's estate. Lord Dartmouth sold his Irish estates in 1698 and a major purchaser was Richard Tenison, Bishop of Meath. Anthony Foster, great-grandfather of Speaker Foster, was one of the original burgesses and during the long minority of Thomas Tenison (born 1707, father Henry Tenison died 1709) the Fosters appear to have consolidated their influence on the borough and their claim to half of it, which was confirmed in a written agreement in 1735 (although Sir Edward Crofton was told in 1786 that it was an unwritten 'gentleman's' agreement). Dixie Coddington (Sr) inherited the Tenison seat on the death of his uncle (Judge) Thomas Tenison, whose only son had predeceased him. At the Union the compensation was equally divided between Dixie Coddington (Jr) and John Foster.

[48] *BNL*, 16–20 Jan. 1784.

[49] *Ibid.*

[50] Henry Bruen married in 1787, died in 1795 leaving two sons, Henry and John Francis, and three daughters who were minors (and were still minors in 1800). A memorial was presented by Bruen's executors, Rt Hon. Henry King and Robert French. Compensation was awarded to the guardians of Henry Bruen.

[51] *DJ*, 23–26 July 1768: in the 1768 election 1,460 votes were cast – Alexander Montgomery 687, Edward Lucas [?]610 and John Corry 165 – but 'there were upwards of 1,000 freeholders not polled'. In the 1776 election 2,467 voted: Alexander Montgomery 1,220, Thomas Tenison 684, C. P. Leslie 563 (*DJ*, 25–27 June). This county had a

considerable Presbyterian population, who may not have
been disposed to vote.
52 1,798 votes were cast in 1776: Hon. John Dawson 696,
Mr Coote 604, Mr Parnell 498 *(DJ*, 1–4 June 1776).
Three years later Dawson succeeded his father as Viscount
Carlow and in the ensuing by-election John Warburton
was reputed to have defeated General Hunt Walsh by 2
votes.
53 See *IHS*, vol. 9 no. 33, pp.53–82, H. F. Kearney, 'A
handlist of the voters of Maryborough, 1760' for an
insight into this (larger) type of electorate.
54 *HP* [1790–1820], vol. 2, p. 681: 63 voted in the 1784
by-election, when Sir Boyle Roche was returned *vice*
Thomas Kelly, Justice of Common Pleas.
55 This figure is an estimate based on adding one-third to
the minimum possible number of voters in 1776 when
1,190 votes were cast for the candidates (see *DJ*, 11–13
June 1776). In 1776, 2,219 votes were cast: Thomas
Mahon (510), Edward Crofton (419) and Arthur French
(361) survived to the close of the poll; some candidates
dropped out. French challenged the election of Crofton
and an Election Committee of the House of Commons
declared the election void. Crofton was returned on re-
election. Contested elections tended to be rowdy, but
Roscommon's appear to have been more so than most.
56 This figure has been calculated by adding one-third to
the minimum possible number of voters in 1776 (see *DJ*,
8–11 June 1776). 1,453 votes were cast: Joshua Cooper
467, Owen Wynne 402, William Ormsby 361 and Sir
Booth Gore 223. *Commons jn. Ire.* 1777. Rt Hon. Owen
Wynne refused to be returned (and in fact was *n.d.e.*);
there was a further election contested by Owen Wynne Jr
and Ormsby; Wynne Jr was returned with a 'respectable'
majority. 753 votes were cast. The election appears to have
lasted from 15 June to 3 July 1778: see *DJ*, issues between
these dates.
57 This county was a palatinate under the jurisdiction of
the Dukes of Ormonde; it was abolished when the 2nd
Duke was attainted in 1715. *DJ*, 30 July–2 Aug. 1768. At
the 1768 election the gross poll was 1,191 and the number
of votes cast was 2,284. PRONI T3318/2 Acc. 12382 gives
a list of the freeholders of Co. Tipperary in 1776.
58 *DJ*, 28 Apr.–2 May 1761 reports that in 1761, 220 votes
were cast (Richard Moore 92, Guy Moore 89, Jeff Walsh
39). *HP* [1790–1820], vol. 2, p. 688. After the Union it
was purchased by John Bagwell.
59 *DJ*, 5–9 May 1761. In this election 697 votes were cast
(Cornelius O'Callaghan 307, Stephen Moore 234, William
Barton 156). 633 votes were cast in the 1768 election
(Cornelius O'Callaghan Jr 236, John Croker 183, William
Barton 156, Lovelace Lowe 58) *(DJ*, 30 July–2 Aug.1768).
60 In the late seventeenth century Sir Archibald Erskine
bequeathed his estates of Augher Castle and Favour Royal
to his two daughters, Mary Richardson and Anne Moutray.
Hon. Richard Rochfort Mervyn (*d.s.p.* 1776) had a claim
on part of the Augher estate (which was divided) through
his wife Letitia Mervyn (*d.s.p.* 1776), and he was thought
to control the return for the Richardson seat during his

marriage (1764–76): see *A narrative of the proceedings of Sir
Edward Crofton relative to his claim to half the borough of
Roscommon*, NLI MS 8826/16, Crofton MSS, pp. 30–2.
61 An attempt was made to subvert the bishop's control in
1783: for how this was checked see PRONI T1566,
Clogher Corporation Book 1783. *HMC Stopford-Sackville*
I, p. 280: The Bishop of Clogher wrote to Lord Sackville
that the citizens of Clogher were all his tenants but that the
Volunteers might be a threat.
62 This is one of the best documented boroughs in the Irish
parliament: see *Historical Studies*, vol. X, A. P. W.
Malcomson, 'The Politics of "Natural Right": The
Abercorn Family and Strabane Borough 1692–1800';
despite its apparent tranquillity, for at least half of this
period the Earl of Abercorn's control was challenged by
local interests and to re-establish his control he eventually,
in 1764, had to buy them out. They were penurious: he
paid one £1,000 and made favourable financial and
political terms with the other.
63 *BNL*, 16–20 Jan. 1784. In 1768 the gross poll was 594:
John Beresford had 154 admitted and 125 questioned
votes, Sir James May had 113 admitted and 60 questioned
votes, and John Congreve had 76 admitted and 66
questioned votes. Nevertheless, the Sheriff decided on the
unusual (and illegal) course of returning two indentures,
coupling Beresford with both of the other candidates. *DJ*,
6–9 Aug 1768.
64 *DJ*, 23–25 May 1776. 105 votes were cast in 1776: 53
for Sir William Osborne, 34 for John Bennett and 18 for
Godfrey Greene.
65 Originally the dominant interest in Co. Waterford and
the boroughs of Dungarvan, Lismore and Tallow was that
of the Earl of Cork. In 1748 the Marquess of Hartington
(4th Duke of Devonshire) married Lady Charlotte Boyle
(died 1754), the sole heiress of Richard, Earl of Cork and
Burlington; her son, the 5th Duke, inherited the Boyle
interest in Waterford.
66 514 votes were cast – Samuel Barker 142, Shapland
Carew 142, Robert Snow 125, William Alcock 105 *(DJ*,
19–23 May 1761). *BNL*, 4–7 June 1776 gives a final poll
of 954 votes: Cornelius Bolton Jr 414, Robert Shapland
Carew 369, William Christmas 171 (the Christmas family
also had an interest in Waterford). *BNL*, 16–20 Jan. 1784
gives the electorate as 1,000.
67 *DJ*, 23–26 May 1761: 1,056 votes were cast in 1761 –
Lord Belfield 452, Hon. Richard Rochfort 343, George
Rochfort 259, Gustavus Lambart 2. *DJ*, 6–9 Aug. 1768:
1,331 votes were cast in 1768 – Lord Belfield 475, Hon.
Col. Rochfort-Mervyn 387, Rt Hon. Anthony Malone
469. *DJ*, 23–25 May 1776: 1,123 votes were cast in 1776
– Hon. Robert Rochfort 523; Benjamin Chapman 350, J.
M. Mason 250.
68 *DJ*, 28 Apr.–2 May 1761: 595 votes were cast in 1761 –
William Handcock 236, H. St George 219, Wentworth
Thewles 140. *DJ*, 2–5 July 1768: in the 1768 election only
195 votes were cast – Sir R. St George 82, William
Handcock 96, Gilbert Holmes 17.
69 *DJ*, 6–9 June 1761: a total of 22 votes were cast in the

1761 election – John Nugent of Clonloft 12, Lord Forbes 8, Hon. John Forbes 2; nevertheless, Forbes Auchmuty, Seneschal of the Manor returned Lord Forbes and the Hon. John Forbes; this return was challenged but confirmed by the House of Commons.

[70] BNL, 16–20 Jan. 1784: electorate unstated, but a large number of electors is implied. 3,626 votes were cast in 1790: John Loftus 1,225, George Ogle 1,072, Sir Frederick Flood 841, Cornelius Grogan 477, Caesar Colclough 11: see T. Powell, 'The background to the rebellion in Co. Wexford 1790–8' (MA thesis, UCD, 1970).

[71] Henry Bruen married in 1787, died in 1795 leaving two sons, Henry and John Francis, and three daughters who were minors (and were still minors in 1800). A memorial was presented by Bruen's executors, Rt Hon. Henry King and Robert French. Compensation was awarded to the guardians of Henry Bruen.

[72] DJ, 16–19 July 1768: the 1768 election results were – Mr Le Hunt 309, Mr Jones-Nevill 263, Mr Grogan 218, Mr Hatton 121 – but the reporter considered that because of the favouritism of the Mayor towards Jones-Nevill's voters, Grogan was deprived of a fair majority of 25. DJ, 4–6 June 1776, reported the 1776 election results as follows: Richard Nevill 332, Richard Le Hunte 293, John Grogan 137.

[73] BNL, 16–20 Jan. 1761. DJ, 2–5 May 1768: c. 1,150 votes were cast in the 1768 election: Ralph Howard 48[?], Hon. Richard Wingfield 355, Richard Chapel Whaley 314. DJ, 4–6 June 1776: in the 1776 election 1,645 votes were cast – Hon. William Brabazon 726, Hon. John Stratford 497, Robert Hoey 422.

[74] Joshua , 2nd Viscount Allen d. 1742 leaving a son who d.s.p. and 2 daughters, Elizabeth who married John Proby, 1st Lord Carysfort and Frances who married William Mayne, 1st Lord Newhaven and d.s.p., so the Allen estates devolved upon Lady Carysfort's (died 1783) heirs.

INDEX

of chapters 1, 2, 6 and 7